HANDBOOK OF
MULTICULTURAL
COMPETENCIES
IN COUNSELING & PSYCHOLOGY

To my students who have motivated me, my colleagues who have challenged me, and my family who have helped me keep things in perspective.

D. B. Pope-Davis

To my students, colleagues, and clients from whom I learn so much and gain great inspiration.

H. L. K. Coleman

To my wife Rossina, my mother Judy, my grandmother, and David and Joe.

W. M. Liu

To Kaiya, Dylan, Phil, all of my family, colleagues, friends, and mentors for their commitment, guidance, and encouragement.

R. L. Toporek

HANDBOOK OF
MULTICULTURAL
COMPETENCIES
IN COUNSELING & PSYCHOLOGY

Editors

Donald B. Pope-Davis
University of Notre Dame

Hardin L. K. Coleman
University of Wisconsin–Madison

William Ming Liu
University of Iowa

Rebecca L. Toporek
San Francisco State University

SAGE Publications
International Educational and Professional Publisher
Thousand Oaks ▪ London ▪ New Delhi

For information:

Sage Publications, Inc.
2455 Teller Road
Thousand Oaks, California 91320
E-mail: order@sagepub.com

Sage Publications Ltd
6 Bonhill Street
London EC2A 4PU
United Kingdom

Sage Publications India Pvt. Ltd.
B-42, Panchsheel Enclave
Post Box 4109
New Delhi 110 017
India

Printed in the United States of America

Library of Congress Cataloging-in-Publication Data

Handbook of multicultural competencies in counseling and psychology /
edited by Donald B. Pope-Davis . . . [et al.].
    p. cm.
Includes bibliographical references and index.
ISBN 0-7619-2306-3
    1 Cross-cultural counseling. I. Pope-Davis, Donald B.
BF637.C6H3173 2003
158′.3—dc21

                                        2003005186

03   04   05   06   07   10   9   8   7   6   5   4   3   2   1

Acquiring Editor:	Arthur T. Pomponio
Editorial Assistant:	Veronica Novak
Production Editor:	Diana E. Axelsen
Copy Editor:	Gillian Dickens
Typesetter:	C&M Digitals (P) Ltd.
Indexer:	Rachel Rice
Cover Designer:	Janet Foulger

Contents

CONCLUSION: REFLECTIONS AND FUTURE DIRECTIONS   589

Foreword

The title of this innovative and comprehensive revised handbook, edited by Professors Pope-Davis, Coleman, Liu, and Toporek, is straightforward and to the point—the focus is entirely devoted to the achievement, maintenance, and application of *multicultural competence* in a variety of domains in psychology. The title, however, begs for an explanation. Why should anyone affiliated with psychology be interested in and concerned about achieving multicultural competence? The answer to this question is not as straightforward as the handbook's title might suggest. A plausible answer must take into consideration the following observations. First, the historical record suggests that psychology has all but ignored the surface- and deep-level meanings and implications of culture and ethnicity for the past 100 years. Second, the mission statement of the American Psychological Association (APA) maintains that the object of the APA shall be to advance psychology as a science and profession and as a means of promoting health and human welfare. The historical record suggests that the profession has not lived up to this statement. Up until 1970 or so, the APA's mission and that of psychology in general appeared to be limited to one segment of the U.S. population, as references to African Americans, Asian Americans, American Indians and Alaska Natives, Hispanics, Pacific Islanders, and Puerto Ricans were almost completely absent from the psychological literature; in fact, the words *culture* and *ethnic* were rarely used in psychological textbooks except in topics dealing with person perception, prejudice and discrimination, and psycholinguistics. Third, the population distribution of the United States has always been portrayed as a "melting pot" consisting of hundreds of uniquely different ethnic and nationalistic groups, with those of Euro-American background constituting the largest demographic concentration. The U.S. Bureau of Census, however, indicates that the variable growth patterns of ethnic minority groups in the United States will stir up and add to the "melting pot" with increasing numbers of different nationalities and ethnic groups for another century or two.

Before these observations are discussed in more detail, attention must be given to the concept of *competence*. At a general level, competence is a state of being psychologically and physically adequate and having sufficient knowledge, judgment, skill, or strength. When this definition is expanded to include *culture,* competence then includes skills reflecting one's understanding and appreciation of cultural differences and similarities. To achieve *multicultural competence,* one must be consciously *willing* to learn and explore other cultural groups; without a conscious intent and desire, the achievement and realization of multicultural competence is not likely to occur. These themes are consistently emphasized in all chapters in this volume. With this in mind, let me move on to discuss the relationship between the three observations and the implications of the handbook for achieving multicultural competence.

In response to the first and second observations, beginning in the 1960s, ethnic minority psychologists began questioning what the APA meant by *human* and to whom the vast body of psychological knowledge applied. Fueled and inspired by the contentious and volatile civil rights movement, America's ethnic minority psychologists forcefully argued that American psychology was not inclusive of what constitutes the U.S. population—they claimed that psychology's research findings and theories were biased, limited to studies involving college and university students and laboratory animals, and therefore not applicable to all humans. Accusations of imperialism, cultural encapsulation, ethnocentrism, parochialism, and, in some circles of dissent, "scientific racism" run the gamut of criticisms hurled at the field of psychology in the past three decades. Comprehensive literature reviews reinforced their accusations and observations.

Before 1976, for example, close to 25 articles and chapters were written on the subject of culture and counseling. Now, close to 500 books, chapters, and journal articles have been written expressing a variety of theoretical and research perspectives on the topic. The accelerated rate of interest and concern generated on the topic in the past 25 years or so is extraordinary but not surprising. The argument and justification for the increased interest rest on the contention that conventional counseling and mental health theories and service delivery approaches do not resonate with many of the lifeways and thoughtways of ethnic minority groups. Because all human thoughts and behaviors are culturally based, accurate assessment, meaningful understanding, and culturally appropriate interventions are required for understanding each context for counseling to effectively occur.

Another response to the question about why anyone affiliated with psychology should be interested in and concerned about achieving multicultural competence concerns the growth of ethnic minority groups in the United States. America never was and likely will not be a *melting pot* of different nationalities and ethnic groups for another century or two. Consider the population projections offered by the U.S. Bureau of the Census. By 2050, the U.S. population will reach more than 400 million, about 47% larger than in the year 2000. The primary ethnic minority groups—specifically, Hispanics, African Americans, Asian Americans, and American Indians and Alaska Natives—will constitute almost 50% of the population in 2050. About 57% of the population younger than age 18 and 34% older than age 65 will be ethnic minorities. Currently, Hispanics number 35.3 million, about 12.5% of the U.S. population, and comprise a diversity of ethnocultural groups from numerous countries. Projections for the year 2010 suggest that Hispanics will be the largest ethnic group, second only to White Americans, and followed by African Americans.

The third observation clearly illustrates that the ethnic and cultural demographic landscape in the United States is increasing to a future point where groups that were once in the numerical minority will be the majority. Conventional and timeworn psychological approaches to understanding the human condition will not be appropriate or relevant unless they can accommodate the heterogeneity generated by ethnic and cultural worldviews.

Cultural and ethnic psychologists increasingly are demonstrating that culture makes a difference in the way people act, perceive, think, and feel so much so that major theories have to be revised to accommodate the new and contradictory results. Although the findings are challenging psychology, the field, in general, is challenging culture in reciprocal ways. Conventional psychologists are pushing us to define what we mean by culture, ethnicity, and the processes and mechanisms that mediate and influence thoughtways and lifeways. Becoming *multiculturally competent* does not imply that one should discard the contributions of past and present psychologists. The challenge for the reader of this handbook is to recognize that we cannot fully understand the human condition without viewing it from a cross-cultural and ethnic perspective, and to do this effectively and efficiently, we must be multiculturally competent. What was learned about the human condition in the past can be reframed and tested with a new set of approaches and procedures in contexts not considered in the past. Similarly, we may find that specific thoughtways and lifeways of certain ethnocultural groups may have some extraordinary value for psychology as a whole and thus assist in improving our understanding of humans and the settings in which we live.

An early version of this handbook with a similar title by Professors Pope-Davis and Coleman was a bold, timely publishing venture set within Sage Publications' Multicultural Aspects of Counseling Series. Seventeen well-written and thought-provoking chapters explored topics dealing with assessment, education and training, and supervision. Since its seminal publication in 1997, interest in cultural and ethnic topics in psychology has mushroomed, thus creating the need for the editors to revise the original handbook to include new and fresh perspectives on a broader range of topics. The current volume has been expanded substantially to include 37 chapters covering a vast landscape of topics in the field.

In the early 1970s, a few ethnic minorities blazed a path through the burgeoning field of psychology by emphasizing the importance of the study of culture and ethnicity. The path is much longer, wider, and unmistakable now. Along the way, several ethnic minority psychologists, through their scholarly publications, left important footprints for others to follow. In 1997, Professors Pope-Davis and Coleman left a small footprint with their first handbook. The publication of this revised and expanded handbook will leave an even more prominent footprint to guide the progressive development of multicultural competence. As readers pore over the chapters, they will come to realize that the attainment of multicultural competence is daunting. The path to attaining multicultural competence is difficult as it is a lifelong journey that involves considerable self-reflection; a critical examination and study of one's cultural and ethnic heritage, including those factors that influence maturation and enculturation; and a willingness to learn about the intricacies and subtleties of other ethnocultural groups with an open mind coupled with an adventuresome spirit.

As a consequence of the accomplishments of the past three decades, cultural and ethnic perspectives are well established in psychology. They are slowly beginning to make a significant mark in the annals of the field. But there is another side to the growth that bears mention. A scan of the offerings of different psychology departments indicates that cultural and ethnic topics are not being given serious attention. A glance at future U.S. population projections suggests that the curriculum for graduate students who work with people from different ethnocultural groups must change. If that does not occur soon, then millions of people will be excluded from what psychology professes as its mission—to advance psychology as a science and profession and as a means of promoting health and human welfare.

Incorporating ethnic and cultural issues into the curriculum is not a matter of political correctness. It is a matter of scientific and professional responsibility. We must remember that culture and ethnicity are important to psychology on a number of levels. Most important of these is that the scope of psychology is aimed at understanding affect, behavior and cognition, and research—education is geared to this purpose. By exploring psychological processes across diverse cultural and ethnic populations and contexts, we gain deeper insights into how these processes operate; the venture can contribute to achieving multicultural competence. The revised handbook leads us in that direction and along a clearly marked path in ways that were not available to the field even a decade ago.

—Joseph E. Trimble, Ph.D.
Professor of Psychology
Western Washington University

Preface

By all possible measures of scholarly research and productivity, it can be easily said that the number of publications on the topic of multiculturalism and multicultural competencies has increased exponentially year after year. What was once a trickle has become a virtual tsunami of scholarship, both theoretical and empirical, that has made a mark on counseling and psychology research and practice. A casual perusal of the leading counseling journals and national and regional conferences will support the fact that there is a steady and increasing focus on culture in our professional practices. And with the recent endorsement of the Guidelines of Multicultural Competencies by the American Psychological Association, multicultural competency has become even more mainstreamed than before.

But within the context of the many successes for multicultural competency in psychology and counseling, it is also important to contextualize our current experience as professionals. Because one of the important hallmarks of multiculturalism is context, it is important that we consider how we may fully understand this book and its meaningfulness within our various communities. Of the numerous contextual issues to consider, we will touch upon a few salient ones. For example, more than a year after the September 11, 2001, terrorist attacks, the United States is in an economic decline marked by enormous white-collar crime, and the country has ended another war with Iraq. Muslim Americans are targeted for interrogation and incarceration, poverty is increasing, and gays and lesbians are still being killed in our streets. These contextual issues pull at the very heart of multicultural competency: our social justice orientation and our hope to transform our communities. And it is within this context that multicultural competency has become more important than ever. Because many of our professional roles situate us at the "front lines" of contact with people and these issues, it is imperative that we better understand and integrate multiculturalism into our practices and become multiculturally competent.

Hence, within this context of multiculturalism's successes and our current situation as a nation, we present the *Handbook of Multicultural Competencies*. We are excited that the handbook, a labor of love for us, has been finally produced. Although many of the chapters were written prior to the events of September 11, 2001, the content is timely to address the role that multicultural competencies have in responding to our world. We are delighted that top scholars in the field of multicultural competency have joined us in contributing their time and energy to this product: a handbook that is the first of its kind to focus specifically on the issue of multicultural competency in our various professional roles. Because we felt that professionals needed a resource that could ground their practice and also provide direction for their growth and development, this book was produced with several goals in mind:

1. to provide readers with a foundation in multicultural competency through historicizing the field and exposure to critical theories,
2. to provide readers with a compendium of the latest theories and research related to multicultural competency,
3. to provide readers with a "hands-on" framework from which they can develop their own practices.

BOOK CONTENTS

The book is organized under five major parts: Concepts and Theories, Assessment, Research, Practice, and Teaching. We also provide at the end a Reflections and Future Directions chapter. We created the five parts because they reflected the essential and fundamental practices within which counselors are involved.

In Part I, Concepts and Theories, the chapters provide the foundation from which we attempt to understand and operationalize multicultural competency. This part historicizes multicultural competency as well as critiques it. The notion of competency versus competencies, major theories and models of feminism and identity development, the philosophy of science, power, school counseling issues, and supervision are among the various issues tackled within this part. Readers are exposed to the difficult dialogues multiculturalists are engaged within as we attempt to develop and reflect on our discipline. The act of Freirian praxis, as readers will understand, is an important endeavor that can only advance the field of multicultural competency.

In Part II, Assessment, the focus narrows on how we understand multicultural competency through our measures and methodology. The important question that weaves the part together is, "How do we assess for and operationalize multicultural competency?" Readers

are provided with a review of major measures of multicultural competency at the individual and environmental levels. In addition, a framework from which to understand demonstrated multicultural competency that shifts away from specific instruments is reviewed. An example of combining both methods of multicultural assessment is used among teachers, showing the importance of multicultural competency at all levels of practice.

The third part, Research, addresses a fundamental element in multicultural competency. The chapters within the part cover important developing issues within the field. For instance, the popularity of empirically supported treatments is reviewed within the schema of multicultural competency. Similarly, the salience of multicultural competency is examined within the counseling relationship. Finally, the part ends with, first, a discussion on the need for qualitative methods in multicultural competency research and, second, a study on multicultural counseling competencies among counseling practitioners.

Part IV, Practice, is one of the most unique for any book on multiculturalism. Within multicultural competency research, the practical applications are often overlooked. Hence, the major focus of this part is the application of multicultural competencies to multiple areas of professional practice. The part first addresses multicultural competencies and accreditation. This is followed by an overview of the ethical implications of multicultural competencies. The remainder of the part examines multicultural competencies within practice dimensions such as consulting, managed health care, counseling centers, supervision, career counseling, schools, health psychology, and rehabilitation counseling. Although not fully capturing all the possible professional settings and responsibilities of counselors and psychologists, the intent of the part was to provide a resource from which people could start their own development.

Part V, Teaching, focuses on teaching multicultural competency. Although there are potentially many resources available to readers, this part aggregates the teaching and pedagogical issues of multicultural competency into one space. The part addresses teaching and multicultural competency within academic achievement, such as in kindergarten through 12th grade (K-12), collegiate undergraduate courses, counseling graduate courses, continuing education, and technology and Internet research. Often overlooked in the multicultural literature or located in discipline-specific journals and books, the intent of this part was to expose readers practicing at various levels to the issues, challenges, and successes that are common among all teachers. Finally, the book ends with a "Reflections and Future Directions" chapter by Drs. Atkinson and Israel.

This book was intended to provide a framework to understand multicultural competencies and to help individuals and groups apply the principles of multicultural competency to their work. Although the contents cover a vast array of topics, the focus is specific: multicultural competencies in all areas of psychological and counseling practice and research. Our hope is that readers will digest the various resources we have gathered and use them to transform themselves and their communities.

William Ming Liu
Donald B. Pope-Davis
Hardin L.K. Coleman
Rebecca L. Toporek

PART I

Concepts and Theories

The purpose of Part I is to help ground readers in the area of multicultural competencies. Certainly, readers can draw from a multitude of resources, but it was important for us to provide readers with, what we believe, are the most salient and important cornerstones to understanding multicultural competency. Building on the work of many scholars, the authors of the various chapters in this section concisely summarize as well as critique the practice of multicultural competency.

In this section, readers are provided with a summative history of multiculturalism along with themes and issues that have arisen and still arise in today's practice. In addition, this section addresses the many frameworks that we use to understand multicultural competency. Specifically, authors review and evaluate the many models of multicultural competency that attempt to capture the essential elements relevant to our practices. Readers will find that the first two chapters of this section provide the necessary cornerstones to understanding multicultural competency through history, issues and themes, and a review of important models. Readers will also find that there is not one model encapsulating multicultural competencies (e.g., Sue, Arredondo, & McDavis, 1992) but many paradigms that have attempted to capture the important facets of competency.

This part also focuses on how people's cultural identities are constructed as well as how those identities, such as gender, affect multicultural competency. Within this section are two theoretical chapters that focus on the philosophy that underlies our practice and an examination of a ubiquitous element in our environment. The chapter addressing our philosophy of science within multiculturalism forces us to explore our assumptions and intent. The chapter that follows focuses on a phenomenon that many people concede is important but ephemeral to psychology and counseling. This issue is power. Hence, the chapter focused on moving from diversity to multiculturalism addresses the operationalization of power in our practice and how differing attention can lead to different outcomes.

Finally, the section closes with an examination of multicultural competency in school settings and issues related to multicultural supervision. First, the chapter on school counseling examines how we can make multicultural competency relevant for practice situations other than college and adult populations. Second, the chapter on multicultural supervision examines the importance of race-related issues on the supervision relationship and, ultimately, the multicultural competency of the trainee.

It is hoped that readers will come away from reading this section with a firm foundation in the area of multicultural competency and the issues related to our professions.

REFERENCE

Sue, D. W., Arrendondo, P., & McDavis, R. J. (1992). Multicultural counseling competencies and standards: A call to the profession. *Journal of Counseling and Development, 70,* 477-486.

1

Multicultural Counseling Competence

History, Themes, and Issues

CHARLES R. RIDLEY
AMY J. KLEINER
Indiana University

Multicultural counseling competence (MCC) has emerged as one of the most important and widely discussed topics in the helping and human service professions. Applied psychology, psychiatry, social work, counseling, health care, and education are among the many professions that acknowledge its importance. Although each of these specialties has contributed to the conversation, the most significant contributions have come from counseling psychology. The purpose of this chapter is to discuss the history, themes, and issues involved in multicultural counseling competence.

The chapter is organized into three major sections. First, we discuss the historical development of MCC. Second, we pinpoint and describe major themes pertaining to the construct. Third, we discuss some critical issues and questions pertaining to multicultural counseling competence.

HISTORICAL DEVELOPMENT

The Vail Conference of 1973 launched an important discussion regarding psychological practice and cultural diversity (Korman, 1974). From this conference came the resolution that providing professional services to culturally diverse individuals is unethical if the counselor is not competent to provide them and that, therefore, graduate training programs should teach appropriate cultural content. A few years later, an article titled "Barriers to Effective Cross-Cultural Counseling" (Sue & Sue, 1977) contributed to the early discussion in multicultural competence. The authors asserted that breakdowns in communication may occur in counseling due to the counselor's inability to clearly understand cultural messages from the client and communicate culturally appropriate information to the client. The article focused on how the values of traditional counseling practices in the United States may conflict with the values of individuals from Third World groups, how these traditional values may serve to distort communications by both clients and counselors in cross-cultural counseling, and what implications these considerations could have for the practice of counseling. Since the publication of this article, the topic increasingly has gained interest and support in applied psychology and related fields. As a result, many psychologists have worked to develop MCC standards and competencies.

Historically, the body of MCC literature began with attempts to define MCC and identify ways in which counselors could become multiculturally competent. In the 1980s, exploration of multicultural competencies began to unfold. In 1982, a landmark paper introduced three cross-cultural counseling competencies (Sue et al., 1982). These competencies—beliefs and attitudes, knowledge, and skills—have served as the foundation for numerous investigations over the past two decades (e.g., Arredondo, Toporek, Brown, Sanchez, & Stadler, 1996; Constantine & Ladany, 2000; Holcomb-McCoy, 2000; Ponterotto & Casas, 1987; Pope-Davis & Dings, 1995; Ramsey, 1995; Sodowsky, Taffe, Gutkin, & Wise, 1994; Sue, Arredondo, & McDavis, 1992; Sue et al., 1998). Ten years later, Sue et al. (1992) issued a call to the profession to implement multicultural counseling competencies and standards in counseling practice and education. Their article provided a rationale for multicultural perspectives in counseling assessment, practice, training, and research; proposed specific standards for a culturally competent counselor; and advocated for the integration of these standards in the

American Association for Counseling and Development (AACD).

Endeavors to define MCC were immediately followed by efforts to provide guidelines for multiculturally competent training programs and curricula. Publications related to training issues began to emerge as early as the mid-1980s. This area of the literature comprises investigations of multiculturally competent training practices, training programs, and supervision. In the early 1990s, literature related to assessment of MCC arose as a critical component of the discussion. This area of the literature encompasses the development of MCC assessment instruments for training, practice, and supervision, as well as the analysis of MCC assessment instruments. Most recently, literature related to specialized applications of MCC has contributed to the conversation. Specialized applications refer to the implementation of MCC strategies in working with distinct populations such as HIV patients, children and families, individuals with disabilities, and children in school settings.

Although the subject of MCC has now gained prominence in the counseling field, the profession was slow to respond to the earliest calls for action. For example, only a few publications on the topic appeared between 1982 and 1994 (e.g., Carney & Kahn, 1984; Isaacs & Benjamin, 1991). In fact, 1994 marked the first time that multiple publications concerning MCC appeared in the literature (e.g., Campinha-Bacote, 1994; Ponterotto, Rieger, Barrett, & Sparks, 1994; Pope-Davis & Dings, 1994; Sodowsky et al., 1994). In 1997 and 1998, the MCC literature blossomed. During this period, the AACD endorsed the guidelines for cultural competence, marking a significant and much needed contribution to MCC. In 1999, Divisions 17 and 45 of the American Psychological Association (APA, 1999) also endorsed the guidelines for cultural competence, marking the association's commitment to culturally competent services and training.

THEMES IN THE LITERATURE

The MCC literature generally falls into five categories: (a) asserting the importance of MCC; (b) characteristics, features, dimensions, and parameters of MCC; (c) MCC training and supervision; (d) assessing MCC; and (e) specialized applications of MCC.

Asserting the Importance of MCC

The claim that MCC is a critical component of counselor training, supervision, and practice resounds throughout the literature. Since Sue and colleagues' (1982) initial assertion, many psychologists have continued to assert the importance of MCC to the counseling profession. Sue et al. (1992) suggested that the field is in need of a philosophical change in the premise of counseling toward inclusivity, altruism, community mindedness, and concern for justice. Accordingly, they outlined a rationale for the necessity of multicultural perspectives in counseling and education, contending that the dramatic increase in the non-White population of the United States requires that mental health professionals be prepared to provide culturally appropriate services to all people.

Similarly, Sue et al. (1992) stated that professionals must work to integrate standards into their practice and training that accurately reflect the diversity that exists in our society. In an effort to respond to the need for extended MCC application in the profession, the authors called for action in the development and implementation of specific multicultural counseling standards throughout the profession. They suggested that professionals who do not have competence in working with individuals from various cultural backgrounds are ethically inappropriate and may be harmful to their clients.

Many psychologists have followed the example of Sue et al. (1992) by extending the rationale for MCC. Silva-Netto (1994)

insisted that the increasing awareness of cross-cultural relationships in the field of counseling underscores the requirement for all counselors to develop cross-cultural competence. Sodowsky et al. (1994) asserted that precisely because the field of counseling psychology has historically claimed to be inclusive, there is a serious need to expand the definition of counseling competencies so that professionals can provide appropriate services to individuals from all cultural backgrounds. More recently, D. W. Sue (2001a) pointed out that mental health services are sometimes oppressive to minority groups and that multicultural counseling competence should be concerned with issues of social justice.

Many psychologists have affirmed the importance of multicultural competence in counselor training programs in particular. Allison, Echemendia, Crawford, and Robinson (1996) noted that current training in the provision of culturally appropriate psychological services to members of ethnic minorities is inadequate, and it is essential for the field to continue to address this issue by promoting cultural competence in all psychologists. Holcomb-McCoy and Myers (1999) recognized the importance of preparing counselors to be multiculturally competent, and Ponterotto and Casas (1987) addressed the need for action in improving counselor training to meet the standards of MCC. Holcomb-McCoy (2000) called for extended research in the specific competencies and factors that are involved in MCC and suggested that this research is particularly important for counselor training programs.

In addition to MCC in training programs, others have argued the importance of MCC in working with specific populations. Lynch and Hanson (1992) and Imber-Black (1997) maintained that regardless of the role a professional plays, it is essential to have the attitudes and skills that facilitate effective cross-cultural interactions when working with children and families. Ka'opua (1998) asserted that in working with special populations such as HIV patients and their families, counselors and professionals need to be culturally competent in their interactions with individuals from varying racial and ethnic backgrounds. Abe-Kim and Takeuchi (1996) challenged mental health professionals to attend to the needs and concerns of ethnic minorities who may feel victimized and deceived by the managed care system and health care professionals in general.

Furthermore, there is the suggestion that counselors should tailor the interactional process to "match to" or complement the individual client's cognitive, behavioral, and emotive abilities and strengths (Hubble, Duncan, & Miller, 1999; Tracey & Ray, 1984). Tracey and Ray (1984) contended that for any relationship to remain functional over a period of time, it must have some level of complementarity. Complementarity and matching to the client can also be thought of as a means of maximizing the likelihood that the client will be responsive to the counselor's suggestions and will remain actively engaged in the counseling process. Because certain groups, such as individuals from low socioeconomic backgrounds, often terminate therapy prematurely (Garfield, 1986), complementarity and matching to clients adds additional support for the necessity of MCC.

Characteristics, Features, Dimensions, and Parameters of MCC

The literature related to identifying the components of MCC covers the exploration of multicultural competencies, the proposal of general definitions of MCC, and models of MCC.

Competencies

As noted earlier, Sue and colleagues originally conceptualized MCC as having three components: beliefs and attitudes, knowledge, and skills (Sue et al., 1982; Sue et al., 1992). *Beliefs and attitudes* refers to the mind-set of counselors about ethnic and racial minorities, as well as the responsibility counselors have to check their biases and stereotypes, develop a positive orientation toward multicultural perspectives, and recognize ways in which personal biases and values can affect cross-cultural counseling relationships. *Knowledge* is the understanding counselors have of their own worldview, their specific knowledge of cultural groups, and their understanding of sociopolitical influences on cross-cultural relationships. Finally, *skills* refers to the specific abilities that are necessary to work with racial and ethnic minorities (Sue et al., 1982; Sue et al., 1992).

A number of scholars have found the three competencies to be a useful framework in which to conceptualize MCC. These competencies were operationalized through the Dimensions of the Personal Identity Model in an effort to assist counselors in seeing people holistically and to increase their ability to recognize the complexity of all individuals (Arredondo et al., 1996). A volume titled *Multicultural Counseling Competencies: Assessment, Education, Training, and Supervision* (Pope-Davis & Coleman, 1997) considered the ways in which counselors can be evaluated for their awareness, knowledge, and skills in working with a wide range of populations. Another book in the same series, titled *Multicultural Counseling Competencies: Individual and Organizational Development* (Sue et al., 1998), again provided a reference for counselors, therapists, and social workers to ground their awareness, knowledge, and skills and also applied these competencies to organizational development. In addition, the three competencies have been supported empirically as being key components of MCC (Holcomb-McCoy, 2000; Sodowsky et al., 1994).

Despite the wide acceptance of the three multicultural counseling competencies, a number of researchers have suggested that beliefs and attitudes, knowledge, and skills are not sufficient for multicultural competence. Sodowsky et al. (1994) developed the Multicultural Counseling Inventory, an instrument designed to operationalize proposed constructs of multicultural counseling competencies. Their factor analysis yielded a fourth factor of MCC: *multicultural counseling relationships,* which refers to the interactional process of a counselor with a client who is a member of an ethnic minority group. Other findings suggest that *multicultural terminology,* referring to the ability of a counselor to understand terminology commonly used to discuss multicultural issues, and *racial identity development* are significant factors in establishing MCC (Holcomb-McCoy, 2000; Holcomb-McCoy & Myers, 1999). Other characteristics that have been suggested as being important to MCC include a special concern for ethically appropriate practices (DeLucia-Waack, 1996), White racial identity development (Neville, Heppner, Thompson, Brooks, & Baker, 1996; Ottavi, Pope-Davis, & Dings, 1994; Richardson & Molinaro, 1996), cultural empathy (Beckett, Dungee-Anderson, Cox, & Daly, 1997; Constantine, 2000; Ridley & Lingle, 1996), avoidance of Eurocentric thinking (Ramsey, 1995), a concern for good science and practice (Castro, 1998; S. Sue, 1998), and a commitment to establishing symmetrical relationships that empower the client within the counseling dynamic (Silva-Netto, 1994).

Constantine and Ladany (2001) suggested the need for a broader conceptualization of the construct of multicultural competence so that counselors can fully understand how it can be achieved. They proposed that MCC consists of six dimensions or competencies: (a) self-awareness, (b) general multicultural knowledge, (c) multicultural counseling self-efficacy, (d) ability to understand unique client variables, (e) effective counseling alliance, and (f) multicultural counseling skills. The authors suggested that the level of a counselor's overall MCC can be determined by identifying what level has been achieved by the counselor in each dimension.

Definitions

In addition to the various competencies, broad definitions of MCC have been offered. Holcomb-McCoy and Myers (1999) defined a multiculturally competent counselor as one who possesses the skills necessary to work effectively and sensitively with clients from various cultural and ethnic backgrounds. To become multiculturally competent, counselors must (a) become aware of their own biases, assumptions, and values related to racial and ethnic minorities; (b) strive to understand the worldview of each client without making negative judgments about the individual; and (c) develop and implement culturally sensitive interventions in their own practice (Sue et al., 1992).

Pope-Davis and Dings (1995) claimed that multicultural counseling competencies are based on three primary factors: (a) an understanding of the different experiences that members of various cultural groups may have, (b) an understanding of the barriers that exist in communication as a result of cultural differences, and (c) a set of abilities that contributes to the cultural skills and proficiencies of a counselor. S. Sue (1998) defined cultural competence as "the belief that people should not only appreciate and recognize other cultural groups, but also be able to effectively work with them" (p. 441). He suggested that counselors have attained cultural competency when they possess the cultural knowledge and skills essential to delivering effective interventions to individuals who are members of cultural groups different from their own.

Ridley, Baker, and Hill (2001) argued that multicultural competence should focus not solely on race issues but on multiple social identities that intersect with individuals, organizations, and society.

Models

Various models have also been introduced as tools that counselors can use to become multiculturally competent. Carney and Kahn (1984) offered a five-stage developmental model for the process of gaining MCC. Beginning with a limited knowledge base of other cultural groups, counselors eventually advance to an activist position, promoting cultural pluralism in our society. Each stage reflects a pattern of growth in three domains: knowledge of cultural groups; attitude, awareness, and sensitivity; and specific cross-cultural counseling skills.

Another model, entitled the "multicultural communication process model," is intended to increase multicultural counseling competence in any counseling relationship (Beckett et al., 1997). This model consists of eight competencies associated with MCC: (a) knowledge of self, (b) acknowledgment of cultural differences, (c) identification and valuation of differences, (d) knowledge of other cultures, (e) identification and avoidance of stereotypes, (f) empathy with people of other cultures, (g) ability to adapt rather than adopt, and (h) ability to acquire recovery skills. The designers suggested that practitioners first use the model to guide their individual growth in multicultural perspectives and then use the model to inform interventions in a multicultural context.

A three-factor model for describing and rating the capacity of mental health practitioners to conduct culturally effective assessments, clinical interventions, and research with members of ethnic minority groups different from their own offers a unique perspective on the concept of competence (Castro, 1998).

Castro (1998) proposed that "cultural capacity" can range from a level of −3, cultural destructiveness, to +3, cultural proficiency. He offered a table that outlines the ways in which counselors can achieve cultural openness and sensitivity (+1), cultural competence (+2), and cultural proficiency (+3) in their clinical practice. *Cultural proficiency* refers to an ideal state that involves high mastery, a commitment to excellence in working with minority populations, and a proactive attitude in designing and implementing strategies with a particular cultural group. By introducing the third level, Castro asserted that a level of cultural capabilities higher than cultural competence exists and that cultural proficiency should be a practitioner's ultimate goal.

Another model of cultural competence emphasizes the importance of recognizing the two cultural perspectives of the counselor and the client and the ability of the counselor to move between both perspectives (López, 1997). López (1997) proposed four aspects of culturally competent therapy as essential for accomplishing this objective. First, he proposed that a counselor must have the ability to balance both perspectives by successfully engaging the client in the therapeutic process and being responsive to the client's actual needs and concerns, rather than the needs and concerns the counselor may initially assume the client to have. Next, he suggested that the collection of information about the client should be culturally responsive, taking into account the many cultural variables that contribute to the results achieved with every assessment tool. In this process, counselors should use multiple instruments, adjust their interpretation based on the client's cultural background, and use clinical judgment in considering all cultural data and deciding how to use it responsibly. In addition, López argued that a counselor's theoretical approach should be responsive to the client's needs and personality. He also suggested that the counselor should adopt a method of intervention that is responsive to the client's personality and skills, rather than rigidly maintaining a single theoretical approach.

Recently, D. W. Sue (2001a) proposed a new model, multiple dimensions of cultural competence (MDCC). The MDCC model provides a framework for organizing culture-specific attributes of competence (including African American, Asian American, Latino American, Native American, and European American cultures), components of cultural competence (awareness of beliefs and attitudes, knowledge, and skills), and foci of cultural competence (including societal, organizational, professional, and individual structures). Referring to a $3 \times 4 \times 5$ factorial combination, Sue suggested that the MDCC model can be used by educators, students, clinicians, and researchers to identify cultural competence within a variety of areas.

MCC Training and Supervision

The literature about multiculturally competent training and supervision generally falls under the categories of identifying training variables, developing guidelines for multiculturally competent counselor training programs, and analyzing issues surrounding multiculturally competent counselor supervision.

Training Variables

A body of the MCC literature related to training and supervision is dedicated to identifying the variables that contribute to a counselor's multicultural counseling competence. One frequently cited variable is exposure to various cultural groups through lived experiences and counseling practice (Allison et al., 1996; Carlson, Brack, Laygo, Cohen, & Kirkscey, 1998; Neville et al., 1996; Salzman, 2000). Trainees who have had client contact with individuals who differ from them culturally

have reported an increase in their MCC as they go through training (Allison et al., 1996; Carlson et al., 1998). In addition, students report that exposure to various multicultural events, such as racially and ethnically diverse speakers and panels, contributed to their sense of multicultural counseling competence (Carlson et al., 1998; Neville et al., 1996).

In a project designed to increase the MCC of Caucasian American counseling students, Salzman (2000) suggested three reasons that exposure to multicultural events leads to increased multicultural competence. First, students gain awareness of the existence of cultural differences. Second, students develop motivation to explore their own cultural influences. Finally, students gain experience with and awareness of the dynamics involved in cross-cultural interactions. In addition to the above factors, other training variables that have been identified as important to the development of MCC include opportunities to explore White racial identity development (Ottavi et al., 1994) and general opportunities to gain direct multicultural counseling training through coursework (Carlson et al., 1998; Steward, Wright, Jackson, & Jo, 1998).

Training Programs

In response to students' need for MCC training, many researchers have addressed the responsibility of counselor training programs to meet specific multicultural competency standards. Pope-Davis and Dings (1995) asserted that to respond to our increasingly diversifying society, we must learn to focus our attention on the ways in which we can provide appropriate clinical training related to multicultural counseling competencies. As a general guideline, McRae and Johnson (1991) suggested that multicultural education should emphasize (a) trainees' awareness and knowledge of themselves as cultural beings, (b) trainees' ability to appropriately and sensitively relate to clients from various cultural backgrounds, (c) trainees' ability to promote accurate perceptions of cultural groups other than their own, and (d) trainees' ability to perform effectively within multicultural counseling relationships.

Other components have been identified as crucial to multiculturally competent training programs. Training programs should integrate throughout the curriculum the three primary competencies—attitudes/beliefs, knowledge, and skills—as well as racial identity development and proficiency in multicultural terminology (Holcomb-McCoy, 2000; Holcomb-McCoy & Myers, 1999). Organizations such as the Council for the Accreditation of Counseling and Related Educational Programs (CACREP), the American Association for Counseling and Development (AACD), and the American Psychological Association (APA) should clarify their definition of MCC and make MCC standards explicit (Holcomb-McCoy & Myers, 1999; Ponterotto & Casas, 1987). This should help to overcome the ambiguity of multicultural competence guidelines. Furthermore, Ponterotto and Casas (1987) recommended that the AACD and APA should assist training programs in incorporating multicultural competence standards into their curricula by offering workshops at annual conferences and forming consultation teams to advise individual programs on how to strengthen their multicultural training practices.

Tomlinson-Clarke and Wang (1999) suggested that training programs adopt a four-part curriculum. First, they conceived a didactic component involving a course that provides knowledge and awareness of community, social, cultural, and political institutions and how they influence human systems. Next, they proposed an experiential component that involves a course building on the didactic course and emphasizing students' self-examination and self-evaluation as racial and cultural beings. Third, they proposed a research practicum in which students carry out multicultural research in the process of participating in a didactic course. Finally, they suggested a clinical practicum as a means of applying in practice the knowledge gained from the didactic and experiential courses.

For counselor training programs to incorporate MCC, they must have specific steps for implementing MCC standards throughout their curricula. The Multicultural Competency Checklist offers a 22-item list to guide training programs in the development of multicultural competence (Ponterotto, Alexander, & Grieger, 1995). The checklist organizes each item into six major themes, including minority representation, curriculum, counseling practice and supervision, research, student and faculty competency assessment, and physical environment. The developmental model of multicultural competence previously mentioned can also be followed to understand the stages students pass through in attaining MCC (Carney & Kahn, 1984). Each stage reflects a pattern of growth in knowledge of cultural groups; attitude, awareness, and sensitivity; and specific skills. The ultimate goal in using this model is to promote counselor trainees' development toward Stage 5 functioning, at which point the counselors assume a self-directed activist posture in expanding their knowledge and promoting cultural pluralism.

Multicultural coursework is an area that has been identified as an important component to multicultural counselor education (Carlson et al., 1998; Neville et al., 1996). One source reported an experiential seminar for training in multicultural competence in which counselors access their own cultural map, access their client's cultural map, and develop an understanding of the consonance and dissonance between the experiences of the two cultural maps (Wisnia & Falendar, 1999). Another evaluation reported the effectiveness of a brief 2-day seminar designed to enhance multicultural competence in ethical and assessment issues (Byington, Fischer, Walker, &

Freedman, 1997). The authors contended that even brief training can have significant effects on counselors' multicultural awareness, knowledge, and skills. Sue (2001a, 2001b) asserted that although workshops and continued education in multiculturalism are helpful to counselor education, training programs must provide learning activities outside the classroom as well. He stated that coursework should integrate learning opportunities that allow students to gain firsthand experience with individuals from various cultural backgrounds.

Supervision

Although training and supervision are often considered a common entity, much of the literature overlooks the factors that contribute to multiculturally competent supervision. It has been suggested that many supervisors are not adequately prepared or trained to work with counselor-trainees who differ from them culturally (Ashby & Cheatham, 1996). One study examined the effect of a supervisee's perceptions of supervisory racial interactions, the supervisor's racial identity, and racial matching in the supervisory working alliance and the development of multicultural competence. Results indicated that supervisee-supervisor racial identity interactions were related to the supervisory alliance, and racial identity interactions and racial matchings influenced supervisees' development of multicultural competence (Ladany, Brittan-Powell, & Pannu, 1997). This evidence further implies the need for supervisors to address their own levels of MCC.

Several general guidelines for multiculturally competent counseling supervisors have been delineated. Supervisors should be concerned not only with promoting their supervisee's level of MCC but also with addressing their own level of multicultural supervision competence (D'Andrea & Daniels, 1997). They

should expand their sensitivity and competence in working with individuals who are ethnically and racially different from themselves, and they should solicit feedback from students about the students' perceptions of the supervisors' efforts to facilitate a positive multicultural relationship within the supervision context. Moreover, individuals who conduct multicultural counseling supervision should have a knowledge base about MCC and should take the initiative to assess their own level of MCC. Other guidelines for multiculturally competent counseling supervision include developing an understanding of oneself as a cultural being, educating oneself about various cultural groups, allowing issues between the counselor and supervisor to surface in supervision, learning to use creative supervisory interventions to meet the needs of the counselor, and seeking out supervision and consultation about multicultural counseling supervision (Ashby & Cheatham, 1996).

Assessing MCC

The literature related to assessment of MCC consists of the presentation and analysis of assessment instruments, as well as a variety of concerns related to the use of self-report measures and limitations of current MCC assessment tools.

Instruments

A number of instruments have been designed to measure the multicultural competence of counselors. The Cross-Cultural Counseling Inventory–Revised (CCCI-R) is a 20-item Likert-type instrument that is intended to assess a counselor's effectiveness with clients of various cultural backgrounds (Ponterotto et al., 1994). Developed by LaFromboise, Coleman, and Hernandez (1991), the CCCI-R was the first instrument designed to test multicultural counseling competence (Ponterotto et al., 1994). Another instrument, developed by Ponterotto, Sanchez, and Magids (1991), is intended to measure a counselor's multiscultural knowledge, skills, and awareness. The Multicultural Counseling Awareness Scale–Form B: Revised Self-Assessment (MCAS:B) involves the use of a 7-point Likert-type format in addition to a demographic questionnaire (Ponterotto et al., 1994). A third instrument, the Multicultural Awareness-Knowledge-Skills Survey (MAKSS), was developed by D'Andrea, Daniels, and Heck (1991) to assess the effects of multicultural instruction on students' development of multicultural counseling competence. The MAKSS involves 8 demographic items and 60 survey items measured on a 4-point scale. Each of the 60 survey items is then divided equally into three subscales that assess a counselor's awareness, knowledge, and skills. All of the above instruments were developed based on Sue et al.'s (1982) tripartite conceptualization of MCC as consisting of awareness, knowledge, and skills (Ponterotto et al., 1994).

The Multicultural Counseling Inventory (MCI), a self-report instrument containing 43 statements, is intended to measure multicultural counseling competencies (Ponterotto et al., 1994; Sodowsky et al., 1994). The MCI was developed to operationalize the proposed constructs of MCC (Sodowsky et al., 1994). Although the MCI was also conceptualized from the three major dimensions of MCC, this instrument identifies a fourth factor, multicultural counseling relationships, as being an additional component to MCC (Sodowsky et al., 1994). Next, the Personal Cultural Perspective Profile (PCPP) is a 14-item cultural continuum intended to serve as an educational and training tool (Ramsey, 1995). The PCPP addresses multicultural awareness, knowledge, and skills by breaking the concept of culture into 14 cultural continua that enable counselors to better understand cultural complexity, avoid Eurocentric thinking, and gain the ability to compare cultures.

Assessment Issues

Researchers have cautioned that the self-report format of MCC assessment instruments has limitations (Ponterotto et al., 1994; Pope-Davis & Dings, 1994). Because counselor self-report is a popular form of assessing MCC, the effect of social desirability is an important variable to investigate (Constantine, 2000; Pope-Davis & Dings, 1994; Sodowsky, Kuo-Jackson, Richardson, & Corey, 1998). Using the MAKSS, MCI, MCAS:B, and the CCCI-R, in addition to the Marlowe-Crowne Social Desirability Scale (MCSDS), Constantine and Ladany (2000) found social desirability to be related to self-reports of MCC, particularly in the MCI Relationship subscale, the CCCI-R, and the MAKSS Skill subscale. Another study examined the assessment of MCC through both self-reported and observer-rated MCC. The findings supported the concept that social desirability and self-reported MCC are positively associated (Worthington, Mobley, Franks, & Tan, 2000). Due to the social desirability problem, there is a need for further investigations that compare the relationship between instrument scores and actual behaviors of counselors (Ponterotto et al., 1994). Another concern that has been raised in regard to MCC assessment instruments is content validity. Pope-Davis and Dings (1994) evaluated the MCAS:B and the MCI for content validity and interinstrument correlations of their respective subscales. They found that the two instruments measure different things because items on the MCI are expressed in behavioral terms, whereas the MCAS:B items are expressed in terms of attitudes and beliefs.

Despite the above-mentioned concerns, appropriate uses for MCC assessment instruments include (a) use of the instruments as self-report measures in counseling supervision, which could improve the level of feedback a supervisor is able to give to supervisees regarding behavior toward and beliefs about clients who differ from them culturally; (b) use of the instruments as tools to measure the effectiveness of multicultural training seminars, workshops, and courses; and (c) use of the instruments by researchers to trace the development of counselors' multicultural competence through training (Pope-Davis & Dings, 1994).

Portfolio assessment offers an alternative to self-reported or supervisor-reported instruments to assess MCC (Coleman, 1997). Some educators in the field of counseling have found that portfolio assessment allows them to determine how a trainee's knowledge and skills about a particular topic have changed over time. Portfolios are thought to promote a sense of ownership and self-reflection that assessment instruments do not. By collecting over time information from students that demonstrates their multicultural awareness, knowledge, and skills, a supervisor or educator can determine students' progress in becoming MCC and can make decisions about what type of feedback would be most helpful to their multicultural counseling development.

Specialized Applications of MCC

A number of papers in the literature address applications of MCC to special populations. The arena of managed care is one application to which MCC components have been applied. Corcoran and Vandeline (1996) asserted that for managed care to work effectively for people from all cultural communities, clinicians and organizations must make efforts to identify the local needs and attitudes about mental health services in their individual communities. Abe-Kim and Takeuchi (1996) explored the impact of health care costs on the delivery of mental health services to ethnic minority populations. They considered cultural competence to be a critical aspect of providing appropriate services to ethnic minorities in a managed care setting and contended

that researchers should explore how structures of the managed care system may affect the delivery of services to various ethnic communities.

It is also recommended that clinicians in managed care settings possess the necessary skills to accomplish needed changes in the accessibility of services to various cultural groups (Corcoran & Vandeline, 1996). Recommendations include (a) defining the client's presenting problem and providing outcomes that make sense to the client, (b) developing culturally sensitive diagnostic impressions to reduce misdiagnosis, (c) bearing in mind the organizational structures that may influence a client's trust in service providers, and (d) ensuring affordable and culturally sensitive services.

Another area of specialized application of MCC is children and families. A recent book, titled *Culturally Competent Family Therapy: A General Model*, provides a guide to culturally competent family therapy and is intended to apply to families from all sociocultural backgrounds (Ariel, 1999). The underlying assumption throughout the book is that every family has a culture that is made up of the communities of membership as well as individual cultural components unique to that family. A related book, titled *Developing Cross-Cultural Competence: A Guide to Working With Young Children and Their Families*, is intended to assist professionals who provide educational, social, and health care services to families with young children who are disabled or at risk for disabilities (Lynch & Hanson, 1992). The underlying assumption in this book is that regardless of the role a professional plays, he or she must possess the necessary attitudes and skills that promote effective multicultural relationships with children and their families. Other specialized applications of MCC in the literature include school counseling (Rogers & Ponterotto, 1997), treatment of Chinese Americans (Fang & Wark, 1998; Shiang, Kjellander, Huang, &

Bogumill, 1998), and treatment of individuals with HIV and their families (Ka'opua, 1998).

IMPORTANT ISSUES AND QUESTIONS

Is a Universally Accepted Definition of MCC Necessary?

Despite the extensive literature on MCC, a universal definition of the construct has not been established (Holcomb-McCoy, 2000; Pope-Davis, Reynolds, Dings, & Nielson, 1995). Several scholars have challenged definitions of the construct (e.g., Constantine & Ladany, 2000; Reynolds, 2001; Ridley et al., 2001; Suzuki, McRae, & Short, 2001). For example, Constantine and Ladany (2000) pondered whether the definition of MCC, based on Sue and colleagues' (Sue et al., 1982; Sue et al., 1992) tripartite conceptualization, adequately captures its presumed meaning. In his rejoinder to questions about his most recent conceptualization of cultural competence, D. W. Sue (2001b) acknowledged problems with his definition. However, he declined to attempt a more precise definition, citing sociopolitical and personal reasons for his stance. He did encourage other scholars to wrestle with this challenge.

Certainly there is some disagreement about the utility of having one all-purpose definition of MCC. In various conversations on the topic, some professionals have suggested that there ought to be a variety of definitions. We disagree. We believe that ultimately one definition should emerge as most reflective of the construct. Although we recognize that MCC is a complex concept that cannot be fully understood through a brief definition expressed in a few sentences, we feel strongly that vague and inconsistent use of the term leads to confusion and erroneous assumptions about its meaning in the field. Moreover, the lack of a universal understanding of MCC stands as a barrier to consistent and systematic integration of MCC concepts into counselor training curricula.

However, we also believe that at this stage of conceptualizing the construct, serious scholarship is the most important need. As various definitions emerge and are subjected to constructive criticism, the specialty should be able to move closer to a precise definition.

Is Cultural Matching a Prerequisite for MCC?

Some professionals believe that counselors and clients must come from the same racial or cultural background for counseling to be effective. However, the research on ethnic/cultural matching in counseling is inconclusive. Ethnic minority clients prefer counselors with similar backgrounds (Atkinson & Lowe, 1995). But there is no evidence that matched dyads yield better outcomes than unmatched dyads. In fact, Vera, Speight, Mildner, and Carlson (1999) found that counselor skills and similarity in personality traits are more critical than ethnic background.

We recognize that ethnic similarity can have a bearing on the ability of a counselor to form a therapeutic alliance with a client. However, we also believe that multicultural competence is not dependent simply on cultural matching. Ridley and Udipi (2002) note a couple of problems that can jeopardize counselors' effectiveness in matched dyads. Counselors may overidentify with their clients, causing them to incorrectly attribute the clients' problems to racism and minimize the clients' psychopathology. On the other hand, counselors may deny identification with their clients, resulting in their discounting clients' legitimate reaction to real racism and overpathologizing clients' psychological presentation.

Furthermore, if cultural matching were a prerequisite for MCC, counselors might be placed in an ethical bind in certain situations. Counselors are bound to ethical codes such as duty to do no harm and responsibility to practice only within their area of competence.

Some counselors may encounter situations in which they are not cultural matches to the client and no counselors are accessible to the client who is a cultural match. In these instances, counselors would be forced to choose between the lesser of two evils: practicing outside their area of multicultural competence or refusing services to a client who does not have access to other counseling resources.

Cultural matching, as we demonstrate, has advantages and potential disadvantages. We offer this rule of thumb on the topic: *multicultural competence first and cultural matching second.* First and foremost, counselors need to acquire the competence to counsel clients of other cultures. This criterion takes precedence over cultural matching. However, in some situations, cultural matching is desirable. This may be the case when a client requests a counselor of the same race or when a counselor is needed who speaks the same language as the client.

Is Culture-Specific Knowledge a Prerequisite for MCC?

Many training programs teach about the various ethnic and cultural groups. Major texts on multicultural counseling often have chapters on major minority populations (e.g., Sue & Sue, 1999). These chapters typically describe predominant norms, values, beliefs, and characteristics of individuals from those populations. The discussions are helpful, especially for counselor-trainees who have limited contact with these populations. They also may be helpful to more seasoned professionals who may not be familiar with subtle cultural idioms. Therefore, culture-specific knowledge should be regarded as essential to MCC.

We argue, however, that culture-specific knowledge is a necessary but insufficient condition for MCC. A frequent criticism of culture-specific knowledge is the inability of practitioners to translate the knowledge into meaningful practice. Another criticism is the

tendency of practitioners to rely solely on culture-specific information to stereotype their clients. In their efforts to match their clients against cultural norms, they may fail to treat them as persons with uniqueness and individuality. It bears repeating that "within-group" differences are always greater than "between-group" differences.

We also consider culture-specific knowledge to be a requisite but not necessarily a prerequisite for MCC in practice. Obviously, there are advantages to understanding the client's culture in advance of counseling, but multiculturally competent counselors have the skills to gather relevant culture-specific information during the counseling process, incorporating the information to facilitate therapeutic change.

Is MCC a Realistic Expectation for Most Practitioners?

As society becomes increasingly diverse and intergroup contacts continue to rise, most practitioners are destined to work with clients from other cultures. In addition to providing direct service, professionals teach, supervise trainees, conduct research, administer programs and organizations, and make social policy. Inevitably, professionals will have direct or indirect contact with members of other groups. Therefore, in our opinion, MCC is not a luxury; it is a necessity. In fact, we argue that part of what it means to be competent as a professional is to be multiculturally competent. It is interesting to note that the ethical standards of the American Psychological Association discuss the importance of working competently with clients of various races, cultures, and ethnic groups.

Is MCC Different From Counseling Competence?

The literature about MCC clearly establishes a rationale for the importance of MCC.

However, it remains unclear how MCC can be distinguished from counseling competence. If MCC were a separate entity from counseling competence, this would suggest that all counseling relationships are not multicultural in nature and/or that certain awareness, knowledge, and skills are applied to multicultural relationships but not to nonmulticultural relationships.

Nevertheless, counseling psychology is concerned with change processes in all counseling relationships. It seems that if we had a thorough conceptualization of therapeutic change to guide our practice, the process of change would apply similarly to all clients. For example, the skills required to be a multiculturally competent counselor would include the ability of counselors to gain important cultural knowledge and to integrate cultural knowledge into appropriate interventions to promote therapeutic change. Similarly, counselors in any situation must be able to gain important information about the client and apply that information in a way that is responsive to the client and promotes the change process. Hence, the distinction between counseling competence and MCC seems to be dependent at least in part on the way in which we conceptualize therapeutic change.

We suggest that the distinction between counseling competence and MCC must be clarified to support the rationale for MCC, as well as enable us to better understand the relationship between counseling competence and MCC. We assert that developing a common theory or map of change processes would allow counselors to use skills and interventions more consistently and purposefully to promote therapeutic change across all counseling situations and in ways that are responsive to all clients. Accordingly, a clear conceptualization of change processes would eliminate much of the confusion about the difference between MCC and counseling competence.

CONCLUSION

We have summarized the major historical developments and primary themes in the literature on multicultural counseling competence. The field of counseling psychology has developed a broad conceptualization of MCC and has provided a convincing rationale for the importance of its application. The field also has promoted MCC in the areas of training, supervision, assessment, and counseling practice. Initially, the profession used the original tripartite multicultural competencies—beliefs and attitudes, knowledge, and skills—as a springboard for understanding the concept. Subsequent models of MCC and additional competencies have since emerged.

The discussion of MCC continues to flourish, as demonstrated by numerous recent publications and conferences dedicated to multicultural competence and multicultural competencies. Nevertheless, some important questions still need to be addressed by scholars in this field. A more universal understanding of dimensions, characteristics, and features of MCC would allow practitioners and educators to apply multicultural competencies in a more systematic and consistent way.

Clarity on important issues such as cultural matching and cultural knowledge would enable counselors in training and practice to more easily identify their areas of competence and more clearly identify potential ethical problems involved in multicultural counseling. Finally, it will be important to distinguish between the features of MCC and those of counseling competence. This distinction should give further support for MCC and clarify the specific skills involved in multiculturally competent counseling practice. We recommend that future scholarship in this area work toward developing a more universal understanding of MCC by addressing the issues and questions raised in this chapter.

REFERENCES

Abe-Kim, J., & Takeuchi, D. T. (1996). Cultural competence and quality of care: Issues for mental health service delivery in managed care. *Clinical Psychology: Science and Practice, 3*, 273-295.

Allison, K. W., Echemendia, R. J., Crawford, I., & Robinson, W. L. (1996). Predicting cultural competence: Implications for practice and training. *Professional Psychology: Research and Practice, 27*, 386-393.

American Psychological Association (APA). (1999). From the vice presidents: Diversity and public interest. *American Psychological Association Division of Counseling Psychology Newsletter, 20*(2), 3-5.

Ariel, S. (1999). *Culturally competent family therapy: A general model.* Westport, CT: Praeger.

Arredondo, P., Toporek, R., Brown, S. P., Sanchez, J., & Stadler, H. (1996). Operationalization of the multicultural counseling competencies. *Journal of Multicultural Counseling and Development, 24, 42-78.*

Ashby, J. S., & Cheatham, H. E. (1996). Multicultural counseling and supervision. In J. L. DeLucia-Waack (Ed.), *Multicultural counseling competencies: Implications for training and practice* (pp. 47-59). Alexandria, VA: Association for Counselor Education and Supervision.

Atkinson, D. R., & Lowe, S. M. (1995). The role of ethnicity, cultural knowledge, and conventional techniques in counseling and therapy. In J. G. Ponterotto, J. M. Casas, L. A. Suzuki, & C. M. Alexander (Eds.), *Handbook of multicultural counseling* (pp. 387-414). Thousand Oaks, CA: Sage.

Beckett, J. O., Dungee-Anderson, D., Cox, L., & Daly, A. (1997). African Americans and multicultural interventions. *Smith College Studies in Social Work, 67*(3), 540-563.

Byington, K., Fischer, J., Walker, L., & Freedman, E. (1997). Evaluating the effectiveness of a multicultural counseling ethics and assessment training. *Journal of Applied Rehabilitation Counseling, 28*(4), 15-19.

Campinha-Bacote, J. (1994). *The process of cultural competence health care: A culturally competent model of care* (2nd ed.). Cincinnati, OH: Transcultural C.A.R.E. Associates.

Carlson, M. H., Brack, C. J., Laygo, R., Cohen, R., & Kirkscey, M. (1998). An exploratory study of multicultural competence of counselors in training: Support for experiential skills building. *Clinical Supervisor, 12*(2), 75-87.

Carney, C. G., & Kahn, K. B. (1984). Building competencies for effective cross-cultural counseling: A developmental view. *The Counseling Psychologist, 12*, 111-119.

Castro, F. G. (1998). Cultural competence training in clinical psychology: Assessment, clinical intervention, and research. In C. D. Belar (Ed.), *Comprehensive clinical psychology: Vol. 10. Sociocultural and individual differences* (pp. 127-140). Oxford, UK: Pergamon/Elsevier Science.

Coleman, H. L. K. (1997). Portfolio assessment of multicultural counseling competence. In D. B. Pope-Davis & H. L. K. Coleman (Eds.), *Multicultural counseling competencies: Assessment, education and training, and supervision* (pp. 43-59). Thousand Oaks, CA: Sage.

Constantine, M. G. (2000). Social desirability attitudes, sex, and affective and cognitive empathy as predictors of self-reported multicultural counseling competence. *The Counseling Psychologist, 28*, 857-872.

Constantine, M. G., & Ladany, N. (2000). Self-report multicultural counseling competence scales: Their relation to social desirability attitudes and multicultural case conceptualization ability. *Journal of Counseling Psychology, 47*(2), 155-164.

Constantine, M. G., & Ladany, N. (2001). New visions for defining and assessing multicultural counseling competence. In J. G. Ponterotto, J. M. Casas, L. A. Suzuki, & C. M. Alexander (Eds.), *Handbook of multicultural counseling* (2nd ed., pp. 482-498). Thousand Oaks, CA: Sage.

Corcoran, K., & Vandeline, V. (1996). *Maneuvering the maze of managed care: Skills for mental health practitioners.* New York: Free Press.

D'Andrea, M., & Daniels, J. (1997). Multicultural counseling supervision: Central issues, theoretical

considerations, and practical strategies. In
D. B. Pope-Davis & H. L. K. Coleman (Eds.),
*Multicultural counseling competencies:
Assessment, education and training, and
supervision* (pp. 290-309). Thousand Oaks,
CA: Sage.

D'Andrea, M., Daniels, J., & Heck, R. (1991).
Evaluating the impact of multicultural coun-
seling training. *Journal of Counseling and
Development, 70*(1), 143-150.

DeLucia-Waack, J. L. (1996). An introduction
to multicultural counseling competencies:
Implications for training and practice. In J. L.
DeLucia-Waack (Ed.), *Multicultural counsel-
ing competencies: Implications for training
and practice* (pp. 1-3). Alexandria, VA:
Association for Counselor Education and
Supervision.

Fang, S. R. S., & Wark, L. (1998). Developing cross-
cultural competence with traditional Chinese
Americans in family therapy: Background information and the initial therapeutic contact.
*Contemporary Family Therapy: An Inter-
national Journal, 20*(1), 59-77.

Garfield, S. L. (1986). Research on client variables
in psychotherapy. In S. L. Garfield & A. E.
Bergen (Eds.), *Handbook of psychotherapy
and behavior change* (3rd ed., pp. 213-256).
New York: John Wiley.

Holcomb-McCoy, C. C. (2000). Multicultural
counseling competencies: An exploratory
factor analysis. *Journal of Multicultural
Counseling and Development, 28*, 83-97.

Holcomb-McCoy, C. C., & Myers, J. E. (1999).
Multicultural competence and counselor training: A national survey. *Journal of Counseling
and Development, 77*(3), 294-302.

Hubble, M. A., Duncan, B. L., & Miller, S. D.
(1999). Directing attention to what works. In
M. A. Hubble, B. L. Duncan, & S. D. Miller
(Eds.), *The heart and soul of change: What
works in therapy* (pp. 407-447). Washington,
DC: American Psychological Association.

Imber-Black, E. (1997). Developing cultural competence: Contributions from recent family
therapy literature. *American Journal of
Psychotherapy, 51*, 607-610.

Isaacs, M. R., & Benjamin, M. P. (1991). *Towards
a culturally competent system of care: Vol. 2.
Programs which utilize culturally competent
principles.* Washington, DC: CASSP Technical
Assistant Center.

Ka'opua, L. S. (1998). Multicultural competence.
In D. M. Aronstein & B. J. Thompson (Eds.),
HIV and social work: A practitioner's guide
(pp. 51-64). New York: Harrington
Park/Haworth.

Korman, M. (1974). National conference on levels
and patterns of professional training in psychology: Major themes. *American Psychologist, 29*, 301-313.

Ladany, N., Brittan-Powell, C. S., & Pannu, R. K.
(1997). The influence of supervisory racial
identity interaction and racial matching on
the supervisory working alliance and supervisee multicultural competence. *Counselor
Education and Supervision, 36*(4), 284-304.

LaFromboise, T. D., Coleman, H. L. K., &
Hernandez, A. (1991). Development and
factor structure of the Cross-Cultural Counseling Inventory—Revised. *Professional
Psychology: Research and Practice, 22*,
380-388.

López, S. R. (1997). Cultural competence in psychotherapy: A guide for clinicians and their
supervisors. In C. E. Watkins Jr. (Ed.),
Handbook of psychotherapy supervision
(pp. 570-588). New York: John Wiley.

Lynch, E. W., & Hanson, M. J. (1992). Steps in
the right direction: Implications for interventions. In E. W. Lynch & M. J. Hanson (Eds.),
*Developing cross-cultural competence: A
guide for working with young children and
their families* (pp. 355-370). Baltimore:
Brookes.

McRae, M. B., & Johnson, S. D. (1991). Toward
training for competence in multicultural
counselor education. *Journal of Counseling
and Development, 70*(1), 131-135.

Neville, H. A., Heppner, M. J., Thompson, C. E.,
Brooks, L., & Baker, C. E. (1996). The
impact of multicultural training on White
racial identity attitudes and therapy competencies. *Professional Psychology: Research
and Practice, 27*, 83-89.

Ottavi, T. M., Pope-Davis, D. B., & Dings, J. G.
(1994). Relationship between White racial
identity attitudes and self-reported multicultural

counseling competencies. *Journal of Counseling Psychology, 41,* 149-154.

Ponterotto, J. G., Alexander, C. M., & Grieger, I. (1995). A multicultural competency checklist for counseling training programs. *Journal of Multicultural Counseling and Development, 23,* 11-20.

Ponterotto, J. G., & Casas, J. M. (1987). In search of multicultural competence within counselor education programs. *Journal of Counseling and Development, 65*(8), 430-434.

Ponterotto, J. G., Rieger, B. P., Barrett, A., & Sparks, R. (1994). Assessing multicultural counseling competence: A review of instrumentation. *Journal of Counseling and Development, 72*(3), 316-322.

Ponterotto, J. G., Sanchez, C. M., & Magids, D. (1991, August). *Initial development of the Multicultural Counseling Awareness Scale.* Paper presented at the annual meeting of the American Psychological Association, San Francisco.

Pope-Davis, D. B., & Coleman, H. L. K. (Eds.). (1997). *Multicultural counseling competencies: Assessment, education and training, and supervision.* Thousand Oaks, CA: Sage.

Pope-Davis, D. B., & Dings, J. G. (1994). An empirical comparison of two self-report multicultural counseling competency inventories. *Measurement and Evaluation in Counseling and Development, 27*(2), 93-102.

Pope-Davis, D. B., & Dings, J. G. (1995). The assessment of multicultural counseling competencies. In J. G. Ponterotto, J. M. Casas, L. A. Suzuki, & C. M. Alexander (Eds.), *Handbook of multicultural counseling* (pp. 287-311). Thousand Oaks, CA: Sage.

Pope-Davis, D. B., Reynolds, A. L., Dings, J. G., & Nielson, D. (1995). Examining multicultural counseling competencies of graduate students in psychology. *Professional Psychology: Research and Practice, 26,* 322-329.

Ramsey, M. (1995). Use of a Personal Cultural Perspective Profile (PCPP) in developing counselor multicultural competence. *International Journal for the Advancement of Counseling, 17*(4), 283-290.

Reynolds, A. L. (2001). Multidimensional cultural competence: Providing tools for transforming

psychology. *The Counseling Psychologist, 29*(6), 833-841.

Richardson, T. Q., & Molinaro, K. L. (1996). White counselor self-awareness: A prerequisite for multicultural competence. *Journal of Counseling and Development, 74*(3), 238-242.

Ridley, C. R., Baker, D. M., & Hill, C. L. (2001). Critical issues concerning cultural competence. *The Counseling Psychologist, 29*(6), 822-832.

Ridley, C. R., & Lingle, D. W. (1996). Cultural empathy in multicultural counseling: A multidimensional process model. In P. B. Pedersen, J. G. Draguns, W. J. Lonner, & J. E. Trimble (Eds.), *Counseling across cultures* (4th ed., pp. 21-46). Thousand Oaks, CA: Sage.

Ridley, C. R., & Udipi, S. (2002). Putting cultural empathy into practice. In P. B. Pedersen, J. G. Draguns, W. J. Lonner, & J. E. Trimble (Eds.), *Counseling across cultures* (5th ed., pp. 317-333). Thousand Oaks, CA: Sage.

Rogers, M. R., & Ponterotto, J. G. (1997). Development of the multicultural school psychology counseling competency scale. *Psychology in the Schools, 34*(3), 211-217.

Salzman, M. (2000). Promoting multicultural competence: A cross cultural mentorship project. *Journal of Multicultural Counseling and Development, 28*(2), 119-124.

Shiang, J., Kjellander, C., Huang, K., & Bogumill, S. (1998). Developing cultural competency in clinical practice: Treatment considerations for Chinese cultural groups in the United States. *Clinical Psychology: Science and Practice, 5,* 182-210.

Silva-Netto, B. R. (1994). Cultural symbols and images in the counseling process. *Pastoral Psychology, 42*(4), 277-284.

Sodowsky, G. R., Kuo-Jackson, P. Y., Richardson, M. F., & Corey, A. T. (1998). Correlates of self-reported multicultural competencies, counselor multicultural social desirability, race, social inadequacy, locus of control, racial ideology, and multicultural training. *Journal of Counseling Psychology, 45,* 256-264.

Sodowsky, G. R., Taffe, R. C., Gutkin, T. B., & Wise, S. L. (1994). Development of the Multicultural Counseling Inventory: A self-report measure of multicultural competencies.

Journal of Counseling Psychology, 41, 137-148.

Steward, R. J., Wright, D. J., Jackson, J. D., & Jo, H. I. (1998). The relationship between multicultural counseling training and the evaluation of culturally sensitive and culturally insensitive counselors. *Journal of Multicultural Counseling and Development, 25*(3), 205-217.

Sue, D. W. (2001a). Multidimensional facets of cultural competence. *The Counseling Psychologist, 29*(6), 790-821.

Sue, D. W. (2001b). The superordinate nature of cultural competence. *The Counseling Psychologist, 29*(6), 850-857.

Sue, D. W., Arredondo, P., & McDavis, R. J. (1992). Multicultural counseling competencies and standards: A call to the profession. *Journal of Counseling and Development, 70,* 477-486.

Sue, D. W., Bernier, J. E., Durran, A., Feinberg, L., Pedersen, P., Smith, E. J., et al. (1982). Position paper: Cross-cultural counseling competencies. *The Counseling Psychologist, 10,* 45-52.

Sue, D. W., Carter, R. T., Casas, J. M., Fouad, N. A., Ivey, A. E., Jensen, M., et al. (1998). *Multicultural counseling competencies: Individual and organizational development.* Thousand Oaks, CA: Sage.

Sue, D. W., & Sue, D. (1977). Barriers to effective cross-cultural counseling. *Journal of Counseling Psychology, 24,* 420-429.

Sue, D. W., & Sue, D. (1999). *Counseling the culturally different* (3rd ed.). New York: John Wiley.

Sue, S. (1998). In search of cultural competence in psychotherapy and counseling. *American Psychologist, 53,* 440-448.

Suzuki, L. A., McRae, M. B., & Short, E. L. (2001). The facets of cultural competence: Searching outside the box. *The Counseling Psychologist, 29*(6), 842-849.

Tomlinson-Clarke, S., & Wang, V. O. (1999). A paradigm for racial-cultural training in the development of counselor cultural competencies. In M. S. Kiselica (Ed.), *Confronting prejudice and racism during multicultural training* (pp. 155-167). Alexandria, VA: American Counseling Association.

Tracey, T. J., & Ray, P. B. (1984). Stages of successful time-limited counseling: An interactional examination. *Journal of Counseling Psychology, 31,* 13-27.

Vera, E. M., Speight, S. L., Mildner, C., & Carlson, H. (1999). Clients' perceptions and evaluations of similarities to and differences from their counselors. *Journal of Counseling Psychology, 46*(2), 277-283.

Wisnia, C. S., & Falender, C. (1999). Training in cultural competency. *Association of Psychology Postdoctoral and Internship Centers Newsletter, 24*(1), 12.

Worthington, R. L., Mobley, M., Franks, R. P., & Tan, J. A. (2000). Multicultural counseling competencies: Verbal content, counselor attributions, and social desirability. *Journal of Counseling Psychology, 47,* 460-468.

2

Models of Multicultural Counseling Competence

A Critical Evaluation

DEBRA MOLLEN
CHARLES R. RIDLEY
CARRIE L. HILL

Indiana University

 ulticultural counseling competence has taken its place among the most important constructs in applied psychology. Researchers, scholars, and practitioners no longer debate the necessity and significance of having this type of competence. Instead, they now assume it. Numerous publications and conference presentations concerned with training, practice, and the development of models underscore the importance of the construct.

The development of models of multicultural competence reflects the advance of scholarship in this specialty. A number of models have been developed, and we are prompted to revisit them in an effort to critically evaluate their merits and shortcomings. In this chapter,

we analyze two major models, eight secondary models, and four implicit models of multicultural counseling competence. Although other models exist, we have chosen a cross section of models that we believe is representative of the field. We distinguish major models from secondary models in that the former are much more elaborate than the latter, and they exert more influence on the field. In addition, we examine models that are not explicitly identified as models of multicultural competence but have implicit assumptions about multicultural competence.

We realized the need for some criteria on which to base our critique. Therefore, we asked ourselves the following questions: What are the critical factors that we use to gauge models' effectiveness? Although empirical validation would certainly provide support for authors' claims, the models we have chosen are relatively new and have not, to the best of our knowledge, been submitted to comprehensive testing. Although empirically validated models are of significant value to the field, at this nascent stage in their development, we must examine models critically using other available criteria. It is our intention to offer such a critique and further stimulate the discussion surrounding multicultural counseling competence.

This chapter is organized into four major sections. In the first section, we describe our criteria for evaluating the major models. In the second section, we describe and critique two major models. In the third section, we describe eight minor models, followed by general critique. In the fourth section, we discuss and critique implicit models. Finally, we offer implications for further research, scholarship, and practice.

CRITERIA FOR EVALUATING MAJOR MODELS

We examined current literature in hopes of finding predetermined criteria for evaluating the effectiveness of models such as the ones we discuss in this chapter. Because no clear, cogent criteria were identified, we decided to establish our own criteria, based on the questions we generated at the outset of the writing of this chapter. The questions we were prompted to ask were as follows: What are the salient features that help determine models' effectiveness? How do the models further stimulate the conversation among researchers, scholars, and practitioners? How do these new models improve on existing models? Here are our six criteria.

1. *A model is characterized by clarity and coherence.* Good models offer sound rationales

for their development and elucidate each facet systematically. In addition, for multidimensional models, clear explanations are given for the relationships between and among parts. For ambiguous terms and phrases, explicit definitions are offered and operationalized as much as possible. This criterion has a dual purpose. First, it lends itself to developing consensus in the field and reduces vagueness. Second, by eradicating multiple, imprecise, and evasive definitions, it can advance discourse.

2. *A model is descriptive as well as prescriptive.* Beyond merely delineating their critical components, effective models—particularly in an applied discipline such as counseling psychology—offer plausible channels for translating theory into action. Ample space should be devoted to making links between the theoretical tenets of the model and the model-in-action, whether intended to inform practice, training, or research or, ideally, all three. For models that aim to inform practice, for example, explicit case examples can be presented so that readers can recognize their clinical utility.

3. *A model makes a unique contribution.* Innovative models may build on previous research, but they need to demonstrate both a rationale for and an explanation of the ways in which they benefit the field. This can be accomplished by acknowledging progress to date, including specific scholars' contributions, and by offering a thorough evaluation of areas needing improvement. Only when discussion is advanced will substantial progress ensue.

4. *A model includes critical facets.* Effective models include those facets widely agreed on by previous researchers and scholars to be essential for the construct they depict. Although models may offer unique vantage points, expanded utility, or certain variations,

they should retain those components deemed most essential by authorities in the field.

5. *A model can be validated.* Validation can be done by using quantitative and/or qualitative methods. It is understood that new models may or may not be based on previous research. However, they are subject to revision as new findings emerge, feedback is offered, and the field continues to advance. Therefore, effective models lend themselves to empirical validation and support by offering testable hypotheses.

6. *A model strikes a balance between simplicity and complexity.* Admittedly, this is a fine line but an important one in any case. Constructs such as multicultural competence should not be oversimplified in the literature. Oversimplification detracts from the operationalization that the field demands. Conversely, the model should not be overly complex. Overcomplexity creates more confusion than clarity.

MAJOR MODELS

Tripartite Model of Multicultural Counseling Competencies

Description of the Model

Landmark works by Sue and colleagues (Sue, Arrendondo, & McDavis, 1992; Sue et al., 1982) are among the most often cited and most frequently discussed by counseling psychologists. In addition to prompting the profession to visit and revisit issues concerning culture as it intersects with therapy, Sue and colleagues' model has been the subject of a great deal of empirical research and scholarly discourse. Both the 1982 and 1992 articles follow a similar format. Each documents problems inherent in using traditional counseling models with racial and ethnic minority groups. Both acknowledge the inclusivity-exclusivity debate with regard to culture, and both favor focusing solely on ethnicity and race to the exclusion of other variables such as gender,

religion, socioeconomic status, sexual orientation, and so on. After laying the groundwork for the need for a new approach to counseling psychology—one that acknowledges the limitations of denying and/or pathologizing culture and seeks to advance the discourse on cultural competence—Sue and his colleagues addressed the arduous task of delineating initial skills, competencies, and objectives that would characterize "culturally skilled" (Sue et al., 1982, p. 49) counseling psychologists.

Sue and his colleagues' works rest on a tripartite framework designed to explain what is meant by *multiculturally competent practice* (Sue et al., 1982; Sue et al., 1992). The components of this framework are knowledge, skills, and beliefs and attitudes. In the 1992 article, the heart of the tripartite model remained, although it was expanded to emphasize the importance of counselor awareness as well. In addition, although the earlier article delineated four critical beliefs and attitudes, four types of "knowledge," and three skills, the latter article devised three major focal points for "proposed cross-cultural competencies and objectives" (Sue et al., 1992, p. 484). The three major focal points included counselor awareness of own cultural values and biases, counselor awareness of client's worldview, and culturally appropriate intervention strategies. Each major focal point was then subdivided into the requisite attitudes and beliefs, knowledge, and skills, reflecting the authors' belief that each was a component of the larger focal point.

Critique of the Model

The following comments analyze the tripartite model in terms of the six criteria presented above.

1. *Characterized by clarity and coherence.* Both of Sue's early works (Sue et al., 1982; Sue et al., 1992) in this area are to be credited for their sound development of the need for new

pathways, not only in the specialty of counseling psychology but also across the many specialties that compose the American Psychological Association. Drawing on then-current and projected demographics as well as historical relevancies, Sue and his colleagues persuasively laid the groundwork for what has arguably become among the most critical features of applied psychology today.

This model, however, though developed with sound rationale, does not always achieve comprehensibility with regard to definitions, clarification of terms, and elucidation of related components. Words and phrases such as *culturally skilled, culturally competent,* and *cultural competency* are used interchangeably. Such definitional ambiguities obfuscate the main purpose of this model: to give researchers and practitioners a guideline for understanding what it means to be culturally competent. For example, an important dimension of multicultural competence is stated as, "Culturally skilled counselors are able to recognize the limits of their competencies and expertise" (Sue et al., 1992, p. 482). The problem with this sort of statement is that it raises more questions than it answers. Is *culturally skilled* synonymous with *culturally competent?* It certainly seems that way from the design of the article. If so, conundrum results when one realizes that *competent* counselors recognize the limits of their *competencies.* Neither term has been sufficiently operationalized, and readers are apt to be puzzled. Furthermore, the word *expertise* is introduced without discussion, prompting us to ask, What is the relationship between competence and expertise? Are they distinct constructs, or do they fall along a continuum?

2. *Descriptive as well as prescriptive.* The tripartite model of cultural competence offers some description in its inventory of stated objectives. The concepts of knowledge, skills, and attitudes and beliefs are given moderate

attention so that readers can glean the basic structure of the authors' intentions. Although the intended objectives are aspirational, the model is limited by the lack of prescription. In some ways, the objectives are like the APA Ethics Code (APA, 1992), which has been critiqued elsewhere for failure to offer clearer guidelines and structure to the profession (Ridley, Hill, & Wiese, 2001). Using the previous example, "Culturally skilled counselors are able to recognize the limits of their competencies and expertise," we can illustrate the limitations of using description to the neglect of prescription. From the standpoint of translating theory into action, we are prompted to ask, How do culturally skilled counselors recognize the limits of their competencies and expertise? What underlying mechanisms need to be developed and strengthened so that counselors are aware of their limitations? Most important, what course of action do counselors take once they have gained this type of awareness? Failing to answer these questions by more extensive model development exalts description into aspiration with insufficient guidance for the counseling psychologist.

3. *Makes a unique contribution.* Undoubtedly, Sue and his colleagues stimulated a great deal of discussion and brought about significant change. Since the 1982 article appeared, there has been a surge of related publications, presentations, monographs, and books. In addition, issues of multicultural competence have begun to be infused in training programs and are more widely reflected in the APA Ethics Code (1992) than they had been previously. The model is to be credited for fulfilling a longstanding need in applied psychology.

4. *Includes critical facets.* The 1982/1992 model focuses exclusively on beliefs and attitudes, skills, and knowledge, which have been subsequently equated with multicultural

counseling competence. As Constantine and Ladany (2000) persuasively asserted, "This historical definition has gone virtually unchallenged by multicultural scholars and practitioners in counseling psychology" (p. 162). In fact, several researchers and scholars have elucidated additional features thought to be crucial for achieving competence, such as the importance of the therapeutic relationship (Sodowsky, Taffe, Gutkin, & Wise, 1994) and racial identity development (Holcomb-McCoy & Myers, 1999). However, these features remain conspicuously absent from the model.

Furthermore, although Sue and colleagues have taken great pains to explain their decision to focus solely on visibly recognizable ethnic minorities (e.g., Sue et al., 1982), we question the validity of this decision. Indeed, for some individuals who are members of the four identified groups—African American, Asian American, Latino/Hispanic, and Native American—other salient parts of their identity such as religion or gender may be at least as critical as ethnicity (Ridley, Baker, & Hill, 2001). Some individuals for whom ethnicity is the most salient feature may not fall neatly into one of the four designated ethnic categories. Some may be biracial or multiracial. Others may be members of ethnic minority groups that do not identify with one of the four categories, yet they may have experienced discrimination and prejudice.

5. *Able to be validated via quantitative and/or qualitative research.* Sue and colleagues' model has been subjected to a wide degree of empirical testing, some of which has lent considerable support for Sue's early works (see, e.g., Ponterotto, Fuertes, & Chen, 2000, for a review). Several instruments based on the original tripartite conceptualization of competence have been devised and studied, and credit should be given for the extensive research on the model. Despite this, several concerns linger about the adequacy of the instruments based

on the tripartite model to fully capture the most salient features of competence. Constantine and Ladany (2000), for example, uncovered a social desirability confound that sheds doubt on the effectiveness of paper-and-pencil self-report methods that have been widely espoused in the literature. In addition, the use of other methods such as grounded theory or consensual qualitative design is sorely needed to more thoroughly assess multicultural counseling competence (Ponterotto et al., 2000).

6. *Strikes a balance between simplicity and complexity.* Wood and Power (1987) persuasively argued that competence involves more than just the aggregate of knowledge and skills. They theorized that a more comprehensive approach to competence is needed—one that rests on an "integrated deep structure" (p. 414). Along similar lines, Lester (2000) traced the rise of the tripartite model to the trend toward positivistic science in the 19th century and found it inadequate to fully represent what it means to be competent.

Discussions in applied psychology call into question the simplicity of the tripartite model approach. Pope and Brown (1996) differentiated between two kinds of competence needed in professional practice: (a) intellectual competence, comprising not only knowledge and ability but also awareness of one's limitations, and (b) emotional competence, consisting of managing sensitive clinical material, managing personal biases, and adhering to self-care. Welfel (1998) commented on the need to consider facets such as diligence and managing burnout when considering competence. In regards to multicultural counseling competence, Sodowsky et al. (1994) identified the importance of the therapeutic relationship as an additional factor. We question Sue and his colleagues' (Sue et al., 1982; Sue et al., 1992) decision to ignore other sources on this topic. Furthermore, we agree with the proposition that the tripartite model, although providing some use in beginning the conversation on competence, may in fact oversimplify the construct to a problematic degree.

Multidimensional Model for Developing Cultural Competence

Description of the Model

D. W. Sue (2001) developed this model in response to a number of issues he felt hindered the incorporation of cultural competence in psychology: (a) a belief in the universality of psychological axioms and theories, (b) the invisibility of monoculturalism in psychological practice, (c) differences in defining cultural competence, and (d) lack of a conceptual framework to organize the multifaceted dimensions of cultural competence.

In an attempt to weave social justice attributes into the discussion, Sue (2001) proposed a new definition of cultural competence:

> Cultural competence is the ability to engage in actions or create conditions that maximize the optimal development of client and client systems. Multicultural counseling competence is defined as the counselor's acquisition of awareness, knowledge, and skills needed to function effectively in a pluralistic democratic society (ability to communicate, interact, negotiate, and intervene on behalf of clients from diverse backgrounds), and on an organizational/societal level, advocating effectively to develop new theories, practices, policies and organizational structures that are more responsive to all groups. (p. 802)

His model consists of three primary dimensions. First, the *components* of cultural competence include awareness, knowledge, and skills. These components are essentially the same as the components of the tripartite model described above. Second, the *foci* of cultural competence include individual, professional,

organizational, and societal levels of intervention. Third, the *racial and culture-specific attributes* of cultural competence pertain to five race-based target groups of intervention: African American, Asian American, Latino/Hispanic American, Native American, and European American. These groups are described against a backdrop of universal, group, and individual levels of personal identity. Sue (2001) described cultural competence as the multifactorial combination and interaction of these three dimensions (see Figure 2.1 for a depiction of Sue's model).

Critique of the Model

1. *Characterized by clarity and coherence.* Sue (2001) fails to develop a strong rationale for his new model in that he neglects to discuss or critique other models related to cultural competence. Although other models might fall short of sufficiently capturing the construct's dimensions, several have been proposed and discussed in the literature (see Ponterotto et al., 2000, for a review). A cogent review and critique of the strengths and limitations of extant models would have helped lay the foundation for the establishment of the new model. Instead, Sue offers no basis for determining why this model is needed or how it is better than existing models. In addition, although Sue is to be applauded for defining cultural competence—an achievement absent from most other models—there are problems with his definition. He creates confusion by equating the phrases *cultural competence* and *multicultural counseling competence*. It is unclear whether cultural competence and multicultural counseling competence are identical or different constructs. Also, Sue's definition is circular in that he uses phrases to define competence that are nearly synonymous with it (e.g., "function effectively" and "advocating effectively"). It is difficult to gain added meaning and significance from the use of these phrases.

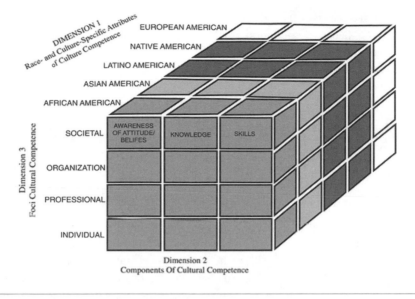

Figure 2.1   A Multidimensional Model for Developing Cultural Competence

2. *Descriptive as well as prescriptive.* Sue's (2001) model is descriptive but not prescriptive. It is descriptive because it depicts a sorely needed, broad representation of cultural competence in psychology. However, although the model portrays several dimensions of cultural competence, it really does not illustrate how these dimensions interact or operate as an aggregate construct. Hence, it is difficult to extract from it clear guidelines about how to execute the model to reflect cultural competence in everyday professional activities.

3. *Makes a unique contribution.* The advances in Sue's (2001) model indicate that he continues to build on the legacy of the landmark publications (Sue et al., 1982; Sue et al., 1992) and ensuing works that he and his colleagues have authored (Sue et al., 1998; Sue, Bingham, Porche-Burke, & Vasquez, 1999; Sue & Sue, 1999). He has made a unique contribution by proposing additional dimensions to the original tripartite model of multicultural competence.

4. *Includes critical facets.* In addition to the tripartite conceptualization of awareness,

knowledge, and skills, Sue's (2001) interpretation of cultural competence includes the issue of social justice. We applaud this interpretation because it reminds us that psychology can and should advance the public interest. In addition, Sue's inclusion of a framework for conceptualizing personal identity is holistic and has the potential for enabling practitioners to integrate all three levels of personal identity—individual, group, and universal—in assessment and case conceptualization. However, there are limitations to Sue's choice to focus his model on a race-based group perspective. The historical neglect of group identity is not itself an adequate rationale for an exclusively race-based model of cultural competence. The development of a comprehensive model in any discipline should be based on the consideration of all the relevant variables, not simply those of interest to the author. In addition, people do not always fit neatly into one of the five race-based groups in Sue's model. It is unclear how the model should be used when the individual, organization, or society of interest spans more than one of the five race-based groups.

5. *Able to be validated via quantitative and/or qualitative research.* Because this model is new, it has not yet been subjected to scientific scrutiny. It appears that the model would best be explored, at least initially, through qualitative methods to describe fully how the components of cultural competence are manifested among different target groups at different levels of intervention. Quantitative studies could then examine the model in more detail.

6. *Strikes a balance between simplicity and complexity.* Sue (2001) is helpful in describing three dimensions of cultural competence and specific aspects of each dimension. Although we would conceptualize the primary dimensions of cultural competence differently, Sue moves the profession in a positive direction. The movement reflects scientist-practitioner principles because of its purposeful simplification. However, as we mentioned in the context of his other model (Sue et al., 1982; Sue et al., 1992), he has moved too far toward simplicity, resulting in the oversimplification of a complex construct. Most professionals would probably find his discussion of the three dimensions of the model too general to use beneficially.

SECONDARY MODELS

A number of secondary models of cultural competence have appeared in the literature. We identify these as secondary models for two reasons: They are far less elaborate than the major models, and they exert less influence in the field. We describe eight of these models, followed by an overall critique of the models.

Carney and Kahn's (1984) Counselor Development Model

The earliest of these secondary models is Carney and Kahn's (1984) five-stage developmental model. Drawing on the work of other scholars as well as their own observations,

these authors claim that cross-cultural change agents acquire their competencies by passage through their identified stages. Each stage has a pattern of growth in three areas: (a) knowledge of cultural groups, (b) attitudinal awareness and cross-cultural sensitivity, and (c) specific cross-cultural counseling skills. In addition, the authors' discussion of each stage is divided into two parts: counselor characteristics and appropriate training environment (which points out the learning tasks for trainees at each stage).

In Stage 1, trainees have a limited knowledge of other cultural groups, and they may harbor ethnocentric attitudes. The learning task for trainees is to recognize the extent to which they may be relying on faulty treatment strategies and goals. In Stage 2, trainees begin to recognize their ethnocentric attitudes and behaviors. The learning tasks for trainees are to develop knowledge of the norms, values, and customs of other cultural groups and also to recognize how ethnocentrism would affect their counseling practice. In Stage 3, trainees may experience internal conflicts derived from feelings of guilt and personal responsibility. The learning task for trainees is self-exploration and resolution of dissonance. In Stage 4, trainees begin to develop self-identity as a cross-cultural change agent. The learning task for trainees is to become autonomous decision makers regarding their personal and professional identities. In Stage 5, trainees assume an activist posture, promoting social equity and protecting cultural pluralism. The learning tasks for trainees are to clarify their commitment and to establish action strategies.

Bennett's (1993) Developmental Model

Bennett (1993) proposed a six-stage developmental model, moving from "ethnocentrism" to "ethnorelativism." The three stages of ethnocentrism are denial, defense, and minimization. The three stages of ethnorelativism are acceptance, adoption, and integration. An individual in the denial stage does not accept cultural differences. An individual in the defense stage acknowledges certain cultural differences but constructs defenses against those differences. An individual in the minimization stage acknowledges cultural differences but trivializes them. An individual in the acceptance stage recognizes and values cultural differences. An individual in the adoption stage develops and improves skills necessary for interacting and communicating with people of different cultures. An individual in the integration stage does more than value other cultures: Such individuals define their own identity and integrate their own cultural perspectives with those of other cultures.

Campenha-Bacote's (1994) Culturally Competent Model of Health Care

Campenha-Bacote (1994) developed the culturally competent model of health care. According to the author, cultural competence is a process that consists of culturally responsive assessments and culturally relevant interventions. The model has four components: cultural awareness, cultural knowledge, cultural skills, and cultural encounters. Cultural awareness is the process of sensitizing oneself to the worldviews of clients from other cultures. The process is deliberate and cognitive, beginning with professionals examining their own prejudices and biases and recognizing how these affect cross-cultural interactions. Cultural knowledge is the process of obtaining information about the illness belief systems and worldviews of other cultures; Campenha-Bacote identified a variety of academic and training experiences by which this knowledge can be obtained. Cultural skill is the process of conducting a cultural assessment; an important benefit of this skill is the avoidance of stereotypical judgments. Cultural encounter is the process of directly engaging in interactions

with diverse cultural groups, enabling health care providers to validate, negate, or modify their cultural perspectives. Campenha-Bacote believes that health care appropriateness in each of these domains can yield culturally responsive services.

Beckett and Colleagues' (1997) Multicultural Communication Process Model

Writing in a social work journal, Beckett, Dungee-Anderson, Cox, and Daly (1997) developed the multicultural communication process model (MCCPM). The authors state that the model defines a two-tiered process for intervention with African American clients. In the first tier, practitioners use the model to guide their individual study and growth in multicultural knowledge. In the second tier, they use the model directly to intervene with a client or indirectly through supervision.

The authors then describe eight components of the MCCPM that they indicate are strategic and interdependent. Because they consider multicultural competence as a process, Beckett et al. (1997) suggest that the components are not sequential or linear. The eight components of the model are as follows: (a) know self, (b) acknowledge cultural differences, (c) know other cultures, (d) identify and value differences, (e) identify and avoid stereotypes, (f) empathize with persons from other cultures, (g) adapt rather than adopt, and (h) acquire recovery skills.

López's (1997) Process Model of Cultural Competence

López (1997) offers a model of cultural competence that he frames as a guide for clinicians and their supervisors. He uses the term *process,* thereby indicating the dynamic and fluid nature of cultural competence. López also asserts that the principles of effective psychotherapy and culturally competent psychotherapy overlap. We should note that this position is not universally held among multicultural scholars and researchers. The essence of cultural competence, according to López, is the ability of clinicians to differentiate their culture-specific frameworks or perspectives from those of their clients and then to move between these different perspectives. By defining cultural competence in this manner, he implies that although the client's cultural perspective is important, it is not the only consideration. The clinician's cultural perspective matters as well.

López (1997) identifies four domains that reflect on cultural competence as a process. In the first domain, *engagement,* therapists get clients to participate in therapy by establishing a positive working relationship. Engaged clients are able to share their culture-specific perspectives on the presenting problem and also help set goals for treatment.

In the second domain, *assessment,* clinicians ascertain the nature of the client's psychological functioning. Recognized as an ongoing process, assessment can be based on formal procedures (e.g., Minnesota Multiphasic Personality Inventory [MMPI-2]) and informal procedures (e.g., clinical interviews). The process requires clinicians to apply the norms of the mainstream culture and those of the client's culture. Balancing cultural perspectives, exercising clinical judgment, and carefully considering all cultural data are integrated into the assessment.

Theory is the third domain. Theory is the explanatory model that explains (a) a client's psychological functioning and (b) how therapy works. Culturally competent therapists realize that clients often have explanatory models of their own, and these may differ from models held by therapists. But therapists respect and validate the clients' theoretical models. At the same time, competent therapists are astute enough to know that the clients' model may reflect dysfunction, not simply an alternative explanation of the presenting problem.

Methods constitute the fourth domain. Methods are the procedures used to facilitate therapeutic change. Culturally competent clinicians adapt their methods and interventions to each client. In making this point, López (1997) seems to draw three implications about treatment. First, individualized treatment planning is essential to cultural competence. Second, a wide range of interventions is potentially usable in treatment. Third, the selected interventions must be compatible with the client's cultural belief system.

Castro's (1998) Three-Factor Model

Castro (1998) argues that the capacity for cultural competence exists along a continuum. Borrowing from the work of other scholars (Cross, Bazron, Dennis, & Isaacs, 1989; Kim, McLeod, & Shantis, 1992; Orlandi, 1992), he modifies and expands the concept of a cultural capacity continuum. His conceptualization consists of six levels of cultural capacity. Each level is assigned a numerical rating, and the continuum ranges from −3 to +3.

The lowest level is cultural destructiveness (−3). Professionals at this level harbor an attitude of superiority about their culture and inferiority about clients from other cultures. The next level is cultural incapacity (−2). This is an orientation that emphasizes separate but equal treatment of clients who are outside of the cultural mainstream. The next level is cultural blindness (−1). This orientation emphasizes that all cultures and individuals are alike and equal. However, professionals who operate at this level discount the importance of culture as well as the need to incorporate multicultural perspectives during treatment. By implication, these three lower levels reflect cultural incompetence.

The next three levels constitute Castro's (1998) three-factor model. He states that the model enables psychologists and other mental health professionals to "conduct culturally effective assessments, clinical interventions, and research with members of ethnic minority populations" (p. 127). He further states that the overall aim of the model is to guide training toward the development of cultural competence.

The first level of the three-factor model is cultural sensitivity or openness (+1). It is an understanding and appreciation of sociocultural factors pertaining to the client and treatment. Cultural sensitivity is also an appreciation of within-group variation, recognizing the considerable heterogeneity within a given ethnic population. The next level of the model is cultural competence (+2). Professionals at this level can work with complex issues and understand cultural nuances. Therefore, they can plan culturally effective interventions. The highest level is cultural proficiency (+3). This is an ideal state and requires a commitment to lifelong learning. This state is indicated by professionals demonstrating excellence and being proficient in the design and delivery of interventions. According to Castro (1998), a professional may be culturally proficient with one target population but not another. He believes that complete cultural proficiency across populations is rare.

Cross's (1988) Model of Cultural Competence

Cross (1988) developed a six-stage model of cultural competence. The model was originally developed for use with organizations, but it has also been adopted for use with individuals. Stage 1 is cultural destructiveness. This stage assumes the superiority of one culture over other cultures. Stage 2 is cultural incapacity. In this stage, there is support for segregation, and there are lower expectations for people of minority cultures. Stage 3 is cultural blindness. In this stage, services and

activities are so ethnocentric that only those who are assimilated benefit from them. Stage 4 is cultural precompetence. In this stage, attempts are made to address diversity issues through hiring and promoting, for example, and offering sensitivity training. Stage 5 is basic cultural competency. In this stage, attempts are made to hire unbiased employees, obtain feedback from communities of color, and assess possible provisions for diverse clients. Stage 6 is advanced cultural competency. In this stage, organizations conduct research, hire culturally competent staff, and advocate on behalf of diversity issues.

Toporek and Reza's (2001) MCCAP

Toporek and Reza (2001) developed the multicultural counseling competency assessment and planning model (MCCAP). The model incorporates the cross-cultural competencies advanced by Sue et al. (1992). The authors describe the MCCAP as an enhancement of Sue et al.'s (1992) model by integrating three additional dimensions: (a) contexts, (b) modes of change, and (c) a process for assessment and planning. The MCCAP model is depicted in Figure 2.2 as a cube that shows all possible interactions among the dimensions.

The base of the model consists of Sue et al.'s (1992) multicultural standards and competencies. Nine standards and competencies are identified, categorized into three areas: (a) having awareness of own assumptions, (b) understanding the client's worldview, and (c) developing appropriate interventions. For each category, competencies are described in terms of a professional's awareness, knowledge, and skills.

The model describes three contexts of multicultural competence. The *personal context* is the professional's identity, beliefs, attitudes, knowledge, and skills as a cultural being. The personal context may affect how professionals conceptualize counseling. The *professional*

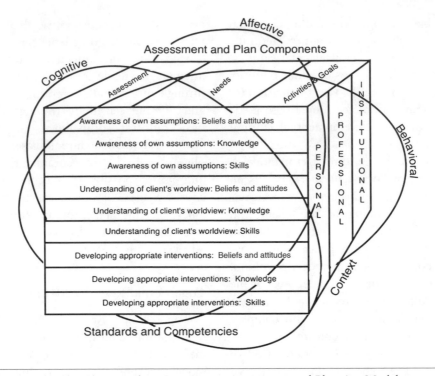

Figure 2.2   Multicultural Counseling Competency Assessment and Planning Model

context is the individual's formal role within the mental health field. The *institutional context* is the individual's membership and participation in a specific organizational setting.

The model describes three modes of change. The *cognitive mode* refers to the process of knowing or perceiving. The *affective mode* refers to the professional's feelings or emotions. The *behavioral mode* refers to the professional's actions and reactions. These modes of change encircle or encompass the other dimensions of the cube.

The model describes three areas of assessment and planning. The purpose of *assessment* is to obtain a comprehensive perspective of the professional's multicultural competence. *Needs* are the areas of awareness, knowledge, and skills requiring further development and learning for the professional. Activities and *goals* help to establish a strategic plan for the professional's development.

Critique of Secondary Models

Collectively, these eight models have added to the conversation about the importance of multicultural competence. Although counseling and clinical psychology continue as the primary platforms for this conversation, these models have helped to extend the conversation into other specialties such as health care and social work. In addition, there have been attempts to apply the construct to specific populations such as African Americans. The models vary greatly along the simplicity-complexity continuum. For example, Bennett's (1993) model is obvious in its oversimplification, whereas Toporek and Reza (2001) propose a much more intricate model. None of the models, regardless of complexity, has been subjected to validation studies. Therefore, we know nothing about their actual efficacy or effectiveness.

Perhaps the most serious limitation of these models pertains to their nondirectiveness. Most of them suggest action to be taken by practitioners that would indicate their cultural competence. These proposed actions identify what needs to occur (e.g., avoiding stereotypes, empathizing with persons from other cultures). For the most part, however, they do not provide concrete guidance in how to achieve these ends. For instance, in Beckett and colleagues' (1997) model, what specific clinical behaviors demonstrate empathizing with clients from other cultures? The authors do not make this clear. Consequently, practitioners who use these models will encounter great difficulty in trying to ascertain whether they have achieved multicultural competence.

To his credit, López (1997) is more helpful than other theorists in bridging theory and practice. He provides case vignettes that illustrate each of the four domains of his process model. The vignettes bring his model into clinical reality, and they are of immense benefit to clinicians. Unfortunately, López's discussion of the various domains in the text of his chapter is still descriptive but not prescriptive. Without the aid of the vignettes, most clinicians would not be able to ascertain from the text how to execute his model of cultural competence.

Some of the secondary models appear to make a less salient contribution than do others. For example, Cross's (1988) and Castro's (1998) models are remarkably similar in regard to the stages that they propose. Although the stages are unique in comparison with other models, neither model really offers a unique perspective when the two are compared to each other. These models would need to be examined empirically to determine their utility and whether their facets are critical to multicultural counseling competence. In general, regardless of the simplicity or complexity of the model, each could be subjected to empirical scrutiny via a combination of qualitative methods. This is highly recommended and would help clinicians comprehend the unique contribution that each model makes to the understanding and development of multicultural competence in psychological practice.

IMPLICIT MODELS

Several models have been advanced that have implicit assumptions about multicultural counseling competence. We discuss these models because they are pervasive in the literature and exhibit powerful influence over the thinking of many practitioners. Despite these factors, they typically are not recognized as models of multicultural competence. In Table 2.1, we outline the assumptions underscoring four of these models.

Ethnic/Cultural Matching

This model maintains that clients should be counseled by counselors of similar ethnic, racial, or cultural backgrounds. The primary assumption implicit in the model is that multicultural competence derives from the common sociocultural experiences of counselors and their clients. Presumably, the common sociocultural experiences enable counselors to identify and empathize with their clients. This type of identification and empathy is assumed to be unavailable to counselors outside the client's group. Two secondary assumptions logically follow: (a) Competence in its cultural aspects is independent of training, and (b) competence requires the counselor's membership in the client's ethnic, racial, or cultural group.

Research indicates ethnic minority clients' consistent and strong preference for ethnically similar counselors (Atkinson & Lowe, 1995). Studies investigating process variables in matched dyads have yielded mixed results. Clients in matched dyads have shown better utilization, and ethnic matching may benefit certain types of clients (S. Sue, 1995).

Table 2.1   Models With Implicit Assumptions of Multicultural Counseling Competence

Models	Assumptions About Competence
Ethnic/cultural matching	Primary: Competence derives from the common sociocultural experiences of counselor and client. Secondary: (a) Competence is independent of training. (b) Competence requires membership in the clients' ethnic, racial, or cultural group.
Conventional counseling	Primary: Competence derives from training in the use of conventional psychotherapy orientations. Secondary: (a) Major psychotherapies are universally applicable and robust enough to account for cultural variation. (b) No additional systemic training is necessary. (c) Counselor's cultural group membership is unimportant.
Conventional counseling with modification	Primary: Competence derives from training in the use of conventional psychotherapy orientations as well as training in cultural sensitivity. Secondary: (a) Conventional psychotherapy orientations are necessary but insufficient. (b) Cultural sensitivity is necessary but insufficient. (c) Counselor's cultural group membership is unimportant.
Cultural-specific counseling	Primary: Competence derives from mastery of change ingredients inherent in the culture of the client. Secondary: (a) The process of change is relativistic. (b) Counselor's membership in the client's culture is advantageous.

However, there is no unequivocal evidence that matching counselors and clients improves the chances of therapeutic gain. Therefore, although there are certain benefits to matching, the implication of competence in this model is not supported by the research.

Conventional Counseling

This model maintains that multicultural counselors should only use conventional counseling approaches. Although the multicultural movement has gained considerable momentum, some professionals—especially those trained years ago—continue to rely almost exclusively on standard person-centered, cognitive-behavioral, and behavioral approaches in their practices. The primary assumption implicit in this model is that multicultural competence derives from training in the use of conventional psychotherapies. Three secondary assumptions logically follow: (a) Major

psychotherapies are universally applicable and robust enough to account for cultural variation among clients, (b) no additional systematic training is necessary, and (c) counselors' cultural group membership is unimportant.

Sue, Zane, and Young (1994) indicated that outcome research on multicultural populations is lacking. Therefore, we do not know whether conventional interventions are efficacious for various cultural groups and whether treatment outcomes differ for majority and minority group clients. In conclusion, there is no evidence that training in conventional interventions is robust enough to account for cultural variations.

Conventional Counseling With Modification

This model maintains that multicultural counselors should use conventional counseling orientations but should modify the treatment by redirecting the focus on the cultural content in the counseling session (Atkinson & Lowe, 1995). The primary assumption implicit in this model is that multicultural competence derives from training both in the use of conventional psychotherapies and in cultural sensitivity. Three secondary assumptions logically follow: (a) Conventional psychotherapies are necessary but insufficient, (b) cultural sensitivity is necessary but insufficient, and (c) counselors' cultural group membership is unimportant.

Atkinson and Lowe (1995) reviewed the research on culturally responsive versus culturally nonresponsive counseling. They found that culturally responsive counselors have credibility with minority clients. They also found that these counselors' clients are more willing to return to counseling and have greater satisfaction with counseling and depth of self-disclosure. However, there is an absence of information on how cultural responsiveness contributes to constructive change.

Cultural-Specific Counseling

This model maintains that some effective interventions are based on the indigenous beliefs and values of specific populations. S. Sue (1992), for instance, recommended the creation of mental health programs/centers or sections of hospitals that would serve ethnic minority populations. The primary assumption implicit in this model is that multicultural competence derives from mastery of change ingredients inherent in the culture of the client. Two secondary assumptions logically follow: (a) The process of change is relativistic, and (b) counselors' membership in the client's cultural group is advantageous.

Constantino, Malgady, and Ragler (1986) provided the only evidence that culturally specific counseling is more effective than conventional counseling. However, many questions remain unanswered. For example, are the mechanisms of change in culturally specific

counseling really unique to the culture of the client? If they are unique, what are these mechanisms? Therefore, there is not enough information to conclude that multicultural competence relates to mastery of culturally specified mechanisms of change.

CONCLUSION

As multicultural counseling competence has taken its place in applied psychology, a variety of models of the construct have emerged. These models have played a key role in furthering the multicultural conversation. In this chapter, we discussed and critiqued two prominent models, eight secondary models, and four models that have implicit assumptions about multicultural competence. Although we have gleaned much insight from these models, further research and scholarship are needed. Using our criteria for evaluating the models, a number of problems persist concerning the utility of the models.

To rectify these problems and advance the field, we offer the following recommendations. First, there needs to be a clear operational definition of the construct, with explicit and cogent description of the relationship between variables. Second, the models should demonstrate a better integration of theory and practice. Third, new models should reflect better grounding in existing theory and science, calling specific attention to their uniqueness and necessity in the field. Fourth, new models should simplify the complexity inherent in the construct, but this should not result in oversimplification. Finally, continual validation research should be conducted to test the effectiveness of the models.

REFERENCES

American Psychological Association (APA). (1992). Ethical principles of psychologists and code of conduct. *American Psychologist, 47,* 1597-1611.

Atkinson, D. R., & Lowe, S. M. (1995). The role of ethnicity, cultural knowledge, and conventional techniques in counseling and psychotherapy. In J. G. Ponterotto, J. M. Casas, L. A. Suzuki, & C. M. Alexander (Eds.), *Handbook of multicultural counseling* (pp. 387-414). Thousand Oaks, CA: Sage.

Beckett, J. O., Dungee-Anderson, D., Cox, L., & Daly, A. (1997). African Americans and multicultural interventions. *Smith College Studies in Social Work, 67*(3), 540-563.

Bennett, M. J. (1993). Towards ethnorelativism: A developmental model of intercultural sensitivity. In R. M. Paige (Ed.), *Education for the intercultural experience* (pp. 21-71). Yarmouth, ME: Intercultural Press.

Campenha-Bacote, J. (1994). *The process of cultural competence in health care: A culturally competent model of care* (2nd ed.). Cincinnati, OH: Transcultural C.A.R.E. Associates.

Carney, C. G., & Kahn, K. B. (1984). Building competencies for effective cross-cultural counseling: A developmental view. *The Counseling Psychologist, 12*(1), 111-199.

Castro, F. G. (1998). Cultural competence training in clinical psychology: Assessment, clinical intervention, and research. In C. D. Belar (Ed.), *Comprehensive clinical psychology: Vol. 10. Sociocultural individual differences* (pp. 127-140). Oxford, UK: Pergamon/Elsevier Science.

Constantine, M. G., & Ladany, N. (2000). Self-report multicultural counseling competence scales: Their relation to social desirability attitudes and multicultural case conceptualization ability. *Journal of Counseling Psychology, 47*, 155-164.

Constantino, G., Malgady, R. G., & Ragler, L. H. (1986). Cuento therapy: A culturally sensitive modality for Puerto Rican children. *Journal of Consulting and Clinical Psychology, 54*, 639-645.

Cross, T. (1988, Fall). Services to minority populations: Cultural Competency Continuum. *Focal Point*, p. 3.

Cross, T. L., Bazron, B. J., Dennis, K. W., & Isaacs, M. R. (1989). *Towards a culturally competent system of care* (Vol. 1).

Washington, DC: Georgetown University Child Development Center.

Holcomb-McCoy, C. C., & Myers, J. E. (1999). Multicultural competence and counselor training: A national survey. *Journal of Counseling and Development, 77*(3), 294-302.

Kim, S., McLeod, J. H., & Shantis, C. (1992). Cultural competence for evaluators working with Asian American communities: Some practical considerations. In M. A. Orlandi, R. Weston, & L. G. Epstein (Eds.), *Cultural competence for evaluators* (pp. 203-260). Rockville, MD: Office of Substance Abuse Prevention.

Lester, S. (2000). The professional accreditation of conservator-restorers: Developing a competence-based professional assessment system. *Assessment & Evaluation in Higher Education, 24*, 407-419.

López, S. R. (1997). Cultural competence in psychotherapy: A guide for clinicians and their supervisors. In C. E. Watkins (Ed.), *Handbook of psychotherapy supervision* (pp. 570-588). New York: John Wiley.

Orlandi, M. A. (1992). Defining cultural competence: An organizing framework. In M. A. Orlandi, R. Weston, & L. G. Epstein (Eds.), *Cultural competence for evaluators* (pp. 293-299). Rockville, MD: Center for Substance Abuse Prevention.

Ponterotto, J. G., Fuertes, J. N., & Chen, E. C. (2000). Models of multicultural counseling. In S. D. Brown & R. W. Lent (Eds.), *Handbook of counseling psychology* (3rd ed., pp. 639-669). New York: John Wiley.

Pope, K. S., & Brown, L. S. (1996). *Recovered memories of abuse: Assessment, therapy, forensics*. Washington, DC: American Psychological Association.

Ridley, C. R., Baker, D. M., & Hill, C. L. (2001). Critical issues concerning cultural competence. *The Counseling Psychologist, 29*, 822-832.

Ridley, C. R., Hill, C. L., & Wiese, D. L. (2001). Ethics in multicultural assessment: A model of reasoned application. In L. A. Suzuki, J. G. Ponterotto, & P. J. Meller (Eds.), *Handbook of multicultural assessment: Clinical, psychological, and educational applications* (2nd ed., pp. 29-45). San Francisco: Jossey-Bass.

Sodowsky, G. R., Taffe, R. C., Gutkin, T. B., & Wise, S. L. (1994). Development of the Multicultural Counseling Inventory: A self-report measure of multicultural competencies. *Journal of Counseling Psychology, 41,* 137-148.

Sue, D. W. (2001). Multidimensional facets of cultural competence. *The Counseling Psychologist, 29,* 790-821.

Sue, D. W., Arrendondo, P., & McDavis, R. J. (1992). Multicultural competencies and standards: A call to the profession. *Journal of Counseling & Development, 70*(4), 477-486.

Sue, D. W., Bernier, J. B., Durran, M., Feinberg, L., Pedersen, P., Smith, E., et al. (1982). Position paper: Cross-cultural counseling competencies. *The Counseling Psychologist, 10,* 45-52.

Sue, D. W., Bingham, R., Porche-Burke, L., & Vasquez, M. (1999). The diversification of psychology: A multicultural revolution. *American Psychologist, 54,* 1061-1069.

Sue, D. W., Carter, R. T., Casas, J. M., Fouad, N. A., Ivey, A. E., Jensen, M., et al. (1998). *Multicultural counseling competencies: Individual and organizational development.* Thousand Oaks, CA: Sage.

Sue, D. W., & Sue, D. (1999). *Counseling the culturally different: Theory and practice* (3rd ed.). New York: John Wiley.

Sue, S. (1992). Ethnicity and mental health: Research and policy issues. *Journal of Social Issues, 48,* 187-205.

Sue, S. (1995). The implications of diversity for scientific standards of practice. In S. C. Hayes, V. M. Follette, R. M. Dawes & K. E. Grady (Eds.), *Scientific standards of psychological practice: Issues and recommendations* (pp. 265-279). Reno, NV: Context Press.

Sue, S., Zane, N., & Young, K. (1994). Research on psychotherapy with culturally diverse populations. In A. E. Bergin & S. L. Garfield (Eds.), *Handbook of psychotherapy and behavior change* (4th ed., pp. 783-817). New York: John Wiley.

Toporek, R. L., & Reza, J. V. (2001). Context as a critical dimension of multicultural counseling: Articulating personal, professional, and institutional competence. *Journal of Multicultural Counseling and Development, 29,* 13-30.

Welfel, E. R. (1998). *Ethics in counseling and psychotherapy: Standards, research, and emerging issues.* Pacific Grove, CA: Brooks/Cole.

Wood, R., & Power, C. (1987). Aspects of the competence-performance distinction: Educational, psychological and measurement issues. *Journal of Curriculum Studies, 19,* 409-424.

3

An Ecological Perspective on Cultural Identity Development

HARDIN L. K. COLEMAN
ROMANA A. NORTON
GINA E. MIRANDA
LAURIE McCUBBIN
University of Wisconsin–Madison

The area of cultural identity development has received considerable attention in the multicultural counseling research literature. Originating with Cross's (1971) theory of Black racial identity development, this area of study has expanded to include various models of cultural identity: racial identity development (e.g., Cross, 1991; Helms, 1990a; Root, 1990; Rowe, Bennett, & Atkinson, 1994), ethnic identity development (e.g., Phinney, 1989), sexual identity development (e.g., Cass, 1979), and womanist identity development (e.g., Helms, 1990b). Of these, models of racial and ethnic identity development continue to dominate cultural identity research. Theory and research on racial and ethnic identity have made many contributions to our understanding

of multicultural counseling competence that cannot be overstated.

Racial identity theorists (e.g., Cross, 1971; Helms, 1990a, 1990b) were the first to problematize the ways in which cultural constructs such as race and ethnicity had been conceptualized and used in psychological research. These researchers challenged researchers to go beyond nominal conceptualizations of race to define and operationalize the psychological and behavioral dimensions underlying these constructs. Models of racial and ethnic identity accomplish this, providing practitioners and researchers with a way of thinking about how racial factors might influence intra- and interpersonal functioning, particularly within the context of counseling and psychotherapy.

Measures of racial and ethnic identity are helping counseling researchers look at how the utility and effectiveness of counseling might be improved for diverse populations.

Racial identity theory has also served as a catalyst for conceptual clarification of the multicultural lexicon. Conceptual confusion around the interrelated constructs of race, ethnicity, and culture has haunted the multicultural counseling competence literature since the multicultural movement began in earnest in the early 1980s. Thanks to the tireless theoretical writings of foundational theorists such as Janet Helms (see, e.g., Helms, 1994, 1995), we seem to be close to reaching a conceptual consensus at the beginning of the new millennium, improving the interpretability and generalizability of multicultural counseling competence research.

Perhaps a less recognized contribution made by racial identity theory to the multicultural counseling competence literature is that it helped narrow the latter's focus from broad, between-group differences (usually White/ non-White) to a focus on in-group diversity. In an effort to broaden the parameters of effective service delivery, the early literature on multicultural counseling competence focused on the combined mental health concerns of various cultural groups (Helms, 1994). Racial and ethnic identity theorists went beyond the etic/emic debate, promoting consideration of individual differences within various cultural groups. The individual difference approach is most evident in foundational racial identity theories that suggest different psychological themes and behaviors for different levels of racial identity development (e.g., Cross, 1971; Helms, 1990a). Theoretically, each of these different levels has different implications for multicultural counseling process and outcome.

Given the theoretical importance of racial and ethnic identity to individuals' functioning and, subsequently, to multicultural counseling competence, it becomes important to identify factors that influence its quality. To date, however, most of these theories have emphasized the content of racial and ethnic identity at the expense of explicating the process of its development. Moreover, what little attention has been paid to the process of racial and ethnic identity development has tended to focus on structural, macrosystemic factors that, taken alone, fail to capture the dynamic nature of a developmental process. It will be our contention that a holistic understanding of racial identity development requires a multisystemic, dynamic conceptualization of racial identity. Such a perspective will help strengthen the multicultural counseling competence literature. We believe that an ecological theory of cultural identity development provides such a conceptualization.

The goal of this chapter is to articulate the rationale and the process needed to develop an ecological theory of cultural identity development. To achieve that goal, we will present the core ideas behind the ecological perspective. That perspective will then be used to discuss the strengths and limitations of current models of cultural identity development, using the racial identity literature as the primary example. It will be our contention that these models, as currently formulated, contribute greatly to our understanding of the processes through which individuals acquire a sense of their cultural identity (i.e., their sense of themselves as a member of a group within their social context). There are limitations, however, to these formulations, and these might be addressed through the development of an ecological perspective. To support this contention, we will use the issues raised by our understanding of how multiracial individuals acquire and develop a sense of racial identity to demonstrate the limitations of current models and, concurrently, the advantages of an ecological perspective on the process of cultural identity development. In social science, a shift in perspective is often accompanied by a shift in methodological focus. In this chapter, we will also outline how a different methodological approach to examine cultural identity development will enhance our understanding of that process. Our conclusion will articulate ideas for future research in this area of human development. It is our core assumption that a sophisticated understanding of cultural identity development is the basic building block of multicultural competence.

THE ECOLOGICAL PERSPECTIVE

The ecological perspective on human development has been explicated in detail by Bronfenbrenner (1979) and applied to issues of development by Lerner and Foch (1986) and to managing cultural diversity by Coleman (1995). Brofenbrenner points out that individuals develop their sense of self within an interlocking web of social systems, some of which exist in immediate proximity to the individual (e.g., parents, family, friends) and some of which are distal to the individual (e.g., government, macroeconomic systems, social and political history). To understand human development, Brofenbrenner argues that we need to examine and understand the meaning of behavior within multiple, interdependent contexts.

The first level of examination is at the level of the organism, or *self-system*. This level is most often the focus of psychology. Examinations at this level would include analyses of the contributions of individual factors (e.g., biology, cognitions) to an individual's sense of self. Closely related to the self-system are systemic factors that involve an individual's interactions with his or her social and personal ecologies (Coleman, 1995). The most immediate influences on an individual's development can be found within the *microsystem* and include those with whom the individual has immediate social contact (e.g., family, school, and neighborhood). A third level of analysis occurs at the level of the *mesosystem*, which comprises reciprocal relationships between microsystem settings. For example, social interactions in one's neighborhood might influence familial interactions, all of which can combine to inform one's sense of self. The fourth level, the *exosystem*, is the combination of several mesosystems (e.g., a school district, city, county, or state). Although individuals do not play a direct role in the exosystem, it nevertheless has an impact on them. The fifth and final level is the *macrosystem*, which is composed of multiple exosystems and includes broad ideological patterns of culture. These patterns consist of a culture's sociopolitical history as well as its current economic, social, and political systems of thought.

The ecological perspective provides a comprehensive and integrated approach to understanding cultural identity. It takes into account both individuals' perceptions of themselves as group members, as well as their experiences of how others within their microsystems, mesosystems, exosystems, and macrosystems understand them. The ecological perspective allows us to move beyond linear explanations of human behavior; it allows us to think in terms of how behavior is organized by and within complex patterns of social and institutional relationships. Moreover, the ecological perspective allows us to examine how factors such as race or gender, which may have vastly different meanings within each ecological level as well as within various cultures (i.e., within various ecologies), can serve to organize an individual's sense of self. This perspective is not possible when one is attempting to examine how factors such as race or gender cause an individual's sense of self as a member of a group.

In this chapter, we will use the concept of *cultural identity* as an umbrella concept for the many types of social identities (e.g., racial, ethnic, gender, or sexual) that comprise our sense of self as a member of a group within the multiple contexts in which we live. Our use of the term *cultural identity* is not meant to replace or minimize the importance of the concepts of racial and ethnic identity. The phrase *cultural identity* is used to emphasize that these social identities are the conceptions we have of ourselves and of others as social beings within a larger social system that we often call culture but that Bronfenbrenner (1979) has called the macrosystem. We believe that the process of cultural identity development is a constant; that is, the processes and mechanisms of acquiring a racial, ethnic, or gender identity function at all times in the development of every specific social identity and in our every sense of lacking or possessing group membership. This chapter will focus on the literature related to racial identity to make a case that we feel is applicable to other social identities (e.g., ethnic, sexual, gender, or class). Moreover, our conversation concerning racial identity will focus on Blacks and Whites, as both the theoretical and research literatures on racial and ethnic identity have focused primarily on these two groups.

CULTURAL IDENTITY

Identity, both personal and cultural, has internal and external qualities. Such an identity involves a coherent sense of internal self—in development over time, in relationship to others—and a sense that others have a consistent sense of who and what we are (Erickson, 1968). This coherent sense is a function of individuals' biological capabilities, their interactions with the contexts that facilitate and constrain their development, and their interpretation of their experience. From this perspective, identity is the acquisition of cognitive coherence and stability, which includes affective and cognitive components, of self in relationship to the context in which one is living. That identity will have both internal qualities (e.g., how one feels about one's self) and external

qualities (e.g., how one feels about one's sense of self in relationship to others and their context). Within the ecological conceptualization of identity that we are attempting to articulate, cultural identity is predominately concerned with how one develops a sense of coherence as a self in relationship to others within particular contexts. It is important, however, not to confuse a sense of coherence with sameness. Having a coherent sense of self does not mean one has to feel that he or she acts and is seen as the same person across contexts. It is integrating the possibility of contextual flexibility into the discussion of cultural identity development that is one of the major contributions of the ecological perspective.

Within this perspective, cultural identity is seen as having internal and external qualities that involve a sense of one's self as a member of a social group (e.g., racial or gender). This identity is achieved over time as one interacts with his or her family, community, and society. Cultural identity involves one's sense of self in relationship to his or her microsystems, mesosystems, exosystems, and macrosystems. The more complex the macrosystems in which an individual develops, the more complex will be the individual's sense of cultural self and the greater challenge an individual will have in achieving that sense. We argue that this coherence will be a function of individuals' contextual or mesosystem stability, their cognitive perspective-taking capability, the history of the group or groups to which they identify or are identified within a particular macrosystem, and their personal goals.

ETHNIC AND RACIAL IDENTITY DEVELOPMENT

It is this complex process of cultural identity development that has engaged theorists concerned with racial and ethnic identity development since Cross (1971) proposed his model of psychological nigrescence. These models (e.g., Atkinson, Morten, & Sue, 1993; Cross, 1991; Helms, 1990a; Phinney, 1995; Rowe et al., 1994) are all concerned with how individuals make sense of their race or ethnicity as those factors represent externally constructed (macrosystemic) beliefs about what the individual can or should believe about himself or herself. All of these models assume that macrosystemic factors such as race, ethnicity, and gender have meaning outside of the individual that the individual must incorporate into his or her identity to achieve a coherent sense of self.

The existing models, however, differ in how they assess the manner in which an individual integrates these factors into his or her sense of self as a group member. The first source of variance is whether the model focuses on the individual's internal or external process of identity development. Those that focus on the internal process are more concerned with learning how the individual thinks or feels about himself or herself as a member of a particular group (e.g., Phinney, 1995). Those that focus on the external process are more concerned with how the individual manages or copes with others or himself or herself as representatives of a particular group (e.g., Helms, 1990a, 1990b). The second source of variance in the existing models is whether the model focuses on achieved identity as an outgrowth of a developmental process (e.g., Helms, 1990a) or as the result of interactions with other cultural groups (Rowe et al., 1994).

Another source of variance between these models is their different understanding of the constructs of race and ethnicity. Although we seem to be close to reaching a consensus about the meaning of these terms, considerable debate and confusion continue to exist in the literature (see Pierce, 2000; Helms, 1995; Spickard & Burroughs, 2000). Some cultural identity theorists feel that, because race is a social fiction, it is best that the concept be done away with altogether and replaced by the term *ethnicity* (e.g., Spickard & Burroughs, 2000). Other theorists see no significant difference between the two concepts (e.g., Phinney, 1990) and use the terms interchangeably. Still others contend that the concept of race, albeit a social construction, continues to have significance for individuals and, as such, should continue to be distinguished from ethnicity (e.g., Helms, 1995; Pierce, 2000). The external focus of race and the internal focus of ethnicity contribute to some of the perceived variance between models of cultural identity development as they differentially focus on the impact of race and ethnicity on the identity development process.

In the literature we reviewed for this chapter, race is often considered to be a social construction of what it means to have certain physical features that have historically been used to categorize individuals into certain groups (e.g., Helms, 1990a). Along with this categorization, race has historically come to be associated with certain levels of privilege, or lack thereof, within particular mesosystems. Ethnicity often refers to allegiance to and involvement with particular cultural traditions, heritages, and customs (e.g., Phinney, 1995). These distinctions allow us to refer to a person as a member of a racial group (e.g., European American or African American) and an ethnic group (e.g., Irish American or Mexican American) and to assume that these distinctions are psychologically and politically meaningful. One way to think of this distinction is to think of race as the signal characteristics that allow others to ascribe meaning to who and what we are. Ethnicity, then, can be thought of as the manner in which we come to include or exclude ourselves from a group that shares a historical/familial relationship; culture, finally, can be thought of as the context in which these external and internal constructions of group membership are made meaningful. A parallel process is the distinction between sex and gender.

In this chapter, *race* will be used when the focus is on how individuals are being characterized as a function of their racial group membership, and *ethnicity* will be used when the focus is on the individual's allegiance to particular group traditions. We will specifically address issues related to this important distinction later in the chapter when we address methodological challenges to research on cultural identity.

Although models of ethnic and racial identity development have resolved the challenge of understanding cultural identity development in different ways, they have all looked at how a macrosystemic factor (e.g., race) has a causal relationship to the individual's sense of self and cultural identity. It is our assertion that the differences between these models of cultural identity do not necessarily reflect significantly different understandings of the nature of cultural identity development but rather are variations on a theme. The core theme that each of these theories share is a belief that cultural identity, whether racial or ethnic, is a function of the individual's acquiring a sense of himself or herself as a member of a particular group within a particular macrosystem. These models differ from each other in their relative emphasis on the degree to which cultural identity is stimulated by external or internal variables.

The models of cultural identity development we have just presented focus on the macrosystemic nature of cultural identity. Even as these models differ on whether the core elements of cultural identity are due to the internal or external nature of that identity, they all assume that membership in a particular racial or ethnic group will have a predictable outcome that will be expressed through an individual's cultural identity. We believe that it is the macrosystemic focus of these models that serves to limit their ability to explain the processes and mechanisms of cultural identity development, particularly within

a pluralistic macrosystem. Given the significant focus on structure, these models may be considered by some to be appropriate for individuals who develop within a homogeneous mesosystem or macrosystem. Within that context, their perceived group membership may have a unitary meaning that is shared by others within the system. For example, within the upper Midwest from 1940 to 1980, the major racial groups were White or Black, with American Indian groups in particular (and mostly isolated) regions. Within that macrosystem, "people of color" were perceived to have certain issues and concerns that were common to the perceived and real cultural norms of African-descended persons. With the post-1975 influx of Southeast Asians and now Latinos into the upper Midwest (U.S. Bureau of the Census, 2000), the perspectives on "people of color" are changing rapidly. This change is leading to significant changes within institutions, such as schools, in their approach to understanding, modeling, supporting, and/or denying cultural identity. Multiculturalism, therefore, demands a more complex understanding of cultural identity development than can be achieved using a purely structural perspective (Oleneck, 2000).

Ecological perspectives on development (Brofenbrenner, 1979; Lerner & Foch, 1986) point the way toward a more expansive model for understanding cultural identity within a pluralistic society. An ecological perspective concurs with traditional approaches in assuming that group membership, particularly membership that is associated with obvious physical characteristics, serves to recruit differential treatment within each mesosystem. It suggests, however, that mesosystems in a heterogeneous society will produce such varied treatments that they will be extremely difficult to understand, except within a schema that focuses on the context-dependent nature of the process. Such a perspective has the ability to be both inclusive of multiple perspectives and objectives, which is to say, context focused. Ecological theorists (e.g., Bronfenbrenner, 1979; Coleman, 1995; Root, 1990, 1999) suggest that an ecological model will address multiple factors to understand the development of a cultural identity. As with traditional models of racial and ethnic identity, an ecological model will recognize the impact of sociopolitical realties that, within a specific history, are replicated across all contexts. Another important element of an ecological model is the role of institutions such as schools, church, and families that, through the enculturation process, teach and model multiple aspects of culture for children to integrate into their sense of self. A third vital agent in the process of cultural identity development, from an ecological perspective, is the meaning-making capability of the individual. It is the individual who is pressed to make sense of the information he or she receives at both the cognitive and affective levels and then to develop behavioral patterns (D. H. Ford, 1987; M. E. Ford, 1992) that both reflect his or her internal sense of self and are effective within his or her microsystems, mesosystems, and macrosystems. The fourth and final element that needs to be accounted for within an ecological model of cultural identity development is an understanding of the reciprocal interaction between the individual and his or her environment. As is central to many theories of family therapy and core feminist theories of identity development (Goldenberg & Goldenberg, 2000), the ecological perspective assumes that we can learn the most about individuals when we understand them in relationship to others.

Because most of the extant research on cultural identity has focused on presumably monocultural groups (e.g., Blacks, Whites, American Indians), the existing models have not been forced to actively consider the role that immediate context plays in the development of cultural identity, and they do not sufficiently account for within-group diversity (Miranda, 2000). We believe that the case of racial identity development among multiracial individuals demonstrates the limitation of foundational models and the value of a context-dependent model. The next section of this chapter discusses the way in which current theory and research on the racial identity development of multiracial individuals demonstrate the limitations of some traditional models of racial identity development and the potential significance of an ecological perspective to this area of cultural identity development.

MULTIRACIAL IDENTITY DEVELOPMENT

Root's (1992) volume, *Racially Mixed People in America,* created a wave of interest in the experiences of multiracial people. A flurry of popular and academic work on the multiracial experience has emerged since the publication of that volume. Focused on experiences thought to be unique to multiracial people, the empirical and theoretical work in this area can be roughly divided into three interrelated research areas: (a) deconstruction of popular and pseudo-scientific conceptualizations of multiraciality, (b) descriptive and empirical investigation of phenomenological experiences that influence the identity development process of multiracial people, and (c) descriptions of the process and content of multiracial identity development.

The works that have been done in all of these areas have been invaluable additions to the social science literature. The first area brought multiracial people to the attention of counseling researchers. This work has inspired discussion about the illogic and the intention of the U.S. racial classification system, as well as the implications that this system has for individuals' identity development. Discussions about the structural forces that serve to regulate racial group membership and identity have helped generate a body of literature that addresses the phenomenological forces that attempt to "manage" (Twine, 1996b) the racial identities of multiracial people (Frankenberg, 1993; Funderberg, 1994, 1998; Phinney & Alipuria, 1996; Renn, 1998; Root, 1992, 1998; Twine, 1996b; Williams, 1996). This research has served as a catalyst for the wholesale reconceptualization of multiracial identity development.

Models of multiracial identity have served at least two functions. First, like their monoracial counterparts, they have functioned to educate racially oppressed peoples about the ways in which social concepts of race manufacture and constrain identity. Second, they have helped legitimize multiraciality, providing multiracial people with a reference group for support (Root, 2000). Models of multiracial identity development can also function to empower multiracial people to define their own racial identities rather than have identifications imposed on them (Root, 1996a). Given that multiracial models of identity were originally conceived with this goal in mind, it is perplexing to witness the development of hierarchical stage models of multiracial identity development (Jacobs, 1992; Kitch, 1992; Poston, 1990) that propose "biracial" identity endpoints. These models appear to replace one kind of "racial tyranny" with another (Appiah, 1996), restricting the identity options of people of mixed-race descent to a single, albeit new and positive, "essential" racial identity. These models prescribe a naturalized process of racial identity development that precludes the possibility of idiosyncratic patterns or context-driven identity choices. Stage models of multiracial identity development make many of the same assumptions that characterize the monoethnic and monoracial models described in the first part of this chapter, particularly concerning the role of interaction and development. One of the purposes of this section is to explore some of the conceptual limitations of stage models of racial identity development.

The conceptual limitations of stage models of racial identity development have led to the development of contextual and ecological conceptualizations of multiracial identity development (Johnson, 1992; Miller, 1992; Root, 1990, 2000). These conceptualizations focus on the widely varying factors that might influence the content and process of multiracial identity development. Such conceptualizations are only concerned with the identity choices that multiracial people might make, insofar as these choices are not overdetermined by contextual factors. As such, ecological models stay true to the original purpose of all racial identity models: to allow racially marginalized people maximal power to define their own identities. To develop a coherent sense of cultural self, a multiracial individual must find a way to integrate multiple racial and ethnic heritages within social contexts that have multiple interpretations of those heritages and varying notions of what it means to be multiracial. The complexity of this task calls for a more complex understanding of the process than can be provided by models that focus primarily on macrosystemic variables such as race. The second purpose of this section is to explore the benefits that ecological approaches to multiracial identity development may have for conceptualizations of cultural identity development.

Erickson (1968) proposed that discomforting events within the individual's environment trigger the identity formation process. This assumption is explicit in the "encounter" phase of most foundational models (e.g., Cross, 1991; Helms, 1990a, 1990b). For multiracial individuals, these events often come from multiple and confusing sources, and their origins can be located in the threat that multiracial people pose to the integrity of the U.S. hierarchical racial classification system and, ultimately, to White paternalistic supremacy

(Omi & Winant, 1994). Multiracial people radically undermine the most vital assumption underlying the racial classification system—the assumption of racial purity. This assumption functions to keep the racial hierarchy intact. The existence of multiraciality, however, suggests that the boundaries erected by the racial classification system are purely cultural, which is to say, artificial and permeable.

The threat that multiraciality poses to the racial hierarchy has historically been managed through the propagation of a multiracial mythology (Nakashima, 1992). Multiracial identity has been constructed, for instance, as inherently pathological. Following the essentialist, purist logic inherent in the social concept of race, multiracial identity has been represented as necessarily confused and fragmented (Nakashima, 1992), the inevitable psychological outcome of an admixture of disharmonious racial essences. Within this logic, multiracial people are fated to experience psychological dysfunction, as it is allegedly impossible for them to develop a coherent sense of self out of oil and water racial essences.

The logic of racial essentialism has also been recruited to construct multiracial people as potentially disloyal (Nakashima, 1992). The alleged presence of nonintegrated, fundamentally opposed racial essences calls into question the multiracial person's sociopolitical allegiances. Thus, the logic of racial purity and racial essentialism functions to erect psychological boundaries between people who differ in terms of phenotype. The construction of multiracial people as potentially disloyal encourages people to police the borders of the racial classification system by which they live. The social adoption of the "one-drop rule," the "law of hypodescent," and racial allegiance testing (Norton, 2000) are all designed to coerce racially ambiguous people into an "appropriate" monoracial category.

Multiracial identity development theorists have noted that monoracial theories of identity development did not capture the unique sociopolitical experiences of multiracial people. Most monoracial identity models, for instance, assume that people of color will seek refuge in their ascribed racial community, most notably during the Immersion/Emersion-like stages (Poston, 1990; Root, 1990). Many multiracial people, however, may not be accepted in the culture of either parent's ascribed race (Root, 2000). Content discrepancies such as this one led to calls for models that might capture the multiracial experience. Several researchers answered this call by proposing models of multiracial identity development that contained racial identity stages that attempted to capture the unique experiences of multiracial people.

Stage models of multiracial identity development differ from those of monoracial identity development in terms of the content of the stages that lead, theoretically, to "healthy" racial identity. They are essentially identical to monoracial models, however, in terms of how they conceive of the process of racial identification. Both models contend that the developmental process of racial identity development is universal—a hierarchical, linear progression, triggered and informed largely by a single macrosystemic level factor (i.e., racism).

The implications that stage model approaches have for the conceptualization of racial identity are far-reaching. The assumption of universality deters these model theorists from considering influences on racial identity development that operate outside of macrosystemic-level factors; microsystem, mesosystem, and exosystem factors that may significantly influence the psychological process and content of racial identification are overlooked (Miller, 1992). This largely decontextualized conceptualization of racial identity development becomes most evident when we look at how within-group differences are conceptualized. Differences within racial groups in terms of racial identification are conceptualized solely in terms of different categories of reaction to racial stimuli. Minimal consideration is given to how other factors that lie outside of racial factors might inform racial identity within racial groups. Indeed, the stage model approach even fails to consider how other macrosystemic-level factors (e.g., socioeconomic status [SES] and sex) might interact with race and inform the process of racial identification. In this sense, stage models of racial identity describe different types of racial identities rather than how racial identity develops.

The assumption of universality is also manifest in the hierarchical nature of stage models of racial identity development. Both monoracial and multiracial stage models posit a linear trajectory of racial identity development that assumes a positively valenced endpoint—an "integrated" monoracial identity or an integrated biracial (or triracial, or quadracial, etc.) identity, respectively. The hierarchical nature of stage models is one of their most troubling aspects. All racial identity theorists seem to agree that a central developmental issue for people of color is overcoming the assaults and constraints of social concepts of race. Moreover, they all agree that healthy resolution of this issue is predicated on the development of positive attitudes about one's racial heritage(s). The assumption of a hierarchical progression toward a "healthy" racial identity, however, seems to make two mistaken assumptions: (a) that one's racial heritage can and must be conceived of as a homogeneous entity and (b) that this homogeneous entity can and must achieve congruence with an individual's racial identity via positive attitudes related to the homogeneous entity (i.e., one's "race").

This seems to suggest that one's racial status, as defined and assigned by society, should determine one's racial identity. This assumption is lodged in the fiction of racial essentialism. Appiah (1996) argued that people marginalized by racism often make strategic use of the logic of racial essentialism to facilitate healing of the self. This strategy involves revising characterizations of collective identities so that they are expressed positively. Once positive, the essential racial identity can be considered a valuable part of who one "centrally" is (Appiah, 1996). This strategy ultimately reinscribes the tyranny of race—the constraining of self-identification through the process of racial essentialism.

Some stage model theorists seem to suggest that the identity endpoint they are proposing is not simply another racial identity but rather a biracial *ethnic* identity (e.g., Kitch, 1992). The debate over whether multiracial people can be described as an ethnic group is ongoing (Nakashima, 1996; Rudin, 1997; Thornton, 1992, 1996; Weisman, 1996). Nevertheless, given our current understanding of ethnic identity and given the inherent heterogeneity within the multiracial population, it seems unlikely that a multiracial ethnic identity could ever be established as a meaningfully persistent category. Even if it could be established, the racial essentialism it implies would remain. We argue that racial essentialism is the logical outcome of all models that use a macrosystemic concept of race. Structural concepts of race imply that an individual's racial heritage produces natural psychological outcomes.

Research findings do not support a linear, hierarchical model of multiracial identity development. Research suggests that multiracial identification can be multiple, highly subjective, and fluid, shifting across contexts as well as the lifetime (Kerwin, Ponterotto, Jackson, & Harris, 1993; Poussaint, 1984; Root, 1990; Stephan, 1991, 1992). We argue that the limitations of stage theories of cultural identity development are problematic for all persons, whether they are defined as multiracial or monoracial. The emphasis on a structural interpretation of race disregards the complex nature of context-dependent processes such as cultural identity development. One of the concerns here is the broad language that is used to describe the construct of interest. There has long been the following question: *How do individuals integrate society's messages concerning their racial or ethnic being?* This question has provoked this answer: *A structural focus on racial or ethnic identity is warranted.* Because, however, this structural identity is often used to explain a wide variety of social phenomena (see, e.g., Helms & Cook's [1999] description of how racial identity affects the supervision process), we argue that the models used to explain the phenomena should be broader, more inclusive, and context focused. We believe an ecological perspective on cultural identity provides a broad enough framework to generate a better understanding of this complex phenomenon.

Several ecological frameworks for understanding multiracial identity have been forwarded (Johnson, 1992; Miller, 1992; Root, 1990), but the most fully developed one has recently been proposed by Root (1999). Root suggests that her model is intended to be a racial identity development meta-model. This model accounts "for the range of ways in which people construct their core identities, and determine the importance of race in them" (Root, 1998). In other words, although her theory primarily deals with the racial identity development of multiracial people, she believes that her model has utility for all racialized people (theoretically, even White people). Three assumptions serve as the foundation of Root's model: (a) There may be many different outcomes of racial identity, and it will become increasingly harder to evaluate these outcomes in a stratified way; (b) racial construction, although historically rooted, is dynamic; and (c) many persons live with multiple secondary statuses that interact with race and necessarily influence the salience of race and the formation of racial identity. Root (1999) is primarily concerned with factors that

influence the process of racial identification. This is a significant departure from foundational stage models of racial identity that, as previously discussed, put little emphasis on the context of the racial identification process. Root's focus on ecological factors that influence racial identity development has several implications. One is that the process of racial identification is not universal either within groups or between groups. Racial identity development occurs within myriad contexts. Moreover, a number of systemic forces drive the identity resolution process (e.g., inherited influences and social experiences). These systems are conceptualized as "lenses through which experiences are filtered" (Root, 1999, p. 77). They are dynamic, reciprocally interacting with each other and the broader ecological context.

Second, the racial identification process is not linear. Gleaning from Parham (1989), Root (1999) describes the identity development process as "a spiraling and circular process by which one resolves tensions and accomplishes identity" (p. 77). Given that this process is not universal within or between groups, and given that individuals' identity processes are differentially affected by various contexts and systems, no single racial identity outcome can be predicted for individuals or groups. Speaking of multiracial identity development in particular, Root posits four possible outcomes of racial identity: (a) acceptance of the ascribed identity, (b) identification with both groups, (c) identification with a single racial group, and (d) identification with a new group. She suggests that all of these identity outcomes may shift across contexts and the life span. Moreover, she suggests there may be additional identity outcomes, as the salience of one's racial identity may be affected by interactions with a person's "secondary statuses" (e.g., gender, class, sexuality).

Root's (1999) conceptualization of racial identity appears to differ dramatically from traditional conceptualizations of racial identity. What Root does not make explicit is the distinction between racial identities and racial roles. Different racial roles might be adopted across different social contexts as a strategy for coping with diverse situations (Coleman, 1995; Nakashima, 1996). A racial identification that a person chooses to use in a specific context may not necessarily reflect a person's "core" identity (Thornton, 1996). On the other hand, fluid, multiple racial identities may actually characterize a person's "core" group identity. Researchers are encouraged to explore this distinction. Ecological models of racial identity development are a welcome addition to the racial identity literature as they come closest to capturing the complexity of the racial identification process. These models, however, need to be more explicit as to how racially marginalized people might develop a positive appreciation for their racial heritages and positive racial identifications, if such positives are possible. That is, it may be that escaping negative racial representations— the constraint on identity development— demands, ultimately, that individuals question the validity of roles based on the fiction of race.

Researchers are also encouraged to explore the applicability of an ecological perspective to the racial identity development process within so-called monoracial populations as a way to move beyond the limitations of structural models and their inherent reliance on an essentialist understanding of group membership. Researchers, moreover, are cautioned in their use of this or any other racial identity model until the key assumptions of the model are empirically validated. This will be a challenging—but not insurmountable—task. Root (1999) suggests that a combination of quantitative and qualitative research methods will need to be employed to flesh out the details of the racial identification process.

METHODOLOGICAL CHALLENGES

In continuing to explore the consequences of dichotomous, decontextualized thinking in the area of race and ethnic identity development, we must examine how these traditions have extended to science and challenge the discovery and construction of knowledge in this area. The study of these constructs rests not only on the methodologies selected but also on the very definitions applied in operationalizing and then "measuring" these variables. This section explores two major methodological dilemmas facing identity research: determining how to conceptualize and measure race and selecting a corresponding epistemological approach to research. Ultimately, this discussion will reiterate the importance of contextualizing emic perspectives throughout the research process within an ecological framework and introduce the extended case method (Burawoy, 1991) as one methodological approach that is simultaneously responsive to contextual variables and can be used to integrate data into theory.

One of the challenges to any study involving variables of race or ethnicity is researchers' ability to account for their myriad definitions and functions in North American society, and therefore in science, as a biological characteristic, a socially constructed human category, a marker for broader group memberships (e.g., class, cultural, and ethnic), and/or as a personal and group identity. The promotion of "race" as a natural and meaningful designation assigned and fixed at birth has a long sociopolitical history as it is reified through contemporary racial classification systems in North American institutions and informs racialized dimensions of human interaction. These conceptualizations are so ingrained in the North American psyche that race has become an uncontested fact of human existence and has ultimately become quantifiable in social science research (through use of racial labels) as an essential variable tied to, or literally causing, myriad life outcomes and personal attributes (e.g., poverty, intelligence). This is evidenced by studies that continue to use race as a main effect for poverty, crime, and intelligence (e.g., *The Bell Curve*; Herrnstein & Murray, 1996). Consequently, it is rare for social scientists to even question the legitimacy of using these same categories as they are laced with taken-for-granted meanings and representations for other constructs, including racial identity and ethnic group membership. Miranda (2000) has discussed the challenges for social scientists in using the labels of *race* and *ethnicity* and how those challenges can serve to confound findings. In the next section of this chapter, we summarize that discussion and present the methodological challenges it represents so that we can shift away from decontextualized and dichotomized approaches to research toward the study and analysis of phenomenological experiences of mixed race and ethnicity in context. Consequently, this becomes an ecological approach to identity research and requires methods that honor both the systemic and idiosyncratic dimensions of this process.

A number of gains could result from a conceptual shift. First, it would challenge researchers to loosen their reliance on predetermined and fixed racial labels that may not be representative of all persons within a given category. For research with multiracial and multiethnic populations, the importance of avoiding the use of a glorified "other" category via a new "multiracial category" cannot be overemphasized. Race, ethnicity, and identity research must honor the diverse social and political histories of people within the United States that inform their personal identities. Lumping all multiracial persons into a single category when studying identity development negates these diverse systemic inputs and reifies essentialist dimensions of pan-ethnic/racial classifications discussed earlier.

Second, the selection of phenomenological or open-ended measures of identity could allow multiracial persons to set the parameters of their own individual racial and ethnic identities, instead of experiencing research as yet another assault on this group's ability to be self-defining. The use of phenomenological data recognizes and values the authority of emic perspectives and resists pathologizing these voices simply because they defy current social constructions or monocentric theoretical frameworks.

Last, using emic perspectives to measure personal expressions of racial and ethnic identity holds the most promise for this area of research in attempting to eradicate decontextualized and essentialist measures, ultimately resulting in a transformation of how this body of research affects race, ethnicity, and identity for populations beyond multiracial/multiethnic people. Consequently, the use of racial labels by an individual may then be understood as the strategic use of language across various contexts to manage daily life tasks and achieve ecological competence. This approach may hold researchers accountable to the myriad functions and locations of one's identity using the socially prescribed terminology. This also acknowledges the entitlement of multiracial people to name their identifications in many ways, including racially and ethnically.

Recent research in the area of multiracial identity development by Rockquemore and Brunsma (2002) is one example of research that has moved in this direction by using mixed-method approaches and asking broad-based phenomenological questions that seek a range of experiences and identity outcomes for biracial persons, rather than having respondents "check a box" of racial categories or preferences that are assumed to measure these domains (and others) independently from context. Not surprisingly, the range of identities reported in their findings clearly confirm the salience of context, within-group variation and social interactions across various environments as significant contributors to the identity development process among this population. In so doing, this approach to researching identity development recognizes "race" itself as a sociopolitical construct but also the formation of an *identity* as a socially and personally constructed process. This reflects the general shift in conceptualizing identity found within other bodies of multiracial literature, which call for fluidity and ecologically contextualized data (see Gaskins, 1999; Johnson, 1992; Renn, 1998).

Limitations in measuring racial heritage, however, are not the only barrier to effective and meaningful research in this area. Given the traditions of dichotomous thinking within a Western culture in general (e.g., Black-White, male-female), it seems natural that we would extend these divisions to the philosophy of science. As the following discussion illustrates, how researchers in this area approach the process of scientific inquiry can have powerful consequences for research with multiracial populations.

To effectively understand the process of cultural identity development, social scientists have myriad methods available to them. Ideally, the method chosen by a researcher complements the research question of interest and one's epistemological stance—the belief in the nature of reality and its accessibility through scientific inquiry (Fisk & Shweder, 1986). Historically, however, there has been a trend within the social sciences to privilege strict positivist philosophies of and approaches to "science" (Harding, 1986; Hill Collins, 2000; Taylor, 1995). Currently, research on cultural identity development has been dominated by postposivitist perspectives that limit our perspective-taking ability.

The identity development models and theories discussed earlier are reflective of traditional positivist thinking. These frameworks often embrace positivistic goals for research findings to empirically validate their models as generalizable truths (as opposed to creating theory with data from the field) and, therefore, uphold dualisms, including the ability to quantify racial identity via racial label variables. Using this approach to research the study of racial and ethnic identity typically renders changes in these identities or reports outside of the discrete categories (including an "achieved" or "foreclosed" multiracial identity) as anomalies, often force-fitting them into these frameworks, pathologizing their meanings, or dismissing their significance.

Advocating for the adoption of philosophies outside of a positivist paradigm typically represents a move away from the use of a priori assumptions and understandings of reality as singular and separate from knowing. The goal of scientific inquiry here is to develop an understanding of a phenomenon through the reconstruction of emic perspectives. Using a more social constructivist approach to science allows for the subjective meaning systems of multiracial/multiethnic individuals to be privileged over existing theoretical frameworks or the meaning systems of the researchers involved. Constructivism is also "anti-essentialist" (Denzin & Lincoln, 1998). Within this paradigm, the social categories Black, White, male, female, as well as their meanings, are understood as socially and individually created, not as markers of real inherent qualities or natural essences (Brewer, 1995; Berger & Luckmann, 1966; Denzin & Lincoln, 1998; Kohn, 1995). This does not methodologically render race or racism an illusion in the lives of persons who experience or perpetuate ongoing microaggressions and racism. It does represent the opportunity to understand race as a social construction that informs interpersonal interactions and creates the sociopolitical contexts in which racial identities are regulated, resisted, and expressed. Adopting a constructivist epistemology would encourage the use of a research method and design that understands racial and ethnic identity development as an interactive process occurring within a society that continues to essentialize and regulate racial group memberships and identity.

Finally, taking a social constructivist perspective in research allows for the exploration of racial identity as a co-creative and subjective process (Anzaldua, 1987; Root, 1998; Twine, 1996a). In other words, it allows for the study of race as a socially constructed "reality," one that is malleable and constantly re-created and/or reified through human interactions and the social structures they uphold or defy. This understanding of multiracial/multiethnic identity development further supports the consideration of methods that fall outside of the traditional approach to measuring racial identity through the use of quantifiable discrete proxy variables (e.g., racial labels, racial preferences).

This chapter, however, has also identified the need for an approach that recognizes the sociopolitical and historical context in which one experiences a given racial position. Macrosystemic aspects of race have real consequences in human lives psychologically, politically, and economically (hooks, 1992; Omi & Winant, 1995; West, 1994). Adopting one-dimensional approaches to research to simply study microlevel dimensions may miss this important variable in its contributions to the ways in which humans experience their daily lives. Future research in this area must not ignore in its final analysis the role of the macrosystem in shaping daily experiences with race and ethnicity. Critical theorists have long challenged mainstream and interpretive science to recognize the historically institutionalized/structural exclusion and individual marginalization of specific human experiences (e.g., those of women and people of color). This agenda for research could certainly be extended to the realities of multiracial/multiethnic populations who are socially and politically marginalized in research and in society. Arguably an inherently "political"

approach to science, the primary goal of critical theory research is the emancipation of oppressed populations through the scientific advancement of these realities (Brewer, 1995; Hill Collins, 2000; Kohn, 1995; McGuigan, 1998). This perspective is a valuable addition to challenging researchers in their assumptions regarding the production of knowledge, as well as historically privileged positions that have advanced one group's worldview of "truth" at the expense of others (Harding, 1986; Hill Collins, 2000; Kincheloe & McLaren, 1998). In its application to racial and ethnic identity research, it calls for understanding phenomenological measures of identity development through the lens of macrolevel structures, including colorism, essentialism, classism, and sexism.

Race, class, and gender researchers are beginning to recognize the need for contextualized phenomenological data that analyze findings in ways that recognize both the structural and psychological dimensions of human existence, particularly for populations of color (Cuàdraz & Uttal, 1999). Informed by critical theory perspectives on power, researchers are then challenged to recognize the multiple and possibly conflicting realities/experiences in a single individual or simultaneous memberships to both privileged and oppressed groups (Anzaldua, 1987; Cuàdraz & Uttal, 1999; Hill Collins, 2000). For example, recent research by Root (1998) and Renn (1998) involving interviews with mixed-race young adults suggests that although these individuals have similar experiences with racial litmus tests and multiple external forces seeking their loyalties to one racial group over another, mixed-race persons themselves contribute to these contexts and develop a wide range of identity outcomes that may shift across contexts and throughout their lifetimes.

Consequently, adopting a solely constructivist perspective would stop at the phenomenological level, thus barring the exploration of context-driven distinctions in the meaning and function of a given label or identity. Likewise, it may ignore the power of one's environment to externally impose a hierarchy of what is valued in any given setting. For example, an individual may use other more privileged social identities (e.g., class) as cultural capital in one context while drawing on other social identities in another. A solely critical theory approach, however, may miss the power of the individual to negotiate his or her environment, transcending the structural constraints placed on personal agency. For these reasons, identity researchers interested in recognizing both macrosystemic and microlevel contributions to racial and ethnic identity development should avoid the tradition of selecting a slice of this process at the expense of examining another. We argue here for adopting the broadest lens through which to view and analyze the range of experiences among multiracial persons and suggest that researchers must be held accountable to these multiple layers when undertaking a study in this area. Again, that lens is the ecological model, which further recognizes the interactional and transformative nature of "reality" at all system levels, allowing for limitless expressions and functions of a private and public racial/ethnic orientation.

Given the rapid growth of research in the area of multiracial identity formation by social scientists and clinicians, it seems important to join with the process of theory and literature development, recognizing the opportunities to promote and expand emic perspectives as represented by both the researcher and the in-depth investigations of this population's experiences as defined by mixed-race persons (see Funderburg, 1994, 1998; Gaskins, 1999; O'Hearn, 1998; Root, 1992, 1996a, 1996b, 1998, 2000). This is an important task for future research, as theory is used not only to develop knowledge for knowledge's sake but is also applied to universal definitions of mental health and "normalcy," making clinical diagnoses and

individual treatments, designing interventions for families, and advancing arguments for "healthy" developmental needs specifically for persons with multiracial/multiethnic backgrounds. This suggests a dire need for future studies to develop and reconstruct meaningful theoretical connections that recognize the diverse contexts in which race and ethnicity are experienced, for use in understanding the process of identity formation across the life course. Consequently, a study that adopts as its primary focus identifying and critiquing the conceptual and theoretical lacunae in this field of research must go beyond the microlevel analysis of phenomenology.

A number of methods are available to interpretive researchers interested in the construction of theory (Creswell, 1998; Denzin & Lincoln, 1998). One such approach is the extended case method (Burawoy et al., 1991), which is a unique approach for social science research that can be extended to the study of multiracial identity development through the use of contextualized data from in-depth interviews to develop theory. The ecological perspective, as discussed earlier, invites researchers to conceptualize racial and ethnic identity as simultaneously socially constructed and structurally imposed. There is also a need, however, to transcend the dualisms of scientific thinking and conceptualizations of race to advantage researchers in using the most appropriate "measures" to challenge and rework theoretical paradigms to better reflect the lived experiences of multiracial/multiethnic populations. This section calls for a shift in methodology toward extending the contextualized analysis of findings to theoretical frameworks.

The extended case method is a relatively new approach to qualitative research (Burawoy, 1998; Burawoy et al., 1991). This method allows the investigator to use primarily participant observation and interviews, not in an attempt to speak for unheard voices or simply describe observations of "others" but rather to share insights resulting from these "interactions" with the participants who informed their research process and contributed to the further understanding of a particular experience or case (Burawoy, 1991, 1998). But the purpose of the research process does not end here. Researchers using this method are expected to expand what are considered "data" to incorporate social and political narratives informing the phenomenon of interest. For researchers interested in multiracial/multiethnic identity development, this calls for designs that use and critique the histories of mixed race, relevant legislation and political movements (e.g., the multiracial movement), pop culture, art/music, and the discourse of race and mixed race across various disciplines. Second, the extended case method uses techniques, including in-depth interviewing and participant observation, while including data from multiple sources to reconstruct theoretical explanations of a given phenomenon. This interplay between technique and theory (re)construction (i.e., analysis) is a unique methodological approach.

Ultimately, this method attempts to reach beyond the limitations of seemingly disparate epistemologies and methods tied to specific techniques, fusing their strengths into a new approach so that preexisting theories can be reconstructed. Consequently, this method represents an unparalleled opportunity for researchers to use a variety of techniques that go beyond describing phenomenological themes and (re)constructing categories or typologies of meaning: Researchers also analyze broader contextual contributions to phenomena, ultimately contributing these findings to theory development (Burawoy, 1998; Denzin & Lincoln, 1998).

The goals for this type of research would include but extend beyond holding the rapidly growing body of multiracial research, literature, and theory accountable to persons whose development occurs on the borders of socially constructed racial and ethnic categories. In using nonessentialist measures to design inquiries within an ecological framework, this method offers a much-needed shift for this field of research. It would allow researchers to respond to the call in the multiracial literature for research that measures race and analyzes identity outcomes as they are experienced and reworked across macro-, meso-, and microlevels. Furthermore, in its ability to contribute to theory, adopting this approach would advance new conceptualizations of race as both psychological and sociological, and various identities may promote or inhibit ecological competence across and interactions within different racial and ethnic contexts. Ultimately, results from research that critically analyzes its findings as proposed have implications beyond theory and literature development to include having a practical application to parenting strategies, creating racially and ethnically relevant interventions, and reworking future conceptualizations of race and ethnicity in North American society, which are essential to the practice of multicultural competence.

CONCLUSION

The goal of this chapter, as the title indicates, was to point us toward an ecological understanding of cultural identity development. Such an understanding would allow us to explore the manner in which an individual's sense of group membership is organized within his or her complex and multilayered social situation. It would allow us to understand how individuals make sense of the group memberships they associate with themselves and the groups to which they find themselves associated. Given the potential fluidity of this experience, an ecological model will attempt to explicate the multiple perspectives that can be taken on an individual's cultural identity. It will seek to understand how that identity is the same and different across the contexts (microsystems, mesosystems, exosystems, and macrosystems) of the individual's life. Such a task appears to overwhelm positivistic methods of analysis, which are forced to impose essentialist notions of macrosystemic factors such as race or ethnicity to create categories for investigation. It also appears to overwhelm constructionist notions of individually generated understandings of self that do not account for the influence of sociohistorical relationships between people and institutions that serve to organize the experience that individuals can have of themselves and each other. An ecological perspective on cultural identity encourages us to find ways of thinking about and systematically investigating ourselves in a way that allows us to simultaneously honor and integrate the meaning-making power of individuals and the role of external forces in organizing their phenomenological experiences.

As we all struggle to understand our place in our worlds, we are aware of the many roles we fill and how those experiences serve to organize our sense of self. Our role as a member of a group is one of those organizing experiences. By taking the time to sit with individuals and allow them to share with us their narrative of self within context, by reading about the role of macrosystemic factors such as race and ethnicity in the history of a culture, and by developing, giving, analyzing, and then integrating reliable measures of cultural identity, we gather all these sources of information that will illuminate the processes and content of cultural identity development.

REFERENCES

Anzaldua, G. (1987). *Borderlands, la frontera— The new Mestiza*. San Francisco: Aunt Lute Books.

Appiah, K. A. (1996). Race, culture, and identity: Misunderstood connections. In K. A. Appiah & A. Gutmann (Eds.), *Color conscious: The political morality of race* (pp. 30-105). Princeton, NJ: Princeton University Press.

Atkinson, D. R., Morten, G., & Sue, D. W. (1993). *Counseling American minorities: A cross-cultural perspective* (4th ed.). Dubuque, IA: Brown & Benchmark/William C. Brown.

Berger, P. L., & Luckmann, T. (1966). *The social construction of reality: A treatise in the sociology of knowledge.* New York: Anchor.

Brewer, R. M. (1995). Knowledge construction and racist science. *American Behavioral Scientist, 39*(1), 62-78.

Bronfenbrenner, U. (1979). *The ecology of human development.* Cambridge, MA: Harvard University Press.

Burawoy, M. (1991). The extended case method. In M. Burawoy, A. Burton, A. Ferguson, K. Fox, J. Gamson, M. Gartrell, et al. (Eds.), *Ethnography unbound: Power and resistance in the modern metropolis* (pp. 271-291). Berkeley: University of California Press.

Burawoy, M. (1998). The extended case method. *Sociological Theory, 16*(1), 4-33.

Burawoy, M., Burton, A., Ferguson, A., Fox, K., Gamson, J., Gartrell, M., et al. (Eds.). (1991). *Ethnography unbound: Power and resistance in the modern metropolis.* Berkeley: University of California Press.

Cass, V. C. (1979). Homosexual identity formation: A theoretical model. *Journal of Homosexuality, 4*, 219-235.

Coleman, H. L. K. (1995). Strategies for coping with cultural diversity. *The Counseling Psychologist, 23*(4), 722-740.

Creswell, J. W. (1998). *Qualitative inquiry and research design: Choosing among five traditions.* Thousand Oaks, CA: Sage.

Cross, W. E., Jr. (1971). The Negro to Black conversion experience: Towards a psychology of Black liberation. *Black World, 20*(9), 13-27.

Cross, W. E., Jr. (1991). *Shades of black.* Philadelphia: Temple University Press.

Cuàdraz, G. H., & Uttal, L. (1999). Intersectionality and in-depth interviews: Methodological strategies for analyzing race, class, and gender. *Race, Gender & Class, 6*(3), 126-186.

Denzin, N. K., & Lincoln, Y. S. (Eds.). (1998). *The landscape of qualitative research.* Thousand Oaks, CA: Sage.

Erickson, E. H. (1968). *Identity, youth and crisis.* New York: W. W. Norton.

Fisk, D. W., & Shweder, R. A. (Eds.). (1986). *Metatheory in social science: Pluralisms and subjectivities.* Chicago: University of Chicago Press.

Ford, D. H. (1997). *Humans as self-constructing living systems.* Hillsdale, NJ: Lawrence Erlbaum.

Ford, M. E. (1992). *Motivating humans.* Newbury Park, CA: Sage.

Frankenberg, R. (1993). *The social construction of whiteness: White women, race matters.* Minnesota: University of Minnesota Press.

Funderburg, L. (1994). *Black, White, other.* New York: Morrow.

Funderburg, L. (1998). Crossing the demographic divide: The otherness of multiracial identity. *American Demographics, 20*(10), 24-25.

Gaskins, P. F. (1999). *What are you? Voices of mixed-race young people.* New York: Henry Holt.

Goldenberg, I., & Goldenberg, H. (2000). *Family therapy: An overview.* Belmont, CA: Brooks/Cole.

Harding, S. (1986). *The science question in feminism.* Milton Keynes, UK: Open University Press.

Helms, J. E. (Ed.). (1990a). *Black and White racial identity: Theory, research, and practice.* Westport, CT: Greenwood.

Helms, J. E. (1990b). *The Womanist Identity Attitudes Scale.* Unpublished scale.

Helms, J. E. (1994). How multiculturalism obscures racial factors in the therapy process. *Journal of Counseling Psychology, 41*(2), 162-165.

Helms, J. E. (1995). The conceptualization of racial identity and other "racial" constructs. In E. J. Trickett, R. J. Watts, & D. Birman (Eds.), *Human diversity: Perspectives on people in context* (pp. 285-311). San Francisco: Jossey-Bass.

Helms, J. E., & Cook, D. A. (1999). Using race and culture in therapy supervision. In J. E. Helms & D. A. Cook (Eds.), *Using race and culture in counseling and psychotherapy: Theory and process* (pp. 277-298). Boston: Allyn & Bacon.

Herrnstein, R., & Murray, C. (1996). *The bell curve: Intelligence and class structure in American life.* New York: Free Press.

Hill Collins, P. (2000). *Black feminist thought: Knowledge, consciousness, and the politics of empowerment.* New York: Routledge Kegan Paul.

hooks, b. (1992). *Black looks: race and representation.* Boston, MA: South End.

Jacobs, J. (1992). Identity development in biracial children. In M. P. P. Root (Ed.), *Racially mixed people in America* (pp. 190-206). Newbury Park, CA: Sage.

Johnson, D. J. (1992). Developmental pathways: Toward an ecological theoretical formulation of race identity in Black-White biracial children. In M. P. P. Root (Ed.), *Racially mixed people in America* (pp. 37-49). Newbury Park, CA: Sage.

Kerwin, C., Ponterotto, J., Jackson, B., & Harris, A. (1993). Racial identity in biracial children: A qualitative investigation. *Journal of Counseling Psychology, 40,* 221-231.

Kitch, G. (1992). The developmental process of asserting a biracial, bicultural identity. In M. P. P. Root (Ed.), *Racially mixed people in America* (pp. 162-178). Newbury Park, CA: Sage.

Kincheloe, J. L. & McLaren, P. L. (1998). Rethinking critical theory and qualitative research. In N. K. Denzin & Y. S. Lincoln (Eds.), *The landscape of qualitative research: Theories and issues* (pp. 260-299). Thousand Oaks, CA: Sage.

Kohn, M. (1995). Science and race matter. *World Press Review, 42*(12), 48-49.

Lerner, R. M., & Foch, T. T. (Eds.). (1986). *Biological-psychosocial interactions in early adolescence.* Hillsdale, NJ: Lawrence Erlbaum.

McGuigan, J. (Ed.). (1998). *Cultural methodologies.* Thousand Oaks, CA: Sage.

Miller, R. L. (1992). The human ecology of multiracial identity. In M. P. P. Root (Ed.), *Racially mixed people in America* (pp. 24-36). Newbury Park, CA: Sage.

Miranda, G. E. (2000). *Negotiating American constructions of race, culture, and family: Theoretical implications for racial and cultural identity development among first generation Black-White biracial adoptees*. Unpublished manuscript, University of Wisconsin–Madison.

Nakashima, C. (1992). An invisible monster: The creation and denial of mixed-race people in America. In M. P. P. Root (Ed.), *Racially mixed people in America* (pp. 162-178). Newbury Park, CA: Sage.

Nakashima, C. (1996). Voices from the movement: Approaches to multiraciality. In M. P. P. Root (Ed.), *The multiracial experience, racial borders as the new frontier* (pp. 79-100). Thousand Oaks, CA: Sage.

Norton, R. A. (2000). *Exploring the relationship between racial essentialism and allegiance testing*. Unpublished manuscript, University of Wisconsin–Madison.

O'Hearn, C. C. (Ed.). (1998). *Half and half: Writers on growing up biracial and bicultural*. New York: Random House.

Oleneck, M. (2000). Can multicultural education change what counts as cultural capital? *American Educational Research Journal, 37,* 317-348.

Omi, M., & Winant, H. (1994). *Racial formation in the United States: From the 1960's to the 1990's* (2nd ed.). New York: Routledge Kegan Paul.

Omi, M., & Winant, H. (1995). Contesting the meaning of race in the post–civil rights movement era. In S. Pedraza & R. Rumbaut (Eds.), *Origins & destinies: Immigration, race, & ethnicity in America* (pp. 470-478). Belmont, CA: Wadsworth.

Parham, T. A. (1989). Cycles of psychological nigrescence. *The Counseling Psychologist, 17*(2), 187-226.

Phinney, J. (1989). Stages of ethnic identity in minority group adolescence. *Journal of Early Adolescence, 9,* 34-49.

Phinney, J. (1990). Ethnic identity in adolescents and adults: A review of research. *Psychological Bulletin, 108,* 499-514.

Phinney, J. (1995). Ethnic identity and self-esteem: A review and integration. In A. Padilla (Ed.), *Hispanic psychology: Critical issues in theory and research* (pp. 57-70). Thousand Oaks, CA: Sage.

Phinney, J., & Alipuria, L. L. (1996). At the interface of cultures: Multiethnic/multiracial high school and college students. *Journal of Social Psychology, 136*(2), 139-158.

Pierce, L. (2000). The continuing significance of race. In P. Spickard & J. Burroughs (Eds.), *We are a people: Narrative and multiplicity in constructing ethnic identity* (pp. 221-228). Philadelphia: Temple University Press.

Poston, W. C. (1990). The biracial identity development model: A needed addition. *Journal of Counseling and Development, 69,* 152-155.

Poussaint, A. P. (1984). Study of interracial children presents positive picture. *Interracial Books for Children Bulletin, 15*(6), 9-10.

Renn, K. A. (1998). *Check all that apply: The experience of biracial and multiracial college students*. ASHE Annual Meeting Paper [Online]. Available: *www.edrs.com/Webstore/Download.cfm?ID=443017&CFID=580102 4&CFTOKEN=26213778*

Rockquemore, K. A., & Brunsma, D. L. (2002). *Beyond Black: Biracial identity in America*. Thousand Oaks, CA: Sage.

Root, M. P. P. (1990). Resolving "other" status: Identity development of biracial individuals. *Women and Therapy, 9*(1-2), 185-205.

Root, M. P. P. (Ed.). (1992). *Racially mixed people in America*. Newbury Park, CA: Sage.

Root, M. P. P. (1996a). A bill of rights for racially mixed people. In M. P. P. Root (Ed.), *The multiracial experience, racial borders as the new frontier* (pp. 3-14). Thousand Oaks, CA: Sage.

Root, M. P. P. (Ed.). (1996b). *The multiracial experience, racial borders as the new frontier*. Thousand Oaks, CA: Sage.

Root, M. P. P. (1998). Experiences and processes affecting racial identity development: Preliminary results from the biracial sibling project. *Cultural Diversity and Mental Health, 4*(3), 237-247.

Root, M. P. P. (1999). The biracial baby boom: Understanding ecological constructions of racial identity in the 21st century. In R. H. Sheets & E. R. Hollins (Eds.), *Racial and ethnic identity in school practices: Aspects of human development* (pp. 67-89). Mahwah, NJ: Lawrence Erlbaum.

Root, M. P. P. (2000). Rethinking racial identity development. In P. Spickard & J. Burroughs

(Eds.), *We are a people: Narrative and multiplicity in constructing ethnic identity* (pp. 205-220). Philadelphia: Temple University Press.

Rowe, W., Bennett, S. K., & Atkinson, D. R. (1994). White racial identity models: A critique and alternative proposal. *The Counseling Psychologist, 19,* 76-102.

Rudin, S. A. (1997). Multiethnicity is divisive and basically a bankrupt ideal. *American Psychologist, 52*(11), 1248-1248.

Spickard, P., & Burroughs, J. (Eds.). (2000). *We are a people: Narrative and multiplicity in constructing ethnic identity.* Philadelphia: Temple University Press.

Stephan, C. W. (1991). Ethnic identity among mixed-heritage people in Hawaii. *Symbolic Interaction, 14,* 261-277.

Stephan, C. W. (1992). Mixed-heritage individuals: Ethnic identity and trait characteristics. In M. P. P. Root (Ed.), *Racially mixed people in America* (pp. 50-63). Newbury Park, CA: Sage.

Taylor, C. (1995). *Philosophical arguments.* Cambridge, MA: Harvard University Press.

Thornton, M. C. (1992). Is multiracial status unique? The personal and social experience. In M. P. P. Root (Ed.), *Racially mixed people in America* (pp. 321-325). Newbury Park, CA: Sage.

Thornton, M. C. (1996). Hidden agendas, identity theories, and multiracial people. In M. P. P. Root (Ed.), *The multiracial experience, racial borders as the new frontier* (pp. 101-120). Thousand Oaks, CA: Sage.

Twine, F. W. (1996a). Brown skinned white girls: Class, culture and the construction of White identity in suburban communities. *Gender, Place & Culture: A Journal of Feminist Geography, 3*(2), 205-224.

Twine, F. W. (1996b). Heterosexual alliances: The romantic management of racial identity. In M. P. P. Root (Ed.), *The multiracial experience, racial borders as the new frontier* (pp. 291-304). Thousand Oaks, CA: Sage.

U.S. Bureau of the Census. (2000). *United States Census 2000.* Washington, DC: U.S. Department of Commerce.

Weisman, J. R. (1996). An "other" way of life: The empowerment of alterity in the interracial individual. In M. P. P. Root (Ed.), *The multiracial experience, racial borders as the new frontier* (pp. 152-164). Thousand Oaks, CA: Sage.

West, C. (1994). *Race matters.* New York: Vintage.

Williams, T. K. (1996). Race as process: Reassessing the "what are you?" encounters of biracial individuals. In M. P. P. Root (Ed.), *The multiracial experience, racial borders as the new frontier* (pp. 191-210). Thousand Oaks, CA: Sage.

4

Gender, Feminism, and Multicultural Competencies

SHARON L. BOWMAN
KEISA D. KING

Ball State University

> *"I am Woman, hear me roar!"*
>
> —Helen Reddy
>
> *"Ain't I a Woman?"*
>
> —Sojourner Truth

What images are evoked when reading these two lines? When Helen Reddy sings "I am Woman, hear me roar!" is she talking about women of color? Certainly, many readers of a certain age would first visualize Ms. Reddy, but who is she singing about? How would that "woman" be described? Probably not as a woman of color; most likely, that roaring woman is White. Now consider the second line. For most of us, this line recalls the image of a Black woman, a Negress, speaking before a women's convention in 1851. Her reminder, her plea, her demand, was that the White women fighting for equal rights recognize that not all women are White and that "colored women" are also deserving of rights and freedoms. It may not be the most-quoted line ever by a woman of color, but it is certainly a well-known one. The line may also evoke the image of bell hooks's 1981 book by the same title. Written well over 100 hundred years later, the message is the same—women come in many shades, not just White, and the focus on "women" should be suitably broadened.

The purpose of this chapter is to examine the place of women of color in psychology's continued progression toward multicultural competence. It has been argued (Gloria, 2001) that multicultural competence in counseling and psychotherapy should be expanded to include "relevant knowledge and skills and the deconstruction of negative attitudes and beliefs about Latinas" (p. 18). Taken even further, acknowledging the different contexts of women of color when discussing multicultural competence is imperative. The experiences of women and men within a racial or ethnic group may be as different as the experiences across groups.

One of the hardest developmental phases is determining where and how one "fits in" with those around them. Children and adults alike seek a peer group with whom they can feel comfortable and understood, be themselves, and not have to explain who they are or be on constant guard. Sometimes one's choice of group connection is based on salient physical characteristics, such as age, gender, race or ethnicity, or disability status. Sometimes it is based on sexual identity. Other times it is based on religious beliefs, occupation, avocational activities, or other interpersonal interactions. What happens when belonging to one group practically demands dissociating from another group? Or when being perceived as a member of one group, fairly or not, leads others to ignore potential membership in other groups? Women of color are under pressure to pledge their allegiance to one side or the other, as though they can easily compartmentalize their identity.

WOMEN OF COLOR: A DOUBLE BIND

The title of Hull, Scott, and Smith's (1982) book says it all: *All the Women Are White, All the Blacks Are Men, but Some of Us Are Brave: Black Women's Studies.* Although the title specifically refers to Black women, the same statement could describe women of other ethnic groups. Women of color have two options: Join with the struggle against racism and subordinate any feelings of discrimination by sex for the greater good of saving the race (in other words, it is more important to protect the men in the community than the women), or join the fight against sexism, meaning separation from the ethnic community and a connection to White feminists fighting the battle of the universal woman, a woman whose issues may not reflect the needs or context of the ethnic community. Ethnic women are, therefore, in a double bind: Choosing to emphasize the sexism in their communities could lead to alienating men and other women who are not interested in confronting their brothers, but choosing to emphasize racism results in a negation of oneself as a woman (Canales, 1997; Gloria, 2001; Jordan, 1997).

Women of Color: Emphasis on Gender

Women of color often find that good models do not exist for race and gender debates. In a gathering of feminists, the tension among the group shifts drastically when a woman of color enters the room (Romany, 1997), whether or not she verbalizes anything race based. If she should choose to enter the discussion, perhaps from a real desire to join the group or from frustration with the group process and her apparent invisibility, the tension will become even more obvious (Bowman et al., 2001). She may be ignored, ridiculed, directly or indirectly challenged about her views, or even subtly dismissed through a topic change by one of the other participants (Grillo & Wildman, 1997; Romany, 1997). These experiences often leave the woman of color feeling disconnected, out of place, saddened, angry, hurt, and confused (Bowman et al., 2001). Most important, she may feel invisible in this group, as though her issues and needs are less important than those of the (White) whole (Grillo & Wildman, 1997).

African American daughters are taught that they must not only survive the oppression of race, class, and gender but also transcend them to succeed (Adams & LaFromboise, 2001; Collins, 1991, 1998). In fact, this is probably true for girls from all ethnic groups. Women of color are invited to join with feminist groups, fight against oppression against women, and join in the demands for equal rights. However, these women often struggle with the connection to a feminist (read: "White feminist") movement, as it does not seem to relate to an ethnic woman's reality. As Reid (1984) noted, the connection to a White feminist description of men as oppressors serves to separate women of color from their ethnic community. Yet that separation from the ethnic community also serves to cut these women off from any support they may need when facing racism in their daily lives. Much to the chagrin of the feminist community, it appears that women of color may indeed consider race more salient than gender and choose to remain connected to their ethnic community (Bowman et al., 2001).

Women of Color: Emphasis on Race/Ethnicity

Women of color participating in a discussion about racial issues may feel equally disconnected if the discussion turns to gender inequities. As women, they are pushed to focus on the needs of the racial or ethnic group (i.e., racism) as the greater danger (Jackson, 2001) and to downplay any perceived gender issues within the community for the greater good (Jordan, 1997). The community, then, ignores the stereotypes that are used to describe ethnic women, or, if not ignored, these stereotypes are almost seen as appropriate and deserved, justifying the mistreatment of women within the community.

For example, Rivera (1997) noted that "the intersection of gender, national origin and race denies Latinas a self-defined, experientially based feminist portrait" (p. 260). Latinas are expected to serve as wives, mothers, and daughters; the needs of the family or community come before their individual needs. Yet they are also stereotyped as highly sensual, sexual beings, as the counterpoint to the stereotype of hot-blooded Latino men. These stereotypes become part of the fabric of institutionalized racism, leaving Latinas with little room to maneuver their own identities as individuals (Gloria, 2001; Rivera, 1997). Gloria (2001) noted that the very nature of the use of *Latina* indicates a political split within the community. Use of this term instead of the generic *Latino* (which holds a connotation of maleness) is one way that Latinas have begun to define their own realities within the community (Dernersesian, 1993, as cited in Gloria, 2001).

African American women are the subject of a similar set of gender based stereotypes, both within and outside of their community. African American female-headed families are generally identified as a social problem; these families are labeled as welfare recipients, and it is often believed that male children are at a disadvantage in such settings (Geiger, 1995). African American women are portrayed as independent, strong-minded, and more assertive or aggressive than their White counterparts (Greene, 1994). Curiously, they are also portrayed either as sexually promiscuous and morally loose or as sexually neutered, motherly figures. These stereotypes allow the dominant society to continue to blame African American women for their second-class status. For example, African American women do not see themselves reflected in American standards of beauty and may even find themselves fighting these standards within the ethnic community. They may struggle with expectations of poor treatment from African American men, being told that their men suffer from racism daily and so should not have to face gender dissension at home (Geiger, 1995). Because they are pushed to support others' needs over their own, it may be difficult for African American women to "selfishly" assert their own needs.

The authors of this chapter have each, at different times and at different universities, served as leaders for support groups for African American women. The group members were undergraduate college students. In each case, a similar group was in operation for African American men, led by an African American man. At the request of the coleaders of the men's groups, an attempt was made to bring the men's and women's groups together for a discussion of intragroup gender issues. Although these groups occurred years apart, on different campuses, and the male coleaders were different men, the dance was the same. The initial step of the dance was a prolonged silence until a brave soul would finally ask a question of the "other" group. Eventually, the discussion moved to finger-pointing and debates over which group was least likely to be listening to the others' needs. An additional step to the dance was a confrontation about imitating the dominant (White) culture: Women claimed that they had no choice but to mimic the long, straight hair and slender body structure of White women because that is what African American men seemed to want. The men, however, countered that the women were doing it out of their own insecurities, not because that was what men wanted. The final step of this dance was for the women to begin to shut down, as their male counterparts would dismiss any gender argument as irrelevant in light of the "overall Black experience." Each of these sessions ended unsatisfactorily for the women (neither author followed up with the male group leaders to ascertain the

men's reactions). The women later noted that they did not feel heard by the men and that their comments were overlooked, dismissed, or ridiculed. Although each group of women was invited to attend a second group meeting, they declined in both cases.

This dance, which pits racism and racial issues against sexism and gender issues, is not as unusual as it might be initially assumed. A relatively recent, high-profile example might be the 1991 U.S. Senate hearings in regard to then–U.S. Supreme Court nominee Clarence Thomas's alleged sexual harassment of Anita Hill (Aldaraca, 1995; Davis & Wildman, 1997; Jordan, 1997; Taylor, 1997). During those hearings, questions were raised about the ulterior motives of feminists and others against Thomas in presenting Hill's case; the relative "damage" done to Hill if these allegations were true, because she took so long to make a formal complaint; and the attempt by White society to "lynch" an African American man (Davis & Wildman, 1997; Jordan, 1997). Although much was made of Thomas's race during the hearings, little if anything was said about Hill's race by the senators involved. In the African American community, on the other hand, much negative commentary was directed toward this Black woman who would dare "air dirty laundry" in public (Taylor, 1997). In other words, according to Jordan (1997), who was one of Hill's attorneys during the hearings, "when there are conflicts between a black man and a black woman, racism 'trumps' sexism" (p. 170). It would seem that this statement could be extrapolated to describe reality for women of all ethnic groups.

Women of Color: Emphasis on Both Identities

Do ethnic minority women think in terms of both their race and their gender? Certainly, many of them do. For many ethnic women, it is nearly impossible to think in terms of one or the other—they are shaped by both of these salient identities. There is no doubt that some women of color will identify more strongly as women, whereas others identify more strongly with their ethnicity, or perhaps neither is as important as some other aspect of their identities (e.g., sexual identity, class, age, disability status). Yet other women will strongly identify themselves as Latinas, as Black women, as Japanese American women, claiming the uniqueness that stems from a uniquely melded identity.

Research supports the idea that ethnic minority women do think in terms of multiple identities. For example, Martin and Hall (1992) measured African American women's attitudes toward feminism, racial identity levels, and belief in the importance of the feminist movement. They found that women who had high scores on the Immersion/Emersion stage held more traditional attitudes about women. In other words, women who were strongly focused on developing their identities as African Americans tended to not hold strong feminist values. However, Martin and Hall also found that 85% of their sample agreed that the feminist movement was important.

Jackson (2001) summarized her individual interviews with five African American women attending a predominantly White women's university. The women revealed that one of the initial attractions of the university was its standing as a women's college and its stated goal of empowering women. As four of the five women interviewed were also lesbian women, they also anticipated feeling support from the campus lesbian community. What they found, however, was that it was a struggle to be an African American woman on this campus. They felt disconnected from their White sisters because of race and from some of their African American sisters because they were lesbians or did not otherwise fit in with the group norms. They did not feel safe on campus or did not feel that they could trust their peers. In fact, the women believed that they needed to prove to other African American women students that they were "Black enough" while also proving to the White women that they were worthy of attending this particular college. The constant strain they described resulted in complicated relationships with both African American and White women on campus.

Espin (1993) noted that feminist therapy as described by Enns (1993) fails to include the contributions and approaches used by women of color. She further stated that "it is not enough to mention in passing that multiculturalism should be considered" (p. 104). It must be integrated into currently developing models instead of waiting for another researcher to add it as an afterthought. Espin sees value in the use of a feminist, ethnospecific approach to counseling. Such an approach requires that White women therapists change their own approaches because it is much more likely that ethnic minority clients will work with White women therapists than minority women therapists.

Malone (2000), on the other hand, reported positively on her use of feminist therapy with aboriginal women. Indeed, whole texts have been penned around ethnic women's connections with both their race and their gender from a feminist perspective. Collins (1991, 1998) has written extensively about Black feminism. Comas-Diaz and Greene (1994) edited a text with chapters on Latinas, American Indian women, and East Indian women, among others; they also invited writers to reflect on various theoretical approaches to counseling and psychotherapy for women of color. Afshar and Maynard's (1994) text was written in a similar vein but from a British standpoint. And, more recently, Landrine (1995) provided a text titled *Bringing Cultural Diversity to Feminist Psychology: Theory, Research and Practice*. These texts, as well as any number of articles in the psychological literature, indicate that women of color are showing more interest in defining themselves not by race or gender alone but by all of their salient, unique identities (which may include class, sexual identity, spirituality, marital status, age, and/or disability status).

WOMEN OF COLOR: FEMINIST OR WOMANIST?

It often comes as a surprise to White women feminists that women of color may not similarly refer to themselves as feminists. In fact, they may be "pro-woman," as one of Jackson's (2001) interviewees reported, but adamant that they are not feminist. Feminism has long been deemed a "White thing," not something relevant to women of color (Gawelek, 1997). Although its roots are in the antislavery and civil rights movements, feminism's focus has been on the universal experience of women, with *universal* being equivalent to *White*. The inherent assumption of feminism, then, is that all women define themselves as women first, regardless of race or class. This assumption ignores the possibility that women of color may view race as the most salient variable in their lives (Brown, 1990). It also ignores the fact that White women in the United States, who live in a culture that provides privilege to those with White skin, have access to power that other women do not (Bowman et al., 2001).

There are women of color who are also feminist. Their perspective on women's issues and women's relation to men, however, is quite different from a White feminist's perspective (Bowman et al., 2001). For example, one of the historical pressure points for the women's movement was the right of married women to work. For African American women, however, working outside the home has always been expected; marriage did not change the need to contribute financially to

the household (Greene, 1994). For women of color, the idea of fighting against men made no sense, as men were allies against the racism experienced by all members of the ethnic minority community. Survival of the community, of the race, remained paramount.

Women of color also held roles in their communities that White women did not hold with White men (Bowman et al., 2001; LaFromboise, Berman, & Sohi, 1994). American Indian women, for example, held leadership roles, were honored members of their communities, and overall had more power and flexibility than White women did in their communities. In studying American Indian communities and other ethnic communities, it is clear that minority women still wield significant influence (Bowman et al., 2001).

Other roles held by women of color in their communities may be perceived as negative by White women feminists, who are not taking into account the whole sociocultural experience of the community (Bowman et al., 2001; Bradshaw, 1994). Perceptions of women of color as abused, submissive to their men, or victimized by their religious beliefs are negative and potentially harmful stereotypes. Women of color who are also pro-woman spend their time justifying their perspective to White feminists; they eventually tire of the struggle to be heard. For example, some years ago, one of the authors led a symposium as a women's conference in which her graduate students were presenting their research projects. One of the presenters was an Orthodox Muslim woman, dressed conservatively and wearing the *hijab*, or head covering. During the question-and-answer period, several White women attendees challenged this particular student's expression of her religion, which they perceived as anti-woman. The student was amazed that her ideas were not heard over the loudness of her appearance.

Women of color who also identify as feminist are fighting issues for which many White women have no basis of understanding. Asian American feminists, for example, may be focused on class issues for the community, immigration concerns, and current manifestations of past racist behaviors in the larger community (Chow, 1991). Chicana feminists may be in a struggle over broad issues of social inequality for their community, difficulties with the educational system, immigration issues, and health care concerns, among other problems (Garcia, 1991). American Indian feminists struggle with keeping their communities strong, especially when more and more members live in urban areas away from reservations (LaFromboise et al., 1994). They also must be concerned with health issues, rampant unemployment, and poor educational resources. African American feminists may be concerned with issues regarding reproductive care, welfare and educational reforms, and safety of their children (Collins, 1998). These issues are not the issues of White feminists, and so the fight is not the same. Women of color also are aware that White feminists have historically been aggressors toward them or have sided with the White male aggressor when it was convenient to do so (Enns, 1997), rendering suspect any attempts at solidarity.

Some women of color have rejected the term *feminist* in favor of the term *womanist*. Walker (1991) used the term *womanist* to describe women of color who are pro-woman but also committed to the survival of all people in their community, men and women alike. Some African American women might feel that identifying as a feminist, which is seen as a "White" thing, might label them as "less Black" than women who identify more strongly with racial issues (Collins, 1998). Kimmel and Garko (1995), describing their data collection for a study of feminist women of color, found that most of the women of color they initially contacted would not respond to their survey. After consulting with an African American woman psychologist, the

authors realized that they would need to make a number of modifications to encourage women of color to participate. One suggestion was to add the term *womanist* to their cover letter and open-ended questions, as the word *feminist* was probably triggering negative connotations. When Kimmel and Garko made the suggested changes, more participants responded, although numbers were still low.

Kimmel and Garko's (1995) survey was a replication of a phenomenological survey of White middle-class feminists. They received responses from 17 women respondents: 12 African Americans, 2 Asian Americans, 2 Hispanic Americans, and 1 American Indian. A majority of the women reported a specific reaction to the word *feminist*. Some rejected it because of its historical connotations and instead used *womanist* or other terms. Other women embraced the term *feminist* and may or may not have had any knowledge about the term *womanist*. Whichever term they used, all held strong convictions about the importance of gender equality. Several respondents related tales of negative interactions with White feminists or of difficulty with other people of color over their support of women's issues.

Overall, when comparing the responses of women of color to those in the previous study of White women, Kimmel and Garko (1995) noted that many of the experiences of feminism/womanism across the groups were similar. Both groups were most aware of their feminist/womanist beliefs while at work and perceived that awareness as more positive than negative. However, women of color provided richer descriptions of their experiences than did White women. Women of color were more likely to discuss the salience of spirituality in their experiences of feminism/womanism, whereas White women generally did not respond to the spirituality question. The former group also perceived race as much more salient and was better able to discuss the tension between gender and race and feminism than did White women. It is clear, then, that researchers cannot make the assumption that women of color who support gender equality will automatically gravitate to the term *feminist* or that their experience of feminism will completely reflect that of White feminist women.

MULTICULTURAL/ FEMINIST COMPETENCIES

Multiculturalism has been described as the fourth force in psychology (Pedersen, 1990). Sue et al.'s (1982) position paper suggested that counseling psychology formally develop multicultural competencies. Sue et al. described three areas of multicultural competency: awareness, knowledge, and skills. Sue, Arrendondo, and McDavis (1992) expanded and revised Sue et al.'s (1982) proposal to create a multicultural competency matrix composed of three characteristics and three dimensions. The three counselor characteristics are (a) counselor awareness of his or her own assumptions, values, and biases; (b) understanding of the worldview of the culturally different client; and (c) development of appropriate intervention strategies and techniques. Infused within each of the characteristics are the three dimensions of awareness, knowledge, and skills.

Critics have recommended that the multicultural competency dialogue expand beyond the development of counseling techniques and competency areas, as well as the relatively limited attention on race and ethnicity (e.g., Coleman, 1997; Helms & Richardson, 1997). Initially, competencies were defined using basic demographic variables and ignored intracultural and intercultural factors (Helms & Richardson, 1997). Demonstrating multicultural competence requires skill mastery and the adoption of a sociopolitical orientation (Helms & Richardson, 1997). Developing multicultural competencies has been described

as a dynamic (Coleman, 1997) and lifelong process (Pope-Davis & Dings, 1995).

Feminist psychology is attempting to eradicate the perception that its gender-focused agenda is oblivious to other oppressions that differentially affect women of color. The infusion of diversity into the traditional feminist agenda can be found in revised definitions of feminist therapy (cf. Brown, 1990, 1995; Chin, 1993; Enns, 1997; Wyche & Rice, 1997), guidelines for feminist curriculum (Chin & Russo, 1997), principles for feminist supervision (Porter & Vasquez, 1997), and research guidelines (Grossman et al., 1997).

Recently, dialogues concerning gender and multicultural competencies have emerged (Atkinson & Hackett, 1995; Enns, 1997; Fassinger & Richie, 1997). Fassinger and Richie (1997) argued that multicultural competency training for counselors should include a focus on both gender and sexual identity, which are nonconscious ideologies as defined by Bem and Bem (1970, as cited in Fassinger & Richie, 1997). Gender-related assumptions such as sexism or heterosexism are so insidious that both the counselor's and the client's worldviews and interpersonal interactions are affected. Fassinger and Richie end with a discussion of how Sue and Sue's (1990, as cited in Fassinger & Richie, 1997) culturally skilled counselor triad of attitudes, knowledge, and skills could be applied to illustrate how nonconscious ideologies of gender and sexual orientation affect multicultural competencies.

Is it possible to join multiculturalism with feminism in a way that will benefit women of color? Is it possible to bring these ideas together in a way that incorporates the best of both ideologies without pushing one agenda over the other? Researchers and theorists assert that it is possible. Gloria (2001) presented a list of multicultural competencies for working with Latinas. Using Sue et al.'s (1992) model, she detailed attitudes and beliefs, knowledge, and skills that are important to counselors wishing to work effectively with Latina women. Williams (1999) discussed both Afrocentric psychology and feminist psychology coming together as Black feminist models as a guide for working with African American women in psychotherapy. Greene and Sanchez-Hucles (1997) described the interactions of a racially mixed group of feminist women charged with "the task of developing guidelines for diversifying feminist psychological theory, research, practice, and training" (p. 180).

Building on the work of Sue et al. (1992) and Gloria (2001) and incorporating the core feminist principles identified by Chin and Russo (1997), we developed the following list of competencies. These competencies are a conceptual foundation for working with women of color. It is assumed that an individual's sociocultural context is shaped by his or her cultural, ethnic, racial, and gender identities. This context, then, determines how the individual perceives members of his or her own group and members of other groups.

Attitudes and Beliefs

Counselors and psychologists must do the following:

1. *Be able to self-reflect (i.e., become aware of their personal attitudes, assumptions, and stereotypes about women of color).* This requires a recognition that all women, or even all women of color, do not experience the world in a uniform manner. This also requires physically interacting with persons of color outside the counseling office. Interactions that occur in tightly prescribed situations do not provide a real sense of the lives of women of color; personal attitudes can only be challenged through broad-based interactions.

2. *Be aware that the "obvious" salient identity characteristic may not be the most salient one to the woman of color.* In other words, a feminist psychologist may assume that a woman of color will be similarly gender focused, whereas a multiculturally focused psychologist may anticipate a woman of color to be similarly focused. A woman of color's reality is often quite complex and may not be easily categorized.

3. *Actively adopt the view that women of color are not inferior or automatically wrong if they espouse beliefs and values that do not conform to the White middle-class norm.* This requires a recognition that one's personal belief system of what is "right" or "wrong" may not be appropriate for the experience of the woman of color. It also requires consideration of the "environmental, social, historical, and political variables" (Gloria, 2001, p. 19) that differentially shape the lives of ethnic minority women.

4. *Be able to recognize that the White middle-class, Western view of psychology taught in most graduate programs may not be appropriate for an individual woman of color.* This lack of appropriateness may stem from fallacies in the model, not necessarily in the woman of color.

Knowledge

Counselors and psychologists must study the following:

1. *The social, historical, environmental, and political factors that differentially affect women of color.* As with any discussion of cultural groups, one must consider the context. What is true for African American heterosexual women may not be true for African American lesbian women, for example. Puerto Rican women may not have the same concerns that are expressed by Cuban American women. This knowledge requires much more than a cursory understanding of race or gender issues.

2. *The concepts of empowerment and social action as they affect women of color.* Knowledge of the current environmental and political climate for a particular group of women of color will provide an understanding of the needs of the ethnic community and the consequences for empowering a woman of color to fight oppression within and outside her community. Competence in this area acknowledges that actively fighting oppression may not seem desirable to every woman of color; the consequences may be too high.

3. *The relationship between gender and ethnicity for the community of women with whom the counselor or psychologist will most likely work.* It is impossible to hold every bit of knowledge about every group of women, but it is important to seek a significant amount of knowledge about the groups with whom one works most often.

4. *The feminist literature, especially as it relates to women of color, and the multicultural literature as it relates to women of color.* An examination of these two literatures should result in developing a unique framework for counseling and psychotherapy with women of color.

5. *The offerings of their environments to identify role models and a resource network appropriate for women of color.* Although women of color may be familiar with the networking possibilities relevant to the salient identity, they may not have knowledge about networking possibilities related to the identities that are not as salient (i.e., she may be familiar with the local civil rights coalition but not the women's rights organization).

Skills

Counselors and psychologists should develop the ability to do the following:

1. *Put aside their personal belief system and empathize with the reality of the woman of color.* Women in general seek connection with another person, and demonstrating genuine empathy is one way to make that connection.

2. *Identify the multiple roles and identities that women of color may hold.* The women themselves may not recognize all the issues connected to these different identities.

3. *Move away from the traditional counselor role when working with women of color.* The traditional concept of therapy designed to foster separation and individuation may not be appropriate for every woman of color, whose ethnic community may not condone such behavior. In addition, institutional manifestations of classism, sexism, and racism sometimes render a woman of color powerless and her needs unheard. A counselor may need to serve as an intermediary to help the woman of color progress through the system.

4. *Serve as a change agent, not just with individual women of color but within the greater community.* Promoting change sometimes means stepping out of the office and into the community to provide services. However, providing services demands that the counselor learn what the community needs, instead of imposing his or her own ideas about what "should" happen onto the community without regard to the acceptability of those ideas.

SUMMARY

Women of color are caught between multiple worlds. The feminist community would ask that they "forget" their ethnic roots for the sake of sisterhood, and the ethnic community would ask that they forsake their gender for the sake of the race. More and more, women of color are refusing to forsake one identity for the other. Instead, they are demanding recognition of the effect of multiple identities in their lives. They prefer to shape their own destinies and define their own realities. As psychology strives to recognize the diversity of both its membership and the public it serves, the demands of these women will become even clearer, and the literature on women of color will grow.

REFERENCES

Adams, V. L., & LaFromboise, T. D. (2001). Self-in-relation theory and African American female development. In D. B. Pope-Davis & H. L. K. Coleman (Eds.), *The intersection of race, class, and gender in multicultural counseling* (pp. 25-48). Thousand Oaks, CA: Sage.

Afshar, H., & Maynard, M. (Eds.). (1994). *The dynamics of 'race' and gender: Some feminist interventions.* London: Taylor & Francis.

Aldaraca, B. A. (1995). On the use of medical diagnosis as name-calling: Anita F. Hill and the rediscovery of "erotomania." In K. M. Vaz (Ed.), *Black women in America* (pp. 206-221). Thousand Oaks, CA: Sage.

Atkinson, D. R., & Hackett, G. (1995). *Counseling diverse populations.* Madison, WI: Brown and Benchmark.

Bowman, S. L., Rasheed, S., Ferris, J., Thompson, D. A., McRae, M., & Weitzman, L. (2001). Interface of feminism and multiculturalism: Where are the women of color? In J. G. Ponterotto, J. M. Casas, L. A. Suzuki, & C. M. Alexander (Eds.), *The handbook of multicultural counseling* (2nd ed., pp. 779-798). Thousand Oaks, CA: Sage.

Bradshaw, C. K. (1994). Asian and Asian American women: Historical and political considerations in psychotherapy. In L. Comas-Diaz & B. Greene (Eds.), *Women of color: Integrating ethnic and gender identities in psychotherapy* (pp. 72-113). New York: Guilford.

Brown, L. S. (1990). The meaning of multicultural perspective in theory building in feminist therapy. In L. S. Brown & M. P. P. Root (Eds.), *Diversity and complexity in feminist theory* (pp. 1-21). New York: Haworth.

Brown, L. S. (1995). Cultural diversity in feminist therapy: Theory and practice. In H. Landrine (Ed.), *Bringing cultural diversity to feminist psychology: Theory, research, and practice* (pp. 14-161). Washington, DC: American Psychological Association.

Canales, M. (1997). Narrative interaction: Creating a space for therapeutic communication. *Issues in Mental Health Nursing, 18,* 477-494.

Chin, J. L. (Ed.). (1993). *Proceedings of the National Conference on Education and Training in Feminist Practice.* Boston: Boston College.

Chin, J. L., & Russo, N. F. (1997). Feminist curriculum development: Principles and resources. In J. Worell & N. G. Johnson (Eds.), *Shaping the future of feminist psychology: Education, research, and practice* (pp. 93-102). Washington, DC: American Psychological Association.

Chow, E. N. L. (1991). The development of feminist consciousness among Asian American women. In J. Lorber & S. A. Fatrell (Eds.), *The social construction of gender* (pp. 255-268). Newbury Park, CA: Sage.

Coleman, H. L. K. (1997). Conflict in multicultural counseling relationships: Source and resolution. *Journal of Multicultural Counseling and Development, 25,* 195-200.

Collins, P. H. (1991). *Black feminist thought: Knowledge, consciousness, and the politics of empowerment.* New York: Routledge Kegan Paul.

Collins, P. H. (1998). *Fighting words: Black women and the search for justice.* Minneapolis: University of Minnesota Press.

Comas-Diaz, L., & Greene, B. (Eds.). (1994). *Women of color: Integrating ethnic and gender identities in psychotherapy.* New York: Guilford.

Davis, A. D., & Wildman, S. M. (1997). The legacy of doubt: Treatment of sex and race in the Hill-Thomas hearings. In A. K. Wing (Ed.), *Critical race feminism: A reader* (pp. 175-182). New York: New York University Press.

Enns, C. Z. (1993). Twenty years of feminist counseling and therapy: From naming biases to implementing multifaceted practice. *The Counseling Psychologist, 21,* 3-87.

Enns, C. Z. (1997). *Feminist theories and feminist psychotherapies: Origin, themes, and variations.* New York: Haworth.

Espin, O. M. (1993). Feminist therapy: Not for or by White women only. *The Counseling Psychologist, 21,* 103-108.

Fassinger, R. E., & Richie, B. S. (1997). Sex matters: Gender and sexual orientation in training for multicultural counseling competency. In D. B. Pope-Davis & H. L. K. Coleman (Eds.), *Multicultural counseling competencies: Assessment, education, training, and supervision* (pp. 83-110). Thousand Oaks, CA: Sage.

Garcia, A. M. (1991). The development of Chicana feminist discourse, 1970-1980. In J. Lorber & S. A. Fatrell (Eds.), *The social construction of gender* (pp. 269-287). Newbury Park, CA: Sage.

Gawelek, M. A. (1997). Women's diversity: Ethnicity, race, class, and gender in theories of feminist psychology. In O. L. Espin (Ed.), *Latina realities: Essays on healing, migration, and sexuality* (pp. 33-50). Boulder, CO: Westview.

Geiger, S. M. (1995). African American single mothers: Public perceptions and public policies. In K. M. Vaz (Ed.), *Black women in America* (pp. 244-257). Thousand Oaks, CA: Sage.

Gloria, A. (2001). The cultural construction of Latinas: Practice implications of multiple realities and identities. In D. B. Pope-Davis & H. L. K. Coleman (Eds.), *The intersection of race, class, and gender in multicultural counseling* (pp. 3-24). Thousand Oaks, CA: Sage.

Greene, B. (1994). African American women. In L. Comas-Diaz & B. Greene (Eds.), *Women of color: Integrating ethnic and gender Identities in psychotherapy* (pp. 10-29). New York: Guilford.

Greene, B., & Sanchez-Hucles, J. (1997). Diversity: Advancing an inclusive feminist psychology. In J. Worell & N. G. Johnson (Eds.), *Shaping the future of feminist psychology: Education, research, and practice* (pp. 173-202). Washington, DC: American Psychological Association.

Grillo, T., & Wildman, S. M. (1997). Obscuring the importance of race: The implication of making comparisons between racism and sexism (or other isms). In A. K. Wing (Ed.), *Critical race feminism: A reader* (pp. 44-50). New York: New York University Press.

Grossman, F. K., Gilbert, L. A., Genero, N. P., Hawes, S. E., Hyde, J. S., & Marecek, J. (1997). Feminist research: Practice and problems. In J. Worell & N. G. Johnson (Eds.), *Shaping the future of feminist psychology: Education, research, and practice* (pp. 573-591). Washington, DC: American Psychological Association.

Helms, J. E., & Richardson, T. Q. (1997). How multiculturalism obscures race and culture as differential aspects of counseling competency. In D. B. Pope-Davis & H. L. K. Coleman (Eds.), *Multicultural counseling competencies: Assessment, education, training, and supervision* (pp. 60-82). Thousand Oaks, CA: Sage.

hooks, b. (1981). *Ain't I a woman?* Boston: South End.

Hull, G. T., Scott, P. B., & Smith, B. (Eds.). (1982). *All the women are White, all the Blacks are men, but some of us are brave: Black women's studies.* New York: Feminist Press.

Jackson, L. R. (2001). The interaction of race and gender in African American women's experiences of self and other at a predominantly White women's college. In D. B. Pope-Davis & H. L. K. Coleman (Eds.), *The intersection of race, class, and gender in multicultural counseling* (pp. 49-70). Thousand Oaks, CA: Sage.

Jordan, E. C. (1997). Race, gender and social class in the Thomas hearings: The hidden fault lines in political discourse. In A. K. Wing (Ed.), *Critical race feminism: A reader* (pp. 169-174). New York: New York University Press.

Kimmel, E. B., & Garko, M. G. (1995). Ethnic diversity in the experience of feminism: An existential-phenomenological approach. In H. Landrine (Ed.), *Bringing cultural diversity to feminist psychology: Theory, research and practice* (pp. 27-53). Washington, DC: American Psychological Association.

LaFromboise, T. D., Berman, J. S., & Sohi, B. K. (1994). American Indian women. In L. Comas-Diaz & B. Greene (Eds.), *Women of color: Integrating ethnic and gender identities in psychotherapy* (pp. 30-71). New York: Guilford.

Landrine, H. (Ed.). (1995). *Bringing cultural diversity to feminist psychology: Theory, research and practice.* Washington, DC: American Psychological Association.

Malone, J. L. (2000). Working with aboriginal women: Applying feminist therapy in a multicultural counselling context. *Canadian Journal of Counselling, 34,* 33-42.

Martin, J. K., & Hall, G. C. N. (1992). Thinking Black, thinking internal, thinking feminist. *Journal of Counseling Psychology, 39,* 509-514.

Pedersen, P. (1990). The multicultural perspective as a fourth force in counseling. *Journal of Mental Health Counseling, 12,* 93 95.

Pope-Davis, D. B., & Dings, J. G. (1995). The assessment of multicultural counseling competencies. In J. G. Ponterotto, J. M. Casas, L. A. Suzuki, & C. M. Alexander (Eds.), *The handbook of multicultural counseling* (pp. 287-311). Thousand Oaks, CA: Sage.

Porter, N., & Vasquez, M. (1997). Co-vision: Feminist supervision, process, and collaboration. In J. Worell & N. G. Johnson (Eds.), *Shaping the future of feminist psychology: Education, research, and practice* (pp. 115-171). Washington, DC: American Psychological Association.

Rivera, J. (1997). Domestic violence against Latinas by Latino males: An analysis of race, national origin, and gender differentials. In A. K. Wing (Ed.), *Critical race feminism: A reader* (pp. 259-266). New York: New York University Press.

Romany, C. (1997). Ain't I a feminist? In A. K. Wing (Ed.), *Critical race feminism: A reader* (pp. 19-26). New York: New York University Press.

Sue, D. W., Arrendondo, P., & McDavis, R. J. (1992). Multicultural counseling competencies and standards: A call to the profession. *Journal of Counseling and Development, 70,* 477-486.

Sue, D. W., Bernier, Y., Durran, A., Feinberg, L., Pedersen, P. B., Smither, E. J., et al. (1982). Position paper: Cross-cultural counseling competencies. *The Counseling Psychologist, 10,* 45-52.

Taylor, K. A. (1997). Invisible woman: Reflections on the Clarence Thomas confirmation hearings. In A. K. Wing (Ed.), *Critical race feminism: A reader* (pp. 183-187). New York: New York University Press.

Walker, A. (1991). *In search of our mother's gardens: Womanist prose.* San Diego: Harcourt Brace.

Williams, C. B. (1999). African American women, Afrocentrism and feminism: Implications for therapy. *Women and Therapy, 22*(4), 1-16.

Wyche, K. F., & Rice, J. K. (1997). Shaping the future of feminist psychology: Education, research, and practice. In J. Worell & N. G. Johnson (Eds.), *Shaping the future of feminist psychology: Education, research, and practice* (pp. 51-71). Washington, DC: American Psychological Association.

5

A Philosophy of Science for Cross-Cultural Psychology

GEORGE S. HOWARD

University of Notre Dame

We have heard about the clashes between modernist-postmodernist styles of thinking in contemporary scholarship and about the related realism-constructivism debates in the philosophy of science. But how many of us truly understand the basic meaning of these warring perspectives and the implications of these controversies for scholarship in cross-cultural psychology?

My effort to unpack these thorny controversies will come in two parts. The first effort, titled, "An Exercise in Intellectual Humility," will concretely show why the modernist ambition of building an edifice of knowledge through a science that is universalizable (or generalizable to all humans everywhere) is doomed to failure. The short answer is that all knowledge is presumptive—that is, it is based on some particular perspective (such as science, religion, etc.). No knowledge is any better than the assumptions on which that

perspective is based (e.g., the existence of lawlike causal influences among theoretical entities, the value of empirical representations of those entities, etc., in some scientific research; the existence of God, the corpus of revealed truths, etc., in some religions). These assumptions are always underjustified (and often completely unknown) to the scientists and religious believers involved—as will be dramatically demonstrated in the first half of this chapter.

But skepticism about obtaining veridical knowledge should not be interpreted as solipsism. It is not. The second half of this chapter traces the outlines of an approach to the philosophy of science (called constructive realism) that capitalizes on the forms of objectivity nurtured by the modernist tradition, for obtaining knowledge of the world and all in it. However, this hybrid approach yields knowledge that is perspective specific (or situation specific, or culture specific) and thus is critically important for cross-cultural approaches. As Gergen (2001) noted, the postmodern approach does not supplant the modern approach— it merely softens its more strident claims to universality and value-neutral knowledge. In fact, the postmodern/constructivist critique of mainstream psychological scholarship actually serves to expand and revitalize our intellectual lives. Finally, the arguments that follow are kept jargon free to help readers gain a concrete, firsthand appreciation for the newer, reinvigorated cross-cultural scholarship of the future.

A number of recent papers (e.g., Flowers & Richardson, 1996; Hong, Morris, Chiu, & Benet-Martinez, 2000) have outlined how multicultural psychology has enabled psychologists to move past the universalisms of mainstream psychological thought. By viewing knowledge as originating in different "frames," one begins to see the wisdom of pluralism as an intellectual strategy.

AN EXERCISE IN INTELLECTUAL HUMILITY

One of the great insights of contemporary scholarship is the perspectival nature of all knowledge claims. That is, one cannot begin to make a knowledge claim unless he or she first makes some fundamental, background assumptions. These assumptions are nested in the paradigm (to use Thomas Kuhn's [1971] phrase) that grounds one's thinking. Kuhn wrote only about different scientific paradigms, but paradigms govern our thinking in all domains (e.g., in economics, one can contrast free market approaches with "Buddhist economics" [see Schumacher, 1973, chap. 4]; in politics, one can compare democratic approaches with communist perspectives; in spirituality, one can contrast Christian with "New Age" perspectives; etc.). Most knowledge claims simply accept a particular worldview as if all of its assumptions were literally

true. This strategy enables people to assert reasonable knowledge claims—but such claims are no better than the assumptions on which they are built. Thus, scholarship cannot produce unvarnished "Truths" but only yields perspectival knowledge claims. Therefore, we ought to state all of our knowledge claims in a tentative manner (e.g., "For a Newtonian physicist . . ."; "To a Freudian psychologist . . ."; "Free market economists believe . . ."; "Believers in liberal democratic values hold . . ."; "All Zoroastricians think that . . ."; etc.).

Unfortunately, most of us forget how limited our own knowledge claims are by the assumptions within our worldviews. Thus, teachers constantly remind students how different the world looks from perspectives that are different from these students' habitual vision of reality. This is easily accomplished by noting how radically reality shifts when it is viewed through the lens of a different perspective. For example, how would an atheist view the Ten Commandments? How would a communist react to the role that lobbyists play in U.S. policy formation? How would a Buddhist economist evaluate the practice of corporate downsizing? Unfortunately, many modernist thinkers miss the more basic epistemological point in this exercise on changing perspectives by blithely asserting that the alternative perspectives (that I just suggested) are simply wrong.

So much for perspectivalism—modernists apparently have truth, wisdom, and beauty by the tail. Checkmate! Intellectual humility loses; hubris wins. Modernist thinkers are generally unimpressed initially with the importance of background assumptions in the "reality" they have created through their web of beliefs.

Fortunately, modernists have an almost unshakable belief in a worldview that can be used to dramatize the role that background assumptions play in creating one's "reality." This unquestioned belief system is mathematics.

Show them the numbers, they seem to say, and it will compel their belief. Thus, my teaching challenge in this chapter is to present modernist thinkers with some carefully crafted mathematical realities that will highlight certain problems with their assumptive worldviews. If I can accomplish this task, I might entice modernists to think about the formative role that background assumptions play in creating *all* knowledge claims. Here goes!

If Money Be Not Thy Slave, It Will Be Thy Master

(Please do *not* turn to Table 5.1 until instructed to do so.)

In my psychology of healthy lifestyles course, I try to help students to make a connection between how their present daily acts will inexorably lead to their lives' destinies. The day-to-day decisions to drink (or not to drink) large quantities of alcohol over time can produce an addiction (or, conversely, a healthy use of distilled spirits). Similarly, conscientiously developed and practiced work habits generally lead to professional success— or failure. And finally, small differences in habits of spending versus saving lead to ___! Exactly what do these small differences in money management styles (i.e., whether to spend or save) lead to over time? Consider the following thought experiment.

Imagine two sets of identical twins (one set of males, [Adam & Bob], one set of females [Alicia & Barbara]) who decided to marry one another (Adam marries Alicia: Couple A; Bob marries Barbara: Couple B) upon graduating from Notre Dame. My reason for imagining pairs of identical twins who marry is that I want to make these pairs equal in every way (e.g., intellectual prowess, motivation and work habits, investment acumen) save one—Couple A likes to spend 95% of their after-tax income,

whereas Couple B chooses to spend 85% of their after-tax income. That one small difference in savings between the pairs of imaginary couples will be responsible for *all* differences in their assets at retirement.

A few realistic starting values (circa 1997) and constants must be determined before we can begin our thought experiment. Notre Dame Arts and Letters graduates average $26,000 for their starting salaries. If both spouses work, the couple would earn $52,000 per year before taxes. The IRS estimates that such a couple would pay approximately 23% for federal, state, local, and Social Security taxes. This estimate is too low if the wage earners are self-employed and for the couples' later working years, when the incomes are much higher. However, the 23% tax bite will be considered constant throughout each couple's working career.

Notre Dame's office of financial aid says that the average level of student loan indebtedness of graduates is now $16,250—or $32,500 for each couple. Students also tend to have about $3,750 ($7,500 per couple) in other debts (e.g., credit card debt, personal loans, auto loans). Thus, the starting value for salaries for Couples A and B is $40,000, and the couples' assets are entered for both as $40,000 of debt. The interest rates on student loans range from 5% to 7.4%, auto loans are around 9%, and my colleagues' credit cards charge from 16% to 21% annually on unpaid balances. An overall interest rate of 10% was chosen for this exercise. My retirement money has averaged 7.15% (TIAA: bonds) and 14.06% (CREF: stocks) in annual returns for the past 10 years—thus a 10% return on investment seems reasonable.

Given these estimates, Couple A saves $2,000 in their first year of work, whereas Couple B saves $6,000. If one chooses different starting values and constants, the net wealth of each couple at retirement will change. (Now estimate the value of each couple's assets at retirement. This represents the heart of this first exercise, so *force yourself* to write an exact estimate of assets after the 43 years of work and savings for Couple A and another estimate for Couple B.)

Because starting values and constants are the same for both the thrifty (B) and spend-thrift (A) couples, the *difference* between the assets (see Table 5.1 now) of Couples A and B at retirement represents the cablelike vise that develops from the fragile thread of a savings habit that persists over 43 years. Table 5.1 reveals that Couple A (5% savings rate) must immediately declare personal bankruptcy if they retire at age 65 because they are $325,987 in debt and no longer have salaries that justify carrying such a high level of personal indebtedness. Couple B (15% savings rate) retires with a positive net worth of $3,841,246. Because all factors (including professional success as measured by annual salary) were equal for both couples, the enormous differences in terminal outcomes (bankruptcy vs. wealth) are due *solely* to the couples' different saving habits (i.e., 5% vs. 15%).

Two stark realities make this thought experiment chilling to Notre Dame students. First, 5½ years ago, the Dow Jones Industrial average finished over 10,000 for the first time in history. An article in the *New York Times* celebrated the event by comparing aspects of November 14, 1972 (the day the Dow first closed over 1,000) with the present. One comparison drew my attention: In 1972, Americans' savings rate was 7.6%—in 1999, it was 0.5%! That is one tenth of the 5% savings rate that landed Couple A in bankruptcy. Second, all other assumptions of the exercise did not employ fictitious estimates specifically designed to dramatize the importance of saving money. Rather, all estimates (e.g., starting salaries, tax rates, investment return rates, interest rates) represent accurate portrayals of what Notre Dame graduates currently face.

Before I explain the assumption that leads to misleading estimates in this first exercise, I'll explain a second exercise. I've found that this second thought experiment in probabilities is quite appropriate for students beginning a course in probability and statistics or a course in philosophical psychology.

Care to Play a Simple Game of Chance?

As you know, a die has the numbers 1 through 6 on each of its six sides. As you can see, I've altered the values on the six sides of four dice. For example, Die A has a value of "5" on three sides and a value of "1" on each of the other three sides; Die B has "3" on each side, and so forth.

Die A	Die B	Die C	Die D
1	3	6	0
1	3	6	0
1	3	2	4
5	3	2	4
5	3	2	4
5	3	2	4

I wager that you do not know enough about probabilities to be able to figure out which is the best of these four dice. When you think you know which is best, let me know and we'll play for a buck. Each of us will roll one of the dice, and the first one to win five rolls gets the buck. Which die would you select? Don't read any further until you've decided which die you'd stake your hard-earned cash on.

Rest assured that I have never lost a cent playing this "game of chance," and I play until all students cry "uncle" (usually not before I'm $15 ahead, and once not until I was almost $100 ahead). Of course, no money ever

Table 5.1   Differences Over Time in Assets for a Couple That Saves 5% of Their After-Tax Income
(Couple A) Versus a Couple That Saves 15% of Their After-Tax Income (Couple B)

	Salaries of A and B	Couple A			Couple B		
		Assets	Interest Expense (yr)	Savings (yr)	Assets	Interest Expense (yr)	Savings (yr)
Start	40,000	−40,000			−40,000		
End Year 1	42,000	−42,000	4,000	2,000	−38,000	4,000	6,000
End Year 2	44,100	−44,100	4,200	2,100	−35,500	3,800	6,300
End Year 3	46,305	−46,305	4,410	2,205	−32,435	3,550	6,615
End Year 4	48,620	−48,620	4,631	2,315	−28,733	3,244	6,946
End Year 5	51,051	−51,052	4,862	2,431	−24,313	2,873	7,293
End Year 10	65,156	−65,156	6,205	3,103	12,032	(248)	9,308
End Year 15	83,157	−83,157	7,920	3,960	84,708	(6,621)	11,880
End Year 20	106,132	−106,132	10,108	5,054	219,804	(18,604)	15,162
End Year 25	135,454	−135,454	12,900	6,450	460,414	(40,097)	19,351
End Year 30	172,878	−172,878	16,465	8,232	877,319	(77,511)	24,697
End Year 35	220,641	−220,641	21,013	10,507	1,586,273	(141,341)	31,820
End Year 40	281,600	−281,600	26,819	13,410	2,775,942	(248,701)	40,229
End Year 43	325,987	−325,987	31,046	15,523	3,841,246	(344,971)	46,570
(Age 65)		$32,598 in interest expenses due every year of retirement without reducing total indebtedness			$384,124 of interest available every year of retirement without touching principal		

Amount in parentheses is the interest expense, which reflects a positive return on investment. Also, all
returns on investments are treated as tax deferred because 15% of earnings can be tax sheltered each year
under combinations of company retirement plans, SEPs, Keoghs, and IRAs.

actually changes hands. However, by the time
the last student surrenders, all are anxious to
know what it is about probability theory that
they don't yet understand.

Explanation of Exercise 1:
To Spend or Not to Spend?

Values obtained for approximately the first
10 years of Table 5.1 generally conform to
students' expectations of how savings and
debt grow. But eventually, the calculated levels
of wealth and debt begin to shock these undergraduates. Why is it that so many people are
shocked by the enormous wealth and debt that
one can accumulate over time? Lend me a
paragraph or two of your time and attention

to milk your intuition regarding how we often
misunderstand growth rates.

Please answer *each* of the three questions
below *before* reading any further. Which of
the following choices would you take in each
case?

A)   A penny that doubled tax deferred every
day for a week, or one million dollars?

B)   A penny that doubled tax deferred every
day for a month, or one million dollars?

C)   A penny that doubled tax deferred every
day for a year, or one million dollars?

Few people take the doubling penny for
a week—as seven time blocks is clearly a

short-term proposition. In fact, the doubling penny is worth only $1.28 after seven doubles. Conversely, intuition usually suggests that a penny that doubles 365 times (Question C) would be quite valuable indeed. It is Question B (an investment that compounds 31 times) that seems to produce a split in college students' intuitions (about half take the doubling penny, the other half take the million dollars). At the end of the second week, the compounding penny rises in value from $1.28 to $163.84. At the end of the third week, the penny is worth $21,611.52, and it grows to $2,782,418.56 by the end of Week 4. So the doubling penny wins after 4 weeks. But the typical month is slightly longer than 4 weeks—it is 31 days. Why quibble over a paltry three more compoundings? Because it makes almost a *$20 million* difference ($22,259,344.48 vs. $2,782,418.56)!

What is wrong with our intuition when many of us select $1,000,000 instead of the $22,000,000 option (the penny that doubles every day for a 31-day month)? Psychologically speaking, we mistakenly think we are dealing with an *arithmetic* progression when, in fact, untaxed, compound interest (and debt also) grows *geometrically*. How can our intuitions be deceived so badly?

Figure 5.1 presents a graph of global human population growth over the past millennium. The two straight lines in Figure 5.1 depict the distinction between future predictions based on the assumptions of arithmetic (straight lines) versus geometric (curved line) growth functions. The dotted line is the theoretical function that depicts the data from year 1000 A.D. to year 1800 A.D.—as if these data were the result of an arithmetic function. Early in a geometric function, one can easily mistake it for an arithmetic growth function, as the predictions do not differ greatly from one another. Humans tend to focus almost solely on short-term impacts, so

assuming linearity (or an arithmetic function) still provides pretty good approximations *in the short run* (even though this assumption is incorrect).

The dashed line is the line of best fit (again assuming linearity) for the data from 1000 A.D. to 1960 A.D. The expected global population in the year 2000 (assuming linearity) would be about 4 billion people. Given that the earth's population is already more than 6 billion, that prediction is wrong. Conversely, assuming that population grows geometrically, the data in Figure 5.1 suggest that the planet's population in the year 2000 will be about 6 billion people. The geometric prediction will undoubtedly prove to be more accurate than the prediction that assumes an arithmetic function (save the occurrence of some worldwide cataclysm—such as the death of every human being in North and South America). The point is that over time, the predictions of geometric functions differ dramatically from predictions that assume linearity. Thus, late in the games of such geometric functions as compounding debt, untaxed compounding interest, global population, and the like, people are likely to be stunned at how quickly the numbers at stake will increase.

Explanation of Exercise 2: On Which Die Will You Die?

In our second exercise, no matter which die you select, I can select one that will beat you the majority of the time. Let me show you how this works. Start with Die B (all 3s) and compare it with Die D (4s and 0s). Because Die B always yields a 3, and Die D delivers a 4 on 66% of the rolls, Die D generally beats Die B. Thus, we can state that B < D. Can we find any die that is superior to Die D? Well, Die A (5s and 1s) is superior to Die D. Half the time, Die A yields a value of 5—which always beats Die D's 4s and 0s. And even when Die A yields a

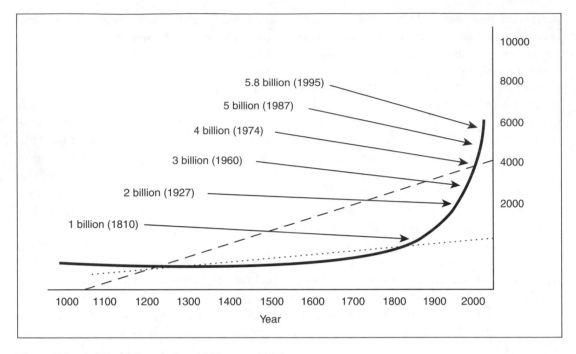

Figure 5.1   World Population 1000 AD to 1995 AD
SOURCE: Population Reference Bureau (1989).

value of 1 (half the time), it still beats Die D's 0s. Thus, A is superior to D, and we can now say that B < D < A. Can we find a die to beat Die A? Die C (6s and 2s) always beats Die A whenever Die A comes up as "1" (half the time). And when Die A comes up as "5" (half the time), it still loses to Die C's 6s. Thus, Die C is superior to Die A, and we now know that B < D < A < C! So we have now proven that Die C is the best die—haven't we? Yes we have—*if and only if probabilities follow the transitive law!*

And what is the transitive law? If you (Y) weigh less than your father (F), and your father weighs less than me (GH), and I weigh less than Refrigerator Perry (RP—a 300 + -pound football player), then we can state that Y < F < GH < RP. The transitive law states that you can safely conclude that you weigh less than Refrigerator Perry. I feel that

conclusion is warranted because I believe the transitive law holds for weights. But is the transitive law a valid assumption in the domain of probabilities? Let's find out.

If the transitive law holds for probabilities, then because B < D < A < C, one could safely conclude that B < C. Sancho Panza declared that "the proof of the pudding is in the eating of it," so let's take his epistemological recommendation and compare Die B with Die C. Die B always produces a "3," whereas Die C produces a "2" on 66% of the throws. Thus, B > C, which is the *opposite* of what the transitive law holds. Thus, in the dice exercise, my students are impaled on the horns of a set of nontransitive dice. No matter which die they chose, there is always a better die left for me to select.

Because my students trusted that the transitive law held for probabilities, they assumed there must be a "best" die to be found. It turned out they were chasing "swamp gas." The ironic part is that many students assume transitivity without even knowing what it is— let alone that they are wagering their hard-earned money on the law's appropriateness for this particular "simple game of change." Once again, my father's warning of years past proves true: "If you're gambling, look around the table. If you don't know who the sucker is—it's you."

But our larger point, about the role of unproven assumptions, is as important as the antigambling message. Our beliefs, knowledge claims, interpretations, rules of thumb, and so forth are only as good as the many background assumptions that undergird our efforts to make sense of the world we inhabit. Donald Campbell (1974) concretizes this reality for research scientists in his doubt-to-trust ratio. To assert any knowledge claim, we are dependent on numerous background assumptions that we often trust implicitly. When the assumptions are wrong, our knowledge claims are hollow.

Perhaps William James's philosophy of pluralism (see *A Pluralistic Universe*, 1907) was the first sustained philosophical treatment of the role that one's perspective plays in the creation of the reality that one experiences. James's vision suggests that we ought to be very humble about our beliefs, views, knowledge, and so forth as one realizes that the world we experience can be expected to shift radically when viewed from a different perspective. All seekers of wisdom should strive for an appropriate level of humility, as it is so easy to fall under the spell cast by our regnant belief systems.

A TEACHING REFLECTION

Many of my reasons for implementing the in-class exercises on savings and probabilities were included in my description of these exercises. My explanation highlights the crucial role of background assumptions in the validity of all knowledge claims. However, two of those reasons deserve a bit more elaboration.

First, American education tends to be too abstract and theoretical for my tastes. I find that students learn concepts much better—and retain these lessons much longer—when they are embedded in a concrete exercise or class demonstration. If students are actually allowed to make the mistakes that one's class is designed to correct, the total experience is one students are less likely to forget. After all, "The proof of the pudding is in the tasting of it" (de Cervantes, 1615/1986). Like Sancho Panza, I feel students learn better by "tasting" than by hearing a lecture. Would you like to hear my hourlong lecture on why chocolate pudding is better than vanilla pudding? Or would you rather be a subject in a pudding taste test? I thought so.

Second, the psychologist Naomi Meara is fond of saying, "Never do anything for only one reason." The teaching corollary for this theorem might be, "Try to develop exercises that teach multiple lessons." In addition to the epistemological lesson on background assumptions, how wonderful it would be if students also took away some life lessons about managing their personal finances and a greater appreciation of how gambling preys on our human shortcomings (both cognitive and emotional) in an almost always successful effort (in the long run) to separate people from their hard-earned money. Those are important lessons for all of us to learn.

Third, multicultural thinkers are used to situations where different cultural sets result in different answers to particular questions. The above examples reinforce the impulse to keep these frames somewhat distinct and to not try to find the "right" answer. Rather, one is encouraged to realize that different frames lead to different truths.

INTERLUDE

I trust I have demonstrated sufficiently why the old modernist ambition of obtaining universalizable truths (in the long run) through scientific methods is no longer tenable. Because there is no perfect perspective (because of the unprovability of background assumptions) from which to view all issues of interest in life, we must be modest pluralists in all our intellectual endeavors. And what does this conclusion suggest for cross-cultural scholarship?

A paper I wrote a decade ago, titled "Culture Tales" (Howard, 1991), argued that each culture that we encounter represents a unique "story" from which we might obtain knowledge and/or wisdom. And although we should expect some degree of coherence and consistency from different perspectives *within* a particular culture, it is absolutely inappropriate to demand consistency *between* knowledge gained from any two cultures. Because each culture represents its own assumptive worldview, any lessons (or facts, or truths) garnered within that perspective are *incommensurable* (in Thomas Kuhn's [1971] sense) with findings from any other culture. We all are urged to be cultural pluralists. Hence, we can see the profound wisdom in William James's handling of the problem of free will by viewing it through the lenses of two incommensurate belief systems (or cultures): "When I think as a religious person, free will is a certainty; when I think as a scientist, it's an impossibility!" (James, 1907).

I could end the chapter here, and readers might believe that my message is rather solipsistic—all cultures are incommensurate, and therefore no answer from any perspective is to be preferred over any answer from another perspective. The extremist postmodernist would then be delighted, but all the ambitions of the extremist modernist would be undercut (as even our glorified science represents but one more perspective from which reality might be viewed). However, that conclusion is far too extreme. There *are* good grounds for preferring some explanations over others. But to make those arguments, I need to turn to the domain of epistemology, where the terms of the postmodernist versus modernist debates morph into the constructivism versus realism controversy in epistemology.

CONSTRUCTIVE REALISM

Many have suggested that a paradigm shift is occurring in the philosophy of the social sciences. The previous paradigm, which dominated the modernist era during the 20th century, could be characterized as objectivism or realism. The new paradigm, which could be described as a constructivist perspective, is based on the assumption that personal realities are socially constructed. This perspective assumes that there can be no observations that are independent of the observer.

As you know, in the constructivism-realism debate, we generally identify ourselves as favoring one or the other pole of this dichotomy. Our intellectual opponents, of course, are fanatically committed to the most extreme interpretation of the opposite pole. So this section's title, "Constructive Realism," might be seen as a ploy on my part to seize the middle ground—which is the position that will enrage the maximum number of combatants? If I only succeed in being controversial in this chapter, I'll consider my effort a failure. I'd like to think that more is going on than "all of us blowing hot air at one another as we pass the time between now and our deaths."

Perhaps when one tries to put opposites together, one will only get incoherence—rather than helpful integration. *Constructive realism* might represent nothing more than a highfalutin oxymoron. I don't think that is the case, but honesty demands that I might be too much of a moron to understand some deep incoherence in my putative solution. Thus, unless I do some serious, insightful work soon, you'll surely vote thumbs down on this chapter. Academics generally get serious by first defining their concepts. How to define constructivism and realism? Well, I'm tenured, so it doesn't really matter if readers think I'm a little less than "properly scholarly." Consequently, I'll offer definitions that are, for me, enormously insightful and fruitful, but they don't look like proper, scholarly definitions. With profound thanks to Efran, Lukens, and Lukens (1988), I offer the following atypical definition of constructivism and realism that, oddly enough, puts an emphasis on different *types of people* rather than on scholarly turf.

> Objectivists are inventors who think they are discoverers—they do not recognize their own inventions when they come across them. Good constructivists, on the other hand, acknowledge the active role they play in creating a view of the world and interpreting observations in terms of it. (Efran, Lukens, & Lukens, 1988, p. 28)

Constructivists are discoverers who think they are inventors—they tend to downplay the role that "real worlds" (either *out there* or [for psychologists] *in here*) play in our experimental (and clinical) observations. Good realists, on the other hand, always strive to appreciate the nature of the objective realities that had a hand in creating the useful but imperfect observations that we experimentally (and clinically) construct.

Do you know what I like about that definition? It allows me to say that I'm a little bit of both—some days I feel more like an explorer; other days I could swear I'm a creator. Similarly, and most important, on some *topics* I could swear I'm creating things, but on other topics I'm virtually certain I'm mostly reading

the real world out there. Would you like an example of that last point? What are you—a realist or a constructivist—on the topic of cold fusion and on the topic of God? I know those are not typical topics for psychologists, but please bear with me, as I am working toward a solution to the constructivist-realist problem that, I hope, applies across the entire landscape of the sciences and the humanities. A solution that says something like the following: "Physicists are almost always better off thinking of themselves as realists; theologians, on the other hand, are better off being constructivists." And what of psychologists? I think we are perched midway between the humanities and the hard sciences—which is why we ought to see ourselves as *constructive realists* and not as extremists on either pole. Unfortunately, it is more difficult to handle the intellectual ambiguity contained in an integrated metaphysics (e.g., constructive realism) than it is to be myopically committed to either extreme position. But I'm afraid that I ran all that by you quite quickly. Let's back up a step and first consider the problems of God and cold fusion a bit more carefully.

A Modest Ode to Realism

In a recent article in the *International Journal of Psychology and Religion,* I was talking about (what else?) cold fusion. As usual, I was making eminently reasonable, totally noncontroversial claims. Because I was discussing a topic in physics, I was leaning toward an objectivist construal of the issue of cold fusion. In discussing the role of reason in science, I said,

> The recent Pons and Fleischmann controversy over "cold fusion" is a good example of a radical concept that the scientific community entertained but (for now) has chosen to reject due to insufficient compelling theoretical articulation and experimental evidence. Although advocates of cold fusion

might feel their ideas have received overly harsh critique by an inappropriately conservative organization, the majority of scientists today believe these innovators were treated fairly—as the background theorizing and experimental evidence are not now sufficiently compelling to warrant altering long-held theories of physics. Finally, it is possible that with a handful of years of additional experimental and theoretical development a number of current physical theories might themselves change in response to the challenge of cold fusion. So although scientists are open to new ideas, they take a very conservative attitude toward them. (Howard, 1994a)

A constructivist reactor (who also happened to be overly enamored by the Edinburg strong program in the sociology of knowledge) took exception to the objectivist construal that I gave to the cold fusion debacle. Because he believed all "facts" are nothing more than social constructions, he found my suggestion—that characteristics of the physical world might be responsible for cold fusion's failure—rather unpalatable. He offered a different view of cold fusion's failure:

> In fact, the cold fusion controversy had amazingly little to do with evidence or theory. It had more to do with such issues as the fact that Pons and Fleischmann were chemists, not physicists, that they announced their findings by press conference and not journal publication, and the fact that their research threatened multimillion dollar high-energy physics grants of those who were working on "hot fusion." In fact, the statements of these two scientists were nearly drowned out by the harrumphing of "regular" scientists dismissing them out of hand. (Donahue, 1994)

Although all the "heat" that the constructivist notes did in fact occur, it was not the *cause* of the scientific community's rejection of cold fusion claims. The reactor's "reasons" serve to explain why professional heat accompanied the rejection, not *why* the scientific claims themselves were rejected. This constructivist sees the effects of bad science (and also bad professional demeanor by Pons and Fleischmann), and he wrongly assumes these reactions were the *cause* of the rejection by the scientific community. Donahue (1994) is wrong in this claim—pure and simple. If virtually unlimited amounts of heat could be produced by passing a weak electric current through a bucket of cold water with salt, only a thorough paranoid would believe that a politically constructed collusion by a powerful scientific elite could cover up such a startling discovery. Don't you think that the University of Utah would now be pursuing cold fusion with complete abandon to cash in on the billions of dollars that would flow from its patents, if only they could make this physical process work? The journal *Philosophy of Science* summarized the lessons to be learned from the cold fusion controversy in the following way:

> In retrospect, it is difficult to draw any conclusions other than that Pons and Fleischmann were careless in their work and announced stunning results based on little and flawed evidence. This was compounded by their refusal to admit their errors and to withdraw their (by then) baseless claims. The most obvious "heavy" in the entire episode is James Brophy, the vice president for research at the University of Utah, who pressed for early announcement by the chemists and who remained active at the center of the financial and legal intrigues that followed. *But what has this to do with the methodology of science?* Not much. What is relevant, though, is the way the scientific community studied the claims and eventually rejected them, in spite of an initial commitment on the part of many investigators to corroborate the claims of Pons

and Fleischmann. This is important if one wants to view science as a social phenomenon shaped by societal forces. For, while it is true that science collectively had a vested interest in the "received" views on nuclear fusion that it had established over the previous fifty years or so, it is also the case that there were great pressures, from industry, financial institutions and the public in general, to substantiate the Pons and Fleishmann claims. But, it just could not be made to fly. While it is undoubtedly so that evidence does not uniquely determine a theory, it is as true that not just anything can be made to go in science. (Cushing, 1994, p. 2)

So what do I want to conclude from this digression into cold fusion? Clearly, the world of physical realities out there represents a most important element in determining *which* scientific theories will pass muster and which won't. If we see physics as nothing more than a socially constructed collusion by a scientific power elite where any old theory can be made to go, then I think we miss a crucial element in why physics works as well as it does.

An Equally Modest Ode to Constructivism

Now let's jump to the opposite extreme. Are you a realist or a constructivist on the problem of God? Well, speaking for myself, I was raised with an oppressively objectivist view of religion. As Sister Stella Regis always said, "There is but One True God, and His only begotten son, Jesus, became man so that we could become faithful members of the One, True, Holy, catholic (small c) and apostolic Catholic (big C) church and if any of you lousy kids don't believe that 100% then when you die you're gonna be *toast*!" As you can see, Sister Stella wasn't a fan of nonobjectivist construals of God—and she also wasn't overly enamored with understatement. But Stella's intellectual tastes aside, we must recognize

that there are currently billions of people who have a completely objectivist construal of God—*they know* God and all of God's characteristics, beliefs, and wishes for us—and they know them right down to the cores of their beings. The obvious intellectual difficulty with this situation is that there have probably been at least a thousand different religions. Thus, for any subgroup of several millions of these theists to be correct in their objectivist construal of God, then several billion of the rest must be wrong in their construal. My reading of the evidence on the existence and characteristics of God is that most of the array of God stories are about equally compelling—and, unfortunately, God has remained conspicuously silent in helping us to pick out the one, true God from the welter of false Gods and religions. So whether or not God created humans—I believe history has shown that *humans construct their Gods*. Although I am largely an objectivist on questions of atomic fission, hot and/or cold fusion, and the like, I am a constructivist on the question of God.

In philosophy of science, I learned one distinction that is quite important indeed. That is the distinction between epistemology and ontology. Epistemology has to do with how we come to know things, and ontology deals with the nature of things in themselves—things like atoms, centers of gravity, brains, selves, rumors, and gods. When I pledged allegiance to realism on the issue of cold fusion and to constructivism on the problem of God, did I mean ontologically, epistemologically, or both? Recall that at the start of this chapter, I claimed that "a constructivist perspective is based on the assumption that social realities are socially constructed. This perspective assumes that there can be no observations that are independent of the observer." So obviously I see us as epistemological constructivists. What I've been examining above is whether we're also to be ontological constructivists. I feel that psychologists take grave risks if they do not realize that there are real forces that form human action—genes, endorphins, neural circuits, physical environments, cultures, kinship systems, and many more. Thus, we ought to be at least partially (and perhaps largely) ontological realists. Extreme ontological constructivism seems to me to be just plain silly. I'll stay near the golden mean on this issue. That is, although we are moved by the socially constructed beliefs of others, we're also affected by genes, endorphins, and so forth.

And although I just suggested that all of us might want to think of ourselves as epistemological constructivists, let's take another, closer look at that possibility. Although I think that there are no observations that are *independent* of the observer, does that imply that *all* observations are created equal? Are we to completely give up the Holy Grail of objectivity?

I'm endorsing a position such as Donald Campbell's (1974) famous, "We are to be ontological realists and epistemological fallabilists." But being a fallabilist is *not* the same as believing that there is no reality out there or that there are not more objective measures possible of that reality. Far from arguing that any old observation was as good as any other—or that any social construction might be as helpful as any other—Campbell himself did the pioneering work on the preeminent technology for actually improving fallable, scientific observations. (Here I refer to construct validity as approximated through the multitrait-multimethod matrix analyzed via structural equation modeling.) I fear I've already made too much ado about metaphysics, so I'll leave it for now.

CONSTRUCTIVE REALISM AND LOOMING ENVIRONMENTAL CRISES

Rather than plowing forward on philosophical issues, I'll instead turn to a general critique of current intellectual styles and then finish with my hope for the type of constructive realist psychological scholarship that might carry us into a better 21st century.

There is a strong tendency in humans to think in dichotomous, either/or terms (Rychlak, 1989). The difficulty with dichotomous thinking is that in asserting the importance of one pole of the dichotomy, one might implicitly downplay the importance of its presumed polar opposite. The history of scholarship in psychology repeatedly demonstrates that thinking in terms of either/or dichotomies can prove unhelpful. For example, is heredity or environment more important to development? Should one adopt masculine or feminine characteristics? Are you a believer in free will or determinism? In these and many other issues, we find some value in the perspectives represented by both polar opposites. Happily, psychological scholarship repeatedly moves past unhelpful dichotomies toward more nuanced appreciations of the ways that oppositional perspectives enrich one another. In such instances, either/or frames might be replaced by both/and conceptualizations. Thus, we now understand the roles of both heredity *and* environment in human development (Plomin, 1990), free will *and* determinism in the genesis of human action (Howard, 1994b), masculinity *and* femininity in sex role orientation (Constantinople, 1973), perspective of rights *and* perspective of care in moral development, both innocent *and* guilty in issues of legal culpability (Howard, 1992), and so forth. Adopting "both/and integrations" whereby society tempts us to see issues in terms of "either/or dichotomies" will make us less likely to fall into the traps of radicalism, fundamentalism, extremism, and maximization that stalk contemporary intellectual life.

Think of this as a general guideline for making intellectual commitments. You ask me if I'm an ontological constructivist or an objectivist? I hope you now better realize how I can say that I am both—more of one than the other if the topic is physics, the opposite if we speak of religion, and generally equal parts of constructivist and objectivist when the topic is psychology. Am I anti-abortion or pro-choice? You guessed it, I'm both. Am I a free willist or a determinist? You've got the pattern by now: I'm both a free willist and a determinist—because that ancient controversy wouldn't have endured for more than 2,000 years if there weren't important truths in both perspectives. Similarly, I am both a realist/objectivist *and* a constructivist because both perspectives contain important insights.

I believe it was Carl Hempel who first exclaimed, "What is the world that the mind can know it? What is the mind that it can know the world?" Let's start with the first part, "What is the world that it can be known by mind?" Well, there are some theories about the world—such as cold fusion—to which the world will simply not acquiesce. Similarly, although the world will not let humans fly, no matter how fast they flap their arms, birds are allowed to fly by flapping their wings. And it's not that the world rejects all attempts by humans to fly because it is opposed to humans flying—the world's laws are neutral in the sense that the workings of aerodynamics are the same for birds as for humans.

In summary, our scientific explanations must not be incompatible with certain aspects of our objects of investigation, or the theory simply will not fly because the world won't let it. However, the world will *not* veto all theories but the One, True Theory of (for example) human nature. Philosophy of science would be a whole lot easier if the world acted only that way. The Truth would then be contained in the one theory (and the only one) that passes scientific muster. What could be easier? We know nothing until we find the Truth. But—alas—the world and science just don't act that way.

Why anyone would assert that one's currently favored scientific theory tells him or her anything about the (Capital T) Truth about the world is a mystery to me. Such people simply don't understand that science doesn't tell us anything about Truths. Rather, currently favored scientific theories are those that are in closest accord with the epistemic criteria for theory choice—such as predictive accuracy, internal consistency, external coherence, unifying power, fertility, and so forth—no more, no less (Howard, 1985; Kuhn, 1971; McMullin, 1983). Thus, the phrase "scientific Truth" is oxymoronic. Why anyone would worry that a "scientific Truth" contradicted a "religious Truth" (an equally oxymoronic phrase) is beyond me.

Let's now address the question, "What is the mind that it can know the world?"

Assume for a moment that there is a real world "out there" (or "in here" for psychologists) that might be known scientifically. What are the chances that *our minds* might come to know it perfectly? Or know it objectively? Or know it at all?

First, let me assert that Donald Campbell (1974) was absolutely correct when he observed wryly, "Cousin to the amoeba, how could we know perfectly?" So—even assuming a knowable world—please forget the dream of a perfect scientific knowledge. Similarly, the extreme relativists' fantasy that "anything goes"—that everyone's opinion on a topic is as valid as anyone else's opinion—is just plain wrong also. This can easily be demonstrated in physics, demonstrated (with difficulty) in psychology, and reasonably argued in religion.

Let me summarize the beliefs that follow from my ruminations thus far:

1. There are some realities out there (and in here) that must be given their due if we want to construct scientifically compelling stories.

2. Being cousins to the amoeba, we cannot know anything perfectly. Thus, all knowledge is flawed. Consequently, all talk about

(Capital T) Truths serves to get us into trouble—whether we speak as scientists or as members of a faith tradition.

3. For me, the key is to be a committed empiricist (à la William James's principle of radical empiricism) in my search for understanding. Were I a physicist, I'd be a researcher who was looking for nature's laws in the traditional way—although always on the alert for the philosophical curve ball (such as Einstein's relativity, Heisenberg's uncertainty, Bohr's interpretation of complementarity) that our scientific excursions might turn up. As a psychologist, I am broadly empiricist (using quantitative and qualitative methods and even, on occasion, developing a few new research approaches to fill holes in our current cadre of methods). I also try to adopt as many conceptual perspectives as possible (e.g., free willist, phenomenologist, narrativist, biological reductionist, radical behaviorist, social learning theorist) to appreciate both the somewhat fixed and somewhat malleable (i.e., constructed) aspects of what it is like to be a human being.

4. I'm even a committed empiricist in my role as a nonprofessional theologian. I am not a believer in Jim Jones's religion (Jonestown) or David Koresch's faith (Waco) because the fruits of these belief systems do not reflect well on these religions (in my opinion).

But there is yet another way in which I'm a committed empiricist in religion. Imagine that at this time next week, I find myself riding on an ass from Jerusalem to Demascus to torture and murder some godless, radical constructivists if they are unwilling to convert to the one, true faith of Constructive Realism. Suddenly, the skies darken and I say, "Whoa assey! This don't look so good." A bolt of lightening then knocks me off the donkey and I think, "No big deal! People get struck by lightening all the time—I'm just glad to be

alive to interpret the experience." But when a booming voice says, "George, George, why doest thou persecute righteous constructivists so?" *That's* when it becomes a nonnatural experience for me. The voice orders, "You are no longer to be called George, henceforth you are to be known as Stupid."

"I've always thought stupidity was an underappreciated characteristic," I reply, "I'm thrilled to be known as 'old stupid.' By the way, Lord, how do your friends address you?" If the voice says, "Yahweh," I'm suddenly Jewish. If God says, "Allah," then I believe in Islam. If "Siddhartha," I'm Buddhist. If "Jesus," I'm Christian. If the voice says, "Zoroaster," I'm momentarily confused. But so great is my commitment to empiricism that eventually I'd be thrilled to be known as "Stupid the Zoroastrian!" Unfortunately, all of the experiences of my life thus far seem to have reasonable, natural (as opposed to supernatural) explanations, so my choice of a religious belief system is of necessity based on more pragmatic considerations. However, I'd love to experience a slightly less dramatic (than my version of the Saul-becoming-Paul story) critical experiment in the religion domain but I haven't—yet. One more point, and then I'll be finished.

What is the import of the constructivism-realism debate for environmental issues? First, we must be ontological realists in our analyses of all looming environmental problems. To paraphrase, realities will not change if we ignore them. Also, we cannot place faith in modern-day versions of the *deus ex machina* slight of hand. Cop-outs such as, "There is no limit to human ingenuity, so someone will find a solution," "All of these problems will be solved by the action of free markets," and so forth are intellectually bankrupt efforts to stop discussions of important (but psychologically troubling) issues. It is disinguous to argue that human ingenuity and free markets worked to create environmental problems (and then the miracle occurs), so that now they will *solve* the problems they just created. The ostrich strategy has always been recognized as impotent by everyone—except the ostrich!

The coming environmental crises—the effects of overcrowding, global warming, loss of biodiversity, overstressed waste sinks, and so on—represent real physical/biological problems that must be dealt with in real, efficacious ways. These problems will not simply be wished away.

Although the past is set in stone, the future is still open to human intervention. The beauty of the constructivist perspective is that it can help us to realize that we are creating our futures day by day. We can explore several possible futures and then choose which one we (both as individuals and as a society) will work to try to create.

In conclusion, this chapter might be seen as an ode to the "golden mean." More and more I've come to distrust extremism, perfectionism, absolutism, and radicalism in almost any form. In fact, I've even adopted a motto of sorts: "Extremism—even in the service of a good cause—is to be deplored by reasonable people." With respect to this realism-constructivism issue, I'd recommend that we all resist the urge to endorse either extreme view—and think seriously about becoming constructive realists.

CONCLUSION:
A MODIFIED VIEW OF EXPERTS

The Baconian revolution in science in the 17th century ushered in the modernist age. At the heart of the Baconian ideal was Laplace's image of the scientist as an "Omniscient Calculator." Scientists were to stand completely apart from the world (their object of investigation) to understand its workings. So ruthlessly committed to objectivity were these idealized scientists to be that if one were able to give them all the causal laws at work on their object of investigation, as well as the starting conditions of the system in question, they then could, with completely accuracy, predict that object's behavior at any point in the future. Of course, Bacon, Laplace, and Newton had inaminate falling bodies, orbiting planets, and combining chemicals in mind for their Omniscient Calculator to understand. However, psychology (and the other social sciences as well) felt that this model of scientific explanation by value-neutral scientists might also be applied with profit to human actions.

To a certain extent, the Baconian model worked well for psychology. However, we now face the limits of this model for what are obviously cross-cultural phenomena. That is, although scientists are the experts in the world of science, they are probably *not* the preeminent experts in nonscientific cultures (e.g., religions, cultures other than their own, genders other than their own, pathologies they have not experienced, etc.). As anthropologists now see themselves as processors or translators of the natives' cultural expertise, so psychologists must realize that their place as scientists affords them little or no special expertise in many of the cultures they seek to understand. The postmodern model of psychological research sees us more as reporters of the insights gleaned by local experts from the culture in question than it sees us as "Omniscient Calculators."

Similarly, the warrant for the validity of our conclusions now no longer comes from the application of proper research method—as it did in the modernist tradition. Rather, the warrant comes from the dedicated history of the investigator in that particular domain. For example, why would you think that my ideas on a philosophy of science might be worth your time and attention? Why is Don Pope-Davis better equipped to edit this handbook than I am? Similarly, if you wish to know about the nature of racism, who knows more, Nelson Mandela or me? Conversely, if you are interested in the phenomenon of growing up in the Irish-Catholic ghetto of Bayonne, New Jersey, in the 1950s, I humbly submit that I am better qualified for that task than either Mandela or Pope-Davis.

The notion of validity as residing in the experience of the local expert is a thoroughly postmodern idea—and flies in the face of the modernist belief that validity resides in the use of proper method. Constructive realism sees a place for both local knowledge and proper method in various types of research. Much to my surprise, Carl Rogers (1973) actually foresaw this shift from modernist to postmodernist views when he claimed that the warrant for any scientific claim lay not in the use of proper methods but in the lengthening shadow of a scholarly, scientific career.

Rogers (1973) asserted that a good deal of subjectivity and intuition are still necessary in science because the first sensing of meaningful patterns comes from very subjective hunches, beliefs, and intuitions of scientists and practitioners who are deeply involved in the phenomena of interest (such as abnormal behavior, education, or industrial relations). Research, then, becomes the elaboration or refinement of the subjective ideas of sensitive and dedicated men and women attempting to understand meaningful patterns of relationships in their areas of interest. In this view, research is not a sterile, uninteresting activity. Rather, the behavioral researcher has much in common with the artist or writer, who also perceives meaning in the world and attempts to express that meaning in a way others can understand and appreciate. The artist might employ the medium of paint or clay, whereas the writer deals in words; the researcher offers insights through experimental demonstrations. In any case, the goal of furthering our understanding and appreciation of meanings in the world is similar in all three of these vocations.

REFERENCES

Campbell, D. T. (1974). Evolutionary epistemology. In P. S. Schlipp (Ed.), *The philosophy of Karl Popper*. LaSalle, IL: Open Court.

Constantinople, A. P. (1973). Masculinity-femininity: An exception to a famous dictum. *Psychological Bulletin, 80,* 389-407.

Cushing, J. (1994). Too hot to handle. *Philosophy of Science, 61,* 1-3.

de Cervantes, M. (1986). *Don Quixote de la Mancha*. New York: Farrar, Straus, & Giroux. (Original work published 1615)

Donahue, M. J. (1994). Reflections on "reflections." *International Journal for the Psychology of Religion, 4,* 151-156.

Efran, J. S., Lukens, R. J., & Lukens, M. D. (1988). Constructivism: What's in it for you? *The Family Therapy Networker, 12,* 27-35.

Flowers, B. J., & Richardson, F. C. (1996). Why is multiculturalism good? *American Psychologist, 51,* 609-622.

Gergen, K. J. (2001). Psychological science in a postmodern context. *American Psychologist, 56,* 803-813.

Hong, Y., Morris, M. W., Chiu, C., & Benet-Martinez, V. (2000). Multicultural minds: A dynamic constructivist approach to culture and cognition. *American Psychologist, 55,* 709-721.

Howard, G. S. (1985). The role of values in the science of psychology. *American Psychologist, 40,* 255-265.

Howard, G. S. (1991). Culture tales: A narrative approach to thinking, cross cultural psychology, and psychotherapy. *American Psychologist, 46,* 187-197.

Howard, G. S. (1992). No middle voice. *Theoretical and Philosophical Psychology, 12,* 12-26.

Howard, G. S. (1994a). Reflections on change in science and religion. *International Journal of Psychology and Religion, 4,* 127-143.

Howard, G. S. (1994b). Some varieties of free will worth practicing. *Journal of Theoretical and Philosophical Psychology, 14,* 50-61.

James, W. (1907). *A pluralistic universe.* New York: Holt.

Kuhn, T. (1971). *The structure of scientific revolutions.* Chicago: Rand McNally.

McMullin, E. (1983). Values in science. In P. D. Asquith & T. Nickles (Eds.), *Proceedings of the 1982 Philosophy of Science Association* (Vol. 2, pp. 3-23). East Lansing, MI: Philosophy of Science Association.

Plomin, R. (1990). *Nature and nurture: An introduction to human behavioral genetics.* Pacific Grove, CA: Brooks/Cole.

Rogers, C. R. (1973). Some new challenges. *American Psychologist, 28,* 379-387.

Rychlak, J. F. (1989). *The psychology of rigorous humanism* (2nd ed.). New York: New York University Press.

Schumacher, E. F. (1973). *Small is beautiful.* New York: Harper & Row.

6

Moving From Diversity to Multiculturalism

Exploring Power and Its Implications for Multicultural Competence

WILLIAM MING LIU
University of Iowa

DONALD B. POPE-DAVIS
University of Notre Dame

Many years ago there was an emperor so exceedingly fond of new clothes that he spent all his money on being well dressed. Two weavers came to town and made it known that not only were their colors and patterns uncommonly fine, but clothes made of this cloth had a wonderful way of becoming invisible to anyone who was unfit for his office, or who was unusually stupid. "Those would be just the clothes for me," thought the Emperor. "If I wore them I would be able to discover which men in my empire are unfit for their posts. And I could tell the wise men from fools." The most trusted wisemen were sent to check on the weavers, but they could not see anything. They thought, "Am I unfit to be the minister?," "Can it be that I'm a fool?" "I mustn't let anyone find it out, though." . . .The emperor tried on the gown and everyone remarked at its beauty, and nobody would confess that he couldn't see anything. But a little child said, "But he hasn't got anything on." The emperor shivered, for he suspected they were right. But he thought, "This procession has got to go on." So he walked more proudly than ever, as his noblemen held high the train that wasn't there at all.

—"The Emperor's New Clothes" by Hans Christian Andersen
(Trans. by J. Hersholt, 1942)

It may seem unusual to begin a discussion on diversity and multiculturalism with a fairy tale, but as a way to illustrate the current status of multiculturalism in psychology, the tale works well. Although it is not our intent to bemoan the slow pace that psychology has taken to transform itself to reflect the principles and vision of multiculturalism, it is important to examine how multiculturalism has been obscured by a focus on diversity, which we consider to be a poor facsimile of multiculturalism. Consequently, psychology has shifted between diversity and multiculturalism in confusing ways, with the overall effect of slowing its incorporation into the practice and science of psychology.

But why focus on the difference between diversity and multiculturalism? Are they not the same things? Inasmuch as people may want to construe diversity and multiculturalism to be opposite sides of the same coin, it is probably more accurate to state that diversity and multiculturalism represent different denominations and have different currency depending on the context. The problem, of course, is that the two cannot be used simultaneously because they represent different paths toward different particular ends. For us, an important distinction is that diversity and multiculturalism have different strategies and objectives for how power is recognized, articulated, and used. This is an important distinction because, for us, power sets the foundation that determines who and what will be recognized and legitimated. Ultimately, as the fairy tale points out, the impression of something occurring even though the essentials have not changed is the difference between diversity and multiculturalism.

For the purposes of this chapter, power will be focused on as a preeminent factor in multiculturalism. Even though power is sometimes alluded to in our multicultural discourse, it has not been linked to the current state of psychology and multiculturalism. And without a clear discernable understanding of power, multiculturalism is destined to remain linked with "diversity." Thus, to understand power in multiculturalism, we will first begin with a personal recollection of power by one of the authors (WML). Second, we will discuss how power can be conceptualized beyond just a singular dimension of "oppressor-oppressed." Third, we will discuss the matrix model of power and action and how these different intersections lead to various consequences. Finally, multicultural praxis will be discussed as a means to recognize power and move toward multiculturalism.

A PERSONAL REFLECTION ON HOW POWER WAS RECOGNIZED

For WML, the idea of power has always been an elusive construct to identify and understand. In his Asian American studies courses as an undergraduate, power was something that was gained, stolen, or forfeited—a reified entity. Power was a predominant theme in these courses on race and culture because as a marginalized scholarly area, power was always at the center—and was about being at the center—and diffuse at the borders where minorities existed. Power was never a topic in his psychology courses. As an objective science, power was unrelated to any of the topics such as psychopathology, assessment, research design, and personality.

In his graduate training, power was related in a simplified and dichotomous manner. In one "in-class" discussion, the instructor stood up to demonstrate her understanding of power as being able to stand on the neck of the oppressed. *Power* and *oppression* were synonymous. Hence, there was an implicit notion that power was the domain of oppressors and that *liberation* necessarily meant the forfeiture of power. Problematically, however, the issue of power was confounded when discussions turned to "empowerment," "agency," and "advocacy" because power is necessary in all those actions. Power also became a topic of discussion among minority students, usually focusing on the dichotomies, disparities, and inequalities of power between the oppressed and oppressor. What never occurred was a discussion of power in resistance and nonoppressive actions. Rather, the focus was on power as an oppressing force to reinforce hierarchical structures, which were believed to be bad and faulty.

Although the focus for most minority students revolved around racial oppression, White women in the class engaged the discourse around their gender and sexism. Other White students who were gay engaged around their sexuality. White men were left out of the discussion altogether because they represented the nexus of symbolic power and oppression. Or at least we thought. Because we did not invite their participation, we disadvantaged ourselves in understanding the socialization process for White men—the roots of entitlement, cultural appropriation, privilege, and dominance were there for the asking.

Further discussions of power in graduate school revolved around the perception of psychology as an objective science and that the introduction of multiculturalism (and diversity) necessarily meant the dissipation of that objectivity. Hence, heated discussions ventured into the topic of power and politics in psychology. Was all science and therapy political, or did it need to remain objective? It was all or nothing, it seemed. And because the oppressor-oppressed framework of power dynamics was taught, the notion of power networks, resistance, and negotiating privileges was not part of the discourse. This became a great limitation in understanding the functions of power in the institution, society, and among individuals. With such confusion, the issue of power was relegated to the realm of theory and not application.

RECONCEPTUALIZING POWER IN MULTICULTURALISM

Defining and Understanding the Complexities of Power

Even though *power* seems to have a putative definition, for us, it is quite possible that people may have different conceptualizations of power. Hence, what is power? What do we mean when we talk about power? For many, power may be understood as a preeminent actor in the exercise of oppression; that is, those who were in power were able to oppress those with lesser power through the restriction of resources and status—a top-to-bottom definition (Foucault, 1977, 1984; Gutting, 1989; Rouse, 1993). Power was reified as an entity and a possession to which some had access and others did not (Omi & Winant, 1994). Many of these notions have been discussed in postmodern literature, critical race studies, and critical feminist discourse.

For psychologists, the definition of power seems to be much more elusive. For instance, Sue and Sue (1990) defined the opposite of power, or powerlessness, as "the expectancy that a person's behavior cannot determine the outcomes or reinforcements he/she seeks" (p. 142). In this dichotomy, though, the individual may be left without agency to act on his or her environment. Other conceptualizations of power have been through self-efficacy. *Self-efficacy* may also be defined as the extent to which an individual believes he or she is able to execute certain behaviors to achieve a goal (Bandura, 1991). Although this is a closer approximation to reconceptualizing "power," there still needs to be an incorporation of a person's context, history, culture, and race as variables associated with self-efficacy. Consequently, self-efficacy alone does not seem to capture the full notion of power.

If we turn away from psychological definitions for a moment and seek our answer in other fields, some elucidation may be found in postmodern philosophy. Foucault (1977, 1984), for example, critiques the concept of oppressor and oppressed and offers the idea of "power" that comes from relationships that are always dynamically changing. Although Foucault was not always clear in his interpretation of power, and his analyses are often problematic (Moussa & Scapp, 1996), it does allow us a point of analysis and examination. Foucault and others (Omi & Winant, 1994; Rouse, 1993) have argued that power should not and cannot be interpreted as a commodity or possessed entity but rather is present only from its exercise within the architecture of society or a particular point in time. The boundaries and institutions (e.g., apparati from which power is exercised such as schools, the police, government, and the media) in society configure power into a network of positions that people can occupy. Within this network, power can be "manifested and sometimes extended by the position of those who are dominated" (Foucault, 1977, pp. 26-27). Thus, power is accessible to everyone, but its application certainly has differential effects depending on who is acting and from what context. Foucault (1980) writes,

> Power must be analyzed as something which circulates, or rather as something which only functions in the form of a chain. It is never localized here or there, never in anybody's hands, never appropriated as a commodity or piece of wealth. Power is employed and exercised through a net-like organization. And not only do individuals circulate between its threads; they are always in the position of simultaneously undergoing and exercising this power. They are not only its inert or consenting target; they are always also the elements of its articulation. (p. 98)

Therefore, in Foucault's analysis, the administration of hegemony and resistance can occur at any time and place and is constantly "shifting and regrouping" (Sarup, 1993, p. 84). For example, those formerly oppressed may find voice in counterdiscourse (or counterhegemony) to fight oppressors (Moussa & Scapp, 1996), and the oppressed can become perceived oppressors themselves eventually. Although abundant historical evidence exists for this claim, it is beyond the scope of this chapter to elaborate on all the examples. But for illustration, one will be used.

The Case of the Oppressed Becoming Oppressors

In 1991, a coalition of Asian Americans staged a demonstration at a Lambda Legal Defense and Education Fund (LLDEF) fundraiser. The point of contention was due to the use of *Miss Saigon* as a source of fund-raising by the LLDEF, even though the Asian American community in New York had written to the LLDEF about their objections to *Miss Saigon*. For Asian Americans, *Miss Saigon* portrayed a racist characterization of Asians in general, was sexist, and obscured what actually occurred during the Vietnam conflict. The LLDEF acknowledged the concerns but noted that the popularity of *Miss Saigon* would allow them to obtain a huge fund to be used for other LLDEF purposes—hence, the fund-raising would continue, but it did acknowledge that it would be more sensitive in the future (Yoshikawa, 1994).

Hence, in this case, the perception that the LLDEF and the Asian American community occupied the same "oppressed" location in the power network is inaccurate. For the LLDEF, engaging and legitimating a dominant hegemonic discourse (e.g., the myth of love in the midst of a racist conflict vis-à-vis *Miss Saigon*'s recapitulation of the *Madame Butterfly* narrative) allowed it a source of legitimacy and funding. The Asian American community in New York City likely perceived the LLDEF as moving from the "oppressed" to the "oppressor" category and experienced the exercise of power by the LLDEF as marginalizing (Yoshikawa, 1994).

Redefining the Exercise of Power

In transforming our understanding of power, we do not want to imply that all oppression (e.g., racism) is the same (Helms & Cook, 1999). Even though it is easy to conclude that everyone has power within the Foucauldian framework of power, for some, the access and exercise of power are easier and have more cultural currency than they do for other people. For example, White supremacy tends to be the most powerful form of oppression and racism in the United States. That is, White supremacy is "far more easily associated with an essentializing (and once very powerful) legacy: that of white supremacy and racial dictatorship in the U.S., and fascism in the world at large" (Omi & Winant, 1994, p. 73). Thus, even though it may be possible to identify Black and White ideologues, White racism still has greater potency because of the historic legacy of racism and its links to the apparati of power in the United States. These apparati (e.g., schools, government, media) also have institutional memories and structures that allow for racism (e.g., perceiving curriculum diversification as a lack of rigor), for example, to easily be activated rather than counterhegemonic actions (e.g., diversifying the curriculum).

Foucault (1977, 1984) also offered an inversion of the idea that "knowledge is power." Specifically, in the original form of "knowledge is power," there is an inability to analyze how knowledge is created and legitimized; it is assumed that those who create knowledge will always act beneficently for others. In this original form, "knowledge" is innocuous, depoliticized, and assumed to be without distortion (objective). But Foucault reversed the relationship, such that "power is

knowledge" (Caputo & Yount, 1993; Sassoon, 1987). Foucault forced an examination of who has the power to create and maintain "knowledge" that allows for the maintenance of certain power relationships. Moreover, as part of the examination, one should understand who benefits from these existing structures. Foucault's reinterpretation of power illuminates the multiple ways power is exercised through people, groups, and institutions. The exercise of power is not uniform and linear but full of contradictions and irregularities that are constantly being challenged and reinterpreted. But how, if power becomes an oppressive force, is it regulated and perpetuated within society? The answer may be a clearer understanding of hegemony and resistance.

HEGEMONY

Power, along with its many manifestations and guises, may be difficult to define. Much like the problem with race and multiculturalism, power has been invested with multiple meanings and definitions that make it formidable to articulate. But what is of interest in this examination of power is its links with how a society functions and how those in society participate in the exercise of power.

An example of Foucault's conceptualization of power and control is found in his theory of domination through the equal application of surveillance. Foucault believed that control does not always come from force but through the consent of those being dominated. In Foucault's (1977) theory of the Panpticon, for instance, prisoners were always under the watchful eye of the guard and therefore acted and "police[d] their own behavior" (Sarup, 1993, p. 68). In effect, the dominant groups could control the actions of subordinated groups, not through abuse or imprisonment but through the subordinated group's inculcation of the dominant group's worldview and expectations. In this way, the least amount of force is applied, and behaviors and attitudes that serve the dominant group are unlinked. That is, there is no cause and effect—supremacy is masked. Consequently, what occurs is the sense that behaviors and attitudes are "natural" rather than constructed, reinforced, and punished.

Thus, *hegemony* is not synonymous with *oppression*. Instead, hegemony is an intricate domain of power relationships that allows for the perpetuation of strategic positions and the greater influence of some people over others through consent or deference (Dobbins & Skillings, 1991; Foucault, 1977, 1984; Hebdige, 1993). Consent becomes a critical aspect of hegemony (Gramsci, 1971; Hebdige, 1993; Omi & Winant, 1994) because for a group of people to remain in a position to exercise control, their position must seem legitimate and natural (Hebdige, 1993).

Within a hegemonic environment, consent is created when people come to accept a "vision of the world that belongs to the rulers" (Fiori, 1970, p. 238). An important mechanism in preserving this facade is to incorporate many of the "key interests of subordinated groups, often to the explicit disadvantage [of those in positions of power]" (Omi & Winant, 1994, p. 66). In psychology, there may be an intimation of accepting multiculturalism through diversification efforts, yet the result of diversity may be hegemonic. That is, acceptance of marginalized groups may be only at a superficial level. One benefit of focusing on diversity may be that institutions may be able to deflect critiques away from its slow incorporation of multiculturalism (D'Andrea & Daniels, 1995). Hence, instead of critiquing relationships of power, focusing on diversity affords a group a semblance of multiculturalism without the struggles inherent in multicultural transformation. Consequently, observers focus on the superficiality of diversity

as progress rather than a sign of some progress and not necessarily transformation.

RESISTANCE AND POWER

The exercise of an individual's agency within a network of power implies that people always have the capacity to resist. Thus, except in "the most absolutist of regimes, resistance to rule itself implies power" (Omi & Winant, 1994, p. 188). This claim is in contradistinction to Sue and Sue's (1990) definition of powerlessness because people are never actually without power. Resistance, however, may take on different forms—active (e.g., militant protest) and passive (e.g., not voting)—and needs to be interpreted within its cultural context.

Reinterpreting power and oppression helps us to understand that, even when opposing one type of oppression, people may participate in other forms (Caputo & Yount, 1993). Hence, a binary view of power relations does not address the problem of being discriminated against by those who might be considered "powerless." Agentic behavior, even resistance in an environment of oppression, may then be a hegemonic negotiation. Specifically, resistance as a form of using power represents compromises wherein privilege may be gained at one level, but discrimination may continue at another. Kandiyoti (1988) suggested that hegemonic negotiation allows one to "maximize security and optimize life options with varying potential for active or passive resistance in the face of oppression" (p. 274). Therefore, in challenging oppression, resistance seems to be a confluence of privilege and power but not totalistic and complete (i.e., cannot resist all forms of oppression or personal "isms" simultaneously). Kondo (1990) assessed this problematic position by stating, "There can be no pristine space of resistance, and . . . subversion and contestation are never beyond discourse and power; . . . [however]

we must remain sensitive to relative degrees of subversiveness" (p. 27).

Consequently, we are constantly negotiating power in our lives regardless of our activity. We cannot assume that resistance implies the complete forfeiture of power; rather, resistance is a type of powerful action in which privileges are exchanged.

Case of Oppression
Within the Context of Resistance

Kim (1993) described how, during the late 1960s and 1970s, when the Asian American community was active within the context of multiple racial minority groups (e.g., African Americans and the civil rights movement, Latino Americans and field workers' rights, and Native Americans and sovereignty and land control), an interesting problem began to emerge. With Asian Americans facing discrimination and racism, the reaction was to focus their energies on creating safe environments for Asian Americans and to look for ways to reinforce the integrity of the Asian American community. What occurred were stringent gender roles in activist organizations where men were the leaders and women took on "domestic" roles, along with the reinforced idea of avoiding interracial dating (especially to Whites). Consequently, some Asian American women started to drift away from these organizations because they only re-created dominant patriarchy, but now under the roof of a minoritied racial group.

But what are people to do if any kind of agentic behavior (e.g., resistance) may reinforce the dominant hegemony? Because any actions may oppose one kind of "ism" while reinforcing another, it seems that it would be impossible to eradicate issues such as racism, sexism, and homophobia. What does this mean for psychology?

POWER IN DIVERSITY
AND MULTICULTURALISM

When we speak of power, we are referring to the various ways in which people, institutions, and cultures engage each other to negotiate perceived competing demands and goals. Because power is implicated in everything we do and is virtually everywhere, it would be impossible to discuss power in every context. Thus, to make our discussion of power relevant for our discussion, we refer to power within the context of people and institutions making efforts to become multicultural. Power, in these instances, is limited to those individuals and institutions (i.e., apparati) that have direct and indirect influence over the multiculturalization of a certain environment and the people within that environment. We also examine the ways that people reinforce a particular way of being (i.e., the status quo) versus embracing multiculturalism.

For us, power is a constant feature between people and within environments, but it is not static or consistent over time and between different contexts. Power is also not automatic but must be nurtured and determined through social and institutional apparati (Foucault, 1977, 1984) that can ensure the maximal opportunities for certain people to have influence and have their goals and interests met. Moreover, it is quite possible that, although power seems externally robust, it is in fact fragile, temporal, and ephemeral. This is in no way to reinforce the notion of power as a reified object, but only to say that "power" may be determined by a particular context and those who participate in that context. For instance, Whiteness can be construed as a type of power that would seemingly be transferable between contexts. Yet, depending on other variables such as social class or location (e.g., urban vs. rural), one's Whiteness does not necessarily ensure participation within "another context's" power structure. Hence, power

Table 6.1   Axes Relevant for Multiculturalism and Power

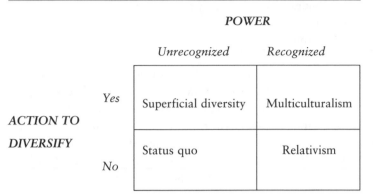

POWER

		Unrecognized	Recognized
ACTION TO DIVERSIFY	*Yes*	Superficial diversity	Multiculturalism
	No	Status quo	Relativism

varies between contexts and people, must be nurtured and developed, and cannot be assumed to be transferred from one context to another.

Because power is sometimes elusive and difficult to identify and articulate, movement toward multiculturalism without recognizing and mapping power within a particular environment will only meet with resistance and failures. For heuristic purposes, we have identified two particular axes that are relevant for multiculturalism and power. The first axis is the recognition of power, and the second is action to diversify (see Table 6.1). As an important first step in becoming multicultural, recognizing the importance of power in people and contexts is crucial in understanding how to develop the most appropriate strategy to become multicultural. The implication of not recognizing power is to leave existing "traditional" ways and frameworks intact without critique and evaluation. The other axis of action to diversify implies that people may or may not acknowledge the importance of diversity. For those who endorse diversity as an important goal, there may be activity to make increased diversity happen, with or without acknowledging power. For those who do not subscribe to the need to diversify, they can either support the status quo or become stuck

in the quagmire of multiple subjectivities (this will be explained below). Thus, combining the two axes produces four different results: superficial diversity, multiculturalism, status quo, and relativism. What follows is a brief explanation of the different results.

Superficial Diversity

First, when power is unrecognized but people move toward "multiculturalism," the result will invariably be a "diverse" community existing on a troubled existing foundation. This cell is entitled *superficial diversity* because old frameworks and structures have not been identified, critiqued, and reconceptualized, and the introduction of "diverse" elements will remain just that—superficial diversity. Consequently, in this cell, diversity is best defined as numbers and representation. Power goes unrecognized and unarticulated. Metaphorically, diversity is reflected as the tiles of a mosaic or ingredients to salads, stews, and stir-frys. In these metaphors, the real power is undisclosed—for whom is the aesthetic object created? Who is the consumer of the mosaic, salad, and stir-fry (Gates, 1992)? Diversity is an attempt by some group or organization to reflect the putative variability of peoples in their environment. It is often a tactic (i.e., a means to an end) that either employs no long-term plan or anticipates only short-term gains. There is no need to critique the power relationships or the status quo when "diversity" is used. Within applied psychology programs, diversity is best illustrated by attending to the "one" multicultural course as an indicator of the program's commitment to multiculturalism. In addition, the burden of diversity and diversification efforts is often placed on the shoulders of "people of color" or those of other "diverse" backgrounds. Consequently, diversity becomes a "minority" or "people-of-color" issue, which often implies that it is a marginal issue.

Multiculturalism

Second, when power is recognized and people move toward diversification, the result will be multiculturalism. For multiculturalism, the definition includes diversity and diversification efforts but moves far beyond it. Multiculturalism is a concerted plan (i.e., strategy) that employs multiple knowledges of people, histories, and contexts in an effort to challenge the current state of mental health practice, theory, and training. Multiculturalism is not just a philosophical worldview (Helms & Richardson, 1997) wherein clinicians take into account similar and different experiences people have and remember to be sensitive to it. Instead, multiculturalism should be omnipresent in every course taught and in the way training is conducted. Multiculturalism is not just remembering to be beneficent for the client: It is a plan of action that employs the knowledge of people, culture, history, and context to affect the way theories are used, diagnoses are done, and treatment plans are made. In training, whether or not an instructor states it explicitly, some psychological theory is invoked. This psychological theory helps the instructor organize and make sense of the client, and these are the learned experiences that he or she wants to impart onto the trainee. When multiculturalism becomes a part of all training, such that it becomes an unconscious schema (i.e., nonexplicit) to organize and make sense of the environment, then multiculturalism will have met the goal of integration. This integration would be beyond the people's ability to point it out because multiculturalism is a part of everything. Finally, multiculturalism would be a part of everyone's life and would not be limited to only diverse groups or "people of color."

Status Quo

Third, when power is unrecognized and there is no movement toward diversity, then this is what we describe as the *status quo*. In this environment, multiculturalism and diversity are not regarded as important, no resources are concentrated toward understanding the importance of diversifying, and the traditional power structures are left intact and in place. People moving into these environments will be expected to assimilate and acculturate toward the norms of the dominant group, and failure to do so will meet with marginalization.

Relativism

Fourth, when power is recognized but there is no concerted action to diversify, the result is relativism. In this cell, power is recognized as an important variable to contend with, but rather than engaging in the struggle, the preference is to stagnate in the discourse over power. Consequently, the belief for people in this environment is that everything is valuable and salient and that we should not have to struggle to determine what this all means for us. Relativism is the belief that virtually anything and everything is tolerable and acceptable because, if a culture values it and sanctions it, then "we" must also recognize its inherent value to that culture. The power in a relativistic worldview accepts the notion that there are competing worldviews at times, but rather than negotiate the complexities of cultural beliefs and practices, power is used to deny the needed struggle. Hence, power is simultaneously recognized and repudiated in relativism. In psychology and counseling courses, this can be experienced as a classroom wherein the instructor legitimates all points of view without analyses or critique. White racism and Black nationalism, for example, are equated as similar and problematic for its "racism." Another example would be a discussion about whether female genital mutilation is regarded as acceptable because it is culturally bound.

OUT OF THE QUAGMIRE: MULTICULTURAL PRAXIS

One possible solution is what we call multicultural praxis. *Praxis,* a notion Paulo Freire (1972) popularized, meant the "action and reflection of men upon their world in order to transform it" (p. 66). Although Freire originally proposed praxis to transform the way people teach and are taught, we can borrow the concept of praxis and adapt it to the exercise of multiculturalism. Because action and reflection are necessary tenets of praxis, we propose that initial acts toward multiculturalism are necessary but should not be viewed as final solutions. Instead, these initial endeavors toward multiculturalism may be viewed as first acts, and periods of reflection (contemplation and evaluation) are necessary before proceeding.

Multicultural praxis works with the understanding that, as actions are made, contexts change and bring in new challenges that need to be assessed. Essentially, any transformative action in a power network changes the original configuration such that new challenges arise and hence new tactics must be developed. For instance, the definition of *race* and *racism* changes over time (Omi & Winant, 1994); thus, what may have worked previously to combat racism in the 1960s may need to be reorganized to meet the new challenges of racism's protean manifestations. Reorganization and evaluation may signify working with people and groups that were previously seen as antagonistic but now have an investment in the goals of a particular movement. When referring to how power operates within the movement toward multiculturalism, any action to recognize power and to transform people and institutions will necessarily change the nature of power relations. Consequently, one cannot readily stay congruent with a long-term plan of multicultural action because contexts change and people and institutions adapt. In multicultural praxis, the notion is to remain fixed on the idea of becoming multicultural, to recognize how power operates within one's environment and among people, but to remain flexible and adaptable to new challenges and the protean manifestations of power.

Case of Contemporary Resistance to Multiculturalism

Although census data and projections show the need for psychology to become more multicultural (Hall, 1997), the transformation of psychology toward multiculturalism has been challenged. From weary administrators and faculty to critical graduate students who challenge the science and need for multiculturalism, resistance takes on various guises. Professionally, two articles stand out as triumphs of resistance to multiculturalisms, albeit in a subterranean manner. First, an article by Fowers and Richardson (1996) asks, "Why is multiculturalism good?" The authors first start by reasoning the importance of multiculturalism in psychology as a necessary transformation. Yet, Fowers and Richardson then reveal the full intention of their argument. The problem as they have seen it is that the multiculturalists have not paid sufficient homage to the "Western" roots of their movement, and if it were not for these rich liberal traditions, multiculturalism may not have ever been founded. Essentially, multiculturalism is in the best traditions of the "West" and thus not originally a challenge made by the subaltern peoples of the "non-West." The second article by Redding (2001) requests multiculturalists to be more open about political diversity. Note here the focus on diversity and not multiculturalism. Redding posits that the movement for multiculturalism has been suffuse with "liberal" bias (i.e., too progressive) and has not been inviting for people with "conservative" political leanings. He argues that the "liberal bias" has consequently led to scientifically erroneous errors such as sanctioning for gay and lesbian parenting. For Redding, political diversity (i.e., conservatism) can coexist side by side with multiculturalism because power is not an issue.

The two examples illustrate how potentially confusing and subtle arguments might be made to reassert the centrality of White dominant thought (i.e., White supremacist worldviews) in psychology. The notion that multiculturalism marginalizes Western traditions or political conservatism is a good example of noncontextualized and ahistorical polemics. Fowers and Richardson (1996) and Redding (2001) do not consider multiculturalism's attempts to move away from and redefine the "center" but would rather just overlay multiculturalism onto the current power structure (i.e., superficial diversity). For multiculturalists, their renewed arguments in favor of re-Westernizing the Western discipline of psychology reflect the potentially protean nature of how racism operates in contemporary society. Although overt situations of racism occur everyday, we also need to be aware of and sensitive to the subtle gestures that continue to reassert one dominant worldview over another. These subtle gestures are difficult to identify because they are couched in the framework of resistance but readily offer more of the same (i.e., the invisible gown of the emperor).

Finally, the argument that multiculturalism must reflect the diversification of the United States could not be sufficiently critiqued and rebutted. Although diversification of the United States was a sufficient argument for initial multicultural movements, as the power

dynamics change, new challenges arise. Hence, multiculturalists are faced with newer and increasingly sophisticated arguments against the need for multicultural transformation. As a result, we must constantly engage and reflect on our actions and environment to achieve the goal of multicultural transformation.

SUMMARY

Unlike the emperor, we cannot continue to proceed with the hopes that people will change to embrace multiculturalism. In fact, we may not use *diversity, cultural relativism,* and *multiculturalism* interchangeably to describe the same phenomenon. Throughout this review, multiculturalism as a cultural discourse has been examined historically and employed to help construct what clients' worldviews may be like from a position within their world. Moreover, it was the aim of this review to reexamine the use of "power" throughout the extant multicultural literature and to decenter the binary conceptualization of power relationships. As seen in the reexamination of client worldviews, binary relationships of power do not address the possibility that individuals, who may be a part of "oppressed" groups, may benefit from privileged aspects of their various cultures and identities (e.g., being male and patriarchy).

The literature also shows that programs and departments are attempting to change to incorporate multicultural issues. However, like the civil rights movement, there does not appear to be an orchestrated and linear progression or change (Bell, 1992). The possibility still exists that, although there is diversity in and around a program and department, multicultural issues and concerns still will not be addressed. That is, diversity may act like an invisible shield to further structural changes. It then becomes important for multicultural advocates to develop the capacity to say, "There isn't anything there."

REFERENCES

Bandura, A. (1991). Human agency: The rhetoric and the reality. *American Psychologist, 46,* 157-162.

Bell, D. (1992). *Faces at the bottom of the well.* New York: Basic Books.

Caputo, J., & Yount, M. (1993). Institutions, normalization, and power. In J. Caputo & M. Yount (Eds.), *Foucault and the critique of institutions* (pp. 3-26). University Park: Pennsylvania State University.

D'Andrea, M., & Daniels, J. (1995). Promoting multiculturalism and organizational change in the counseling profession: A case study. In J. G. Ponterotto, J. M. Casas, L. A. Suzuki, & C. M. Alexander (Eds.), *Handbook of multicultural counseling* (pp. 17-33). Thousand Oaks, CA: Sage.

Dobbins, J. E., & Skillings, J. H. (1991). The utility of race labeling in understanding cultural identity: A conceptual tool for the social science. *Journal of Counseling and Development, 70,* 37-44.

Fiori, G. (1970). *Antonio Gramsci: Life of a revo lutionary.* New York: Verso.

Foucault, M. (1977). *Discipline and punish: The birth of the prison* (A. Sheridan, Trans.). New York: Random House.

Foucault, M. (1980). *Power/knowledge: Selected interviews and other writings, 1972-1977* (C. Gordon, Ed. and Trans.). New York: Pantheon.

Foucault, M. (1984). The body of the condemned. In P. Rabinow (Ed.), *The Foucault reader* (pp. 170-178). New York: Pantheon.

Fowers, B. J., & Richardson, F. C. (1996). Why is multiculturalism good? *American Psychologist, 51,* 609-621.

Freire, P. (1972). *Pedagogy of the oppressed.* New York: Herder and Herder.

Gates, H. L., Jr. (1992). *Loose canons: Notes on the culture wars.* New York: Oxford University Press.

Gramsci, A. (1971). *Selections from prison notebooks.* New York: International Publisher.

Gutting, G. (1989). *Michel Foucault's archaeology of scientific reason.* Cambridge, UK: Cambridge University Press.

Hall, C. C. I. (1997). Cultural malpractice: The growing obsolescence of psychology with the changing U.S. population. *American Psychologist, 52,* 642-651.

Hebdige, D. (1993). From culture to hegemony. In S. During (Ed.), *The cultural studies reader* (pp. 357-367). New York: Routledge Kegan Paul.

Helms, J. E., & Cook, D. A. (1999). *Using race and culture in counseling and psychotherapy: Theory and process.* Boston: Allyn & Bacon.

Helms, J. E., & Richardson, T. Q. (1997). How "multiculturalism" obscures race and culture as differential aspects of counseling competency. In D. B. Pope-Davis & H. L. K. Coleman (Eds.), *Multicultural counseling competencies: Assessment, education and training, and supervision* (pp. 60-82). Thousand Oaks, CA: Sage.

Kandiyoti, D. (1988). Bargaining with patriarchy. *Gender & Society, 2,* 274-290.

Kim, E. H. (1993). Mediations on the year 2020: Policy for women. In J. D. Hokoyama & D. T. Nakanishi (Eds.), *The state of Asian Pacific America: Policy issues to the year 2020* (pp. 253-262). Los Angeles: Asian Pacific American Public Policy Institute and UCLA Asian American Studies Center.

Kondo, D. K. (1990). M. Butterfly: Orientalism, gender, and a critique of essentialist identity. *Cultural Critique, 16,* 5-29.

Moussa, M., & Scapp, R. (1996). The practical theorizing of Michel Foucault: Politics and counter-discourse. *Cultural Critique, 33,* 87-112.

Omi, M., & Winant, H. (1994). *Racial formation in the United States: From the 1960s to the 1990s* (2nd ed.). New York: Routledge Kegan Paul.

Redding, R. E. (2001). Sociopolitical diversity in psychology: The case for pluralism. *American Psychologist, 56,* 205-215.

Rouse, J. (1993). Foucault and the natural sciences. In J. Caputo & M. Yount (Eds.), *Foucault and the critique of institutions* (pp. 137-162). University Park: Pennsylvania State University Press.

Sarup, M. (1993). *An introductory guide to post-structuralism and post-modernism* (2nd ed.). Athens: University of Georgia Press.

Sassoon, A. S. (1987). *Gramsci's politics* (2nd ed.). Minneapolis: University of Minnesota Press.

Sue, D. W., &, Sue, D. (1990). *Counseling the culturally different: Theory and practice* (2nd ed.). New York: John Wiley.

Yee, A. H., Fairchild, H. H., Weizmann, F., & Wyatt, G. E. (1993). Addressing psychology's problems with race. *American Psychologist, 48,* 1132-1140.

Yoshikawa, Y. (1994). The heat is on Miss Saigon coalition: Organizing across race and sexuality. In K. Aguilar-San Juan (Ed.), *The state of Asian America: Activism and resistance in the 1990s* (pp. 275-294). Boston: South End.

7

Multiculturally Competent School Counseling

HARDIN L. K. COLEMAN
THOMAS BASKIN

University of Wisconsin–Madison

A school counselor reports that 85 of the 300 students for whom she is responsible are getting Ds or Fs. She works in a community that is changing from a rural economy to being a bedroom community for a midsized city in the Midwest. The community is 98% European American, and there is a relatively low percentage of students receiving free or reduced lunches at the school. Her failing students are mostly European American and reflect the economic distribution of the town. They are, however, more likely to be boys than girls, in the same way that students in the top 20% of the class are more likely to be girls than boys.

A counselor in an urban area about 70 minutes away is working in a middle school that is 98% African American; there is a 70% mobility rate in the school, and the percentage of students receiving free or reduced lunch at the school is more than 90%. The school has a strong and focused principal who, along with the staff, is highly committed to the success of all children. The school is orderly, there is a lot of communication among the staff, and the staff work hard to create a relevant curriculum for their children within the confines of state-required proficiency examinations. Recently, only 5% of the eighth grade demonstrated sufficient proficiency to merit graduation to the ninth grade.

Although these are very different schools in very different communities, the counselors share a similar challenge. Specifically, they both have to understand how the context in which their students strive, or do not strive, for academic and social success both facilitates and constrains the achievement of that goal. They need to understand how cultural factors such as race, gender, and class organize behavioral expectations within and for individuals and design interventions that address the needs of individuals within the context in which they are being served. We believe that the ability to serve the needs of students within their ecological context is the essence of multiculturally competent school counseling. As Oleneck (2000) has identified, it is the school personnel's responsibility to facilitate the sufficient transfer of cultural capital to allow all children to succeed in schools.

School counselors are in a unique position to facilitate academic and social success through ecologically relevant interventions (Coleman & Tuescher, in press). In this chapter, we outline the manner in which the role and skills of the school counselor can be used to meet the needs of culturally diverse students as an integral part of the schooling process. We first describe the role of the school counselor and how that role can be used to facilitate the social and emotional development of children. Then we describe the particular skills of the school counselor and articulate how these skills can be used in a culturally relevant manner. To show how these roles and skills can be integrated to serve the needs of children, we describe an integrated intervention to motivate adolescents that uses a focus on belongingness as the key component (Bina, Finn, & Sowle, 2001).

THE SCHOOL COUNSELOR'S ROLE

The professional school counselor's role is multifaceted. On a day-to-day if not hourly basis, counselors work with children, parents, teachers, administrators, and community agencies. Depending on the focus and competence of the counselor, he or she will spend time teaching a class, counseling an individual or group, consulting with a teacher or parent, or monitoring a lunchroom. Counselors will

facilitate an abuse report to social services, and then they will help prepare an application to college. They will run a friendship group one period, develop a special education referral the next, and then advise the student council during lunch. Given the multiple tasks that the professional school counselor performs, it is often hard to understand the coherent philosophy underlying the role.

When one steps back from the day-to-day functions of school counselors, it becomes readily apparent that they are the ones in the school who have the primary responsibility for organizing, implementing, and evaluating the development of socioemotional competence among school-age children, specifically as it applies to the acquisition of academic accomplishment and a successful transition from school to the world or work. Increasingly, the profession of school counseling argues that these goals are best met through the creation, implementation, and maintenance of a comprehensive developmental guidance program. According to *The Wisconsin Developmental Guidance Model: A Resource and Planning Guide* (1997), an effective program has certain characteristics. It will (a) be systematic, sequential, and comprehensive; (b) be founded on developmental psychology, educational philosophy, and counseling methodology; (c) focus on individual, process, and product; (d) emphasize cognitive, affective, behavioral, experiential, and environmental domains; (e) be directed toward consolidation of the present and preparation for the future; (f) facilitate the individualization and transfer of learning; and (g) provide evaluation of student performance and corrective feedback. The goal of such a program is to facilitate the acquisition of certain competencies within children. Table 7.1 presents the nine competencies that are the desired outcomes of the Wisconsin comprehensive developmental guidance program. The underlying assumption is that those children who possess these competencies are better prepared to take advantage of educational

Table 7.1   Wisconsin Developmental
                  Guidance Model Competencies

1. Connect family, school, and work

2. Solve problems

3. Understand diversity, inclusiveness, and fairness

4. Work in groups

5. Manage conflict

6. Integrate growth and development

7. Direct change

8. Make decisions

9. Set and achieve goals

opportunities and successfully complete the school-to-work transition.

Olneck (2000) recently suggested that one of the challenges to effective multicultural education is changing what counts for cultural capital (Bourdieu, 1973, 1986). It is Olneck's contention that we face a difficult choice between helping students acquire social and academic competence, as those have been defined by the Eurocentric education establishment (see, e.g., Bennett, 1996; Hirsch, 1994), or helping children acquire their culturally relevant developmental competencies (Garcia Coll et al., 1996). The effective professional school counselor does not see these goals as mutually exclusive. The multiculturally competent school counselor seeks to use his or her skills to help the child acquire those competencies that are necessary to be successful within the school and within the child's community. Such a counselor will be aware of how to adjust his or her practice as a function of the continuity between the culture of the school, the culture of the school's community, and the culture of the child. If these cultures are the same, the counselor will practice differently than if these cultures are different. Acquiring the necessary skills to make these adjustments is a primary responsibility of the professional school counselor.

Skills of the School Counselor

It is the professional school counselor's responsibility to manage a comprehensive developmental guidance program (Campbell & Dahir, 1997; Paisley & Borders, 1995). It is also the counselor's job to work with teachers, parents, and administrators to help students acquire the competencies presented in Table 7.1. To achieve these ends, the school counselor must acquire a certain set of professional competencies (Coleman, James, Hellman, & Tuescher, 1995). These skills, presented in Table 7.2, are the focus of most counselor training programs. One of the dilemmas in school counselor education is that the necessary focus on skills acquisition as a precursor to effective performance supercedes the focus

Table 7.2   Skills of the Professional School
                  Counselor

Assessment and intervention

Developmental guidance

Consultation

Program planning and management

Multicultural competence

Professional identity

on the content of an actual guidance program. The latter, therefore, is often the focus of post-degree training (Holcomb-McCoy, 2001). In the following section, we articulate, from an ecological perspective, how school counselors can address the needs of children in a pluralistic society. One of the core skills that a professional school counselor needs to develop is how to adapt programming to meet the universal and culturally specific needs of the students in his or her school (Constantine & Yeh, 2001).

Assessment and Intervention

One of the primary roles of the school counselor is to assess the needs of students and plan and then implement relevant interventions. One of the dangers facing counselors in a pluralistic society is an overreliance on standardized measures that do not take into account cultural variability. A traditional approach is to evaluate the skills and abilities of students based on seemingly objective criteria such as grades or performance on high-stake tests. A multiculturally competent (MCC) school counselor will look at this information in relation to other contextual variables. For example, when determining the academic promise of a fifth grader who is on free or reduced lunch, a school counselor will work with teachers to see that such a child who is performing above grade level in math and social studies (work that can be performed in school) but at grade level in reading most likely does not have an ability deficit in relationship to his middle-income peers but might be living in a situation that does not allow for or facilitate reading time outside of school. The school counselor would not allow this relatively lower performance to inhibit the child's entrance into programs for the talented or gifted and would help the teacher find ways to reinforce the child's time on the reading task. The school counselor would also help the child, the teacher, and the librarian find reading material that is relevant to the everyday reality of the child. The MCC school counselor would also learn how to integrate an understanding of context into information provided through standardized academic or psychological assessments. He or she would include a more clinical interview into any battery of tests to identify contextual and cultural factors that could serve to give a more accurate interpretation of test results than could be achieved through a traditional understanding of test results.

In addition to integrating a contextual understanding into test interpretation, an MCC school counselor would integrate that understanding into the interventions that she

or he plans and implements. Let's take, for example, an African American school counselor counseling a recently immigrated Chinese American student. According to the traditional model of school counseling, if the student came to the counselor because he was anxious in school and did not feel that he fit in, the counselor could assess him using a standardized belongingness scale. An MCC school counselor would want to use a scale that had been standardized for culturally Chinese students. Next, in his subjective assessment as a traditional counselor, he would be looking for how the student made friends and how he fit in with other students. An MCC school counselor would understand that the student's view of friendship might be different. He may spend more time with his nuclear family than other students, and he may have more family commitments. Furthermore, he may spend more time with his extended family than other students might otherwise. In this way, he might be disconnected at school but very connected with his family, whereas the typical European American student who does not have many friends at school may typically be fairly isolated and disconnected from his family and from others in his community. A traditional intervention might include a social skills and assertiveness training program, whereas the multiculturally competent counselor would be sensitive to the difference between mental health and acculturation. A more systemic intervention might include making an exception to the school district's transfer policy and allowing the student to transfer to another school that he would prefer because many of his cousins go there.

Developmental Guidance

In the traditional model of school counseling, developmental guidance involves bringing each student along in developmentally appropriate ways toward a school-to-work transition.

The added dimension of culture causes the MCC school counselor to understand that different cultures may emphasize different values in students. What is developmentally appropriate at one level, for one culture, may be different for another culture. In grade school, it may be appropriate for European American students to think of career aspirations relatively independent of what their families are doing, yet for many other cultures, it would be more culturally appropriate for the students to be largely concerned with family goals for their future career. Consequently, a grade-school classroom guidance intervention might appropriately ask not only what students' interests are but also what their families' needs and expectations are for their future career goals. In another example, students from certain cultures may have family expectations such that they are required to spend considerable time and energy working in their families' business. Effective developmental guidance programs could incorporate an understanding for the students of how the tasks they are doing for their families can be building blocks for possible other future careers. Helping in a family's restaurant builds skills related to the eventual attainment of an MBA, and working at a family grocery may contain many skills similar to a future accountant. Counselors can be culturally sensitive by supporting the families' present goals of having their children work in the family business while advocating for the students' future career goals in a way that shows possibilities, without mandating that the students ever need to leave the family business, if they ultimately choose not to do so.

Consultation

In the traditional model of consultation, the counselor assists teachers, administrators, and others in dealing with the social and emotional needs of students. MCC school counselors see how culture adds to this task in at least two important ways. First, they see how recommendations and goals for a student from one culture may be different from those of another culture. For example, the ability to afford and wear the clothes of a peer group may affect one student differently than another. Although a solution for all might be the implementation of uniforms for all students, this would affect students differently. For immigrant families, the students may not be aware of the current style of dress of their school-age peers. Uniforms would remove from them the social pressure to either figure out what the popular clothing styles are among their peers or face the stigma of being inappropriately dressed. On the other hand, students from single-parent families may be well aware of the current style of their peers, but a policy of school uniforms may remove the financial pressure from the family of trying to maintain this current clothing style. Second, MCC school counselors understand how the ethnicity of teachers, administrators, counselors, parents, students, and others may all interplay in complicated ways. An African American principal may have certain values concerning optimal goals for African American students. A European American teacher may see these same goals as rigid and not in the best interest of the student. The MCC school counselor understands the differing cultural views of other school staff members and helps in the consultation process to illuminate these different viewpoints. Other school staff members may be unaware of different cultural norms and standards, whereas some may be very aware of these differences. In consultation, the MCC school counselor is able to both make culturally appropriate recommendations and help school staff members in seeing their own cultural goals and perspectives. In another example of this, a school counselor might observe school administrators trying to motivate students toward a certain behavior by promising a school dance if the students follow certain guidelines. This information may be communicated to faculty, students, and parents. However, the view of which appropriate sexual nuances and behaviors are acceptable at the dance may be very different from culture to culture. Some recent Russian immigrants have relatively liberal views of the sexual practices of young teenagers, but some traditional Asian families may deem any sexual nuances to be inappropriate at this age. The MCC counselor works effectively with administrators, faculty, students, and parents to ensure that schoolwide social events are both rewarding and culturally appropriate for everyone involved.

Program Planning and Management

The traditional school counselor plans and manages programs that meet the developmentally appropriate needs of the student population (Coleman, 1995). The MCC counselor understands the cultural assumptions that can be a part of any program. All goals and values within a program are subject to cultural scrutiny. A program that encourages high school students to attend college may include the cultural assumption that everyone who can attend college should attend college. Although this goal may be rooted in a sincere desire to advocate for and empower students of all cultures, there may be some students who prefer to not go to college. They may have values that keep them close to their friends, families, and partners, such that going away to a college would be considered foolish on their part. A program that pressures them to go away to the "best" college they are able to be admitted to may be doing them a disservice. The MCC counselor is sensitive to these variations. This can mean a modification of a program's goals. It may also mean an increased sensitivity in the implementation of programs, such that a counselor prepares for those students who do

not fit neatly into the goals and values of the program and is careful to ensure that they receive the culturally sensitive support that they need. Consequently, a student who could be admitted to a more prestigious college far away from his or her home might be supported in going to a nearby college that is more consistent with other priorities. In another example, a high school may promote a program whereby students are offered opportunities to participate in interpersonal support groups. These groups may promote interpersonal skills that include eye contact, voicing of one's feelings, and so forth. For certain Native American tribes, cultural norms around eye contact are very different from those of the dominant European American cultural paradigm in the United States. The MCC school counselor understands the importance of knowing both the cultural differences present in the student body and the ultimate goals of the program (in this case, the advancement of self-esteem and not acculturation), such that program tasks can be modified to be culturally appropriate for all students.

Professional Identity

As part of their professional identity, MCC school counselors maintain that they themselves have their own cultural background and identity, that they personally will promote healthy counseling from a multicultural perspective, and that it is the responsibility of the counseling profession as a whole to promote multiculturally sensitive counseling. MCC school counselors recognize the importance of their own cultural identity. They seek to grow in knowledge and understanding of their own background and how that background affects the exercise of their profession. They seek to balance participation of activities specific to their own culture with an openness to, and participation in, activities of other cultures. In addition, MCC counselors personally promote counseling from a multicultural perspective. They seek to develop their counseling skills and abilities, with a constant mind toward the importance of culture. They participate in workshops and trainings that integrate multicultural awareness within counseling. Furthermore, MCC school counselors advocate for counseling professionals to be multiculturally competent. They support their schools and professional groups in sponsoring trainings and professional educational experiences that include sensitivity toward multicultural issues.

BELONGING TO SCHOOL: A KEY OUTCOME OF A CULTURALLY RELEVANT SCHOOL COUNSELING PROGRAM

Key to helping all students acquire the competence they need to succeed in school and in the school-to-work transition is developing programming that is relevant to the needs of students in a pluralistic society. Two of the greatest needs that students have are developing a sense of belonging or connectedness to the school and the socioemotional skills necessary to undertake the challenge of school. In this section, we outline the manner in which programming that addresses the belonging needs of students can be systematically developed and implemented in a manner that is culturally relevant.

Individual Counseling

In the context of individual counseling, it is especially important to understand the unique cultural view of the person being counseled. This unique cultural view finds significant expression in schools through the belongingness needs of individual students. Although belongingness is seen as a universal need (Baumeister & Leary, 1995; Maslow, 1954), the expression of this need may look entirely different in different cultures. For example, in Afghani culture, the father tends to hold most of the power in making decisions for the family. If an Afghani student is trying to make decisions about after-school activities that he or she is interested in but is concerned about his or her father's opinion, it may be vital to secure the approval of the father for successful participation in the activity. In individual counseling, it is especially important to be sensitive to the struggles of the individual, as this will be the root of connection and trust with the student. It will be very important to listen to the nuances of the students' opinions and of what they communicate about the culture in which they are from. To make the individual counseling session successful concerning belongingness, the counselor will need to understand the meaning and importance of belongingness generally, how it is commonly expressed in the student's culture, how the individual student expresses this need, and what the current assets and deficits are that the student is currently experiencing around belongingness. Only then can the counselor guide the student toward a more rewarding sense of belongingness.

Group Counseling

In a group context, MCC school counseling is generally more complicated, but it can also be aided by this group context. The complexity of the group is important when one realizes that there may be a group composed of students from multiple cultural backgrounds. Furthermore, even those from the same cultural group may have differences, such as different levels of acculturation, which lead them to have different views of what it means to belong. In addition, beyond the cultures of the individual group members, there is the culture of the community, the culture of the school, and the culture formed of the group itself. This causes a very complicated system, as there will be multiple cultural views, multiple levels of belongingness, and multiple opinions of what the path to a greater sense of belongingness will be. Given this, it is important in group counseling that the MCC school counselor understand this complexity around belongingness and mediate the potential for multiple solutions to students' issues around belongingness. This complicated system, however, may include some built-in checks and balances that help the counselor increase the belongingness of group members. In having a diverse set of group members, individuals may make an effort to bridge the gaps between one another. This may lead to the expression of belongingness needs in ways that are expressed and explained more clearly than students might not otherwise do if they were in a group with only persons from their own culture. For example, a student from Africa might miss playing a certain after-school game that she used to play in her home country but that is not available in her current school. In a group setting with people from other cultures, she may need to describe the game, why she misses it, and what she feels was valuable about the experience. In this way, the group can both help her to discover other activities that may meet her needs in her new school; also, in her process of describing what she is missing, she may articulate to herself and to others some of what her felt belongingness needs are. Furthermore, as the group itself forms a supportive culture, members may learn the group's ways and norms and be able to accommodate these into their understanding and sense of belongingness. Finally, however, this potential positive of group norms may again become complicated and potentially negative as members may pick up on the expectations of the group and subsume their true concerns to the norms of the group. In this case, it is important for the MCC school counselor to encourage integration over assimilation (Coleman, 1995). This would mean the inclusion of a means by which all members' views of belongingness could be valued and incorporated (integration) rather than merely having all members be expected to buy into one dominant monocultural view (assimilation).

Developmental Guidance

In developmental guidance, a counselor focuses on developmentally appropriate guidance concerns for each student. The MCC school counselor understands how culture adds an important dimension to a student's development. In belongingness, this means that cultural views and culturally appropriate tasks may vary greatly according to the age of the individual. For example, imagine a culture that expects a man to be independent and individualistic and a woman to be community oriented and collaborative. This culture may expect the same behaviors of boys as it does of men and of girls as it does of women, or, alternatively, it may have an entirely different view of what it means for children to belong. Children may be given great latitude in how they relate to others and may not be expected to conform to adult norms until they are older. In this developmental process, the counselor must understand cultural pressures so that he or she can help students understand that what worked for them as children may be what their culture is pressuring them away from as they get older. Students may then need to choose whether to conform to the pressure of their culture of origin or continue on against these cultural pressures. This might be the case for a collaborative young man who is being pushed toward more independence.

In a similar example, an understanding of the developmental dimension of culture is again important. Parents may hold great influence over the lives of students from certain cultures. However, as a student ages into his or her teen years, the parent's role becomes greatly reduced in some cultures, but in others, it remains strong well into a student's 20s. Around belongingness, this may mean that students from certain cultures may be discouraged by their parents from participating in school-sponsored activities independent from the family in their middle school years but may be free to participate in these same activities while in high school. When thinking of the belongingness of a student, the MCC school counselor considers culture, developmental level, and the interaction of the two when trying to understand what a student is experiencing and what interventions may aid the particular student.

Bina et al. (2001) articulated that a key to motivating students to achieve in school is to systematically improve their sense of belongingness or connectedness to school. Using an ecological perspective (Bronfenbrenner, 1979; see also Chapter 3, this volume), they showed how belongingness needs to be addressed across multiple areas of a student's life with a specific focus on community factors, peer factors, and school factors. To stimulate a sense of community-school connection in adolescents, they recommended the use of service learning (Billing, 2000; Melchior, 2000) as a low-cost method for building the connection between home and school that can often be absent in both multi- and monocultural communities. A second vital approach to fostering this connection is through the active process of parent education workshops, which can focus on a wide range of issues that collectively serve to lead teachers and parents into a collaborative relationship around the education of the children within the school (Maeroff, 1998; Scales, Blyth, Berkas, & Kielsmeier, 2000). A third community-school activity that leads to an enhanced sense of belonging is mentoring (Barton-Arwood, Jolivette, & Massey, 2000; Karcher, Davis, & Powell, 2002; Karcher & Lindwall, in press; Miller, 1997; Rockwell, 1997).

Bina et al. (2001) also identified small group work with the school as an effective way to facilitate a sense of belonging in the school for a diverse range of students. Not only is group work an efficient use of counselor time (Zinck & Littrell, 2000) and effective at helping children acquire targeted concepts and skills (Page & Chandler, 1994), it also provides a source for support and connectedness within the school (Campbell & Myrick, 1990). This is particularly true for at-risk students who do not have positive relationships with adults in the building. After participating in groups, students are more likely to use the counselor and other adults as a source of support and are less likely to drop out (Bauer, Sapp, & Johnson, 2000; Schnedeker, 1991). Although group work can focus on many different issues (e.g., academic motivation, resilience, or substance use), multiculturally competent counselors will see that groups can also help them build relationships with a diverse group of students, help those students develop relationships with each other, and enhance the sense among students that they are valued members of the community, regardless of their race, class, or academic status.

The third area that Bina et al. (2001) proposed as a focus to facilitate belongingness in schools is through classroom activities. In addition to standard classroom guidance, they advocated a focus on training teachers to improve their skills at establishing personal connections with each student. Multiple authors (e.g., Alderman, 1999; Goodenow & Grady, 1993; Roeser, Midgley, & Urdan, 1996) have identified that a teacher's ability to create an atmosphere of connectedness within the classroom has a positive effect on students' attitudes toward school and, subsequently, their performance in school. Bina et al. outlined a workshop that trains teachers to establish positive working relationships with students through the use of both listening skills and explicit strategies for promoting belongingness. Although these are central parts of the training of counselors, they are too often absent from teacher education curriculum. Somehow, it is assumed that teachers have these skills naturally or will acquire them on the job. An effective school counselor will develop training modules that seek to explicitly help teachers gain these skills and to help teachers maintain them over time.

CONCLUSION

After more than a century of advocacy for progressive social change that has fostered the labor, civil rights, and feminist movements, we still find ourselves at the crossroads of creating an equitable and just society. Having tried to create this change through macroeconomics, large-scale reform, and even technology, American society is coming to realize that the true source of change will come through substantive educational reform. It is our contention that this reform will not be achieved through high-stakes performance tests, vouchers, or even merit pay to teachers. Nor will it be achieved solely through curricular innovations. It is our central thesis that reform will occur when we pay attention to the social and emotional needs of each child in each classroom as the major building block for personal accomplishment. By taking this responsibility seriously, we will achieve, in the aggregate, true social change.

The skills and roles of the school counselors provide them with the opportunity to be a major agent in this process of change. In this chapter, we have advocated that school counselors need to understand that to be successful in this endeavor, they must use these skills and complete their role in a manner that is relevant to the contextual and cultural needs of their students. At the core of the multiculturally competent school counselor's success is his or her ability to facilitate in each child a sense of belongingness in the school community that will stimulate that child's motivation to set and accomplish prosocial goals such as academic achievement and career attainment.

REFERENCES

Alderman, M. K. (1999). *Motivation and achievement: Possibilities for teaching and learning.* Mahwah, NJ: Lawrence Erlbaum.

Barton-Arwood, A., Jolivette, K., & Massey, N. G. (2000). Mentoring with elementary-age students. *Intervention in School & Clinic, 36,* 36-40.

Bauer, S. R., Sapp, M., & Johnson, D. (2000). Group counseling strategies for rural at-risk high school students. *The High School Journal, 83,* 41-50.

Baumeister, R. F., & Leary, M. R. (1995). The need to belong: Desire for interpersonal attachment as a fundamental human motivation. *Psychological Bulletin, 117,* 497-529.

Bennett, W. J. (1996). *The book of virtues: A treasury of great moral stories.* New York: Touchstone.

Billing, S. H. (2000). Research on K-12 school-based service learning: The evidence builds. *Phi Delta Kappan, 81,* 658-664.

Bina, C., Finn, L., & Sowle, G. (2001). *Methods for increasing student motivation.* Unpublished manuscript, University of Wisconsin–Madison.

Bourdieu, P. (1973). Cultural reproduction and social reproduction. In R. Brown (Ed.), *Knowledge, education, and cultural change* (pp. 71-112). London: Tavistock.

Bourdieu, P. (1986). The forms of capital. In J. Richardson (Ed.), *The handbook of theory and research in the sociology of education* (pp. 241-258). New York: Greenwood.

Bronfenbrenner, U. (1979). *The ecology of human development.* Cambridge, MA: Harvard University Press.

Campbell, C. A., & Dahir, C. A. (1997). *The National Standards for School Counseling Programs.* Alexandra, VA: American School Counseling Association.

Campbell, C. A., & Myrick, R. D. (1990). Motivational group counseling for low-performing students. *Journal for Specialists in Group Work, 15,* 43-50.

Coleman, H. L. K. (1995). Cultural factors and the counseling process: Implications for school counselors. *The School Counselor, 42,* 180-185.

Coleman, H. L. K. (1996, August). *Heuristics for choosing cultural specific treatment.* Paper presented at the meeting of the American Psychological Association, Toronto, Canada.

Coleman, H. L. K., & Tuescher, K. D. (in press). *School-based interventions for psychological disorders.* Alexandria, VA: American School Counseling Association.

Coleman, H. L. K., James, A., Hellman, S., & Tuescher, K. (1995). *Portfolio assessment of school counselor competence.* Unpublished manuscript, University of Wisconsin– Madison.

Constantine, M. G., & Yeh, C. (2001). Multicultural training, self-construals, and multicultural competence of school counselors. *Professional School Counseling, 4,* 202-207.

Garcia Coll, C., Lamberty, G., Jenkins, R., McAdoo, H. P., Crnic, K., Wasik, B. H., et al. (1996). An integrative model for the study of developmental competencies in minority children. *Child Development, 67,* 1891-1914.

Goodenow, C., & Grady, K. E. (1993). The relationship of school belonging and friends' value of academic motivation among urban adolescent students. *Journal of Experimental Education, 62,* 60-71.

Hirsch, E. D. (Ed.). (1994). *What your third grader should know.* New York: Delta.

Holcomb-McCoy, C. (2001). Exploring the self-perceived multicultural counseling competence of elementary school counselors. *Professional-School-Counseling, 4,* 195-201.

Karcher, M. J., Davis, C., & Powell, B. (2002). Developmental mentoring in schools: Testing connectedness as a mediating variable in the promotion of academic achievement. *The School Community Journal, 12,* 36-52.

Karcher, M.J., & Lindwall, J. (in press). Social interest, connectedness, and challenging experiences: What makes high school mentors persist? *Journal of Individual Psychology.*

Maeroff, G. I. (1998). Altered destinies: Making life better for school children in need. *Phi Delta Kappan, 79,* 425-439.

Maslow, A. H. (1954). *Motivation and personality.* New York: Free Press.

Melchior, A. (2000). Service learning at your service. *Education Digest, 66,* 26-32.

Miller, D. (1997). Mentoring structures: Building a protective community. *Preventing School Failure, 41,* 105-110.

Olneck, M. (2000). Can multicultural education change what counts as cultural capital? *American Educational Research Journal, 37,* 317-348.

Page, R. C., & Chandler, J. (1994). Effects of group counseling on ninth grade at-risk students. *Journal of Mental Health Counseling, 16,* 340-351.

Paisley, P. O., & Borders, L. D. (1995). School counseling: An evolving specialty. *Journal of Counseling and Development, 74,* 150-153.

Rockwell, S. (1997). Mentoring through accessible, authentic opportunities. *Preventing School Failure, 41,* 111-115.

Roeser, R. W., Midgley, C., & Urdan, T. C. (1996). Perceptions of the school psychological environment and early adolescents' psychological and behavioral functioning in school: The mediating role of goals and belonging. *Journal of Educational Psychology, 88,* 408-422.

Scales, P. C., Blyth, D. A., Berkas, T. H., & Kielsmeier, J. C. (2000). The effects of service-learning on middle school student's social responsibility and academic success. *Journal of Early Adolescence, 20,* 332-358.

Schnedeker, J. A. (1991). Multistage group guidance and counseling for low achieving students. *The School Counselor, 39,* 47-51.

The Wisconsin developmental guidance model: A resource and planning guide. (1997). Madison: Wisconsin Department of Public Instruction.

Zinck, K., & Littrell, J. M. (2000). Action research shows group counseling effective with at-risk adolescent girls. *Professional School Counseling, 4,* 50-59.

8

Multicultural Supervision

The Influence of Race-Related Issues in Supervision Process and Outcome

ROMANA A. NORTON
HARDIN L. K. COLEMAN
University of Wisconsin–Madison

The development of multicultural competency is now understood as essential to the repertoire of therapeutic competencies that counselors are expected to hone during counselor training (e.g., Ponterotto, Casas, Suzuki, & Alexander, 1995; Pope-Davis & Coleman, 1997). The development of such competencies may be seriously compromised, however, in supervisory relationships that are marked by racial and cultural conflict. The negative influence that conflictual multicultural supervisory relationships might have on the outcome of supervision might negatively affect counselor trainees' expectations of multicultural counseling encounters, affecting their overall professional development. Indeed, the process and outcome of multicultural counseling may be affected by issues arising from both perceived and real differences related to supervisees' and supervisors' race and culture. Given the triadic relationship between the supervisor, supervisee, and client (Brown & Landrum-Brown, 1995), it is conceivable that such issues could bleed into the supervisee-client relationship, having a negative impact on its outcome.

Ironically, although the multicultural counseling literature has expounded on multicultural counseling issues, showing that unresolved issues related to race and culture can influence the counseling process, these issues have only recently been addressed in the supervision literature. Following Leong and Wagner's (1994) critical review of the multicultural supervision literature, the number of conceptual articles and chapters that addressed the various issues and challenges that can arise in multicultural supervision increased significantly. Although this work sheds more light on the process of multicultural supervision, most of the assertions made in the recent multicultural supervision literature have not been empirically investigated. Given the relatively recent emergence of this topic area, the paucity of empirical research is perhaps understandable. Nevertheless, given assertions that race- and culture-related conflicts within the context of multicultural supervision can have pernicious effects on both supervision and counseling outcomes (e.g., Constantine, 1997), it is incumbent on counseling researchers to devote more energy to the empirical investigation of multicultural supervision issues. One of the purposes of this chapter is to review the literature that addresses the impact that race-related issues have on the multicultural supervision process and outcome. The review that we have conducted here is selective rather than exhaustive. Our intention was to illuminate either issues that have been raised repeatedly but have little or no empirical support or issues that seem particularly salient to this topic but to which scant theoretical and research attention has been paid. We chose to focus on race-related issues because the overwhelming majority of the conceptual and empirical research in the multicultural supervision literature focuses on this difference factor.

A second purpose of this chapter is to review two conceptual frameworks that, when combined, help explain *why* race-related conflicts might arise in multicultural supervisory dyads (i.e., Helms's [1990] racial identity interaction model) and *how* such conflicts might have an impact on the supervision process (Bordin's [1983] working alliance model). These two models might serve to guide research inquiry on obstacles to successful multicultural supervision. Recommendations

for future research are discussed in the discussion section of this chapter.

CONCEPTUAL ISSUES

As suggested earlier, the field of multicultural supervision is a relatively new field of interest in counseling psychology, and it is in its infancy in terms of how it conceptualizes and, subsequently, languages itself and its concerns. Whether or not useful knowledge is to come out of this field of study, however, hinges in large part on the extent to which conceptual and terminological consensus exists within the field. Only then can researchers have meaningful discussions and conduct meaningful investigations about the concerns of this field. Although several researchers have discussed some of the conceptual and terminological issues salient to multicultural supervision (e.g., D'Andrea & Daniels, 1997; Leong & Wagner, 1994), and some of what is said here is a reiteration of those discussions, our purpose here is twofold. First, we seek to broaden the discussion about conceptual and terminological issues. Second, we seek to encourage multicultural supervision researchers to come to consensus about the conceptual issues that surround this field of study.

Multicultural Supervision

Counselor researchers continue to use the terms *cross-cultural supervision* and *cross-racial supervision* interchangeably to describe supervisory relationships in which the supervisor and supervisee, and sometimes the supervisee's client, are from different racial (e.g., Black) or ethnic groups (e.g., Latino). Although the debate about how to refer to this field of scholarship appears to be ongoing (Brown & Landrum-Brown, 1995; D'Andrea & Daniels, 1997; Leong & Wagner, 1994), we agree with researchers who advocate for the use of the umbrella term *multicultural supervision*

(D'Andrea & Daniels, 1997; Leong & Wagner, 1994).

D'Andrea and Daniels (1997) advocated for the use of this term to describe "situations in which supervisors and supervisees are involved in examining a variety of cultural/ethnic/racial issues pertinent to effective counseling with clients from diverse backgrounds" (p. 294). In other words, the umbrella term *multicultural supervision* captures the myriad challenges with which supervisory dyads must contend, including perceived racial, ethnic, and cultural differences between supervisors, supervisees, and clients.

Although it is true that counselors who pursue this field of interest are primarily focused on the effect that a specific difference factor (e.g., race) has on the supervisory process (Brown & Landrum-Brown, 1995), there are at least two reasons why these supervisory dyads cannot be simply characterized and subsequently understood as, say, *cross-racial*. First, counselor researchers are reminded that supervision—indeed, any interpersonal interaction—is always already *multi*cultural (Pedersen, 1991). The generic term *multicultural supervision* serves to remind us of two things:

1. Rarely, if ever, is a single difference factor (e.g., race) between the supervisor and supervisee responsible for challenges in supervisory relationships; rather, intersections between such factors, including gender, sexual orientation, and class, are usually at work.
2. Given that a triadic relationship exists between supervisor, supervisee, and client, the supervisory relationship may also be affected by the client's unique cultural configuration.

Although our ability to identify and understand intersections of difference factors and their impact on supervisory relationships is currently constrained by methodological and statistical limitations, counselor researchers should, at the very least, acknowledge the complexity of multicultural supervision.

Second, terms such as *cross-racial* seem to imply that there is some inevitable, fundamental difference between people who have been assigned to different racial categories. As we will see later in this chapter, people who have been assigned to different racial categories may not differ with regard to their attitudes and feelings about race and other perceived difference factors.

Researchers should qualify the specific focus of their work in this field of study as we have done. That said, the present chapter examines research literature that focuses on the influence that race-related issues have on the multicultural supervision process.

Race and Ethnicity

There has been much discussion and controversy over the past decade about the meaning of the constructs *race* and *ethnicity* (Betancourt & Lopez, 1993; Beutler, Brown, Crothers, Booker, & Seabrook, 1996; Helms, 1994a, 1994b; Helms & Richardson, 1997; Spickard & Burroughs, 2000; Yee, Fairfield, Weizman, & Wyatt, 1993; Zuckerman, 1990). Although a proper understanding of the conceptual confusion surrounding these constructs requires an understanding of the historical and sociopolitical forces that have shaped popular understandings about these variables, this discussion is beyond the scope of this chapter. Nevertheless, a few words will be devoted to the conceptual and methodological aspects of this issue given its salience to the topic of multicultural supervision.

Although social scientists generally agree that *race* is a sociopolitically motivated construction, it continues to be popularly understood as a biological entity that determines innate dispositions, including "race-specific" aptitudes, preferences, attitudes, and behaviors.

For social scientists, the social construction of race is evidenced in the use of nominal conceptualizations of race as a proxy variable for ethnic group allegiances and cultural commitments (e.g., ethnicity or ethnic identity). If you have identified the racial category to which an individual has been assigned, you have identified that person's ethnocultural characteristics. In other words, nominal conceptualizations of racial and ethnic differences that depend on race and ethnicity as demographic variables encourage researchers to conflate race with ethnicity and ethnicity with race (Helms, 1996). Moreover, such conceptualizations reify between-group differences and tend to ignore within-group differences. Acknowledging this issue, several researchers have challenged researchers to tap the psychological and social correlates underlying these constructs (Fouad & Brown, 2001; Helms, 1994a).

Although race, as popularly understood, is a fiction, it nevertheless continues to carry social and political significance (Pierce, 2000). We share the view that race is a sociopolitical construction that, nonetheless, has social and psychological implications for individuals (Helms, 1996). Individuals' attitudes about their own and others' ascribed race (i.e., racial identity or racial consciousness) can influence their interpersonal interactions as well as their feelings about themselves. This understanding of race suggests that individuals' perceptions of the meaning and salience of race can vary among and between individuals assigned to specific racial categories. Note also that this conceptualization of race does not necessarily imply cultural affiliation or commitments (i.e., ethnicity or ethnic identity).

RACE-RELATED ISSUES WITHIN THE MULTICULTURAL SUPERVISION

A number of clinicians and counselor researchers have speculated about specific issues that can arise in multicultural supervision (e.g., Bradshaw, 1982; D'Andrea & Daniels, 1997; Fong & Lease, 1997; Morgan, 1984; Peterson, 1991; Priest, 1994; Vargas, 1989). Although there is some evidence for a few of the assertions that these researchers have made, most have not been investigated. We have divided the literature into three broad but somewhat artificial categories. Researchers are reminded that all of these categories and subcategories intersect with one another as well as other difference factors, such as class or gender.

Much of the multicultural supervision literature focuses on Black and White supervisory dyads, with primary emphasis placed on White supervisor/Black supervisee configurations. Given that the racial and ethnic composition of supervisory dyads is becoming increasingly diverse (D'Andrea & Daniels, 1997), it is not clear if the assertions made about Black-White supervisory dyads generalize to supervisory dyads composed of different racial configurations. The emphasis placed on White supervisors, however, may not be misplaced. Although the number of supervisors of color is increasing, recent polls suggest that supervision provided by White counselors continues to be the norm (Duan, Roehlke, & Matchisky, 1998; Fong & Lease, 1997). Nevertheless, given that theory and research that address issues specific to supervisors of color are meager at best, we have included what little information exists on this topic area as a separate category.

Three broad categories of issues related to multicultural supervision have been consistently identified in the clinical and research literature: (a) institutional issues, (b) issues related to minority supervisors, and (c) issues related to supervisor multicultural competencies.

Institutional Issues

Although at first glance, an institution's policies regarding multiculturalism may not appear to be related to the multicultural supervision process, researchers have cogently argued that an institution's expressed and demonstrated commitments to multiculturalism can have a significant impact on multicultural supervisory dyads (Peterson, 1991; Priest, 1994).

Peterson (1991) speculated at length about the systemic link between the supervisor and the institution. Institutional environments that do not promote and value cultural diversity may have both direct and indirect effects on the supervision process. Supervisees of color may be suspicious of training sites that purport to value diversity (i.e., in mission statements and orientation speeches) but do not have a culturally diverse administrative and professional staff that reflects such an appreciation. The sincerity of supervisors' efforts to be sensitive to cultural and racial issues may be questioned when the institutional environment in which supervisees must train is not reflective of supervisors' espoused values.

Institutions that lack diversity policies that transcend affirmative action policies may also unwittingly promote race-related conflicts. For instance, training sites that do not have formal procedures in place for resolving race-related conflicts that might erupt between supervisees and their supervisors place trainees of color in a particularly difficult position. Given the social and evaluative power of supervisors (Bernard & Goodyear, 1998; Holloway, 1995), these supervisees might be understandably reluctant to work through such difficulties with supervisors, much less "go over their head" to have the conflict addressed by the supervisors' superiors.

Training sites should also have mechanisms in place for dealing with race-related issues that can arise between trainees. McNeil, Hom, and Perez (1995) provided examples of the different sorts of race-related conflicts that can occur between White supervisees and supervisees of color. They cited examples in which White supervisees directly challenged the qualifications of supervisees of color, suggesting

that their placements were earned through affirmative action policies. They noted that such interactions put in place a "we versus them" atmosphere within the institution. These attitudes may spill over into supervision, particularly when supervisors are not actively involved in challenging racist stereotypes and misinformation. Supervisors not only convey knowledge to supervisees but also serve as role models for supervisees' professional identification (Bradshaw, 1982). As such, one of the supervisor's tasks is to promote diversity at the institutional level so that discussions about multicultural competency are systematically reinforced (Peterson, 1991; Priest, 1994). In doing so, supervisors assume the role of "change agent" for counselor-trainees as well as the system (Peterson, 1991).

Only one study could be found that addressed the institutional experiences of counselor supervisees. Fukuyama (1994) conducted a study of critical incidents with interns of color who had completed a doctoral internship year. When asked to describe positive and negative organizational factors that influenced their professional development, interns cited the following positive factors: (a) "support to be myself," (b) "having people from different cultures working together provided the support I needed," and (c) "having another intern from the same ethnic background who could validate the respondent's concerns." Negative factors included (a) "social isolation felt by new intern" and (b) "need for mentoring." Study respondents offered the following institutional recommendations:

1. "use all of the available personnel resources in the agency for multicultural training, including culturally diverse practicum students and support staff";
2. "provide more multicultural supervisors";
3. "discuss cross-cultural issues in an intern seminar under the training director's guidance"; and

4. "provide more training for supervisors in working with multicultural issues," including "[training] supervisors to respect and accept cultural differences."

Fukuyama's (1994) findings clearly suggest that supervisees of color feel that the knowledge, commitment, and appreciation for diversity demonstrated within their training institutions have an impact on their supervision and training experiences. It is unclear, however, what kind of impact multicultural competency has on the supervisory process. Clearly, more studies need to be conducted on the role that institutional environments play in the multicultural supervision process and outcome issues.

Issues Related to Supervisors of Color

Researchers have warned that supervisors of color may be the targets of supervisee misconceptions and prejudices (Bradshaw, 1982; Priest, 1994). Acting on racial stereotypes and prejudice, supervisees may judge minority supervisors as less competent than White supervisors and resist their authority. One study offers some support for this conjecture.

McRoy, Freeman, Logan, and Blackmon (1986) examined the working relationships of social work field instructors and supervisees involved in multicultural supervisory dyads. Several Black and Hispanic supervisors reported instances when supervisees questioned their competence and authority.

Although the investigators of this study did not explore how supervisors of color responded to such challenges, several researchers have speculated about this.

Priest (1994) suggested that supervisors of color may feel compelled to "prove themselves" when they perceive that their authority and competence are being challenged by supervisees. If this is true, how do such attempts manifest in multicultural supervision? What

kind of impact do such perceptions have on the supervisory relationship? Bradshaw (1982) speculated that supervisors of color who come to multicultural supervision with negative expectations might misinterpret supervisees' behaviors. Supervisee anxiety, for instance, might be wrongly attributed to discomfort with cross-racial supervision instead of supervisee experience level. Relatedly, the findings of the McRoy et al. (1986) study suggest that individuals' expectations of multicultural supervision and what actually transpires within multicultural supervision may be discrepant. Specifically, although supervisors reported that they expected more problems with multicultural supervision than advantages, the majority of these supervisors (72%) reported that they had not experienced any problems during multicultural supervision. Later in this chapter, we show that a similar discrepancy was found for supervisees involved in multicultural supervision. Researchers should take note of the importance of making distinctions between individuals' expectations of multicultural supervision and what actually transpires in multicultural supervision, as McRoy et al. did. The discrepancy found between expectancies and outcomes raises interesting questions that may have implications for future research. For instance, do negative expectations of multicultural supervision affect the supervision outcome? If so, how? What accounts for these discrepancies?

One plausible explanation for the discrepancy found between supervisors' expectations and those supervisors' actual experiences within supervision is that many acts of racism are covert and "unintentional" and, therefore, difficult to pinpoint. Although purely speculative, it may be that some supervisors who reported negative expectations of multicultural supervision but reported no actual problems within the context of such supervision chose not to report subtle or unintended acts of racism because such acts could not be supported with "hard" evidence. Some researchers, for instance, have suggested that supervisees of color may be reluctant to raise issues of racism in supervision for fear of being labeled "paranoid" (e.g., Fong & Lease, 1997). Despite the position of power held by supervisors of color within the supervisory dyad, their minority status in the predominantly White institutions in which they work may make them reluctant to confront White supervisees about racist attitudes for fear of being marked as "troublemakers" (Peterson, 1991). Speculations such as this point to the need for alternative methods of evaluating multicultural supervision process issues (e.g., phenomenological or social critical) than have been used historically. We will briefly discuss the question of supervision process methodology at the end of this chapter.

Another issue pertaining to supervisors of color and multicultural supervision issues is whether supervisors of color serve as models of cultural diversity. Some researchers have asserted that White supervisees' counselor training might be augmented when they are supervised by Black supervisors (Bradshaw, 1982; Vargas, 1989). Following this logic, cross-racial supervisory dyads provide White supervisees with the opportunity to work with supervisors whose knowledge and social position resist racial stereotypes (Bradshaw, 1982). This assertion implies that direct exposure to racially and culturally different supervisors serves to counteract supervisees' latent racial stereotypes and biases. Bradshaw (1982) proposed that Black supervisors might "enhance the white resident's concrete knowledge and capacity to be empathetic to blacks and other minorities who seem alien to them" (p. 211). It has also been asserted that supervisors of color might also serve as support agents or mentors to supervisees (Bradshaw, 1982; Fukuyama, 1994). Following this logic, same-race supervisors might be particularly helpful to minority supervisees who have had either little exposure to predominately White institutions or negative experiences in these institutions.

Although these assertions may have some merit—indeed, supervisees of color have indicated that they would like to have more supervisors of color available to them (e.g., Fukuyama, 1994)—we take issue with the essentialist assumptions underlying it. Specifically, the assertion that supervisors of color can serve as role models of diversity is predicated on the assumption that as racial beings (as opposed to nonracial beings, i.e., White), supervisors of color are necessarily more multiculturally competent than White supervisors. This may not be the case. As we will discuss later, supervisors' (White or "non-White") degree of racial consciousness may be a function of their racial identity status rather than a function of the racial category to which they have been assigned.

Unfortunately, research on minority supervisors' supervision experiences is virtually nonexistent. We could not locate a single study in the counseling literature that explored this experience. One can only speculate as to why this is the case. As briefly discussed earlier, although supervisors of color are growing in number, White supervisors continue to be the norm. The experiences of supervisors of color may be overlooked simply because the trend historically has been to focus on White supervisors' role in the multicultural supervisory dyad. Nevertheless, the mere fact that supervisors of color are growing in number should suggest to researchers that this growth might be accompanied by unique issues that were previously overlooked or absent before. Researchers are encouraged to investigate the issues that may be unique to this neglected population.

Issues Related to Supervisor Multicultural Competencies

Most of the theoretical and research literature on multicultural supervision addresses issues related to supervisors' multicultural competence. Supervisors' lack of multicultural knowledge and awareness seems to be of particular concern to researchers because of the direct impact that an absence of these competencies can have on the quality of multicultural supervision. Numerous researchers have asserted that many supervisors may not have the same level of multicultural competency that their supervisees have (Brown & Landrum-Brown, 1995; D'Andrea & Daniels, 1997; Fukuyama, 1994; Midgette & Meggert, 1991; Priest, 1994). This discrepancy has been attributed to the relatively recent emergence of the field of multiculturalism and the even more recent emergence of the field of multicultural supervision (D'Andrea & Daniels, 1997). The discrepancy between supervisors' and supervisees' levels of multicultural competence is thought to be particularly problematic because of the hierarchical structure of the supervisory relationship (Holloway, 1995).

Supervisors' expert and evaluative roles afford them greater power in the supervisory relationship (Bernard & Goodyear, 1998; Holloway, 1995). The resulting power differential between supervisors and supervisees may make supervisees reluctant to raise issues related to race and culture in the context of multicultural supervision—issues that they may believe the supervisor is well aware. Supervisors, however, may not be aware of the salience of these issues; worse still, they may be aware of these issues but minimize or ignore these issues because of a lack of multicultural knowledge. Ignoring the hierarchical nature of supervision and failing to address racial and cultural issues may have deleterious effects on both the outcome and process of supervision. Specifically, supervisees' professional and personal development might be attenuated because an important aspect of their professional training has been neglected. Furthermore, supervisees of color, acutely aware of the salience of multicultural issues,

may be wary of supervisors who fail to address such issues. These supervisees may question both the expert credibility and intentions of these supervisors. Reluctant to raise these issues because of their vulnerable position, these supervisees might psychologically withdraw from the supervision process.

The majority of the work in this area assumes that multicultural supervisory dyads are primarily constituted of White supervisors and supervisees of color. Researchers have subsequently focused on how White supervisors' lack of multicultural competency influences the quality of cross-cultural supervisory relationships. The emphasis on White supervisors' multicultural knowledge is justified for two reasons. First, power differences between supervisors and supervisees may be particularly salient in White supervisor–supervisee of color supervisory dyads (Brown & Landrum-Brown, 1995). The history of ethnic and racial relations in the United States has been and remains a history of power differentials; as such, supervisees of color may be particularly sensitive to the power imbalances inherent to supervision. Second, the emphasis on White supervisor cultural competence is reflective of historical reality—most clinical supervisors are White (Constantine, 1997; Duan & Roehlke, 2001). As discussed in the previous section, however, we take issue with the virtual nonexistence of theory and research on minority supervisors' multicultural competence. As we will later see, Helms's (1990, 1995) model of racial identity development suggests that supervisors of color may not be exempt from issues that arise from insufficient multicultural competency.

Supervisees of color may be particularly sensitive to supervisors' failures to acknowledge and raise multicultural issues. Supervisors who ignore power differentials in supervision and lack cultural knowledge and awareness risk placing their supervisees in a double bind. If they ignore their supervisors' lack of cultural knowledge and awareness, they risk compromising their personal and professional development. If they address their supervisors' limitations, they potentially face interpersonal and professional repercussions. In this latter scenario, the supervisee is discouraged from freely participating in supervision, and the supervisory working relationship will be severely compromised. In effect, the supervisors' lack of sensitivity to power differentials and lack of multicultural competency function to silence and, quite possibly, demoralize supervisees of color.

Given the power differentials and salience of issues related to race and culture for supervisees of color, researchers (Fong & Lease, 1994; Fukuyama, 1994; Helms & Cook, 1999; Morgan, 1984; Priest, 1994) have repeatedly asserted that it is incumbent on supervisors to (a) be aware of the limits of their multicultural competency and (b) initiate discussions about racial and cultural issues. The anecdotal and research literature suggests, however, that some supervisors continue to avoid or ignore discussions about race and culture.

Avoidance of Racial and Cultural Issues

Bradshaw (1982) suggested that the minimization or avoidance of racial and cultural issues might be one of the most pernicious problems in multicultural supervisory dyads. Almost two decades later, counseling researchers continue to reiterate these concerns (Brown & Landrum-Brown, 1995; Cook, 1994; Fong & Lease, 1997; Helms & Cook, 1999). Researchers have suggested that supervisors' lack of attention to or avoidance of cultural issues may lead to a variety of problems in multicultural supervision, including decreased supervisee disclosure and increased mistrust (Fong & Lease, 1997). Supervisors who ignore or minimize these issues may unwittingly reinscribe systems of racial and ethnic oppression.

Speaking specifically about supervisory dyads composed of White supervisors and supervisees of color, Fong and Lease (1997) proposed that "issues of trust and vulnerability interact with issues of power and racial oppression in the cross-cultural supervisory relationship" (p. 393). They asserted that White supervisors who ignore supervisory power dynamics and their potential interaction with racial and cultural factors might engender mistrust in supervisees of color. Indeed, mistrust of White Americans is rooted in hundreds of years of racial and ethnic oppression. Chronically aware of this history, some supervisees of color may question the goodwill and expertise of supervisors who minimize or avoid racial and cultural issues.

Constantine (1997) solicited interns' and supervisors' perceptions about the extent to which multicultural issues were discussed and addressed in their supervision relationships. Several interns indicated that they felt that their supervisors seemed reluctant to bring up multicultural issues. More disturbingly, however, several supervisors indicated that they did not feel that multicultural issues were important or necessary to counselor supervision. In addition, a few other supervisors indicated that they had never given thought to multicultural issues. Although these supervisors' attitudes did not appear to be shared by the majority of supervisors who participated in the study, the mere existence of these attitudes is cause for concern. One wonders what kind of impact such attitudes had on the supervision process.

The findings of a recent descriptive study conducted by Duan and Roehlke (2001) raise additional questions about the extent to which issues related to race and culture are addressed in supervision. The researchers solicited interns' and supervisors' perceptions about whether supervisors addressed cultural issues within the context of multicultural supervision. Significant differences between supervisors' and supervisees' perceptions were reported. Specifically, although more than 93% of supervisors reported that they had addressed cultural issues that arose within the supervisory relationship, only 50% of supervisees reported receiving such acknowledgment (Duan & Roehlke, 2001). Moreover, supervisors were significantly more likely than supervisees to report that they had (a) asked their supervisees for help and made efforts to understand their supervisees' culture, (b) initiated discussions about the cultural differences between them, and (c) acknowledged the power differential between them (Duan & Roehlke, 2001).

The researchers also found that supervisees' satisfaction with multicultural supervision was related to how comfortable they were with self-disclosure and whether they felt that their supervisors held positive attitudes about them. Although the methodological design employed by the researchers precludes any conclusions about how these factors might be related to the supervisors' level of multicultural competence, critical incidents elicited from supervisees suggest that there may be a direct relationship between the two. A significant number of supervisees indicated that the supervisors' cultural knowledge and sensitivity were seen as having a positive impact on the supervisory relationship. A few supervisees, however, indicated that a lack of sensitivity to cultural issues, coupled with a lack of acknowledgment of racial and cultural differences, had a negative impact on their thinking, learning, and development.

Researchers are encouraged to investigate the origins of the differences between supervisor and supervisee perceptions regarding supervisors' efforts to address cultural differences. Moreover, the impact that these differing perceptions have on the multicultural supervision process also requires further investigation.

Two studies shed additional light on how supervisors' failure or reluctance to address racial issues affects supervisees. Kleintjes and Swartz (1996) conducted interviews with a group of Black clinical psychology trainees from a predominantly White university in South Africa. Many of these trainees' supervisors failed to address issues related to race in supervision. The trainees gave reasons for why they, in turn, failed to raise these issues with their supervisors. The following explanations were provided by supervisees: (a) They experienced the university as a "colorless zone" where anti-apartheid sentiments encouraged faculty to acknowledge race, (b) they feared being seen as using their Blackness as an excuse for poor performance, (c) they feared being seen as using their Blackness as a defense against other issues, (d) they feared being seen as pathologically preoccupied with the issue of color and discrimination, (e) they were uncertain whether these issues were best shared or dealt with personally, and (f) they acknowledged their own personal insecurities as the reason for not bringing up the issue of race (cf. Bernard & Goodyear, 1998, p. 41). These responses reflect the lack of power felt by the supervisees interviewed. The trainees clearly felt that they could not address issues of race in the supervisory and institutional contexts in which they operated, even though issues of race were painfully salient for these trainees. This study shows how the failure to effectively address issues of race at the institutional and relational levels can serve to impede professional development (see Chapter 11, this volume).

The McRoy et al. (1986) study discussed earlier also examined whether supervisees experienced problems in multicultural supervision. Supervisees, like their supervisors, expected more problems than benefits in their multicultural supervisory relationships. Moreover, the number of supervisees who reported having actually experienced problems in multicultural supervision was low. Most supervisees who did experience problems, however, chose not to address these problems with their supervisors. Those who did address these problems, however, reported that they were satisfied with the outcome. These findings strongly indicate the need for supervisors to initiate discussions about race and culture in supervision. The salience of race and culture to both supervisors and supervisees, manifest in their negative expectations of multicultural supervision, should compel supervisors to adopt a preventative rather than a remedial approach to multicultural supervisory issues. Given the potential salience of race- and culture-related issues in supervision, it is a sign of incompetence if a supervisor continues to ignore or avoids addressing such issues in supervision.

Proctor and Davis (1989) proposed that White helping professionals may deny awareness of or feign blindness to issues of race and culture by simplistically insisting that they are able to treat the minority client like "any other client." This practice has been coined the "illusion of color-blindness" (cf. Proctor & Davis, 1989). Although the "color-blind" practitioner may actually be well intentioned, his or her reasoning conveys a gross lack of cultural knowledge and awareness. Specifically, "any other client" implies "any other White client," betraying the fact that the helping professional is using White cultural values and norms as the standard of comparison for everyone else (Proctor & Davis, 1989). Cultural critics (e.g., Bell, 1992; Hacker, 1992) have recently described the post-1980s climate as "race neutralizing" (cf. Thompson & Jenal, 1994). These writers argue that "a confluence of forces has created an atmosphere in which many Americans experience discomfort with the continued reality of racial inequality and yet succumb to denying, avoiding, and minimizing this reality" (Thompson & Jenal, 1994, p. 484). This trend is a vicious circle, and supervisors who avoid race- and culture-related issues may be construed by supervisees as advocates of this race-neutralizing trend.

Indirect evidence suggests that some supervisors may evoke color-blind strategies when confronted with supervisees of color. Learning to address issues of race in both counseling and supervision should become a major responsibility of clinical training programs (see Chapter 11, this volume, for an in-depth discussion of these training issues).

Summary of Theoretical and Research Literature

As is apparent from the literature we have reviewed, research on multicultural supervision has focused on how race has or has not been addressed within supervision, particularly between White supervisors and supervisees of color. This research has helped us to see that there are potential problems in multicultural supervision, but it has not led us to understand how these problems arise or provided us with a conceptual framework to guide our problem solving. In the next section of this chapter, we propose that integrating our understanding of racial identity development in the supervision (see Chapter 11, this volume; Cook, 1994; Helms, 1990) and working alliance (Bordin, 1983; Holloway, 1995) provides an excellent conceptual framework to guide future research on multicultural supervision.

CONCEPTUAL FRAMEWORKS

Racial Identity Theory

Much of the current dialogue about racial and cultural issues in supervision reduces these complex constructs to nominal demographic variables (Helms, 1994a; Helms & Cook, 1999). Such conceptualizations do not accurately indicate how a person's racial or ethnic status informs his or her attitudes about interactions with others. Indeed, nominal conceptualizations of race and ethnicity imply that, in "cross-racial" multicultural supervisory dyads, there is an inherent and/or essential conflict between persons who are racially or ethnically different. Such an implication is misleading as it ignores the fact that persons inhabit racial and ethnic identities in many different and even contradictory ways. The foundation of a person's racial or ethic identity is not something inherent—it is historical. It not only varies widely but is also constantly under revision (see Chapter 3, this volume). To suggest that the composition of a supervisory dyad is impeding the supervision process, then, is not to suggest that there is an inherent inclination toward conflict between individuals—it is to suggest that if specific histories are in place, they *might* affect the supervision process in conflictual ways. There are certainly cases in which a dyad's racially and/or ethnically differing histories do not create conflict, and cases such as these remind us that race and ethnicity are not the only factors—perhaps not even the most important factors that need to be considered.

Helms (1990) contended that attitudinal similarities between supervisory members determine their attraction for one another. Although group members may differ in terms of their racial or ethnic group membership, they may not differ with regard to their racial attitudes. Recent conceptual work (Cook, 1994) and empirical work (Ladany, Brittan-Powell, & Pannu, 1997) have addressed this problem by defining race in terms of Helms's racial identity construct.

According to Helms (1990, 1995), racial identity is a multidimensional psychological construct comprising a number of ego statuses that pertain to the feelings, thoughts, and behaviors that an individual has in relation to his or her own race and to people assigned to different racial categories. For both Whites and people of color, racial attitudes are thought to range between obliviousness to the salience of race (and of racism) to awareness of racism and an appreciation for diversity.

Helms (1990) proposed a racial identity interaction model that speculated about the quality of relationships between clients and counselors at different stages of racial identity development. Helms suggested that the interpersonal interactions that take place between people at different stages of racial identity development, despite shared racial status, might be conflictual. She proposed that specific types of interpersonal interactions or relationship types resulted from specific racial identity attitude pairings. Moreover, she proposed that relationship type would be more predictive of interpersonal process and outcome than either level of racial identity development or racial status alone.

Cook (1994) extended Helms's (1990) racial identity interaction model to help explain the ways in which racial attitudes might affect the supervision process and outcome. She suggested that the racial identity attitudes of supervisors and supervisees affect how they interact with one another, whether or not they address racial issues, and how they conceptualize and relate to their clients (Cook, 1994). According to Cook's adaptation, supervisory relationships can be characterized as "parallel" when supervisors and supervisees from either the same or different racial or ethnic groups demonstrate similar attitudes about Whites and people of color. Although parallel supervisory dyads are the least contentious of the dyadic interaction types proposed by Helms, they may also be associated with the least growth. Cook proposed that certain parallel pairs could also have negative implications for supervisory relationships. For instance, White supervisors at the Contact level of racial identity development, paired with a supervisee of color at the Conformity level, may both ignore the race of their clients (i.e., exhibit color blindness) and subscribe to universalistic problem and treatment approaches. Overreliance on a universalistic approach might lead to erroneous conceptualizations of a client's presenting problems and inappropriate treatment strategies (Pedersen, 1996). Moreover, supervisees' personal and professional development may stagnate in terms of their multicultural counseling competency.

Supervisory pairs are considered "crossed" when supervisors and supervisees from either the same or different racial or ethnic group(s) have different and/or conflicting attitudes about Whites and people of color (Cook, 1994). Generally speaking, the extent to which these supervisory dyad members' racial attitudes differ determines the degree to which the dyads will experience conflict over race-related issues. There are two categories of crossed pairs—"progressive" and "regressive." A crossed pair is considered "progressive" when the racial identity attitudes of the person with the most power (i.e., the supervisor) are more developed than those of the person with the least power (i.e., the supervisee). "Regressive" pairs occur when the racial identity attitudes of the supervisor are less developed than those of the supervisee. The implications for both types of crossed pairs seem fairly obvious. In progressive crossed pairs, supervisors are in the position to help supervisees develop more sophisticated racial attitudes. Some resistance might be expected on the part of supervisees who find themselves in progressive supervisory relationships, particularly if the supervisors' and the supervisees' racial attitudes are more than one stage apart (Cook, 1994). Nevertheless, if the supervisor has established a good working alliance with the supervisee, progressive relationship types would be expected to promote counselor personal and professional development.

In regressive crossed supervisory pairs, however, supervisors may actually thwart their supervisees' efforts to address racial and cultural issues in supervision. The further apart the supervisors' and supervisees' racial attitudes, the more conflictual the supervision relationship. Supervisors with relatively unsophisticated racial identity attitudes may refuse to acknowledge the importance or even the existence of racial issues. This relationship type might be expected to compromise the quality of the supervisory relationship, resulting, perhaps, in a number of negative outcomes. Supervisees who challenge supervisors to address issues related to race and culture might be perceived as hostile and receive poor evaluations. Alternatively, supervisees might resist bringing culturally relevant counseling issues to the supervisory session, attenuating their professional development and quite possibly leading to less than optimal counseling outcomes.

There are at least two advantages to Cook's (1994) adaptation of Helms's work. First, Cook's work is theory driven. Grounded in Helms's (1990) racial identity interaction model, her account of multicultural supervision helps explain why race-related issues can affect the process and outcome of counselor supervision. Second, it offers a way to examine individual differences in racial identity attitudes, avoiding the conceptual pitfalls inherent in defining race as a nominal demographic variable. At least one study has garnered support for Cook's extension of Helms's racial identity interaction model.

Ladany et al. (1997) conducted a study that examined the influence of supervisor-supervisee racial identity interactions on the supervisory working alliance and supervisee multicultural competence. The results revealed that supervisory alliances were weakest when supervisees held more sophisticated racial identity attitudes than their supervisors. Perhaps not surprisingly, supervisees who engaged with supervisors who shared more developed racial attitudes reported the strongest supervisory alliances. The authors also found that supervisors who had racial attitudes as developed or more developed than their supervisees were more capable of promoting supervisee multicultural competence than supervisors whose racial attitudes were less sophisticated. Taken together, these findings suggest two things. First, it seems that supervisors who are more aware of issues of race and racism can influence their supervisees' awareness and knowledge of issues related to race and culture. This finding also suggests that multicultural supervisory relationships can specifically influence how counselors-in-training perform in multicultural counseling as well. Second, the results suggest that supervisor and supervisee racial attitudes can create specific interpersonal dynamics that can affect the quality of the supervisory relationship.

Although Cook's (1994) extension of Helms's (1990) racial identity interaction theory helps explain why different racial attitudes can influence supervisory relationships, it falls short of providing an explanation for how these attitudes affect the process of supervision. A theoretical framework that explains both why and how racial attitudes influence supervisory relationships might provide the means for practicing racially and ethnically sensitive supervision. The working alliance model of supervision (Bordin, 1983) may provide the other half of such a framework. Specifically, the working alliance model articulates *how* racial identity attitudes can affect the supervision process.

The Supervisory Relationship: The Working Alliance

The findings of the Ladany et al. (1997) study suggest that the success of supervision (e.g., supervisee professional growth) may be contingent on the quality of one aspect of the supervisory relationship—the working alliance. The working alliance has been broadly conceptualized as a change mechanism in both therapy and supervision (Bordin, 1983; Frank & Frank, 1991; Torrey, 1972). Bordin (1983) suggested that supervisee

change or development is a function of two factors: "the strength of the alliance between the person seeking change and the change agent, and the power of the tasks that are incorporated in the alliance" (p. 35). He defined the supervisory working alliance as a collaboration for change that involves three aspects: "(1) mutual agreements and understandings regarding the goals sought in the change process; (2) the tasks of each of the partners; (3) the bonds between the partners necessary to sustain the enterprise" (p. 35). Strong working alliances are forged in part through the mutual establishment of clear and explicit supervisory goals. Strong working alliances are also determined by the mutual establishment of tasks or activities that enable the demonstration and accomplishment of the goals of supervision. Supervisory bonds are forged from the experience of association and shared activity (Bordin, 1994). Strong supervisory alliances should promote supervisee professional and personal development. As we will discuss below, the working alliance facilitates or constrains the (a) acquisition of goals, (b) accomplishment of tasks, and (c) development of bonds in supervision. To use a mechanistic metaphor, the working alliance is the oil in the engine of supervision.

Research (Burkard, Ponterotto, Reynolds, & Alfonso, 1999) has demonstrated a significant relationship between a counselor's racial identity and his or her ability to effectively address issues of race within a counseling relationship. It is our contention that there is a powerful interaction between a supervisor's ability to address issues of race within multicultural supervision and that supervisor's ability to develop an effective working alliance. We also hypothesize that the racial identity of the supervisor and the supervisee will affect both the handling of racial issues in supervision and the working alliance. At this time, there is insufficient research to predict the direction of these relationships. In the following discussion on the goals, tasks, and bonds in supervision, we suggest ways in which racial issues can be handled within successful multicultural supervision. Verification of these suggestions will be an important focus of future research.

The Goals of Supervision

Supervisors are responsible for inducting supervisees into the culture of supervision. This induction process involves educating supervisees about the purposes and goals of supervision. Supervisees who are not provided with a clear explanation of supervision and the various expectations that are associated with it may have difficulty integrating their supervision experiences. Supervisors often assume that supervisees "know" what supervision is. This might be untrue not only for novice supervisees but for seasoned supervisees as well. This is because supervisory experiences differ across supervisors and contexts. Educating supervisees about what to expect from supervision entails discussion about the goals of supervision. This becomes especially important in relationships that may contain ambiguities, as is possible in multicultural supervision.

The goals of supervision broadly include personal goals (e.g., increasing awareness about personal attitudes and values), skill-related goals (e.g., mastery of counseling skills and techniques), and knowledge-related goals (e.g., increasing knowledge about various populations and theories) (Bernard & Goodyear, 1998). Supervisees are not simply passive recipients of supervision; they often have their own expectations and goals for supervision. Supervisors who fail to consider their supervisees' expectations for supervision presuppose that their expectations for supervision are congruent with their supervisees when this may not be the case. Supervisees come to supervision with different histories and experiences in place. Bordin (1983) suggested that strong supervisory alliances are forged when supervisory dyads discuss one another's expectations for supervision. This collaborative process may help supervisors and supervisees reach agreements about the goals of supervision. A hallmark of successful multicultural supervision may include explicit discussions of how the goals of the supervisor and supervisee are culturally derived.

Supervisors and supervisees with dissimilar and/or conflicting racial identity attitudes might have incongruent expectations of supervision. Theoretically, this situation would occur in regressive supervisory dyads (e.g., a Contact-Internalization combination). Supervisors who express Contact stage racial attitudes may ignore or minimize racial and cultural issues, compelling supervisees with Internalization stage racial attitudes to suppress such concerns. Supervisees who suspect that such supervisors are not sensitive to racial and/or cultural issues are likely to suppress their race- and culture-related supervision expectations because of evaluative pressures.

Given that supervisors have more social power than supervisees, they are responsible for creating an atmosphere in which such issues can be openly and safely explored (Helms & Cook, 1999). Supervisors need to make their willingness to address racial and cultural issues explicit from the start of supervision. Helms and Cook (1999) suggest that supervisors can achieve this by

> [allowing] race and culture to enter into the room; that is, to discuss the various implications of the supervisor's, the supervisee's, and the client's racial and cultural socialization, and the effects of the interactions among these dimensions on the supervision process. (p. 283)

This goal, of course, cannot be obtained unless supervisors are willing to examine and share their own racial and cultural perspectives outside of and within supervision. To be effective, supervisors should explore their own racial and cultural attitudes, values, and behaviors outside of supervision (Coleman, 1997). Supervisors might begin this process by evaluating their own racial identity attitudes using one of the widely available racial identity scales (e.g., White Racial Identity Attitude Scale [WRAIS]) (Helms & Carter, 1990).

Supervisors should make it clear that one of the goals of supervision is to address and manage racial and cultural issues. This discussion should be integrated into a general discussion about the goals of supervision. Racial identity models can provide a relatively nonthreatening focus for discussing racial attitude differences and how they can affect the supervisory and counseling process (Helms & Cook, 1999). Such models permit the examination of individual differences, avoiding sweeping generalizations about various racial and ethnic groups. It is important that discussions of racial identity attitudes take place within a general discussion of the principles of professional growth and development rather than in the history of casting and denying blame (Helms & Cook, 1999). Supervisors, therefore, need to explore supervisee expectations and assumptions about supervision, their previous supervisory experiences, and their personal goals for supervision.

Supervisors will also want to explicitly address what their expectations and goals of the supervisee will be. Goals specific to racial and cultural issues might be gleaned from Sue, Arredondo, and McDavis's (1992) operationalized list of multicultural competencies (Arredondo et al., 1996) and adapted to supervision. The result of these initial discussions should be a written list of mutually agreed-on goals (Bordin, 1983). Having established these goals, the supervisor should turn to linking goals to the specific tasks of supervision.

The Tasks of Supervision

The tasks of supervision, which comprise the second component of the working alliance model, should be closely linked to the established goals of supervision. Specifically, supervisors should make clear conceptual connections between the established goals and the tasks of supervision (Bordin, 1983). This will help supervisees make sense of their supervisory experiences. Like the goals established for supervision, supervisory tasks must be mutually established and agreed on.

The tasks that supervisors assign to supervisees can be drawn from a variety of formats. Supervisors, however, should consider supervisees' level of racial identity development before deciding on a particular format. Some formats are more challenging than others, and supervisors must determine if a given supervisee is prepared for particular challenges. For instance, one complementary supervisee task that is linked to the goal of increasing awareness and understanding of one's racial/cultural self may be a review of videotapes of counseling sessions with culturally different clients. Although this format offers supervisees the opportunity to observe nonverbal cues and nonverbal exchanges that they may be unaware of, it is also renders supervisees more vulnerable to supervisor scrutiny (Watkins, 1997). Watkins (1997) suggested that supervisors should "anticipate the degree and type of resistance the supervisee might feel regarding the taping" (p. 337). For instance, majority supervisees at the Contact level of racial identity development may be resistant to feedback about their videotaped interactions with minority clients early in cross-cultural supervision. This may be especially true when minority supervisors supervise majority supervisees. In this instance, minority supervisors may want to consider using didactic formats that build up to more challenging, experiential formats.

The various tasks assigned to supervisees require that they (and supervisors) inhabit various roles (Holloway, 1995). Part of inducting supervisees into the culture of supervision involves apprising supervisees of the different roles that they will be asked to inhabit. Some of these roles will be unfamiliar to the supervisee and, therefore, anxiety provoking. The content of individual supervision, for instance, tends to have a personal-emotional emphasis (Bartlett, 1984). Compared to some other supervision modalities (e.g., practicum training), this supervision modality tends to put more emphasis on increasing supervisee self-awareness. Accordingly, supervisees are often implicitly required to assume the role of "client" in addition to the role of "learner." The "client" role that the supervisee is asked to assume in supervision is different, however, from the role that actual clients assume. Unlike the actual client, the supervisee is playing multiple roles—"learner" and "client." The evaluative pressures of the former may make it difficult for the supervisee to assume the responsibilities of the latter (e.g., self-disclosure). This is particularly true when the function of the role has not been clarified— that is, when the role has not been adequately linked to a goal.

The client-learner role combination may be more anxiety provoking for some supervisees than others. Supervisees of color, for instance, who express Immersion/Emersion racial attitudes may mistrust White supervisors and be reluctant to discuss deeper process issues. Supervisors at the Reintegration stage of racial identity development may mislabel such supervisees as "difficult" and thus perpetuate a downward spiral of interpersonal conflict. Supervisees of color who express Immersion/Emersion racial attitude ego statuses may resist disclosing to White supervisors with more sophisticated racial identity attitudes as well. Research suggests that some people of color are more mistrusting of whites than others (e.g., Nickerson, Helms, & Terrell, 1994; Watkins, Terrell, Miller, & Terrell, 1989). The historical mistreatment of minorities has fostered a perception of all Whites as potentially racist and not to be trusted (cf.

Fong & Lease, 1997). Supervisees of color who hold such beliefs may be less inclined to reveal emotional concerns in supervision, hindering the development of the working alliance (Fong & Lease, 1997). One way that supervisors can help build trust is by minimizing supervisee role difficulties. This can be achieved by drawing explicit conceptual linkages between the goals of supervision and the specific roles that the supervisee will be asked to adopt.

The Bonds of Supervision

Working alliance bonds refer to the feelings of liking, caring, and trust that develop from establishing a collaborative relationship with supervisees (Bordin, 1983). The bonds established within the working alliance are an outgrowth of the tasks and goals established in supervision (Bordin, 1983). Issues of race and culture, if they are not addressed, can serve as barriers to the development of working alliance bonds in multicultural supervision. As previously discussed, however, a collaboration to identify the goals and tasks related to racial and cultural issues demonstrates supervisors' sensitivity to such issues, subsequently demonstrating respect and care for the supervisee. Strong supervisory bonds are also associated with less role conflict and greater overall satisfaction with supervision (Ladany & Friedlander, 1995).

CONCLUSION

Over the past 30 years, we have become increasingly sensitized to the effect of culture on the counseling process (Sue et al., 1992). Much of the research on multicultural counseling has focused on development issues such as racial identity or client issues such as expectations or preferences (Coleman, Wampold, & Casali, 1995). The field has only just begun to examine the challenges of developing effective treatment for people of color (Wampold, Ahn, & Coleman, 2001). As has been historically true of counseling research (Holloway, 1995), we have paid insufficient attention to the role of supervision in the provision of effective clinical services. It is the core contention of this chapter that effective multicultural supervision is the building block of multicultural counseling competence, which will lead to effective clinical services in a pluralistic society.

The model for effective multicultural supervision that we have proposed requires the supervisor to pay balanced attention to the manner in which cultural issues (we specifically examined the issue of racial attitudes in this chapter) serve to facilitate or constrain the development of an effective working alliance. We have integrated the theoretical work of Helms (1990, 1995), Cook (1994), and Bordin (1983) to suggest that we need to systematically investigate the manner in which the racial identity of the supervisor and supervisee interacts to affect the relationship within supervision and, ultimately, outcomes in the lives of clients. In this chapter, we have suggested several ways in which cultural issues can be explicitly integrated in the process of supervision to both enhance the relationship and facilitate the acquisition of multicultural competence in the supervisee and the expression of multicultural competence in the supervisor. We hope that these ideas serve as a stimulus for more systematic research in this area.

We want to conclude with the suggestion that the complex relationship called multicultural supervision demands the use of conceptual frameworks and related methodologies that allow the investigator to examine multiple factors using multiple methods within a coherent framework. As Coleman, Norton, Miranda, and McCubbin have suggested (see Chapter 3, this volume), an ecological perspective using the extended case method (Buroway et al., 1991) is extremely useful for such research. Such an approach would allow the investigator to integrate data derived from surveys of racial identity and working alliance with phenomenologically derived data (e.g., interviews), observational data (e.g., microanalysis of tape sessions), and contextual data (e.g., information about the institution within which the multicultural supervision is occurring). It is our contention that meaningful progress in this area of research will require that we step beyond research that focuses on a parsimonious explanation of the relationship between two factors in supervision (e.g., racial identity and working alliance) and learns to focus on the interaction between such factors and the context within which the interaction occurs. Such an approach will provide us the information we need to develop increasingly effective training programs that, at the end of the day, will allow us to provide better clinical services to a culturally diverse clientele.

REFERENCES

Arredondo, P., Toporek, R., Brown, S. P., Jones, J., Locke, D. C., Sanchez, J., et al. (1996). Operationalization of the multicultural counseling competencies. *Journal of Multicultural Counseling and Development, 24*, 42-78.

Bartlett, W. E. (1984). A multidimensional framework for the analysis of supervision of counseling. *The Counseling Psychologist, 11*(1), 9-18.

Bell, D. A. (1992). *Faces at the bottom of the well: The permanence of racism*. New York: Basic Books.

Bernard, J. M., & Goodyear, R. K. (1998). *Fundamentals of clinical supervision* (2nd ed.). Needham Heights, MA: Allyn & Bacon.

Betancourt, H., & Lopez, S. R. (1993). The study of culture, ethnicity, and race in American psychology. *American Psychologist, 48*, 629-637.

Beutler, L. E., Brown, M. T., Crothers, L., Booker, K., & Seabrook, M. K. (1996). The dilemma of factitious demographic distinctions in psychological research. *Journal of Consulting and Clinical Psychology, 64*, 892-902.

Bordin, E. S. (1983). A working alliance based model of supervision. *The Counseling Psychologist, 11*(1), 35-42.

Bordin, E. S. (1994). Theory and research on the therapeutic working alliance: New directions. In A. O. Horvath & L. S. Greenberg (Eds.), *The working alliance: Theory, research, and practice* (pp. 13-37). New York: John Wiley.

Bradshaw, W. H., Jr. (1982). Supervision in Black and White: Race as a factor in supervision. In M. Blumenfield (Ed.), *Applied supervision in psychotherapy* (pp. 199-220). New York: Grune & Stratton.

Brown, M. T., & Landrum-Brown, J. (1995). Counselor supervision: Cross-cultural perspectives. In J. G. Ponterotto, J. M. Casas, L. A. Suzuki, & C. M. Alexander (Eds.), *Handbook of multicultural counseling* (pp. 263-286). Thousand Oaks, CA: Sage.

Burawoy, M., Burton, A., Ferguson, A., Fox, K., Gamson, J., Gartrell, M., et al. (Eds.). (1991). *Ethnography unbound: Power and resistance in the modern metropolis.* Berkeley: University of California Press.

Burkard, A. W., Ponterotto, J. G., Reynolds, A. L., & Alfonso, V. C. (1999). White counselor trainees' racial identity and working alliance perceptions. *Journal of Counseling and Development, 77*(3), 324-329.

Coleman, H. L. K. (1997). Conflict in multicultural counseling relationships: Source and resolution. *Journal of Multicultural Counseling and Development, 25,* 195-200.

Coleman, H. L. K., Wampold, B. E., & Casali, S. L. (1995). Ethnic minorities' ratings of ethnically similar and European American counselors: A meta-analysis. *Journal of Counseling Psychology, 42,* 55-64.

Cook, D. A. (1994). Racial identity in supervision. *Counselor Education and Supervision, 34,* 132-141.

Constantine, M. G. (1997). Facilitating multicultural competency in counseling supervision: Operationalizing a practical framework. In D. B. Pope-Davis & H. L. K. Coleman (Eds.), *Multicultural counseling competencies: Assessment, education, and training, and supervision* (pp. 310-324). Thousand Oaks, CA: Sage.

Cook, D. A., & Helms, J. E. (1988). Visible racial/ethnic group supervisees' satisfaction with cross-cultural supervision as predicted by relationship characteristics. *Journal of Counseling Psychology, 35,* 268-274.

D'Andrea, M., & Daniels, J. (1997). Multicultural counseling supervision: Central issues, theoretical considerations, and practical strategies. In D. B. Pope-Davis & H. L. K. Coleman (Eds.), *Multicultural counseling competencies: Assessment, education, and training, and supervision* (pp. 290-309). Thousand Oaks, CA: Sage.

Duan, C., & Roehlke, H. (2001). A descriptive "snapshot" of cross-racial supervision in university counseling center internships. *Journal of Multicultural Counseling & Development, 29*(2), 131-147.

Duan, C., Roehlke, H., & Matchisky, D. J. (1998, August). *National survey of cross-cultural supervision: When the supervisor and the supervisee are different in race.* Paper presented at the annual meeting of the American Psychological Association, San Francisco.

Fong, M. L., & Lease, S. H. (1997). Cross-cultural supervision: Issues for the White supervisor. In D. B. Pope-Davis & H. L. K. Coleman (Eds.), *Multicultural counseling competencies: Assessment, education, and training, and supervision* (pp. 387-405). Thousand Oaks, CA: Sage.

Fouad, N. A., & Brown, M. T. (2001). Role of race and social class in development: Implications for counseling psychology. In S. D. Brown & R. W. Lent (Eds.), *Handbook of counseling psychology* (3rd ed., pp. 379-410). New York: John Wiley.

Frank, J. D., & Frank, J. B. (1991). *Persuasion and healing: A comparative study of psychotherapy* (3rd ed.). Baltimore: Johns Hopkins University Press.

Fukuyama, M. A. (1994). Critical incidents in multicultural counseling supervision: A phenomenological approach to supervision research. *Counselor Education and Supervision, 43,* 142-151.

Hacker, A. (1992). *Two nations: Black and White, separate, hostile, unequal.* New York: Ballantine.

Helms, J. E. (Ed.). (1990). *Black and White racial identity: Theory, research, and practice.* Westport, CT: Greenwood.

Helms, J. E. (1994a). The conceptualization of racial identity and other "racial" constructs. In E. J. Trickett, R. J. Watts, & D. Birman (Eds.), *Human diversity: Perspectives on people in context* (pp. 285-311). San Francisco: Jossey-Bass.

Helms, J. E. (1994b). How multiculturalism obscures racial factors in therapy process: Comment on Ridley et al. (1994), Sodowsky et al. (1994), Ottavi et al. (1994), and Thompson et al. (1994). *Journal of Counseling Psychology, 41*(2), 162-165.

Helms, J. E. (1995). An update of Helm's White and people of color racial identity models. In J. G. Ponterotto, J. M. Casas, L. A. Suzuki, & C. M. Alexander (Eds.), *Handbook of multicultural counseling* (pp. 181-198). Thousand Oaks, CA: Sage.

Helms, J. E. (1996). Toward a methodology for measuring and assessing racial as distinguished from ethnic identity. In G. R. Sodowsky & J. Impara (Eds.), *Multicultural assessment in counseling and clinical psychology* (pp. 143-192). Lincoln, NE: Buros Institute of Mental Measurement.

Helms, J. E., & Carter, R. T. (1990). Development of the White Racial Identity Inventory. In J. E. Helms (Ed.), *Black and White racial identity: Theory, research, and practice* (pp. 67-80). Westport, CT: Greenwood.

Helms, J. E., & Cook, D. A. (1999). Using race and culture in therapy supervision. In J. E. Helms & D. A. Cook (Eds.), *Using race and culture in counseling and psychotherapy: Theory and process* (pp. 277-298). Boston: Allyn & Bacon.

Helms, J. E., & Richardson, T. Q. (1997). How multiculturalism obscures race and culture as differential aspects of counseling competency. In D. B. Pope-Davis & H. L. K. Coleman (Eds.), *Multicultural counseling competencies: Assessment, education, and training, and supervision* (pp. 60-79). Thousand Oaks, CA: Sage.

Holloway, E. L. (1995). *Clinical supervision: A systems approach.* Thousand Oaks, CA: Sage.

Kleintjes, S., & Swartz, L. (1996). Black clinical psychology trainees at a "White" South African university: Issues for clinical supervision. *Clinical Supervisor, 14*(1), 87-109.

Ladany, N., Brittan-Powell, C. S., & Pannu, R. K. (1997). The influence of supervisory racial identity interaction and racial matching on the supervisory working alliance and supervisee multicultural competence. *Counselor Education and Supervision, 36,* 284-304.

Ladany, N., & Friedlander, M. L. (1995). The relationship between the supervisory working alliance and trainees' experience of role conflict and role ambiguity. *Counselor Education and Supervision, 34,* 220-231.

Leong, F. T. L., & Wagner, N. M. (1994). Cross-cultural supervision: What do we know? What do we need to know? *Counselor Education and Supervision, 34,* 117-132.

McNeil, B. W., Hom, K. L., & Perez, J. A. (1995). The training and supervisory needs of racial and ethnic minority students. *Journal of Multicultural Counseling and Development, 23*(1), 246-259.

McRoy, R. G., Freeman, E. G., Logan, S. L., & Blackmon, B. (1986). Cross-cultural field supervision: Implications for social work education. *Journal of Social Work Education, 22,* 50-56.

Midgette, T. E., & Meggert, S. S. (1991). Multicultural counseling instruction: A challenge for faculties in the 21st century. *Journal of Counseling and Development, 70,* 136-141.

Morgan, D. W. (1984). Cross-cultural factors in the supervision of psychotherapy. *The Psychiatric Forum, 12*(2), 61-64.

Nickerson, K. J., Helms, J. E., & Terrell, F. (1994). Cultural mistrust, opinions about mental illness, and Black students' attitudes toward seeking psychological help from White counselors. *Journal of Counseling Psychology, 41,* 378-385.

Pedersen, P. B. (1991). Multiculturalism as a generic approach to counseling. *Journal of Counseling and Development, 20,* 6-12.

Pedersen, P. B. (1996). The importance of both similarities and differences in multicultural counseling: Reaction to C. H. Patterson. *Journal of Counseling and Development, 74,* 236-237.

Peterson, F. K. (1991). Issues of race and ethnicity in supervision: Emphasizing who you are, not what you know. *The Clinical Supervisor, 7*(1), 27-40.

Pierce, L. (2000). The continuing significance of race. In P. Spickard & J. Burroughs (Eds.), *We are a people: Narrative and multiplicity in constructing ethnic identity* (pp. 221-228). Philadelphia: Temple University Press.

Ponterotto, J. G., Casas, J. M., Suzuki, L. A., & Alexander, C. M. (Eds.). (1995). *Handbook of multicultural counseling.* Thousand Oaks, CA: Sage.

Pope-Davis, D. B., & Coleman, H. L. K. (Eds.). (1997). *Multicultural counseling competencies: Assessment, education, and training, and supervision.* Thousand Oaks, CA: Sage.

Priest, R. (1994). Cross-cultural supervision: An examination of clinical reality. *Counselor Education and Supervision, 34*(2), 152-158.

Proctor, E. K., & Davis, L. E. (1989). *Race, gender, and class: Guidelines for practice with individuals, families, and groups.* Englewood Cliffs, NJ: Prentice Hall.

Spickard, P., & Burroughs, J. (Eds.). (2000). *We are a people: Narrative and multiplicity in constructing ethnic identity.* Philadelphia: Temple University Press.

Sue, D. W., Arredondo, P., & McDavis, R. J. (1992). Multicultural competencies and standards: A call to the profession. *Journal of Multicultural Counseling and Development, 20*, 64-88.

Thompson, C. E., & Jenal, S. T. (1994). Interracial and intraracial quasi-counseling interactions when counselors avoid discussions of race. *Journal of Counseling Psychology, 41*(4), 484-491.

Torrey, E. F. (1972). *The mind game: Witchdoctors and psychiatrists.* New York: Emerson Hall.

Vargas, L. A. (1989, August). *Training psychologists to be culturally responsive: Issues in supervision.* Paper presented at a symposium at the 97th annual convention of the American Psychological Association, New Orleans, LA.

Wampold, B. E., Ahn, H., & Coleman, H. L. K. (2001). Medical model as metaphor: Old habits die hard. *Journal of Counseling Psychology, 48*(3), 268-273.

Watkins, C. E., Jr. (1997). *Handbook of psychotherapy supervision.* New York: John Wiley.

Watkins, C. E., Jr., Terrell, F., Miller, F. S., & Terrell, S. L. (1989). Cultural mistrust and its effects on expectational variables in the Black client–White counselor relationship. *Journal of Counseling Psychology, 36*, 447-450.

Yee, A. H., Fairchild, H. H., Weizman, F., & Wyatt, G. E. (1993). Addressing psychology's problem with race. *American Psychologist, 48*, 1132-1140.

Zuckerman, M. (1990). Some dubious premises in research and theory on racial differences: Scientific, social, and ethical issues. *American Psychologist, 45*, 1297-1303.

PART II

Assessment

One of the critical issues that has permeated research and training in multicultural counseling competencies has been assessment. As the literature has grown in this area, the types of assessment tools available have become more sophisticated and varied. This section endeavors to provide readers with state-of-the-art information regarding assessment of counselors and counselor trainees, the training environment, teachers, and supervisors. Some of the authors have provided updated user information for existing measures of multicultural competencies, whereas other authors have presented comprehensive proposals for assessing multicultural competence in various settings.

This section is comprised of six chapters. The first and second chapters in this section (Chapters 9 and 10) present updated research and user information for two widely used measures of multicultural competence. By presenting this information in tandem, we hope to provide readers with the information necessary to evaluate and identify which measure may be best suited for their research or training needs.

In Chapter 11, the authors describe a comprehensive model for assessing trainees' multicultural competence throughout the counseling training program. Such a model addresses earlier criticism that multicultural training is often relegated to one course or one semester. The authors of this chapter propose a model of integrating and assessing trainees' multicultural competence through coursework, practica, and research. As a result, both the student and program are involved in an ongoing process of learning, assessing, and applying tools for appropriate multicultural counseling.

Chapter 12 addresses the need to assess the multicultural competence of the training environment itself. The authors of this chapter provide updated psychometric and user information for an instrument designed to assess aspects of curriculum, supervision, climate, and research. They also discuss a variety of uses for the instrument, including formative and summative evaluation, research, and program development.

The authors of Chapter 13 describe an array of tools that may be used in assessing the multicultural competence of teachers. A burgeoning area of application of multicultural competence has been in the area of teacher training. The authors of this chapter discuss the goals of such an assessment, the issues in conducting this assessment, and the benefits of using a variety of approaches.

The findings of recent research assessing multicultural supervision competence in counseling are presented in Chapter 14. Updated psychometric information is presented for an established measure of multicultural supervision. In addition, findings are discussed regarding the extent to which multicultural supervision competence and multicultural counseling competence were found to be related. The authors discuss a variety of implications and suggestions for assessing supervisory competence.

9

The Multicultural Counseling Knowledge and Awareness Scale (MCKAS)

Validity, Reliability, and User Guidelines

JOSEPH G. PONTEROTTO
JODI C. POTERE
Fordham University at Lincoln Center

This past year's American Psychological Association (APA) convention in San Francisco (August, 2001) marked the 10-year anniversary of the Multicultural Counseling Awareness Scale (MCAS), which was first introduced to the research community at the 1991 APA convention, which was also held in San Francisco (Ponterotto, Sanchez, & Magids, 1991). During the past decade, the MCAS has undergone a moderate degree of psychometric testing and a number of revisions. Along with the Multicultural Awareness-Knowledge-Skills Survey (MAKSS) (D'Andrea, Daniels, & Heck, 1991) and the Multicultural Counseling Inventory (MCI) (Sodowsky, Taffe, Gutkin, & Wise, 1994), the

MCAS is a frequently used paper-and-pencil self-report measure of perceived multicultural counseling competency. The purpose of this brief chapter is to bring together all available psychometric data on the instrument with the goal of clarifying for readers the uses, strengths, and limitations of the MCAS. The reader is urged to first read Ponterotto et al. (1996) and Ponterotto, Gretchen, et al. (2002) before absorbing the present chapter.

THEORETICAL BASE AND INSTRUMENT EVOLUTION

MCAS items are anchored in the multicultural counseling competency model, first put forth by Sue et al. (1982) and then expanded in Sue, Arredondo, and McDavis (1992) and Sue et al. (1998). This model explicates the competencies prerequisite to effective multicultural counseling practice in the culturally heterogeneous United States. The competency model posits three levels of competence that are sequential and additive. First, counselors need to be aware of their own values, biases, stereotypes, and assumptions about human behavior and "appropriate" counseling process and outcome. Second, counselors must have specific knowledge of the worldviews of the culturally diverse groups with whom they plan to work. Finally, counselors must possess a wide repertoire of specific communication, assessment, and intervention skills targeted to culturally diverse groups (see review and empirically based critique of the competency model in Ponterotto, Fuertes, & Chen, 2000).

The MCAS has undergone a number of iterations and revisions. The prototype instrument included 70 items (42 knowledge/skills items and 28 awareness items), which was reduced to 45 items (28 knowledge/skills items, 14 awareness items, and 3 social desirability test items) after psychometric testing (Ponterotto et al., 1996). The latest version of the instrument has been renamed the Multicultural Counseling Knowledge and Awareness Scale (MCKAS) and consists of 32 items (20 knowledge items and 12 awareness items) (Ponterotto, Gretchen, et al., 2002). The revisions were primarily the result of exploratory and confirmatory factor analyses and independent tests and critiques of the instrument. Across all factor-analytic studies, a two-factor extraction has remained the best-fit model.

Critiques of the MCAS and MCKAS are found in a number of publications (e.g., Constantine & Ladany, 2000, 2001; Constantine, Gloria, & Ladany, 2002; Ponterotto & Alexander, 1996; Ponterotto et al., 2000; Ponterotto, Rieger, Barrett, & Sparks, 1994; Ponterotto, Gretchen, et al.,

2002; Pope-Davis & Dings, 1994, 1995). We now turn to a summary and integration of psychometric data on the MCAS/MCKAS.

PSYCHOMETRIC EVIDENCE FOR THE MULTICULTURAL COUNSELING AWARENESS SCALES (MCAS/MCKAS)

This section on psychometric evidence reviews the characteristics of participant samples, measures of central tendency and variance, and validity and reliability data. In keeping with the latest guidelines of the joint task force in testing standards (American Educational Research Association, American Psychological Association, and National Council on Testing in Education [AERA/APA/NCTE], 1999), the validity sections are organized along newly recommended subheadings.

Participant Samples and Measures of Central Tendency, Variance, and Skewness

Table 9.1 summarizes sample descriptions across a number of studies incorporating the MCKAS or its precursor, the MCAS. The sample sizes/location, age ranges, gender composition, and racial/ethnic composition are also listed. Participant samples varied widely and included art therapists (Dizon, 1997), marriage and family therapists (Constantine, Juby, & Liang, 2001), predoctoral interns in counseling and clinical psychology (Manese, Wu, & Nepomuceno, 2001; Pope-Davis, Reynolds, & Dings, 1994), distinguished national experts and seasoned school counselors (Ponterotto et al., 1996), and multiple, geographically dispersed samples of master's- and doctoral-level counseling students. It is also readily evident from Table 9.1 that more females than males, as well as more Caucasian Americans than racially diverse Americans, have completed the MCAS/MCKAS over the past decade.

Table 9.1   MCKAS/MCAS Sample Descriptions

Source	n	Sample	Mean Age	Age Range	Sex Composition	Racial/Ethnic Composition
Alpert (1995)[a]	53	Counselor trainees from Florida	33.71	23-54	76% F; 25% M	73% W; 12% B; 15% H
Bidell (2001)[b]	287	Students recruited from universities in California, Nevada, Texas, and Ohio.	—	—	0% F; 100% M	60% W; 12% H; 11% A; 7% B; 5% biracial; 2% other; 2% NR; 1% NA
Carrillo (1997)[a]	56	Master's-level counselors and psychologists from Texas	—	—	45% F; 55%M	43% W; 57% H
Constantine (2000)[b]	255	American Counseling Association (ACA) members, counseling students, and faculty	42.7	22-73	56% F; 43% M	83% W; 8% H; 3% B; 2% A; 1% biracial
Constantine, Juby, and Liang (2001)[b]	113	Members of the American Association for Marriage and Family Therapy	51.6	25-78	50% F; 50% M	100% W
Constantine, Gloria, and Ladany (2002)[b]	260	Members of a professional counseling association and individuals recruited through personal contacts	39.1	22-73	66% F; 33% M	78% W; 7% H; 5% B; 4 % A; 2% biracial; .4% NA; .4% international respondent
Constantine and Ladany (2000)[b]	135	Members of the American Counseling Association and students in counseling	35.8	22-65	75% F; 25% M	77% W; 8% B; 7% H; 5% A; 1% NA; 2% biracial
Detabali (1995)[a]	63	Vocational rehabilitation counselors—Tennessee	44.06	23-62	58% F; 42% M	86% W; 13% B; 2% other
Dizon (1997)[a]						
Conference attendees	102	Art therapists	—	—	90% F; 6% M	77% W; 14% O; 6% B; 2% A; 1% H
Mailing participants	195	Art therapists	—	—	91% F; 9% M	76% W; 18% O; 3% H; 2% A; 1% B; 1% NA
Kocarek, Talbot, Batka, and Anderson (2001)[a]	120	Master's-level counseling students	32.7	22-63	88% F; 12% M	74% W; 13% B; 6% H; 5% multiracial; 2% A; 1% NA

(Continued)

139

Table 9.1 Continued

Source	n	Sample	Mean Age	Age Range	Sex Composition	Racial/Ethnic Composition
Manese, Wu, and Nepomuceno (2001)[a]	35	Predoctoral interns	31.34	25-50	67% F; 31% M	67% W; 8% B; 15% A; 5% H
Ponterotto et al. (1996)[a]						
Study 1	126	Counseling students, school counselors, and multicultural counseling experts	36	22-63	79% F; 18% M	71% W; 10% H; 9% B; 6% A; 1% NA; 2% O; 2% NR
Study 2	72	Counseling/counseling psychology students in the Northeast	34.69	22-61	72% F; 28% M	67% W; 17% B; 13% H; 3% O
	42	Counseling/counseling psychology students in the Northeast	30.71	21-56	88% F; 12% M	83% W; 7% A; 10% O
	45	Counseling/counseling psychology students in the Northeast	31.11	22-50	67% F; 33% M	80% W; 11% B; 9% O
Study 4	29	Students enrolled in multicultural course in New Mexico	37.38	21-61	65% F; 35% M	72% W; 17% H; 10% O
Ponterotto, Gretchen, et al. (2002)						
Study 1[a]	525	Students and professionals in counseling and counseling psychology	35	21-69	67% F; 33% M	83% W; 7% B; 6% H; 2% A; 1% NA; 1% O
Study 2[b]	199	Northeastern counselors in training	30	—	75% F; 25% M	45% W; 18% B; 16% H; 2% A; 1% NA
Pope-Davis and Dings (1994)[a]	92	Predoctoral interns	33.4	26-48	76% F; 24% M	83% W; 17% non-White
Pope-Davis, Reynolds, and Dings (1994)[a]	141	Predoctoral interns	32.91	23-48	71% F; 29% M	84% W; 16% non-White
Vinson and Neimeyer (2000)[a]	87	Counseling psychology students	27.8	—	64% F; 36% M	75% W; 9% A; 4% B; 3% H; 1% NA; 7% O

NOTE: Dashes indicate data not reported. F = female; M = male; W = White; B = Black; H = Hispanic; A = Asian; NR = not reported; NA = Native American; O = other.

a. 45-item scale.
b. 32-item scale.

Table 9.2 summarizes central tendency and variance data across the MCAS/MCKAS samples. Both total mean and standard deviation data and scaled mean and standard deviation are presented across subscales. The scaled mean data allow for meaningful score comparisons across subscales as they have differing numbers of items. To calculate the scaled means (and standard deviations), the total subscale score (addition of all subscale items) is divided by the number of items making up the particular subscale, resulting in the standard metric range of 1 (*not at all true*) to 7 (*totally true*), characteristic of actual item response choices on the MCAS/MCKAS.

A review of scaled mean data for the Knowledge/Skills subscale shows that scores ranged from 2.95 (Detabali, 1995) to 6.5 (Ponterotto et al., 1996), with a mean of 4.54 across all studies. This indicates a fairly normal distribution of scores across samples. From a clinical perspective, these data indicate that the collective sample self-rated as having moderate levels of multicultural counseling knowledge. Looking at the Awareness subscale, scaled mean scores ranged from a low of 4.40 (Detabali, 1995) to a high of 6.23 (Manese et al., 2001), with the mean falling at 5.65. This indicates a negative skew, with the collective sample perceiving themselves as quite aware of multicultural issues in the counseling process.

Validity

Evidence Based on Test Content. Content validity was established through multicultural expert ratings of item clarity and domain appropriateness, independent card-sort procedures, and use of a graduate student focus group (Ponterotto et al., 1996).

Evidence Based on Internal Structure. In their initial factor analysis of MCAS items, Ponterotto et al. (1996) examined one-, two-, three-, and four-factor extractions using principal component methods and oblique rotations. The authors found that the two-factor extraction (Knowledge and Skills items loading together, as well as Awareness items) represented the best-fit model, accounting for 28% of the common variance. In a later principal components analysis (Ponterotto, Gretchen, et al., 2002, Study 1), the two-factor orthogonal model accounted for 32.2% of common variance.

In a confirmatory factor analysis incorporating aggregate variables (or item parcels) (as recommended in Bagozzi & Heatherton, 1994), Ponterotto, Gretchen, et al. (2002) found that the two-factor oblique and orthogonal models had identical fits, which were superior to the null and global models. The two-factor models had a goodness-of-fit index (GFI) of .90, a Tucker Lewis index (TLI) of .91, and a relative noncentrality index (RNI) of .93.

Evidence Based on Relations to Other Variables: Convergent and Discriminant Evidence and Test Criterion Relationships. Table 9.3 summarizes the statistical relationship of MCAS/MCKAS subscales to other measures. This database informs the convergent, discriminant, and criterion-related evidence of the MCAS/MCKAS subscales. This section first presents evidence for the Knowledge subscale and then moves to an assessment of the Awareness subscale.

Convergent evidence for the Knowledge subscale is indicated by its significant correlation with the Knowledge subscales of the MCI and the MKASS (Constantine & Ladany, 2001; Kocarek, Talbot, Batka, & Anderson, 2001; Ponterotto, Gretchen, et al., 2002; Pope-Davis & Dings, 1994), as well as with a self-report version of the Cross-Cultural Counseling Inventory–Revised (Constantine & Ladany, 2001; Ponterotto et al., 1996). Discriminant evidence is indicated by the

(text continued on p. 147)

Table 9.2 Means and Standard Deviations of Total MCKAS/MCAS and Subscale Scores in Various Studies

Source	n	Total		Knowledge/Skills		Awareness	
		M	SD	M	SD	M	SD
Alpert (1995)[a]							
Pretest	53	192.00 (4.27)	26.90 (0.60)	114.81 (4.10)	20.46 (0.73)	77.19 (5.51)	8.32 (0.59)
Posttest	53	196.50 (4.37)	27.90 (0.62)	122.86 (4.39)	21.76 (0.78)	78.77 (5.63)	8.15 (0.58)
Carillo (1997)[a]	56	228.86 (5.09)	20.51 (0.46)	—	—	—	—
Constantine (2000)[b]—Total	225	177.87 (5.56)	21.22 (0.66)	106.20 (5.31)	15.63 (0.78)	71.67 (5.97)	9.99 (0.83)
Males	53	171.52 (5.36)	23.03 (0.72)	102.39 (5.12)	16.58 (0.83)	69.13 (5.76)	9.89 (0.82)
Females	70	182.68 (5.71)	18.50 (0.58)	109.09 (5.45)	14.32 (0.72)	73.59 (6.13)	9.70 (0.81)
Constantine, Juby, and Liang (2001)[b]	113	163.36 (5.11)	19.25 (0.60)	97.01 (4.85)	15.50 (0.78)	66.35 (5.53)	8.53 (0.71)
Constantine, Gloria, and Ladany (2002)[b]	259	180.16 (5.63)	20.16 (0.63)	107.00 (5.35)	15.60 (0.78)	73.08 (6.09)	8.76 (0.73)
Constantine and Ladany (2000)[b]—Total	135	182.00 (5.69)	19.12 (0.60)	107.68 (5.38)	15.81 (0.80)	74.32 (6.19)	7.05 (0.59)
Detabali (1995)[a]—Total	63	153.38 (3.41)	31.12 (0.69)	89.22 (3.19)	25.99 (0.93)	64.15 (4.58)	12.28 (0.88)
White males	23	144.08 (3.20)	35.75 (0.79)	82.47 (2.95)	29.14 (1.04)	61.60 (4.40)	12.08 (0.86)
White females	30	155.76 (3.46)	25.12 (0.56)	92.53 (3.30)	21.12 (0.75)	63.23 (4.52)	11.92 (0.85)
Minority participants	9	170.00 (3.78)	33.42 (0.74)	97.11 (3.47)	31.81 (1.14)	72.88 (5.21)	11.68 (0.83)
Dizon (1997)[a]							
Conference attendees	102	191.90 (4.26)	25.30 (0.56)	114.60 (4.09)	20.70 (0.74)	77.30 (5.52)	9.80 (0.70)
Mailing participants	195	188.50 (4.19)	26.50 (0.59)	111.00 (3.96)	20.30 (0.73)	77.50 (5.54)	12.80 (0.91)
Kocarek, Talbot, Batka, and Anderson (2001)[a]	79	190.70 (4.24)	28.64 (0.64)	112.08 (4.00)	22.71 (0.81)	78.62 (5.62)	11.54 (0.82)
Manese, Wu, and Nepomuceno (2001)[a]							
Pretest	35	—	—	129.86 (4.64)	21.11 (0.75)	87.23 (6.23)	7.21 (0.52)
Posttest	28	—	—	148.21 (5.29)	16.34 (0.58)	86.18 (6.16)	7.41 (0.53)
Ponterotto et al. (1996)[a]							
Study 1—Multicultural experts	10	—	—	182.00 (6.50)	10.06 (0.36)	81.20 (5.80)	3.64 (0.26)
Study 1—School counselors	31	—	—	127.24 (4.54)	18.76 (0.67)	68.32 (4.88)	11.76 (0.84)
Study 1—Counseling students	85	—	—	128.92 (4.64)	26.88 (0.96)	74.06 (5.29)	9.52 (0.68)
Study 1—White participants	86	—	—	128.53 (4.62)	26.32 (0.94)	—	—
Study 1—Minority participants	32	—	—	143.47 (5.13)	27.44 (0.98)	—	—

(Continued)

142

Table 9.2   Continued

Source	n	Total		Knowledge/Skills		Awareness	
		M	SD	M	SD	M	SD
Study 3—Pretest	19	—	—	108.64 (3.88)	19.60 (0.70)	84.00 (6.00)	15.12 (0.54)
Study 3—Posttest	19	—	—	150.92 (5.39)	19.04 (0.68)	87.50 (6.25)	11.48 (0.41)
Study 4—Sample 1 pretest	8	—	—	112.00 (4.00)	27.44 (0.98)	81.20 (5.80)	9.24 (0.66)
Study 4—Sample 1 posttest	8	—	—	140.00 (5.70)	20.44 (0.73)	88.20 (6.30)	9.80 (0.70)
Study 4—Sample 2 pretest	30	—	—	98.00 (3.50)	27.44 (0.98)	75.60 (5.40)	11.34 (0.81)
Study 4—Sample 2 posttest	24	—	—	117.60 (4.20)	23.52 (0.84)	77.00 (5.50)	11.62 (0.83)
Study 4—Sample 3 pretest	26	—	—	106.40 (3.80)	16.24 (0.58)	74.20 (5.30)	11.34 (0.81)
Study 4—Sample 3 posttest	29	—	—	134.40 (4.80)	18.76 (0.67)	82.60 (5.90)	8.82 (0.63)
Ponterotto, Gretchen, et al. (2002)							
Study 1[a]	525	211.50 (4.70)	63.00 (1.40)	115.92 (4.14)	28.00 (1.40)	79.80 (5.70)	9.94 (0.71)
Study 2[b]	196	—	—	99.20 (4.96)	16.00 (0.80)	60.72 (5.06)	13.68 (1.14)
Pope-Davis and Dings (1994)[a]	92	—	—	132.25 (4.72)	19.74 (0.71)	86.26 (6.16)	6.98 (0.50)
Pope-Davis, Reynolds, and Dings (1994)[a]	141	—	—	126.57 (4.52)	21.93 (0.78)	86.55 (6.18)	5.93 (0.42)
Vinson and Neimeyer (2000)[a]	87	—	—	—	—	—	—
White students	65	—	—	119.92 (4.28)	24.32 (0.87)	83.70 (5.98)	9.23 (0.66)
Students of color	22	—	—	146.36 (5.23)	22.13 (0.80)	85.50 (6.11)	6.32 (0.45)

NOTE: Dashes indicate data not reported. Scaled means and scaled standard deviations are reported in parentheses and are calculated by totaling the subscale score and dividing by the number of items on the subscale.

a. 45-item scale.
b. 32-item scale.

Table 9.3   Convergent, Discriminant, and Criterion-Related Evidence for the MCKAS/MCAS
Subscales

Source	Variable	Total	Knowledge/Skills	Awareness
Alpert (1995)[a]— Gain scores	WRIAS—Contact	0.05	−0.05	0.19
Gain scores	WRIAS—Disintegration	−0.24	−0.33*	0.07
Gain scores	WRIAS—Reintegration	−0.23	−0.28	0.01
Gain scores	WRIAS—Pseudo-independence	0.15	0.18	−0.01
Gain scores	WRIAS—Autonomy	0.16	0.24	−0.08
	Counseling credits completed	—	0.18	0.23
	Multicultural training	—	0.45**	0.31
Pretest scores	WRIAS—Contact	—	0.00	−0.29
Pretest scores	WRIAS—Disintegration	—	−0.45**	−0.35*
Pretest scores	WRIAS—Reintegration	—	−0.47**	−0.46**
Pretest scores	WRIAS—Pseudo-independence	—	0.45**	0.19
Pretest scores	WRIAS—Autonomy	—	0.36*	0.12
Bidell (2001)[b]	SOCCS—Skills subscale	0.36**	0.46**	0.14*
	SOCCS—Awareness subscale	0.22**	0.07	0.41**
	SOCCS—Knowledge subscale	0.51**	0.56**	0.29**
	SOCCS—Total	0.47**	0.50**	0.33**
	ATLGMS	−0.22**	−0.07	−0.47**
	Counselor Self-Efficacy Scale	0.58**	0.60**	0.28**
	Beck Depression Inventory	−0.26**	−0.24**	−0.19**
Constantine (2000)[b]	IRI-EC	0.42**	0.38**	0.29**
	IRI-PT	0.25**	0.22*	0.18*
	SDS	−0.04	0.01	−0.11
Constantine, Juby, and Liang (2001)[b]	SDS	−0.07	0.14	−0.42***
	NRS	−0.33***	−0.18*	−0.43***
	WRIAS—Contact	0.06	0.08	0.00
	WRIAS—Disintegration	−0.37***	−0.32***	−0.25**
	WRIAS—Reintegration	−0.43***	−0.31***	−0.41***
	WRIAS—Pseudo-independence	0.38***	0.44***	0.05
	WRIAS—Autonomy	0.30***	0.32***	0.10
Constantine, Gloria, and Ladany (2002)[b]	MAKSS—Total	0.68**	0.32**	0.70**
	MAKSS—Awareness	0.67**	0.45**	0.61**
	MAKSS—Knowledge	0.59**	0.27**	0.61**
	MAKSS—Skills	0.49**	0.15*	0.55**
	MCI—Total	0.63**	0.25**	0.68**
	MCI—Relationship	0.22**	0.07	0.25**
	MCI—Knowledge	0.68**	0.39**	0.66**
	MCI—Skills	0.45**	0.16*	0.49**
	MCI—Awareness	0.53**	0.13*	0.62**
Constantine and Ladany (2000)[b]	CCCI-R	0.61**	0.65**	0.19*
	MAKSS—Awareness	0.67**	0.64**	0.40**
	MAKSS—Knowledge	0.67**	0.68**	0.31**
	MAKSS—Skills	0.59**	0.63**	0.20*

(Continued)

Table 9.3   Continued

Source	Variable	Total	Knowledge/Skills	Awareness
	MAKSS—Total	0.76**	0.77**	0.34**
	MCI—Awareness	0.52**	0.60**	0.08
	MCI—Knowledge	0.64**	0.66**	0.27**
	MCI—Skills	0.46**	0.52**	0.08
	MCI—Relationship	0.22*	0.32**	−0.12
	MCI—Total	0.61**	0.69**	0.11
	SDS	−0.05	0.07	−0.31**
	MCC—Etiology	0.16	0.15	0.09
	MCC—Treatment	0.19*	0.15	0.18*
Kocarek, Talbot, Batka, and Anderson (2001)[a]	MAKSS—Knowledge	0.45**	0.55***	-0.02
	MAKSS—Skills	0.57***	0.62***	0.12
	MAKSS—Awareness	0.53***	0.43**	0.45**
	GSEDS—Knowledge	0.69***	0.71***	0.39**
	GSEDS—Skills	0.47*	0.62***	0.03
	GSEDS—Comfort	0.36*	0.21	0.49***
Manese, Wu, and Nepomuceno (2001)[a]	Premulticultural course	—	0.12	−0.08
	Preworkshop hours	—	0.30	0.02
	Pre-MC clients supervised	—	−0.06	0.13
	Postmulticultural course	—	0.12	0.01
	Postworkshop hours	—	0.09	0.36
	Post-MC clients supervised	—	0.16	0.06
Ponterotto et al. (1995)[a]	QDI—Factor 1	—	0.41**	0.50**
	QDI—Factor 2	—	0.34*	0.21
	QDI—Factor 3	—	0.23	0.39**
Ponterotto et al. (1996)[a]	CCCI-R	0.38**	0.44**	0.15
	NRS	0.31	0.16	0.49**
	SDS	0.18	0.22	0.00
Ponterotto, Gretchen, et al. (2002)[b]	MCI—Awareness	—	0.44**	−0.06
	MCI—Knowledge	—	0.49**	0.10
	MCI—Skills	—	0.43**	−0.10
	MCI—Relationship	—	−0.12	0.74**
	MEIM—Ethnic identity	—	0.31*	0.03
	MEIM—Other group orientation	—	0.12	0.20
	SDS	—	−0.39*	0.07
Pope-Davis and Dings (1994)[a]	MCI—Awareness	—	0.55**	0.16
	MCI—Knowledge	—	0.58**	0.17
	MCI—Skills	—	0.27**	0.29**
	MCI—Relationship	—	0.09	0.03

(Continued)

Table 9.3   Continued

Source	Variable	Total	Knowledge/Skills	Awareness
Pope-Davis, Reynolds, and Davis (1994)[a]	Year in program	—	0.07	0.13
	MC workshop hours	—	0.35**	0.05
	MC coursework	—	0.34**	−0.05
	MC supervision	—	0.49**	0.18*
Pope-Davis, Dings, and Ottavi (1995)[a]	Year in program	—	−0.12	−0.36***
	MC workshop hours	—	0.40***	0.09
	MC coursework	—	0.32***	0.11
	MC supervision	—	0.05	0.07
Vinson and Neimeyer (2000)[a] White students	WRIAS—Contact	—	−0.22	−0.30*
	WRIAS—Disintegration	—	−0.17	−0.29*
	WRIAS—Reintegration	—	−0.31*	−0.38*
	WRIAS—Pseudo-independence	—	0.25*	0.12
	WRIAS—Autonomy	—	0.31*	0.11
	Number of courses	—	0.27*	0.07
	Number of workshops	—	0.38**	0.01
	Self-reported counseling competency	—	0.52**	0.26*
	Self-reported MC counseling competency	—	0.57**	0.23
Students of color	POCRIAS—Contact	—	−0.08	−0.38
	POCRIAS—Dissonance	—	−0.34	−0.22
	POCRIAS—Immersion/ Emersion	—	−0.25	−0.09
	POCRIAS-Internalization	—	0.33	0.23
	Number of courses	—	0.26	0.17
	Number of workshops	—	0.60**	0.24
	Self-reported counseling competency	—	0.34	0.01
	Self-reported multicultural counseling competency	—	0.42	0.17

NOTE: Dashes indicate data not reported. WRIAS = White Racial Identity Attitude Scale; SOCCS = Sexual Orientation Counselor Competency Scale; ATLGMS = Attitudes Toward Lesbians and Gay Men Scale; IRI-EC = Interpersonal Reactivity Index–Empathic Concern; IRI-PT = Interpersonal Reactivity Index-Perspective Taking; SDS = Social Desirability Scale; CCCI-R = Cross–Cultural Counseling Inventory-Revised; POCRIAS = People of Color Racial Identity Attitude Scale; MEIM = Multiethnic Identity Measure; MC = multicultural counseling; QDI = Quick Discrimination Index; MCC = Multicultural Counseling Competency; NRS = New Racism Scale; MAKSS = Multicultural Awareness-Knowledge-Skills Survey; MCI = Multicultural Counseling Inventory; GSEDS = Graduate Students' Experiences With Diversity Scale.

*$p < .05$; **$p < .01$; ***$p < .001$.

subscale's negligible correlation with a measure of socially desirable responding (Constantine & Ladany, 2000; Constantine et al., 2001; Ponterotto et al., 1996).

Criterion-related evidence for the Knowledge subscale is indicated through its significant correlation in expected directions with White racial identity theory (Alpert, 1995; Constantine et al., 2001; Vinson & Neimeyer, 2000), subtle and overt racist views (Constantine et al., 2001; Ponterotto et al., 1995), ethnic identity development (Ponterotto, Gretchen, et al., 2002), empathic ability (Constantine, 2000), counselor self-efficacy and sexual orientation counselor competency (Bidell, 2001), experiences with diversity (Kocarek et al., 2001), and various training variables (e.g., multicultural courses, workshops, etc.) (Alpert, 1995; Vinson & Neimeyer, 2000). Importantly, the lack of criterion-related evidence was established when scores of the Knowledge subscale failed to correlate with independent ratings of counselor case conceptualization skills (Constantine & Ladany, 2000).

Regarding the Awareness subscale, convergent evidence was established through significant correlations with the Awareness subscale of the MAKSS (Kocarek et al., 2001), though the MCKAS Awareness subscale did not correlate with the like-named Awareness subscale of the MCI (Constantine & Ladany, 2001). Examining discriminant evidence, we note that the Awareness subscale was not significantly correlated to social desirability in the Constantine (2000) or Ponterotto et al. (1996) studies but was in the most recent Constantine et al. (2001) study. Constantine et al. interpreted this finding as those who are low in multicultural awareness have a particularly high need to appear desirable to others. This explanation seems plausible to us.

With reference to the Awareness subscale, criterion-related evidence is indicated through

significant relationships, in expected directions, with White racial identity statuses (Alpert, 1995; Constantine et al., 2001; Vinson & Neimeyer, 2000), empathic ability (Constantine, 2000), counselor self-efficacy, attitudes toward lesbians and gays, sexual orientation counselor competence (Bidell, 2001), experiences with diversity (Kocarek et al., 2001), and overt and subtle racial bias (Constantine et al., 2001; Ponterotto et al., 1995). Given that a defining characteristic of the Awareness subscale is its measurement of counselor cultural bias, it would be expected that this subscale would correlate more highly than the Knowledge subscale with measures of racial bias. From Table 9.3, it is evident that the magnitude of the correlations between the Awareness subscale and the New Racism Scale (Constantine et al., 2001) and the Quick Discrimination Index (Ponterotto et al., 1995) was in fact higher in most instances. Raising some doubt regarding the criterion-related evidence for the subscale was the fact that it did not correlate significantly to ratings of case conceptualization skills (Constantine & Ladany, 2000).

The most recent AERA/APA/NCTE (1999) testing standards recommend calculating effect sizes for criterion-based studies. Incorporating the correlations listed in Table 9.3 and using Cohen's (1988) effect size classifications— where $r < .3$ equals a small effect size, $r = .3$ to .49 equals a medium effect size, and $r = .5 +$ equals a large effect size—it was found that for the Knowledge subscale, 44% of correlations had small effect sizes, 36% were medium effect sizes, and 20% were large effect sizes. Regarding the Awareness subscale, 69% of correlations had small effect sizes, 22% were medium effect sizes, and 9% were large effect sizes. From the effect size analysis, it is clear that the Knowledge subscale exhibited stronger criterion relationships with expected variables than did the Awareness subscale.

RELIABILITY

Ten-month test-retest reliability coefficients for the MCAS were .70 for the Knowledge/ Skills subscale and .73 for the Awareness subscale (Manese et al., 2001). Given the length of the test-retest period, these coefficients are deemed very satisfactory.

Internal consistency reliability (using coefficient alpha) data across the subscales are summarized in Table 9.4. Coefficient alphas for the Knowledge subscale ranged from a low of .78 (New Mexico sample in Study 4 in Ponterotto et al., 1996) to a high of .93 (in Studies 1, 2, and 5 [New York sample] in Ponterotto et al., 1996). With the exception of the small New Mexico sample, all coefficient alphas for the Knowledge subscale fell at .85 or higher, where the mean was .90 (across 22 samples, $N = 3,304$) and the median was .91. With regard to the Awareness subscale, coefficient alphas ranged from a low of .67 (Study 5 in Ponterotto et al., 1996) to a high of .89 (Constantine & Ladany, 2000; Constantine et al., 2002). With the exception of one study in Ponterotto et al. (1996), all coefficient alphas fell above .70, where the mean was .78 (across the 22 samples, $N = 3,304$) and the median was .78.

The pattern of coefficient alphas across the subscales indicates that the Knowledge subscale is more reliable (internally consistent) than the Awareness subscale. There are two reasons for this finding, in our view. First, given the principal component factor analysis construction of the MCAS/MCKAS, the first factor, with its higher eigenvalue and greater number of items (refer to Ponterotto et al., 1996), is likely to be more internally consistent. Second, the Knowledge susbscale is more defined and focused and less broad and "fuzzy" than the Awareness subscale. Broad constructs result in lower coefficient alphas than narrow constructs (see discussions in Ponterotto et al., 2000; Tracey, 2000). We believe that the Awareness construct has been more elusive to scale developers, as evidenced by the lower correlation of this construct across multicultural competency instruments relative to the Knowledge subscale across the same instruments (see Constantine & Ladany, 2000; Ponterotto et al., 2000; Pope-Davis & Dings, 1995).

SUBSCALE INDEPENDENCE

The model of multicultural counseling competence (i.e., Sue et al., 1992; Sue et al., 1998) on which the MCAS/MCKAS and other such instruments are based hypothesizes that the separate components or factors—in this case, Knowledge and Awareness—are only moderately related. Low to moderate correlations among the subscales justify the independent interpretations of the factors or subscales in research studies.

Table 9.5 presents the subscale intercorrelations among the Knowledge, Awareness, and total scores of the MCAS/MCKAS. Understandably, one would expect high correlations between the instrument total score and its subscales, particularly the Knowledge subscale, as that factor possesses a majority of instrument items. Reviewing Table 9.5, it is evident that the expected pattern of correlations is borne out. The MCAS/MCKAS total score is very highly correlated with the Knowledge subscale and highly correlated with the Awareness subscale. Most important, the Knowledge and Awareness subscales evidenced lower to moderate intercorrelations. Specifically, these correlations ranged from a low of .04 (Ponterotto, Gretchen, et al., 2002, Study 2) to a high of .50 (Vinson & Neimeyer, 2000). The mean subscale intercorrelation across studies was .36, with the median falling at .37. This pattern of correlations between the Knowledge and Awareness subscales supports the interpretation that the two constructs are fairly independent and should be analyzed separately in research studies.

Table 9.4   Coefficient Alphas for Total MCKAS/MCAS and Subscale Scores

Source	n	Total	Knowledge/ Skills	Awareness
Bidell (2001)[a]	287	0.93	0.92	0.78
Constantine (2000)[a]	225	0.91	0.90	0.89
Constantine, Juby, and Liang (2001)[a]	113	0.85	0.85	0.75
Constantine, Gloria, and Ladany (2002)[a]	259	0.89	0.90	0.89
Constantine and Ladany (2000)[a]	135	0.89	0.90	0.75
Detabali (1995)[b]	63	—	0.92	0.77
Kocarek, Talbot, Batka, and Anderson (2001)[b]	120	0.91	0.91	0.83
Manese, Wu, and Nepomuceno (2001)[b]—Pretest	35	—	0.90	0.76
Posttest			0.88	0.78
Ponterotto et al. (1996)[b]—Study 1	126	0.93	0.93	0.78
Study 2—Sample 1	72	0.93	0.93	0.81
Study 2—Sample 2	42	0.90	0.91	0.76
Study 2—Sample 3	45	0.92	0.93	0.78
Study 5—Total	414	0.92	0.92	0.79
Study 5—Iowa	126	0.91	0.92	0.75
Study 5—National	141	0.90	0.91	0.67
Study 5—New Mexico	29	0.75	0.78	0.78
Study 5—New York	118	0.92	0.93	0.78
Ponterotto, Gretchen, et al. (2002)—Study 1[b]	525	—	0.92	0.79
Study 2[a]	196	—	0.85	0.85
Pope-Davis and Dings (1994)[b]	92	—	0.90	0.72
Pope-Davis, Reynolds, and Dings (1994)[b]	141	—	0.92	0.75

NOTE: Dashes indicate data not reported.

a. 32-item scale.
b. 45-item scale.

SUMMARY AND RESEARCHER GUIDELINES

The Multicultural Counseling Awareness Scales (MCAS and MCKAS) are frequently used self-report measures of perceived multicultural counseling knowledge and awareness. It is recommended that the latest 32-item, two-factor version known as the Multicultural Counseling Knowledge and Awareness Scale be used for subsequent research. The MCKAS is brief (relative to the MAKSS and MCI),

possessing a moderate degree of validity and a moderate to high degree of both internal consistency and test-retest reliability. Furthermore, according to a recent comparison of multicultural competency instruments, "The MCKAS may be the least influenced by high social desirability attitudes on the part of respondents" (Constantine & Ladany, 2000, p. 161).

At present, there is little available research on the relationship between MCKAS scores and actual skill and success in counseling

Table 9.5   MCKAS/MCAS Subscale Intercorrelations

Source	n	Total	Knowledge/ Skills	Awareness
Alpert (1995)[a]				
Knowledge/skills	35	—	—	0.49**
Bidell (2001)[b]				
Knowledge/Skills	287	0.95**	—	—
Awareness	287	0.74**	0.42**	—
Constantine (2000)[b]				
Knowledge/Skills	225	0.90**	—	—
Awareness	225	0.34**	0.34**	—
Constantine, Juby, and Liang (2001)[b]				
Knowledge/Skills	113	0.90***	—	—
Awareness	113	0.62***	0.22**	—
Constantine, Gloria, and Ladany (2002)[b]				
Knowledge/Skills	259	0.62**	—	—
Awareness	259	0.13*	0.32**	—
Constantine and Ladany (2000)[b]				
Knowledge/Skills	135	0.94**	—	—
Awareness	135	0.61**	0.30**	—
Kocarek, Talbot, Batka, and Anderson (2001)[b]				
Knowledge/Skills	120	0.93***	—	—
Awareness	120	0.66***	0.33**	—
Ponterotto et al. (1996)[a]				
Knowledge/Skills-Study 1	126	0.96***	—	—
Awareness-Study 1	126	0.58***	0.37**	—
Knowledge/Skills—Study 2, Sample 1	72	—	—	0.45**
Knowledge/Skills—Study 2, Sample 2	42	—	—	0.35*
Knowledge/Skills—Study 2, Sample 3	45	—	—	0.47**
Knowledge/Skills—Study 5	414	0.96**	—	—
Awareness—Study 5	414	0.69**	0.44**	—
Ponterotto, Gretchen, et al. (2002)				
Knowledge/Skills-Study 2[b]	196	—	—	0.04
Pope-Davis and Dings (1994)[a]				
Knowledge/Skills	92	—	—	0.39**
Pope-Davis, Dings, and Ottavi (1995)[a]	126			
Knowledge/Skills		—	—	0.39***
Pope-Davis, Reynolds, and Dings (1994)[a]				
Knowledge/Skills	141	—	—	0.37**
Vinson and Neimeyer (2000)[a]				
Knowledge/Skills—White students	65	—	—	0.31**
Knowledge/Skills—Minority students	22	—	—	0.50*

NOTE: Dashes indicate data not reported.

a. 45-item scale.
b. 32-item scale.

*$p < .05$; **$p < .01$; ***$p < .001$.

culturally diverse clients. This is a much-needed area for further investigation. Future research can also focus on updating the conceptual base for the knowledge items as the field continues to mature (e.g., Ponterotto, Casas, Suzuki, & Alexander, 2001) and on bolstering and revising the Awareness subscale given its skewed distribution and minimal criterion-related evidence.

Given the limitations of the MCKAS and other self-report instruments, psychologists should only use the scales for group research purposes. The instruments can also be used as pretest/posttest measures in evaluating programs and training interventions. The MCKAS should not be used as a tool for individual decision making as, for example, in the case of merit pay and promotion decisions, graduate student applicant evaluation, and so forth. Recently, the senior author of this chapter was contacted by a large managed care company requesting to use the MCKAS to screen mental health providers for their approved listing. The request was denied as the MCKAS is not validated for individual selection purposes.

It is recommended that researchers using the MCKAS include the following information in their written reports:

1. a detailed description of the respondents completing the instrument;
2. careful elaboration of the conditions and mechanisms of testing, including administration and collection procedures, prebriefing and debriefing content, and ethical care;
3. for every use of the MCKAS, researchers should report the mean and standard deviation, as well as the coefficient alphas for each subscale;
4. researchers should not lose sight of the limitations of paper-and-pencil self-report measures.

Recently, qualitative research methods were characterized as "The Fifth Force" in psychology (cf. Ponterotto, 2002; Ponterotto, Costa, & Werner-Lin, 2002), and we urge researchers to adopt such methods, particularly intensive interviewing (in constructivist and critical theory paradigms) and participant observation, into the study of counseling competency, process, and effectiveness.

REFERENCES

Alpert, L. M. (1995). *Comparing effects of didactic versus experiential training strategies on counselor trainees' multicultural awareness and knowledge.* Doctoral dissertation, School of Education, Barry University, Miami, FL.

American Educational Research Association, American Psychological Association, National Council on Measurement in Education (AERA/APA/NCTE). (1999). *Standards for educational and psychological testing.* Washington, DC: American Educational Research Association.

Bagozzi, R. P., & Heatherton, T. F. (1994). A general approach to representing multifaceted personality constructs: Application to state self-esteem. *Structural Equation Modeling, 1,* 35-67.

Bidell, M. P. (2001, August). *Extending multicultural counselor competency to lesbian/gay/bisexual clients: The development and validation of the Sexual Orientation Counselor Competency Scale (SOCCS).* Poster presented at the annual meeting of the American Psychological Association, Washington, DC.

Carrillo, P. (1997). *The relationship of multicultural sensitivity of the psychotherapist on length of treatment.* Doctoral dissertation, Department of Psychology, Our Lady of the Lake University, San Antonio, TX.

Cohen, J. (1988). *Statistical power analysis for the behavioral sciences* (2nd ed.). Hillsdale, NJ: Lawrence Erlbaum.

Constantine, M. G. (2000). Social desirability attitudes, sex, and affective and cognitive empathy as predictors of self-reported multicultural counseling competence. *The Counseling Psychologist, 28,* 857-872.

Constantine, M. G., Gloria, A. M., & Ladany, N. (2002). The factor structure underlying three self-report multicultural competence scales. *Cultural Diversity and Ethnic Minority Psychology, 8,* 334-345.

Constantine, M. G., Juby, H. L., & Liang, J. J. C. (2001). Examining self-reported multicultural counseling competence and race-related attitudes among White marital and family therapists. *Journal of Marital and Family Therapy, 27,* 353-362.

Constantine, M. G., & Ladany, N. (2000). Self-report multicultural counseling competence scales: Their relation to social desirability attitudes and multicultural case conceptualization ability. *Journal of Counseling Psychology, 47,* 155-164.

Constantine, M. G., & Ladany, N. (2001). New visions for defining and assessing multicultural counseling competence. In J. G. Ponterotto, J. M. Casas, L. A. Suzuki, & C. M. Alexander (Eds.), *Handbook of multicultural counseling* (2nd ed., pp. 482-498). Thousand Oaks, CA: Sage.

D'Andrea, M., Daniels, J., & Heck, R. (1991). Evaluating the impact of multicultural counseling training. *Journal of Counseling and Development, 70,* 143-150.

Detabali, R. M. (1995). *Cultural diversity awareness of vocational rehabilitation counselors in the state of Tennessee.* M.S. thesis, University of Tennessee, Knoxville.

Dizon, V. F. (1997). *How culturally aware are art therapists? Assessing the general multicultural knowledge and awareness of art therapists.* M.S. thesis, Art Therapy, Eastern Virginia Medical School, Norfolk, VA.

Kocarek, C. E., Talbot, D. M., Batka, J. C., & Anderson, M. Z. (2001). Reliability and validity of three measures of multicultural competency. *Journal of Counseling and Development, 79,* 486-496.

Manese, J. E., Wu, J. T., & Nepomuceno, C. A. (2001). The effect of training on multicultural counseling competencies: An exploratory study over a ten-year period. *Journal of Multicultural Counseling and Development, 29,* 31-40.

Ponterotto, J. G. (2002). Qualitative research methods as the fifth force in psychology. *The Counseling Psychologist, 30,* 394-406.

Ponterotto, J. G., & Alexander, C. M. (1996). Assessing the multicultural competence of counselors and clinicians. In L. A. Suzuki, P. Meller, & J. G. Ponterotto (Eds.), *Handbook of multicultural assessment* (pp. 651-672). San Francisco: Jossey-Bass.

Ponterotto, J. G., Burkard, A., Rieger, B. P., Grieger, I., D'Onofrio, A., Dubuisson, A., et al. (1995). Development and initial validation of the Quick Discrimination Index (QDI). *Educational and Psychological Measurement, 55,* 1026-1031.

Ponterotto, J. G., Casas, J. M., Suzuki, L. A., & Alexander, C. M. (Eds.). (2001). *Handbook of multicultural counseling* (2nd ed.). Thousand Oaks, CA: Sage.

Ponterotto, J. G., Costa, C. I., & Werner-Lin, A. (2002). Research perspectives in cross-cultural counseling. In P. B. Pedersen, J. G. Draguns, W. J. Lonner, & J. E. Trimble (Eds.), *Counseling across cultures* (5th ed., pp. 395-420). Thousand Oaks, CA: Sage.

Ponterotto, J. G., Fuertes, J. N., & Chen, E. C. (2000). Models of multicultural counseling. In S. D. Brown & R. W. Lent (Eds.), *Handbook of counseling psychology* (3rd ed., pp. 639-669). New York: John Wiley.

Ponterotto, J. G., Gretchen, D., Utsey, S. O., Rieger, B. P., & Austin, R. (2002). A revision of the Multicultural Counseling Awareness Scale (MCAS). *Journal of Multicultural Counseling and Development, 30,* 153-180.

Ponterotto, J. G., Rieger, B. T., Barrett, A., Harris, G., Sparks, R., Sanchez, C. M., et al. (1996). Development and initial validation of the Multicultural Counseling Awareness Scale. In G. R. Sodowsky & J. C. Impara (Eds.), *Multicultural assessment in counseling and clinical psychology* (pp. 247-282). Lincoln, NE: Buros Institute of Mental Measurements.

Ponterotto, J. G., Rieger, B. T., Barrett, A., & Sparks, R. (1994). Assessing multicultural counseling competence: A review of instrumentation. *Journal of Counseling and Development, 72,* 316-322.

Ponterotto, J. G., Sanchez, C. M., & Magids, D. (1991, August). *Initial development of the Multicultural Counseling Awareness Scale.* Paper presented at the annual meeting of the

American Psychological Association, San Francisco.

Pope-Davis, D. B., & Dings, J. G. (1994). An empirical comparison of two self-report multicultural counseling competency inventories. *Measurement and Evaluation in Counseling and Development, 27*, 93-101.

Pope-Davis, D. B., & Dings, J. G. (1995). The assessment of multicultural counseling competencies. In J. G. Ponterotto, J. M. Casas, L. A. Suzuki, & C. M. Alexander (Eds.), *Handbook of multicultural counseling* (pp. 287-311). Thousand Oaks, CA: Sage.

Pope-Davis, D. B., Dings, J. G., & Ottavi, T. M. (1995). The relationship of multicultural counseling competency with demographic and educational variables. *Iowa Psychologist, 40*(1), 12-13.

Pope-Davis, D. B., Reynolds, A. L., & Dings, J. G. (1994). Multicultural competencies of doctoral interns at university counseling centers: An exploratory investigation. *Professional Psychology: Research and Practice, 25*, 466-470.

Sodowsky, G. R., Taffe, R. C., Gutkin, T., & Wise, S. L. (1994). Development of the Multicultural Counseling Inventory: A self-report measure of multicultural competencies. *Journal of Counseling Psychology, 41*, 137-148.

Sue, D. W., Arredondo, P., & McDavis, R. J. (1992). Multicultural counseling competencies and standards: A call to the profession. *Journal of Multicultural Counseling and Development, 20*, 45-52.

Sue, D. W., Bernier, J. B., Durran, M., Feinberg, L., Pedersen, P., Smith, E., et al. (1982). Position paper: Cross-cultural counseling competencies. *The Counseling Psychologist, 10*, 45-52.

Sue, D. W., Carter, R. T., Casas, J. M., Fouad, N. A., Ivey, A. E., Jensen, M., et al. (1998). *Multicultural counseling competencies: Individual and organizational development.* Thousand Oaks, CA: Sage.

Tracey, T. J. G. (2000). Issues in the analysis and interpretation of quantitative data: Reinstitutionalization of the null hypothesis test. In S. D. Brown & R. W. Lent (Eds.), *Handbook of counseling psychology* (3rd ed., pp. 177-198). New York: John Wiley.

Vinson, T. S., & Neimeyer, G. J. (2000). The relationship between racial identity development and multicultural counseling competence. *Journal of Multicultural Counseling and Development, 28*, 177-192.

10

New Developments in the Assessment of Multicultural Competence

The Multicultural Awareness-Knowledge-Skills Survey–Teachers Form

MICHAEL D'ANDREA
JUDY DANIELS
MARY JO NOONAN
University of Hawaii

Multiculturalism has emerged as a powerful sociopolitical and theoretical force in our society in general and in the fields of counseling (D'Andrea & Daniels, in press; Ponterotto, Casas, Suzuki, & Alexander, 2001), education (Banks & McGee-Banks, 1997), psychology (Pedersen, Draguns, Lonner, & Trimble, 2002), and social work (Brueggemann, 1996) in particular. Much of the impetus for the emergence of multiculturalism as a new and powerful sociopolitical and professional force comes from (a) the unprecedented demographic changes that are occurring in our contemporary society and (b) a growing awareness that counselors, teachers, psychologists, and social workers must acquire new competencies if they are to work effectively, ethically, and respectfully within the context of a rapidly changing, culturally diverse 21st-century society (D'Andrea, 2000; Lewis, Lewis, Daniels, & D'Andrea, 2003).

THE CULTURAL-RACIAL TRANSFORMATION OF THE UNITED STATES

The unprecedented nature of the demographic changes that are occurring in our society is rooted in the fact that the United States is rapidly shifting from a nation that has historically been composed of a majority of people who come from White, Western European, English-speaking backgrounds to a country in which most of its residents will come from non-White, non-European, non-English-speaking groups (D'Andrea & Daniels, 2001). Although most researchers agree that this unprecedented demographic shift is likely to be completed by 2050, the results of the 2000 census indicate that we are already well on our way to becoming a much more pluralistic society than at any other time in U.S. history. As the results of the 2000 census indicate, more than 30% of the total number people in the United States presently come from African American, Asian American, Latino/Latina, Native American, and Pacific Island backgrounds (U.S. Bureau of the Census, 2001). This represents a 6% increase in the 24% of the total number of persons who reported themselves as coming from non-White backgrounds during the 1990 census.

A more detailed analysis of the most recent census indicates a significant increase in the number of U.S. cities that are currently composed of a majority of persons who come from non-White, non-European backgrounds in comparison to 1990. This includes millions of African American, Asian American, Latino/Latina, Native American, and Pacific Islander children and adolescents whose educational and psychological needs are routinely placed in the hands of U.S. public school teachers and counselors (Pedersen & Carey, 2003). Numerous multicultural counseling researchers point to differential birth rates among persons from White and non-White groups and the dramatic increase in the number of immigrants coming from Asia, Mexico, and South America as major factors that underlie the demographic changes taking place in the United States (Atkinson, Morten, & Sue, 1998).

As a result of these changes, counselors, teachers, psychologists, and social workers are increasingly being called on to work with persons who are culturally and racially different from themselves. These differences extend far beyond the obvious phenotypic distinctions that distinguish persons from different cultural, racial, and ethnic backgrounds and include more fundamental worldview, value, attitudinal, interpersonal style, and other behavioral differences as well. These latter differences result in significant variations in the way culturally and racially diverse persons construct the meaning of, associate value with, and respond to many of the traditional public education and mental health care services that are offered to them in the United States (Daniels, Arredondo, & D'Andrea, 2001a, 2001b; Pedersen & Carey, 2003).

RECOGNIZING THE NEED TO BECOME CULTURALLY COMPETENT

The rapid increase in the number of persons from diverse cultural-racial groups who hold different views about education and adhere to different constructions of what constitutes "mental health" presents educators and mental health practitioners with a host of new challenges. Although these challenges have been discussed in detail by numerous multicultural advocates over the past 30 years, they essentially require counselors, teachers, psychologists, and social workers to acquire new professional competencies that will enable them to work more effectively, respectfully, and ethically among persons from culturally and racially diverse populations.

Several multicultural theorists and researchers have also suggested that educators and mental health practitioners who fail to acquire these kinds of professional competencies do much more than lower their own ability to work effectively and ethically with persons from diverse student and clientpopulations. In elaborating on this point, these theorists and researchers insist that the failure of U.S. public schools and mental health care systems to effectively address the educational and psychological needs of millions of children, adolescents, and adults from culturally and racially diverse backgrounds can be directly linked to the lack of cultural competence by teachers, counselors, psychologists, and social workers (Banks & McGee-Banks, 1997; Pedersen & Carey, 2003; U.S. Department of Health and Human Services, 2001). This systemic failure

(a) prevents many children and adolescents from realizing their educational and intellectual potential during their formative years;
(b) impedes their ability to secure the resources necessary to achieve a heightened sense of mental health and personal well-being; and
(c) in much broader and abstract terms, compromises the spiritual health and psychological well-being of our democratic society as important values and principles on which our nation was founded are denied or ignored (D'Andrea & Daniels, in press; U.S. Department of Health and Human Services, 2001; West, 1999).

To increase their future viability, relevance, and respectability, educators and mental health professionals have been strongly urged to become more culturally competent so they might be able to work more effectively and ethically with individuals from diverse cultural-ethnic groups in general, especially among persons who come from non-White, non-European backgrounds, as they will soon constitute the majority of people in the United States (Sue & Sue, 1999; U.S. Department of Health and Human Services, 2001). Although this suggestion seems reasonable in light of the rapid cultural-racial transformation of the United States, several obstacles impede a fuller integration of cultural competencies into the

fields of counseling, education, psychology, and social work.

Among these obstacles include various forms of resistance and apathy that continue to be manifested by many educators and mental health practitioners when it comes to dealing with the issue of multicultural competence (D'Andrea & Daniels, 1996; Kiselica, 1999; Pedersen & Carey, 2003). These forms of resistance and apathy are commonly exhibited in a number of ways, including the following:

(a) a general resistance to direct the sort of time, energy, and individual/institutional resources that are necessary to foster a greater level of multicultural competence in the fields of education and mental health;
(b) inaccurate and negative comments regarding what some persons in these fields perceive to be ambiguous and unclear definitions of the meaning of multicultural competence;
(c) a reluctance to acknowledge the tremendous strides that have been made in defining and operationalizing the term *multicultural competence* over the past 25 years; and
(d) criticisms about the lack of valid and reliable assessment tools that are available to measure teachers' and mental health professionals' level of multicultural competence (Pedersen et al., 2002; Pope-Davis & Coleman, 1997).

Given the serious problems that teachers and mental health professionals will predictably encounter if they fail to acquire the types of professional competencies that would otherwise enable them to work more effectively and ethically in our contemporary society, we believe that they are presented with two critical options. On one hand, educators and mental health professionals can decide to make a heightened commitment to invest the time and energy that are necessary to become more culturally competent, or they can run the risk of becoming increasingly viewed in negative and even hostile terms by many persons from diverse cultural-racial groups who have constructed different thoughts and feelings about education and mental health care in general and teaching, learning, and personal wellness in particular (Banks & McGee-Banks, 1997; Locke, Myers, & Herr, 2001; Pedersen et al., 2002).

DEFINING, OPERATIONALIZING, AND ASSESSING MULTICULTURAL COMPETENCE

To effectively meet the challenges of multi-culturalism, leaders in the fields of education and mental health must do much more than simply become knowledgeable of the various ways in which their work is affected by the demographic changes that are taking place in our society. In short, they need to become more knowledgeable about what it means to be *culturally competent* and provide the types of institutional resources that will enable educators and mental health practitioners to continue their professional development in this area.

Although these fields have made progress in terms of increasing their constituents' awareness of the need to become culturally competent, the counseling profession has taken a clear lead in defining, institutionalizing, and operationalizing the multicultural competence construct during the past decade (Daniels et al., 2002; Sue et al., 1998). The Association for Multicultural Counseling and Development (AMCD), a division within the American Counseling Association (ACA), has arguably been the most significant professional organizational entity to promote a clearer definition of *multicultural competence* during this time period.

Among its most significant contributions in this area is the AMCD's efforts to develop, endorse, and publish a set of 31 multicultural counseling competencies that represent minimum standards counselors are expected to acquire prior to working with persons from culturally and racially different backgrounds (Sue, Arredondo, & McDavis, 1992). Since being published in 1992, these competencies have had and continue to have a reverberating impact in the fields of counseling and psychology. This reverberation is in part reflected in the fact that (a) six other ACA divisions have formally endorsed these competencies, and (b) they have become the cornerstone of many multicultural development training efforts (Pope-Davis & Coleman, 1997; Sue et al., 1998).

The AMCD competencies were further enhanced when Arredondo and her colleagues published an article in 1996 that outlines specific strategies for operationalizing these competencies. Although the development, institutionalization, and operationalization of the AMCD competencies represent major advancements that help clarify the meaning of this complex construct, it is important to acknowledge that all of the persons who are responsible for these scholarly and organizational advancements have repeatedly emphasized that the definition and operationalization of multicultural competence need to be viewed as an ongoing, fluid, and developmental process. In other words, rather than viewing the AMCD competencies in static terms, it has repeatedly been stressed that they need to be thought of as an initial starting point that will evolve and change as the multicultural counseling knowledge base expands and our collective understanding of cultural competence matures.

In addition to these advancements, several researchers have also developed a number of instruments that are designed to assess counseling practitioners' and trainees' multicultural competence. These measures include the (a) Multicultural Awareness-Knowledge-Skills Survey–Counselor Edition (MAKSS-CE) (D'Andrea, Daniels, & Heck, 1991), (b) Multicultural Counseling Knowledge and

Awareness Scale (MCKAS) (Ponterotto, Gretchen, Utsey, Rieger, & Austin, 2001), (c) Multicultural Counseling Inventory (MCI) (Sodowsky, Taffe, Gutkin, & Wise, 1994), and (d) Cross-Cultural Counseling Inventory– Revised (CCCI-R) (LaFromboise, Coleman, & Hernandez, 1991). Although all of these assessment tools provide counselors with a useful means to evaluate their own and others' level of multicultural competence, the MAKSS-CE has been used extensively since its publication in 1991. Commenting on the extensive use of the MAKSS-CE, Kim and his colleagues explain that this instrument has been used by more than 600 researchers in over 600 universities, mental health agencies, and businesses in six different countries since its development, thus making it one of the most widely used instruments of its kind (Kim, Cartwright, Asay, & D'Andrea, 2002).

Given the popularity of the MAKSS-CE and being aware of the research that has been done to ascertain its validity and reliability (D'Andrea et al., 1991; Kim et al., 2002), we decided to develop modified versions of this instrument to serve the needs of colleagues in other professional fields. The new versions of the MAKSS-CE were specifically designed to assess teachers' and social workers' level of multicultural competence. Although efforts are currently under way to test the validity and reliability of a newly developed instrument that was designed for social workers (D'Andrea, Fong, & Daniels, 2003), we have completed a study that explores the effectiveness of a modified version of the MAKSS-CE that measures the multicultural competence of public school teachers and undergraduate and graduate students in teacher education programs. This modified version of the MAKSS-CE is called the Multicultural Awareness-Knowledge-Skills Survey for Teachers (MAKSS–Form T) (D'Andrea, Daniels, & Noonan, 1994).

In developing the MAKSS–Form T, we hoped to provide a useful and practical tool that would (a) aid educators in evaluating their own level of multicultural competence and (b) provide school counselors with a valid and reliable instrument to evaluate their efforts to foster teachers' competence in this area. In addition to these considerations, three other factors led us to develop and test the validity and reliability of the MAKSS–Form T.

First, we recognize that school counselors are well positioned to help teachers develop the kinds of multicultural competencies that are necessary to work more effectively, respectfully, and ethically with culturally and racially diverse student groups. We are also aware that many educators are indeed interested in becoming more culturally competent and would welcome help from counselors in this regard (Pedersen & Carey, 2003).

Second, despite the interest that many educators demonstrate in terms of wanting to increase their current level of cultural competence and the important role that counselors can play in assisting them in this area, little progress has been made in terms of developing and testing instruments that effectively measure teachers' multicultural competence (D'Andrea, 1995).

Third, school counselors have told us that their own efforts to help educators develop an increased level of multicultural competence are hampered by the lack of available assessment tools in this area. These persons have further pointed out that such instruments would indeed be very useful in helping teachers and counselors (a) accurately identify the specific strengths they have already developed in this area and (b) specify those competency areas that need to be further developed in the future. By having assessment tools available that provide this sort of information, counselors would be better able to use their role as consultant-trainers (Baker & Gerler, 2001) to support teachers in their quest to become more culturally competent.

AN EXPANDED VIEW OF COUNSELORS' ROLES IN THE SCHOOLS

Counselors play numerous roles in the school setting. Besides providing direct counseling services to students in need of personal or academic assistance (Lewis et al., 2003; Schmidt, 1993), many offer classroom-based instructional services that fall under the general rubric of *guidance activities* (Baker, 2000). These activities are primarily designed to foster the psychological development and personal well-being of large numbers of students who have not manifested personal difficulties within the school setting (Baker & Gerler, 2001; Muro & Kottman, 1995). In addition to these roles, school counselors also serve an important role as a professional consultant-trainer for those teachers who are interested in learning more effective ways of dealing with their students (Duncan, 1995; Lewis et al., 2003).

Although all of these roles are indeed important, several surveys that have been conducted over the past 25 years indicate that teachers view the consultant trainer role as one of the most important functions that counselors play in schools (Baker & Gerler, 2001; Bardon, 1976; Curtis & Zins, 1981; Duncan, 1995; Gutkin, 1980). A particular area that is increasingly becoming the focus of much counselor-teacher consultation and training interactions involves a growing demand for counselors to help teachers develop the kinds of cultural competencies that will enable them to work more effectively and respectfully among culturally and racially different students (Pedersen & Carey, 2003). For these services to be useful in fostering teachers' growth in this area, they must be provided by counselors who have themselves acquired the types of multicultural competencies that have been outlined by the AMCD.

CULTURALLY COMPETENT SCHOOL COUNSELORS: A VALUABLE RESOURCE FOR TEACHERS

Culturally competent school counselors serve as valuable resources to teachers who are interested in developing new knowledge and skills in multicultural education. Besides offering individual consultation services for teachers who are interested in becoming more culturally competent, school counselors are encouraged to use group consultation training services so that they might be able to assist larger numbers of teachers in expanding their current level of multicultural proficiency (Lewis et al., 2003).

To effectively implement and evaluate these types of group consultation training services, counselors need to be able to accurately assess teachers' present level of multicultural competence (D'Andrea, 1995). In doing so, counselors are better able to tailor group consultation training services to meet educators' specific needs and avoid underestimating or overestimating their current level of multicultural competence.

Education experts have suggested that efforts to promote teachers' multicultural competence through the use of counselor-led consultation and training activities should focus on a number of specific components. This includes using a strength-based approach to consultation and training that builds on teachers' current level of multicultural awareness, knowledge, and skills (Burstein, Cabello, & Hamann, 1993; Fox, Kuhlman, & Sales, 1988; Lynch & Hanson, 1992).

Although it is important to evaluate teachers' level of multicultural competence in these three areas prior to providing multicultural group consultation and training services, counselors are also urged to assess the impact of these services by conducting posttest evaluations to determine the degree to which teachers report an increase in their multicultural awareness, knowledge, and skills as a result of participating in these kinds of professional development interventions. The results of such evaluative efforts can also be shared with school administrators to (a) demonstrate the positive value of these kinds of group consultation and training projects and (b) solicit administrative and fiscal support for the continuing implementation of these services in the future.

Although there are many reasons to assess teachers' multicultural competence when implementing consultation training services in the school setting, even the most conscientious and committed counselor is hampered by the lack of instruments that are currently available to measure educators' level of competence in this area. In fact, upon reviewing the counseling and teacher education literature, we were only able to locate three instruments that were specifically developed to measure teachers' competencies in this area (Burstein & Cabello, 1989; Burstein et al., 1993; Tran, Young, & DiLella, 1994). We also noticed several major shortcomings with all three of these instruments.

One of the major problems with these instruments lies in the operational definition of the construct that they were designed to measure (i.e., multicultural competency). Although multicultural education experts generally agree that teachers need to demonstrate competency in three distinct areas (multicultural awareness, knowledge, and skills) to be considered "culturally competent" (Burnstein & Cabello, 1989; Pedersen & Carey, 2003), none of the instruments currently available was designed to measure all three of these areas. In addition to this limitation, it was disconcerting to note that no research had been done to test the validity or reliability of any of these instruments. In light of the need to develop and test the validity and reliability of other instruments that are intentionally designed to provide school counselors and teachers with an accurate measure of their

current level of multicultural competence, we undertook the following study.

METHOD

Participants

Participants in this study included 171 undergraduate and graduate students attending a large, public, research-based university in the western part of the United States. All of the research participants were enrolled in various teacher education programs (e.g., elementary education, secondary education, and special education) at the university. Of the participants, 102 were experienced educators who had worked or were currently working in public schools.

The participants' cultural backgrounds were representative of the diverse student body at the university where they were enrolled. A breakdown of the cultural-ethnic-racial backgrounds of the sample group is as follows: 78 (46%) Japanese Americans, 34 (19%) Caucasians, 12 (7%) Filipinos, 11 (7%) Hawaiians, 8 (4%) Chinese Americans, 2 (1%) from Hispanic backgrounds, 12 (7%) biracial persons, and 14 (9%) participants who indicated that they were from some "other" cultural-ethnic-racial background but did not provide any more specific information.

A breakdown of the participants' gender resulted in 46 (27%) males and 125 (73%) females participating in this investigation. Of the participants, 53 (31%) were undergraduate students in education, 16 (10%) were enrolled in a special postbaccalaureate professional development program for teachers, 98 (57%) were enrolled in a master's degree program in special education, and 4 (2%) were completing their doctoral degree studies in secondary education.

Instrument

The MAKSS–Form T is a self-administered test that was developed to measure teachers' level of multicultural competence (D'Andrea et al., 1994). This instrument is divided into two sections. The first section consists of a set of items that provide descriptive information about the individual who completes the MAKSS–Form T (e.g., the individual's gender, educational level, cultural-ethnic-racial background, etc.). The second section consists of 60 survey items that were equally divided into three subscales. These subscales were designed to provide a measure of teachers' multicultural education awareness, knowledge, and skills, respectively. All of the items are presented in a multiple-choice format in which the individual is asked to choose between one of four possible responses to each question or statement contained on the survey. The content and format of the MAKSS–Form T were largely taken from a similar instrument (MAKSS-CE) that was described earlier in this chapter.

Procedure

The MAKSS–Form T was administered in group settings by the researchers and other colleagues in the College of Education where they were employed. Students in seven different education classes were explained the purpose of the study and asked if they would voluntarily agree to complete the survey. All of the students agreed to complete the survey and did so at the beginning of one of their regularly scheduled class meetings. It took the participants between 15 and 20 minutes to complete the MAKSS–Form T.

RESULTS

Testing the Validity of the MAKSS–Form T

To test the construct validity of the MAKSS–Form T, we used a principal axis extraction and orthogonal (varimax) rotation of the participants' responses to the 60 survey

items. This generated a three-factor model that constituted 62% of the variance. Only those items that had high factor loadings (greater than .30) were included in the three factors (see Table 10.1).

As noted in Table 10.1, 8 items met the statistical criteria on the first factor. It was further noted that all of the items that loaded well on the first factor were designed to measure teachers' level of multicultural awareness. Thus, we referred to this factor as the multicultural Awareness subscale. In contrast, 13 items loaded well (.30 or above) and highly correlated with one another on the second factor. Upon examining the content of these items, we decided to label this factor the multicultural Knowledge subscale. Finally, the results of the factor analysis indicated that all 20 of the original items on what was referred to as the multicultural Skills subscale met the predetermined criteria described above. Thus, in conducting this statistical test, we were able to provide evidence that tentatively supported the construct validity of the MAKSS–Form T. A listing of the 41 survey items that met the statistical criteria described above and were included in the final design of the survey can be found in Appendix 10.A.

Testing the Reliability of the MAKSS–Form T

Separate Cronbach alpha reliability coefficients were calculated using the 8 items that comprised the multicultural Awareness subscale, the 13 items that made up the multicultural Knowledge subscale, and the 20 items on the multicultural Skills subscale. These tests resulted in the following reliability coefficients: .73 (Awareness subscale), .86 (Knowledge subscale), and .93 (Skills subscale).

Finally, we proceeded to test the intercorrelation of all three subscales. This resulted in the following intercorrelation coefficients: .62

Table 10.1   Summary of the Item Loadings Based on Conducting a Factor Analysis of the Three
MAKSS-A Subscales

Item Numbers	Awareness (MA)	Knowledge (MK)	Skills (MS)
Multicultural awareness (MA)			
MA-3	.47		
MA-4	.67		
MA-6	.67		
MA-8	.71		
MA-9	.59		
MA-10	.43		
MA-17	.37		
MA-19	.58		
Multicultural knowledge (MK)			
MK-1		.70	
MK-2		.70	
MK-3		.69	
MK-4		.57	
MK-5		.71	
MK-6		.70	
MK-7		.71	
MK-8		.69	
MK-9		.40	
MK-10		.53	
MK-11		.65	
MK-12		.57	
MK-19		.33	
Multicultural skills (MS)			
MS-1			.64
MS-2			.64
MS-3			.49
MS-4			.63
MS-5			.72
MS-6			.55
MS-7			.66
MS-8			.63
MS-9			.56
MS-10			.65
MS-11			.76
MS-12			.68
MS-13			.66
MS-14			.64
MS-15			.69
MS-16			.70
MS-17			.69
MS-18			.69
MS-19			.69
MS-20			.77

(Awareness and Knowledge), .54 (Knowledge and Skills), and .50 (Awareness and Skills). These findings suggest that the three subscales are related but distinct in terms of the global construct under investigation (i.e., multicultural competency).

DISCUSSION

Although the data generated in this study provide initial evidence that tentatively supports the validity and reliability of the MAKSS–Form T, it is important to point out a number of limitations in this study. First, the statistical procedures that were used in this study represent basic approaches in testing the validity and reliability of a newly developed instrument. With this limitation in mind, researchers are encouraged to use more sophisticated statistical methods to test other dimensions of the MAKSS–Form T's reliability (e.g., test-retest, interscorer reliability) and validity (e.g., concurrent, predictive validity) in future studies.

In thinking specifically about the importance of testing the predictive validity of this new instrument, researchers are encouraged to design future studies that compare teachers' self-reported scores on the MAKSS–Form T with independent ratings of their overall level of multicultural competence in classroom settings that are composed of students from diverse cultural-racial backgrounds (Pedersen & Carey, 2003). This recommendation would require researchers to implement a combination of quantitative and qualitative observational research strategies when testing for the predicative validity of the MAKSS–Form T.

Another important limitation of the present study involves the external validity of the reported results. Because the sample selected for this study was restricted to a nonrandomized group of experienced teachers and students who were enrolled in various undergraduate and graduate teacher education training programs at a large public university in the western part of the United States, the generalizability of the reported results is limited. One way to address this limitation is to have researchers use larger sample groups that are composed of experienced teachers as well as undergraduate and graduate students in education courses who are randomly selected from various parts of the United States.

Despite these limitations, it is important to acknowledge that results of this exploratory study represent the first time researchers have generated statistical evidence that provide tentative support for the validity and reliability of an instrument that was specifically designed to measure teachers' multicultural competence. Recognizing that these efforts represent small but important advancements in this area, professional educators and counselors are encouraged to consider using the MAKSS–Form T as a way to assess teachers' multicultural competence until other instruments are tested and prove to be effective in providing valid and reliable measures of this complex construct.

School counselors are particularly encouraged to think about the potential benefits that might be derived by using the MAKSS–Form T when offering consultation and training services among teachers who are interested in acquiring new cultural competencies. Besides offering teachers with a practical means of assessing their own multicultural strengths as well as helping them identify specific areas that are in need of improvement, counselors could use the results of the MAKSS–Form T to tailor their services in ways that best meet educators' needs. For instance, a group of teachers may have scored high on the multicultural education Awareness and Knowledge subscales but low on the multicultural education Skills subscale. When providing consultation training services with this particular group of educators, it would be important to present information and use activities (i.e., role-plays, demonstrations, etc.) that are intentionally aimed at fostering the development of new instructional skills that would enhance their overall effectiveness when working with students from culturally and racially diverse backgrounds. This assessment strategy can also be employed by faculty members in teacher education programs to more effectively and respectfully stimulate the multicultural competence of undergraduate and graduate students.

In closing, we believe that it would be a serious mistake for educators and mental health practitioners to view multiculturalism as a new "fad" that will soon pass from our attention. Thinking about multiculturalism in this overly simplistic way will undermine our ability to effectively face the important challenges that accompany the unprecedented demographic changes that are taking place in our nation. Instead, educators and mental health practitioners are urged to develop the kinds of professional competencies that will enable them to work more effectively, respectfully, and ethically within the context of a culturally and racially diverse society. It is hoped that the information presented in this chapter is helpful for those teachers and mental health professionals who are interested in both (a) gaining a clearer understanding as to why it is important to become more culturally competent and (b) becoming knowledgeable about assessment tools that can be used to measure one's level of multicultural competence.

APPENDIX 10.A

ITEMS ON THE MULTICULTURAL AWARENESS-KNOWLEDGE-SKILLS SURVEY–TEACHERS FORM (MAKSS–FORM T)

Multicultural Awareness Subscale

1. At this point in your life, how would you rate yourself in terms of understanding how your cultural background has influenced the way you think and act?
2. At this point in your life, how would you rate your understanding of the impact of the way you think and act when interacting with persons of different cultural backgrounds?
3. In general, how would you rate your level of awareness regarding different cultural institutions and systems?
4. At the present time, how would you generally rate yourself in terms of being able to accurately compare your own cultural perspective with that of a person from another culture?
5. How well do you think you could distinguish "intentional" for "accidental" communication signals in a multicultural classroom situation?
6. Ambiguity and stress often result from multicultural situations because people are not sure what to expect from each other.
7. Teachers need to change not just the content of what they think but also the way they handle this content if they are to accurately account for the complexity in human behavior.
8. How would you rate your understanding of the concept of "relativity" in terms of the goals, objectives, and methods of working with culturally different students and their families?

Multicultural Knowledge Subscale

How would you rate your understanding of the following terms?

1. Culture
2. Ethnicity
3. Racism
4. Mainstreaming
5. Prejudice
6. Multicultural education
7. Ethnocentrism
8. Pluralism
9. Contact hypothesis
10. Attribution
11. Transcultural
12. Cultural encapsulation
13. The difficulty with the concept of "integration" is its implicit bias in favor of the dominant culture.

Multicultural Skills Subscale

1. How would your rate your ability to teach students from a cultural background significantly different from your own?
2. How would you rate your ability to effectively assess the needs of students and their families from a cultural background different from your own?
3. How well would you rate your ability to distinguish "formal" and "informal" teaching strategies?
4. In general, how would you rate yourself in terms of being able to effectively deal with biases, discrimination, and prejudices directed at you by students and/or their families?
5. How well would you rate your ability to accurately identify culturally biased assumptions as they relate to your professional training?
6. How well would you rate your ability to discuss the role of "method" and "context" as they relate to teaching?
7. In general, how would you rate your ability to accurately articulate a student's behavioral problem when the student is from a cultural group significantly different from your own?
8. How well would you rate your ability to analyze a culture into its component parts?
9. How would you rate your ability to identify the strengths and weaknesses of standardized tests in term of their use with students from different cultural-racial-ethnic backgrounds?
10. How would you rate your ability to critique multicultural research?
11. In general, how would you rate your skill level in terms of being able to provide appropriate educational services to culturally different students and their families?
12. How would you rate your ability to effectively consult with another professional concerning the educational and behavioral needs of students whose cultural background is significantly different from your own?
13. How would you rate your ability to effectively secure information and resources to better serve culturally different students and their families?
14. How would you rate your ability to accurately assess the behavioral and educational needs of female students?
15. How would you rate your ability to accurately assess the behavioral educational needs of male students?
16. How would you rate your ability to accurately assess the behavioral and educational needs of older students?
17. How would you rate your ability to accurately assess the behavioral and educational needs of boys who may be homosexual?
18. How would you rate your ability to accurately assess the behavioral and educational needs of girls who may be lesbians?
19. How would you rate your ability to accurately assess the behavioral and educational needs of students with mental health disorders?
20. How would you rate your ability to accurately assess the behavioral and educational needs of students who come from very poor socioeconomic backgrounds?

REFERENCES

Arredondo, P., Toporek, R., Brown, S. P., Jones, J., Locke, D. C., Sanchez, J., et al. (1996). Operationalization of the multicultural counseling competencies. *Journal of Multicultural Counseling and Development, 24,* 42-78.

Atkinson, D. R., Morten, G., & Sue, D. W. (Eds.). (1998). *Counseling American minorities: A cross-cultural perspective* (5th ed.). Boston: McGraw-Hill.

Baker, S. B. (2000). *School counseling for the twenty-first century* (3rd ed.). Upper Saddle River, NJ: Merrill/Prentice Hall.

Baker, S. B., & Gerler, E. R. (2001). Counseling in schools. In D. C. Locke, J. E. Myers, & E. L. Herr (Eds.), *The handbook of counseling* (pp. 289-318). Thousand Oaks, CA: Sage.

Banks, J. A., & McGee-Banks, C. A. (1997). *Multicultural education: Issues and perspectives* (3rd ed.). Boston: Allyn & Bacon.

Bardon, J. (1976). The state of the art (and science) of school psychology. *American Psychologist, 31,* 785-791.

Brueggemann, W. G. (1996). *The practice of macro social work.* Chicago: Nelson-Hall.

Burstein, N. D., & Cabello, B. (1989). Preparing teachers to work with culturally diverse students: A teacher education model. *Journal of Teacher Education, 40,* 9-16.

Burstein, N. D., Cabello, B., & Hamann, J. (1993). Teacher preparation for culturally diverse urban students: Infusing competencies across the curriculum. *Teacher Education and Special Education, 16,* 1-13.

Curtis, M. J., & Zins, J. E. (1981). Consultative effectiveness as perceived by experts in consultation and classroom teachers. In M. J. Curtis & J. E. Zins (Eds.), *The theory and practice of school consultation* (pp. 88-96). Springfield, IL: Charles C Thomas.

D'Andrea, M. (1995, March). *RESPECTFUL counseling: An integrative model for professionals in the field.* Paper presented at the annual convention of the American Counseling Association, Denver, CO.

D'Andrea, M. (2000). Postmodernism, social constructionism and multiculturalism: Three forces that are shaping and expanding our thoughts about counseling. *Journal of Mental Health Counseling, 22,* 1-16.

D'Andrea, M., & Daniels, J. (2001). Facing the changing demographic structure of our society. In D. C. Locke, J. E. Myers, & E. L. Herr (Eds.), *Handbook of counseling* (pp. 529-539). Thousand Oaks, CA: Sage.

D'Andrea, M., & Daniels, J. (in press). *Multicultural counseling: Empowerment strategies for a diverse society.* Pacific Grove, CA: Brooks/Cole.

D'Andrea, M., Daniels, J., & Heck, R. (1991). Evaluating the impact of multicultural counseling training. *Journal of Counseling and Development, 70,* 143-150.

D'Andrea, M., Daniels, J., & Noonan, M. J. (1994). *The multicultural awareness, knowledge, and skills survey–Teachers Form (MAKSS–Form T).* Honolulu: University of Hawaii, College of Education.

D'Andrea, M., Fong, R., & Daniels, J. (2003). *The multicultural awareness, knowledge, and skills survey for social workers (MAKSS–Form SW).* Unpublished manuscript, University of Hawaii, Honolulu.

Daniels, J., Arredondo, P., & D'Andrea, M. (2001a, July). An African-centered perspective of mental health. *Counseling Today, 44,* 39, 44.

Daniels, J., Arredondo, P., & D'Andrea, M. (2001b). Expanding definitions of mental health. *Counseling Today, 43,* 31, 35.

Daniels, J., Arredondo, P., D'Andrea, M., Ivey, M. B., Ivey, A., Locke, D. C., et al. (2002, March). *Culturally competent social justice counseling: Promoting unity through diversity.* A symposium presented at the annual meeting of the American Counseling Association, New Orleans, LA.

Daniels, J., & D'Andrea, M. (1996). Implications for ameliorating ethnocentrism in counseling. In D. W. Sue, A. E. Ivey, & P. D. Pedersen (Eds.), *A theory of multicultural counseling and therapy* (pp. 157-173). Pacific Grove, CA: Brooks/Cole.

Duncan, C. F. (1995). Cross-cultural school consultation. In C. C. Lee (Ed.), *Counseling for diversity: A guide for school counselors and related professionals* (pp. 129-141). Boston: Allyn & Bacon.

Fox, C. L., Kuhlman, N. A., & Sales, T. B. (1988). Cross-cultural concerns: What's missing from special education training programs. *Teacher Education and Special Education, 11,* 155-161.

Gutkin, T. B. (1980). Teacher perceptions of consultation services provided by school psychologists. *Professional Psychology, 11,* 637-642.

Kim, B. S. K., Cartwright, B. Y., Asay, P. A., & D'Andrea, M. (2002). *Multicultural Awareness, Knowledge, and Skills Scale–Counselor Edition–Revised: factor analysis, reliability, and validity.* Manuscript submitted for publication.

Kiselica, M. (Ed.). (1999). *Confronting prejudice and racism during multicultural training.* Alexandria, VA: American Counseling Association.

LaFromboise, T. D., Coleman, H. L. K., & Hernandez, A. (1991). Development and factor structure of the Cross-Cultural Counseling Inventory–Revised. *Professional Psychology: Research and Practice, 22,* 380-388.

Lewis, J. A., Lewis, M. D., Daniels, J. A., & D'Andrea, M. (2003). *Community counseling: Empowerment strategies for a diverse society* (3rd ed.). Pacific Grove, CA: Brooks/Cole.

Locke, D. C., Myers, J. E., & Herr, E. L. (2001). *The handbook of counseling.* Thousand Oaks, CA: Sage.

Lynch, E. W., & Hanson, M. J. (1992). *Developing cross-cultural competence: A guide for working with young children and their families.* Baltimore: Brookes.

Muro, J. J., & Kottman, T. (1995). *Guidance and counseling in the elementary and middle schools: A practical approach.* Madison, WI: WCB Brown & Benchmark.

Pedersen, P., & Carey, J. C. (2003). *Multicultural counseling in the schools: A practical handbook* (2nd ed.). Boston: Allyn & Bacon.

Pedersen, P. B., Draguns, J. G., Lonner, W. J., & Trimble, J. E. (Eds.). (2002). *Counseling across cultures* (5th ed.). Thousand Oaks, CA: Sage.

Ponterotto, J. G., Casas, J. M., Suzuki, L. A., & Alexander, C. M. (Eds.). (2001). *Handbook of multicultural counseling* (2nd ed.). Thousand Oaks, CA: Sage.

Ponterotto, J. G., Gretchen, D., Utsey, S. O., Rieger, B. T., & Austin, R. (2001). *A revision of the multicultural counseling awareness scale (MCAS).* Unpublished manuscript.

Pope-Davis, D. B., & Coleman, H. K. C. (Eds.). (1997). *Multicultural counseling competencies: Assessment, education and training, and supervision.* Thousand Oaks, CA: Sage.

Schmidt, J. J. (1993). *Counseling in the schools.* Boston: Allyn & Bacon.

Sodowsky, G. R., Taffe, R. C., Gutkin, T., & Wise, S. L. (1994). Development of the multicultural counseling inventory: A self-report measure of multicultural competencies. *Journal of Counseling Psychology, 41,* 137-148.

Sue, D. W., Arredondo, P., & McDavis, R. J. (1992). Multicultural counseling competencies and standards: A call to the profession. *Journal of Counseling and Development, 70,* 477-486.

Sue, D. W., Carter, R. T., Casas, J. M., Fouad, N. A., Ivey, A. E., Jensen, M., et al. (1998). *Multicultural counseling competencies: Individual and organizational development.* Thousand Oaks, CA: Sage.

Sue, D. W., & Sue, D. (1999). *Counseling the culturally different: Theory and practice* (3rd ed.). New York: John Wiley.

Tran, M. L. T., Young, R. L., & DiLella, J. D. (1994). Multicultural education courses and the student teacher: Eliminating stereotypical attitudes in our ethnically diverse classroom. *Journal of Teacher Education, 45,* 183-189.

U. S. Bureau of the Census. (2001). *Profiles of general demographic characteristics: 2000 Census of Population and Housing, United States.* Retrieved August 11, 2001, from www2.census.gov/census 2000/datasets/demographicprofile/0National Summary/

U.S. Department of Health and Human Services. (2001). *Mental health, culture, race, and ethnicity: A report of the Surgeon General.* Washington, DC: Government Printing Office.

West, C. (1999). *The Cornel West reader.* New York: Basic Civitas.

11

Multicultural Counseling Competency and Portfolios

HARDIN L. K. COLEMAN
JULIE M. HAU
University of Wisconsin–Madison

The current ethnic and racial demographics of the United States are shifting, with projections estimating that within the next 20 years, racial and ethnic minorities will become a majority in the United States (Sue, 1991). The American Psychological Association, Office of Ethnic Minority Affairs (1993) has articulated guidelines for providers of psychological services to ethnic, linguistic, and culturally diverse populations. Therefore, it is essential that mental health professionals acquire the necessary multicultural counseling competencies to serve an increasing diverse society. Furthermore, portfolios can assist with the training of multicultural counseling competencies in mental health training programs.

Mental health training programs have a role in facilitating the acquisition of multicultural counseling competencies with trainees who have various experiences, expectations, career goals, and levels of competency as they enter training programs. In training programs, trainees have a diverse array of academic and professional experiences as well as opportunities to serve culturally diverse clientele. Some trainees may have significant personal and professional experiences with people from various abilities, ages, ethnic and racial groups, sexual orientations, and socioeconomic classes. Others may have had more homogeneous experiences working with a specific group. Furthermore, trainees' goals and aims beyond graduate school may be varied. That is, some trainees may prefer to work with specific cultural groups on a particular issue providing culture-specific interventions, whereas other trainees may demonstrate an interest in acquiring a variety of skills to work with several cultural groups. Given the variety of experiences and career goals among trainees, how do mental health training programs provide the experiences and the training necessary to facilitate the development of multiculturally competent mental health professionals? Moreover, how does a program assess the acquisition and encourage the self-awareness necessary for the development of multicultural counseling competency?

The purpose of this chapter is to describe how using portfolios within the structure of training programs can contribute to the acquisition and development of multicultural counseling competence for counselor trainees (Coleman, 1999). After a brief review of the literature on the role and function of portfolios, attention will be paid to how portfolios can be used to address a major challenge to multicultural counseling competency: the trainee's ability to become reflective and to articulate the manner in which his or her own racial identity development can influence his or her growth and effectiveness as a clinician. Suggestions for the incorporation of portfolios in the development and assessment of multicultural counseling competencies in training programs are provided.

THE ROLE AND FUNCTION OF PORTFOLIOS

The portfolio is "a purposeful collection of trainee work that tells the story of the student's efforts, progress and achievement in a given area" (Arter & Spandel, 1992, p. 3). This collection demonstrates a trainee's growth across time. For instance, the portfolio can be an avenue through which the trainee demonstrates an emerging competence (e.g., multicultural counseling competence). The portfolio creator ideally integrates multicultural counseling competencies across multiple areas of competency such as case conceptualizations, consultation, clinical skills, professional

identity, and scholarship. At various stages in an individual's career, the portfolio may demonstrate varying levels of competencies. The novice mental health professional may demonstrate a breadth of general counseling awareness, knowledge, and skills, whereas the experienced professional may demonstrate depth in working with culturally specific interventions. For an example of such a portfolio, see the Web site of a preservice school counselor at http://careers.education.wisc.edu/samples. Furthermore, the portfolio may be used for different purposes at different times.

Grosvenor (1993) defined three types of portfolios—showcase, descriptive, and evaluative. First, the showcase portfolio is designed to present trainees' highest level of competency and best work. This type of portfolio could be most useful to a trainee in a job interview or presentation in which he or she is asked to demonstrate succinctly and expediently his or her current level of competency. Second, a portfolio demonstrating trainees' progress across time is defined as a descriptive portfolio. Trainees can examine and demonstrate their growth through self-reflection on the awareness, knowledge, and skills acquired across time—specifically, addressing how they have changed and how they can evidence their changes. A descriptive portfolio is especially relevant in multicultural training, as will be discussed later. The third type of portfolio is created for the purposes of evaluation. Often examined by a preset rubric or criterion, this type of portfolio can be useful in evaluating trainees' acquisition of competence at particular points in their development. It may reflect a combination of the showcase and descriptive portfolio, focusing on trainees' development across some particular area of competency for the purposes of evaluation. Baltimore, Hickson, George, and Crutchfield (1996) encouraged counselor training programs to include all three types of portfolios in training programs based on the needs of the trainees and trainers. Hence, the portfolio can be of utility for multiple purposes and across different contexts.

Although there is considerable debate concerning the use of portfolios in terms of their reliability, validity, and utility versus standardized forms of assessment, Birrell and Ross (1996) argued that portfolios could be used to complement standardized forms of assessment without dichotomizing the value of each form of assessment. They suggested that powerful evaluative information can be gleaned from each mode of evaluation. An analogy we find useful is that if standardized assessments provide a single snapshot of trainees' current competency, portfolios reflect the picture album with a narrative demonstrating the actual process across time of becoming and continuing to explore multicultural counseling competencies. We contend that the use of portfolios encourages trainees to self-reflect on the snapshot nature of many assessment instruments, the strengths and limitations of standardized instruments, and the examination of potential biases around contexts within which tests are written and used.

Developing the critical thinking skills to analyze the validity, reliability, and utility of assessment instruments is a component of multicultural counseling competency. The American Psychological Association (1993) listed examining the norms and context in the creation and evaluation of standardized assessment instruments for use with racial and ethnic minorities and people of various socioeconomic statuses as a standard for the delivery of ethical services. Through the portfolio, the trainees examine the roles of multiple modes of assessment in context through selecting various exhibits to be evaluated. In addition, trainees self-reflect on the relative value of each exhibit to explicate how each exhibit demonstrates their awareness, knowledge, and skills as developing counselors. From engagement in this process, trainees can generalize

this experience to that of their clients. They can explore how their clients make meaning of various instruments to help describe who they are and how they interact with the world. We argue that engaging in the examination and questioning of testing instruments and the status quo encourages trainees to work on becoming lifelong critical thinkers examining the sociopolitical contexts within which we all live.

We have explored the role and function of portfolios—three types of portfolios and one example of the role of the portfolio in developing one aspect of multicultural competent counseling (i.e., the use of standardized instruments). We now spotlight the descriptive portfolio. The descriptive model of a portfolio, as proposed by Grosvenor (1993), is used to reflect the lifelong praxis model that can specifically address the development of multicultural counseling competencies endorsed by many others (Ridley, Mendoza, & Kanitz 1994; Sue, 1997; Sue, Arredondo, & McDavis, 1992; Toporek & Reza, 2001). Praxis in the training of mental health professionals is a philosophy of education that assumes that the development of multicultural counseling competencies is a lifelong endeavor in which competency includes the continued process of practice and examination of one's awareness, knowledge, and skills. The descriptive portfolio is an ideal way to demonstrate the process of praxis because, by definition, the descriptive portfolio's purpose is to provide a narrative of development. Furthermore, the portfolio, as a performance-based form of evaluation, requires trainees to demonstrate lifelong learning outcomes (Baltimore et al., 1996).

Portfolios can assist in the development and evaluation of multicultural counseling competency as trainees directly demonstrate the learning outcomes of awareness, knowledge, and skills from various learning experiences across time. The portfolio is a work in progress of trainees' performance, evaluated across time as a dynamic reflection of the trainees' development throughout the course of a training program. Trainees can, therefore, use the portfolio to reflect on their progress toward multicultural competency, demonstrate acquired multicultural competence, and identify areas requiring further development. Examples for the demonstration of multicultural counseling competencies include such exhibits as case conceptualizations, transcriptions, or taped sessions, wherein trainees provide written commentary on their awareness, knowledge, and skills. If trainees have the opportunity to select multiple cases across time, they can further explore the within- and between-group differences across clients' cultural contexts and in their own counseling awareness, knowledge, and skills (Carter, 1991). See Coleman, Morris, and Norton (in press) for an example of instructions for creating a portfolio.

Portfolios have been used as a means of having trainees demonstrate their competence across a variety of contexts, including psychology (Beers, 1985; Ricabaugh, 1993), cross-cultural courses for international students (Jacobson, Sleicher, & Burke, 1999), career development for returning adult trainees (Mark & Menson, 1982), and counselor education (Baltimore et al., 1996; Coleman, 1996, 1997; Coleman et al., in press; Tuescher, 1997). Examples of online counselor-in-training portfolios can be viewed at http://careers.education.wisc.edu/samples. Furthermore, Coleman (1996, 1997) has suggested that the portfolio can be a valuable tool in the assessment of multicultural counseling competence. Portfolios, as a performance-based form of assessment, provide a means for trainees to exhibit their development of multicultural awareness, knowledge, and skills. Whereas the majority of research on and examination of multicultural counseling competencies has reflected self-reports (Ottavi, Pope-Davis, &

Dings, 1994; Parker, Moore, & Neimeyer, 1998), the portfolio is a form of assessment that includes self-reports of awareness and knowledge, as well as the demonstration of clinical skills with clients.

Tuescher and Coleman (2000) suggested that a major benefit of a portfolio is to stimulate self-reflection. Their model of counselor competence development argued that a competent counselor is one who successfully integrates awareness, knowledge, and skills to effectively provide services to a client within a particular context. They contended that competence looks different in novice, intermediate, and expert counselors, as the counselor develops a broader perspective on his or her clinical practice as a function of experience and reflection on that experience. Tuescher and Coleman also articulated that portfolios facilitate this process in several ways. Preparing evidence for a portfolio becomes the trigger for self-reflection on the counselors' part, therefore stimulating a broader perspective on their work. Viewing the evidence in the portfolio enhances the counselors' sense of ownership over their competence, which supports their clinical self-efficacy and, therefore, facilitates the integration of their awareness, knowledge, and skills. By consistently reworking their portfolios, clinicians acquire greater sophistication in their self-reflection and a deeper level of clinical skills and performance.

Tuescher (1997) conducted a study examining self-reflection related to portfolios for counselors in training. In this study, counselors in training were assigned to two conditions (portfolio, nonportfolio) and to three different supervisors. Under each supervisor, the trainees who completed the portfolio demonstrated higher levels of self-reflection than those who did not complete the portfolio. What prevented a significant difference to emerge between the control and experimental groups was that the trainees with one supervisor had increased self-reflection that surpassed those in the other groups, regardless of condition (portfolio, nonportfolio). Tuescher interpreted this to suggest that there are many ways to improve counselor competence and that portfolios are one useful tool.

This interpretation has been supported in subsequent research by Coleman et al. (in press). In addition, a trainer who encourages self-reflection in a facilitative environment and the creation of the portfolio may have combined effects leading to greater self-awareness. Furthermore, future researchers could examine the independent effect that can be attributed to using portfolios in supervision, as the supervisor appears to have a significant effect on the development of counselor competence.

Coleman, Morris, and Norton (2000) demonstrated that portfolios have a positive impact on the development of multicultural counseling competence. Specifically, they examined the influence of ecological case conceptualization and portfolios on the development of multicultural counseling competency for counselors in training. In the creation of an ecological case conceptualization, the trainee considers the context of the client's individual factors: microsystem, mesosystem, exosystem, and macrosystem—that is, understanding the self within the context of the multiple social systems (Coleman & Tuescher, in press; see Chapter 10, this volume). Both training techniques increased multicultural counseling competency, but different modalities influenced different aspects of multicultural counseling competency. The ecological case conceptualization group demonstrated an increased ability to analyze clinical material, whereas the portfolio group demonstrated higher multicultural competency when working with a confederate client. That is, the process of creating an ecological case conceptualization facilitated increased knowledge, whereas portfolios facilitated multicultural counseling skills in counselors when working with clients, as hypothesized by Tuescher and Coleman (2000).

It appears necessary for training programs to include multiple means of developing multicultural counseling competence in training as different tasks influence different aspects of multicultural counseling competence. The portfolio does just that as it requires the trainee to exhibit multiple modes of learning. The trainee could include an ecological case conceptualization wherein the trainee reflects on the process of creating a case conceptualization. The benefits of this are twofold. The individual increases his or her skills in case conceptualization while increasing his or her awareness and knowledge concerning the assessment and treatment of diverse clients. Moreover, self-reflection is an important component of racial identity development, an identity that is closely related to the acquisition of multicultural counseling competency. This will be discussed in further detail regarding implications for training programs.

IMPLICATIONS FOR TRAINING PROGRAMS

Many training models have been implemented to assist trainees and training programs with the process of developing multicultural counseling competencies (Ridley et al., 1994; Sue, 1997; Toporek & Reza, 2001). In addition, Sue et al. (1992) outlined guidelines for multicultural counseling competencies and standards for the profession. They identified three dimensions of multicultural counseling competencies: awareness, knowledge, and skills. Counselor awareness involves awareness of how cultural heritage influences worldview, which is expressed in values, beliefs, assumptions and biases, and effects of interpersonal behavior for both the client and the counselor. Furthermore, the act of becoming self-aware requires counselors to examine how their worldviews influence the clients they serve. Counselors who demonstrate knowledge and understanding of historical systems of oppression and racism are keenly aware of the historical context of their clients. Multicultural competent counselors demonstrate skills that are culturally congruent with the needs and historical contexts of the clients they serve.

Ridley et al. (1994) have argued for a process-oriented approach to multicultural training, whereby multiculturalism is integrated across all course content. In this approach, the emphasis is on "becoming" a part of an ongoing process of professional development. The portfolio has implications for such programs as it mirrors the integrative nature of the program by encouraging trainees to integrate multicultural counseling competencies across multiple professional experiences through the process of praxis. As faculty encourage the integration of material from other courses and integrate the portfolios into coursework, self-reflection on multicultural awareness, knowledge, and skills becomes a focus of trainees' development. For example, as aforementioned, exhibits may include multiple modes such as case conceptualizations, journals, videotaped interviews, tests, papers, and self-assessment inventories that demonstrate trainees' integration of multicultural counseling competence and growth across time. Trainees then reflect on their developmental process, articulating how each exhibit demonstrates their development of multicultural counseling competencies. This process stimulates further perspective taking and sets the stage for enhanced competence.

Although the role of the trainee is one of the core factors in the development of multicultural counseling competency, Toporek and Reza (2001) argued for the development of institutional awareness concerning multicultural competence and to understand the role of the multicultural competent counselor as change agents at the institutional level. Therefore, not only is it important for training programs to explore the individual responsibilities of the mental health professional (i.e., trainee) in the assessment of multicultural counseling competence, but it is also ideal for

the training program to collectively develop institutional awareness, knowledge, and skills around the training of its trainees. To achieve this end, training programs must consider their role in the creation of learning environments where multicultural competencies are addressed. This includes facilitating the creation and maintenance of environments that value difference. Thus, training programs can model multicultural counseling competency to their trainees by including an integrative and multimodel method of assessment: the portfolio. Many have argued that one-shot training, in-services, and courses are inadequate in the training of multicultural competent counselors (Ridley et al., 1994; Toporek & Reza, 2001). There have been several calls for an integrated approach to multiculturalism across the curriculum (Ridley et al., 1994; Sue, 1997). Furthermore, the implicit and explicit value of multiculturalism is evident to trainees by the emphasis placed on one source such as a specific course, professor, or workshop versus the integration of multiculturalism into every aspect of trainees' educational experience.

Gloria and Pope-Davis (1997) discussed the role of cultural ambience in training programs. They reflected on the ways training programs can create learning environments that value multiple perspectives. To develop cultural learning environments that foster the development of multicultural competency, trainers can create pluralistic environments where multiple perspectives are respected, honored, and validated, just as trainees must do for their clients. Actual behavioral representations of the value of multiculturalism can be evidenced by the integration of portfolios across the curriculum because it shows that the training programs value a variety of ways of learning. Furthermore, trainees can select the form of evaluation that best reflects their way of learning and self-reflect on those that pose challenges to their learning, with the opportunity to reflect on the important distinctions between "knowing that and knowing how" (Johnson, 1987). Trainees have the option of selecting empirical or theoretical papers, standardized examinations, professional presentations, case conceptualizations, essay exams, taped sessions with clients, transcriptions, or multiple variations of each of these to reflect what meaning they have made out of their learning experience.

This model requires trainers and trainees to work together to build environments where multiculturalism is integrated as an ongoing developmental value in training. The role of the portfolio as a self-defined means of assessing trainees' competency level, which includes a program-facilitated rubric, encourages trainees and trainers to collectively take responsibility for multicultural competency development. This further models the need for trainees to define themselves professionally and begin a process of continued exploration of their multicultural competency development. In addition, the portfolio provides a space where trainees can determine which aspects influence their development, as well as extending this conversation to their interactions with supervisors to facilitate the dialogue of communication around the trainees' developmental processes. As trainees explore understanding themselves (e.g., ethnic identity) and the influence of understanding their cultural self in relation to others, the portfolio can be a powerful meaning-making format in which trainees can tell stories of their experiences with training and its influence on their multicultural competency development. One aspect of this process that is a key component of multicultural counseling competency is the counselor's racial identity development.

RACIAL IDENTITY DEVELOPMENT IN RELATION TO MULTICULTURAL COUNSELING COMPETENCIES

Over the past 500 years in U.S. history, racism has reflected many forms, including blatant racism, enlightened racism, symbolic racism, paternalistic racism, liberal racism, and unintentional racism (Barrett & Swim, 1998; Crocker & Major, 1989; Jhally & Lewis, 1992; Ridley, 1995). Although many of the laws that perpetuated and maintained racism have been abolished, racism continues in contemporary U.S. society in numerous individual and institutionalized forms (Winant, 1998). To serve as multiculturally competent health professionals, trainees face the challenge of examining individual and institutional racism, White privilege, racial identity development, and the influence of these phenomena on their development and interactions with clients (Barrett & Swim, 1998; Corvin & Wiggins, 1989; Crocker & Major, 1989). We suggest that portfolios serve as an excellent tool for stimulating increasingly complex understandings of trainees' racial identity, as well as its role in trainees' multicultural counseling competence. In the next section, we present ways in which this development can be facilitated within training programs.

This section focuses on White racial identity development because the majority of research on multicultural counseling competencies for mental health trainees has been in relation to White racial identity development, with the exception of Manese, Wu, and Nepomuceno (2001). As more racial and ethnic minorities enter mental health professions, it is critical for multicultural competency research to extend it focus to intragroup and intergroup racism, in relation to the service of clients. For example, a racial and ethnic minority could work with an ethnic majority. Furthermore, intragroup differences between a Hmong American clinician and a Japanese American client, or a Mexican American clinician with a Puerto Rican American client, require research attention.

Trainees not only require education about race-based systems of oppression for racial and ethnic minorities in the United States but also need to explore the role of White society and institutions in perpetuating these systems (Brandt, 1991; Corvin & Wiggins, 1989; Ponterotto, 1991). Ignoring racism, racial identity development, and White privilege in training models for professionals suggests that White trainees do not need to discover more about themselves and that this is a task only for clients, further pathologizing racial and ethnic minorities as the problem to be explored instead of examining the contextual and systematic influence of oppression for racial and ethnic minorities in the United States. That is, omission of these concepts in the development of multicultural counseling competencies relinquishes the individual and collective responsibility of White racism (Ridley et al., 1994).

Researchers have proposed many models of racial identity development (Helms, 1992; Rowe, Bennett, & Atkinson, 1994) to assist counselors in understanding themselves and the clients they serve. Feagin and Vera (1995) suggested, "The key to understanding White racism is to be found not only in what White people think of people of color but also what Whites think of themselves" (p. xi). White racial identity models examine the processes by which White people develop a consciousness of their Whiteness and its associated sociopolitical privileges in relation to racial and ethnic minority groups in the United States (Helms, 1992; Rowe et al., 1994).

Helms (1992) presented a theory of White identity development with five original ego stages with an update of six stages, including Contact, Disintegration, Reintegration, Pseudo-Independence, Immersion/Emersion, and Autonomy. The Contact stage exemplifies a White individual's unawareness of the sociopolitical meanings of race in the United States. Disintegration represents a growing awareness of race-related issues propelling the individual into confusion or cognitive dissonance about his or her previous ignorance

about the roles of race in the United States. Reintegration reflects a period of idealization of White culture with negative attitudes toward members of racial and ethnic minority groups. Pseudo-Independence signifies a stage of cognitive intellectualization whereby White culture is used as a means of converting racial and ethnic minorities to think, feel, and behave in ways that are congruent with White culture. In the Immersion/Emersion stage, individuals conceptualize their notions of Whiteness in a nonracist vein and begin the process of redefining their definition of Whiteness. The Autonomy stage exemplifies an internalization of a nonracist positive White perspective, joined with a rejection of the benefits of racism and a respect for other racial and ethnic groups without imposition of White perspectives.

Rowe et al. (1994) argued that other models of White identity development focus on Whites' attitudes toward other groups without incorporating White attitudes toward their own group. They hypothesized two categories of White consciousness—unachieved and achieved. Unachieved consciousness includes three types—avoidant, dependent, and dissonant. The avoidant type avoid examination of White identity and concern for racial and ethnic minority issues. The dependent type explore some attitudes of White consciousness but depend on others' understanding of race for their conceptualizations. The dissonant type struggle with uncertainty when their previously colorblind White racial consciousness conflicts with the unfair treatment that they observe racial and ethnic minorities experience. Achieved White consciousness includes four types—dominative, conflictive, reactive, and integrative. The dominative type justify the mistreatment of racial and ethnic minority groups through a White ethnocentric ideology. The conflictive type oppose individual discriminatory behaviors but often disagree with systematic changes to eliminate racism. The reactive type contend that Whites benefit from and hold responsibility for racism in the United States. Finally, the integrative type understand the moral responsibility of valuing a multicultural society and develop a deepening understanding of the sociopolitical forces affecting the lives of racial and ethnic minorities while maintaining realistic understandings of their individual capacity to challenge the system.

Theorists have provided models for various stages for the process of developing White racial identity development, and researchers have demonstrated the influence of racial identity development on the acquisition of multicultural counseling competency (Burkard, Ponterotto, Reynolds, & Alfonso, 1999; Ottavi et al., 1994; Sabnani, Ponterotto, & Borodovsky, 1991). Burkard et al. (1999) found that the relationship between White racial identity stage, working alliance, and client race/ethnicity influences multicultural counseling competency. Participants were randomly assigned to view an African American or White 12-minute counseling videotape vignette, instructed to imagine themselves as the counselor in the vignette, self-reported on the working alliance they imagined experiencing with the client, completed the Working Alliance Inventory (WAI) (Horvath & Greenberg, 1986), and responded to the White Racial Identity Attitude Scale (WRIAS) (Helms & Carter, 1990). The results demonstrated that trainees' performance was related to their own racial identity stage and not to the clients' ethnicity/race. Increased levels of racial identity led to stronger working alliances with both White and African American clients. White counselors' examination of their racial identity appears to influence the counselor-client relationship, regardless of race/ethnicity of the client; therefore, training programs must facilitate the development of racial identity awareness for trainees so that they can increase their multicultural counseling competence. For suggestions on teaching strategies

during each stage of identity development, consult Corvin and Wiggins (1989). Furthermore, Coleman (1998) demonstrated that multicultural counseling competency and general counselor competence have been identified as closely related, making the former an essential competency for counselors to develop in their work with all clients.

Ottavi et al. (1994) suggested that information about White racial identity development and multicultural counseling competencies could be collected at different points in trainees' development but did not propose a method for effectively integrating this information into counselors' development as multicultural competent professionals. We argue that this is precisely the role portfolios can play within a training program. Portfolios could enhance the mental health profession's understanding of the identity processes in relation to the development of multicultural counseling competencies because they require trainees to demonstrate both the process and the outcome of their training. Not only do counselors in training demonstrate their awareness, knowledge, and skills by using portfolios, but they also self-reflect on the process of developing these competencies. Course instructors and training programs can encourage trainees to reflect on changes in their development and observe the actual results of trainees' self-reflections. Evaluators can rate trainees' development across time with instruments such as the Cross-Cultural Counseling Inventory–Revised (CCCI-R) (LaFromboise, Coleman, & Hernandez, 1991).

The emotion-laden nature of exploring one's owns beliefs, values, and prejudices often invokes anxiety for trainees (Gloria & Pope-Davis, 1997; Gloria, Rieckmann, & Rush, 2000). In fact, Toporek and Reza (2001) argued for training programs to stimulate the cognitive, affective, and behavioral shifts for developmental change in relation to multicultural counseling competencies. Self-awareness through the process of creating a portfolio and examining one's racial identity development provides a place for trainees to explore their thoughts, feelings, and behaviors and how it influences their work with clients.

Croteau (1999) and Kiselica (1998) reflected on the importance of normalizing the multiple reactions that White counselors may have as they begin to examine their beliefs, values, and attitudes. It is hoped that supervisors can normalize the process that developing professionals encounter by challenging and confronting beliefs, values, and assumptions while providing a supportive and empathetic environment when exploring understandings of racial social realities (Kiselica, 1998). As Norton and Coleman (Chapter 8, this volume) have suggested, this is an excellent and appropriate function for supervision, with the use of portfolios facilitating the acquisition of multicultural counseling competencies in a collaborative manner. Portfolios, therefore, can be considered a useful pedagogical tool, an assessment device, a self-reflection vehicle, and a stimulant to the development of an effective working alliance between trainer and trainee.

This chapter has focused on the racial identity development of White counselors in training because a majority of the research on multicultural counseling competency focuses on White racial identity development models in relation to the acquisition of this. Furthermore, the history of oppression by White people through mental health care systems makes this exploration paramount. The exploration of White racial identity development in relation to multicultural counseling competencies has been an important contribution to the multicultural literature as the mental health field has been historically and politically plagued by both intentional and unintentional classism, homophobia, racism, and sexism. However, we see this as a significant limitation as it is important to examine racial identity development for racial and ethnic minorities as they acquire multicultural counseling competencies. As more racial and ethnic minority trainees enter the mental health professions, more research on the role of racial identity development in relation to people of color in multicultural counseling competency is needed. In addition, we need to attend to the importance of trainees' and trainers' (see Norton & Coleman, Chapter 8, this volume) understanding of the intersection of multiple contexts and cultural identities (such as ability, age, class, gender, geography, country of origin, race, ethnicity, culture, and sexual orientation) that trainees must learn to integrate for the delivery of multiculturally competent service (Pope-Davis & Coleman, 2001). Other factors such as age, gender, education level, clinical experience, multicultural coursework, multicultural client contact, and clinical supervision influence the development of multicultural counseling competencies (D'Andrea, Daniels, & Heck, 1991; Pope-Davis & Ottavi, 1994).

In training programs that are serious about preparing its graduates to be competent professionals in a pluralistic society, trainees will explore the role of multiple experiences and culture in shaping their beliefs, values, and biases. In such programs, trainees will come to understand how their multiple identities influence their interactions with others. The role of the entire ecology of experience, as proposed by Coleman, Norton, Miranda, and McCubbin (Chapter 3, this volume), provides an in-depth explanation of the ecological model in relation to cultural identity development. As Coleman et al. argued for the use of mixed methods for the in-depth analysis of the complex interactions between cultural identity and social systems, we call to future researchers to examine the multiple contextual factors of trainees' cultural identity development in relation to the development of multicultural counseling competencies. The portfolio provides an ideal

Table 11.1   Suggestions for the Use of Portfolios to Facilitate Multicultural Counseling Competencies

Students	Trainers	Training Programs
Use the portfolio as a place to verbalize your growth process. Consider class assignments, practicum experiences, and out-of-class experiences that may help demonstrate how you have grown.	Incorporate portfolio and self-reflection assignments in each of your classes. Include portfolio assignments across courses and in multiple contexts. For instance, trainees can demonstrate their multicultural counseling competency in academic contexts through coursework, clinical contexts through practicum, and personal contexts through self-reflection.	Examine the value of portfolios for the entire training program.
Be open to discussing and examining areas of growth and share with peers, faculty, supervisors, and advisers.	Set aside class time when students meet in small groups to discuss their progress on making their portfolios. Ask students about the portfolio process in supervision, advisee meetings, and as part of an exit interview.	The descriptive portfolio is a demonstration of growth across time. Therefore, providing the opportunity for the students to use the portfolio as a capstone to course completion can serve to assess competencies and provides an opportunity for students to have a conversation with trainers about their overall experiences in the program, their growth across time, and as a sort of exit interview for the training process (Baltimore, Hickson, George, & Crutchfield, 1996; Grosvenor, 1993).
Explore technological options in the creation of portfolios.	Collaborate with technological specialists to create secure and efficient resources for students.	Explore the availability and creation of larger systems for supporting the use of technology in portfolios.
Include work from your first experiences to later experiences that reflect your growth across time.	Integrate a developmental approach in creating the portfolio, as reflected in the descriptive portfolio.	Discuss as a team theories of mental health trainee multicultural counseling competency development and how portfolios can be an assessment tool in this process.
Inquire about the expectations and ask for ongoing supervision on the progress of your portfolio.	Share expectations with students, advisees, and trainees on general outlines for what is expected in the portfolio.	Provide trainees clarity on grading standards while providing space for creativity (Beers, 1985). Creating a departmental rubric outlining general guidelines and suggestions for the portfolio could be useful in alleviating ambiguity about training program expectations for trainees and trainers. Evaluation rubrics can serve as a guiding template toward trainees' progress while providing flexibility for individual differences.

(Continued)

Table 11.1   Continued

Students	Trainers	Training Programs
Include a diverse array of experiences.	Value multiple forums students incorporate in the portfolio.	Faculty should evaluate trainees' progress across time and contexts. The portfolio can serve as a springboard for further dialogue whereby trainees, trainers, advisees, advisers, supervisees, and supervisors can dialogue around areas for growth and mark developmental milestones across the training experience (Coleman, Morris, & Norton, in press).
Attend activities outside of your usual frame of reference (e.g., attending cultural events, interacting with a diverse array of colleagues, and reading diverse literary as well as educational books).	Suggest that trainees use the portfolio as a place for trainees to examine their cultural identity development. Provide support and challenge in the training process. Be open to multiple ways of learning.	Discuss the role of cultural identity development in training of mental health professionals.
Prepare for the evaluative process by rereading past exhibits. Write comprehensive as well as context-specific pieces on your growth across time.	Throughout the training, experience periodic and capstone evaluations with feedback and to serve as empowering conversations about creating and integrating course materials and practicum experience in the portfolio.	Facilitate a space of collaboration for the entire training program so that faculty and students can share in the purpose, evaluation, expectations, and growth of each student and the training program.

assessment tool to conduct mixed-method research with qualitative analyses of the portfolio as well as quantitative examination of actual behavioral outcomes with clients and attitudinal outcomes for trainees. In addition, the portfolio can be used to examine multiple personal and professional identities in relation to the acquisition of multicultural counseling competence. As trainees provide narratives of their meaning-making processes and performance outcomes in their work with clients, the portfolio serves as a valuable assessment and research tool of counselors' developmental processes and multicultural competence outcomes (Coleman, 1996, 1997, 1999).

Preparing trainees to be effective clinicians in a culturally diverse society is a challenging, complex, and rewarding task—a task that requires trainers to assist trainees in being aware of their cultural selves and how that interacts in their clinical practice. It also forces trainees to think complexly to learn and acquire the awareness, knowledge, and skills to work effectively with clients who come from multiple cultural perspectives, have varied historical contexts, and have a variety of presenting problems and different types of resiliencies. Even in training programs that integrate multiculturalism throughout their coursework, trainees struggle to find a way to integrate their learning into a coherent framework they can use to guide their practice as clinicians and scholars. It is our contention that creating a portfolio can provide an integrative experience for trainees. The process of identifying and presenting evidence of their professional competence stimulates self-reflection in trainees, which leads to an integrative understanding of their competence. To achieve this end, however, training programs will have to implement portfolios in a systematic manner. We want to conclude with some recommendations for trainees and trainers in the implementation of portfolios in training programs that strive to develop multicultural counseling competency in their graduates. Table 11.1 presents these suggestions.

We have examined the role and function of portfolios in training programs. Furthermore, the validity, reliability, and utility of portfolios for the demonstration and evaluation of multicultural counseling competencies have been explored. A key component to the development of multicultural counseling competencies—cultural identity development—has been reviewed. As a medium for self-reflection, the portfolio is an ideal tool to use in trainees' examinations of their cultural identity development. We recommend that researchers consider incorporating portfolios in future research endeavors to examine our contentions and past research, which suggests that portfolios enhance the self-reflective processes necessary to acquire the awareness, knowledge, and skills necessary in developing multicultural counseling competence. In addition, the role of the portfolio as a learning experience on which trainees reflect to have increased levels of cognitive, emotional, and behavioral complexity surrounding their cultural identity development requires empirical exploration. In closing, the suggestions we have provided for programs are just that—suggestions. The flexibility of several types and uses for portfolios enables training programs to incorporate portfolios to meet their diverse needs and those of an increasingly diverse society.

REFERENCES

American Psychological Association, Office of Ethnic Minority Affairs. (1993). Guidelines for providers of psychological services to ethnic, linguistic, and culturally diverse populations. *American Psychologist, 48*(1), 45-48.

Arter, J. A., & Spandel, V. (1992, September). Using portfolios of trainee work in instruction and assessment. *Educational Measurement: Issues and Practice*, pp. 36-44.

Baltimore, M. L., Hickson, J., George, J., & Crutchfield, L. B. (1996). Portfolio assessment: A model for counselor education. *Counselor Education and Supervision, 36*(2), 113-121.

Barrett, L. F., & Swim, J. K. (1998). Appraisals of prejudice and discrimination. In L. F. Barrett & J. K. Swim (Eds.), *Prejudice: The target's perspective* (pp. 12-36). San Diego: Academic Press.

Beers, S. E. (1985). Using a portfolio writing assignment in a course on developmental psychology. *Teaching of Psychology, 12*, 94-96.

Birrell, J. R., & Ross, S. K. (1996). Standardized testing and portfolio assessment: Rethinking the debate. *Reading Research and Instruction, 35*, 285-297.

Brandt, J. (1991). *Dismantling racism: The continuing challenge to White America*. Minneapolis, MN: Augsburg Fortress.

Burkard, A. W., Ponterotto, J. G., Reynolds, A. L., & Alfonso, V. C. (1999). White counselor trainees' racial identity and work alliance perceptions. *Journal of Counseling and Development, 77*(3), 324-329.

Carter, R. T. (1991). Cultural values: A review of empirical research and implications for counseling. *Journal of Counseling and Development, 70*, 164-173.

Coleman, H. L. K. (1996). Portfolio assessment of multicultural counseling competency. *The Counseling Psychologist, 24*(2), 216-229.

Coleman, H. L. K. (1997). Portfolio assessment of multicultural counseling competency. In D. Pope-Davis & H. L. K. Coleman (Eds.), *Multicultural counseling competencies: Assessment, education and training and supervision* (pp. 43-59). Thousand Oaks, CA: Sage.

Coleman, H. L. K. (1998). General and multicultural counseling competency: Apples and oranges? *Journal of Multicultural Counseling and Development, 26,* 147-156.

Coleman, H. L. K. (1999). Training for multi-cultural supervision. In E. Holloway & E. Carroll (Eds.), *Training counseling supervisors* (pp. 130-161). London: Sage.

Coleman, H. L. K., Morris, D., & Norton, R. A. (2000, August). *Developing multicultural counseling competence through the use of portfolios.* Paper presented at the meeting of the American Psychological Association, Boston.

Coleman, H. L. K, Morris, D., & Norton, R. A. (in press). Developing multicultural counseling competence through the use of portfolios. *Journal of Multicultural Counseling and Development.*

Coleman, H. L. K., & Tuescher, K. D. (in press). *School-based interventions with psychological disorders.* Alexandria, VA: American School Counseling Association.

Corvin, S. A., & Wiggins, F. (1989). An antiracism training model for White professionals. *Journal of Multicultural Counseling and Development, 17,* 105-114.

Crocker, J., & Major, B. (1989). Social stigma and self-esteem: The self-protective properties of stigma. *Psychological Review, 96,* 608-630.

Croteau, J. M. (1999). One struggle through individualism: Toward an antiracist White racial identity. *Journal of Counseling and Development, 77,* 30-32.

D'Andrea, M., Daniels, J., & Heck, R. (1991). Evaluating the impact of multicultural counseling training. *Journal of Counseling and Development, 70,* 143-150.

Feagin, J. R., & Vera, H. (1995). *White racism.* New York: Routledge Kegan Paul.

Gloria, A. M., & Pope-Davis, D. B. (1997). Cultural ambience: The importance of a culturally aware learning environment in the training and education of counselors. In D. B. Pope-Davis & H. L. K. Coleman (Eds.), *Multicultural counseling competencies: Assessment, education and training, and supervision* (pp. 242-262). Thousand Oaks, CA: Sage.

Gloria, A. M., Rieckmann, T. R., & Rush, J. D. (2000). Issues and recommendations for teaching an ethnic/culture-based course. *Teaching of Psychology, 27*(2), 102-107.

Grosvenor, L. (Ed.). (1993). *Student portfolio.* Washington, DC: National Education Association Professional Library.

Helms, J. E. (1992). *A race is a nice thing to have: A guide to being a White person or understanding the White persons in your life.* Topeka, KS: Content Communications.

Helms, J. E., & Carter, R. T. (1990). Development of the White Racial Identity Inventory. In J. E. Helms (Ed.), *Black and White racial identity: Theory, research, and practice* (pp. 67-80). Westport, CT: Greenwood.

Horvath, A. O., & Greenberg, L. S. (1986). The development of the Working Alliance Inventory. In L. S. Greenberg & W. Pinsof (Eds.), *The psychotherapeutic process: A resource handbook* (pp. 529-556). New York: Guilford.

Jacobson, W., Sleicher, D., & Burke, M. (1999). Portfolio assessment of intercultural competence. *International Journal of Intercultural Relations, 23,* 467-492.

Jhally, S., & Lewis, J. (1992). *Enlightened racism.* Boulder, CO: Westview.

Johnson, S. D. (1987). Knowing that versus knowing how: Toward achieving expertise through multicultural training for counseling. *The Counseling Psychologist, 15*(2), 320-331.

Kiselica, M. S. (1998). Preparing Anglos for the challenges and joys of multiculturalism. *The Counseling Psychologist, 26*(1), 5-21.

LaFromboise, T. D., Coleman, H. L. K., & Hernandez, A. (1991). Development and factor structure of the Cross-Cultural Counseling Inventory–Revised. *Professional Psychology: Research and Practice, 22,* 380-388.

Manese, J. E., Wu, J. T., & Nepomuceno, C. A. (2001). The effect of training on multicultural counseling competencies: An exploratory study over a ten-year period. *Journal of Multicultural Counseling and Development, 29,* 31-40.

Mark, M., & Menson, B. (1982). Using David Kolb's experiential learning theory in portfolio development courses. *New Directions for Experiential Learning: Building on Experiences in Adult Development, 16,* 65-74.

Ottavi, T. M., Pope-Davis, D. B., & Dings, J. G. (1994). Relationship between White racial identity attitudes and self-reported multicultural counseling competencies. *Journal of Counseling Psychology, 41*(2), 149-154.

Parker, W. M., Moore, M. A., & Neimeyer, G. J. (1998). Altering White racial identity and interracial comfort through multicultural training. *Journal of Counseling and Development, 76,* 302-310.

Ponterotto, J. G. (1991). The nature of prejudice revisited: Implications for counseling intervention. *Journal of Counseling and Development, 70,* 216-224.

Pope-Davis, D. B., & Coleman, H. L. K. (Eds.). (2001). *The intersection of race, class, and gender: Implications for multicultural counseling.* Thousand Oaks, CA: Sage.

Pope-Davis, D. B., & Ottavi, T. M. (1994). Relationship between racism and racial identity among White Americans: A replication and extension. *Journal of Counseling and Development, 72,* 293-297.

Ricabaugh, C. A. (1993). The psychology portfolio: Promoting writing and critical thinking about psychology. *Teaching of Psychology, 20*(3), 170-172.

Ridley, C. R. (1995). *Overcoming unintentional racism in counseling and theory: A practitioner's guide to intentional intervention.* Thousand Oaks, CA: Sage.

Ridley, C. R., Mendoza, D. W., & Kanitz, B. E. (1994). Multicultural training: Reexamination,

operationalization, and integration. *The Counseling Psychologist, 22*(2), 227-289.

Rowe, W., Bennett, S. K., & Atkinson, D. R. (1994). White racial identity models: A critique and alternative proposal. *The Counseling Psychologist, 22,* 129-146.

Sabnani, H. B., Ponterotto, J. G., & Borodovsky, L. G. (1991). White racial identity development and cross-cultural counselor training: A stage model. *The Counseling Psychologist, 19,* 72-102.

Sue, D. W. (1991). A conceptual model for cultural diversity training. *Journal of Counseling and Development, 70,* 99-105.

Sue, D. W. (1997). Multicultural training. *International Journal of Intercultural Relations, 21*(2), 175-193.

Sue, D. W., Arredondo, P., & McDavis, R. J. (1992). Multicultural counseling competencies and standards: A call to the profession. *Journal of Counseling and Development, 70,* 477-486.

Toporek, R. L., & Reza, J. V. (2001). Context as a critical dimension of multicultural counseling: Articulating personal, professional, and institutional competence. *Journal of Multicultural Counseling and Development, 29*(1), 13-30.

Tuescher, K. D. (1997). *The effect of portfolios on self-reflection in counseling trainees.* Unpublished doctoral dissertation, University of Wisconsin–Madison.

Tuescher, K. D., & Coleman, H. L. K. (2000, August). *The self-reflection scale.* Paper presented at the annual meeting of the American Psychological Association, Boston.

Winant, H. (1998). Racial dualism at century's end. In W. Lubiano (Ed.), *The house that race built* (pp. 87-115). New York: Vintage.

12

Assessing Multicultural Competence of the Training Environment

Further Validation for the Psychometric Properties of the Multicultural Environment Inventory–Revised

REBECCA L. TOPOREK
San Francisco State University

WILLIAM MING LIU
University of Iowa

DONALD B. POPE-DAVIS
University of Notre Dame

There have been two primary forces behind the attention to multiculturalism in counseling and psychology training programs. First, acknowledging that multicultural issues are an important component of counseling and psychology implies that training is necessary in multicultural issues. Various authors have argued that there is a need to increase the provision of culturally relevant services to clients (Arredondo et al., 1996; Bernal & Castro, 1994; D. W. Sue, 2001), increase the quality of culturally relevant research (Graham, 1992; Quintana, Troyano, & Taylor, 2001; S. Sue, 1999), and minimize

AUTHORS' NOTE: The MEI-R is a copyrighted measure (2000). If you are interested in obtaining a copy of the measure, contact Donald B. Pope-Davis, Ph.D., 118 Haggar Hall, University of Notre Dame, Notre Dame, IN 46656; e-mail: dpd@nd.edu.

negative effects of inappropriate and biased mental health services on culturally diverse clients (Hall, 1997; Pedersen, 1997; Sue & Sue, 1990). Second, increasing the cultural diversity and multicultural competency of psychologists and counselors necessarily means increasing the diversity of students and evolving the training environment to embrace cultural issues and topics. Both of these concerns have been identified as practical and ethical issues (American Psychological Association [APA], 1997; Atkinson, Brown, & Casas, 1996).

Although there has been notable research examining the degree to which psychology training programs are attending to multicultural training, most of this research has focused on multicultural course offerings, other curricular aspects of training, and the demographic diversity of faculty and students (e.g., Constantine & Gloria, 1999; Constantine, Ladany, Inman, & Ponterotto, 1996; Dinsmore & England, 1996; Hills & Strozier, 1992). Limited research has examined multicultural aspects of the training environment both attitudinally and holistically. Pope-Davis, Liu, Nevitt, and Toporek (2000) identified a need for a tool to assess multicultural environments and developed the Multicultural Environment Inventory–Revised (MEI-R). Pope-Davis et al. presented exploratory information regarding the initial development and validation of the MEI-R. This chapter presents updated information regarding the psychometric properties and appropriate applications for the MEI-R.

The MEI-R was developed in the context of two significant publications: the Multicultural Competency Checklist for Counseling Training Programs (MCC) (Ponterotto, Alexander, & Grieger, 1995) and the APA's (1997) publication, *Diversity and Accreditation*. Both documents outlined important areas that training programs needed to address to be multiculturally competent. Reflecting the meaningful aspects of these reports, Ponterotto et al. (1995) proposed the MCC to assist graduate psychology programs in attending to various aspects of multicultural training and milieu within training programs. This checklist consisted of 22 items in a checklist format covering six themes: minority representation, curriculum issues, counseling practice and supervision, research considerations, student and faculty competency evaluation, and physical environment. The MCC has proven useful in multicultural training research (e.g., Constantine et al., 1996; Ponterotto, 1997). The limitation, however, is that the checklist format provides an opportunity to indicate only whether a condition is present and not the degree to which a condition may be present in training.

The APA also recognized the need to address multiple aspects of multicultural training in a publication on diversity and accreditation (APA, 1997). This publication outlined a set of guidelines for programs to use to address diversity issues within graduate training. The guidelines primarily reflected the themes presented by Ponterotto et al. (1995) and suggested that the accreditation process should examine these aspects in addition to the traditional criteria for program accreditation.

THE DEVELOPMENT OF THE MEI-R

In an effort to provide an instrument that could be used in program evaluation and quantitative research, Pope-Davis et al. (2000) developed the MEI. Initially, the MEI consisted of 53 Likert-type items that were appropriate for responses by either faculty or students. In the development process, an analysis sample was used for item reduction and preliminary psychometric examination. The resulting instrument consisted of 27 items with four interpretable factors, including curriculum and supervision, climate and comfort, honesty in recruitment, and multicultural research. A validation sample was then used to test the revised version of the MEI (MEI-R) and provide psychometric data. Pope-Davis et al. reported internal consistency using Cronbach's alpha (α = .94) for the total 27-item scale. Internal consistency was reported for the following factors: Curriculum and Supervision (α = .92), Climate and Comfort (α = .92), Honesty in Recruitment (α = .85), and Research (α = .83). Pope-Davis et al. reported significant relationships between all factors except Honesty in Recruitment and Research. This preliminary data provided adequate support for the validity and reliability of the MEI-R.

The purpose of this chapter is to present the results of recent research that provided further psychometric support for the MEI-R. In addition, we discuss the strengths of the MEI-R as a tool for program evaluation and training environment research.

METHOD

Participants

Of the 336 participants, including 312 graduate students and 24 faculty of varying ranks, 245 were women (73%) and 59 were men (27%). The racial profile of the participants was as follows: White (n = 192; 57%), Black (n = 44; 12%), Asian American (n = 36; 11%), Latino (n = 31; 9%), Native American (n = 6; 2%), biracial/multiracial (n = 4; 3%), international (n = 4; 3%), and other (n = 18; 5%). The participants ranged in age from 20 to 66 years (M = 31.5; SD = 8.76).

Participants were solicited via e-mails on various multicultural, cross-cultural, course-specific, organizational, and internal listservs. Students and faculty who agreed to participate were provided the Internet link to the survey and also given log-on and passwords to access the surveys. No compensation was given in exchange for participation. The data for this study were combined from two different studies

to conduct the confirmatory analyses. Data from the first sample were collected specifically to assess psychometric properties of the MEI-R and included 155 participants. The MEI-R data from the other 181 participants were collected as part of a larger study examining multicultural research training self-efficacy. The combined data set resulted in a total of 336 participants.

Measures

Multicultural Environment Inventory–Revised (MEI-R; Pope-Davis et al., 2000)

The MEI-R is a 27-item Likert-type measure designed to assess people's attitudes and perceptions of their training environment as it pertains to multiculturalism. There are four subscales in the MEI-R. The first relates to the individual's belief that his or her training environment provides multicultural curriculum and supervision (11 items; score range from 11-55). The second subscale relates to the individual's belief that he or she feels comfortable as a multicultural person in the training environment (11 items; score range from 11-55). The third subscale refers to the individual's honesty about multicultural issues when recruiting new people to the training program (3 items; score range from 3-15). Finally, the fourth subscale is the individual's belief that the training environment supports multicultural research (2 items; score range from 2-10). The MEI-R can be scored according to each subscale or a total score. Subscale scores are derived from summing all items of a particular subscale. A total score is the sum of all items in the MEI-R. As mentioned earlier, Pope-Davis et al. (2000) found adequate internal consistency for the total scale and the four separate subscales.

RESULTS

The results of a confirmatory factor analysis suggested that the model and subscales of the

MEI-R established by Pope-Davis et al. (2000) provided an adequate fit for the data. We used maximum likelihood estimation with the Satorra-Bentler scaled chi-square (Satorra & Bentler, 1994) to correct for nonnormality in the data. The goodness-of-fit indices included the Satorra-Bentler scaled chi-square statistic ($\chi^2 = 858.34$, $df = 318$), the comparative fit index (CFI = .92), and the root mean square error of approximation (RMSEA = .071) values, based on a 90% confidence interval (.065, .077). Figure 12.1 presents the confirmatory factor structure with standardized solutions and correlations between factors.

The MEI-R demonstrated a high estimate of internal consistency using Cronbach's alpha for the total scale ($\alpha = .96$) as well as for the individual subscales. Cronbach's alphas for the individual subscales were as follows: Curriculum and Supervision ($\alpha = .95$), Climate and Comfort ($\alpha = .92$), Honesty in Recruitment ($\alpha = .92$), and Multicultural Research ($\alpha = .89$).

DISCUSSION

The MEI-R was developed to assist programs and faculty in assessing the multicultural training environment both for research and program development purposes. This study supported the construct validity of the original factor structure and subscales described by Pope-Davis et al. (2000) and also supported internal consistency for the instrument. We will describe the subscales in greater detail and then discuss some of the applications in which the MEI-R may prove useful.

Subscales of the MEI-R

The subscale that focuses on curriculum and supervision contains 11 items and assesses the respondent's perceptions of various aspects of training, including the inclusion of multicultural issues in coursework, multicultural

supervision, overall evaluations, exams, and multiculturalism as an attitudinal value in the program. The Climate and Comfort subscale of the MEI-R contains 11 items assessing the respondent's comfort in all courses and supervision in practicum. This subscale reflects an individual's comfort with both faculty and the training program. In addition, this subscale queries diversity in evaluation methods and teaching strategies as well as the respondent's feelings of safety, support, and being valued. The subscale regarding honesty in recruitment is relatively straightforward and assesses the respondent's comfort with providing open and honest information to prospective students, staff, and faculty. Three items on this subscale essentially state that an individual is "honest" with potential hires and recruits (i.e., faculty, staff, and students) about the multicultural valuing in the respondent's training program. The final subscale contains 2 items and assesses the involvement of faculty in multicultural research both generally and as a specific research agenda. Although it does not exhaust all potential areas that a training program could focus on to become multicultural and to value multiculturalism, the MEI-R does reflect the salient areas outlined by Ponterotto et al. (1995) and the APA (1997).

Applications of the MEI-R

Given the support for the validity and reliability of the MEI-R, we suggest that training programs and researchers should use this instrument in a variety of ways. The remainder of this chapter discusses some examples of the utility of the MEI-R in assessing the multicultural training environment.

Program Development Toward Multiculturalism

Counseling and psychology programs may choose to conduct an assessment of the

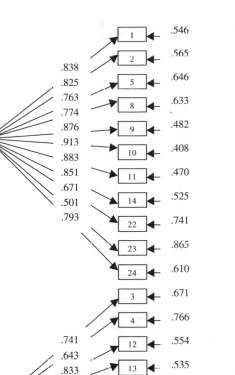
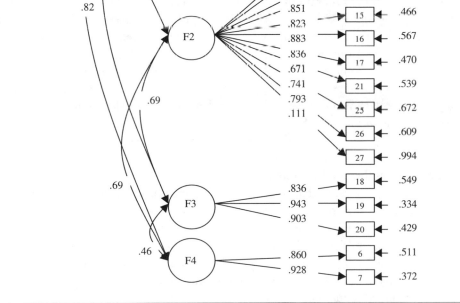

Figure 12.1 Confirmatory Factor Structure With Standardized Solutions and Correlations Between Factors for the MEI-R

multicultural environment for formative or summative evaluations. The MEI-R, much like any other assessment tool, needs to be used

with intention. Specifically, training programs need to first conduct some preliminary work prior to using the MEI-R as a measure or reflection of an environment's multiculturalism. A program's faculty, students, and support staff should engage in a discussion about what constitutes multicultural competency for their environment, what are the salient issues members are struggling with, and what are some potential routes to achieve their goal. First and foremost, members of a training program need to be informed about a program's intention to evolve and change, and the members need to support such a move. Hence, the MEI-R is to be used by training programs with the intent to involve all members of a training program, with an initial vision of becoming multicultural, and with avenues and spaces for discourse and dialogue to occur.

Applying the MEI-R without the necessary preparation may lead to resentment, resistance, confusion, and frustration by members of a training program who (a) may not feel that anything is amiss with the program or (b) may believe that they were not asked for input into issues that are directly meaningful to them. Consequently, results from the MEI-R, or any other multicultural competency measure, may reflect biased responses, errors, or nonresponses. All these data problems could potentially frustrate the implementation of programmatic changes.

The MEI-R may be used in conjunction with objective data such as the number of multicultural courses offered, diversity of faculty and student body, multicultural research and publications produced, and the presence of formal organizations (e.g., multicultural committee) and multicultural events. Depending on the goals of the evaluation, either the subscale scores or scores on individual items may be used. When used as part of a formative evaluation, the MEI-R may be most helpful in assessing perceptions about a program's strengths and weaknesses in multicultural training to identify areas in need of attention. As a component of a summative evaluation, the MEI-R may be used to assess whether programmatic changes resulted in changes in perceptions about the multicultural climate, curriculum, supervision, research, and recruitment. The MEI-R can provide a snapshot of faculty and student perceptions or be used as a pretest and posttest of the influence of changes on perceptions.

Maintaining a Multicultural Focus

Similar to programs seeking to become more multiculturally valuing than their original state, other programs will likely find themselves achieving aspects of their vision toward multiculturalism. In that respect, training programs need to have some format to continually reflect on their progress. The MEI-R can be used in such a manner.

As new students enter or leave a program or as faculty enter and leave training programs, it is important to understand their perceptions of the environment. This is especially true for new members entering (or returning members) into a particular environment. Although a multicultural vision can be articulated to new members, the perceptions of new members can provide valuable information about the relative strengths and challenges of a program seeking to be multicultural. Information gathered on the MEI-R that reflects new member perceptions can help existing members gauge success and future challenges, as well as areas needing attention. All of these aspects could possibly contribute to retention of faculty, students, and staff and the continual development of the training program.

Multicultural Research

Research in multicultural counseling and training is acknowledging the need to account for complex relationships among variables. One such variable that is not often addressed is the training environment. There is a need to advance multicultural research to include multilevel sources (see Chapter 14, this volume). For example, when investigating factors that influence the effect of multicultural supervision, students' perceptions of the multicultural climate may provide information about the context within which supervision occurs. This is particularly relevant when we consider that the multicultural competence of supervisors may be influenced by the support and resources provided by the training program.

In addition, the MEI-R can be used as part of survey research that examines specific multicultural competencies of respondents and its relationship with various outcomes such as supervision, clinical applications, and attitudes toward diversity. Researchers should explore the ways in which a respondent's environment potentially helps or inhibits the full actualization of multicultural competency (i.e., feeling of self-efficacy in multicultural issues) and competencies (i.e., specific demonstrable multicultural proficiencies). This is one area that the extant research has yet to explore.

Future Research and Development of the MEI-R

Currently, the MEI-R has been used in selective counseling research. Future research could potentially use the MEI-R in other training programs outside of counseling. For instance, the MEI-R could be used in clinical psychology training programs because the constructs in the MEI-R tend to be generalizable to clinical psychology. Beyond clinical psychology, the authors envision its use within all fields of psychology. Although the MEI-R is focused specifically on applied psychology programs, evolution of the MEI-R could occur such that experimental, theoretical, and research areas of psychology could also become multiculturally competent. For the nonapplied areas of psychology, it would be important to articulate a vision of

multicultural competency and competencies for a particular field because demands vary across disciplines.

As the MEI-R is used in research, additional constructs or items may be needed. One way to potentially gather these important data would be through a qualitative analysis. These data can be gathered either through narratives at the end of a survey (either electronic or paper and pencil) or through qualitative follow-up of selective participants. Qualitative information has been identified as an important piece of data in multicultural research (Pope-Davis, Liu, Toporek, & Brittan-Powell, 2001). With respect to the MEI-R, qualitative data could provide valuable perceptions about a respondent's environment not yet assessed.

CONCLUSION

The updated empirical evidence provides further information and support for the usefulness and strength of the MEI-R. Building on the recent validation, we provided a sample of potential ways that researchers, psychologists, and training programs might use the MEI-R. We would like to emphasize that the instrument is not limited to only these applications and encourage readers to consider its potential usefulness in their research. Fundamentally, we hope that the MEI-R serves as an effective tool in the service of increasing training environments' multicultural valuing and enhances the experience of students, faculty, staff, and, ultimately, clients.

REFERENCES

American Psychological Association, Commission on Ethnic Minority Recruitment, Retention, and Training in Psychology. (1997, January). *Diversity and accreditation.* Washington, DC: American Psychological Association.

Arredondo, P., Toporek, R., Brown, S. P., Jones, J., Locke, D. C., Sanchez, J., et al. (1996). Operationalization of the multicultural counseling competencies. *Journal of Multicultural Counseling & Development,* 24(1), 42-78.

Atkinson, D. R., Brown, M. T., & Casas, J. M. (1996). Achieving ethnic parity in counseling psychology. *The Counseling Psychologist, 24,* 230-258.

Bernal, M. E., & Castro, F. G. (1994). Are clinical psychologists prepared for service and research with ethnic minorities? Report of a decade of progress. *American Psychologist, 49,* 797-805.

Constantine, M. G., & Gloria, A. M. (1999). Multicultural issues in predoctoral internship programs: A national survey. *Journal of Multicultural Counseling and Development,* 27(1), 42-53.

Constantine, M. G., Ladany, N., Inman, A. G., & Ponterotto, J. G. (1996). Students' perceptions of multicultural training in counseling psychology programs. *Journal of Multicultural Counseling and Development, 24,* 241-253.

Dinsmore, J. A., & England, J. T. (1996). A study of multicultural counseling training at CACREP accredited counselor education programs. *Counselor Education and Supervision, 36,* 58-76.

Graham, S. (1992). "Most of the subjects were White and middle class": Trends in published research on African Americans in selected APA journals, 1970-1989. *American Psychologist, 47,* 629-639.

Hall, C. C. I. (1997). Cultural malpractice: The growing obsolescence of psychology with the changing U.S. population. *American Psychologist, 52,* 642-651.

Hills, H. I., & Strozier, A. L. (1992). Multicultural training in APA-approved counseling psychology programs: A survey. *Professional Psychology: Research and Practice, 23,* 43-51.

Pedersen, P. B. (1997). *Culture-centered counseling interventions: Striving for accuracy.* Thousand Oaks, CA: Sage.

Ponterotto, J. G. (1997). Multicultural counseling training: A competency model and national survey. In D. B. Pope-Davis & H. L. K. Coleman (Eds.), *Multicultural counseling competencies: Assessment, education and training, and supervision* (pp. 111-130). Thousand Oaks, CA: Sage.

Ponterotto, J. G., Alexander, C. M., & Grieger, I. (1995). A multicultural competency checklist for counseling and training programs. *Journal of Multicultural Counseling and Development, 23,* 11-20.

Pope-Davis, D. B., Liu, W. M., Nevitt, J., & Toporek, R. L. (2000). The development and initial validation of the Multicultural Environmental Inventory. *Cultural Diversity and Ethnic Minority Psychology,* 6(1), 57-64.

Pope-Davis, D. B., Liu, W. M., Toporek, R. L., & Brittan-Powell, C. (2001). How do we identify cultural competence in counseling? Review, introspection, and recommendations for future research. *Cultural Diversity and Ethnic Minority Psychology, 7,* 121-138.

Quintana, S. M., Troyano, N., & Taylor, G. (2001). Cultural validity and inherent challenges in quantitative methods for multicultural research. In J. G. Ponterotto, J. M. Casas, L. A. Suzuki, & C. M. Alexander (Eds.), *Handbook of multicultural counseling* (2nd ed., pp. 604-630). Thousand Oaks, CA: Sage.

Sue, D. W. (2001). Multidimensional facets of cultural competence. *The Counseling Psychologist,* 29(6), 790-821.

Sue, D. W., & Sue, D. (1990). *Counseling the culturally different: Theory and practice* (2nd ed.). New York: John Wiley.

Sue, S. (1999). Science, ethnicity, and bias. *American Psychologist, 54,* 1070-1077.

13

Assessing Teacher Multicultural Competence

Self-Report Instruments, Observer
Report Evaluations, and a Portfolio Assessment

JOSEPH G. PONTEROTTO
JACLYN MENDELSOHN
LONETTE BELIZAIRE
Fordham University at Lincoln Center

As the demography of the United States continues to shift rapidly, and as multicultural issues continue to form an essential component of the teacher education mission, there will be an increasing need to develop and test tools to assess the multicultural competence of teachers at all educational levels. Despite a burgeoning general literature in multicultural education over the past decade, there is surprisingly little attention in this literature devoted to accountability in preparing and evaluating teachers for service in an increasingly culturally diverse society. Therefore, it is timely at this point to review the status of multicultural education in teacher training, particularly with regard to available tools to assess the preparedness of teachers for work in U.S. schools.

This chapter is organized along three major sections. First, we review the status of multicultural education in teacher preparation programs vis-à-vis demographic shifts in the P-12 school population and the recent mandates of leading professional organizations of teacher preparation. Second, we build a rationale for the need for valid and reliable quantitative tools and credible qualitative tools to monitor and assess teacher trainees' readiness for work in a heterogeneous society. As part of this second section, we review four self-report instruments and one observer report evaluation, and we introduce a new guided portfolio assessment for P-12 teachers. Finally, we close the chapter by positing specific research needs in the area of assessing multicultural competence of teachers.

SHIFTING DEMOGRAPHIC REALITIES

It is common knowledge that the demography of the U.S. population is shifting rapidly from a predominantly Anglo, European American citizenry to a predominantly non-Anglo, non–European American population. A recent *New York Times* (Schmitt, 2001) analysis of the 2000 U.S. Census reports that non-Hispanic Whites now constitute a numerical minority of the total population of the country's 100 largest cities. Looking specifically at P-12 school districts, the Council of the Great City School, which represents the nation's 47 largest school systems, estimates that 25% of its students are European American; .5% are American Indian, Eskimo, or Aleut; 6% are Asian American/Pacific Islanders; 26% are Hispanic; and 42% are African American (www.ncrel.org/sdrs/cityschl/city1_1a.htm, as cited in Ragle, Szakaly, & Zygmunt-Fillwalk, 2001).

For more precise present and projected population demographics, we present Table 13.1, which summarizes the latest data from U.S. Census reports. The most recent fully available data (1999 counts) indicate that White Americans represent 72% of the U.S. population; by the year 2025, this proportion will decrease to 62%; and by 2050, Whites will represent roughly 53% of the total U.S. population. At present, looking at the percentage of school-age children (5-17 years), Whites represent roughly 65% (see row 2 of Table 13.1). Furthermore, Whites are the oldest racial group in the United States (median age = 38.1), with Hispanics (median age = 26.5) and American Indians (median age = 28.2) representing the

youngest racial cohorts in the United States. Perhaps the most remarkable statistic summarized in Table 13.1 is the average population growth rate per decade over the next 50 years. During this time, Asian Americans will grow in population by close to 30% and Hispanics by 28%, but Whites will grow at a rate of only 2% per decade.

The rapid race-based demographic changes currently under way among the general population are not matched by changes in the nature of the P-12 teaching workforce. Table 13.1, row 2 reveals that 34.68% of school-age children represent racial/ethnic minority groups, yet according to the National Council on the Accreditation of Teacher Education Programs (NCATE, 2001), less than 15% of the teaching workforce represents minority groups. Although we expect the representation of minority teachers to increase in coming decades, we do not anticipate that representational growth will come near the general growth rates of racial/ethnic minority populations.

Also, we do not maintain that teachers necessarily need to represent the racial/ethnic groups that they teach, but it is clear from related research in the counseling field (Atkinson, Brown, & Casas, 1996) that increased minority representation in the profession markedly enhances the quality of and satisfaction with services. Furthermore, a question can be raised as to the "real-life" preparedness of many new White teachers to work within culturally heterogeneous environments. For example, Gomez (1993) cited an American Association for Colleges of Teacher Education (AACTE) survey of 3rd- or 4th-year teacher education students enrolled in 42 AACTE member institutions, which found that the overwhelming majority of White students were raised in European American neighborhoods, attended predominantly White universities, had primarily White friends, and indicated a strong preference to work in a

Table 13.1   Current and Anticipated Population Demographics by Hispanic Origin and Race: 1999-2050

		Not of Hispanic Origin			
	Hispanic Origin[a]	*White*	*Black*	*Asian, Pacific Islander*	*American Indian, Eskimo, Aleut*
% of total population: 1999	11.49	71.89	12.14	3.73	.74
% of 5- to 17-year-olds: 1999	14.86	65.32	14.84	3.98	1.0
Median age: 1999	26.5	38.1	30.3	32.0	28.2
Projections					
% of total population: 2025	18.19	61.97	12.89	6.17	.79
% of total population: 2050	24.33	52.67	13.24	8.86	.80
Average growth (%) by decade: 2000-2050	27.62	2.42	10.82	29.96	10.84

SOURCE: Data extracted from U.S. Bureau of the Census (2000, Tables 16-18).

a. Hispanic origin persons may be of any race.

majority setting upon graduation. The reality is, given demographic shifts and the paucity of minority teachers, that a good number of teachers in this AACTE survey will in fact educate many pupils of racial/ethnic minority backgrounds.

MULTICULTURAL MISSION INHERENT IN PROFESSIONAL TEACHING ASSOCIATIONS

Part of the upsurge in attention to multicultural training in teacher education programs stems from the rapid demographic shifts currently under way in the United States. Perhaps an even more direct influence on the rapidly evolving curriculum of teacher education programs is the mandate from influential teacher preparation and accreditation organizations. Taking the lead in highlighting the increasing salience of multicultural competence to all teacher trainees are the NCATE and the Interstate New Teacher Assessment and Support Consortium (INTASC). Working collaboratively, the NCATE and INTASC

have devised accreditation and licensing standards for teachers. The NCATE/INTASC guidelines focus not only on traditional cognitive and knowledge-focused domains but also on the affective domain through the area of personal "dispositions" thought to characterize successful teachers.

Directly relevant to our content coverage in this chapter is the following INTASC standard:

The teacher understands how students differ in their approaches to learning and creates instructional opportunities that are adapted to diverse learners. (INTASC, 2001, p. 7)

Personal dispositions directly tied to this principle would include the belief that all children can learn, a valuing of human diversity, and sensitivity to cultural and community norms (Ragle et al., 2001).

The following two NCATE professional standards also speak directly to the need for cultural competence in all teachers:

Candidates preparing to work in schools as teachers or other professional school personnel know and demonstrate the content, pedagological, and professional knowledge, skills, and dispositions necessary to help all students learn. (NCATE, 2001, p. 14, Standard 1)

The unit (teacher education program) designs, implements, and evaluates curriculum and experiences for candidates to acquire and apply the knowledge, skills, and dispositions necessary to help students learn. These experiences include working with diverse higher education and school faculty, diverse candidates, and diverse students in P-12 schools. (NCATE, 2001, p. 29, Standard 4)

The above professional standards, coupled with the acknowledgment of evolving demographics and the reality of disproportionate school achievement levels across racial/ethnic groups (see Webb-Johnson, Artiles, Trent, Jackson, & Velox, 1998), have led many teacher education programs to design multicultural education courses and attempt to infuse multicultural issues across the curriculum. However, little is known about the profession's recent effectiveness in this revised mission, given lack of both systematic research and reliable and valid assessment tools (Sleeter, 2001). In the next section, we present brief reviews of multicultural assessment tools for teachers, and then we end the chapter by positing specific research directions for the field.

SELF-REPORT TOOLS TO ASSESS TEACHERS' MULTICULTURAL COMPETENCE

This section reviews briefly four quantitative, paper-and-pencil self-report instruments of teachers' multicultural competence. During our computer and manual searches for such instruments, we were surprised by how few well-validated instruments were available.

Most measures that we located across a wide teacher education literature base were one-time use scales, often developed for a particular dissertation or study. Interestingly, the minimal attention devoted to psychometric properties of teacher multicultural competency scales stands in sharp contrast to the parallel literature in the counseling field (see reviews in Constantine & Ladany, 2001; Ponterotto, Fuertes, & Chen, 2000).

The instruments reviewed below are the Cultural Diversity Awareness Inventory (CDAI) (Henry, 1986), the Multiethnic Climate Inventory (MCI) (Johnson & Johnson, 1996), the Multicultural Teaching Concerns Survey (MTCS) (Marshall, 1996), and the Teacher Multicultural Attitude Survey (TMAS) (Ponterotto, Baluch, Greig, & Rivera, 1998). These instruments were selected because they are among the more recently developed assessments, all witnessing use in the 1990s; were published in peer-reviewed national journals; and appear to have at least initial levels of content validity.

Cultural Diversity Awareness Inventory (CDAI)

The CDAI was initially designed by Henry (1986) to examine attitudes, beliefs, and behavior toward culturally diverse young children. The target audience was adults (e.g., teachers, school administrators, therapists) being trained for direct service to culturally diverse youth. The CDAI includes 28 self-report items arranged on a 5-point Likert-type scale using anchor points of *strongly agree* to *strongly disagree*.

Since Henry's (1986) original work, the CDAI has been slightly modified (Deering & Stanutz, 1995; Larke, 1990), with the 28 items now organized conceptually (though not factor analytically) into five areas: (a) general cultural awareness (e.g., "uncomfortable with people who have values different from mine"),

(b) the culturally diverse family (e.g., "should include family view of school and society in school program planning"), (c) cross-cultural communication (e.g., "uncomfortable with people who speak nonstandard English"), (d) assessment (e.g., "give standardized or intelligence test in child's dominant language"), and (e) the multicultural environment (e.g., "teachers should provide opportunities for children to share cultural differences") (Larke, 1990, pp. 26-27).

Larke (1990) used the CDAI in a posttest-only design with 51 female elementary preservice teachers who had completed one multicultural education course. The author used descriptive statistics (percentages) to examine students' levels of agreement or disagreement across the 28 items. Deering and Stanutz (1995) used the CDAI in a pretest-posttest design to assess the impact of a middle school field experience in a culturally diverse setting for 16 female secondary preservice teachers. As in the Larke study, Deering and Stanutz examined percentages of agreement and disagreement across items. The results of this study indicated attitude change across some items but not others. In both studies, only descriptive statistics were presented, and no psychometric evidence regarding the CDAI was examined.

Multiethnic Climate Inventory (MCI)

The MCI is a 20-item, 5-point Likert-type survey (with the anchor points of *strongly disagree* to *strongly agree*) introduced by Johnson and Johnson (1996). According to these authors, the 20-item MCI was developed from a 45-item pilot instrument. The authors noted that the final 20 items were selected though the use of a factor analysis, although the analysis itself is not presented.

The MCI includes the following four subscales of five items each: (a) Cultural Encapsulation (e.g., "I want most people in my school to be the same race and culture as I am"), (b) Cultural Hostility (e.g., "I don't trust people whose race is different from mine"), (c) Majority Dominance (e.g., "Minorities should learn to work in the majority world but retain their own identity"), and (d) Minority Suppression (e.g., "I believe that the White majority will never fully accept minorities as equals") (Johnson & Johnson, 1996, p. 136).

Johnson and Johnson (1996) incorporated the MCI to examine its relationship with concrete-abstract thinking levels in 123 middle school teachers in the Southeast. The findings were generally consistent with conceptual systems theory (cf. Harvey, Hunt, & Schroder, 1961) and indicated that concrete thinkers had significantly stronger agreement with Cultural Encapsulation and Majority Dominance attitudes than did middle-level or abstract thinkers. This finding provides some initial criterion validity evidence for the MCI.

The only additional psychometric data presented in Johnson and Johnson (1996) are reliability as assessed through coefficient alpha. The results were satisfactory, with coefficient alphas being .77 for Cultural Encapsulation, .71 for Cultural Hostility, .73 for Majority Dominance, and .77 for Minority Suppression.

Multicultural Teaching Concerns Survey (MTCS)

The MTCS (Marshall, 1996) is a 64-item self-report measure of teachers' concerns regarding working with diverse student populations. Development of the MTCS was conceptually anchored in Locke's (1988) multicultural awareness model and in Fuller and Brown's (1975) three-tier concern conceptualization: concerns about self, tasks, and teaching impact. MTCS items are presented to participants (teacher trainees and teachers, P-12 focus) on a 5-point Likert-type scale with the anchors of *an extremely important concern for me at this time* and *an extremely unimportant concern for me at this time.* The MTCS includes four factor analytically derived subscales: Cross-Cultural Competence, Strategies and Techniques, School Bureaucracy, and Familial/Group Knowledge.

Marshall (1996) used a fairly systematic procedure to develop the MTCS. To generate content for item development, the author presented four open-ended questions to 206 preservice and experienced teachers. These participants generated more than 300 concerns and questions, from which Marshall retained 243 after sorting. A theme analysis by the author revealed four major themes represented in the concerns. Next, descriptions of these categories were developed, and three independent judges successfully matched specific questions with defined categories. To reduce the pool of 243 questions, Marshall conducted a three-round modified Delphi poll across three judges, eventually decreasing the question pool to 64 questions, which formed the content items for the MTCS. Marshall developed separate MTCS forms for preservice and experienced teachers.

Administering the 64-item MTCS to 146 preservice and experienced teachers, Marshall (1996) conducted an exploratory factor analysis using the maximum likelihood method with a varimax (orthogonal) rotation. Four interpretable factors emerged, accounting for 51% of the common variance. The four-factor solution was consistent with the categories emanating from the theme analysis of the initial 300 questions. In interpreting the four-factor solution, Marshall selected factor loadings of > .30 while eliminating items with multiple high loadings.

The resulting structure included 11 items assessing Cross-Cultural Competence (e.g., "Will culturally diverse students perceive me as biased simply because my background is different from theirs?"), 11 items assessing Strategies and Techniques (e.g., "How do I

make lessons and content relevant to diverse students?"), 4 items assessing School Bureaucracy (e.g., "How do I deal with attitudes of intolerance toward diverse students as expressed by my colleagues?"), and 5 items assessing Familial/Group Knowledge (e.g., "In what specific ways does family culture affect diverse students' performance in school?").

Marshall's (1996) MTCS is an interesting tool to assess multicultural concerns held by both preservice and practicing teachers. The MTCS has content validity, given the systematic item development and elimination procedures incorporated by Marshall. Furthermore, initial exploratory factor analysis supports a four-factor model. However, the research on the MTCS is still in its infancy, and Marshall did not present any reliability evidence or convergent or criterion validity evidence for the MTCS.

Teacher Multicultural Attitude Survey (TMAS)

The TMAS (Ponterotto et al., 1998) is a unidimensional 20-item self-report inventory of teachers' multicultural awareness and sensitivity. TMAS items are situated on a 5-point Likert-type scale with response anchors being *strongly disagree* to *strongly agree.* Teachers scoring higher on the TMAS are aware of multicultural issues in education; are open, receptive, and embracing of cultural diversity; and believe cultural diversity and multicultural education enhance the learning environment for all students.

The TMAS was developed and validated over two studies (both reported in Ponterotto et al., 1998) using 429 teachers and teacher education students from three states in the Northeast (Study 1) and 227 teacher education students in New York (Study 2). Content validity was established through expert ratings of item clarity and domain appropriateness and the use of two focus groups with urban and suburban teachers. A prototype 30-item TMAS was reduced to the current 20 items through item analysis and factor analysis. Study 2 in Ponterotto et al. (1998) subjected the revised 20-item TMAS to another factor analysis, which resulted in a dominant first factor (eigenvalue = 6.5; 32.5% of common variance). A forced one-factor extraction found that 18 of the 20 items had structure coefficients of .35 or greater, and 17 items had structure coefficients of .40 or higher.

Coefficient alpha for the 20-item TMAS was .86, and theta coefficient was .89. A 3-week test-retest reliability coefficient of .80 was achieved with 16 teacher education students. With regard to criterion-related validity, the TMAS correlated significantly in predicted directions with the Multiethnic Identity Measure (Phinney, 1992) and the Quick Discrimination Index (Ponterotto et al., 1995; Utsey & Ponterotto, 1999). Importantly, the TMAS evidenced no social desirability contamination in a correlation with the popular Crowne and Marlowe (1960) Social Desirability Scale. Additional criterion-related validity evidence was noted in the Group Differences Approach (Walsh & Betz, 1990), which found that participants who had completed workshops on multicultural education scored significantly higher than those who had not.

Of the four instruments reviewed briefly in this section, the TMAS has amassed the most psychometric evidence. However, we would consider the collective group of instruments to be in relatively early stages of psychometric testing. Appendix 13.A lists all 20 items of the TMAS.

OBSERVER REPORT ASSESSMENT

The limitations of self-report instruments are well known: They may be subject to response bias and socially desirable responding, there is concern whether self-report correlates significantly to actual behavior, and in regression models, self-report instruments often account for very small percentages of variance in the defined construct (see related discussion in Krosnick, 1999).

A quantitative alternative to self-report instruments is observer report evaluations. Observer report assessments most often entail "experts" (e.g., master teachers, seasoned counselors) evaluating novice professionals (e.g., student teachers, counselor trainees) on predetermined and quantified content categories. In our review of the literature, we located one observer report measure with good promise for multicultural assessment—the Racial Ethical Sensitivity Test (REST).

The Racial Ethical Sensitivity Test

Conceptually, the REST (Brabeck et al., 2000) was anchored in Rest's (1983) theory of ethical development and the professional ethical principles of multiple professional organizations (teaching, administration, counseling, psychology, nursing, social work). Brabeck et al. (2000) identified six principles common to these professional organizations: professional competence, integrity, professional and scientific responsibility, respect for others' rights and dignity, concern for others' welfare, and social responsibility. These principles helped form the foundation of vignettes depicting acts of racial/ethnic and gender intolerance.

The vignettes were developed systematically through (a) a review of newspaper and magazine articles from the popular press, (b) the use of four culturally diverse focus groups, and (c) consultation with a professional playwright. This process led to the development of five videotaped vignettes titled Faculty Lounge, Math Class, Northside High, Residence Hall, and Basketball Practice. For example, the Faculty Lounge vignette was as follows:

> Two teachers are discussing a student in front of a new faculty member. The two

veteran teachers discuss the student's academic and private life in stereotypical and derogatory ways. They show no concern for her privacy and a complete disregard for her rights to confidentiality. In addition, it is clear they have no understanding of her culture. When the new faculty member tries to share her thoughts and stand up for the student, she is met with hostility and ridicule. (Brabeck et al., 2000, p. 125)

Structured interview protocols were written for each video vignette, and scoring criteria were developed. The specific questions in the protocols were designed to assess the participants' awareness of the ethical issues highlighted earlier and violated in the vignette. Each vignette portrays from five to nine complex ethical issues. Each issue can be scored 1 (*participant did not identify the behavior*), 2 (*participant identified the targeted behavior*), or 3 (*the participant recognized and elaborated upon the targeted unethical behavior*). Across all vignettes, there was a total of 37 ethical violations, so REST total scores can range from 37 to 111.

Brabeck et al. (2000) conducted a series of reliability checks in developing the scoring system. Interrater agreement across five judges in a pilot study ranged from .80 to 1.00 for 77% of items rated. In a second study, interrater agreement was .70 and .72 across two time trials, with a 2-week test-retest stability coefficient of .65. Coefficient alphas were also calculated and ranged from .46 to .69 at Time 1 and from .27 to .74 at Time 2. These alphas are low, but given the nature of the structured interview protocol, coefficient alpha is not a relevant reliability index. Interestingly, 42 participants were shown two of the five vignettes and also completed a self-report measure of multicultural counseling competency, the Multicultural Awareness-Knowledge-Skills Survey (D'Andrea, Daniels, & Heck, 1991). There was a negligible and nonsignificant correlation between the self-report and

observer report measure. This finding highlights our point at the start of this section that self-report may not be indicative of actual behavior.

In summary, the REST is a carefully developed, conceptually anchored observer report measure of multicultural ethics in school practice. Initial indices of interrater agreement and test-retest stability are satisfactory, and the REST shows promise for objective assessment of school personnel's multicultural ethical awareness and knowledge. Understandably, as a new measure, the REST is in need of additional testing, particularly in regard to test-retest stability, interrater agreement, and criterion-related validity.

PORTFOLIO ASSESSMENT

Developing multicultural competence is an evolving process that is continuous and ongoing. One limitation of both self-report and observer report assessments of multicultural competence is that they are static, measuring perceived competence at one point in time. A more flexible alternative to quantitative assessments of teachers' multicultural competence is qualitative and experiential assessment tools. One example is the portfolio, defined by Arter and Spandel (1992) as "a purposeful collection of student work that tells the story of the student's efforts, progress, or achievement in a given area(s)" (p. 36; also cited in Coleman, 1997, p. 46). Portfolio assessments help determine not only what a student has learned about a particular topic but also how the student's awareness and knowledge evolve over time. Importantly, portfolio assessments promote self-reflection about learning and greater ownership over one's learning process and goals (Coleman, 1997). There is now a significant literature on portfolio assessments in teacher education, and the following sources are highly recommended to readers: Coleman, Norton, Miranda, and McCubbin (Chapter 3, this volume); Mick (1996);

Pleasants, Johnson, and Trent (1998); and Wade and Yarbrough (1996).

The Multicultural/Diversity Teaching Competencies Portfolio

In this section, we introduce a new portfolio designed by the present authors. The 12-page portfolio centers on 20 specified competencies and is designed for P-12 teacher education students. The origins of the portfolio stem primarily from the experiences of the senior author, who has been teaching multicultural education and multicultural counseling courses since 1985. The portfolio contents reflect the biases of the chapter's authors, who are counseling psychologists by training and who have used portfolio assessments in multicultural counseling training. Chief among these biases is the definition and goals of multicultural education and the view that multicultural competence develops parallel to one's "multicultural personality" development. First, we define *multicultural education* and then we move to a brief discussion of the "multicultural personality."

Our definition of multicultural education is synthesized from various sources (e.g., Nieto, 2000; Ponterotto, Lewis, & Bullington, 1990; Ponterotto & Pedersen, 1993) and includes three components:

- an education whereby all students, regardless of race, ethnicity, religion, gender, or sexual orientation, feel equally welcome, valued, empowered, and challenged in school;
- an education whereby issues of diversity are infused throughout the curriculum, and learning includes knowledge about diverse groups (e.g., worldview, acculturation levels, sociocultural history, immigration and migration patterns) as well as a focus on examining one's own socialization, personal biases, and worldview; and
- an education whereby issues of White and male privilege, internalized racism and homophobia, and oppression are honestly and accurately addressed.

The second bias reflected in our portfolio is that to teach effectively in a heterogeneous society, one has to develop as a multicultural person. Ponterotto discussed the construct of the "multicultural personality," reflecting a personality disposition embracing (and seeking) cultural diversity (see Ponterotto, Costa, & Werner-Lin, 2002; Ponterotto, Jackson, & Nutini, 2001; Ponterotto & Pedersen, 1993). Our conception of the multicultural personality parallels to some degree the constructs of the "multicultural person" (Nieto, 2000), the "multicultural citizen" (Banks, 2001), and the "multicultural orientation to life" (Ramirez, 1999).

Nieto (2000) believes that teachers must transform themselves into multicultural persons, which involves personal reeducation in three areas: (a) learning more about cultural pluralism, (b) confronting one's own racism and biases, and (c) learning to see reality from a variety of perspectives. Banks (2001) sees a teacher with multicultural citizenship as (a) having a balance of cultural, national, and global identifications and understanding multiple ways in which knowledge is constructed; (b) becoming knowledge producers; (c) being thoughtful, caring, and reflective; and (d) being socially active in efforts to create a more humane nation and world. Ramirez (1999) believes that a professional with a multicultural orientation to life (a) strives for maximum personality development, in part achieved by interacting with diversity; (b) adapts well to different environmental situations; (c) enjoys leadership roles in diverse groups and develops innovative solutions for resolving conflict in diverse groups; (d) works for social justice for all citizens; and (e) seeks exposure to as much diversity as possible through friendships, colleagues, readings, travel, and so on.

Building on the work of these authors and incorporating our own experiences and perceptions, we define the multicultural personality as being

> characterized by an individual who embraces diversity in her or his personal life; makes active attempts to learn about other cultures and interact with culturally different people (e.g., friends, colleagues); understands the biases inherent in his or her own worldview and actively learns about alternate worldviews; and is a social activist, empowered to speak out against all forms of social injustice (e.g., racism, homophobia, sexism, ageism, domestic violence, religious stereotyping).

At present, we hypothesize that the "multicultural personality" may be correlated with the following variables: satisfaction with and quality of life, existential meaning, psychological hardiness, psychological resiliency and flexibility, increased cognitive complexity and critical thinking skills, enhanced perceptual acuity, reduced discomfort with ambiguity, reduced general anxiety, and better physical health. Naturally, we believe that the multicultural personality will be correlated with more effective and successful teaching at all levels (see Ponterotto et al., 2002, for research hypotheses related to the multicultural personality).

Organization of the Portfolio

With our above-stated definitions of multicultural education and the multicultural personality serving as conceptual building blocks of the portfolio, we have organized the portfolio competencies into three distinct, though not mutually exclusive, categories: Teacher Personal Dispositions (6 competencies), Teacher Knowledge (7 competencies), and Teacher Skill (7 competencies). The broad categories stem from longstanding literature in multicultural counseling (Sue et al., 1998), coupled with evolving NCATE standards. The specific content inherent in the competencies stems from related literature in multicultural

counseling (Ponterotto, Casas, Suzuki, & Alexander, 2001; Sue et al., 1998), a review of the multicultural education literature (e.g., Banks, 2001; Gomez, 1993; Ladson-Billings, 1999; Nieto, 2000; Noordhoff & Kleinfeld, 1993; Ponterotto et al., 1990; Sleeter, 2001; Webb-Johnson et al., 1998), and the authors' collective experiences in the area.

Appendix 13.B lists the 20 competencies included in the portfolio, and Appendix 13.C presents one page depicting the actual portfolio layout. As can be seen in Appendix 13.C, the portfolio layout includes three columns. Column 1 lists the specific competency, column 2 requests that the student reflect on specific class activities that help him or her process and digest the competency, and column 3 asks the student to consider events and experiences outside of class that address the competency. In the next sections, we describe how we use the portfolio.

Completing the Portfolio

Although initially designed for courses on multicultural education, the portfolio can be used and adapted for any course in the curriculum. The portfolio is given out the first week of class in a 15-week semester. Students work on the portfolio for the entire semester, handing it in on the 13th week and getting it back with the professor's reflective comments on the 14th or 15th week of the semester. Students are instructed to fill in the portfolio in any way that best helps them reflect and express themselves regarding their multicultural development. They may write in pen or pencil, use the back of the portfolio, or include art, diary entries, pictures, newspaper/magazine clippings, and so forth. Students are told that some experiences may address multiple competencies, and overlap is fine and to be expected given that the competencies are understandably interrelated.

Throughout the semester, the professor shares examples of how a class activity (see

Appendix 13.C, column 2), role-play, debate, discussion, or "class tension" applies to various competencies. The professor may also mention a movie seen or a novel just read and how it led her or him to consider a particular competency and fill in column 3. The professor's active modeling alleviates some anxiety held by students regarding how the portfolio is to be completed. This process also sends the clear message that the portfolio is to be worked on continuously throughout the semester and not saved as an assignment for the last few weeks of the semester.

We encourage the professor to complete the entire portfolio contiguous to the students and therefore model, in part, the first competency (regarding continuing education; see Appendix 13.B). Also, at various points in the course, the professor invites (does not require) students to share a recent portfolio entry to help classmates see the variety of ways in which various competencies are addressed and processed on the portfolio. However, only the professor sees the students' completed portfolios as they are considered personal documents; it is left up to individual students to decide whether they might want to share the portfolio with another student, prospective employer, and so forth. The senior author's experience in using this portfolio and a 34-item multicultural counseling portfolio reveals that the entries are often highly personal and emotive, as students reflect on personal upbringing, race/ethnic-based messages from parents, experiences with privilege or racism, and so forth.

Challenges With and Grading of Portfolios

For students who have never worked with portfolio assessments before, the Multicultural/Diversity Teaching Competencies Portfolio can cause some anxiety and frustration. Many students are not accustomed to the flexibility and lack of specific directions on how the portfolio needs to be completed. The professor purposely provides only general guidelines so as to promote the individual reflective and expressive creativity of the students. Around the 3rd or 4th week of classes, students often note that the portfolio is time-consuming, is emotionally draining, and lacks explicit directions; they are also unsure of what should be included in the portfolio and uncertain as to the level of personal self-disclosure suggested. Our experiences with portfolio assessments in education and counseling parallel those noted by Pleasants et al. (1998) and Wade and Yarbrough (1996), who report similar challenges.

Invariably, after some initial confusion and resistance with completing the portfolio, students come to highly value the portfolio activity. In fact, over the years, we have found consistently that students evaluate this assignment as one of most fruitful in the class (and in the entire program). In addition to learning about specific competencies for multicultural development as professionals, students report that working on and processing the portfolio helped them get in touch with their own socialization and family/community history, their own worldviews and racial identity development, their own experiences with oppression and/or privilege, the need to be more active in social justice issues as frontline professionals, and the connection between their own multicultural development and their work as teachers or counselors in a heterogeneous society. Grading of the portfolio is based primarily on completeness, attention to task, and the professor's perception of seriousness with which the assignment was completed and the level of personal processing and reflection undertaken.

SOME RESEARCH NEEDS IN ASSESSING TEACHERS' MULTICULTURAL COMPETENCE

Recent reviews (e.g., Sleeter, 2001; Webb-Johnson et al., 1998) of research assessing the multicultural competence of teachers reveals a number of important trends. First, the majority of research focuses on preservice teacher education students. Second, many studies are anecdotal, with authors describing and evaluating their own multicultural education courses. Third, many studies rely on pretest and posttest assessments of students' multicultural awareness/knowledge using Likert-type rating scales. The accumulated knowledge on how to best train and assess teachers' multicultural competence is limited. Furthermore, despite two decades of research in the area, the reviews cited above note that we still do not know the most effective ways to prepare teachers for work in an increasingly diverse society. Specifically, pretest-posttest studies of competence after a multicultural course appear mixed, although studies assessing coursework in collaboration with field experiences appear more positive, and more positive still are training methods that include community partnerships and community-based learning (see Gomez, 1993; Sleeter, 2001).

Our own reading of select studies in the area supports the conclusions of the research reviews cited above. It appears to us that relatively little research is theoretically grounded, making it difficult to integrate findings from a varied and fragmented literature. We end this chapter with five directions for needed research in the area.

1. There is a need to study professional teachers actively engaged in teaching in both racially heterogeneous and homogeneous communities. For example, master multicultural teachers can be nominated by parents, students, and peers and observed using both qualitative and quantitative methods. Multicultural learning is central to mixed and homogeneous classrooms; how does a master multicultural teacher work similarly and dissimilarly teaching an all-White class, an all-Black class, or a racially mixed class? Also of value in this vein would be participant-observation studies of model multicultural schools and life story studies of

pioneers in multicultural teaching (e.g., Ponterotto, Jackson, et al., 2001).

2. If research is to evaluate the impact, challenges, and success of a specific multicultural class or intervention, researchers should expand on pretest-posttest designs, as multicultural learning is not a linear process. That is, there are peaks and valleys of multicultural growth, and testing students just the first and last days of the semester is limited contextually. For instance, paper-and-pencil measures can be distributed four times per semester, and students could also be interviewed at various points in the semester so researchers can better assess the evolution of multicultural competence and the multicultural personality.

3. Greater research sophistication is needed in assessing multicultural competence, preferably using multimethod (qualitative and quantitative) designs. Recent studies using dialogue journals (Garmon, 1998), concept maps (Trent, Pernell, Mungai, & Chimedza, 1998), and portfolio assessments (Pleasants et al., 1998) help broaden the scope of research inquiry in the area.

4. If research is to focus on preservice college and university education students, then attempts can be made to follow and assess the students in field experiences and on the job.

5. It would behoove the state of knowledge in the field if more quantitative researchers would ground their hypotheses in relevant theory. Theoretical anchors could include worldview, racial/ethnic identity, oppression and privilege, the multicultural personality, and bilingualism (see theoretical updates in Ponterotto, Casas, et al., 2001).

CONCLUSION

This chapter has highlighted the recent momentum in multicultural competency accountability that is grounded in evolving demographic trends and professional associa-tion mandates. Assessment tools inclusive of teacher self-report surveys, observer report evaluations, and a portfolio assessment were reviewed. Finally, important research areas and methodologies warranting increased attention were put forth. It is hoped that this chapter will stimulate increased critical think-ing and research on the assessment of teachers' multicultural competence.

APPENDIX 13.A

TEACHER MULTICULTURAL ATTITUDE SURVEY (TMAS)

1. I find teaching a culturally diverse student group rewarding.
2. Teaching methods need to be adapted to meet the needs of a culturally diverse student group.
3. Sometimes I think there is too much emphasis placed on multicultural awareness and training for teachers.
4. Teachers have the responsibility to be aware of their students' cultural backgrounds.
5. I frequently invite extended family members (e.g., cousins, grandparents, godparents, etc.) to attend parent teacher conferences.
6. It is not the teacher's responsibility to encourage pride in one's culture.
7. As classrooms become more culturally diverse the teacher's job becomes increasingly challenging.
8. I believe the teacher's role needs to be redefined to address the needs of students from culturally diverse backgrounds.
9. When dealing with bilingual students, some teachers may misinterpret different communication styles as behavioral problems.
10. As classrooms become more culturally diverse, the teacher's job becomes increasingly rewarding.
11. I can learn a great deal from students with culturally different backgrounds.
12. Multicultural training for teachers is not necessary.
13. In order to be an effective teacher, one needs to be aware of cultural differences present in the classroom.
14. Multicultural awareness training can help me work more effectively with a diverse student popu-lation.
15. Students should learn to communicate in English only.
16. Today's curriculum gives undue importance to multiculturalism and diversity.
17. I am aware of the diversity of cultural backgrounds in my classroom.
18. Regardless of the racial and ethnic makeup of my class, it is important for all students to be aware of multicultural diversity.
19. Being multiculturally aware is not relevant for the subject I teach.
20. Teaching students about cultural diversity will only create conflict in the classroom.

Do you have any thoughts or comments about this survey or about the research topic?

APPENDIX 13.B

CONTENT ITEMS COMPRISING THE MULTICULTURAL/DIVERSITY TEACHING
COMPETENCIES PORTFOLIO

I. TEACHER PERSONAL DISPOSITIONS

1. I understand that becoming a multicultural teacher is a continuous process that all teachers must address. I personally have progressed in my development by moving from being less culturally aware to becoming more aware and sensitive to my own cultural heritage and to valuing and respecting differences. I am aware of how my own cultural background and experiences, attitudes, values, and biases influence my views of education and social processes.

2. I am comfortable with differences that exist between students and myself in race, ethnicity, culture, gender, sexual orientation, beliefs, and so on. Part of this process includes recognizing my preconceived notions, stereotypes, and negative emotional reactions toward historically oppressed groups (as well as other groups) and understanding how these reactions may prove detrimental to my students in their education and social development. I am willing to contrast my beliefs and attitudes with those of my culturally different students in a nonjudgmental fashion.

3. I possess knowledge and understanding about how oppression, racism, discrimination, and stereotyping affect me personally and in my work. In addition to recognizing how I am discriminated against based on my group memberships, I must acknowledge my own discriminatory attitudes, beliefs, and feelings about race, sexual orientation, class, gender, and so on. I understand how I may have experienced privilege in my own life and how I may have directly or indirectly benefited from individual, institutional, and cultural racism/sexism.

4. As a teacher, I am aware that I have the potential for tremendous social influence on my students, as well as their families. As an employee of the board of education, I recognize the education system and the school as being extremely powerful socializing agents. I also understand how this socializing process may act to oppress minorities.

5. I view diversity in my classroom as an asset to my students' educations, as well as my own. I understand diversity benefits the learning of all the students in my classroom. I am aware of the need, and have the ability, to incorporate the multitude of human experiences in my lesson plans and course materials.

6. I am committed to becoming more socially active to fight oppression in my classroom, my school, my community, and my personal life.

II. TEACHER KNOWLEDGE

1. I possess specific knowledge and information about the particular groups with which I am working. I am aware of the cultural heritages and historical backgrounds of my culturally different students. I understand that a superficial knowledge of other cultures may further my stereotyping and therefore seek an in-depth knowledge of other cultures, beliefs, values, and lifestyles.

2. I understand how variables such as culture, race/ethnicity, sexual orientation, gender, and so forth may affect the educational processes (i.e., learning styles, educational choices, the identification of learning disorders, relationships with teachers, elders, and authority figures, help-seeking behavior, etc.). Furthermore, I am able to apply information from various racial, ethnic, gender, and sexual orientation identity development models to assist in my understanding of my relationships and communications with individual students. Educators can take such variables into account when determining a variety of teaching approaches.

3. I understand and have knowledge of sociopolitical influences that impinge on the life of minorities. Immigration issues, poverty, racism, stereotyping, institutional barriers, and powerlessness all leave major scars that may influence the education and social development process.

4. I value differences in communication styles, including bilingualism, and view them as assets to education. I recognize the challenges that students may face within our education system when English is not the native language. I encourage all my students to develop bilingual skills, and I work to improve my own bilingual competence.

5. I am aware that various forms of testing and assessment may be culture and class bound and therefore may place certain students at a disadvantage. I attempt to ameliorate the negative impact of standardized testing by creating varied forms of testing and evaluation within my classroom. Furthermore, I recognize the large-scale affects of biased assessment, such as over-representation of minorities in special education and lower level tracks.

6. I have knowledge and respect for minority family structures, hierarchies, values, and beliefs. I am knowledgeable about the community characteristics and the resources in the community as well as the family. I understand how this may affect my students and how I communicate with them and their families. I understand the great heterogeneity existing within cultural groups.

7. I understand that being a multicultural teacher must be pervasive through all facets of my professional work. It extends to all of my students, the faculty with whom I work, my lesson plans, my classroom environment, and so forth to create a more open place for students from various backgrounds to thrive. On a personal level, I strive to develop a multicultural personality.

III. TEACHER SKILL

1. I am able to incorporate various teaching styles, course materials, and lesson plans that benefit all of my students. I understand the limitations of using only one instructional method and that teaching styles and approaches may be culture bound. When I am unable to provide appropriate instruction, I take the appropriate steps, which may include consultation, supervision, and coteaching. Furthermore, I continuously seek to further my skills by seeking consultation, supervision, and continuing education.

2. I am able to implement various forms of assessment within my classroom, in ways that will allow the students from various backgrounds to thrive in their education. I use both individualistic and collectivistic evaluation tools.

3. I attend and work to eliminate biases, prejudices, and discriminatory practices within the education system. I am cognizant of sociopolitical contexts in conducting evaluations and providing education and am developing sensitivity to issues of oppression, sexism, elitism, and racism. I am a social activist on behalf of my students and their families.

4. I am able to engage in advocacy or systems intervention roles, in addition to my teaching role. Although the conventional teaching roles are valuable, other roles such as the consultant, advocate, adviser, facilitator (of indigenous education models), and so on may also prove more culturally appropriate.

5. I am able to create a multicultural environment in my classroom, both physically and emotionally. My students, their caregivers, and other faculty can see in my classroom setup, as well as my teaching methods, that various cultural, racial, ethnic, religious, gender, etc. backgrounds are valued in my space.

6. I am a skilled communicator and respect the differences in communication styles between culturally different faculty members and myself. I take responsibility for communicating to my students who do not speak English (or speak limited English); this may mean appropriate use of outside resources.

7. I am able to communicate multiculturalism to my students. I understand the negative impact of discriminatory peer interactions, and I continuously promote appreciation of diversity in student relations with one another.

APPENDIX 13.C

SAMPLE PAGE FROM THE PONTEROTTO ET AL. MULTICULTURAL/DIVERSITY TEACHING COMPETENCIES PORTFOLIO

III. TEACHER SKILL	*Class Activity*	*Date*	*Nonclass Activity*	*Date*
4. I am able to engage in advocacy or systems intervention roles, in addition to my teaching role. Although the conventional teaching roles are valuable, other roles such as the consultant, advocate, adviser, facilitator (of indigenous education models), and so on may also prove more culturally appropriate.	(refers to anything that happened in class: lecture, debate, discussion, guest speakers, films, experiential exercises, role-plays, etc.)		(refers to anything helping you become multiculturally aware and competent outside of class: other professional activities such as workshops, lectures, conferences, personal experiences, etc.)	
5. I am able to create a multicultural environment in my classroom, both physically and emotionally. My students, their caregivers, and other faculty can see in my classroom setup, as well as my teaching methods, that various cultural, racial, ethnic, religious, gender, etc. backgrounds are valued in my space.				
6. I am a skilled communicator and respect the differences in communication styles between culturally different faculty members do not speak English (or speak limited English); this may mean appropriate use of outside resources.				

REFERENCES

Arter, J. A., & Spandel, V. (1992, September). Using portfolios of student work in instruction and assessment. *Educational Measurement: Issues and Practice*, pp. 36-44.

Atkinson, D. R., Brown, M. T., & Casas, J. M. (1996). Achieving ethnic parity in counseling psychology. *The Counseling Psychologist, 24*, 230-258.

Banks, J. A. (2001). Citizenship education and diversity: Implications for teacher education. *Journal of Teacher Education, 52*, 5-16.

Brabeck, M. M., Rogers, L. A., Sirin, S., Henderson, J., Benvenuto, M., Weaver, M., et al. (2000). Increasing ethical sensitivity to racial and gender intolerance in schools: Development of the Racial Ethical Sensitivity Test. *Ethics & Behavior, 10*, 119-137.

Coleman, H. L. K. (1997). Portfolio assessment of multicultural counseling competence. In D. B. Pope-Davis & H. L. K. Coleman (Eds.), *Multicultural counseling competencies: Assessment, education and training, and supervision* (pp. 43-59). Thousand Oaks, CA: Sage.

Constantine, M. G., & Ladany, N. (2001). New visions for defining and assessing multicultural counseling competence. In J. G. Ponterotto, J. M. Casas, L. A. Suzuki, & C. M. Alexander (Eds.), *Handbook of multicultural counseling* (2nd ed., pp. 482-498). Thousand Oaks, CA: Sage.

Crowne, D. P., & Marlowe, D. (1960). A new scale of social desirability independent of psychopathology. *Journal of Consulting Psychology, 24*, 349-354.

D'Andrea, M., Daniels, J., & Heck, R. (1991). Evaluating the impact of multicultural counseling training. *Journal of Counseling and Development, 70*, 143-150.

Deering, T. E., & Stanutz, A. (1995). Preservice field experience as a multicultural component of a teacher education program. *Journal of Teacher Education, 46*, 390-394.

Fuller, F. F., & Brown, O. H. (1975). Becoming a teacher. In K. Ryan (Ed.), *Teacher education* (pp. 25-52). Chicago: National Society for the Study of Education.

Garmon, M. A. (1998). Using dialogue journals to promote student learning in a multicultural teacher education course. *Remedial and Special Education, 19*, 32-45.

Gomez, M. L. (1993). Prospective teachers' perspectives on teaching diverse children: A review with implications for teacher education and practice. *Journal of Negro Education, 62*, 459-474.

Harvey, O. J., Hunt, D. E., & Schroder, H. (1961). *Conceptual systems and personality organization*. New York: John Wiley.

Henry, G. B. (1986). *Cultural Diversity Awareness Inventory* (Rep. No. PS 016 636). East Lansing, MI: National Center for Research on Teacher Learning. (ERIC Document Reproduction Service No. ED 282 657)

Interstate New Teacher Assessment and Support Consortium (INTASC). (2001). *Core standards for teacher accreditation* [Online]. Available: www.ccso.org/intasc.html

Johnson, P. E., & Johnson, R. E. (1996). The role of concrete-abstract thinking levels in teachers' multiethnic beliefs. *Journal of Research and Development in Education, 29*, 134-140.

Krosnick, J. A. (1999). Maximizing questionnaire quality. In J. P. Robinson, P. R. Shaver, & L. S. Wrightsman (Eds.), *Measures of political attitudes* (Vol. 2, pp. 37-57). San Diego: Academic Press.

Ladson-Billings, G. (1999). Preparing teachers for diversity. In L. Darling-Hammond & G. Sykes (Eds.), *Teaching as the learning profession* (pp. 86-123). San Francisco: Jossey-Bass.

Larke, P. J. (1990). Cultural Diversity Awareness Inventory: Assessing the sensitivity of preservice teachers. *Action in Teacher Education, 12*, 23-30.

Locke, D. C. (1988). Teaching culturally-different students: Growing pine trees or bonsai trees? *Contemporary Education, 59*, 130-133.

Marshall, P. L. (1996). Multicultural teaching concerns: New dimensions in the area of teacher concerns research? *Journal of Educational Research, 89*, 371-379.

Mick, L. B. (1996). Using portfolios to help elementary education majors gain insight into disabilities and the family system. *Intervention in School and Clinic, 31*, 290-296.

National Council on the Accreditation of Teacher Education Programs (NCATE). (2001). *Professional standards for the accreditation of schools, colleges, and departments of education*. Washington, DC: Author.

Nieto, S. (2000). *Affirming diversity: The sociopolitical context of multicultural education* (3rd ed.). New York: Longman.

Noordhoff, K., & Kleinfeld, J. (1993). Preparing teachers for multicultural classrooms. *Teaching and Teacher Education, 9*, 27-39.

Phinney, J. S. (1992). The Multigroup Ethnic Identity Measure: A new scale for use with diverse groups. *Journal of Adolescent Research, 7*, 156-176.

Pleasants, H. M., Johnson, C. B., & Trent, S. C. (1998). Reflecting, reconceptualizing, and revising: The evolution of a portfolio assignment in a multicultural teacher education course. *Remedial and Special Education, 19*, 46-58.

Ponterotto, J. G., Baluch, S., Greig, T., & Rivera, L. (1998). Development and initial score validation of the Teacher Multicultural Attitude Survey. *Educational and Psychological Measurement, 58*, 1002-1016.

Ponterotto, J. G., Burkard, A. W., Rieger, B. P., Grieger, I., D'Onofrio, A., Dubuisson, A., et al. (1995). Development and initial validation of the Quick Discrimination Index (QDI). *Educational and Psychological Measurement, 55*, 1026 1031.

Ponterotto, J. G., Casas, J. M., Suzuki, L. A., & Alexander, C. M. (Eds.). (2001). *Handbook of multicultural counseling* (2nd ed.). Thousand Oaks, CA: Sage.

Ponterotto, J. G., Costa, C. I., & Werner-Lin, A. (2002). Research perspectives in cross-cultural counseling. In P. B. Pedersen, J. G. Draguns, W. J. Lonner, & J. E. Trimble (Eds.), *Counseling across cultures* (5th ed., pp. 395-420). Thousand Oaks, CA: Sage.

Ponterotto, J. G., Fuertes, J. N., & Chen, E. C. (2000). Models of multicultural counseling. In S. D. Brown & R. W. Lent (Eds.), *Handbook of counseling psychology* (3rd ed., pp. 639-669). New York: John Wiley.

Ponterotto, J. G., Jackson, M. A., & Nutini, C. D. (2001). Reflections on the life stories of pioneers in multicultural counseling. In J. G. Ponterotto, J. M. Casas, L. A. Suzuki, & C. M. Alexander (Eds.), *Handbook of multicultural counseling* (2nd ed., pp. 138-161). Thousand Oaks, CA: Sage.

Ponterotto, J. G., Lewis, D. E., & Bullington, R. (1990). *Affirmative action on campus*. San Francisco: Jossey-Bass.

Ponterotto, J. G., & Pedersen, P. B. (1993). *Preventing prejudice: A guide for counselors and educators*. Thousand Oaks, CA: Sage.

Ragle, B. K., Szakaly, C. H., & Zygmunt-Fillwalk, E. M. (2001). *Implications of multicultural interventions on early childhood educators' attitudes toward diversity*. Unpublished manuscript, Teachers College, Ball State University.

Ramirez, M. (1999). *Multicultural psychotherapy: An approach to individual and cultural differences* (2nd ed.). Boston: Allyn & Bacon.

Rest, J. R. (1983). Morality. In J. Lavell & E. Monkmam (Eds.), *Handbook of child psychology: Vol. 3. Cognitive development* (pp. 556-629). New York: John Wiley.

Schmitt, E. (2001, April 30). Whites in minority in largest cities, the census shows. *New York Times*, pp. A1, A12.

Sleeter, C. E. (2001). Preparing teachers for culturally diverse schools: Research and the overwhelming presence of whiteness. *Journal of Teacher Education, 52*, 94-106.

Sue, D. W., Carter, R. T., Casas, J. M., Fouad, N. A., Ivey, A. E., Jensen, M., et al. (1998). *Multicultural counseling competencies: Individual and organizational development*. Thousand Oaks, CA: Sage.

Trent, S. C., Pernell, E., Mungai, A., & Chimedza, R. (1998). Using concept maps to measure conceptual change in preservice teachers enrolled in a multicultural education/special education course. *Remedial and Special Education, 19*, 16-31.

U.S. Bureau of the Census. (2000). *Statistical abstract of the United States*. Washington, DC: Government Printing Office.

Utsey, S. O., & Ponterotto, J. G. (1999). Further factorial validity assessment of scores on the Quick Discrimination Index (QDI). *Educational and Psychological Measurement, 59*, 325-335.

Wade, R. C., & Yarbrough, D. B. (1996). Portfolios: A tool for reflective thinking in teacher education? *Teaching and Teacher Education, 12,* 63-79.

Walsh, W. B., & Betz, N. E. (1990). *Tests and assessment* (2nd ed.). Englewood Cliffs, NJ: Prentice Hall.

Webb-Johnson, G., Artiles, A. J., Trent, S. C., Jackson, C. W., & Velox, A. (1998). The status of research on multicultural education in teacher education and special education. *Remedial and Special Education, 19,* 7-15.

14

Assessing Supervisors' and Supervisees' Perceptions of Multicultural Competence in Supervision Using the Multicultural Supervision Inventory

DONALD B. POPE-DAVIS
University of Notre Dame

REBECCA L. TOPOREK
San Francisco State University

LIDETH ORTEGA-VILLALOBOS
University of Notre Dame

There are several benefits of increased competence in multicultural supervision, including improvement of the quality of services to supervisees' clients, enhancement of the training experience for supervisees, and development of a more satisfactory supervision relationship. Because attention to multicultural supervision is relatively new, most literature has served to form a foundation, create definitions, and explore relevant influences in multicultural supervision. As this foundation becomes more established, the next step will be to critically examine how multicultural supervision may improve counseling and

AUTHORS' NOTE: The MSI is a copyrighted measure (2000). If you are interested in obtaining a copy of the measure, contact Donald B. Pope-Davis, Ph.D., 118 Haggar Hall, University of Notre Dame, Notre Dame, IN 46656; e-mail: dpd@nd.edu.

enhance the training experience. The objectives of this chapter are to (a) discuss a study of the intersection of multicultural supervision competence, multicultural counseling competence, and satisfaction with supervision; (b) examine an instrument designed to assess supervisors' and supervisees' perceptions of multicultural supervision competence; and (c) propose critical issues relevant to the next generation of multicultural counseling supervision assessment for practice and research.

Literature addressing theoretical aspects of multicultural supervision has focused on models (e.g., D'Andrea & Daniels, 1997; Martinez & Holloway, 1997; Porter, 1995) and issues to consider in multicultural supervision (Fong & Lease, 1997; Priest, 1994; Stone, 1997). In addition to the theoretical literature, qualitative and quantitative research exploring various aspects of multicultural supervision has increased greatly in the past decade. The majority of these studies have focused on the expectations and perspectives of supervisees (Cook & Helms, 1988; Daniels, D'Andrea, & Kim, 1999; Fukuyama, 1994; Hird, Cavalieri, Dulko, Felice, & Ho, 2001; Ladany, Brittan-Powell, & Pannu, 1997; McNeill, Hom, & Perez, 1995). A few studies have considered the perspective of both supervisors and supervisees (e.g., Constantine, 1997; Duan & Roehlke, 2001). A limited number of studies have investigated matched dyads in supervision (e.g., Duan & Roehlke, 2001). Most of the existing literature in multicultural supervision has focused on cross-racial or cross-ethnic supervisory relationships. There is limited literature that uses an inclusive definition of multicultural supervision attending to race, ethnicity, gender, sexual orientation, social class, religion, and physical disabilities.

Given a review of the literature, several areas would benefit from exploration. First, there is a need for assessment tools that can more systematically measure multicultural supervision for practical use in research, practice,

and training. Second, it would be useful to better understand the relationship between multicultural supervision competence and multicultural competence in counseling. Third, assessing the respective perceptions of the supervisor and the supervisee engaged in multicultural supervision relationships would be valuable, particularly as they relate to multicultural supervision competence, satisfaction with supervision, and multicultural competence. To address these issues, we begin our discussion by briefly reviewing relevant literature and presenting the findings of a recent study that examined the relationship between multicultural counseling competence, multicultural supervision, and satisfaction with supervision from the perspective of supervisors and supervisees. We then examine a structured assessment instrument: the Multicultural Supervision Inventory (MSI) (Pope-Davis, Toporek, & Ortega, 1999). This is an instrument designed to assess supervisees' and supervisors' perspectives of multicultural competence in supervision. Finally, we will present a host of issues that we believe are critical for the next generation of research and assessment in multicultural supervision.

MULTICULTURAL SUPERVISION IN THE CONTEXT OF MULTICULTURAL COUNSELING COMPETENCIES AND SATISFACTION WITH SUPERVISION

Many of the models of multicultural supervision assume that the supervisor has a higher level of multicultural competence and awareness than the trainee for whom he or she is providing supervision. For example, models that are designed to facilitate a supervisor's ability to foster multicultural growth in a supervisee provide recommendations for encouraging supervisee awareness, knowledge, and skills (e.g., D'Andrea & Daniels, 1997; Martinez & Holloway, 1997; Porter, 1995). This requires some relatively sophisticated multicultural awareness, knowledge, and skill on the part of the supervisor. Given the findings of Constantine (1997), this assumption may not be accurate. She found that among predoctoral interns and their supervisors, the majority of supervisors (70%) had not completed a formal multicultural or cross-cultural counseling course. However, the majority of interns (70%) had completed such a course. Even when a supervisor has received multicultural training, the level of multicultural competence is still uncertain. However, existing literature does not provide information regarding the extent to which multicultural supervision competence is related to the supervisor's demonstration of general multicultural counseling competence. This gap in the literature can lead us to theorize that multicultural competence in supervision could be influenced by the supervisor's competence in multicultural counseling. However, the nature and strength of this relationship have not yet been explored empirically.

Few studies have reported on the assessment of multicultural supervision or the relationship between the multicultural competence of the supervisor, as perceived by both the supervisor and supervisee, and the supervisee's reports of general satisfaction in supervision. Pope-Davis, Toporek, et al. (2000) reported the need for structured instruments to assess supervisors' multicultural competence and the supervision relationship. They emphasized the need to attend to multiple levels of analysis, including the client, counselor, and supervisor. In addition, they asserted that multicultural supervision may be inclusive of differences in race, ethnicity, gender, sexual orientation, religion, disabilities, and other dimensions of identity along which supervisors and supervisees may differ. To address counselor/supervisee and supervisor perspectives, they proposed the Multicultural Supervision Competence Scale–Revised (MSC-R; later renamed MSI) and provided some preliminary findings. The instrument used multicultural knowledge, awareness, and skills to provide a framework to define supervisory competencies. Additional aspects were also integrated, including multicultural relationship issues and social desirability. Pope-Davis, Toporek, et al. reported finding a significant relationship between supervisees' self-reported satisfaction with supervision and the ratings of multicultural supervision competence they assigned their supervisors ($r = .68$, $p < .001$). In addition, they found that general multicultural competence was significantly related to supervisors' self-rating of multicultural supervision competence and supervisees' ratings of the multicultural supervision competence of their supervisors. Pope-Davis, Toporek, et al. emphasized that these findings were preliminary and should be considered with caution given the small sample size.

Duan and Roehlke (2001) recently presented findings of a study of predoctoral interns and their supervisors. They developed a cross-racial survey that included questions about supervisors' previous experience and knowledge of cross-racial supervision, supervisors' behavior and personal characteristics, supervisors' expectations for supervisee self-disclosure, supervisee comfort in self-disclosure, and overall satisfaction. They found that supervisees and supervisors held parallel perceptions of agreement of goals, experiences of conflict, and assessment of attention to conflict in supervision. However, supervisors, more so than supervisees, felt that they addressed cultural issues related to the supervision relationship, acknowledged their lack of cross-racial supervision experience, made efforts to understand their supervisees' culture, initiated discussions of cultural differences in the relationship, acknowledged the power differential in the relationship, and valued differences in learning styles. This study is useful in that it assessed supervisor and supervisee perceptions of cross-racial supervision. Aside from the MSI, this study presented one of the few formal instruments for use in multicultural supervision.

ASSESSING SUPERVISORS' AND SUPERVISEES' PERCEPTIONS

Given the complexity of multicultural supervision, a more thorough examination of supervisees' and supervisors' perceptions and experiences would be helpful. The following study is an extension and elaboration of the original study reported by Pope-Davis, Toporek, et al. (2000). Currently, most graduate counseling programs offer at least one multicultural counseling course. The goals of this type of course are to increase students' multicultural competence through awareness, knowledge, or skill or all of the above. Increasing students' multicultural counseling competence may influence their expectations of supervision and the extent to which they are able to solicit guidance regarding multicultural counseling issues. Likewise, the ability of a supervisor to adequately address a supervisee's multicultural training needs may be influenced by the supervisor's general multicultural counseling competence. As stated in the introduction, we believe that the goals of increased competence in multicultural supervision are to improve the quality of services to supervisees' clients, enhance the training experience for supervisees, and foster a more satisfactory supervision relationship.

Participants, Measures, and Procedures

A total of 160 supervisors ($n = 74$) and supervisees ($n = 86$) at American Psychological Association (APA)–approved internship sites across the United States participated in the study. Table 14.1 provides demographic and multicultural training information for the sample. Packets containing the MSI, the Multicultural Competence Inventory (MCI) (Sodowsky, Taffe, Gutkin, & Wise, 1994), the Supervision Satisfaction Questionnaire (SSQ) (Ladany, Hill, Corbett, & Nutt, 1996), the Short-C form of the Marlowe-Crowne Social Desirability Scale (Reynolds, 1982), and a demographics questionnaire were sent to training directors of internship programs. Training directors were asked to distribute packets to pairs of supervisors and supervisees. Packets were counterbalanced and coded to differentiate trainee and supervisor pairs.

The MSI (Pope-Davis et al., 1999) consisted of 43 Likert-type self-report items. The supervisee version was designed to measure supervisees' perceptions of the multicultural supervision competence of their supervisor within a counseling or clinical supervision context. The supervisor version was designed to measure supervisors' perceptions of their own multicultural supervision competence. Each item is a declarative statement about some aspect of the supervisor's behavior or some aspect of the supervisory relationship. Participants are asked to rate the degree to which they believe the statement is reflective of their experience with supervision (1 = *strongly disagree,* 5 = *strongly agree*). Sample items for supervisees include the following: "My supervisor helped me to understand ethnic identity and how that relates to my counseling" and "I would feel comfortable telling my supervisor if we had misunderstandings due to our cultural differences." The respective items on the supervisor version are as follows: "I helped my supervisee to understand his/her ethnic identity and how that relates to counseling" and "My supervisee would feel comfortable telling me if we had misunderstandings due to our cultural differences." Scores range from 43 to 215, with high scores indicating a greater degree of multicultural competence demonstrated by the supervisor in supervision. Pope-Davis, Toporek, et al. (2000) reported preliminary coefficient alphas of .92 (supervisor version) and .97 (supervisee version). Divergent validity was supported in that no significant correlation was found between the participants' scores on the MSI (supervisor and supervisee versions) and the Social Desirability Scale.

Table 14.1 Demographic and Multicultural Training Background of Supervisors and Supervisees Participating in the Study (in percentages)

	Supervisors	*Supervisees*
Sex		
Male	34	29
Female	66	71
Race		
Asian American/Pacific Islander	9	7
African American/Black	12	11
Latino(a)/Hispanic	3	2
Native American/American Indian	0	0
White/Caucasian	72	69
Biracial/multiracial	0	0
Jewish	4	8
Other	0	2
Training		
Never completed multicultural course	50	14
Completed one or more courses	50	86
Total number	75	86

The MCI (Sodowsky et al., 1994) is a self-report measure of counselor multicultural competence. The inventory was designed to measure the qualities of multiculturally skilled counselors. It has four scales: Multicultural Counseling Skills, Awareness, Knowledge, and Relationship. The items are self-report statements that are rated on a 4-point Likert-type scale (4 = *very accurate*, 1 = *very inaccurate*). The authors reported internal consistency reliabilities (Cronbach's alpha) ranging from .67 to .81 for the four scales.

The SSQ (Ladany et al., 1996) was created to assess supervisee perceptions of the quality and outcomes of supervision. The SSQ is an eight-item self-report inventory with a 4-point scale ranging from 1 (*low satisfaction*) to 4 (*high satisfaction*). A sample item for this measure is, "To what extent does supervision fit your needs?" Ladany et al. reported internal consistency coefficient alphas of .96.

In an effort to address social desirability, the Short-C form of the Marlowe-Crowne Social Desirability Scale (Reynolds, 1982) was used to measure socially desirable patterns of responding. This instrument consists of 13 true false items. Reliability for this scale was reported as Kuder-Richardson 20 = .74.

Finally, participants were asked to complete a demographic questionnaire regarding supervisors' and supervisees' age, gender, ethnic background, counseling experience, experience with supervision, and their differences with their supervisors along ethnicity, gender, physical ability, religion, sexual orientation, or other relevant cultural characteristics. This demographic questionnaire also asked participants to describe their level of multicultural training in terms of coursework as well as workshops and seminars. Last, the questionnaire asked participants to describe the emphasis on multiculturalism at their site, the diversity of clients and supervisors, and the extent to which multicultural issues were intentionally addressed in their program.

Findings

The results of the study provided information regarding preliminary psychometric properties of the MSI as well as supervisor and supervisee perspectives of multicultural supervision experiences. Of the participants, we were able to identify 36 matched dyads, allowing for comparison of two levels of analysis for each of these supervisory experiences. We will first present the findings regarding the supervisees' perspectives generally, then supervisors' perspectives, and then comparison data from the matched dyads. This will be followed by a presentation of the results regarding the psychometric properties of the MSI.

Multicultural Competence and Satisfaction in Supervision and Counseling

Several research questions were addressed through the analyses using parallel methods for both supervisors and supervisees. Stepwise regression was used to determine the extent to which the participants' own multicultural counseling competence predicted ratings of multicultural supervision competence of the supervisor. For supervisees, we also used a stepwise regression method to determine the extent to which their multicultural counseling competence and their ratings of their supervisors' multicultural supervision competence predicted the supervisees' satisfaction with supervision. Analyses of variance (ANOVA) were conducted to examine group differences in the dependent variables. The independent variables considered in the ANOVAs included participant demographic and training variables as well as site characteristics. The mean scores and standard deviations for the MCI, SSQ, MSI, and the three factors derived from a principal components analysis are presented later in Table 14.4.

The results of regression analysis, in which social desirability was entered in the first step and MCI scores were entered in the second step, indicated that supervisees' ratings of their own multicultural counseling competence was a significant predictor of their ratings of their supervisors' competence ($B = .885$, $SE\ B = .393$, $\beta = .321$, $p < .05$) and accounted for 10.2% of the total variance.

A stepwise regression analysis indicated that, when entered in the same step, supervisees' multicultural counseling competence and their ratings of their supervisors' multicultural supervision competence significantly accounted for a significant portion (17%) of the variance of supervisees' satisfaction with supervision. However, in the final regression equation, only the supervisees' multicultural counseling competence served as a significant predictor of satisfaction with supervision, accounting for 11% of the variance ($B = 38.17$, $SE\ B = 6.41$, $\beta = -.338$, $p < .05$). A univariate analysis of variance indicated a significant relationship between perceived supervisor competence and the extent that supervisees reported that multicultural issues were intentionally addressed in supervision, $F = 13.79(4, 77)$, $p = .001$. Pairwise comparisons reflected significant mean differences between supervisees who perceived that these issues were addressed a lot or above average and rated their supervisors as more competent than did supervisees who perceived less attention to multicultural issues and less supervisor competence ($p < .05$).

Supervisees rated the multicultural supervision competence of supervisors who belonged to cross-racial dyads significantly higher than those who belonged to a racially similar pair, $F(1, 73) = 5.05$, $p < .05$. No significant differences were found in supervisees' competence ratings of supervisors belonging to dyads that differed on sex, religion, and sexual orientation. No significant relationships were found between supervisees' ratings of their supervisors' multicultural competence and the following factors: supervisees' race, supervisees' gender, years of counseling experience, months of supervision experience, and type of degree or program of enrollment. In addition, characteristics of supervisors (e.g., gender, race, age, and position in the institution) and site characteristics (e.g., diversity of clients and supervisors and emphasis placed on multicultural training) were not significantly related to supervisees' ratings of their supervisors' multicultural supervision competence. Self-reported importance of multicultural training for supervisees, level of multicultural training completed, and number of hours of multicultural training in workshops or seminars attended were not significantly related to MSI scores and SSQ scores.

The results of regression analysis in which social desirability was entered in the first step and MCI scores were entered in the second step indicated that supervisors' ratings of their own multicultural counseling competence were a significant predictor of their ratings of their supervision competence ($B = 1.219$, $SE B = .197$, $\beta = .672$, $p < .001$) and accounted for 44.2% of the total variance. In addition, significant relationships were found between supervisors' multicultural competence and the number of multicultural courses completed, $F(3, 63) = 7.02$, $p < .01$, as well as the importance of multicultural training for the supervisor, $F(3, 63) = 6.52$, $p < .001$, such that supervisors who completed two courses or more had significantly higher means than those who never completed a formal course (mean difference = 31, $p = .001$). Furthermore, supervisors who rated the importance of multicultural training as "above average" and "a lot" had significantly higher means than supervisors who rated multicultural training of "average" importance (mean difference "above average" = 20, $p < .05$, mean difference "a lot" = 27, $p = .001$). In addition, there were significant differences between individuals who had attended multicultural counseling workshops or seminars and those who had not completed such training, $F(1, 63) = 5.418$, $p < .05$. Finally, there were significant differences in multicultural supervision competence between supervisors based on the degree to which they reported that multicultural issues were intentionally addressed in supervision, $F(3, 63) = 4.164$, $p < .01$. No significant relationships were found between supervisors' ratings of their multicultural supervision competence and their gender, race, years of counseling and supervision experience, length of the supervisory relationship, emphasis of site on multicultural training, extent of racial diversity of clients and supervisors at sites, and degree of experience in working with supervisees from a different race, sex, religion, and sexual orientation.

To examine the differences in the means of the matched dyads, we conducted paired-samples t tests for the MSI total score. In addition, a paired-samples t test was conducted to examine the differences in MCI scores. The scores of matched pairs of supervisees and supervisors were not significantly correlated for the MSI or the MCI. The mean scores did not differ significantly across the pairs.

Psychometric Findings

Although the current sample size is not adequate to draw conclusions about the psychometric properties of the MSI, we were interested in a preliminary exploration of its factor structure and possible subscales. A reverse-scored item was recoded to ensure that all items analyzed were on uniform scaling; two other items were excluded from the analysis because their purpose was to gauge the relevance of cultural issues in supervision. A principal components factor analysis was run with an oblique rotation because the factors were not assumed to be independent. The principal components factor analysis resulted in the extraction of seven factors that met Meineigein criteria of values greater than 1.0, a solution that accounted for 68% of the variance. A scree plot analysis indicated that factor solutions ranging from three to five factors would be adequate. Initially a four-factor solution was chosen because it accounted for 58% of the variance, was consistent with the scree plot analysis, and was theoretically

Table 14.2   MSI Preliminary Three-Factor Solution Component Correlation Matrix

Component	Component 1	Component 2	Component 3
1	1.0	.466	.240
2	.466	1.0	.346
3	.240	.346	1.0

NOTE: Extraction method: principal component analysis. Rotation method: promax with Kaiser normalization.

Table 14.3   MSI Preliminary Three-Factor Solution Pattern Matrix

Item	Component 1	Component 2	Component 3
MSI 2			.661
MSI 3	.842		
MSI 6	.791		
MSI 7	.816		
MSI 9			.777
MSI 11			.589
MSI 12	.869		
MSI 14	.841		
MSI 16	.849		
MSI 20	.788		
MSI 21	.819		
MSI 23	.802		
MSI 26	.758		
MSI 27			.789
MSI 28	.738		
MSI 34	.750		
MSI 35	.604		
MSI 38		.901	
MSI 39		.890	
MSI 40		.787	

NOTE: Extraction method: principal component analysis. Rotation method: promax with Kaiser normalization.

interpretable. Next, items were methodically removed that met the following exclusion criteria: factor loadings less than .40 and cross-factor loadings greater than .30. We repeated the extraction three times and removed items that met exclusion criteria. The resulting four-factor solution accounted for 69% of the total variance, but the fourth factor extracted only included 1 item. Further assessment of the factor loadings and the scree plot indicated that a three-factor solution might be appropriate. A three-factor solution was specified. This extraction led to a final scale that included 20

items, with factor loadings ranging from .60 to .90. The final solution accounted for 65% of the total variance. Table 14.2 presents the preliminary solution's component correlation matrix, and Table 14.3 presents the component pattern matrix. Factor 1 accounted for 46% of the variance, and its loadings ranged from .60 to .87. Based on the 13 items that loaded on Factor 1, this factor was interpreted as the supervisor's competence in addressing the impact of culture in supervision, including the role of counselor cultural identity. Factor 2 consisted of 3 items accounting for 12% of the

Table 14.4   Means and Standard Deviations

		Total Sample		Matched Pairs	
		Supervisors	*Supervisees*	*Supervisors*	*Supervisees*
MSI	M	157.42	151.10	153.68	160.52
	SD	19.89	31.72	22.17	28.63
	n	64	78	34	33
MSI Factor 1	M	47.77	40.40	46.85	45.20
	SD	8.39	12.93	9.49	11.59
	n	66	81	34	35
MSI Factor 2	M	13.65	12.96	13.36	13.36
	SD	1.81	2.10	2.18	1.71
	n	68	85	36	36
MSI Factor 3	M	13.85	16.39	13.81	16.74
	SD	2.60	2.84	2.49	2.31
	n	67	83	36	35
MCI	M	120.61	124.36	120.90	123.63
	SD	10.97	11.51	10.74	11.11
	n	51	53	29	27
SSQ	M	21.55	—	—	—
	SD	4.20	—	—	—
	n	86	—	—	—

NOTE: Dashes in columns indicate "not calculated" because the SSQ was not given to supervisees. MSI = Multicultural Supervision Inventory; MCI = Multicultural Competence Inventory; SSQ = Supervision Satisfaction Questionnaire.

total variance, with factor loadings ranging from .79 to .90. The theme of the items in Factor 2 centered on the supervisor's ability to foster a collaborative learning relationship. Factor 3 accounted for 7% of the total variance, with loadings that ranged from .59 to .79. The theme of the four items on this factor revolved around the supervisor's support of the supervisee, including confidence and understanding. The internal consistency reliability estimate for the final 20-item MSI scale was $\alpha = .92$. The reliability estimates for each of the three factors were as follows: Factor 1 ($\alpha = .96$), Factor 2 ($\alpha = .80$), and Factor 3 ($\alpha = .68$).

Discussion of the Findings

This study was conducted to examine multicultural supervision from the perspective of supervisees and supervisors. In particular, we were interested in the relationship between multicultural counseling competence, satisfaction with supervision, and multicultural supervision experiences. In addition, we wanted to consider whether supervisee characteristics, supervisor characteristics, or training environment characteristics were influential in perceptions of multicultural supervision. The findings provided some insight into the complex relationships between the constructs and implications for the evaluation of multicultural supervision.

The findings highlighted the significant role of multicultural counseling competence, its relationship to a supervisor's own perceived multicultural supervision competence, and the ratings of supervisees. In general, competence with multicultural issues in the counseling setting seemed to color the lens through which supervisors were assessed and assessed themselves. We found that, for both supervisors and supervisees, higher levels of self-perceived multicultural counseling competence were related to higher ratings of supervisors' effectiveness with culture in supervision; this was reflected by multicultural counseling competence scores, perceptions in intentionality of addressing multicultural issues in supervision, and the extent of the supervisors' multicultural training. Characteristics of the supervisors' general counseling and supervision experience and site characteristics were not significantly related to supervisors' competency ratings. This was interesting on several different levels. First, multicultural training and multicultural behaviors (e.g., intentionality in supervision) were more important than supervisors' general experiences. These findings provide support for multicultural supervision training, which includes attention to multicultural counseling competence and confirms that experience in counseling and supervision alone does not necessarily lead to better multicultural supervision. Second, the finding that degree of attention a site places on multicultural issues was not significantly related to multicultural supervision competence engages an interesting discussion. Although it is recognized that the attention that training environments give to multicultural issues is critical in students' academic experiences, this does not seem to influence the ratings given to multicultural supervision. This finding can highlight individual supervisors' roles in enhancing their own multicultural competence independent of their sites' emphasis. Supervisors may choose to intentionally address multicultural issues in supervision or pursue multicultural training through self-study or external opportunities to increase their multicultural competence as supervisors. The importance placed on multicultural issues in a training program's philosophy and mission may encourage and influence whether supervisees and supervisors value this

training or receive support and resources for these professional development activities. This finding raises questions regarding the level of analysis of these questions. For example, supervisees' and supervisors' perceptions of the sites' involvement and commitment to multicultural issues may not have accurately reflected the actual state of the training program, a phenomenon that would need to be measured beyond the individual perspective. For an institutional level of analysis and programmatic evaluation, another means of collecting site data may be necessary (Pope-Davis, Liu, Nevitt, & Toporek, 2000).

The one personal characteristic that appeared to be significant in this study was that supervisees who had racially different supervisors rated their supervisors as more competent than those who had racially similar supervisors. This might suggest that cross-racial supervisory relationships could serve as avenues to foster supervisees' perceptions of greater supervisor competence. It is important to note that the data did not allow for an examination of differences between assumptions about White supervisors versus supervisors of color.

The findings regarding satisfaction with supervision indicated that, as individual variables, perceptions of multicultural supervision competence did not significantly predict satisfaction. However, supervisees' multicultural counseling competence predicted satisfaction with supervision such that trainees with less multicultural competence tended to be more satisfied with supervision. It is possible that trainees who perceive themselves as having high multicultural competence have higher expectations or tend to be more critical of supervision in general. Although this is plausible, one finding seems to contradict this hypothesis: Supervisees' ratings of the importance of multicultural training and level of multicultural training completed were not significantly related to ratings of supervisors' multicultural supervision competence and satisfaction with supervision. Clearly, more research is needed to understand the complexity of the supervision experience.

Finally, the examination of the matched pairs of supervisors and supervisees produced some interesting results. Supervisors and supervisees did not differ significantly in their ratings of the supervisors' multicultural supervision competence. This may indicate that perceptions of multicultural supervision competence are relatively congruent given the types of questions asked by the MSI.

Limitations of the study should be noted. First, the study relied on self-report measures and thus is subject to limitations common to all self-report measures. Second, the MSI is a relatively new measure and would benefit from additional validity studies. Finally, the overall sample size and the number of matched dyads were relatively low, suggesting that the findings should be considered with caution.

ISSUES AND RECOMMENDATIONS FOR FUTURE EVALUATION OF MULTICULTURAL SUPERVISION

Attention to multicultural supervision is relatively recent and can serve as a foundation to develop knowledge in this area. For knowledge and practice to advance, we must focus on several issues and recommendations that are critical. The study discussed above suggests that there is a relationship between general multicultural counseling competence, multicultural supervision competence, and satisfaction with supervision. We would like to now go beyond these findings and make recommendations for the advancement of assessment in supervision. We have organized our discussion into four parts: the role of multicultural training of supervisors, programmatic recommendations, multiple levels of analysis, and three types of assessment in supervision.

Multicultural Training of Supervisors

Several areas may lead to greater multicultural supervision competence. First, the development of a set of guidelines for multicultural supervision competence similar to those proposed by Sue, Arredondo, and McDavis (1992) would be one step toward providing direction for training, supervisors' self-assessment, and evaluation. Second, increasing supervisors' multicultural competence in the counseling setting can provide a foundation through which supervisors have greater awareness, knowledge, and skill from which to draw when observing the counseling scenarios of their supervisees. Third, multicultural supervision training may address the following skill areas: (a) addressing multicultural issues in supervision, (b) providing guidance regarding multicultural counseling interventions, (c) fostering supervisees' multicultural growth and awareness, and (d) assessing the supervisory relationship in terms of support, cultural respect, and challenge for the supervisees.

Programmatic Recommendations

Counseling training programs may address multicultural supervision competence in several ways. First, programs need to clearly communicate a commitment to providing multicultural clinical training that includes a component specifically devoted to supervision. Second, programs can provide supervisees and supervisors with a structure for discussing and assessing relevant multicultural aspects of supervision. This may be a formal evaluation component or guidelines for structuring supervision. Third, providing resources to facilitate supervisors' multicultural counseling competence may help increase supervisors' clinical skills, thereby increasing their ability to recognize multicultural issues in their supervisees' counseling sessions and provide guidance. Resources may include providing workshops and case conferences for supervisors. Fourth, opportunities for supervisors to consult with other supervisors who have multicultural expertise could help them address difficult issues in supervision. Fifth, in cases in which supervision is provided by advanced students, supervision training should be provided that addresses multicultural counseling and supervision issues. As with any multicultural training, information or knowledge regarding racial identity issues, social class, sexual orientation, oppression, and other relevant content areas should be included. Supervisors must also be aware of how power differentials may influence supervision and counseling, particularly when cultural differences are involved. In addition, training should attend to supervisors' feelings, attitudes, and beliefs about cultural differences. Equally important is the need for training to provide a forum for exploring different behaviors that would be critical for the supervision context. Behavioral or skill training may address situations such as initiating and conducting discussions about cultural differences as well as approaches to cultural impasses that may arise in supervision.

Levels of Analysis

Counseling training takes place in a complex system, providing knowledge and experience to students. Therefore, it is reasonable to assume that supervision may be best evaluated within its appropriate context. In the study presented above, supervisors' and supervisees' perceptions of the training sites' attention to multiculturalism were not related to supervision competence. However, evaluation that directly assesses the sites' attention to multicultural training and competence may produce different results. Given the possible discrepancy between perceptions and reality, we assert that the analysis of multicultural supervision and training should be done from at least four levels, including the perspective of

the supervisor, supervisee, training program, and client. This may involve a complement or compilation of several measures, including actual multicultural courses required in the program, attention to multicultural issues in supervision training, inclusion of multicultural training in the mission of the program, the degree to which multicultural issues are infused into required coursework, and a more thorough assessment of the multicultural training environment (see Pope-Davis, Liu, et al., 2000). To assess supervision from the client perspective, we should attend to the degree to which a supervisor's guidance regarding multicultural issues translates into increased counselor multicultural understanding or competence from the perspective of the client.

Three Types of Assessment

In addition to multiple levels of analysis, there are also three types of assessment to integrate into multicultural supervision: self-reflection, process-oriented assessment, and evaluative assessment. Although good supervision typically uses these three forms of assessment, multisource assessment is particularly relevant for multicultural supervision. We recommend that these three components be systematically included in supervision both for supervisors and trainees.

Self-Reflection

This component requires that supervisors and supervisees reflect on their expectations for supervision, their attitudes and beliefs about multicultural issues, their existing knowledge, their multicultural counseling and supervision experience and intervention skills, and their thoughtful examination of the challenges and areas for growth. A set of guidelines for multicultural supervision competence could provide a structure for examining these questions. This self-reflection can then inform the next component of assessment, process-oriented assessment.

Process-Oriented Assessment

This component is often integrated into supervision as a foundation for supervision. This begins a discussion between the supervisor and supervisee, in which they share their expectations, previous experience, and existing knowledge. This component is important to ensure that supervision is developmentally appropriate for the supervisee and to examine issues that may arise later in the supervision process. In multicultural supervision, this component would use the areas discussed in the self-reflection section and may help in collaboratively setting supervision goals that will optimize the development of multicultural competence for the supervisee. In addition, it can help the supervisor identify areas in which he or she may need to gain consultation or do additional research.

Evaluative Assessment

In multicultural supervision, the evaluation of the supervisee would attend to multicultural issues as an integral part of the clinical evaluation. The criteria for evaluation should be discussed early in supervision, with clarification of terms and competency areas. In addition, evaluation of the supervisor can enhance his or her multicultural supervision competence. This component may use structured guidelines as recommended in this chapter or a more formal instrument such as the MSI.

CONCLUSION

The objectives of this chapter were to discuss the assessment of multicultural supervision through a discussion of previous literature; an examination of the relationship between multicultural supervision competence, multicultural counseling competence, and satisfaction with supervision; the presentation of a formal instrument for measuring multicultural supervision competence; and recommendations for the future of evaluation and assessment in multicultural supervision. Although attention to multicultural supervision has increased dramatically, a tremendous amount of development is still needed. The next generation of research and design will need to take multicultural supervision assessment to a deeper level of complexity and sophistication.

REFERENCES

Constantine, M. G. (1997). Facilitating multicultural competency in counseling supervision: Operationalizing a practical framework. In D. B. Pope-Davis & H. L. K. Coleman (Eds.), *Multicultural counseling competencies: Assessment, education and training, and supervision* (pp. 310-324). Thousand Oaks, CA: Sage.

Cook, D. A., & Helms, J. E. (1988). Visible racial/ethnic group supervisees' satisfaction with cross-cultural supervision as predicted by relationship characteristics. *Journal of Counseling Psychology, 35,* 268-274.

D'Andrea, M., & Daniels, J. (1997). Multicultural counseling supervision: Central issues, theoretical considerations, and practical strategies. In D. B. Pope-Davis & H. L. K. Coleman (Eds.), *Multicultural counseling competencies: Assessment, education and training, and supervision* (pp. 290-309). Thousand Oaks, CA: Sage.

Daniels, J., D'Andrea, M., & Kim, B. S. K. (1999). Assessing the barriers and changes of cross-cultural supervision: A case study. *Counselor Education and Supervision, 38,* 191-204.

Duan, C., & Roehlke, H. (2001). A descriptive "snapshot" of cross-racial supervision in university counseling center internships. *Journal of Multicultural Counseling and Development, 29*(2), 131-146.

Fong, M. L., & Lease, S. H. (1997). Cross-cultural supervision: Issues for the White supervisor.

In D. B. Pope-Davis & H. L. K. Coleman (Eds.), *Multicultural counseling competencies: Assessment, education and training, and supervision* (pp. 387-405). Thousand Oaks, CA: Sage.

Fukuyama, M. A. (1994). Critical incidents in multicultural counseling supervision: A phenomenological approach to supervision research. *Counselor Education, 34*(2), 142-151.

Hird, J. S., Cavalieri, C. E., Dulko, J. P., Felice, A. A. D., & Ho, T. A. (2001). Visions and realities: Supervisee perspectives of multicultural supervision. *Journal of Multicultural Counseling and Development, 29*(2), 114-130.

Ladany, N., Brittan-Powell, C. S., & Pannu, R. K. (1997). The influence of supervisory racial identity interaction and racial matching on the supervisory working alliance and supervisee multicultural competence. *Counselor Education and Supervision, 36*, 284-304.

Ladany, N., Hill, C. E., Corbett, M. M., & Nutt, E. A. (1996). Nature, extent and importance of what psychotherapy trainees do not disclose to their supervisors. *Journal of Counseling Psychology, 43*(1), 10-24.

Martinez, R. P., & Holloway, E. L. (1997). The supervision relationship in multicultural training. In D. B. Pope-Davis & H. L. K. Coleman (Eds.), *Multicultural counseling competencies: Assessment, education and training, and supervision* (pp. 325-349). Thousand Oaks, CA: Sage.

McNeill, B. W., Hom, K. L., & Perez, J. A. (1995). The training and supervisory needs of racial and ethnic minority students. *Journal of Multicultural Counseling and Development, 23*, 246-258.

Pope-Davis, D. B., Liu, W. M., Nevitt, J., & Toporek, R. L. (2000). Multicultural Environment Inventory: Initial development and validation. *Cultural Diversity and Ethnic Minority Psychology, 6*(1), 57-64.

Pope-Davis, D. B., Toporek, R. L., & Ortega, L. (1999, March). *The Multicultural Supervision Scale.* College Park, MD: Author.

Pope-Davis, D. B., Toporek, R. L., Ortega, L., Bashshur, M., Liu, W. M., Brittan-Powell, C. S., et al. (2000, August). *Supervisee and supervisor experiences of multicultural supervision.* Symposium presented at the annual meeting of the American Psychological Association, Washington, DC.

Porter, N. (1995). Supervision of psychotherapists: Integrating anti-racist, feminist, and multicultural perspectives. In H. Landrine (Ed.), *Bringing cultural diversity to feminist psychology: Theory, research and practice* (pp. 163-175). Washington, DC: American Psychological Association.

Priest, R. (1994). Minority supervisor and majority supervisee: Another perspective of clinical reality. *Counselor Education and Supervision, 34*, 152-158.

Reynolds, W. M. (1982). Development of reliable and valid short forms of the Marlowe-Crowne Scale of Social Desirability. *Journal of Clinical Psychology, 38*(1), 119-125.

Sodowsky, G. R., Taffe, R. C., Gutkin, T. B., & Wise, S. L. (1994). Development of the Multicultural Counseling Inventory: A self-report measure of multicultural competencies. *Journal of Counseling Psychology, 41*, 137-148.

Stone, G. L. (1997). Multiculturalism as a context for supervision. In D. B. Pope-Davis & H. L. K. Coleman (Eds.), *Multicultural counseling competencies: Assessment, education and training, and supervision* (pp. 263-289). Thousand Oaks, CA: Sage.

Sue, D. W., Arredondo, P., & McDavis, R. J. (1992). Multicultural counseling competencies and standards: A call to the profession. *Journal of Counseling and Development, 70*, 477-486.

PART III

Research

Research is probably the facet in multi-cultural competency that helps establish our credibility in the eyes of people outside the field of multicultural competency and allows us to further our scientific, professional, and political goals. Although legitimacy is not the goal of multicultural research, it is one of the many important by-products of our efforts. Similarly, it is through research that we better understand our environment, ourselves, and our community and how our actions and behaviors create change.

This part is composed of four chapters. The first chapter (Chapter 15) examines a vital and salient issue that professionals and trainees alike are debating: the relevance of developing a culturally relevant, empirically supported treatment. Speedier treatments and the call for measurable outcomes for treatments and interventions have become an issue in training and practice. However, with the addition of culture into the empirically supported treatment movement, the debate and scientific issues only become more complex than before.

Next, Chapter 16 focuses on using a relational approach or perspective to conduct multicultural competency research. The authors of this chapter address the important client and counselor variables and provide a rationale and method for a relational approach in multicultural competency research.

The third chapter in this part, Chapter 17, argues for the need to include qualitative research methods into our current science. Typically, individual-level measures on multicultural competency are used, but the author suggests that important nuances of multicultural competency are missed from this positivistic approach. Hence, the use of qualitative methods can be used effectively to understand the meaningfulness of multicultural competency in people's lives.

This part closes with Chapter 18, which addresses a population that is often overlooked in the multicultural competency literature: private practitioners. The chapter presents original research on the issue of multicultural competencies among private practitioners. Although a preliminary study, the results suggest, nonetheless, important issues that must be addressed at the posttraining level of education.

PART III

Research

15

Challenges to the Development of Culturally Relevant, Empirically Supported Treatment

HARDIN L. K. COLEMAN
BRUCE E. WAMPOLD
University of Wisconsin–Madison

Aconsult with a colleague captured the challenge of establishing empirically supported treatments that are either culturally specific or sensitive. While working in a school-based clinic, a young (late 20s) mother was referred to our Jewish colleague to address concerns about her child's behavior. The mother came into the clinic with Aryan Nation paraphernalia and proceeded to share a complex history that included being sexually abused by her father, with whom she shared intense ideologies concerning the superiority of Caucasians even though the woman, through her maternal heritage, had relatives who were ethnic minorities. She also lived in an ethnically diverse area. The mother reported having a difficult time managing her child and felt threatened by her neighbors but was resistant to treatment and was unconvinced that her child needed counseling. Using traditional diagnostic perspectives, our colleague was considering an adjustment disorder with anxiety and depression as the one most likely to be understood by the woman's health maintenance organization (HMO).

This diagnosis reflects our traditional understanding of mental health and psychological treatment. This understanding promotes the interpretation that mental health is a function of intrapsychic and behavioral factors. Using the medical model, the assumption has been that once you determine the behavioral manifestations of a disorder, you can make assumptions about the cause and recommend treatment based on a normative understanding of the disorder. Increasingly, the mental health establishment has sought, through controlled experimentation, to determine what treatment protocols work best with which mental health disorders. The mother described above highlights the challenges to our reliance on empirically supported treatment.

To be empirically supported, a treatment needs specific qualities. The problem or behavioral disorders needs to be clearly defined (e.g., depression or academic underachievement). The goals and processes of the treatment need to be explicit. What counts as change needs to be identified and measurable as well as the techniques that are used to stimulate change. Another key ingredient of empirically supported treatment is that it is evaluated in direct comparison to alternate forms of treatment that are also systematically applied. At the very least, an empirically supported treatment (EST) is theory driven, systematically applied to a specific population, and systematically evaluated using reliable and valid measures of change (Chambless et al., 1998; Chambless & Hollon, 1998; Chambless et al., 1996; Crits-Christoph, 1998; Henry, 1998; Wampold, 1997).

The purpose of this chapter is to critically examine whether the factors that lead to becoming an EST challenge the development of culturally relevant, empirically supported treatments (CRESTs). We suggest that the challenges to the creation of culturally relevant or specific ESTs include the following:

1. difficulty using standard processes for establishing ESTs to determine the efficacy or effectiveness of treatments;
2. an absence of received or achieved theory concerning effective and culturally relevant treatment;
3. a lack of information as to what combination of cultural factors (e.g., gender, class, ethnicity, or sexual orientation), emotional disturbance (e.g., depression, posttraumatic stress disorder [PTSD], or conduct disorder), and context (e.g., rural, urban, in

school, or psychiatric ward) can be used to define the "specific population";
4. a difficulty establishing culturally relevant definitions of what constitutes psychological or behavioral change; and
5. a lack of measurements that have been normed on difficult-to-define specific populations to make accurate assessments of a client's psychological status prior to and after treatment.

In this chapter, we discuss how an ecological perspective on clinical work can lead us toward a culturally relevant practice and to the methodological challenges to evaluating treatment efficacy. In the second section, the challenges to developing empirical support for culturally relevant treatments using current methodological approaches are discussed. The third section outlines the factors that can make a treatment culturally relevant, along with examples. We end the chapter with a proposal for an alternate model for the evaluation of effective and culturally relevant counseling services.

As our colleague struggled with assessing and developing a treatment plan for her client, she realized that a traditional diagnosis and treatment plan would be insufficient for the client's needs, let alone help the client resolve her issues as a sexual abuse victim (which was neither her presenting problem nor a diagnostic category that leads to third-party payment) or work through the parenting issues that brought her into counseling. Our colleague also recognized the social aspects of the client's difficulties—namely, deep-seated, generational hatred that created barriers to her emotional development and for her community. Knowing the difficulty of getting reimbursed for an adjustment disorder, realizing that the client did not have the resources or motivation to engage in traditional office-based treatment, and holding the belief that this client needed to have her cultural perspective taking challenged, our colleague facilitated her enrollment in a parenting group with other low-income women who had a variety of cultural backgrounds. Our colleague believed that such an intervention would have several benefits. This intervention would allow the client to come into treatment with less resistance as the manifest focus would be on her child and the skills she needed to serve that child well. In the group, she would come into contact with ethnic minorities as individuals, which *could* serve to expand her perspective on issues of racial hierarchy. Just as important, our colleague knew that one of the ongoing topics of conversation in the group concerned how a substantial percentage of the mothers' history as sexual assault/abuse victims affected their parenting. Our colleague's assumption was that this conversation could trigger her client's reevaluation of her relationship with her father, which our colleague saw as reinforcing the client's rigid approach to parenting—one source of the parent-child conflict. What our colleague needs is a coherent perspective to guide her clinical choices. Current standards suggest that she should turn to the approved list of ESTs and apply the one that best fits her client's diagnoses. We have already discussed the clinical challenges to that process; in the next section, we want to address the methodological issues that suggest that ESTs may not be as useful as the clinical science establishment would have us believe (e.g., Hall, 2001).

METHODOLOGICAL CHALLENGES TO CULTURALLY RELEVANT, EMPIRICALLY SUPPORTED TREATMENTS

Recent examinations of empirically supported treatments (Atkinson, Bui, & Mori, 2001; Wampold, 2001) have identified that the effective ingredient in treatment may not be stressed in the treatment protocol and derived from theory but depends on the clinician. These findings suggest that the recent emphasis on multicultural competence in the clinician

(see Chapter 11, this volume) may be the core factor that influences treatment outcome. What follows is a discussion concerning the challenges of culturally relevant treatment in developing empirically supported treatment. Three approaches to identifying and developing psychological interventions are applicable to diverse groups. We will examine each of these approaches, their underlying assumptions, and their usefulness for multicultural counseling.

Examine Generalizability Across Various Populations

More than 450 approaches to counseling and psychotherapy have been identified—it seems reasonable that some of these therapies will be more effective for some types of people than for others. The goal of the generalizability strategy is to examine the relative efficacy of treatments with types of persons. This strategy has a long history in psychology and education; essentially, the goal is to answer Paul's (1967) question, "What treatment, by whom, is most effective for this individual with that specific problem, under which set of circumstances, and how does it come about?" (p. 111). We first discuss this strategy from a general research perspective and then examine the assumptions and usefulness of it in creating CRESTs.

Suppose that there are two treatments, such as the cognitive-behavioral and interpersonal process for depression, and two types of people, such as male and female. Relative efficacy can be examined by randomly assigning one half of the men and one half of the women to the two treatments in the usual factorial design (i.e., a 2 × 2 design). The main effect for treatment indicates which of the two treatments is more efficacious. That is, if type of person is ignored, then the design is a treatment comparison design (Heppner, Kivlighan, & Wampold, 1999; Wampold, 2001). The main effect for type of person indicates whether men or women are more psychologically distressed, have fewer symptoms, or are better adjusted (i.e., depending on the focus of the treatment and choice of the effect constructs in the study). The important effect for generalizability purposes is the interaction between treatment and type of person—that is, is one of the treatments more efficacious with one type of person and the other treatment more efficacious for the other type of person? For example, the interpersonal process may be more efficacious with women (who are stereotypically believed to be relationship focused) and the cognitive-behavioral treatment may be more efficacious with men (who are believed to be more rational)—such a result would be tremendously informative.

The generalizability strategy has been recommended as a vital means in multicultural counseling to determine which treatments work best for various racial, ethnic, cultural, and other nonmajority groups (e.g., Hall, 2001; Maltzman, 2001; Quintana & Atkinson, 2002). With the generalizability strategy, however, there are several assumptions about (a) how treatments work, (b) the epistemological status of the characteristics of people, and (c) the homogeneity of disorders across types of persons.

The first assumption involved in the generalizability strategy is related to the efficacious aspects of treatments. The anticipated interaction between the treatment and the characteristics of people assumes that specific ingredients of the treatment work better with one type of individual than another. Consider how this translates into the multicultural arena. If cognitive treatments work better with European Americans and interpersonal treatments work better with African Americans, then there is the assumption that the cognitive ingredients somehow are effective with European Americans and the interpersonal ingredients are effective with African Americans. However, this assumption ignores the overwhelming evidence that the specific ingredients of treatments per se do not create the beneficial outcomes of counseling (Wampold, 2001). If, as Wampold (2000, 2001) proposed, the benefits of counseling are derived from the healing context, the belief in the treatment and its rationale, the therapeutic relationship, and other factors common to most counseling approaches, then the search for interactions between specific treatments and characteristics of people will be futile and will unjustifiably elevate the importance of specific ingredients of treatments.

A second assumption of the generalizability strategy is that therapists are unimportant to the outcome relative to the importance of differences among treatments. However, the evidence indicates that much more of the variability in outcomes in treatments is due to the therapist (within treatments) than to differences among treatments; moreover, ignoring therapist effects leads to an overestimate of the true effects due to treatments (Wampold, 2001; Wampold & Serlin, 2000). In the generalizability strategy, the situation is ripe for therapists to influence the results. The validity of the factorial design, whereby treatments are crossed with types of persons, depends on the therapists in each treatment condition being equally skilled generally and equally skilled with each type of person. If the study examines the relative efficacy of two treatments for, say, African Americans and Asian Americans, then the therapists would need to be equally skilled with both groups, a condition not easily satisfied.

A third assumption of the generalizability strategy is that persons can be classified on constructs relevant to their response to treatment. When a researcher examines the relative efficacy of treatments across racial groups (e.g., African Americans, Asian Americans, Hispanic Americans, European Americans), then the construct of race, as defined in the research, is elevated in importance vis-à-vis treatments (see Chapter 3, this volume, for a discussion of this issue in social science). Whether one considers race to be a socially constructed or a biologically determined phenomenon, it is necessary to theorize how this construct makes a difference in treatment outcome. If race is a proxy for cultural values and attitudes, it is obvious that racial classifications contain subgroups with very different attitudes and values (e.g., for Hispanics, there are Puerto Ricans in New York City, Cubans in Florida, Mexican Americans in California, etc.). Despite the admonition to consider the heterogeneity of racial groups, stratifying by the relevant constructs, such as socioeconomic status (SES), generational status, racial identity, degree of acculturation, country of origin, gender, and so on, is literally impossible. A related problem is present in the generalizability strategy vis-à-vis the research design because the grouping variable related to the type of person cannot be randomly assigned and thus is a status variable (Heppner et al., 1999). In the continuing example, it is obviously not possible to randomly assign participants to racial groups. Consequently, the participants in the racial groups either must be matched on relevant variables (e.g., gender, SES, degree of severity of disorder), or attempts must be made to adjust means by considering these variables (e.g., analysis of covariance), a statistical strategy of dubious distinction (e.g., Porter & Raudenbush, 1987).

Examining generalizability across groups is intuitively appealing but theoretically impoverished and pragmatically impossible. Indeed, to our knowledge, no studies have compared two treatments with types of persons whereby the classification of persons was relevant to multicultural counseling. However, a few studies have examined the relative efficacy of a single treatment with racial/ethnic groups. An examination of one of these studies will demonstrate how such designs are impoverished in theory and in design. Chambless and

Williams (1995) tested the efficacy of in vivo exposure with African Americans and European Americans with agoraphobia. They found that although the treatment was beneficial for both groups, it was less beneficial to the African Americans than to the European Americans. However, there were many confounding variables, including therapist-client ethnic match (of the 19 therapists, only 2 were African American), the socioeconomic status of the participants (SES of African Americans was lower), the severity of the disorder (African Americans' agoraphobia was more severe), and the location of treatment (the African Americans received more in-home therapy because of transportation problems). In addition, because the treatment had been validated predominantly on European Americans, the treatment was not culturally relevant to African Americans. Consequently, it is not possible to know whether differences were due to one of the treatments being less effective for African Americans, one of the confounds, or the cultural relevance of the treatment. There was no attempt to understand if any of the African Americans' fears of public spaces were connected with their history of discrimination and racism in such places. In this study, no theoretical hypothesis was made about the specific ingredients of in vivo exposure that would indicate or contraindicate this treatment for African Americans, leaving this study simply as a exemplar of blind empiricism searching for relative efficacy. The many design issues in this study surely lead one to believe that such misguided searches will not be informative.

Culturally Specific Treatments

At first glance, culturally specific treatments that are created as modified standard treatments or novel treatments designed for various racial, ethnic, or cultural groups have great appeal, but they also have several drawbacks.

Although culturally specific treatments appear to be superior theoretically to the blind empiricism applied with the generalizability strategy, there remain problematic assumptions. The primacy of racial, ethnic, or cultural group designations is just as troublesome in this context as it was in the generalizability strategy. If a particular treatment is adapted or designed to treat agoraphobia with African Americans, then the racial or ethnic classification of "African American" assumes that (a) the variability within African Americans is less important than the difference between African Americans and other racial and ethnic groups; (b) racial or ethnic group designation is isomorphic with or more important than other person characteristics such as SES, gender, attitudes, and values; and (c) race and ethnicity are salient constructs that determine how therapy should be designed and delivered. Exploration of these assumptions will reveal the flaws with the seemingly respectful and purportedly efficacious strategy related to culturally specific treatments.

One of the perspicuous criticisms of identifying empirically supported treatment is the "one-size-fits-all" nature of such an endeavor. However, designing or adapting a treatment for a particular racial, ethnic, or cultural group falls into the same trap. Advocating culturally specific treatment for a certain cultural group is logically isomorphic to recommending cognitive-behavioral treatment for depression—the only difference being that person characteristics related to the disorder are substituted for person characteristics related to race, ethnicity, or culture. Consider the challenge of selecting a single culture-specific treatment for Asian Americans based on Eastern philosophy, even though Asian Americans have diverse countries of origin, religions, spiritual and philosophical beliefs, racial identification, levels of acculturation, and so forth.

Designing culturally specific treatments can lead to a conflict between values. To illustrate, consider how one would design such treatments for a cultural group that, according to current thinking, oppresses women. How does one design a treatment that is consonant with and respects this culture without denigrating the status of women? To illustrate a similar dilemma, consider a situation that one of the authors faced in a multicultural counseling class. Each of the class members gave a presentation on a different cultural group and drew the implications for counseling and education. All went well during the presentation as the class, being particularly sensitive to the needs of diverse populations, understood the characteristics and history of the population (knowledge), felt the appropriate empathy for the oppression of each group (awareness), and stated that they were able to work with the population (skills). That is, until a young European American woman, who had been teaching in a village in northern Alaska, gave a presentation on working with Alaskan indigenous people. As part of the presentation, she offered the class a delicacy shared as they would in the Alaskan community—whale meat. Not one person would taste the offering, with various defenses (e.g., "I don't eat meat," "Whales should be protected"). Her explanation that the people in her village would be offended by their refusal and that they would be not be taken seriously as healers or teachers fell on deaf ears. Requiring that a treatment be culturally specific precludes, as it did in the class discussion, an open, meaningful, and collaborative dialogue between the cultures of the therapist and the client.

A fuller understanding of the problems with culturally specific treatments can be gained by examining research and research strategies in this area. First, consider a study by Rosselló and Bernal (1999), who tested the efficacy of cognitive-behavioral therapy and interpersonal treatments of depression with Puerto Rican adolescents. As part of this test, they created culturally relevant adaptations of these treatments and used Puerto Rican therapists. They found that both treatments were effective vis-à-vis a waiting-list control group, but neither of the treatments was demonstrably superior to the other. On the surface, it appears that this study provided evidence that these are culturally specific and efficacious treatments for a particular non-White cultural group. Although a case can be made that this study adds to the literature, little is learned about delivering services to such groups. Because the researchers used culturally relevant treatment models, we do not know whether the treatments were effective due to their cultural relevance, to the specific ingredients that are theoretically derived from the treatment models, or to the common factors contained in the treatments. After all, the results replicated the predominant findings in all comparative outcome studies conducted over the past four decades that bona fide treatments are superior to no treatment but are equally efficacious (Wampold, 2001). Moreover, we do not know if non–Puerto Rican therapists using either culturally adapted or nonculturally adapted models would have been equally effective. Finally, as with all treatments, there were clients who did not get better and clients who terminated prematurely.

Interestingly, we could not find in the literature a study that compared a culturally adapted treatment to the treatment delivered without the cultural adaptation. Is this an oversight by researchers? We think not. Consider such a study that compares culturally adapted treatment (CAT) to the modal model treatment (MMT), the latter of which will be administered as indicated in the treatment manual, with the therapists being proscribed from responding in any way that recognizes the race, ethnicity, or culture of the clients. Is this a fair comparison? Not really: The MMT is not an appropriate comparison because the therapists are required to ignore a major aspect of the client. Culturally neutral or insensitive approaches are not "good"

counseling, and thus the comparison is unfair. If the therapists in the MMT are permitted to be culturally sensitive and respond accordingly, then what is the difference between "culturally specific treatment" and "culturally sensitive treatment"? To address this question, we argue that a more inclusive understanding of clinical practice needs to be integrated into the EST movement. Rather than relying on symptoms to dictate the choice of treatment, we believe that the etiology of psychological disorders and the choice of appropriate treatment need to be understood within a contextual understanding of clinical practice. In the next section, we articulate such an understanding.

Ecological Perspectives on Clinical Practice

Given the perspective that clinicians should limit their practice to ESTs in order to practice ethically (Crits-Christoph, 1998), how can our colleague working with the mother we mentioned earlier in this chapter know that she is doing the right thing? How can we, as scientists, assist her in managing the needs of such a client with confidence and ethics? We contend that developing best clinical practices in a pluralistic society must incorporate a context-driven model of treatment that goes beyond theories of treatment (e.g., cognitive-behavioral or psychodynamic), as well as beyond theories of individual development, so that a ecological perspective can be used to articulate the manner in which the multiple layers of context interact to organize the behavior and potential of the counselor and the client as they collaborate in attempts to stimulate change in the client's life. As clinical practice has learned to address issues related to culture and context within the therapeutic process, theorists have begun to integrate an ecological perspective into our understanding of clinical work (e.g., Coleman & Tuescher, in press; Neville & Mobley, 2001). Various representations of the ecological perspectives on human development and behavior (Brofenbrenner, 1979; Lerner, 1995; Lerner & Kauffman, 1985; see also Chapter 3, this volume) share common assumptions that are useful in developing a contextual model of psychological intervention.

One of the core assumptions of an ecological perspective is that reducing our understanding of human behavior, particularly behavior that results from interpersonal interaction, to the linear relationship between proximal factors provides an insufficient explanation of how that behavior is organized within the complex interactions between an individual and his or her immediate (e.g., family, community, and peers) and general (e.g., society, institutions, and heritage) environment. Within an ecological framework, therefore, the search is not purely for causal relationships between factors but for how those factors are systematically organized to facilitate particular behavioral patterns. This assumption is core to Donovan and Marlatt's (1988) understanding of addictions within a biopsychosocial rather than a medical model. The medical model of addiction seeks a proximal or immediate explanation for a person's addiction. This search has led to an emphasis on trait theories of addictions, with a focus on biological, genetic, or familial explanations for addictions. The biopsychosocial model suggests that addictive behavior is the result of a complex interactions between biological, psychological, and social factors that are organized within an individual's life to facilitate the acquisition of an addiction. Within this framework, the addiction is not caused by the individual's biology, psychology, or social situation but is organized through the interaction of these factors.

The ecological perspective goes a step beyond the biopsychosocial model (BPS). In the BPS, the focus is still on the individual and looking at the behavior patterns in terms of how the individual manages (or mismanages)

his or her context. The ecological perspective assumes that a person's behavior is organized within and by his or her context. From this perspective, the influence of what Brofenbrenner (1979) referred to as the macrosystem has as much effect on the organization of an individual's behavior as do microsystemic variables such as the individual's parents or biology.

Another assumption of the ecological perspective is that core human processes involving issues related to such factors as affect, cognitive development, or perception are shared by people across contexts, but to understand how these processes are organized within an individual's life, one has to understand how the individual has made sense of his or her context and used that understanding to develop a repertoire of behavior that can effectively manage the demands of the context in which he or she lives (Cohen, 2001). This means that we need to understand normative behavior as it relates to the shared context in which a group of individuals have been raised. For example, a child's taste in food is deeply influenced by the smells and taste that surround that child from time of birth. As those smells and tastes are varied, so will the child's taste in food be varied. As those smells and tastes are limited, so will be the child's taste in food. If, however, the child has positive or negative personal experiences with particular tastes or smells, that will influence his or her idiosyncratic development. It is possible and valuable, therefore, to help an individual explore the significant events that have influenced his or her developmental trajectory, but it is equally important and valuable to understand how the context in which these events occurred served to organize the manner in which they became significant to the individual. This process should not discount the power of the individual when interpreting the meaning of that event for himself or herself. Another shared assumption across ecological perspectives is that the idiosyncratic interpretations and responses of individuals lead to change throughout the ecosystem.

A final core assumption of the ecological perspective that is important to the clinical process is the understanding, shared by all systems theories, that change in one part of the ecosystem will lead to changes in other parts of the system. This process is evident among immigrants. Changing the physical, social, and institutional context in which an individual is embedded will lead to changes in language, values, dress, customs, and behaviors. LaFromboise, Coleman, and Gerton (1993) have identified the multiple ways in which individuals can engage in the process of second-culture acquisition and made clear that the process will have a profound effect on how people think about themselves, raise their children, and interact with others. Although it is a dramatic example of how change in one part of a system creates changes in others, the process is an important part of the ecological perspective.

The implications of the ecological perspective for clinical practice are profound (Neville & Mobley, 2001). Its greatest value is that it provides a heuristic for integrating intra- and interpersonal factors that influence behavior with macrosystemic factors, which influence the individual who may be a client and organize the nature of the relationship that is therapy. As a context-driven theory of treatment, this perspective violates the assumptions of most ESTs that ask for specificity in client problems and a manualized treatment format that is replicated across each course of treatment. A theory that suggests that treatment needs to adjust to both the individual's personal and cultural realities will have difficulty making a priori decisions about either the focus or outcome of treatment. Such a treatment would need to make context-driven assessments as to the role of depression or cultural identity development in the challenges that bring a client into treatment. It would also

have to provide guidelines for how the clinician works with a client when those factors may take prominence in the work.

The dilemma that we face is the recognition (Sue, Ivey, & Pedersen, 1996) that cultural factors have not been well integrated into traditional models of treatment and that, even though we have an increasingly well-thought-out understanding of multicultural counseling competence, we have not developed models of culturally relevant treatments that have empirical support or articulated standards as to what those treatments should include or when to use those treatments. In the next section, we articulate a heuristic for choosing treatment approaches based on idiosyncratic needs of the client and share several examples of culturally relevant treatment.

HEURISTICS FOR CHOOSING CULTURE SPECIFIC TREATMENT

Tyler, Brome, and Williams (1991) described three models for understanding counseling relationships in a pluralistic society: the universalist, particularist, and transcendent models. Universalists suggest that cultural differences are secondary to the universals of human development. Particularlists suggest that human development is culturally defined. Transcendents posit that human development must be understood in the interaction between cultural contexts and individual experience. Much of the current debate in the field of multicultural counseling (see Coleman, 1995; Draguns, 1996; Helms & Richardson, 1997) is over the validity of these three models. Figure 15.1 represents the multiple levels in which culture affects the counseling process according to the transcendent model.

The questions for the practitioner concern what type of treatment best addresses the needs of a client. At what point should a client be referred to treatment that will focus on issues related to his or her disorder and address

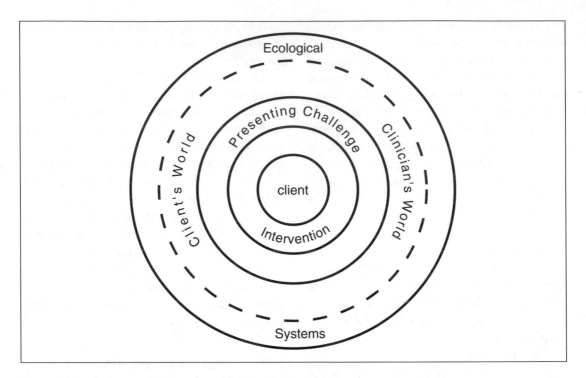

Figure 15.1   Contextual Framework for Counseling Interventions

culturally specific issues as the core of the treatment process? In this section, we identify characteristics of culturally specific treatment and discuss when such a referral is appropriate.

What Is Culture-Specific Treatment?

Treatment that is culture specific has certain characteristics and assumptions. One way to think about these characteristics and assumptions is to realize that treatments we refer to as traditional are really culturally specific. In this case, the culture is European, male, and middle-class centric. These treatments tend to place tremendous emphasis on internal factors in the etiology of the disorder and the individual's ability to develop control over the change process. In the treatment process, the primary mode of interaction is verbal and abstract, with the use of linear thinking as the hallmark for healthy thinking. Within this culturally specific treatment

format, there are assumptions of resources (making the treatment middle class) and motivation to join the mainstream (which makes it assimilationalist).

Culture-specific treatments do the following:

1. respect and use the culture's definitions of psychological and sociological distress,
2. respect the culture's assumptions about personal control and responsibility,
3. use the culture's dominant modes of interaction,
4. align with the culture's worldview,
5. emphasize developing constructive relationships with other cultural group members,
6. recognize and address the exogenous as well as endogenous sources of behavior,
7. emphasize the development of a positive cultural identity as a core strategy for coping with psychological and sociological distress.

These characteristics lead to common foci of treatment in culturally specific treatment:

1. There is an emphasis on the traditional strengths of the culture, both in terms of how the program is structured and the models of effective functioning that are presented to the client.
2. There is a focus on exploring the client's status as a member of a cultural group within a particular ecosystem.
3. There is a focus on learning the positive qualities that are core components of the client's culture.
4. There is an emphasis on learning how to cope as a member of one cultural group within contexts that facilitate contact with other cultural groups.
5. There is an emphasis on group solidarity (often practiced in group sessions within the treatment program).
6. There is an attempt to include techniques that are relevant to the cultural group receiving the intervention.

As these guidelines indicate, to be culturally relevant, an intervention has to do more than adapt existing treatments to meet the needs of particular groups or just change the type of person who participates in the treatment. To be culturally relevant, a treatment needs to be embedded into the assumed worldview of the participants (Wampold, 2001). As a result of this embeddedness, most culturally relevant interventions may not be generalizable. Unlike ESTs, they may be so context specific and so responsive to the needs of the individual participant that evaluation of the intervention may also need to be done within the context on a case-by-case basis. Such treatments may not be able to establish manuals to dictate the treatment, but guidelines could be developed to lead the clinician and client through the growth process.

EXAMPLES OF CULTURALLY SPECIFIC PROGRAMMING: KWANZA, UJIMA, AND PROJECT EUNICE

To show how these principles can be put into practice, we describe three programs that are used in a small midwestern city to address the culture-specific needs of African Americans. All three of these programs assume that there are two major burdens in the lives of African Americans who are in need of mental health services. The first is that they have significant experiences of oppression and discrimination within mainstream institutions, primarily involving schools and the field of employment. The second is that they have not received systematic enculturation into traditional African American culture. When these two burdens are present, African Americans lack the emotional and social resources needed to respond to traumatic and stressful events in their lives. These experiences leave African Americans stressed, distrustful, and feeling like there is little they can do to take control of events in their lives. The psychological and behavioral sequelae of this process include depression, school and job failure, addiction, and a tendency to use aggression to resolve conflict. The programs described below explicitly took these factors into account as they were designed.

Kwanza

Bass and Coleman (1997) designed an in-school program for African American male adolescents who were at risk for academic underachievement or failure. The program ran for 20 weeks. During the first 10 weeks, 6 participants were introduced to the Kwanza principles of (a) *Umoja* (unity), (b) *Kujichagulia* (self-determination), (c) *Ujima* (collective work and responsibility), (d) *Ujamaa* (cooperative economics), (e) *Nia* (purpose), (f) *Kuumba* (creativity), and (g) *Imani* (faith). These seven principles represent the core of Africentric values (Karenga, 1980). The other focus of the first 10 weeks was on developing a sense of group unity. During the second 10 weeks of the program, the focus changed to exploring how the participants were applying these principles within their school and home community. Bass and Coleman found that behavioral change did not occur until the adolescents made a commitment to themselves and each other to apply these principles in their lives. This suggests that teaching about cultural identity is, in itself, insufficient to promote change. To get people to change, one must explore the interaction between their belief systems and their environment.

Ujima

Ujima is a family program that is based on Meyers et al.'s (1991) conceptualization of an optimal worldview that is rooted in traditional Africentric values. This program is designed to work with families that have a history of substance abuse and at least 6 months of sobriety. The goal of the program is to help clients understand how the interaction between their ethnic status, their personal history, and their current situation produces behavior that is counterproductive to their personal well-being. Of the families participating in this program, 95% are headed by single women, so the program has evolved to serve the needs of persons with those gender-specific needs. At intake, all members of the family are assigned an individual therapist and to groups that are gender and age specific. The mothers in the program enter a 10-week starter group in which they are introduced to the conceptualizations of Meyers et al., the principles of psychological colonization, and a program-specific model called the cycle of pain, which is used to describe the pressure to retreat to traditional coping strategies when psychologically trying situations arise. They are also introduced to belief systems analysis (BSA), in which they are taught to critically examine their assumptions for evidence of internalized oppression (racist, sexist, and classist) and explore more optimal conceptualizations. Upon graduation from the starters group, the

mothers enter into a weekly group until the family leaves the program. This group focuses on the multilevel sources of distress and explores useful solutions for the participants. In individual therapy, these issues are explored in more depth and discussed in terms of the mothers' particular cases. This pattern is repeated for the children, who are in adolescent- or latency-aged groupings by gender. These groups use a significant amount of play and art therapy to help the children become more articulate about the cultural and personal pressures in their lives and solutions to these pressures. Family sessions are run on a regular basis to explore issues related to communication and family functioning. Great efforts are made to ensure that these sessions are used to reinforce the parental hierarchy as it replicates traditional African American values of responsibility and wisdom.

Project Eunice

This project was explicitly designed to be an early intervention program for single mothers with adolescent sons who were at risk for involvement with the juvenile justice system. The program was driven by the awareness that more than 80% of the African American adolescent males in corrections facilities came from households headed by a single mother. Participants for this project were recruited from families that had been referred to traditional support programs (e.g., parent education, in-school group guidance) but had not engaged with those services. This program assumed that these families had no reason to trust social service systems, that they might not have the emotional and social resources needed to access this system, and that there had been gaps in communications between the family and service providers. Unlike many prevention and early intervention programs, this project did not have particular starting dates, and the length of the program was relatively long (6-9 months). The program operated on a series of phases of treatment that were not time limited.

Phase 1: Relationship Building. The clinicians who did the treatment also did the recruitment and intake. Families were given the time they needed in deciding to enter the program. A clinician would make repeated visits to get to know and be known by the client.

Phase 2: Assessment and Treatment Planning. This phase took place in the client's home on a biweekly basis. The family was formally interviewed concerning their history and what changes they wanted to make; the family also worked with the staff to determine a plan that would work for them. This process allowed the family to feel known and respected for their strengths.

Phases 3 and 4: Group and Family Meeting. During this phase, the families received weekly family sessions, and then all adolescent males in the family attended a group meeting while the mothers attended a meeting among themselves. Transportation was arranged to the group meetings. The mothers met at a participant's house and shared a meal as the goal was to create a traditional support system that would extend beyond the length of the program. The focus of the conversation was on gender and the types of challenges the participants faced as individuals and as members of their culture. Solutions were discussed from this multileveled perspective as well. One focus of the groups and a significant focus of the family sessions were on the developmental challenges faced by African American families when a male reaches adolescence.

Phase 5: Multifamily Meetings. As the families engaged with the program, they participated in multifamily meetings. These meetings were organized around a potluck where each family brought food. The focus of these meetings was to share common challenges and solutions to raising African American male adolescents. This was often a good opportunity to discuss issues such as gang involvement and relationships with school personnel.

Phase 6: Mentoring. Once a family felt they had reached their goals in the program, they were invited into the mentoring phase of the program. During this phase, the mothers and boys were invited to attend the group-specific meetings to act as mentors for new families coming into the program. This served to replicate traditional patterns of transmitting information across generations.

When to Refer?

What is common across these culturally specific interventions is the assumption that there is an interaction between the emotional or behavioral disturbance the client is experiencing, the client's cultural group membership, and the context in which the client is experiencing this interaction. Understanding this interaction is a key component of multicultural counseling competence (Sue et al., 1996), as is understanding when a client might benefit from a culturally specific treatment. Particularlists would argue that matching by culture is always the best form of treatment. Not only is that not always possible, but there is little empirical evidence to support such a claim. Clinical expertise, however, suggests that culture-specific treatment has utility. We hypothesize that one of the sources of this utility is the manner in which involvement in such a program can serve as a motivator for the participant. The model for motivation in clinical relationships that the first author developed (Coleman, 1992) and a transtheoretical model of change developed by Prochaska and DiClemente (1982) combine to give insight into how and when culture-specific treatment can be effective.

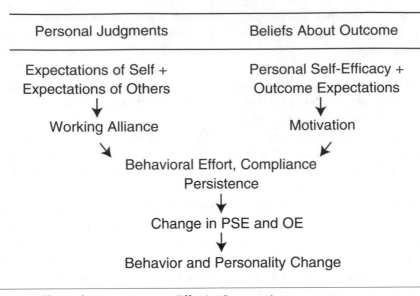

Figure 15.2   Effects of Expectations on Effective Interventions

SOURCE: Coleman (1992).

Motivation is a key element in successful counseling (Bandura, 1986; Miller & Rollnick, 1991). Many factors stimulate motivation in clients. A major one is the ability to establish an effective working relationship with the therapist, and another is developing faith in the types of activities that are involved in the therapy (Wampold, 2001). Figure 15.2 represents the relationship between these two factors. As Coleman, Wampold, and Casali (1995) have suggested, when you have a therapist who is matched with you on a salient cultural factor (e.g., ethnicity, gender, or class), the client tends to ascribe to that therapist values and perspectives that are similar to the client's. Information that such a therapist provides can have a credibility that may not be readily available to a therapist from a different cultural group (Sue & Zane, 1987). In a culture-specific treatment program, this credibility is enhanced as it asks the client to use his or her cultural framework to both understand the nature of the problem and to generate solutions for change. One of the reasons, therefore, that culture-specific treatment may be effective is

that it stimulates motivation in the client by providing a naturally credible therapist who uses techniques that call upon the client's culturally developed strengths (Wampold, 2001). Coleman (1992) and Wampold (2001) have suggested that effective treatment simultaneously meets the client's expectations for himself or herself and the clinician while also providing treatment that meets his or her outcome expectations. This combination of positive working alliance and treatment efficacy is what can be provided through a culturally specific program.

Prochaska and DiClemente (1982) have developed a model for explaining the change process (see Figure 15.3) that addresses the role of motivation in the therapy process that may have utility in understanding when to refer clients to culturally specific treatment. They argue that there are six stages of change. In the precontemplation stage, the client does not even recognize having a problem. In the contemplation stage, the client begins to see the nature of his or her problems but has not committed to making a change. In the determination stage,

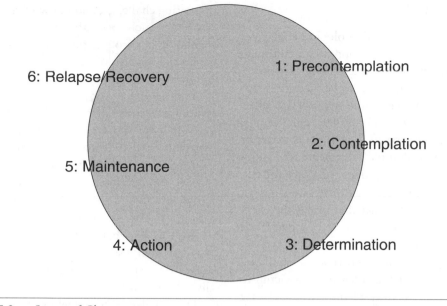

Figure 15.3   Stages of Change

SOURCE: Prochaska and DiClemente (1982).

the client makes a decision to change. In the action stage, he or she makes a change. In the maintenance stage, the client learns how to allow those changes to become stable factors in his or her life. Prochaska and DiClemente also recognized that we all relapse, which is Stage 6.

A client can make these changes in a culture-specific or a generic (read: Eurocentric) treatment program. When, however, a person is having difficulties getting motivated to change or making commitments to change, a referral to a culture-specific treatment program may well be in order. In such a case, the focus on external factors and the sense of group solidarity can serve to reduce the stigma associated with recognizing problems as a function of a personal deficit and provides clients a new perspective on concerns. The educational piece helps clients contextualize their problems, helps them feel less alone, and provides models—people who look and think like they do—for dealing with these problems. These factors serve to reduce the client's

ambivalence concerning change that Miller and Rollnick (1991) have identified as a major obstacle to motivation. Culture-specific treatment may, therefore, be particularly appropriate for clients in the precontemplation stage to determination phases of treatment, as well as during the maintenance stage.

The complex interaction of factors (e.g., client's presenting concern, program of intervention, stage of change, therapist competence) that make up the therapeutic process is at times overwhelming. When we attempt to develop empirically supported treatments using the rigorous standards presented at the start of this chapter, we are forced to wonder what we are evaluating. The fact that most treatments that are empirically supported are cognitive or behavioral is not surprising because these theories lend themselves to clear problem definition and manualized treatment. Even these treatments, however, are challenged when we strive to integrate the effects of culture on the treatment process.

CONCLUSION

We have presented methodological challenges to developing empirical support for culturally relevant treatment, characteristics of culture-specific treatment, and some heuristics for deciding when that is the appropriate treatment modality for a client. The claim here is not that culture-specific treatment is better or worse than traditional treatment. The argument is that there is a time and place for culture-specific work, just as there is a time for focusing on the disorder that brings the client to treatment in the first place. To determine the effectiveness of these treatments, however, we need to develop a process for acquiring empirical support that does not fall victim to the problems we have identified in ESTs yet can allow clinicians more than a gut-level comfort with using one treatment rather than another. We want to conclude by presenting guidelines for developing and evaluating culturally relevant treatments.

Articulate a Theory of Culturally Relevant Treatment

The first step in developing culturally relevant ESTs is articulating a theory. In the consultation we presented at the beginning of the chapter, our colleague needed an articulate rationale for why she chose to treat the combination of social (race hatred) and interpersonal (victimization) issues in her client rather than the adjustment disorder. We have come a long way from a rigid focus on intrapsychic issues and a unidimensional understanding in counseling. What we still need to train clinicians to do is have an articulate and systematically derived theory of how culture affects the counseling process. To develop a theory-driven practice, clinicians need to articulate precisely how they think cultural factors affect the client's development of a presenting challenge, have a contextual understanding of that

presenting challenge, and know what works in resolving such a challenge for particular clients. It is through the systematic maintenance and analysis of case notes that clinicians can derive their theory.

As a field, we need to have access to these grounded theories of culturally relevant practice. Ongoing efforts need to be made so that clinicians and students of the clinical process have access to these systematic case studies so that we can develop an aggregate understanding of effective practice. On the basis of that aggregate understanding, we can develop theories as to what works well with whom. We can then use those theories to develop standardized protocols as the basis of culturally relevant ESTs.

The challenge to developing a coherent theory of culturally relevant or specific counseling is very similar to developing a useful understanding of the addictions process. As Donovan and Marlatt (1988) have indicated, addictions represent a complex pattern of behavior that results from multiple factors in the individual's life. To explain this pattern of behavior, addictions specialists have developed a biopsychosocial model. This model suggests that addictions are the outcome of a complex interaction between our biological, psychological, and social selves. What is evident from this description of the biopsychosocial model of addictions is that this complex behavior pattern, even with identifiable biological processes, resists a linear causal explanation. We suggest that attempts to identify a causal relationship between cultural group membership and emotional disturbance are equally difficult. If this is the case, establishing empirical support for culturally relevant or specific treatments will be equally difficult. To do so will demand using an ecological perspective on the counseling process that seeks to understand the manner in which particular phenomena, such as therapeutic outcomes, are organized through the interactions between

Culturally Relevant, Empirically Supported Treatment   243

the individual and his or her immediate and cultural context (Brofenbrenner, 1979; see also Chapter 3, this volume).

Value Ecological Validity

Another step in the development of CRESTs is the willingness of journal editors to value ecological validity. Current standards for ESTs emphasize manualized treatment for specific disorders. The outcome of this standard both limits the type of individual who participates in the investigation and does not allow for an evaluation of the role that context may play in the etiology and resolution of the disorder. A focus on ecological validity would allow empirical investigations to focus on determining that treatment is effective at helping clients achieve contextually relevant goals that are established within a collaborative relationship that is the hallmark of competent multicultural counseling. A focus on ecological, rather than internal, validity would allow the focus in research to move away from attention on techniques to a focus on process.

Focus on Nonspecific or Common Factors in EST

We need more research in the clinical literature on those issues that have been addressed in analogue research such as ethnic matching or cultural empathy. ESTs place substantial focus on the techniques of treatment. From a cultural perspective, it is also important to evaluate the relationship between competent techniques and other counseling variables such as relationship building. We need to know how members of different cultural groups experience a phenomenon such as relationship building, how it is affected by context, and how it affects outcome. Process-focused clinical research would focus more on how the client experiences change within the clinical relationship than on the effect of particular

techniques on reducing particular symptoms. It should be noted that the approach taken here is consistent with the approach to EST taken by the field of counseling psychology (Wampold, Lichtenberg, & Waehler, 2002).

Own Our Values

We want to end with an acknowledgment that we need to be aware of and own the values that we bring to this topic and to address them explicitly in both our clinical and scientific endeavors. Let us give you a concrete example. One of our colleagues (Bass, 2000) completed an investigation in which he compared a culturally specific intervention with African American academic underachievers to a traditional social skills intervention with the same population. On measures of academic self-efficacy, classroom behavior, academic achievement, and general school conduct, both interventions were equally effective, with substantive changes pretreatment and post-treatment. One might say that we do not need to do the culturally specific treatment because the general treatment is good enough. Of course, there is the other voice that will argue for the value-added nature of the cultural information the students receive. It is here that we need to be honest about our political values and articulate them as we choose the treatments we value.

Systematically Evaluate the Treatment's Effectiveness

Suggesting that culturally relevant treatment is a challenge to empirical validation is not to say that it is quixotic. In fact, one of the strengths of the ecological perspective is that it allows for the use of mixed methodologies in the process of program evaluation. Clinical research needs to address the effectiveness of interventions designed to meet the needs of particular individuals using a variety of contextually relevant measures. Certainly, symptom reduction is an important goal of all treatment. Within culturally relevant interventions, however, there is the implicit assumption that cultural identity development is also a valuable outcome from the process, as is an increased understanding of one's sociopolitical status. Some of these outcomes may be easily assessed using standardized measures or context-appropriate ones such as the Goal Attainment Scale (Kiresuk, Smith, & Cardillo, 1994). Attention must also be paid to process variables as well as the client's experience of the process, which may be better acquired using a critical ethnographic approach to treatment evaluation (Burawoy et al., 1991; see also Chapter 3, this volume). Determining the method and standards for evaluation is a key component of a CREST.

In summary, we advocate a process for determining the effectiveness of culturally relevant treatments that are context driven; respect the interaction among context, the disorder, and the individual; and systematically use evaluation methods that can capture that complexity.

REFERENCES

Atkinson, D. R., Bui, U., & Mori, M. (2001). Multiculturally sensitive empirically supported treatments—An oxymoron? In J. G. Ponterotto, J. M. Casas, L. A. Suzuki, & C. M. Alexander (Eds.), *Handbook of multicultural counseling* (2nd ed., pp. 542-574). Thousand Oaks, CA: Sage.

Bandura, A. (1986). *Social foundations of thought and action: A social cognitive theory.* Englewood Cliffs, NJ: Prentice Hall.

Bass, C. K. (2000). Effects of a culturally relevant intervention on the academic achievement of African American adolescent males (Doctoral dissertation, University of Wisconsin– Madison). *Dissertation Abstracts International, 61,* 3064.

Bass, C. K., & Coleman, H. L. K. (1997). Enhancing the cultural identity of early adolescent male African Americans. *The School Counselor, 1,* 48-51.

Bronfenbrenner, U. (1979). *The ecology of human development.* Cambridge, MA: Harvard University Press.

Burawoy, M., Burton, A., Ferguson, A. A., Fox, K. J., Gamson, J., Gartell, N., et al. (1991). *Ethnography unbound: Power and resistance in the modern metropolis.* Berkeley: University of California Press.

Chambless, D. L., Baker, M. J., Baucom, D. H., Beutler, L. E., Calhoun, K. S., Daiuto, A., et al. (1998). Update on empirically validated therapies, II. *The Clinical Psychologist, 51,* 3-16.

Chambless, D. L., & Hollon, S. D. (1998). Defining empirically supported therapies. *Journal of Consulting and Clinical Psychology, 66,* 7-18.

Chambless, D. L., Sanderson, W. C., Shoham, V., Johnson, S. B., Pope, K. S., Crits-Christoph, P., et al. (1996). An update on empirically validated therapies. *The Clinical Psychologist, 49*(2), 5-18.

Chambless, D. L., & Williams, K. E. (1995). A preliminary study of African Americans with agoraphobia: Symptom severity and outcome of treatment with in vivo exposure. *Behavior Therapy, 26,* 501-515.

Cohen, D. (2001). Cultural variation: Considerations and implications. *Psychological Bulletin, 127,* 451-171.

Coleman, H. L. K. (1992). Impact of ethnicity on expectations of counselor competence. *Dissertation Abstracts International, 53,* 3106.

Coleman, H. L. K. (1995). Culture in the counseling process: Implications for school counselors. *The School Counselor, 42,* 180-185.

Coleman, H. L. K., & Tuescher, K. D. (in press). *School-based interventions for psychological disorders.* Alexandra, VA: American School Counseling Association.

Coleman, H. L. K., Wampold, B. E., & Casali, S. L. (1995). Ethnic minorities' ratings of similar and European American counselors. *Journal of Counseling Psychology, 42,* 55-64.

Crits-Christoph, P. (1998). Training in empirically validated treatments. In K. S. Dobson & K. D. Craig (Eds.), *Empirically supported therapies: Best practice in professional psychology* (pp. 3-26). Thousand Oaks, CA: Sage.

Donovan, D. M., & Marlatt, G. A. (1988). *Assessment of addictive behaviors.* New York: Guilford.

Draguns, J. G. (1996). Humanly universal and culturally distinctive: Charting the course of cultural counseling. In P. B. Pederson, J. G. Draguns, W. J. Lonner, & J. E. Trimble (Eds.), *Counseling across cultures* (4th ed., pp. 1-20). Thousand Oaks, CA: Sage.

Hall, G. C. N. (2001). Psychotherapy research with ethnic minorities: Empirical, ethical, and conceptual issues. *Journal of Consulting and Clinical Psychology, 69,* 502-510.

Helms, J. E., & Richardson, T. Q. (1997). How "multiculturalism" obscures race and culture as different aspects of counseling competency. In D. Pope-Davis & H. L. K. Coleman (Eds.), *Multicultural counseling competence: Assessment, education, and training and supervision* (pp. 60-82). Thousand Oaks, CA: Sage.

Henry, W. P. (1998). Science, politics, and the politics of science: The use and misuse of empirically validated treatments. *Psychotherapy Research, 8,* 126-140.

Heppner, P. P., Kivlighan, D. M., Jr., & Wampold, B. E. (1999). *Research design in counseling* (2nd ed.). Belmont, CA: Brooks/Cole.

Karenga, M. (1980). *Kawaida theory: Kwanzaa, origin, concepts, and practice.* Inglewood, CA: Kawaida Publications.

Kiresuk, T. J., Smith, A., & Cardillo, J. E. (1994). *Goal attainment scaling: Applications, theory, and measurement.* Englewood Cliffs, NJ: Lawrence Erlbaum.

LaFromboise, T. M., Coleman, H. L. K., & Gerton, J. (1993). Psychological impact of biculturalism: Evidence and theory. *Psychological Bulletin, 114,* 395-412.

Lerner, R. M. (1995). *America's youth in crisis.* Thousand Oaks, CA: Sage.

Lerner, R. M., & Kauffman, M. B. (1985). The concept of development in contextualism. *Developmental Review, 5,* 309-333.

Maltzman, S. (2001). The specific ingredients are in the match: Comments on Ahn and Wampold (2001). *Journal of Counseling Psychology, 48,* 258-261.

Meyers, L. J., Speight, S. L., Highlen, P. S., Cox, C. I., Reynolds, A. L., Adams, E. M., et al. (1991). Identity development and worldview: Toward an optimal conceptualization. *Journal of Counseling and Development, 70,* 54-63.

Miller, W. R., & Rollnick, S. (1991). *Motivational interviewing: Preparing people to change addictive behavior.* New York: Guilford.

Neville, H. A., & Mobley, M. (2001). An ecological model of multicultural counseling psychology processes. *The Counseling Psychologist, 29,* 471-486.

Paul, G. A. (1967). Outcome research in psychotherapy. *Journal of Consulting and Clinical Psychology, 31,* 109-118.

Porter, A. C., & Raudenbush, S. W. (1987). Analysis of covariance: Its model and use in psychological research. *Journal of Counseling Psychology, 34,* 383-392.

Prochaska, J. O., & DiClemente, C. C. (1982). Transtheoretical therapy: Toward a more integrated model of change. *Psychotherapy: Theory, Research, and Practice, 19,* 276-288.

Quintana, S. M., & Atkinson, D. R. (2002). A multicultural perspective on principles for empirically-supported intervention. *The Counseling Psychologist, 30,* 281-291.

Rosselò, J., & Bernal, G. (1999). The efficacy of cognitive-behavioral and interpersonal treatments for depression in Puerto Rican adolescents. *Journal of Consulting and Clinical Psychology, 67,* 734-745.

Sue, D. W., Ivey, A. E., & Pedersen, P. B. (1996). *A theory of multicultural counseling and therapy.* Pacific Grove, CA: Brooks/Cole.

Sue, S., & Zane, N. (1987). The role of culture and cultural techniques in psychotherapy: A critique and reformulation. *American Psychologist, 42,* 37-45.

Tyler, F. B., Brome, D. R., & Williams, J. E. (1991). *Ethnic validity, ecology, and psychotherapy: A psychological competence model.* New York: Plenum.

Wampold, B. E. (1997). Methodological problems in identifying efficacious psychotherapies. *Psychotherapy Research, 7,* 21-43.

Wampold, B. E. (2000). *The great psychotherapy debate: Model, methods, and findings.* Mahwah, NJ: Lawrence Erlbaum.

Wampold, B. E. (2001). Contextualizing psychotherapy as a healing practice: Culture, history, and methods. *Applied and Preventive Psychology, 10,* 69-86.

Wampold, B. E., Lichtenberg, J. W., & Waehler, C. A. (2002). Principles of empirically-supported interventions in counseling psychology. *The Counseling Psychologist, 30,* 197-217.

Wampold, B. E., & Serlin, R. C. (2000). The consequences of ignoring a nested factor on measures of effect size in analysis of variance. *Psychological Methods, 5,* 425-433.

16

Multicultural Research on Counselor and Client Variables

A Relational Perspective

GARGI ROYSIRCAR
ROBERT HUBBELL
GREGORY GARD

Antioch New England Graduate School

Multicultural counseling is a professional response to individuals from racial and cultural minority groups based on the assumptions that cultural heritage and norms influence the worldviews of clients and counselors; U.S. race/ethnic relations, prejudice, stereotyping, and discrimination account for substantial client stress; and the exploration of racial and cultural issues is relevant to treatment. Multicultural counseling is not just individual and group psychotherapy, as defined by mainstream counseling theories. It may include mentoring, tutoring, life skills coaching, empowering clients to retain their cultural identifications, providing information about U.S. life, guidance with adaptation and daily life skills, advocacy, and affirmation of biculturalism. Along these same lines of thought, Atkinson, Thompson, and Grant (1993) provided eight possible roles of the counselor: adviser, consultant, advocate, change agent, facilitator of indigenous support systems, facilitator of indigenous healing methods, counselor, and psychotherapist. So the expectation is that in multicultural counseling, counselors are able to help with real-world problems (e.g., welfare system) as well as assist with psychological problems.

Within this framework of providing multicultural therapy and outreach, interventions might also include building self-esteem and social skills; being supportive when clients refer to experiences of oppression and marginalization, wars in their country of origin and their accompanying hurts, or family interactions that are different from U.S. societal expectations; evaluating the negative aspects of fighting, bullying, and gang participation for schoolchildren; and exploring career interests. This type of culturally consistent help has been shown to be effective by counselor self-reports, client evaluations of outcome, and observation reports (Roysircar, 2003; Roysircar, Gard, & Hubbell, in press; Roysircar, Gard, Hubbell, & Ortega, 2003; Roysircar, Webster, et al., 2003; Sweet & Estey, 2003; Wilczak, 2003).

By extension, multicultural counseling competence (Arredondo et al., 1996; Roysircar, Arredondo, Fuertes, Ponterotto, & Toporek, 2003; Roysircar, Sandhu, & Bibbins, 2003; Sue, Arredondo, & McDavis, 1992) pertains to the effective delivery of counseling services to minorities. Multicultural competencies include a broad constellation of awareness of counselor attitudes and values, knowledge, and skills; chief among its components are the following:

- having good self-awareness of the attitudes or worldviews into which the counselor has been socialized;
- recognizing and being sensitive to the client's worldviews and attitudes;
- having knowledge of the cultural groups with which one works;
- understanding the effects of racial identity, acculturation, ethnic identity, minority stress, and coping with minority status on the individual;
- understanding the impact of sociopolitical influences on minority persons;
- possessing proficiencies to work with culturally different groups;
- having the ability to be culturally responsive and to translate mainstream interventions into culturally consistent strategies, understanding, skills, and interactional proficiency.

Thus, multicultural competence, as currently advanced, is a standard indicating that people should not only appreciate other cultural groups but also be able to effectively work with them (Roysircar, 2003; Toporek, 2003). The focus is on actual clinical interactions, relationships, skills, and ultimately outcome (Coleman, 2003; Fuertes & Ponterotto, 2003).

In this chapter, we discuss research concerning the impact of counselor variables on the multicultural process and outcome in terms of counselor cultural and racial awareness, counselor application of cultural knowledge, counselor recognition of dyadic racial dynamics, and counselor interface with minority client mistrust. Implications of research findings for these counselor variables are discussed. Another section addresses the current research on multicultural counseling competencies and its future directions. A final section looks at counseling process and outcome from the general factors model, showing its relevance to multicultural counseling.

CULTURALLY CONSISTENT COUNSELING: COUNSELOR RESPONSE TO MINORITY CLIENT PRESENTATIONS

Sue and Zane (1987) recommended that cultural knowledge is made proximal to therapy when it is translated into clinical skills, such as case conceptualization, strategies for problem resolution, and formulation of counseling goals. These clinical skills advance the process toward a positive outcome. Several studies since the 1990s have investigated the counseling process when counselors have used culturally responsive approaches. These are presented as follows.

Counselor Cultural and Racial Awareness

In a study (Fuertes, Mueller, Chauhan, Walker, & Ladany, 2002) that interviewed

White American therapists of African American clients, representing nine dyads, therapists' awareness of the privilege associated with being White in the United States, the historical legacy of White oppression of others, and the historical and contemporary existence of racism were significant. Skills that appeared to be used by the therapists were also ones of awareness: of having been oppressed in some way themselves, of having been oppressors, of having a one-up position with their clients, and of recognizing that the reality of racism and tension between White Americans and African Americans is reflected in the counseling hour. Specifically, skills included being direct but sensitive to issues pertaining to race, conveying a sense of openness, and showing acceptance of the historic effects of racism. Therapists had knowledge of racial identity and its central role in their clients' lives, and they were aware of and able to make statements about their clients' racial identity. Therapists approached in a sensitive way other variables salient to the clients' identity, such as gender, socioeconomic status, physical disability, and sexual orientation. All nine therapists reported in interviews appreciable gains for their clients, including lifts in depression, reduced anxiety, and decrease in panic attacks. They reported in clients an increase in insight and racial identity awareness and a better sense of direction for their clients. Therapists reported better rapport, increased intimacy, and disclosure on the part of their clients; some risk taking with respect to the clients' disclosure of aspects of their lives never before discussed; and overall improved client participation and involvement in therapy. It is important to note that the therapists did not develop tunnel vision by focusing exclusively on the race of the client or by overestimating its relevance to the exclusion of other factors. In fact, therapists described their clients' interpersonal concerns as deeply intertwined with factors such as sexism, homophobia, and poverty.

Although Fuertes et al.'s (2002) study gave therapists' perspectives about their racial sensitivity when counseling, another interview study (Pope-Davis et al., 2002) provided clients' ($N = 10$) perceptions of their experiences in multicultural counseling. Each client identified multicultural counseling competence as critical; however, in situations when the clients felt that other needs were more significant, they forgave their counselors for a lack of cultural knowledge or sensitivity. These clients worked to adapt to their counselors' abilities and approaches, limiting the amount of material that they were willing to discuss with their counselors. The study highlighted the integral role clients may play in determining how, what, and when cultural issues might be explored in therapy. A key finding was that clients whose counselors lacked cultural understanding blamed themselves and thus may have accumulated additional psychological baggage from therapy. An important implication is that counselors could benefit from regular feedback from their clients regarding their effectiveness. The types of cultural knowledge that clients identified as important included culturally specific knowledge of family relationships and expectations, racism and discrimination, acculturation, sexism and gender role issues, communication styles, cultural beliefs about counseling, cultural issues related to sexual orientation, ethnic and cultural identity, and norms for behavior.

Cultural responsiveness results from shared attitudes between the counselor and the client. Counselor trainees' 8th session, out of 10 counseling sessions with minority middle school students, was randomly chosen for taping; these tapes were qualitatively analyzed (Roysircar, 2002). Content and process analyses done consensually by a team indicated a matching of counselor responses and client verbal behaviors. As counselors guided the clients through a structured drawing exercise and made probing remarks and reflections that were consistent with clients' cultural understandings, clients made many self-disclosures, some of which were intimate. Clients gave positive reactions at termination on several indices: liking-satisfaction, perceived effectiveness, client well-being change, and help-seeking attitudes. Similarly, in another study (Pomales, Claiborn, & LaFromboise, 1986), African American college students, regardless of their racial identity development, rated racially sensitive counselors higher on credibility. Racial sensitivity meant that the counselor discussed racial aspects of the client's problem with the client.

Wade and Bernstein (1991) investigated African American female clients' perceptions of experienced African American counselors and White counselors who either received cultural sensitivity training or did not receive this type of training. Training in culture sensitivity included a summary of the concerns presented by culturally diverse clients, discussion on counselor self-awareness and minority clients, and acquisition of skills through experiential training. After three sessions, client ratings of counselors who had received culturally sensitive training were significantly higher for credibility, empathy, unconditional regard, and client satisfaction compared to counselors who had not received such training. Even though half of the counselors were White and half Black, positive client ratings were not affected by counselor race but rather by sensitivity. However, it is to be noted that more clients returned to see African American counselors than White counselors, supporting what has been demonstrated by the empirical literature that many African Americans prefer African American counselors.

Counselor Application of Cultural Knowledge

Culture-specific knowledge about ethnic minority groups must not be applied stereotypically to a client who comes from an ethnic minority or culturally diverse group (DeFrino, 2003; Wilczak, 2003). Constantine and Ladany (2001) have added understanding of unique client variables as a multicultural counseling competency. Roysircar (2003) stated that the multiculturally competent counselor does not resolve but explores, processes, and holds the paradox, existentially speaking, between an ethnic minority person's individual identity and multiple reference group identifications and contexts. As an example of cultural stereotyping, there is a tendency in conceptual writings to see Asians as being collectivistic in their thoughts and attitudes. In reality, with regard to coping responses to environmental stresses, collectivism and individualism might be situation specific and affected by the individual Asian's acculturation, religious affiliation, generation status, or length of stay in the United States, as indicated by one study (Roysircar & Gard, 2002). In another study, Hong Kong college students used both internal (self-referenced) and external (other-referenced) attributions about causes of mental health problems, although they mostly used internal attributions (self-responsibility) for curing the problems, which might also involve using interpersonal resources (Luk & Bond, 1992).

Similarly, although Japanese Americans were more likely than White Americans to view mental illness as having social causes, they wanted to resolve the problems on their own, possibly with help from family and friends (Narikiyo & Kameoka, 1992). The expectation that a Japanese sample in the United States would show a tendency for interdependence with others was not supported in another study (Kawanishi, 1995). Japanese participants were more likely than Anglo-Americans to see the cause of stress as their own responsibility. In addition, both Anglo-American and Japanese participants agreed that successful coping depends mostly on one's own effort. Japanese participants' internal attributions may have been related to a cultural tendency for self-blame and self-criticism. Values of modesty and being reserved, enculturated by Japanese socialization, may have also resulted in unwillingness to see others as causing stress or successful coping. However, Japanese participants also agreed much more strongly than White Americans with the statements that stressful coping depends mostly on luck and that stressful events are brought on by bad luck. Thus, internal attributions were not exclusive of external attributions and vice versa. Research needs to show the normal distributions of individualism and collectivism for Asian samples and the complex interactions of individualism and collectivism with various cultural and individual variables, such that the application of cultural knowledge in counseling Asian Americans is not stereotypic.

Sodowsky (1991) tested whether applying cultural understanding to counseling would affect Asian Indian international students' perceptions of counselor credibility. In one tape, a White counselor tailored the tasks of case conceptualization, treatment methods, and goals to the collectivistic family values of an Asian Indian male international student client. The client presented himself as a responsible person with a lot of initiative but expressed hesitation in changing his major from computer science to his new interest in the social sciences. The client referred to family expectations back home about his economic success and to his U.S. relatives' personal-social support while he attended college in the States. In a second tape, the same counselor used a practice that demonstrated Western value biases of individualistic needs and personal choice in vocational interests. With regard to the counseling perspectives of the two tapes, Asian Indian international students, South Korean international students, and White American students were randomly assigned to watch one

of the two tapes. Asian Indian students rated the counselor using culturally consistent tasks as significantly more expert and trustworthy than the culturally discrepant counselor. White Americans rated the counselor using mainstream methods as significantly more expert and trustworthy. There was an interaction effect, with Asian Indian scores being higher than White American scores for the culturally consistent counselor. Koreans did not react as Asian Indians, suggesting that Asian nationality groups might hold some distinct values that are different from each other as well as from those of the host society.

Teresa LaFromboise (1992) developed five vignettes of American Indian families with few lines of initial dialogue between a client and a counselor. Subsequently, the counselor made three sets of responses: affinity attempts, clarifications, and helpfulness. Affinity attempts include the counselor disclosing personal information to establish a connection with the client. The intention of such an affinity response is to be submissive and friendly. Clarifications establish exactly what is being said and felt for both the client and the counselor. The intention of clarification is to be friendly and submissive. Helpfulness refers to making suggestions or offering advice. The intention of helpfulness is to be dominant and friendly. American Indians rated on various scales the impressions that the three sets of responses made on them. Affinity responses clustered around affiliation, agreeableness, and nurturance domains. Affinity statements were seen as submissive, with counselors remaining affiliated with clients when differences would yield confrontation. Clarification responses clustered on agreeableness and nurturance domains and were seen as friendly and submissive counselor intentions. Helpful responses clustered around competitive, mistrusting, and hostile domains and were seen as a negative counselor intention. The findings agreed with earlier studies in the 1980s that American Indians pay more attention to potential indicators of insincerity when assessing a counselor. The helpful response, although intending to show friendly dominance, was perceived negatively. The implication of this finding is that a counselor who makes suggestions is perceived as hostile, manipulative, and competitive by a person who comes from a minority group that has been oppressed and deceived by people in power.

Trimble, Fleming, Beauvais, and Jumper-Thurman (1996) said that knowledge and awareness of American Indian cultural legacy and historical and present-day influences on Indian life are essential to counseling effectiveness. Such knowledge is translated into culturally consistent therapist responses. For example, the therapist needs to develop comfort with silence, as silence often represents the client's acknowledgment that what the therapist has said requires considered thought and reflection. It is seen as a gesture of respect and careful listening and is not viewed as classic "resistance."

Counselors must have knowledge about the cultures that they work with. They cannot expect their clients to educate them when, in fact, the clients have come to them for help. Counselors could also consult with professionals who have expertise in specific cultures. Other than counselors and psychologists, the experts could include anthropologists, historians, political scientists, people in international industry and businesses, and well-traveled individuals. However, asking clients to share their understanding of their cultural beliefs, religion, and practices may translate into client empowerment, as well as into the counselor's understanding of the client's worldview. Engaging the client to describe cultural issues of significance to him or her also helps in assessing the client's unique characteristics that interface with multiple cultural contexts and identifications.

Dyadic Racial Dynamics in the Counselor-Client Relationship

Richardson and Helms (1994) examined the perceptions that Black men have of parallel dyads involving a Black male client and a White male counselor. Parallel dyads are defined as involving a client and a counselor who share similar racial identity attitudes about themselves relative to Blacks and Whites as reference groups. Two parallel dyads were selected in which the White counselor's autonomy attitudes and the Black client's parallel internalization attitudes were predominant; these positive racial attitudes are at the most advanced developmental level. In one audiotaped dyad, the client reported a problem with coworkers' insensitivity to cultural differences; in the other dyad, the client reported being cut from the university basketball team because of the client's race. Black undergraduate students in a predominantly White university were shown the tapes in a counterbalanced order, in which half of the participants heard each of the tapes first. Participants' racial identity attitudes predicted their reactions to the counseling session. Higher levels of participant encounter attitudes, which were developmentally less mature than the attitudes indicated in the tape, were predictive of negative reactions to the counseling; that is, the higher the participants' encounter attitudes, the more anxious the participants felt. Using Helms's (Richardson & Helms, 1994) interaction model, the authors stated that participants may have responded to the counselors in a negative manner when encounter attitudes were high because the counselor's manner of addressing race-related concerns did not properly focus on issues (e.g., confusion) associated with the encounter stage.

The Richardson and Helms (1994) study reveals significant differences from studies previously cited in this chapter (LaFromboise, 1992; Pomales et al., 1986; Sodowsky, 1991).

Helms's model of Black-White counseling interactions proposes that it is the interface of counselor and client racial identity attitudes, rather than session cultural content per se, application of cultural knowledge, or multicultural skills, that influences client perceptions of the counseling process. The implication of research on dyadic racial dynamics is that counselors must not only understand how racial identity attitudes affect the Black client; they must also understand how their own racial identity is a variable that influences counseling dynamics. Second, counselors must be able to accurately assess racial identity variables that influence the counseling relationship. Third, counselors need to use interventions that are sensitive to salient characteristics in the racial identity development process while addressing race-related concerns for Black clients.

Minority Client Mistrust. Studies in the 1970s and early 1980s focused on racial similarities in counseling as there was an assumption that racial or ethnic similarity between the client and the counselor would influence positive process and outcome. On the other hand, Watkins and Terrel (1988) showed that Black people who scored high on the Cultural Mistrust Inventory expected less from counseling regardless of counselor race. Client mistrust became a more salient variable of interest in the 1990s owing to research interest in client self-disclosure and premature termination.

Thompson, Worthington, and Atkinson (1994) studied the interactions of counselor race-based versus universal statements, counselor race (Black, White), and client mistrust. Although Black clients found counselors in both statement conditions equally credible, they were more willing to self-refer and to disclose more intimately when the counselor responded with racial content than were clients who were exposed to universal content. Low levels of mistrust were associated with a

greater number of disclosing statements to Black counselors, whereas high levels of mistrust were associated with a lesser number of disclosing statements to White counselors. It is important to note the interaction between mistrust and the race of the counselor and client.

Because interpersonal trust is a constant concern in the client-counselor multicultural relationship, not having been modeled by minority-majority group relations, LaFromboise and Dixon (1981) specified seven negative counselor responses through experimental manipulation that create an atmosphere of distrust for American Indians: (a) an abrupt shift in topic, (b) purposeful inaccurate paraphrasing, (c) mood and interest change, (d) a break in confidentiality, (e) exposure of a hidden agenda, (f) a stereotyping statement, and (g) a broken promise. The antithetical trustworthy responses included being attentive, structured, directive (mainstream responses), and respectful of cultural identity (culture-specific response). American Indian students (LaFromboise & Dixon, 1981) clearly gave more positive ratings to both the American Indian counselor and the White counselor who demonstrated trustworthy behaviors. However, generalization from this study is cautioned regarding the importance or unimportance of ethnic similarity between the counselor and client because the stimulus sample of counselors was limited to one non-Indian and one Indian counselor.

It is suggested that both Black and White counselors have to contend with the mistrust factor of Black clients, with high levels of mistrust being related to superficial exploration and potential early termination. This suggestion is in line with the writings of authors who propose an emic or culture-specific approach to counseling. In particular, Black psychologists have advocated this approach to assist troubled Black clients in the context of a deracinated social climate, a climate that minimizes or even questions the significance of the Black experience as a positive or even growth-promoting aspect of their psyche. Also from the emic framework, it can be argued that studying perceived counselor credibility, which is based on mainstream studies of the social influence of authority figures, may be limited in explaining the dyadic multicultural client-counselor process. For example, highly skilled counselors, trained in conventional relationship skills, may be perceived as credible by Black clients. However, these same counselors may not elicit the depth of disclosure required for meaningful work with Blacks because they do not use culturally responsive methods, such as addressing issues of race.

Implications

In the studies reviewed to this point, counselors were culturally or racially responsive to client concerns, such as the importance of congruent client-counselor shared attitudes, counselor cultural sensitivity, counselor respect for minority client individuality, counselor knowledge of cultural variables, counselor-client racial dynamics, and counselor awareness of client racial mistrust. Cultural and racial responsiveness obviously improves client perceptions of the counselor. It increases client willingness to return for counseling, satisfaction, disclosure, and depth of disclosure. Although the studies mentioned earlier are very informative, additional research is needed to determine that including cultural content and observing a facilitative racial and cultural dyadic process produce a positive effect on and outcome for minority clients. More directions are needed on how counselors can (a) use cultural content in counseling and (b) observe a facilitative racial and cultural dyadic process with their clients. The first author, through her experiences in providing multicultural training, is currently developing such directions in her outcome studies on training (e.g., Roysircar, 2003; Roysircar, Gard, et al., 2003; Roysircar et al., in press; Roysircar, Webster,

et al., 2003), which are summarized in the next section. Information is also needed on diverse client attitudes and behaviors that are affected by the use of cultural content and process (e.g., Pope-Davis et al., 2002). The question for culture-specific services is whether it will encourage segregation. Will the mental health system use the above type of research findings and justify the segregation of ethnic minority mental health services to separate and, consequently, unequal clinics? How will managed care respond to culturally responsive care leading to longer treatment? Likewise, will managed care use these data to argue against culturally responsive treatment to reduce cost? These are the dilemmas of multicultural counseling research. The history of U.S. race relations makes ethnic minority research volatile. The complexity of issues in multicultural counseling research must be recognized, and the potential side effects of such research must be anticipated.

ASSESSMENT OF MULTICULTURAL COUNSELING COMPETENCIES

The multicultural process and outcome research reviewed to this point has tended to focus on client characteristics, with very few of the analyses focused on therapist characteristics. This neglected area is being attended to by more recent multicultural competency research literature that studies therapist variables specifically.

Since the mid-1990s, multicultural counseling competence has received growing interest. It represents a philosophical shift in defining ethnic and race relations, traditionally seen as involving a conflict between assimilation and separatism and later seen as a melting pot where racial and cultural differences were expected to blend in. In the current philosophical shift to multiculturalism and pluralism, the notion that minority group members are inferior to majority group members is questioned, accompanied with an expectation for respectful interracial and interethnic interactions and effective cross-cultural communications. From the professional perspective, the philosophical shift means that cultural differences are recognized by research to affect the validity of assessment, the therapist-client alliance, and treatment effectiveness (Sodowsky & Impara, 1996). The inadequacy of mainstream services for members of ethnic and racial groups, as evidenced by the under-use of therapy and early termination, has become the impetus for the competency effort (Sue et al., 1982). Multicultural competencies have culture- specific elements (Sue et al., 1982; Sue et al., 1992; see item contents of instruments by D'Andrea, Daniels, & Heck, 1991; LaFromboise, Coleman, & Hernandez, 1991; Ponterotto et al., 1996; Sodowsky, Taffe, Gutkin, & Wise, 1994). Chief among these culture-specific elements are the following:

- Counselors have a good understanding of their own worldviews and attitudes in which they are socialized, so the counselors approach minority clients with cultural self-awareness.
- Counselors have a good understanding of clients' worldviews and attitudes.
- Counselors have specific knowledge of the cultural groups with which they work.
- Counselors know about individual effects in racial identity, acculturation, ethnic identity, minority stress, and coping.
- Counselors have an understanding of sociopolitical influences.
- Counselors possess specific skills needed in working with culturally different groups.
- Counselor have the ability to use culturally based interventions and to translate interventions into culturally consistent strategies.

When studying counselor characteristics, Sodowsky, Kuo-Jackson, Richardson, and Corey (1998) considered it important to first control for the contributions of counselor race and multicultural social desirability. The effect of race needed attention because of repeated evidence, as indicated by this review, about racial and ethnic differences among people in the United States. The authors also intended to show that multicultural counseling competency can hold its own outside multicultural social desirability, or what is popularly called "political correctness." *Multicultural social desirability* is defined as a preference to make a good impression on others by self-reporting that one is very responsive and attentive in all personal and social interactions with racial and ethnic minorities and that one always favors institutional policies for diversity. Constantine and Ladany (2000) and Ponterotto et al. (1996) have also recommended that self-report multicultural competency measures be accompanied by measures of social desirability.

After partialing out the significant contributions of counselor race and multicultural social desirability, counselor personality traits and training were shown to be significant predictors of multicultural competency ($R^2 = .34$ for the full model), as measured by Sodowsky et al.'s (1994) Multicultural Counseling Inventory (MCI) measure. Counselor racial ideology is a belief system about personal versus external control of race relations in the United States. For example, it includes racist explanations, such as, "African Americans can overcome racism by working harder." Racial ideology was a significant negative predictor of multicultural competency. Social inadequacy is the opposite of social self-esteem, indicating a lack of openness to social influences and to favorable and unfavorable social feedback. Social inadequacy was a significant negative predictor of multicultural competency. All racial and ethnic minority counselors had significantly lower scores than White counselors in racial ideology and social inadequacy. Counselors who perceived themselves as multiculturally competent indicated a preference for externality (with regard to racial ideology) and collectivism (with regard to social self-esteem), as opposed to internality and individualism, which are assumed to be White American worldviews. All minority group counselors scored higher than White counselors in multicultural awareness. Blacks had the highest multicultural relationship score, and Whites had the lowest. Hispanics and Asians had the highest scores in multicultural knowledge. Counselors' actual clinical work and research with minority populations, unlike multicultural workshop attendance, were significant predictors of increasing multicultural competency.

Ongoing examination by the author of multicultural services provided by counselor trainees has enabled the identification of an average range of scores on multicultural social desirability and self-reported multicultural counseling competency (Roysircar, Gard, et al., 2003; Roysircar et al., in press; Sodowsky et al., 1998). This permits in the future the identification of very high and very low social desirability scores that might imply questionable validity of self-reported competency of certain participants. Benchmarks for high and low self-reported multicultural counseling competencies have also been developed on the basis of several studies that have used the MCI measure (Roysircar, Gard, et al., 2003).

Other studies (e.g., Constantine & Yeh, 2001; D'Andrea et al., 1991; Pope-Davis & Ottavi, 1994; Roysircar et al., in press; Sodowsky et al., 1998) have shown that greater exposure to multicultural training that includes classroom didactics, experiential training, and practicum increases self-reported multicultural competencies. Themes derived from counselor trainees' ($N = 16$) process notes about barriers to and connections with their minority clients were significantly related to the multicultural counseling competencies (Roysircar, Webster, et al., 2003). Those who were categorized as low scorers on the MCI endorsed more frequently the themes of barriers, frustrations with barriers, preoccupation with cultural similarities or differences, and anxiety about progress than those who were categorized as higher scorers. Overall, these negative themes had negative correlations with MCI subscale scores. Thus, these themes were labeled *negative multicultural thoughts*. Those trainees who were categorized as high scorers on the MCI endorsed more frequently the themes of other awareness and reflection, self-awareness and reflection, empathy and self-disclosure, treatment planning and implementation, analyses of counselor biases, and intentional exchange of cultural information. Overall, these positive themes had positive correlations with MCI subscale scores. Thus, these themes were called *positive multicultural thoughts*. The negative multicultural thoughts showed the most number of significant negative correlations with multicultural skills and multicultural relationship. The positive multicultural thoughts showed the most number of significant positive correlations with multicultural relationship and multicultural awareness. Thus, training experience with actual minority clients involved trainees in the process of the multicultural relationship-building competency, in addition to working on multicultural skills and awareness building (Roysircar, Webster, et al., 2003).

In a second study by the first author (Roysircar, Gard, et al., 2003), two raters were educated on the meaning of positive and negative multicultural themes that were derived qualitatively from counselors' reactions to their culturally diverse clients, as stated in the counselors' process notes. The negative themes were environmental barriers, frustrations with environmental barriers, unintegrated differences, overgeneralization of similarities, and stereotypes. The positive themes were as follows: differences integrated, cultural empathy–cognitive, affective connection with the client's subjective culture, counselor self-disclosure, and counselor self-reflection. The two raters (a) identified each theme and (b) counted the frequency of each theme in each counselor's process notes across 10 sessions (sample of counselors = 67). For the 10 process notes of each counselor, the sum of the frequencies of positive multicultural thoughts was subtracted from the sum of the frequencies of negative multicultural thoughts to arrive at a total positive-negative multicultural thoughts (P-NMCT) score for each counselor. P-NMCT was higher for counselors who showed reliable and clinically significant MCI change scores, in the improved direction, after 10 sessions than for counselors whose MCI change scores were not high enough at posttest to be considered reliably and clinically significant. In addition, *t* tests for minority clients (sample of clients = 67), who were paired with their counselors, showed significantly stronger help-seeking attitudes, well-being change, satisfaction, and effectiveness scores for the counselors in the reliable MCI change group than for counselors in the no-change group. This study indicated that when studying self-reported increased multicultural competence over time, which was evaluated as reliable and clinically significant change, counselor self-evaluation could be corroborated by external sources, their minority clients, and other counselor observers.

In a third study by the first author (Roysircar et al., in press), a multicultural alliance/relationship framework was used, focusing on training variables. These training variables included session process notes, in which counselor trainees wrote reflections on their cultural self-awareness in response to the dyadic interactional process with clients, and counselor trainees' self-reports on three measures: the White Racial Identity Attitudes Scale (WRIAS) (Helms, 1990), the MCI (Sodowsky et al., 1994), and the Multicultural Social Desirability Scale (Sodowsky et al., 1998).

Counselor expressions of Connection/Closeness thoughts toward their clients increased in the later sessions, whereas expressions of Disconnection/Distance thoughts declined concomitantly. Connection/Closeness and MCI full-scale scores predicted trainees' WRIAS Pseudo-Independence and Autonomy combined subscale scores, which represent positive White racial identity attitudes. A multicultural socially desirable response bias did not relate significantly to the Connection/Closeness thoughts, Disconnection/Distance thoughts, positive White racial identity attitudes of the trainees, or self-reported multicultural counseling competencies.

In another study that also investigated the relationship of White racial identity attitudes and multicultural counseling competencies (Ladany, Inman, Constantine, & Hofheinz, 1997), White supervisees who had high pseudo-independence were likely to report high multicultural competence. High levels of dissonance and awareness in White supervisees were also related to high self-reported multicultural competence. However, there appeared to be a more direct translation between racial identity and self-reported multicultural competence for supervisees of color, who were assessed on their persons-of-color racial identity statuses, than for Whites. Self-reported multicultural competence, however, was not related to multicultural case conceptualization ability. The authors imply that the supervisees may have been overconfident of their multicultural abilities. In addition, some of the respondents who were instructed to include racial factors in their conceptualizations noted that although the supervisor instructed them to include racial factors, these issues were not relevant to the case conceptualization, and they thus chose not to include them (Roysircar, Gard, et al., 2003). Therefore, the authors state that a supervisor's interventions may prove ineffective unless a supervisee believes cultural differences are important to therapy.

A one-semester multicultural counseling course taught at three predominantly White state universities in the Midwest and on the East and West Coasts (Neville et al., 1996) was related to White counseling students' adoption of more positive White racial identity attitudes. Pseudo-independence and autonomy racial identity attitudes were associated with stronger endorsement of multicultural competency, as measured by D'Andrea et al.'s (1991) Multicultural Awareness-Knowledge-Skills Survey (MAKSS) measure. Higher levels of contact and disintegration of racial identity attitudes were related to lower levels of reported multicultural competency. Changes in racial identity attitudes were sustained over a 1-year period. Qualitative analyses underscored the importance of ethnically diverse speakers and panels in promoting multicultural competency.

Constantine (2001) has similarly shown that increased multicultural training and counselor race or ethnicity were significant predictors of observer-rated multicultural counselor competencies, as measured by an observer-rated adaptation of LaFromboise et al.'s (1991) Cross-Cultural Counseling Inventory–Revised (CCCI-R). In another study, Constantine (2002) found that client attitudes about counseling, client ratings of perceived counselor credibility, and client ratings of multicultural competencies (use of an adapted CCCI-R measure) accounted for significant variance ($R^2 = .58$) on a measure of client satisfaction. Client rating of multicultural competency specifically contributed significant variance (R^2 change $= .07$) over and above perceived counselor credibility. Similar to Constantine (2002), Fuertes and Brobst (2002) have shown that White counselors' multicultural competence on an adapted CCCI-R measure, as assessed by counseling psychology students who reported being recipients of therapy, accounted for significant variance in client satisfaction. White counselor multicultural competence was not a significant contributor to client satisfaction of the White American sample, but it was significant for the minority sample, offering support for multicultural counseling's perspective that minority clients seek multicultural competencies in their counselors. Worthington, Mobley, Franks, and Tan (2000) found that after taking social desirability into account, observer-rated therapist multicultural competency, as measured by the CCCI-R, was significantly correlated with the therapist being able to conceptualize client distress as being possibly symptomatic of external/systemic sources such as sociopolitical forces (e.g., racism), to attribute the locus of cause of client distress outside of the client, and to verbalize multicultural issues in session. In addition, these authors found that therapist self-reported multicultural counseling knowledge, as measured by a subscale of the MCI, was significantly predictive ($R^2 = .20$) of observer-rated scores on the CCCI-R, even after social desirability had been controlled.

Self-report ratings and observer report ratings in multicultural counseling competencies are relevant, depending on the purpose of the said evaluation. Counselor self-report of multicultural competencies is methodologically appropriate and distinct, capturing a phenomenon that is not identified by observer-rated checklists of behavior. Similarly, client evaluations of counselors are methodologically appropriate and distinct. Thus, it should be noted that a recent qualitative study (Pope-Davis et al., 2002) on client experiences of multiculturally competent counseling suggests that clients do not conceptualize multicultural competency in the same ways clinicians and researchers do.

Multicultural courses include an experiential component in the course work to personalize didactics, research, and discussions. Multicultural training curriculum and clinical practicum have a strong emphasis on counselor trainees' and supervisees' reflections on their personal biases that form a barrier between them and their minority clients (Arredondo et al., 1996; DeFrino, 2003; Roysircar, 2003; Roysircar, Gard, et al., 2003; Roysircar et al., in press; Roysircar, Webster, et al., 2003; Sodowsky, 1996; Sweet & Estey, 2003; Sue et al., 1982; Sue et al., 1992; Wilczak, 2003). Therefore, counselor self-reports of multicultural competencies, which are used to study change scores over time and training, are methodologically appropriate. Although observer ratings can provide a checklist of counselor behaviors, these cannot gauge counselors' intrapersonal processes. Counselors, like clients, know best their experiences and issues on which supervisors provide feedback.

Multicultural Counseling Relationship

The research on multicultural competencies has provided considerable information on multicultural awareness, knowledge, and skills but not on the relationship between the counselor and the minority client. Sodowsky and her colleagues (Roysircar, 2003, 2004; Roysircar, Gard, et al., 2003; Roysircar et al., in press; Roysircar, Webster, et al., 2003; Sodowsky, 1996; Sodowsky et al., 1994) have considered the multicultural counseling relationship to be the human element in counselor-client interactions, which they have described as "ethnotherapeutic empathy" that entails the integration of "cultural knowledge with a dynamic experience of the client's subjective culture" (Sodowsky et al., 1998, p. 262). Her research on the multicultural counseling relationship is finding concurrent validity in recent multicultural competency studies. In interviews (Fuertes et al., 2002), White Americans reporting on their work with African American clients described using core relationship-building skills, such as listening, attending, paraphrasing, asking open-ended questions, and conveying open and accepting

nonverbal cues, to engage the client in therapy. In addition, a communication of empathy from the therapists seemed to strengthen rapport and deepen the level of affect and work from the client. All of the therapists mentioned the importance of collaboratively setting up goals to engage and empower the client. In another interview study, in this case with clients (Pope-Davis et al., 2002), it was found that clients' interpersonal process with the counselor and the client-counselor relationship were active processes in which the client was engaged. These studies lend empirical support to include the counseling relationship in the conceptualization of multicultural counseling competencies. It is to be noted that Constantine and Ladany (2001) expanded the multicultural counseling competency model to add two additional factors: counselors' understanding of unique client variables and establishment of an effective working alliance. Fuertes and Ponterotto (2003) stated the following about the working alliance with culturally diverse individuals:

> They are able to establish core conditions in counseling, regardless of their preferred theoretical and technical conditions in counseling. They are able to establish rapport and working alliances with their clients; they can heal ruptures in the alliance; they are open to criticism from or to being tested by the client; and they can establish goals and formulate tasks with the client. They are able to communicate openness to and are able to discuss issues associated with gender, race, ethnicity, culture, socio-economic background, sexual orientation, and other human diversity factors with their clients. They can sensitively process differences in race and culture. They are able to name or identify for their clients experiences that may be of a racist or oppressive nature. They are able and willing to modify their theoretical and technical styles and/or interventions to meet the client psychologically, including knowing when not to discuss race

or salient cultural differences with their clients. And they are able to continually evaluate the process of counseling, the progress being made on mutually agreed upon goals, and the quality of the relationship with their clients. (pp. 55-56)

McRae and Johnson (1991) said, "Aside from understanding one's self as a racial-ethnic cultural being, it is important for counselors to examine the counselor-client relationship" (p. 131), which is characterized "with similar and different cultural values, racial identity attitudes, [and] issues of power, control, and oppression" (p. 135). In Martinez and Holloway's (1997) supervision model for multicultural counseling, power is viewed as a vehicle for the counselor to construct a mutually empowering relationship, indicating a shift from a perspective of "power over" to one of "power with." As the counselor commits to the process of multicultural self-awareness, power becomes a shared property of the multicultural relationship and not of one individual. In addition to shared power, involvement is an affiliative dimension that is integral to the relationship, carrying the meaning of forming intentional attachments as each member uses the other as a source of self-affirmation, relating freely as individuals rather than in stereotyped roles (Martinez & Holloway, 1997) (see Table 16.1).

CONNECTIONS TO THE GENERAL PSYCHOTHERAPY OUTCOME LITERATURE

A major goal of this chapter is to review the relevant research concerning the impact of therapist variables on multicultural process and outcome. To demonstrate the broad generalizability of the multicultural research presented here, we conclude this chapter by discussing a salient feature of current psychotherapy outcome literature as it relates to multicultural counseling.

In an extensive review of meta-analytic data, Wampold (2001) has demonstrated that the variance in psychotherapy outcome is largely a product of the therapeutic relationship. The evidence for factors specific to a particular treatment model (e.g., technique, manualized treatment or program) being responsible for the effectiveness of psychotherapy has not been convincingly demonstrated. This, of course, is contrary to the empirically supported treatment (EST) movement within psychology, which looks to determine a set of best practices or preferred treatments for specific disorders based on rigorously controlled efficacy studies. The methodology used to determine treatment efficacy involves comparing two or more highly controlled and standardized treatments and/or a control group. Adherence to a manualized protocol is essential to ensure the validity of a study attempting to validate a particular treatment and its specific ingredients (e.g., eye movement as a specific ingredient in eye movement desensitization and reprocessing, or EMDR). However, in the process of controlling for the relational factors affecting treatment (hope, expectancy, support), the impact of the therapist and the therapeutic relationship is minimized and rendered subordinate to technique. In the empirically supported treatment model, the primary role of the therapist is to administer the treatment package. We argue that this represents an etic approach to counseling and psychotherapy, which fails to consider the significance of the multiculturally competent therapist and the culture of the client and, as such, is insufficient in terms of counselor cultural and racial awareness, counselor application of cultural knowledge, counselor recognition of dyadic racial dynamics, the counselor interface with minority client mistrust, and counselor multicultural competencies. These therapist variables have been addressed in this chapter, indicating a relational perspective in multicultural research.

Table 16.1   Summary of Major Themes in Multicultural Research on Process and Outcome

Major Sections in This chapter	*Reference*
Introduction	Sodowsky, Taffe, Gutkin, and Wise (1994)
• Multicultural competencies include general and multicultural skills, cultural self-awareness and other awareness, multicultural relationship, and cultural knowledge.	Atkinson, Thompson, and Grant (1993); Roysircar, Gard, Hubbell, and Ortega (2003); Roysircar, Gard, and Hubbell (in press); Stevenson and Renard (1993)
• Clinical work with multicultural clients is not limited to individual and group modalities but includes many forms of community-based and skills training interventions. These latter interventions are culturally consistent with the collectivistic approaches of many minorities.	Constantine (2002); LaFromboise and Dixon (1981); Pomales, Claiborn, and LaFromboise (1986); Roysircar, Gard, et al. (2003); Sodowsky (1991); Toporek (2003); Wade and Bernstein (1991)
Culturally Consistent Counseling: Therapist Response to Minority Client Presentations	
• Cultural responsiveness/sensitivity results from shared attitudes between therapist and client and is a better predictor of client ratings of satisfaction, empathy, unconditional regard, and therapist credibility than race.	LaFromboise (1992); Pope-Davis et al. (2002); Sodowsky (1991); Trimble, Fleming, Beauvais, and Jumper-Thurman (1996)
• Therapists must have knowledge of the cultures that they work with and cannot expect their clients to educate them when it is the client who has come for help.	Fuertes, Mueller, Chauhan, Walker, and Ladany (2002); Greene (1995); Richardson and Helms (1994); Thompson, Worthington, and Atkinson (1994)
• Research on racial dynamics in the counseling dyad suggests that the therapist must be aware of how both his or her own as well as the client's racial identity affects the client.	LaFromboise and Dixon (1981); Watkins and Terrel (1988)
• With regard to minority client mistrust, seven therapist responses have been identified as potentially creating an atmosphere of distrust: (a) an abrupt shift in topic, (b) purposeful inaccurate paraphrasing, (c) mood and interest change, (d) a break in confidentiality, (e) exposure of a hidden agenda, (f) a stereotyping statement, and (g) a broken promise.	Pope-Davis et al. (2002); Roysircar, Gard, et al. (2003); Roysircar et al. (2001); this chapter
• More research needs to be done in the area of how therapists use cultural content and how a therapist's culturally facilitative dyadic process affect client attitudes and outcome. A potential downside to such research and culture-specific services is increasing segregation.	Fuertes et al. (2002); Pope-Davis et al. (2002); Roysircar, Arredondo, Fuertes, Ponterotto, and Toporek (2003); Roysircar, Sandhu, and Bibbins (2003); Sodowsky and Impara (1996); Sue, Arredondo, and McDavis (1992)
Assessment of Multicultural Counseling Competencies	
• Since the mid-1990s, multicultural counseling competence has been increasingly recognized as affecting the validity of assessment, the therapeutic alliance, and treatment effectiveness. The latter was of particular interest, given high rates of early termination and underutilization of treatment services by racial and ethnic minorities.	Constantine (2001, 2002); Constantine and Yeh (2001); D'Andrea, Daniels, and Heck (1991); Neville et al. (1996); Ponterotto et al. (1996); Pope-Davis and Ottavi (1994); Roysircar, Gard, et al. (2003); Roysircar et al. (in press); Roysircar, Webster, et al. (2003); Sodowsky, Kuo-Jackson, Richardson, and Corey (1998); Worthington, Mobley, Franks, and Tan (2000)
• Multicultural training increases both self-reported and observer-reported ratings of multicultural counseling competencies.	

(Continued)

Table 16.1 Continued

Major Sections in This Chapter	*Reference*
• Use of observer ratings of multicultural counseling competencies is a new development in this area.	Constantine (2001); Roysircar, Gard, et al. (2003); Roysircar et al. (in press); Sodowsky (1996); Worthington et al. (2000)
• Use of client ratings of therapist competencies, variables, and outcome is also a new development.	
• Assessment of multicultural therapist competencies remains ultimately an individual, self-reflective experience as the therapist must assess his or her own awareness of cultural influences, racial oppression, the sociopolitical nature of counseling, and similarity of values related to acculturation, racial and ethnic identity, and worldview with each new client of color.	Constantine (2002); Fuertes and Brobst (2002); Pope-Davis et al. (2002); Roysircar, Gard, et al. (2003) This Chapter
• Controlling for social desirability or multicultural social desirability in self-reported multicultural competencies is a current methodological practice.	Constantine (2001); Constantine and Ladany (2000); Ponterotto et al. (1996); Roysircar, Gard, et al. (2003); Roysircar et al. (in press); Sodowsky et al. (1998); Worthington et al. (2000)
• Multicultural training curriculum and clinical practicum have a strong emphasis on therapist trainees' and supervisees' reflections on their personal biases that form a barrier between them and their minority clients. Although observer ratings can provide a checklist of therapist behaviors, these cannot gauge therapists' intrapersonal processes.	Roysircar (2003); Roysircar, Gard, et al. (2003); Roysircar et al. (in press); Roysircar, Webster, et al. (2003); Sodowsky (1996); Arredondo et al. (1996); Sue et al. (1982)
• The multicultural counseling relationship emphasizes the human element in therapist-client interactions, which can be described as "ethnotherapeutic empathy," entailing the integration of "cultural knowledge with a dynamic experience of the client's subjective culture."	Constantine and Ladany (2001); Fuertes et al. (2002); McRae and Johnson (1991); Pope-Davis et al. (2002); Roysircar (2003); Roysircar et al. (in press)
• As the therapist commits to the process of multicultural self-awareness, power becomes a shared property of the multicultural relationship and not of one individual. In addition to shared power, involvement is an affiliative dimension that is integral to the relationship, carrying the meaning of forming intentional attachments as each member uses the other as a source of self-affirmation, relating freely as individuals rather than in stereotyped roles.	Roysircar, Webster, et al. (2003); Sodowsky (1996); Sodowsky et al. (1994); Sodowsky et al. (1998, p. 262); Martinez and Holloway (1997); this chapter
• Multicultural counseling competencies are related to White racial identity statuses	Fuertes et al. (2002); Ladany, Inman, Constantine, and Hofheinz (1997); Neville et al. (1996); Roysircar et al. (in press)
• The consistent findings in the general psychotherapy outcome literature demonstrate the broad generalizability of the multicultural research on process and outcome.	Wampold (2001); this chapter

Wampold (2001) argued that effective counseling and psychotherapy are characterized by the therapist's ability to provide a treatment marked by congruence of client beliefs, attitudes, and values with the context and shared meaning of the treatment. A therapist forms his or her case conceptualization and chooses techniques and interventions informed by cultural and idiographic data rather than as a response to a set of symptoms or a diagnosis. As such, we conclude that the relationship forms the center of the treatment, and appropriate emphasis is placed on a broad set of multicultural skills, knowledge, attitudes, and experiences of the counselor or therapist. Therefore, effective treatment is treatment that is culturally consistent and a product of multicultural competence.

In conclusion, data need to be drawn from multiple sources and perspectives without privileging (a priori) one against another in an attempt to understand the interactional nature of the multicultural counseling relationship. As such, each rater (i.e., client, counselor, and observer/supervisor) remains the expert of his or her own experience and perspective. This standard must be not only respected in our clinical work, where it is most prevalent, but also extended to the realm of research methodology. The relative importance of the various perspectives hinges on the question being asked. Likewise, the methodology to find answers to proposed questions is diverse. The ensuing investigations may be quantitative (e.g., Constantine, 2001, 2002; Fuertes & Brobst, 2002; Worthington et al., 2000), qualitative (e.g., Fuertes et al., 2002; Pope-Davis et al., 2002), or of a mixed design (e.g., Roysircar, Gard, et al., 2003; Roysircar et al., in press; Roysircar, Webster, et al., 2003).

REFERENCES

Arredondo, P., Toporek, R., Brown, S. P., Jones, J., Locke, D. C., Sanchez, J., et al. (1996). Operationalization of the multicultural counseling competencies. *Journal of Multicultural Counseling and Development, 24,* 42-78.

Atkinson, D. R., Thompson, C. E., & Grant, S. (1993). A three-dimensional model for counseling racial/ethnic minority clients. *The Counseling Psychologist, 21,* 257-277.

Coleman, H. L. K. (2003). Culturally relevant empirically supported treatment. In G. Roysircar, P. Arredondo, J. N. Fuertes, J. G. Ponterotto, & R. L. Toporek (Eds.), *Multicultural counseling competencies 2003: Association for Multicultural Counseling and Development* (pp. 79-86). Alexandria, VA: Association for Multicultural Counseling and Development.

Constantine, M. G. (2001). Predictors of observer ratings of multicultural counseling competence in trainees. *Journal of Counseling Psychology, 48,* 456-462.

Constantine, M. G. (2002). Predictors of satisfaction with counseling: Racial and ethnic minority clients' attitudes toward counseling and ratings of their therapists' general and multicultural counseling competence. *Journal of Counseling Psychology, 49*(2), 255-263.

Constantine, M. G., & Ladany, N. (2000). Self-report multicultural counseling competence scales: Their relation to social desirability attitudes and multicultural case conceptualization ability. *Journal of Counseling Psychology, 47,* 155-164.

Constantine, M. G., & Ladany, N. (2001). New visions for defining and assessing multicultural counseling competence. In J. G. Ponterotto, J. M. Casas, L. A. Suzuki, & C. M. Alexander (Eds.), *Handbook of multicultural counseling* (2nd ed., pp. 482-498). Thousand Oaks, CA: Sage.

Constantine, M. G., & Yeh, C. J. (2001). Multicultural training, self-construals, and multicultural competence of school counselors. *Professional School Counseling, 4,* 202-207.

D'Andrea, M., Daniels, J., & Heck, R. (1991). Evaluating the impact of multicultural counseling training. *Journal of Counseling and Development, 70,* 143-150.

DeFrino, B. (2003). Multicultural interactions with Jewish American adolescents. In G. Roysircar, P. Arredondo, J. N. Fuertes, J. G. Ponterotto, & R. L. Toporek (Eds.), *Multicultural counseling competencies 2003: Association for Multicultural Counseling and Development* (pp. 121-130). Alexandria, VA: Association for Multicultural Counseling and Development.

Fuertes, J. N., & Brobst, K. (2002). Clients' perspectives of therapist multicultural competence. *Cultural Diversity and Ethnic Minority Psychology, 8,* 214-223.

Fuertes, J. N., Mueller, L. N., Chauhan, R. V., Walker, J. A., & Ladany, N. (2002). An investigation of Euro-American therapists' approach to counseling African-American clients. *The Counseling Psychologist, 30,* 763-789.

Fuertes, J. N., & Ponterotto, J. G. (2003). Culturally appropriate intervention strategies. In G. Roysircar, P. Arredondo, J. N. Fuertes, J. G. Ponterotto, & R. L. Toporek (Eds.), *Multicultural counseling competencies 2003: Association for Multicultural Counseling and Development* (pp. 51-58). Alexandria, VA: Association for Multicultural Counseling and Development.

Greene, B. (1995). African American women. In L. Comaz-Diaz & B. Greene (Eds.), *Women of color: Integrating ethnic and gender identities in psychotherapy* (pp. 10-29). New York: Guilford.

Helms, J. E. (Ed.). (1990). *Black and White racial identity: Theory, research, and practice.* Westport, CT: Greenwood.

Kawanishi, Y. (1995). The effects of culture on beliefs about stress and coping: Causal attribution of Anglo-American and Japanese persons. *Journal of Contemporary Psychotherapy, 25,* 49-60.

Ladany, N., Inman, A. G., Constantine, M. G., & Hofheinz, E. W. (1997). Supervisee multicultural case conceptualization ability and self-reported multicultural competence as functions of supervisee racial identity and supervisor focus. *Journal of Counseling Psychology, 44,* 284-293.

LaFromboise, T. D. (1992). An interpersonal analysis of affinity, clarification, and helping responses with American Indians. *Professional Psychology: Research and Practice, 23,* 281-286.

LaFromboise, T. D., Coleman, H. L., & Hernandez, A. (1991). Development and factor structure of the Cross-Cultural Counseling Inventory–Revised. *Professional Psychology: Research and Practice, 22,* 380-388.

LaFromboise, T. D., & Dixon, D. N. (1981). American Indian perception of trustworthiness in a counseling review. *Journal of Counseling Psychology, 28,* 135-139.

Luk, C. L., & Bond, M. H. (1992). Chinese lay beliefs about the causes and cures of psychological problems. *Journal of Social and Clinical Psychology, 11,* 140-157.

Martinez, R. P., & Holloway, E. L. (1997). The supervision relationship in multicultural training. In D. B. Pope-Davis & L. K. H. Coleman (Eds.), *Multicultural counseling competencies: Assessment, education and training, and supervision* (pp. 325-349). Thousand Oaks, CA: Sage.

McRae, M. B., & Johnson, S. D. (1991). Toward training for competence in multicultural counselor education. *Journal of Counseling & Development, 70,* 131-135.

Narikiyo, T. A., & Kameoka, V. A. (1992). Attributions of mental illness and judgements about help seeking among Japanese-American and White American students. *Journal of Counseling Psychology, 39,* 363-369.

Neville, H. A., Heppner, M. J., Louie, C. E., Thompson, C. E., Brooks, L., & Baker, C. E. (1996). The impact of multicultural training on White racial identity attitudes and therapy competencies. *Professional Psychology: Research and Practice, 27,* 83-89.

Pomales, J., Claiborn, C. D., & LaFromboise, T. D. (1986). Effects of Black students' racial identity on perceptions of White therapists varying in cultural sensitivity. *Journal of Counseling Psychology, 33,* 57-61.

Ponterotto, J. G., Rieger, B. P., Barrett, A., Sparks, R., Sanchez, C. M., & Magids, D. (1996). Development and initial validation of the Multicultural Counseling Awareness Scale. In G. R. Sodowsky & J. C. Impara (Eds.), *Multicultural assessment in counseling and clinical psychology* (pp. 247-282). Lincoln, NE: Buros Institute of Mental Measurements.

Pope-Davis, D. B., & Ottavi, T. M. (1994). Examining the association between self-reported multicultural counseling competencies and demographic and educational variables among therapists. *Journal of Counseling and Development, 72,* 651-654.

Pope-Davis, D. B., Toporek, R. L., Ortega-Villalobos, L. D., Ligiero, D., Brittan-Powell, C. S., Liu, W. M., et al. (2002). Client perspectives of multicultural counseling competence: A qualitative examination. *The Counseling Psychologist, 30*(3), 355-393.

Richardson, T. Q., & Helms, J. E. (1994). The relationship of the racial identity attitudes of Black men to perceptions of "parallel" counseling dyads. *Journal of Counseling and Development, 73,* 172-177.

Roysircar, G. (2002). *Multicultural cases: Conceptualization, assessment, and practice.* Unpublished manuscript.

Roysircar, G. (2003). Counselor awareness of own assumptions, values, and biases. In G. Roysircar, P. Arredondo, J. N. Fuertes, J. G. Ponterotto, & R. L. Toporek (Eds.), *Multicultural counseling competencies 2003: Association for Multicultural Counseling and Development* (pp. 17-38). Alexandria, VA: Association for Multicultural Counseling and Development.

Roysircar, G. (2004). Counseling and psychotherapy for acculturation and ethnic identity concerns with immigrants and international student clients. In T. B. Smith (Ed.), *Practicing multiculturalism: Affirming diversity in counseling and psychology* (pp. 248-268). Boston: Allyn & Bacon.

Roysircar, G., Arredondo, P., Fuertes, J. N., Ponterotto, J. G., & Toporek, R. L. (Eds.). (2003). *Multicultural counseling competencies 2003: Association for Multicultural Counseling and Development.* Alexandria, VA: Association for Multicultural Counseling and Development.

Roysircar, G., & Gard, G. (2002, August). *Predictors of acculturation and coping for Asian international students.* Paper presented at the annual convention of the American Psychological Association, San Francisco.

Roysircar, G., Gard. G., & Hubbell, R. (in press). Counselor trainee self-reflection in process notes on multicultural services: Within and between session analyses of alliance for clients. *Professional Psychology: Research and Practice.*

Roysircar, G., Gard, G., Hubbell, R., & Ortega, M. (2003). *Relationships of client evaluations of outcome, observer reports, and counselor self-reports of multicultural counseling competencies: Evaluation of multicultural training.* Unpublished manuscript submitted for publication.

Roysircar, G., Gard, G., Taliouridis, C., Potter, B., Huynh, U. K., Utsch, H., et al. (2001, August). *Multicultural counseling competencies: An outcome evaluation study.* Paper presented at the annual convention of the American Psychological Association, San Francisco.

Roysircar, G., Sandhu, D. S., & Bibbins, V. (2003). *Multicultural competencies: A guidebook of practices.* Alexandria, VA: American Counseling Association.

Roysircar, G., Webster, D. R., Germer, J., Palensky, J. J., Lynne, E., Campbell, G. R., et al. (2003). Experiential training in multicultural counseling: Implementation and evaluation. In G. Roysircar, D. S. Sandhu, & V. E. Bibbins Jr. (Eds.), *A guidebook: Practices of multicultural competencies* (pp. 3-15). Alexandria, VA: American Counseling Association.

Sodowsky, G. R. (1991). Effects of culturally consistent counseling tasks on American and international student observers' perception of therapist credibility. *Journal of Counseling and Development, 69,* 253-256.

Sodowsky, G. R. (1996). The Multicultural Counseling Inventory: Validity and applications in multicultural training. In G. R. Sodowsky & J. C. Impara (Eds.), *Multicultural assessment in counseling and clinical psychology* (pp. 283-324). Lincoln, NE: Buros Institute of Mental Measurements.

Sodowsky, G. R., & Impara, J. C. (Eds.). (1996). *Multicultural assessment in counseling and clinical psychology.* Lincoln, NE: Buros Institute of Mental Measurements.

Sodowsky, G. R., Kuo-Jackson, P. Y., Richardson, M. F., & Corey, A. T. (1998). Correlates of self-reported multicultural competencies: Therapist multicultural social desirability, race, social inadequacy, locus of control, racial ideology, and multicultural training. *Journal of Counseling Psychology, 45,* 256-264.

Sodowsky, G. R., Taffe, R. C., Gutkin, T. B., & Wise, S. L. (1994). Development of the

Multicultural Counseling Inventory: A self-report measure of multicultural competencies. *Journal of Counseling Psychology, 41*, 137-148.

Stevenson, H. C., & Renard, G. (1993). Trusting ol' wise owls: Therapeutic use of cultural strengths in African American families. *Professional Psychology: Research and Practice, 24*, 433-442.

Sue, D. W., Arredondo, P., & McDavis, R. J. (1992). Multicultural counseling competencies and standards: A call to the profession. *Journal of Multicultural Counseling and Development, 20*, 64-68.

Sue, D. W., Bernier, J. E., Durran, A., Feinberg, L., Pedersen, P., Smith, E. J., et al. (1982). Position paper: Cross-cultural counseling competencies. *The Counseling Psychologist, 10*, 45-52.

Sue, S., & Zane, N. (1987). The role of culture and cultural techniques in psychotherapy: A critique and reformulation. *American Psychologist, 42*, 37-45.

Sweet, S. G., & Estey, M. (2003). A step toward multicultural competencies: Listening to individuals with multiple sclerosis and cerebral palsy. In G. Roysircar, P. Arredondo, J. N. Fuertes, J. G. Ponterotto, & R. L. Toporek (Eds.), *Multicultural counseling competencies 2003: Association for Multicultural Counseling and Development* (pp. 103-120). Alexandria, VA: Association for Multicultural Counseling and Development.

Thompson, C. E., Worthington, R., & Atkinson, D. R. (1994). Therapist content, orientation, therapist race, and Black women's cultural mistrust and self-disclosure. *Journal of Counseling Psychology, 41*, 155-161.

Toporek, R. L. (2003). Counselor awareness of client's worldview. In G. Roysircar, P. Arredondo, J. N. Fuertes, J. G. Ponterotto, & R. L. Toporek (Eds.), *Multicultural counseling competencies 2003: Association for Multicultural Counseling and Development* (pp. 39-50). Alexandria, VA: Association for Multicultural Counseling and Development.

Trimble, J. E., Fleming, C. M., Beauvais, F., & Jumper-Thurman, P. (1996). Essential cultural and social strategies for counseling Native American Indians. In P. Pedersen, J. G. Draguns, W. J. Lonner, & J. E. Trimble (Eds.), *Counseling across cultures* (pp. 177-209). Thousand Oaks, CA: Sage.

Wade, P., & Bernstein, B. L. (1991). Culture sensitivity training and therapist's race: Effects on Black female clients' perceptions and attrition. *Journal of Counseling Psychology, 38*, 9-15.

Wampold, B. E. (2001). *The great psychotherapy debate: Models, methods, and findings.* Mahwah, NJ: Lawrence Erlbaum.

Watkins, C. E., & Terrel, F. (1988). Mistrust level and its effects on counseling expectations in Black-White therapist relationships: An analogue study. *Journal of Counseling Psychology, 35*, 194-197.

Wilczak, C. (2003). A counselor trainee's conversations with a Colombian immigrant woman. In G. Roysircar, P. Arredondo, J. N. Fuertes, J. G. Ponterotto, & R. L. Toporek (Eds.), *Multicultural counseling competencies 2003: Association for Multicultural Counseling and Development* (pp. 89-101). Alexandria, VA: Association for Multicultural Counseling and Development.

Worthington, R. L., Mobley, M., Franks, R. P., & Tan, J. A. (2000). Multicultural counseling competencies: Verbal content, counselor attributions, and social desirability. *Journal of Counseling Psychology, 47*, 460-468.

17

Qualitative Research and Multicultural Counseling Competency

An Argument for Inclusion

DEVIKA DIBYA CHOUDHURI

Eastern Michigan University

Qualitative research seems deceptively simple. The researcher, who needs no expensive laboratory, goes out unarmed with painstakingly constructed and tested instruments to meet persons and strive to understand the ways in which they understand and experience their world. The skills involved in data collection are no more than a keenly attentive ear and a self examined for blindsiding assumptions. In truth, such a description sounds no more fearsome and scientific than the process of multicultural counseling, whereby we seek to meet persons across from their own phenomenological ground. The three aspects of competency in multicultural counseling of awareness, knowledge, and skills apply as readily to competency in qualitative research.

In this chapter, I lay out an overview of the qualitative research paradigm and then explore the intersections with multicultural counseling competency, arguing for its unique applicability in this arena. Following this, I present a brief description of qualitative methods that are particularly compatible with research in multicultural issues, discuss some of the challenges of conducting and presenting such research, and end with an examination of an example of multicultural qualitative research, describing the process of developing and carrying out one particular project.

OVERVIEW OF QUALITATIVE RESEARCH

Unlike quantitative methods that come out of the physical sciences, qualitative research methodology is rooted in anthropology and sociology (Hoshmand, 1989) and provides an alternate way of exploring social science phenomena. It is considered by many researchers to go beyond simply a different methodology than quantitative research, presenting an alternate paradigm or worldview that implies a different notion of reality and of how reality is known (Lincoln & Guba, 1985). Other researchers see the two methodologies as complementary, providing different kinds of information, and may strive to combine them in research to triangulate and assess the strength of findings (Firestone, 1987). Less concrete and more contextual than quantitative methods, the methodology is therefore harder to definitively categorize. However, describing the general characteristics of the qualitative paradigm may be a place to start.

All qualitative researchers use a phenomenological standpoint, attempting to understand the meaning of events, interactions, and relationships that occur from the perspective of those involved (Bogdan & Biklen, 1992). The underlying assumptions of such positions include (a) the ontological one that reality (as known by human beings) is subjective and multiple; (b) the epistemological assumption that there is a relationship between the researcher and the researched, and such relationship is therefore necessary to explore and articulate; (c) the axiological assumption that research is value laden and that biases will always be present; (d) the rhetorical assumption that the ways in which research is described is intimately connected with the research itself; and (e) a methodological assumption that the process of research is integral to the ends of the research.

Within this broad description, a number of different traditions of qualitative inquiry depict different theoretical and philosophical positions regarding the nature of inquiry, purposes of such inquiry, and use of findings. According to Creswell (1998), the five traditions

are biography, phenomenology, grounded theory, ethnography, and case studies. Of these traditions, researchers interested in psychological phenomena have tended to use the phenomenological approach, concerned with questions of belief and consciousness. Case studies also have a long history in psychology, most outstandingly used by Freud to develop psychoanalytic theory (Creswell, 1998).

All researchers are guided by theory. In qualitative research, some of the most common theoretical foundations include symbolic interactionism (Blumer, 1969, in Bogdan & Biklen, 1992), critical theory first developed by the Frankfurt school (Creswell, 1998), feminist research (Olesen, 1994), and a broad array of postmodernist theoretical approaches. It is important that qualitative researchers describe and articulate the theoretical underpinnings of their research, as well as contextualize their own positions in the context of such theory vis-à-vis their research.

In terms of design, qualitative research is more fluid than quantitative research, so that although the research purpose is explicit prior to the research, the research questions developed to guide the research are acknowledged to be shifting in response to the data collected. In essence, the researcher must be willing to be surprised by the data collected and to be informed by the data to pursue that which is emerging as important rather than sticking to the original design if no longer compatible. Qualitative research questions tend to be more open-ended and exploratory and are based on discovery rather than verification. Rather than asking if some phenomena are true, the question seeks to understand what the phenomena are. The approach is therefore holistic rather than reductionist.

Other aspects of this research exemplify the philosophical assumptions referred to earlier. With the perspective that the social reality of human beings is constructed, subjective, and multiple, there is less of an attempt to verify the truth of a person's perceptions as in understanding what such perceptions are and how they came to be. The emphasis is therefore on how persons make meaning of their environment as opposed to the reality of the environment itself, which in a postmodernist context would be posited to be unknowable except through the lens of the perceiver. In qualitative research, there are no subjects but rather participants, informants, collaborators, and, sometimes, coresearchers. This reflects the assumption that differentiating between researcher and those under scrutiny submerges the profound ways in which a researcher is a part of the research. In ethnographic research, the researcher may take on the position of a participant observer, interacting with participants and the environment over a period of time. In document analysis, interviewing, observation, or other more distant methods, there may not be the same close relationship. Regardless, participants in qualitative research play an active and egalitarian role.

According to Glesne and Peshkin (1992), "The voice of subjectivity takes an I, the first-person singular, the attestation that a particular person is in a particular place for a particular purpose" (p. 101). One's person and position as researcher being inextricably interwoven, the researcher's voice needs to be articulated not just in descriptions of others but in locating the direction from which such descriptions are made. The relationship between researcher and researched, once acknowledged, surfaces as value laden. In quantitative research, this would be considered a threat to validity. In qualitative research, validity and reliability are questions that lie with the reader. The reader makes such judgments based on the articulation of the researcher's subjectivity and sufficient description to allow the reader to be informed (McWilliam, 2000). The purpose is not to disallow bias but to expose it so that it can be taken into consideration when evaluating the

findings. The instrument under scrutiny is the researcher, and the same degree of attention given in quantitative research to evaluating the reliability and validity of an instrument is here directed at the person of the researcher and the process of the research.

Finally, the steps of data analysis and reporting are also significantly different from quantitative methodologies. Here, the process of data analysis is inductive and recursive and permeates the process of data collection rather than being an end step, performed once all data are gathered. Because the goal is not to verify a hypothesis but to generate rich and meaningful descriptions of discovered phenomena and process, the field notes, transcripts, researcher memos, and documents are all part of the data collection and analysis. In the process of analysis, triangulation as a means of using multiple data sources as well as methods of analysis, validation by outside readers, and member checks by which participants can comment and critique analyses, returning to the data source to verify themes, are all procedures to help in the generation of thoughtful findings that are convincing to the reader. It is the story told through the reporting—the narration that seeks to convince the reader that the phenomenon described is meaningful, interesting, and understandable—that decides the quality of the research. Ultimately, qualitative research requires a high degree of writing skill, needing a means of articulating the theories that informed the study, the process of the study in terms of the methods, the data collection, the analysis, and the findings in such a way as to present itself as trustworthy.

MULTICULTURAL COUNSELING AND QUALITATIVE RESEARCH

In the history of psychology, research traditions were typically drawn from the sciences of biology and chemistry, with researchers striving to emulate the modernist, objectivist stance of such sciences. The best research was that which most carefully controlled for threats to internal and external validity. The fledgling science of psychology, concerned with respectability in the scientific arena while dealing with the variability of human behavior, strove to create laws and theories that had the force and stability of physical knowledge. The overlap with biology also resulted in distancing from other social sciences such as sociology and anthropology. Unlike most social sciences that have looked at humans as social beings, counseling and psychology typically held notions of humans as individuated selves in isolation (McLeod, 1996). Qualitative research was used primarily in clinical case studies to generate further understanding, and such research was usually presented in ways that implied objectivity and authoritative expertise on the part of the researcher.

Multicultural counseling research has had a similar history, with quantitative methods dominating the field. It too has struggled with issues of legitimacy. Although psychology and counseling have historically accepted the twin notions of human individuality and universality, the idea of social groups being significant has been less acceptable. Groundbreaking researchers such as Vontress (1969, 1972), Sue and Sue (1977), or Helms (1979), to name a few, who sought to examine areas such as the ways in which race affects experience, often found it an uphill battle (Sue, Arredondo, & McDavis, 1992). Even recently, multicultural counseling research, theory, and the importance of competency are still questioned (Weinrach & Thomas, 1996, 1998). The struggle to be heard implied that researchers would have to use the most respectable forms of research, and qualitative research methods would be even more contested. In addition, most of the researchers came from psychology, where the training is often exclusively in quantitative methodology. It is understandable that

multicultural counseling researchers would rarely use qualitative methods.

Over the past few decades, there has been a shift in the dominance of quantitative methods. Some part of this was through the realization that qualitative methods might be useful in answering particular kinds of questions (Rennie, 1996; McLeod, 1994). Greenberg (1986, in Heppner, Kivlighan, & Wampold, 1992) argued that counseling psychology should place more emphasis on discovery than on verification because otherwise, poorly understood constructs would be investigated to little understanding. In addition, when there is little known about a field, qualitative inquiry is useful for generating themes that may be operationalized by later quantitative research (Mathews & Paradise, 1988).

However, specifically in multicultural counseling research, I argue that there is a rationale for using qualitative methodology that goes beyond notions of usefulness. Merchant and Dupuy (1996) have commented that there is a basic epistemological fit between multicultural counseling and qualitative inquiry because of the emphasis on identity as variable, shifting, and primarily understood through the eyes of the beholder. Social identities are complex and multiple, intersecting with each other as well as with the context and the shifting meanings ascribed to them by both the perceiver and the perceived. An area of identity, such as gender, cannot be understood as a pure construct from other aspects of identity; in effect, gender is raced and classed. Identities of race, class, gender, culture, sexual orientation, age, religion, or disability have a sociohistorical and political focus but are held by individuals who make meaning of them in contextual and shifting ways. Although it cannot generate one-size-fits-all answers, qualitative inquiry is peculiarly suited to explicate such complexity in the construction and experience of identity.

One of the compelling reasons for research aimed at developing multicultural counseling competency in counselors is because of the long history of marginalization and oppression of certain groups of people in society (Pedersen, 1994). The counseling field has been as culpable as any other in this regard. The ill service done to clients who have membership in such groups has been documented through their lack of use of counseling services, low retention in treatment, and maltreatment (Atkinson, Morten, & Sue, 1993). Research in multicultural counseling appears to have gone through a set of waves, each serving a different purpose. In the beginning, research focused on demonstrating that there were differences in the experience and perceptions of women and people of color (those who had African, Asian, Latino, or Native American heritage) versus normatively studied and universalized European American male experience. After this, research focused on developing theories to explain and understand the differences found such as theories of racial identity development (e.g., Helms, 1990) or sociopolitical experience (e.g., Constantino & Malgady, 1998). The third wave focused on examining the differences within specific groups, examining perhaps the racial and ethnic variations in help-seeking attitudes (Leong, Wagner, & Tata, 1995) or the effect of the counselor's disability on the client's experience of counseling (Leirer, 1996). In the practice of multicultural counseling, there is far more theory generated than research. Suggestions and prescriptions are based on philosophical assumptions more so than on empirical data. For instance, Ridley (1989) developed a groundbreaking argument for racism as an active component of the normative counseling process. In many ways, the argument carries conviction based on the recognition of its applicability rather than on supporting empirical data. On the other hand, the argument presents a cogent format for what not to do in counseling but is less helpful in providing a framework within which to act.

Pope-Davis, Liu, Toporek, and Brittan-Powell (2001) made a cogent argument that the body of multicultural competency research has largely focused on counselors, but the perspectives of clients have been given short shrift.

Qualitative research, by focusing on the meaning of experience, may be helpful in generating more ideas about what clients find helpful, useful, nonoppressive, and empowering while taking the diversity of clients and the context of their interactions with counselors into account. Qualitative research by Thompson and Jenal (1994); Thompson, Worthington, and Atkinson (1994); and Watkins and Terrell (1988) has been helpful in highlighting some of the complexities of client expectations and the impact of ethnicity. Pope-Davis et al. (2002) used grounded theory to develop a model of client perspectives of multicultural counseling, which was generated through the narratives of clients rather than the constructs of counselors. As compellingly, qualitative approaches can give us information about multicultural counselor development and supervision (Fukuyama, 1994) and inform us regarding identity development as multicultural counselors (Constantine, 1999).

The multicultural counseling competencies developed by Sue et al. (1992) require that counselors have awareness, knowledge, and skills of the cultural contexts that their clients come from as well as interrogate their own worldviews and perspectives. Similarly, qualitative research requires an articulation of one's own position and stance, a scrutiny of one's relationship with the Other, and an attempt to understand the Other's position. Like counseling, qualitative research also requires a comfort or at least tolerance with the messiness and complexity of human variability. With regard to the complexity of diversity, it has become increasingly necessary to attend to the social contexts within which people live as opposed to studying individuals in an effort to inscribe explanations of phenomena within the person. When meeting with clients, we seek to understand how clients experience the world. To do this, we go directly to clients and understand what we can from them about their experiences. Qualitative research tends to ask the kinds of questions that clinicians ask and can explore such questions in ways that are clinically meaningful. It makes an elegant equation to do in counseling research what is done in counseling practice, and the commonality between the approaches may infuse new understandings across both. Process research that emphasizes the study of change (Greenberg & Pinsof, 1986) may be better answered by qualitative methods because significant change events are often infrequent, complex, and context specific. In essence, we would be using such research to develop microtheories, rather than global frameworks, both respecting complexity and accepting the futility of seeking stable answers. We would be seeking pattern discoveries, one of the strengths of qualitative research, as opposed to the frequency/aggregate approach to data that may be less suitable for our purposes.

CHALLENGES TO QUALITATIVE MULTICULTURAL RESEARCH

The challenges of using qualitative methods in multicultural research lie for the most part in the very flexibility of qualitative research. Because of the reliance on the data to direct the research, the methods are less clearly defined than in quantitative research. Questions drawn from quantitative paradigms of validity, reliability, sample size, objectivity, and analysis can be misapplied to qualitative research. Because the majority of researchers are still trained primarily in quantitative methods, shifting to a qualitative approach may be difficult, with researchers and reviewers feeling uncertain about this approach. Another factor is the time and effort required as well as funding and publication challenges of conducting

qualitative research. A study can take much longer than a comparable quantitatively focused project, require greater labor in both the data collection and analysis, demand higher writing skills, and have more trouble securing funding and getting published (Moon, Dillon, & Sprenkle, 1990).

Particularly in conducting multicultural research, however, issues arise that are peculiar to qualitative inquiry. On one hand, qualitative research can be explicitly designed to be action research, focused on historical problems of domination, alienation, and social struggle. On the other hand, a research method that strives to capture the richness and complexity of experience may also be extremely intrusive and potentially harmful. The notion of sensitivity in counseling research (McLeod, 1996), in which the focus of research is on areas of vulnerability with the concurrent potential for impeding and doing harm to clients, has been raised. This is particularly true when examining areas of social identity such as race, gender, sexual orientation, or class, where the researcher is treading on sensitive ground, mined by the experiences of oppression and discrimination. Beyond asking unsafe questions, ethical issues arise because anonymity is more difficult to maintain in a smaller sample in which stories told are saturated by unique markers, risks are harder to determine in advance given the exploratory nature of the inquiry, and the close contact between researcher and participant blurs traditional boundaries (Grafanaki, 1996). As pointed out by Hallbrook and Ginsberg (1997), the issues of ethnographic transference and countertransference become an issue in qualitative mental health research.

In multicultural counseling, the reflexivity of the counselor is essential, with the self-scrutiny of one's own biases within the counseling relationship very much a part of the process. This challenge is replicated in qualitative multicultural research, whereby the researcher must interrogate the power dynamics in terms of the relationships of who asks and who answers, for what purpose, and to whose benefit in conducting any research with participants who have historically been exploited and marginalized. These questions are highlighted for the researcher who holds membership in those groups, as well as the researcher who holds conflicting memberships. For instance, an African American male researcher examining the meaning made of religious affiliations within the African American community must interrogate his own purposes for engaging in the study, as well as his relationship with participants and how they will perceive him. Similarly, a European American woman researcher examining the experiences of women of color in counseling must scrutinize the impact of her project (Gerrard, 1995). The perceived trustworthiness of the researcher is crucial to the openness of the participants, and the researcher may well have to "prove" himself or herself to the suspicious participants by investing time and effort, as well as by developing a relationship before engaging in inquiry. Particularly for researchers who hold membership in the groups they study, the questioning of their legitimacy may be harder to bear. For instance, a researcher of color who pursues questions of ethnicity and racism may be accused of being emotionally invested in the research to the extent that such investment is distorting objectivity. The very intimacy of qualitative research lends itself to such delegitimizing accusations and is harder to disprove when contrasted with the normative distance between researcher and subject customary in quantitative research. On the other hand, norms in many cultural groups are to establish the relationship before engaging in business, and members of such groups may be more open and informative in a qualitative research process. Ultimately, the challenges of conducting multicultural qualitative research are commensurate with the rewards of new

understandings of the experiences of people, who are portrayed with regard to their complexity rather than despite their diverse identities. The goal is to generate new understandings of the ways in which people make sense of their experience with such understandings.

EXAMPLE OF MULTICULTURAL QUALITATIVE RESEARCH

In this section, I describe a qualitative research project I conducted that may bring to life some of the concerns and issues discussed earlier. The focus of this section is on the project itself and conducting the inquiry, with spatial restrictions denying coverage of the findings themselves. The language of this section also reflects the personalized, localized characteristic of qualitative research in which the researcher is actively present.

Rationale

Over the course of 2½ years, I carried out a study investigating the perspectives of clients of color about their experiences in counseling. I defined clients of color as those persons of African, Asian, Latino, and indigenous heritage who had participated in or experienced counseling. It is important to state that my selection of such persons assumed that although cultural experiences are diverse within and between groups, there is a commonality of experience across such groups based on their relative status in society. For example, an African American man and a Puerto Rican woman would have in common some experience that would be distinguishably dissimilar from the experience of an Irish American man. Because the element of culture is present for all three persons, it is not a sufficient distinction. What is involved is a common experience of White racism, whereby being African American carries a connotation very different than being from an ethnic minority group such as Irish Americans.

My rationale for this study was that although much of the recent literature on multicultural issues in counseling had examined a number of issues, the perspective and voice of the clients themselves have often been missing. As Pope-Davis et al. (2001) have pointed out, most of the existing research has used pseudo-clients rather than actual clients and tended to focus on variables based on expectations rather than experience. Most counseling research has been quantitative in nature, and client experiences of counseling have typically been measured using experimental studies in laboratory conditions or through surveys with specific research questions in mind. Although clients' behavioral or psychological change might be measured to check effectiveness, their interactions analyzed, or their opinions sought on certain researcher-generated constructs, their narratives of the experience and meaning of counseling were often unheard. I found this troublesome because the result was that the clients around whom the process of counseling centered were left on the margins of their own stories. When one considered the sociopolitical experience of clients of color in being marginalized, this overlooking of their voices while assuming the characteristics of their stories seemed an oppressive replaying of supremacy. Many clients of color wanted to make their own meaning about counseling, but their voices were absent, which seems doubly ironic given the marginalization of people of color from the construct creation in psychology and counseling.

Locating Subjectivity

It was important to locate myself as the researcher prior to data collection (Gerrard, 1991). As an Asian Indian woman of an immigrant generation, I had experienced incidents of prejudice and discrimination in this society. However, I also believed that an immigrant experience carried a different weight than that of a generationally American person of color. I wanted to acknowledge the points of commonality but also those areas where I must not assume I understood. For instance, there is an important difference between an immigrant who is optimistic that struggle will bring reward and an American of generational minority status who has learned that achievement may be considered presumption and punished. Beyond that, I wanted to acknowledge that to many of the people I interviewed, I may have been perceived simply as a "foreigner," exoticized by difference of national origin and shades of orientalism, regardless of my status as a person of color in the United States.

It is also important to delineate and confess that the political stance I took was activist, which can be seen in my choice of this research; this study was qualitative instead of acceptably quantitative, focusing on clients of color in the community rather than some convenient university sample of largely White undergraduates. My self-image took some blows in the course of this research project as my participants taught me about the privileges of my position.

A particular point was that as a professional counselor speaking with those who had been in the position of clients, I did not want to replay those dynamics of expertise that responded to vulnerability. Here, the participants were the experts on their experience and construction, and I wanted to be careful not to infringe by applying authoritative frames to make sense of their narratives.

Philosophical Foundations

Theoretically, my inquiry straddled three major areas: (a) the experience of clients from ethnic minority groups who have historically not been helped by traditional modes of counseling, (b) the recognition of the centrality of the counseling relationship in counseling, and

(c) the social constructivist perspective of the nature of meaning and knowledge co-constructed through interaction. I used a phenomenological approach, which inquires into the structure and essence of experiencing a particular phenomenon for a set of people (Patton, 1990). The three assumptions in such a mode of inquiry are that how people experience and make meaning is important, that the only ways to know such meaning is to go directly to the people who experienced the phenomenon, and that a set of meanings can be mutually understood and have some consistency that cuts across the heterogeneity of experience. In addition, my perspective was also informed by symbolic interaction theory (Blumer, 1969). The basic premises of this theory are that we know things by their meaning, these meanings are constructed through social interaction, and meanings change through interaction. Symbolic interaction theory views human activity as focused on interpreting the symbols making up their environment and then developing meanings to guide their actions. Social interaction is a system of definitions and interpretations that operate to construct, sustain, and transform patterns of conduct (Woods, 1992). I thus perceived participant narratives as constructed along several dimensions of ongoing meaning making rather than as pieces of objective reality or data, which directed not only the focus of this study but also the questions I asked and the analysis of the data gathered.

Participants

I worked with 16 participants: 8 were of African descent, 3 of Asian descent, 4 of Latino heritage, and 1 Native American. Of these participants, 12 were born and raised in the United States, and 4 were born in other countries. They ranged from 19 to 51 years of age. Only 1 participant disclosed that he was gay, whereas the majority explicitly informed me that they were heterosexual or implied it

with their experiences. Although 7 participants had received psychiatric diagnoses of chronic conditions, only 1 considered herself as having a disability. Of those who had a religious affiliation, 7 participants associated themselves with one or another Christian group, 2 were Buddhist, and 1 was exploring indigenous belief systems.

Socioeconomic status is an imprecise definition because it can be defined by income, family upbringing, present circumstance, past conditions that have shaped one's outlook, and access to opportunity or sense of control. It is especially difficult in qualitative research, where it is dependent on constructed and related experience and cannot be relegated to one overall quantitative coding. On the basis of their narratives and, in some cases, their explicit self-definition, I assumed that 3 of the participants had been raised in upper-middle-class environments and were currently within that class bracket or at least middle class. Of the participants, 5 appeared to have middle-class backgrounds, and 7 seemed to be working class in that they had limited resources but some kind of support and some access to opportunity or at least the hope of it. One participant was homeless and living in a shelter at the time of the interviews. Although 7 participants experienced counseling primarily through practitioners in private practice, 7 experienced it through entering the mental health system—an umbrella of community and mental health agencies, substance abuse and rehabilitation clinics, prisons, and court-ordered counseling services where they had little choice in whom they received services from. Two participants had experienced counseling through the support system provided by schools.

Procedures

The process of data collection was very long, with one of the major obstacles being recruitment of participants. Often, it was the institutional structures of agencies that blocked access to clients in the name of protection. Interestingly, community-based sites such as grocery stores and activity centers where I simply posted announcements brought in far more participants. I offered monetary compensation for time spent being interviewed because I wanted to draw on a population that was both socioeconomically and ethnically diverse. I also wanted to honor the inverting of the counselor-client dynamic, acknowledging that participants were helping me.

Participants first made contact by phone and left a message. I would return the call, and we would speak on the phone as I described the study along with my needs and answered their questions. We would set up a place to meet. Although my office was often the interview site, I also met participants in their homes, in parks, and in community centers. When possible, I tape-recorded all interviews and transcribed the interviews. When the interview took place in high noise or outdoor sites, I took notes and developed detailed interview notes immediately following the interview. Memos and field notes on descriptions of the phone contacts, my reactions and responses, and issues that arose were also part of the data.

I used intensive multiple interviews with the participants, exploring their experiences, understandings, and lives. I wanted to know how they entered the counseling relationship, their perceptions of themselves and the counselor, their understandings of the process and content of counseling, and their ideas about successful and unsuccessful counseling. The questions I asked were open-ended and dependent on the flow of conversation between us, led by the participant rather than myself.

The interview process was complex and constantly surprised me, disturbing many assumptions that I had gone in with. I was surprised at the openness and candor of the participants. I seemed to be visibly sufficiently of color (recognizably brown-skinned and dark of hair and eye) to be given the space to demonstrate and prove my credibility. Paradoxically, that I was not from the participant's ethnic group seemed to also enhance the interview on some levels. In a way, I was perceived as trustworthy but because I was not "in"; it could not be taken for granted that I would automatically understand. Instead of relying on in-group verbal shorthand, the participant would articulate more with me, which was immensely helpful in later data analysis. Knowing that I was a counselor made these veterans of counseling relax with me on some level that seemed very similar to counseling. I knew it had to be related because I felt very close to the boundary myself and often caught myself crossing over from interviewer to counselor. One time, a participant said to me as she was leaving after an interview, "Well [I think] that you were a great counselor today," when I had not noticed myself behaving like a counselor. Sensitized by the participants, I began to hear the counselor in the reflections I gave, the trick of offering a conclusionary statement that summarizes what the participant said. The participants heard it too or at least recognized on a meta-level the manner of my interaction, which then shaped and influenced their response to me. I learned to pick up on my urges to respond in therapeutic ways during the interview itself and then make choices. In some situations, I pulled back from the empathic response, but in others, I gave it but then moved back into the interview mode.

Data Analysis

The process of data analysis was not defined within a certain time frame or stage of the research. As I collected data, I was thinking about what I was finding and writing memos about my observations and thoughts, which in turn affected future interviews and the directions I went with participants. Thus, analysis was an ongoing process throughout the study. On a more structured note, when I felt saturated with the interviewing process and the participants I had spoken with, I laid out the full texts of the interviews, as well as the accompanying field notes and memos in chronological order, and read them over several times. There were three major dimensions to this process, which included organization, categorization, and interpretation (Patton, 1990). The sheer amount of data in the form of written material was overwhelming, and my first step was to organize it. To do this, I had to immerse myself within it. This immersion process led me to realize a couple of areas where I had raised questions but never followed up, and I ended up arranging a couple more follow-up interviews with participants. This is the method of returning to the data source. I also used some member checks by asking a few of the participants who had the time, energy, and desire to discuss with me their reactions to some of the themes that I saw emerging.

Following the first ordering, I went over the data and entered in rudimentary codes in the margins of the notes as I started the process of naming and categorizing. At this point, I had two other readers read through the raw transcripts of four interviews and generate their own codes for verification of my reading. The sheer bulk of the data was often exhausting, but as I began wading through it and assigning codes, it went faster as I saw codes repeated. Glesne and Peshkin (1992) referred to this as "entering the code mines" (p. 132), and it often felt like a dimly illuminated process that made both my back and head hurt. At the end of this process, I seemed to have hundreds of codes, which I then collapsed into larger categories. For instance, I had several terms of *rapport, friendliness, greeting, warmth, attentiveness, concentration, remembering,* and *climate,* which all collapsed into a larger

category of establishing relationship. At the same time, I had other major categories that also included several of these subcodes. So, for instance, under the larger category of socioeconomic class-based interactions, I included some of the subcodes for the climate, which were also present in the earlier code category.

The step from categorization to interpretation seemed gigantic, and it was a step that I did not take for the longest time. My head was full of themes, and it felt difficult to articulate. I could not assign primacy to any aspect because they were all simultaneously present. It was here that the assistance through conversations I had with others became critical. Being able to begin the process of stumbling through and picking words to describe themes in conversations with advisers and peers who were engaged in their own qualitative research was invaluable. The step toward interpretation was difficult because it seemed such a risk to impose meaning, something I had not really perceived myself as doing when assigning code categories. Of course, the truth is that I had been assigning meaning all along, but in this step, such meaning making was public and open to scrutiny as opposed to a private process of narrowing down constructs. Reading others' work, whether it be qualitative research studies, clinical case studies, or theoretical perspectives, was very helpful.

The final step in data analysis was writing the findings. I found that the writing was a reflective and corrective process for me. Sometimes, a category that I had blithely worked out could not be written and had to be revised. I saw places where there were gaps in my analysis because the writing did not flow. The writing and the revising of that writing over and over were the final steps in polishing the apple. Other readers were especially helpful at this stage with their suggestions, concerns, questions, and clarifications. In a sense, this was the stage where I was establishing the trustworthiness of the study and the findings.

This was also the point where I saw the limitations of the study with the greatest clarity. The small sample size, the kinds of experiences and ethnicities and life stages that were missing from the narratives, the questions I did not ask, and the responses that were not given were all highlighted at this point. I needed to come to terms with the project as being about partial, contextual understanding rather than revealed truth based on any objective, externalized fact.

Many of the participants had multiple experiences of counseling, and their perspectives were varied, complex, dynamically shifting, and context dependent. Their voices and experiences were the heart of the study.

> It wasn't that I had gone to see her and that she was a professional helping me but she knew me, I had told her things . . . no one else knew, or I guess, knows about me. Even today, so much time has gone by, I sometimes think she still knows me better than anyone else. (Chia-Peng, Chinese American woman)

> He didn't know me . . . he couldn't care less who I was. I mean, he was probably a good guy, but who knew . . . he didn't take the time to show me and I didn't take the time to find out. (Jimmy, Native American man)

> One time, I was tired of being in prison and I was going to go hang myself in the shed. I had it all set up because nobody comes in that shed at a certain time during the day. And my friends told me, go talk to this counselor. . . . So, I go in there and I set up an appointment and I go in and talk to him. I'm sitting there talking and he falls asleep! (David, African American man)

> She actually. . . . She gave me feedback, where I didn't feel anyone else did. No one else. You know, no one else actually let me know that they were listening to me and knew what was going on. (Laura, Mexican American woman)

The voices of the participants echoed with the complexity of pain and need, of alienation and connection, of counseling encounters that met their concerns, whereas others ignored or betrayed their grief. Through the lens of client narratives, I perceived counselors playing roles of abusers, rescuers, teachers, and authority figures but also symbols of possible help—healers in the mythic sense. For Margaret, to not see a counselor meant the following:

> I just am wilting away, I'm isolating myself, I'm not talking to people, you know. 'Cause I know when I talk to people, I feel so much better. Think better. Like even just sitting here, talking with you . . . things are starting to click in my head about what I need to do. And yet when I don't talk to somebody, I feel like I'm closing up, and I don't want to.

Adegbisi, who was frustrated with her White female counselor, stayed with her out of that aching need for connection:

> Because I really had no one else to talk to! In a way I felt like—she wasn't my mother, no way was she ever going to be like my mother—but it was so nice to hear an older woman.

Reminiscing about her first visit to a counselor after seeing scores of doctors, Della said,

> She was very attentive. I had . . . someone there to hear me, and nobody ever heard me [before] and I was just shown the door. You know, nobody ever paid me no attention and it was very frustrating and it's been 40 years.

Whether they were helped or not, the clients I spoke to had an astonishing faith in the possibility of counseling. In their stories, clients characterized themselves as consumers, patients, prisoners, addicts, victims, people who are "just normal," mixed up, troubled, or "going through bad times." The plots of their stories about counseling were multiple and complex, with strands of redemption and corruption, subjugation and resistance, and indifference and intimacy. On one hand, Laura described her experience with one counselor as follows:

> She just wanted me to tell her things like that and when I'd tell her "I don't know what you mean," she got like mad at me, like almost yelled at me type of thing. And then after a while, I just started telling her things she wanted to hear. I would say, "I'm mad at my mom," and she's like, "Well, how do you know you're mad?" And I'd make something up and she'd be like, "Well what did you want to do?" And I have never wanted to hit my mom, but I'd tell her that. And she would be glad.

Laura would please the counselor, often at the expense of her own truth, which can be read as submissive. Yet, in giving the counselor what she wanted, Laura could be subversively powerful because she was able to read the counselor more accurately than the counselor could read her and, in doing so, meet the counselor's needs, whereas the counselor could not meet hers.

Counseling was constructed as a complex space, both alien and desirable. David, who distrusted counselors and yet loved his present one, had heard counseling defined as a White space. He mourned,

> My family don't understand it! They think about it in two terms—either you're normal or you're nutty as a fruitcake! If you're normal you can hang out, if you're nutty and you ain't that nutty, you can still hang out. Real nutty and needs some help—well, you'd better go talk to those White folks! We don't know nothing about that!

Similarly, Menomee also had counseling constructed as oppositional to her life. When her husband complained, she gave up counseling, thinking,

> You know, what's wrong with you that you can't get a friend? Why you got to go pay this woman to listen to you? You know, and uh, later on, as I thought about it, I said to myself, well, that's just not good if I'm taking money that could be used for some other purposes and maybe I'm depriving my family, you know.

Yet she mourned the loss of counseling from her life while still believing it was unsuitable for her.

Overall, I believe the findings of this study could hold particular messages about the experiences of clients of color in counseling in this part of the world, during this period in history. Through the reflections of participant narratives, this study also explored the larger ramifications of thinking through how we position and understand ourselves vis-à-vis others who have power and authority, offer healing, and offer connection or distance in terms of our resistances and accommodations, our acquiescence and opposition.

CONCLUSION

Qualitative research is exhausting and draining, demanding immersion, growth, and readiness to change on the part of the researcher. It is also enlightening and stimulating, and it offers possibilities of new knowing and understanding leading, in turn, to greater growth. Much the same could be said about committing to developing competency in multicultural counseling. In this chapter, I have sought to provide an introduction to qualitative research and argue as persuasively as I know how that this method of inquiry is profoundly suitable for multicultural counseling research.

In an old teaching tale, six blind men are asked to define an elephant by touch. Each of them touches a different aspect and comes up with six different identifications of the animal. In a postmodernist context, the point of the story might be that regardless of our particular disabilities, we all hold partial truths derived from our subjective locations. Such little truths are not definitive and cannot speak for the whole, but neither are they wholly false; after all, there are times an elephant can have the striking speed of a serpent or the strength of trees. Indeed, collecting partial truths and placing them beside each other enables us to understand the diversity of contexts and possibilities inherent in any endeavor. In the field of multicultural counseling, qualitative research offers another perspective: a partial truth about counseling and identities in relationship that may be useful in shifting our lens. To be competent, we need to be able to approach multicultural counseling as a complex endeavor, letting go the desire for objectivist frameworks that reduce persons to a collection of demographic variables. Qualitative research encourages us in such pursuits because it produces the kind of understanding that is incomplete and partial, disallowing us from being comfortable in our certainties that we can understand race, culture, gender, sexual orientation, class, disability, age, or religion in any consistent framework that holds true across context. In the future, I hope there will be more such troubling research in the field.

REFERENCES

Atkinson, D. R., Morten, G., & Sue, D. W. (1993) *Counseling American minorities* (4th ed.). Dubuque, IA: Brown.

Blumer, H. (1969). *Symbolic interactionism: Perspective and method.* Englewood Cliffs, NJ: Prentice Hall.

Bogdan, R. C., & Biklen, S. K. (1992). *Qualitative research for education* (2nd ed.). Boston: Allyn & Bacon.

Constantine, M. G. (1999). Racism's impact on counselors' professional and personal lives: A response to the personal narratives on racism. *Journal of Counseling & Development,* 77(1), 68-72.

Constantino, G., & Malgady, R. (1998). Overcoming cultural and linguistic bias in diagnostic evaluation and psychological assessment of Hispanic patients. In R. Javier & W. Herron (Eds.), *Personality development and psychotherapy in our diverse society: A sourcebook* (pp. 465-486). Northvale, NJ: Jason Aronson.

Creswell, J. W. (1998). *Qualitative inquiry and research design: Choosing among five traditions.* Thousand Oaks, CA: Sage.

Firestone, W. A. (1987). Meaning in method: The rhetoric of quantitative and qualitative research. *Educational Researcher, 16,* 16-21.

Fukuyama, M. A. (1994). Critical incidents in multicultural counseling supervision: A phenomenological approach to supervision research. *Counselor Education and Supervision, 34*(2), 142-151.

Gerrard, N. (1991). Racism and sexism, together, in counselling: Three women of color tell their stories. *Canadian Journal of Counselling, 25*(4), 555-566.

Gerrard, N. (1995). Some painful experiences of a White feminist therapist doing research with women of color. In J. Adleman & G. Engudanos (Eds.), *Racism in the lives of women: Testimony, theory and guides to antiracist practice* (pp. 55-64). New York: Haworth.

Glesne, C., & Peshkin, A. (1992). *Becoming qualitative researchers: An introduction.* White Plains, NY: Longman.

Grafanaki, S. (1996). How research can change the researcher: The need for sensitivity, flexibility, and ethical boundaries in conducting qualitative research in counselling/psychotherapy. *British Journal of Guidance and Counselling, 24*(3), 329-338.

Greenberg, L. S., & Pinsof, W. M. (1986). Process research: Current trends and future perspectives. In L. S. Greenberg & W. M. Pinsof (Eds.), *The psychotherapeutic process: A research handbook* (pp. 3-20). New York: Guilford.

Hallbrook, B., & Ginsberg, R. (1997). Ethnographic countertransference in qualitative research: Implications for mental health counseling. *Journal of Mental Health Counseling, 19*(1), 87-93.

Helms, J. E. (1979). Black women. *Counseling Psychologist, 8*(1), 40-41.

Helms, J. E. (1990). *Black and white racial identity: Theory, research, and practice.* Westport, CT: Greenwood.

Heppner, P. P., Kivlighan, D. M., & Wampold, B. E. (1992). *Research design in counseling.* Pacific Grove, CA: Brooks/Cole.

Hoshmand, L. T. (1989). Alternate research paradigms: A review and teaching proposal. *The Counseling Psychologist, 17*(1), 3-79.

Leirer, S. J. (1996). The effect of counselor disability, attending behavior, and client problem on counseling. *Rehabilitation Counseling Bulletin, 40*(2), 82-95.

Leong, F. T., Wagner, N. S., & Tata, S. P. (1995). Racial and ethnic variations in help-seeking attitudes. In J. G. Ponterotto, J. M. Casas, L. A. Suzuki, & C. M. Alexander (Eds.), *Handbook of multicultural counseling* (pp. 415-438). Thousand Oaks, CA: Sage.

Lincoln, Y., & Guba, E. (1985). *Naturalistic inquiry.* Beverly Hills, CA: Sage.

Mathews, B., & Paradise, L. V. (1988). Toward methodological diversity: Qualitative research approaches. *Journal of Mental Health Counseling, 10*(4), 225-234.

McLeod, J. (1994). *Doing counseling research.* London: Sage.

McLeod, J. (1996). Qualitative approaches to research in counseling and psychotherapy: Issues and challenges. *British Journal of Guidance and Counselling, 24*(3), 309-316.

McWilliam, R. A. (2000). Reporting qualitative studies: Author and reviewer guideline series. *Journal of Early Intervention, 23*(2), 77-80.

Merchant, N., & Dupuy, P. (1996). Multicultural counseling and qualitative research: Shared worldview and skills. *Journal of Counseling and Development, 74*(6), 537-542.

Moon, S. M., Dillon, D. R., & Sprenkle, D. H. (1990). Family therapy and qualitative research. *Journal of Marital and Family Therapy, 16*(4), 357-373.

Olesen, V. (1994). Feminisms and models of qualitative research. In N. K. Denzin & Y. S. Lincoln (Eds.), *Handbook of qualitative research* (pp. 158-174). Thousand Oaks, CA: Sage.

Patton, M. Q. (1990). *Qualitative evaluation and research methods.* Newbury Park, CA: Sage.

Pedersen, P. (1994). *A handbook for developing multicultural awareness* (2nd ed.). Alexandria, VA: American Counseling Association.

Pope-Davis, D. B., Liu, W. M., Toporek, R. L., & Brittan-Powell, C. S. (2001). What's missing from multicultural competency research: Review, introspection, and recommendations. *Cultural Diversity and Ethnic Minority Psychology, 7*(2), 121-138.

Pope-Davis, D. B., Toporek, R. L., Ortega-Villalobos, L., Ligiero, D. P., Brittan-Powell, C. S., Liu, W. M., et al. (2002). Client perspectives of multicultural competence: A qualitative examination. *The Counseling Psychologist, 30*(3), 355-393.

Rennie, D. L. (1996). Fifteen years of doing qualitative research on psychotherapy. *British Journal of Guidance and Counselling, 24*(3), 317-327.

Ridley, C. (1989). Racism in counseling as an adversive behavioral process. In P. Pedersen, J. Draguns, W. Lonner, & J. Trimble (Eds.), *Counseling across cultures* (3rd ed., pp. 55-77). Honolulu: University of Hawaii Press.

Sue, D. W., Arredondo, P., & McDavis, R. J. (1992). Multicultural counseling competencies and standards: A call to the profession. *Journal of Counseling & Development, 70*(4), 477-486.

Sue, D. W., & Sue, D. (1977). Barriers to effective cross-cultural counseling. *Journal of Counseling Psychology, 24*(5), 420-429.

Thompson, C. E., & Jenal, S. T. (1994). Interracial and intraracial quasi-counseling interactions when counselors avoid discussing race. *Journal of Counseling Psychology, 41*(4), 484-491.

Thompson, C. E., Worthington, R., & Atkinson, D. R. (1994). Counselor content orientation, counselor race, and Black women's cultural mistrust and self-disclosures. *Journal of Counseling Psychology, 41*(2), 155-161.

Vontress, C. E. (1969). Cultural barriers in the counseling relationship. *Personnel and Guidance Journal, 1*(1), 11-17.

Vontress, C. (1972). The Black militant as counselor. *Personnel and Guidance Journal, 50*(7), 576-580.

Watkins, C. E., Jr., & Terrell, F. (1988). Mistrust level and its effects on counseling expectations in Black client–White counselor relationships: An analogue study. *Journal of Counseling Psychology, 35,* 194-197.

Weinrach, S. G., & Thomas, K. R. (1996). The counseling profession's commitment to diversity-sensitive counseling: A critical reassessment. *Journal of Counseling & Development, 74*(5), 472-477.

Weinrach, S. G., & Thomas, K. R. (1998). Diversity-sensitive counseling today: A postmodern clash of values. *Journal of Counseling & Development, 76*(2), 115-122.

Woods, P. (1992). Symbolic interactionism: Theory and methods. In M. D. LeCompte, W. L. Millroy, & J. Preissle (Eds.), *The handbook of qualitative research in education* (pp. 337-404). Durham, NC: Academic Press.

18

Objectively Measured Multicultural Counseling Competencies

A Preliminary Study

SHELLEY RUELAS

Arizona State University

An accumulation of critiques, recommendations, general information, and theoretical conceptualizations has supported the notion that professional psychologists need to acquire specialized counseling skills to effectively meet the needs of clients with diverse experiences and backgrounds (American Psychological Association, 1993; Ponterotto, Casas, Suzuki, & Alexander, 1995; Pope-Davis & Coleman, 1997; Sue, Arredondo, & McDavis, 1992). In response, considerable empirical research identifying both the individual characteristics and training experiences that facilitate psychologists' acquisition of these specialized counseling skills has been generated (Ladany, Inman, Constantine, & Hofheinz, 1997; Neville, Heppner, Thompson, Brooks, & Baker, 1996; Pope-Davis, Reynolds, Dings, & Nielson,

1995; Sodowsky, Kuo-Jackson, Richardson, & Corey, 1998). These studies have provided empirical evidence supporting the premise that multicultural counseling competencies are critical to successfully meet the needs of diverse populations. However, it has also been noted that research findings are potentially limited in that self-report measures of multicultural counseling competencies have been used in a majority of these studies, thus leaving us to question whether psychologists' *actual* competence in working with diverse populations indeed parallels their *anticipated* level of skill (Constantine & Ladany, 2001; Pope-Davis & Dings, 1995).

Given this current dilemma, it is arguable that research using behaviorally based measures of multicultural counseling competence, as opposed to self-report measures, would contribute to the knowledge base regarding multicultural counseling at this time. The study presented in this chapter was conducted with this aim in mind. Building on previous research identifying individual characteristics, educational training, and clinical experiences as related to psychologists' self-reported multicultural counseling competency, the current study explored how these variables were related to psychologists' demonstrated multicultural counseling skill. This was accomplished by the development and use of an instrument that assessed psychologists' ability to identify counseling strategies that would be most appropriate for use with ethnic minority clients.

The first portion of this chapter reviews past studies identifying individual characteristics, including personality and demographic variables, as well as educational and professional experiences that have been linked with the development of multicultural counseling competencies among psychologists. The limitations of self-report assessments will then be summarized briefly, followed by a presentation of the conceptual framework from which the instrument used in this study to measure psychologists' demonstrated multicultural counseling competence was based. After a review of the study procedure and methodology, the resulting research findings will be presented and discussed.

VARIABLES RELATED TO MULTICULTURAL COUNSELING COMPETENCE

Individual Characteristics

Psychologists' ethnic background is perhaps one of the most common variables of interest for multicultural research. Several studies investigating the influence of ethnicity on psychologists' multicultural counseling competence have found a significant relationship between ethnicity and self-reported multicultural competence. Specifically, ethnic minority counselors tend to score higher on self-reported multicultural competencies than do European American counselors (Pope-Davis et al., 1995; Pope-Davis & Ottavi, 1994). However, other studies in this area have failed to find support for the relationship between ethnic background (or other demographic factors, including age and gender) and ability to work effectively with diverse populations (Ottavi, Pope-Davis, & Dings, 1994; Pope-Davis, Reynolds, Dings, & Ottavi, 1994).

One possible explanation for these mixed findings lies in the common assumption that ethnic group membership equates with culturally diverse life experiences, which in fact may not be the case. Indeed, the term *ethnicity* has often been narrowly defined within our society, yet at the same time can represent complex political, social, religious, and personal views and experiences. Given this ambiguity, it was hypothesized that ethnic group membership would not be positively related to psychologists' multicultural counseling competence but, rather, that ethnic and racial identity constructs (developed as a function of one's life experiences, sociopolitical views, etc.) would be a more viable measure of how racial, cultural, and ethnic characteristics can influence multicultural counseling competence. Several studies have examined the relationship between racial and ethnic identity constructs and the capacity to adequately serve culturally diverse clients. In their attempts to measure racial identity among European American psychologists, the large majority of these studies have used Helms's White Racial Identity Attitude Scale (WRIAS) (Helms & Carter, 1990). However, it should be noted that there is some controversy regarding the construct validity of the WRIAS. Specifically, it has been suggested that the WRIAS is not a multidimensional measure of racial identity and that the factor structure of the WRAIS does not measure all five of the hypothesized stages of racial attitude development proposed by Helms (Behrens, 1997; Pope-Davis, Vandiver, & Stone, 1999; Tokar & Swanson, 1991).

Despite measurement limitations, research on the influence of racial and ethnic identity development on various counseling competencies has shown a consistent and significant relationship between racial/ethnic identity development and self-reported multicultural counseling skill. In general, as White racial identity attitudes approached higher levels of racial consciousness, so did self-perceived multicultural counseling competence (Burkard, Ponterotto, Reynolds, & Alfonso, 1999; Ottavi et al., 1994). In studies that also looked at the relationship between multicultural competence and racial identity development among ethnic minority psychologists, findings were mixed. Self-perceived multicultural competence appeared to be positively correlated with racial/ethnic identity in some studies (Ladany, Brittan-Powell, & Pannu, 1997; Ladany, Inman, et al., 1997). However, when a third-party rating of multicultural competence was used in a similar study, further support for the relationship between ethnic minority racial identity and multicultural counseling competence was not established (Ladany, Inman, et al., 1997).

Some authors have also hypothesized that there is a critical relationship between counselors' level of dogmatism and their ability to implement effective counseling interventions (Brannon, 1977; Carlozzi, 1985; Carlozzi, Campbell, & Ward, 1982; Stair, 1988; Walton, 1986; Wright, 1975). Highly dogmatic persons are said to "exhibit a closed way of thinking . . . [and have] an authoritarian perspective, and an intolerant attitude towards those with dissimilar values or beliefs" (Carlozzi et al., 1982, p. 228), whereas low dogmatic persons are thought to be more open-minded toward thoughts and beliefs that

differ from their own. Researchers have found a significant inverse relationship between dogmatism and perceived counseling skill, defined by such constructs as ability to empathize (Carlozzi, 1985; Carlozzi et al., 1982; Victor, 1976; Wright, 1975). This inverse relationship might also exist with regard to psychologists' multicultural counseling competencies, in that highly dogmatic psychologists may be less likely to try alternative counseling roles than psychologists who are less dogmatic in their personality style. Although studies examining the relationship between dogmatism and counseling competence specific to work with multicultural populations were not found in a review of the research literature, dogmatism was included as a variable of interest in the current study given the above consideration.

Training Experiences

In addition to examining psychologists' individual characteristics as they are related to multicultural counseling competence, researchers have investigated the extent to which educational coursework (including professional development) and clinical experience influence the development of multicultural counseling competencies. It is not surprising that several publications in the counseling literature support the premise that training program attributes and components such as program philosophy, curriculum, research, and clinical opportunities are critical to the development of multicultural counseling competencies (Bernal & Padilla, 1982; Hills & Strozier, 1992; Ponterotto, Alexander, & Grieger, 1995; Ponterotto & Casas, 1987; Ridley, Mendoza, & Kanitz, 1994; Speight, Thomas, Kennel, & Anderson, 1995). With specific regard to multicultural curriculum and research experience on multicultural topics, it has been empirically shown that multiple educational experiences with a focus on diversity issues (i.e., educational courses, psycho-educational workshops and seminars, involvement in research projects, etc.) have had a positive impact on psychologists' self-reported multicultural competence (Neville et al., 1996; Ottavi et al., 1994; Pope-Davis et al., 1994; Pope-Davis et al., 1995; Sodowsky et al., 1998). Although these studies fail to provide complete consensus regarding the positive association between classroom, workshop, and other experiences and multicultural counseling competencies, their findings in general support this notion.

Empirical support for the relevancy of direct clinical experience in relation to multicultural counseling competence, specifically with multicultural populations, has also been established in the research literature. Several studies reviewed here operationalized "direct" or "experiential" clinical experiences by calculating (a) the number of minority clients seen, (b) the number of hours spent providing clinical services to ethnically diverse clients, (c) the number of "multicultural supervision" hours (i.e., supervisory sessions with specific regard to multicultural counseling dynamics between the counselor and client), and (d) the number of supervisory experiences with supervisors of color (Ladany, Inman, et al., 1997; Ottavi et al., 1994; Pope-Davis et al., 1995; Sodowsky et al., 1998). Some evidence suggests that there is indeed a positive relationship between multicultural counseling competencies and direct clinical experience with clients of color (Ottavi et al., 1994; Sodowsky et al., 1998). However, other studies have failed to provide further evidence of this relationship. Similarly, researchers exploring the relationship between self-reported multicultural counseling competencies and supervision received from supervisors of color have failed to reveal a significant relationship between these two variables (Ladany, Inman, et al., 1997; Ottavi et al., 1994; Pope-Davis et al., 1995).

ASSESSMENT ISSUES

Despite the valuable contributions made by these and other similar research studies, the field of psychology has been limited in the assessment of what contributes to multicultural competence, given the nearly exclusive reliance of researchers in this area on self-report instruments as indices of multicultural counseling competencies. These self-report scales include the Multicultural Counseling Awareness Scale–Form B (MCAS-B) (Ponterotto, Sanchez, & Magrids, 1991), the Multicultural Awareness-Knowledge-Skills Survey (MAKSS) (D'Andrea, Daniels, & Heck, 1990), and the Multicultural Counseling Inventory (MCI) (Sodowsky, Taffe, Gutkin, & Wise, 1994).

These instruments have contributed greatly to the counseling literature through their operationalization of the multicultural counseling competence construct, but they have also been criticized for their limitations as self-report measures (Constantine & Ladany, 2001; Ponterotto, Rieger, Barrett, & Sparks, 1994; Pope-Davis & Dings, 1995). Specifically, these self-report instruments have been criticized for their failure to address the potentially confounding effect that social desirability has on research participants' responses to these surveys (Pope-Davis & Coleman, 1997). Indeed, Sodowsky et al. (1998) found empirical support for the hypothesis that psychologists' desire to be perceived as competent in this area may need to be taken into account with self-reported assessments of their multicultural counseling competence. Similarly, some researchers have speculated that self-report measures of multicultural competence are better indices of self-perceived or anticipated counseling skills than they are indices of actual competence (Constantine & Ladany, 2001; Pope-Davis & Dings, 1995). Findings from a study conducted by Ladany, Inman, et al. (1997) confirmed the validity of this concern. In their empirical study comparing self-reported multicultural competence and multicultural case conceptualization ability, defined as the ability to integrate cultural factors in the conceptualization of clients' presenting concerns, no relationship was found between participants' self-reported multicultural competence and their actual multicultural case conceptualization ability.

Constantine and Ladany (2000) also recently examined the relationship between several self-report multicultural counseling competency measures and a behavioral index of multicultural counseling competence, as measured by multicultural case conceptualization ability. After accounting for social desirability, they found that none of the self-report measures was significantly related to demonstrated multicultural counseling competence. This finding suggests that self-reported multicultural competence may be a better index of psychologists' self-efficacy rather than actual competence. The outcome of this study also highlights a third criticism of current self-report measures of multicultural counseling competencies—namely, the notion that these instruments are lacking in their exclusion of what might be key aspects of competence, such as multicultural case conceptualization skills or perhaps the ability to build rapport within a multicultural counseling relationship (Constantine & Ladany, 2001).

TOWARD AN OBJECTIVE MEASURE OF MULTICULTURAL COMPETENCE

As previously noted, the limitations of self-report measures in the assessment of multicultural counseling competence suggest that researchers should devote greater attention to the development and use of behavioral indices of multicultural competence. Toward this aim, the instrument used in this study to assess multicultural competence required psychologists to select and rate highly counseling strategies that have been deemed appropriate for use with ethnic minority clients who have various presenting circumstances and characteristics. This instrument was based on Atkinson, Thompson, and Grant's (1993) conceptual framework of effective multicultural counseling approaches. In their model, Atkinson et al. presented a framework consisting of eight different "helping roles" that are appropriate to adopt when working with ethnically diverse clients. Depending on the client's presenting problem etiology, goal of counseling, and acculturation level, psychologists may choose to engage in any one of following eight helping roles: *advocate, change agent, consultant, adviser, facilitator of indigenous support systems, facilitator of indigenous healing methods, counselor,* and/or *therapist.* For the purposes of this study, counseling strategies representative of the eight counseling roles were incorporated into an instrument that required respondents to rate how useful they perceived the various strategies to be when working with diverse clients who varied in terms of their acculturation level, problem etiology, and goal of counseling.

The major aim of this study was to expand on previous research in the area of multicultural competence by determining if the demographic, individual characteristic, and educational/training variables that have been linked to psychologists' self-reported multicultural counseling competence were in fact significantly related to psychologists' demonstrated multicultural counseling competence. This was accomplished by using a rigorous and objective method of assessing multicultural competence, defined as the ability to select and rate highly those counseling strategies that have been deemed as most appropriate for use with particular ethnic minority clients. The hypotheses and research questions of this study were as follows:

- Psychologists' ethnic group membership would not be predictive of their multicultural counseling skill.

- Psychologists' racial/ethnic identity development level would be predictive of their multicultural counseling skill.
- Psychologists' clinical experiences would be predictive of their multicultural counseling skill.
- Psychologists' didactic educational experiences would be predictive of their multicultural counseling skill.
- Psychologists' training and professional experiences would be predictive of multicultural counseling skill above and beyond the extent to which their individual characteristics are predictive of multicultural counseling skill.
- Is the degree to which psychologists are open-minded (i.e., level of dogmatism) related to their multicultural counseling skill?
- Do psychologists' multicultural counseling skills vary as a function of particular client characteristics and circumstances?

METHOD

Participants

Study materials were sent to a random sample of 400 psychologists across the United States who had a counseling or clinical related training background. Potential participants were members of the American Psychological Association (APA) and active practitioners. APA members were chosen as the target sample to provide more variability with respect to clinical experience than samples recruited for similar studies in the past (e.g., studies that included students or interns as participants). Of the usable surveys, 149 were returned, resulting in a 43% return rate.

The ages of participants in this study ranged from 30 to 78 years old, with the mean age being 51. Regarding ethnic background, 67% ($n = 100$) of the participants self-identified as European American. Of the respondents, 15% ($n = 22$) were Latino(a)/ Hispanic, 7% ($n = 11$) were Asian American, 5% ($n = 7$) were African American, and 1% ($n = 2$) were

of Native American heritage. The remaining 5% ($n = 7$) self-identified as having an "other" ethnic group membership than those listed above.

Of the respondents, 47% ($n = 70$) were male and 52% ($n = 77$) were female. Two respondents had missing information for this question. Psychologists with a clinical training background comprised a majority of the sample (55%), followed by psychologists with a counseling training background (39%). The remaining 6% of respondents reported a school, neuropsychology, health psychology, or other psychology-related background. Finally, regarding participants' work setting, 59% of respondents reported that their primary workplace was in private practice. Eight percent reported working in an outpatient hospital setting, 7% in a community counseling center setting, 6% in a university counseling center setting, 5% in an academic department setting, and another 5% in an inpatient hospital setting. One percent reported their primary workplace as being in a K-12 school setting, whereas the remaining 9% of participants described their primary work setting as being something other than those listed above.

Materials

Vignettes

Based on the three-dimensional (3-D) counseling model presented by Atkinson et al. (1993), Atkinson, Kim, and Caldwell (1998) developed eight vignettes depicting ethnically diverse clients whose circumstances and clinical presentation would require a counselor to adopt one of eight multicultural counseling roles. For each of the eight conditions depicted in the vignettes, the 3-D model specifies that counselors employ a unique counseling role. Four of the eight vignettes developed by Atkinson et al. (1998) were chosen for use in this study because they called for counselors to adopt nontraditional counseling roles. The specific roles called for by these four vignettes included the following: consultant, change agent, facilitator of indigenous support systems, and facilitator of indigenous healing systems.

Each vignette reflects a particular client problem varying along three dimensions: acculturation level, source of problem, and goal of counseling. Each dimension is considered a continuum, but for heuristic purposes, Atkinson et al. (1998) dichotomized each dimension into two levels. The acculturation dimension is reflected by "high" or "low" levels of acculturation, the source of problem (problem etiology) dimension refers to either "external" or "internal" sources, and the goal of counseling dimension refers to "prevention" or "remediation" of the problem.

These dimensions are operationalized as follows. A low-acculturated client is portrayed as a recent U.S. immigrant who has limited English-proficiency skills. A high-acculturated client is portrayed as a fifth-generation person, that is, someone whose immigrant family has been living in the United States for at least four generations, who has "largely adopted the beliefs, values, customs, and institutions of the dominant culture" (Atkinson et al., 1993, p. 261). A client with an internal source of problem is portrayed as someone dealing with depression caused by the loss of a loved one, whereas a client with an external source of problem is portrayed as someone dealing with workplace discrimination. A client with a remediation goal of counseling is portrayed as a client who is currently experiencing problems. In contrast, a client with a prevention goal of counseling is portrayed as one who is not currently in distress but presumably could encounter future difficulties given his or her current circumstances.

Data reported by Atkinson et al. (1993) suggest that all three dimensions on which the vignettes are intended to vary were adequately represented in all of the original vignettes. However, support for the "goal of counseling" dimension was not as strong as was support for the remaining dimensions on one of the four vignettes selected for this study. This vignette, developed to elicit the "facilitator of indigenous support" role, was modified to strengthen the prevention/remediation goal dimension. The remaining three vignettes remained as they were originally developed. The ethnicity of the clients portrayed in the vignettes was either "Hispanic" or "Asian" to maintain the generalizability of the vignettes and the external validity of the study. A manipulation check was performed to ensure that the salient and distinct characteristics of each vignette (i.e., the characteristics intended to elicit a particular multicultural counseling response) were not compromised given the above modifications; results supported the validity of the modified vignettes.

Instruments

Counseling Strategy Rating Scale (CSRS). The CSRS is a shortened version of the Helper Activity Scale (HAS), developed by Atkinson et al. (1998). For each of the eight counseling roles recommended by the 3-D counseling model, the authors of the HAS designed three "helping activities" representative of the actions that a counselor in that role would take. Respondents are asked to rate each statement on a 5-point Likert-type scale, ranging from 1 = *not at all helpful* to 5 = *very helpful*. For example, "encourage person to seek support from family, friends, or a community organization to prevent problems anticipated in the future" is one of the three helper activity statements associated with the "facilitator of indigenous support systems" counseling role. For the purpose of this study, the helper activity statements were modified to characterize the help-seeker/help-giver relationship as an actual counseling relationship. In addition, only those 12 items from the HAS associated with the four roles under investigation in this study were included in the CSRS.

The CSRS incorporated all four vignettes described earlier. For each vignette, three multiculturally appropriate counseling strategies were embedded within three other counseling strategies that represent traditional "counselor" or "psychotherapy" roles. Thus, after reading a given vignette, a participant had to rate six counseling strategies. Three of these strategies comprised an appropriate multicultural counseling role (to be incorporated in the dependent variable), and three comprised a traditional counseling role (neutral stimuli that were not analyzed).

Reliability coefficients were calculated for the modified CSRS instruments using participant responses from this study. The validity of the total CSRS scale and the CSRS subscales was adequately supported in this study. The CSRS full-scale alpha coefficient equaled .67, the Consultant subscale equaled .76, the Facilitator of Indigenous Support System subscale equaled .70, and the Change Agent subscale equaled .74. A correlation was performed between the two items of the Facilitator of Indigenous Healing Systems subscale to estimate the internal reliability of this subscale. Due to an editing error, not all three strategies associated with this vignette were included in the survey sent to participants. These two items were significantly correlated ($r = .48$, $p < .01$), thus providing support for the reliability of this particular subscale.

Multigroup Ethnic Identity Measure (MEIM). The MEIM assesses ethnic identity achievement based on the conceptualization that ethnic identity is composed of ethnic behaviors and practices, feelings of belonging within a given ethnic group, the process of exploration and commitment toward learning more about one's background, and the process of becoming aware of attitudes toward and interactions with ethnic groups other than one's own (Phinney, 1992). It consists of 23 items requiring respondents to indicate the degree to which they agree or disagree with each item using a 4-point Likert-type scale. The two major subscales of the instrument include the (a) Affirmation and Belonging subscale (representing the respondents' feeling of attachment to and positive regard for their particular ethnic group) and (b) the Ethnic Identity Achievement subscale (representing the developmental process of exploring and becoming secure with one's own ethnic status). Only the 14 items comprising these two subscales (i.e., the total ethnic identity score of the MEIM) were used in this study.

In a study conducted by Phinney (1992) that examined the reliability of the MEIM, Cronbach's alpha was calculated among two different research samples. The overall reliability for MEIM was .81 for the first sample (high school students) and .90 for the second sample (college students), thus supporting the use of the MEIM as a reliable measure of ethnic identity. On the Affirmation and Belonging subscale, Phinney reported Cronbach's alphas of .75 for the high school sample and .86 for the college sample. On the Ethnic Identity Achievement subscale, reliability coefficients were reported to be .69 and .80, respectively (Phinney, 1992). Reliability coefficients were calculated using responses from participants in the current study and further established the MEIM's reliability. Cronbach's alpha coefficient for all 14 items of the scale was .89. On the Affirmation and Belonging subscale, Cronbach's alpha equaled .86. On the Ethnic Identity Achievement subscale, Cronbach's alpha equaled .84.

Dogmatism Scale. The Dogmatism Scale–Short Form (DS-Short) is a 20-item instrument developed by Troldahl and Powell (1965) based on Rokeach's (1960) 40-item dogmatism scale. The lengthy amount of time required to complete the original instrument (approximately 20 minutes) limited its utility in field studies. Troldahl and Powell thus modified Rokeach's scale by eliminating more than half of the original items, thus creating the DS-Short. Reliability of the DS-Short was established in Troldahl and Powell's study, in which they established a split half reliability of .79 (the original scale = .84). Validity for the DS-Short was also assessed using responses from participants in the current study. Cronbach's alpha was calculated and found to equal .79, thus further establishing internal validity for the scale.

Demographic Questionnaire. In this section of the survey, participants were asked to provide the following information: age, gender, ethnicity, psychology specialty area, specific degree type, primary workplace, and years of post-doctoral professional experience.

Clinical and Educational History Questionnaire. In this section of the survey, participants were asked to provide information concerning their clinical training experiences and professional activities in conjunction with ethnic minority populations. Questions included were estimated percentage of ethnic minority clients/students with whom they have worked with (or are currently working with) in a direct service capacity; the estimated number of supervision hours involving diverse clients; the estimated number of seminars, workshops, and research projects oriented toward work with diverse populations; and the estimated number of courses relating to counseling diverse populations completed during clinical training.

RESULTS

A hierarchical regression analysis was conducted to (a) examine the influence of participants' individual characteristics and training/professional experiences on their ability to identify an appropriate multicultural counseling role and (b) determine if training/professional experiences significantly influenced participants' multicultural counseling competence once the influence of their individual characteristics had already been accounted for. Participants' scores on the Affirmation and Belonging and Ethnic Identity Achievement subscales of MEIM, in addition to their ethnic group membership status, were entered as predictor variables in the first step of the hierarchical regression model. The number of direct service hours participants had rendered to diverse clients, the number of supervision hours that participants had received (in which issues pertaining to ethnically diverse clients were addressed), the number of educational courses involving multicultural issues that participants had taken, and the number of educational workshops/seminars involving multicultural issues that participants had engaged in were entered as predictor variables in the second step of the hierarchical regression model. Participants' CSRS score was entered as the criterion variable.

The amount of variance accounted for by the predictor variables in the overall regression model approached statistical significance, $R^2 = .11$, $F(7, 125) = 2.02$, $p = .06$, yet did not attain the conventional probability level of .05. However, it does appear that training experiences do significantly contribute to psychologists' multicultural counseling competence above and beyond organismic characteristics, as seen in the significant ΔR^2 statistic reported in Table 18.1.

The unique contributions of each predictor variable in both steps of the regression model are also reported in Table 18.1. The amount of unique variance accounted for by participants' organismic characteristics—specifically, ethnic group membership and ethnic identity—was not statistically significant. The contributions of these variables remained nonsignificant in

Table 18.1   Summary of Hierarchical Regression Analysis of the Influence of Training Variables, Above and Beyond Organismic Variables, on Psychologists' Multicultural Counseling Ability

Variable	B	SE B	β	t
Step 1				
EID—Affirmation and achievement	−.09	.099	−.105	−.93
EID—Achievement	.147	.091	.183	1.61
Ethnic group membership	−.153	.108	−.131	−1.41
Step 2				
EID—Affirmation and achievement	−.109	.098	−.124	−1.11
EID—Achievement	.171	.090	.214	1.89
Ethnic group membership	−.169	.108	−.144	−1.57
Direct service hours	−1.806E-06	.000	−.021	−.21
Supervision hours received	7.021E-05	.000	.237	2.61*
Educational courses	−7.504.E-03	.014	−.048	−.55
Workshops/training seminars	−2.048.E-03	.001	−.136	−1.48

NOTE: $R^2 = .032$ for Step 1; $\Delta R^2 = .075^*$ for Step 2 ($p < .05$). EID = ethnic identity development.
$^*p < .001$.

Step 2 of the model, where it was also observed that the unique proportion of variance accounted for by the number of direct service hours that participants had rendered to diverse clients was nonsignificant. Similarly, education coursework and educational seminars/workshops were not statistically significant in terms of their unique contributions to the regression model. However, the variance accounted for by the number of multicultural supervision hours that participants received was statistically significant, as seen in Table 18.1.

Multicollinearity statistics calculated for this model indicated that intercorrelations among the predictor variables of this analysis, originally observed in the preliminary analysis, did not unduly influence the hierarchical regression model.

To determine if participants' scores varied across the four subscales of the CSRS (i.e., if scores on one particular subscale were significantly higher as compared to the remaining subscales), a one-way repeated-measures ANOVA, was conducted with the four subscale scores of the CSRS as the repeated factors. The overall repeated-measures ANOVA was found to be significant, $F(3, 444) = 12.27$, $p < .001$. As can be seen in Table 18.2, the source of this effect can be attributed to participants' scores on the fourth subscale, which were significantly higher than participants' scores on the first through third subscales. As displayed in Table 18.3, participants' mean scores on the fourth subscale were the highest ($M = 3.75$), followed by the first subscale ($M = 3.35$), the second subscale ($M = 3.24$), and the third subscale ($M = 3.18$).

Finally, a correlation matrix was constructed to determine the strength of relationship, if any, between psychologists' degree of open-mindedness toward thoughts and beliefs that differ from their own, as measured by their level of dogmatism, and their ability to identify an appropriate multicultural counseling strategy. Dogmatism was not observed to have a statistically significant relationship with

Table 18.2   Pairwise Comparisons of Participants' Scores Across All Four Subscales of the CSRS

	M(1)	*M(2)*	*M(3)*	*M(4)*
M(1)	0			
M(2)	.112	0		
M(3)	.172	.06	0	
M(4)	−.394*	−.506*	−.566*	0

NOTE: $M(1)$ = mean on Consultant subscale, $M(2)$ = mean on Facilitator of Indigenous Healing Systems subscale, $M(3)$ = mean on Change Agent subscale, $M(4)$ = mean of Facilitator of Indigenous Support Systems subscale.

*$p < .001$.

Table 18.3   Means of Participants Scores on Subscales of the CSRS

Subscale	*M*	*SD*	*n*
1. Consultant	3.54	.9382	149
2. Facilitate Indigenous Healing	3.24	.9857	149
3. Change Agent	3.18	.9637	149
4. Facilitate Indigenous Support	3.75	.8825	149

the total CSRS score ($r = .007$, p = ns), indicating a lack of association between these two variables.

DISCUSSION

The Influence of Psychologists' Personal Characteristics on Multicultural Counseling Competence: Findings and Recommendations for Research

Ethnicity and Racial/Ethnic Identity. Findings from this study support the notion that psychologists' ethnic background does not, in and of itself, influence their demonstrated multicultural counseling ability. This finding could be a reflection of the complexities involved in accurately capturing the political, social, and personal experiences that are commonly associated with the experience of being an ethnic minority. As such, racial/ethnic identity level was hypothesized to be a better predictor of multicultural counseling competency (as compared to ethnicity) based on the assumption

that it provides a more direct index of the extent to which one has reflected on the personal meaning that racial diversity, racism, oppression, and privilege has in one's life. Interestingly, ethnic identity level was not significantly related to psychologists' ability to select an appropriate multicultural counseling role. Perhaps psychologists who score high on ethnic identity development have given substantial thought to issues of diversity such as "cultural differences" and "group membership" but have not pondered at length the more controversial, and conceivably more uncomfortable, aspects of diversity such as racism, oppression, and discrimination. Alternatively, these nonsignificant findings could be a result of methodological limitations. That is, given that 75% of the psychologists included in this study reported moderate to high levels of ethnic identity development, there may not have been sufficient variance on participants' ethnic identity scores to detect a significant relationship between ethnic identity level and demonstrated multicultural counseling skill.

The inability to detect a relationship between racial/ethnic identity and multicultural counseling competence in the current study has important implications for research in this area as well as for racial/ethnic identity theory. Racial identity theory might be expanded to incorporate other potentially important constructs that are not currently included in these theoretical models. For example, the construct regarding "how much one has reflected on racism and power differential issues" might be equally important to consider in conjunction with current theoretical constructs such as ethnic identity belonging and achievement. Replication studies might improve on the methodological challenges of the current study by targeting specific racial/ethnic identity groups and using assessment instruments developed specifically for these ethnic groups. However, considering the methodological challenge of having statistically adequate numbers of ethnically diverse research participants, researchers might also focus on the improvement and refinement of current multigroup racial/ethnic identity development inventories.

Dogmatism. The nonsignificant relationship between dogmatism and multicultural counseling competence may be an indication that the instrument used to measure dogmatic personality traits does not tap into current social representations of "rigid" or "inflexible" thought processes and personality traits. That is, although Rokeach's (1960) dogmatism scale has been shown to be a valid and reliable instrument, most of the research confirming the psychometric properties of this scale was conducted shortly after the scale's publication. It is conceivable that the nonsignificant findings of the current study are a function of outdated criteria used to define dogmatic personality style. Perhaps an updated version of the scale,

reflecting current sociocultural sentiment, would provide a better index of the relationship between dogmatic personality traits and multicultural counseling competence.

The Influence of Training and Experience on Multicultural Counseling Competence: Findings and Recommendations for Training and Research

Multicultural Coursework and Professional Development Seminars. As reviewed previously, several authors have found a significant relationship between didactic classroom training experiences, such as educational courses and professional development workshops, and self-reported multicultural counseling experience. It was surprising in this study to find that educational coursework did not significantly influence psychologists' ability to choose an appropriate counseling strategy for use with an ethnic minority client. One possible explanation for this finding is that, despite increasing attention to multicultural issues within professional training programs, a majority of psychologists still receive minimal exposure to multicultural training opportunities that facilitate the acquisition of multicultural counseling *awareness* and *knowledge,* much less *skills,* for use with diverse clients. Findings from this study support this notion, as roughly 60% of the participants in the current study reported having taken only one educational course that involved multicultural issues. It is doubtful that such limited training enabled participants to acquire substantial multicultural counseling competencies, particularly multicultural intervention skills such as the selection of appropriate multicultural counseling strategies. Indeed, participation in a course *entirely* devoted to the study of racial/ethnic minority groups might help participants to gain considerable knowledge and awareness of multicultural issues yet still fail to address specific multicultural counseling intervention issues given practicalities such as time restrictions and participants' readiness level.

Based on this possibility, it could be recommended that training programs include multicultural course *series* within their curriculum. In this way, trainees would be able to build on their multicultural *knowledge* and *awareness* (typically covered in introductory courses) with the acquisition of multicultural counseling *skills* (the opportunity of which usually arises in more advanced courses). In fact, to the degree that this study found support for the positive influence of multicultural counseling supervision on the development of multicultural counseling skills, it may be advisable that multicultural courses incorporate strategies similar to those used in the supervision setting. Presumably, these courses provide the opportunity to engage in personally interactive training experiences eliciting self-assessment and reflection. Similar strategies in the classroom might include experiential classroom exercises (e.g., open discussion of emotional reaction in response to such videos as *The Color of Fear* and *Last Chance for Eden*) that would afford trainees the opportunity to actively process what they are learning as it applies to both their personal value system, their clinical work, and/or research endeavors.

Direct Clinical Service and Clinical Supervision Experiences. In addition to didactic educational experiences, the influence of clinical experiences on multicultural counseling competence was also assessed in the current study. Clinical experiences included the number of clinical hours rendered to diverse clients and hours spent addressing issues of diversity in clinical supervision. The number of direct service hours that participants reported having worked with diverse clients was not significantly related to participants' multicultural counseling ability in the current study. Pope-Davis et al. (1995) and Ladany, Inman, et al. (1997) also failed to find support for the relationship between self-reported multicultural counseling skill and clinical hours rendered to diverse clients. In addition, despite their use of a more objective measure of multicultural counseling competence, Ladany, Inman, et al. (1997) found that there was no significant relationship between clinical hours with diverse clients and multicultural case conceptualization ability. These findings are in direct contrast to other studies (Ottavi et al., 1994; Sodowsky et al., 1998), which have found empirical support for the relationship between experience working with ethnically diverse clients and self-reported multicultural counseling competence. One possible explanation for why the current study failed to find a significant relationship is that an objective measure of multicultural counseling competence was used in this study, whereas those studies that found significance used self-report measures (Ottavi et al., 1994; Sodowsky et al., 1998). However, considering Ladany, Inman, et al.'s (1997) findings, it is also possible to hypothesize that clinical experiences with diverse clients do not influence the acquisition of multicultural counseling skill in and of itself. Although initially surprising, this finding can be explained if one were to assume that the process of *reviewing and reflecting* on one's work with clients is the critical "learning" element of direct clinical experiences with clients. Perhaps psychologists engaged in clinical work with diverse clients did not process how effective they actually were with these clients. Extending this argument, it would follow that to have an impact on the acquisition of multicultural counseling skill, direct service experiences would need to occur in conjunction with supervision experiences in which issues of diversity and their impact on the counseling relationship could be addressed.

Findings from the current study do provide some evidence in support of the significant role that actively reviewing one's clinical work with diverse clients has on the acquisition of multicultural counseling competency. These findings should be interpreted cautiously as the analysis on which they are based closely approached but did not reach conventional levels of statistical significance. Nonetheless, the findings suggest there may be a relationship between multicultural counseling competence and time spent addressing issues of diversity during clinical supervision (i.e., multicultural supervision). In short, it appears that the number of multicultural supervision hours that psychologists in this study received during their training had a positive influence on their ability to identify appropriate multicultural counseling strategies for use with diverse clients, as measured by the CSRS.

The apparently critical role that multicultural supervision plays in the development of multicultural counseling skills is important, especially considering the finding in this study that direct service experiences with ethnically diverse clients seem to have an insignificant impact on multicultural counseling competence. Taking both findings into consideration, it appears that regardless of the number of hours that participants rendered to ethnically diverse clients, it is the *time that participants spent in supervision discussing issues of diversity in relation to their clients* that influences the acquisition of multicultural counseling skills. Even though clients may have multiple experiences working with ethnically diverse clients, these experiences may not be useful in the development of rigorously measured multicultural counseling *skill* unless they are processed in a supervisory or perhaps consultation context.

Arguably, the active processing, attitude of open exploration, reflection, creative thinking, and sharing of ideas, which take place in a supervisory exchange, are critical factors in facilitating the development of both general and multicultural counseling skills. Supporting this notion is research in the field of counseling supervision. Investigators have found that

the acquisition of strong counseling skills and the experience of a positive supervisory interaction are positively influenced by supervisees' willingness to disclose, their interest in receiving the supervisor's feedback, and their willingness to confront personal areas of weakness (Kennard, Stewart, & Gluck, 1987; Rabinowitz, Heppner, & Roehlke, 1986). Although relatively few studies have been conducted on these issues as they relate to multicultural supervision (Leong & Wagner, 1994; Stolenberg, McNeill, & Crethar, 1994), findings from the current study suggest that this is viable area of continued research and exploration. For example, given Kiselica's (1998) argument that effective multicultural training might entail the disclosure of personal and possibly anxiety-provoking multicultural experiences, continued research in this area might include instruments that measure the degree to which supervisors/supervisees "risk take" within the supervision exchange.

The Importance of Clinical and Educational Training Experiences

In this study, it was hypothesized that training variables, such as educational coursework and direct clinical service, were more influential than organismic characteristics on the development of multicultural counseling competencies. The overall regression model testing this hypothesis approached but did not reach the conventional level of significance. A higher subject-to-variable ratio within the regression model might have improved the statistical outcomes of this analysis; that is, with more participants, the level of significance may have exceeded .05. Nonetheless, this finding still provides marginal evidence in support of the above hypothesis.

Likewise, the significant change in R^2 for training variables, after organismic variables had already been entered into the equation, also provides tentative support for the above hypothesis in this analysis. Given the equivocal nature of these statistical results, as well as the minimal amount of variance accounted for by the overall regression model, this finding should be interpreted cautiously. Still, considering the numerous efforts the field of psychology is making to train multiculturally competent psychologists from mainstream and majority backgrounds, it is encouraging to find some support for the significant influence of training variables, above and beyond organismic variables, on multicultural counseling competence. Additional research may be able to establish that educational and clinical experiences, presumably those fostering personal reflection on issues of diversity, can contribute to the development of multicultural competence, even when psychologists lack some of those personal attributes that are commonly associated with cultural sensitivity.

The Need for Multiple Indices of Multicultural Counseling Competence: Assessment Issues and Recommendations for Future Research

A research question was posed in this study to ascertain if psychologists' demonstrated skill with counseling diverse populations might vary depending on the particular presenting concerns of the client. Use of the CSRS provided an opportunity to assess psychologists' multicultural counseling skill in response to four different client circumstances, in which each circumstance called for a unique, specific, and culturally sensitive counseling approach. Findings from this study did in fact indicate that psychologists' ability to identify an appropriate multicultural strategy differed, depending on the specific characteristics of diversity displayed by the clients described in each vignette. Specifically, psychologists scored significantly higher when responding to the Facilitator of Indigenous Support subscale of the CSRS than on all other three subscales of

the instrument (Consultant, Change Agent, and Facilitator of Indigenous Healing Support). This finding suggests that psychologists may only be comfortable expanding their traditional counseling strategies when dealing with a counseling situation that calls for preventative intervention strategies. Under the well-intentioned yet misguided concern that alternative counseling strategies might not provide immediate relief, perhaps psychologists become more cautious in their application of alternative counseling when a client is actively in distress. Certainly, further research exploring the circumstances under which psychologists most readily apply alternative and culturally sensitive counseling strategies is needed.

Extending this argument, research focused on the identification of multiple and varied indices of multicultural counseling competence could provide critical information needed to fully understand the development of these competencies. The use of a stringent instrument that measured demonstrated, not self-perceived, multicultural counseling competence was an important methodological strength of this study. However, multicultural counseling competencies most likely encompass more than just skill at selecting an appropriate multicultural counseling strategy, and future research using several indices of multicultural counseling would be beneficial. For example, it might also be useful for researchers to broaden their operationalization of multicultural counseling competence to include aspects of competence, including *relationship* variables, such as rapport-building skills with clients from different cultures and socioeconomic backgrounds, as well as intervention techniques, such as selection of counseling strategies.

It is recommended that researchers engaged in this effort continue to focus their attention on rigorous and specifically defined indices of multicultural counseling competencies. The

CSRS focuses on psychologists' skill level—in short, their ability to choose appropriate counseling strategies for use with ethnically diverse clients. Self-report measures of multicultural competence appear to have a wider focus in their aim of assessing one's attitude and knowledge, in addition to skill, in relation to multicultural counseling issues. It is possible that the CSRS could be a far more rigorous test of multicultural counseling competence than self-report measures. The use of such an instrument with participants who lack extensive training in multicultural counseling issues could fail to produce significant findings, as may have been the case in the current study. However, future studies might produce significant results based on this rigorous test of demonstrated multicultural counseling competence with a few methodological variations. For example, it would be recommended that such research investigations sample recent graduate or current psychology students given the presumption that less recent graduates would have limited exposure to the theoretical underpinnings of the CSRS.

Finally, it is recommended that researchers continue with the development of not only rigorous but also *behaviorally based* indices of multicultural counseling competence. Increasing evidence supports the concern that self-report measures of multicultural counseling competence are at best measures of psychologists' anticipated or desired competencies. Use of instruments requiring psychologists to provide *demonstrated* markers of their *actual* multicultural counseling competence would considerably diminish this concern. The CSRS is presented as a viable instrument to help researchers accomplish this goal of assessing actual, rather than self-perceived, multicultural counseling competencies. However, it should be noted that although the CSRS appears to be a valid measure of multicultural competence based on one's ability to choose an appropriate counseling strategy, it may

benefit the field to continue discussion regarding what constitutes appropriate multicultural counseling strategies.

REFERENCES

American Psychological Association, Office of Ethnic Minority Affairs. (1993). Guidelines for providers of psychological services to ethnic, linguistic, and culturally diverse populations. *American Psychologists, 48,* 45-48.

Atkinson, D. R., Kim, B. K. S., & Caldwell, R. (1998). Ratings of helper roles by multicultural psychologists and Asian American students: Initial support for the 3-dimensional model of multicultural counseling. *Journal of Counseling Psychology, 45,* 414-423.

Atkinson, D. R., Thompson, C. E., & Grant, S. K. (1993). A three-dimensional model for counseling racial/ethnic minorities. *The Counseling Psychologist, 21,* 257-277.

Behrens, J. T. (1997). Does the White racial identity scale measure racial identity? *Journal of Counseling Psychology, 44,* 3-12.

Bernal, M. E., & Padilla, A. M. (1982). Status of minority curricula and training in clinical psychology. *American Psychologist, 37,* 780-787.

Brannon, V. A. (1977). The influence of White counselor dogmatism in counseling Black clients who present differing problem situations (Doctoral dissertation, East Texas State University, 1977). *Dissertations Abstracts International, 38*(6a), 3281-3282.

Burkard, A.W., Ponterotto, J. G., Reynolds, A. L., & Alfonso, V. C. (1999). White counselor trainees' racial identity and working alliance perceptions. *Journal of Counseling & Development, 77,* 324-329.

Carlozzi, A. F. (1985). Dogmatism and the person of the counselor. *The High School Journal, 68,* 147-153.

Carlozzi, A. F., Campbell, J. J., & Ward, G. R. (1982). Dogmatism and externality in locus of control as related to counselor trainee skill in facilitative responding. *Counselor Education and Supervision, 21,* 227-236.

Constantine, M. G., & Ladany, N. (2000). Self-report multicultural counseling competence scales: Their relation to social desirability attitudes and multicultural case conceptualization ability. *Journal of Counseling Psychology, 47,* 155-164.

Constantine, M. G., & Ladany, N. (2001). New visions for defining and assessing multicultural counseling competence. In J. G. Ponterotto, J. M. Casas, L. A. Suzuki, & C. A. Alexander (Eds.), *Handbook of multicultural counseling* (2nd ed., pp. 482-498). Thousand Oaks, CA: Sage.

D'Andrea, M., Daniels, J., & Heck, R. (1990). *The Multicultural Awareness-Knowledge-Skills Survey.* Honolulu: University of Hawaii–Manoa.

Helms, J., & Carter, R. T. (1990). Development of the White Racial Identity Attitude Inventory. In J. Helms (Ed.), *Black and White racial identity: Theory, research, and practice* (pp. 67-80). Westport, CT: Greenwood.

Hills, H. I., & Strozier, A. L. (1992). Multicultural training in APA-approved counseling psychology programs: A survey. *Professional Psychology: Research and Practice, 23,* 43-41.

Kennard, B. D., Stewart, S. M., & Gluck, M. R. (1987). The supervision relationship: Variables contributing to positive versus negative experiences. *Professional Psychology: Research and Practice, 18,* 172-175.

Kiselica, M. S. (1998). Preparing Anglos for the challenges and joys of multiculturalism. *The Counseling Psychologist, 26,* 5-21.

Ladany, N., Brittan-Powell, C. S., & Pannu, R. K. (1997). The influence of supervisory racial identity interaction and racial matching on the supervisory working alliance and supervisee multicultural competence. *Counselor Education and Supervision, 36,* 284-304.

Ladany, N., Inman, A. G., Constantine, M. G., & Hofheinz, E. W. (1997). Supervisee multicultural case conceptualization ability and self-reported multicultural competence as functions of supervisee racial identity and supervisor focus. *Journal of Counseling Psychology, 44,* 284-293.

Leong, F. T. L., & Wagner, N. S. (1994). Cross-cultural counseling supervision: What do we know? What do we need to know? *Counselor Education & Supervision, 34,* 117-131.

Neville, H. A., Heppner, M. J., Thompson, C. E., Brooks, L., & Baker, C. E. (1996). The impact of multicultural training on White racial identity attitudes and therapy competencies. *Professional Psychology: Research and Practice, 27,* 83-89.

Ottavi, T. M., Pope-Davis, D. B., & Dings, J. G. (1994). Relationships between White racial identity attitudes and self-reported multicultural counseling competencies. *Journal of Counseling Psychology, 44,* 284-293.

Phinney, J. S. (1992). The multigroup ethnic identity measure: A new scale for use with diverse groups. *Journal of Adolescent Research, 7,* 156-176.

Ponterotto, J. G., Alexander, C. M., & Grieger, I. (1995). A multicultural competency checklist for counseling training programs. *Journal of Multicultural Counseling & Development, 23,* 11-20.

Ponterotto, J. G., & Casas, J. M. (1987). In search of multicultural competence within counselor education programs. *Journal of Counseling and Development, 65,* 430-434.

Ponterotto, J. G., Casas, J. M., Suzuki, L. A., & Alexander, C. M. (1995). *Handbook of multicultural counseling.* Thousand Oaks, CA: Sage.

Ponterotto, J. G., Rieger, B. P., Barrett, A., & Sparks, R. (1994). Assessing multicultural counseling competence: A review of instrumentation. *Journal of Counseling and Development, 72,* 316-322.

Ponterotto, J. G., Sanchez, C., & Magrids, D. (1991, August). *Initial development and validation of the Multicultural Counseling Awareness Scale (MCAS-B).* Paper presented at the annual convention of the American Psychological Association, San Francisco.

Pope-Davis, D. B., & Coleman, H. L. K. (1997). *Multicultural counseling competencies: Assessment, education and training, and supervision.* Thousand Oaks, CA: Sage.

Pope-Davis, D. B., & Dings, J. G. (1995). The assessment of multicultural counseling competencies. In J. G. Ponterotto, J. M. Casas, L. A. Suzuki, & C. M. Alexander (Eds.), *Handbook of multicultural counseling* (pp. 287-311). Thousand Oaks, CA: Sage.

Pope-Davis, D. B., & Ottavi, T. M. (1994). Examining the association between self-reported multicultural counseling competencies and demographic variables among counselors. *Journal of Counseling and Development, 72,* 651-654.

Pope-Davis, D. B., Reynolds, A. L., Dings, J. G., & Nielson, D. (1995). Examining multicultural counseling competencies of graduate students in psychology. *Professional Psychology: Research and Practice, 26,* 322-329.

Pope-Davis, D. B., Reynolds, A. L., Dings, J. G., & Ottavi, T. M. (1994). Multicultural competencies of doctoral interns at university counseling centers: An exploratory investigation. *Professional Psychology: Research and Practice, 25,* 466-470.

Pope-Davis, D. B., Vandiver, B. J., & Stone, G. L. (1999). White racial identity attitude development: A psychometric evaluation of two instruments. *Journal of Counseling Psychology, 46,* 70-79.

Rabinowitz, F. E., Heppner, P. P., & Roehlke, H. J. (1986). Descriptive study of process outcome variables of supervision over time. *Journal of Counseling Psychology, 33,* 292-300.

Ridley, C., Mendoza, D., & Kanitz, B. (1994). Multicultural training: Re-examination, operationalization, and integration. *The Counseling Psychologist, 22,* 227-289.

Rokeach, M. (1960). *The open and closed mind.* New York: Basic Books.

Sodowsky, G. R., Kuo-Jackson, P. Y., Richardson, M. F., & Corey, A. T. (1998). Correlates of self-reported multicultural competencies: Counselor multicultural social desirability, race, social inadequacy, locus of control racial ideology, and multicultural training. *Journal of Counseling Psychology, 45,* 256-264.

Sodowsky, G. R., Taffe, R., Gutkin, T., & Wise, S. (1994). Development of the multicultural counseling inventory: A self-report measure of multicultural competencies. *Journal of Counseling Psychology, 41,* 137-148.

Speight, S., Thomas, A. J., Kennel, R. G., & Anderson, M. E. (1995). Operationalizing

multicultural training in doctoral programs and internships. *Professional Psychology: Research and Practice, 26,* 401-406.

Stair, C. E. (1998). The relationship between counselor and subject dogmatism and the subject's perception of counselor expertness, attractiveness, and trustworthiness (Doctoral dissertation, Oklahoma State University, 1998). *Dissertation Abstracts International, 49*(1A), 42.

Stolenberg, C. D., McNeill, B. W., & Crethar, H. C. (1994). Changes in supervision as counselors and therapists gain experience: A review. *Professional Psychology: Research and Practice, 25,* 416-449.

Sue, D. W., Arredondo, P., & McDavis, R. J. (1992). Multicultural counseling competencies and standards: A call to the profession. *Journal of Counseling & Development, 70,* 477-486.

Tokar, D. M., & Swanson, J. L. (1991). An investigation of the validity of Helms' (1984) model of White racial identity development. *Journal of Counseling Psychology, 38,* 296-301.

Troldahl, V. C., & Powell, F. A. (1965). A short-form dogmatism scale for use in field studies. *Social Forces, 44*(2), 211-215.

Victor, J. B. (1976). Peer judgments of teaching competence as a function of field independence and dogmatism. *Journal of Experimental Education, 44,* 10-13.

Walton, L. M. (1986). The relationship between dogmatism and skill in discriminating among facilitative and nonfacilitative responses to client crisis statements (Doctoral dissertation, University of Virginia, 1986). *Dissertation Abstracts International, 47*(2A), 426.

Wright, W. (1975). Counselor dogmatism, willingness to disclose, and clients' empathy ratings. *Journal of Counseling Psychology, 22,* 390-394.

PART IV

Practice

One of the goals for this book was to provide readers with a comprehensive tool for addressing multiple contexts within which multicultural competencies are relevant. This section is an example of one context that often does not receive its due attention. The majority of people who experience counseling will do so through a relationship with a counseling practitioner. In fact, the greatest diversity of people who come into contact with counseling will be with professionals practicing through agencies, schools, hospitals, and private practitioners. The goal of this section is to provide practitioners and educators with a resource to address the myriad issues that arise in the application of multicultural competence in counseling. We are pleased to present chapters focusing on a wide range of settings within which counseling practice occurs.

Twelve chapters comprise this part. The first two chapters address professional issues faced by practitioners and the counseling profession as a whole—namely, accreditation and ethics. The chapter on accreditation (Chapter 19) discusses the issues that have shaped the place that multicultural competence has in current accreditation and considers its future as accreditation and training evolve. The chapter on ethics (Chapter 20) examines the shift in the construct of ethics in response to

the need for multicultural competent counseling practice.

The next two chapters discuss multicultural competence in relation to two often neglected arenas: consultation and managed care. In Chapter 21, the author focuses on complexities of integrating multicultural competence in psychologists' work as consultants. This chapter provides readers with insights that they may implement in developing and demonstrating competence in this work. Chapter 22 addresses the challenge and importance of multicultural counseling competencies, given the influence of managed care in the clinical setting. Because managed care is becoming more prevalent as a third party in the therapeutic process, the author of this chapter discusses the unique challenge of providing culturally competent counseling within the structure inherent in this type of system.

The fifth chapter in this part (Chapter 23) discusses the role of multicultural competence in counseling center services. Counseling centers often have dual functions, providing a wide range of services to students and providing a training environment for counseling trainees. Although counseling centers may vary widely in the types of services they offer and in the diversity of their clientele, this chapter illuminates issues and challenges in multicultural competence that are common within this type of environment.

The sixth chapter in this section (Chapter 24) focuses on multicultural competencies in the practice of supervision. This chapter recognizes the distinct contribution that supervision makes to practice and seeks to facilitate readers' understanding of the issues involved in the process and outcome of supervision.

The next five chapters in this section attend to the role of multicultural counseling competence in specific areas of counseling, including career counseling (Chapter 25), school counseling (Chapter 26), health psychology (Chapter 27), rehabilitation counseling (Chapter 28), and group counseling (Chapter 29). Multicultural competencies suggest many principles that are applicable to all counseling. However, there are also specific issues and concerns defined by the scope and presenting concerns typically seen by counselors and psychologists practicing in these specialties. It is hoped that by providing focused discussions, practitioners will be better able to apply and develop increased multicultural competence in their work.

The final chapter (Chapter 30) explores the issues that arise in counseling practice with clients who have been affected by discrimination and harassment in the workplace. Using two case examples as a foundation, the author provides a discussion of clinical issues that may arise as a result of experiencing discrimination in the workplace as well as during the subsequent evaluation and legal process.

19

Multicultural Competence and Accreditation in Professional Psychology

ELIZABETH M. ALTMAIER

University of Iowa

For the past 50 or so years, beginning in 1947, the American Psychological Association (APA) has "accredited" doctoral programs in professional psychology. The history of this activity has its roots in the articulation of standards for education in professional programs in law and medicine (Nelson & Messenger, 2003), where education was transformed from an apprentice-based system to a formalized structure with input from both those doing the training (faculty) and those receiving the products (the professional communities). Within the APA, specialized accreditation began with a request from the Veterans Administration (VA) in December 1945 to the Board of Directors of the APA for a list of institutions that, with some additional financial assistance from the VA, would be able to provide an adequate education for the psychologists needed by the VA to provide clinical services for its returning veterans. The then-named Committee on Graduate and Professional Training defined "domains" of training having primarily to do with staff, curriculum, and departmental facilities; considered applications from programs that wished to be defined as accredited; and published lists of such programs in publicly available documents. In 1947, a special committee authorized by the APA Board of Directors submitted what has come to be known as the Shakow Report (Committee on Training, 1947). This report, a predecessor to our current *Guidelines and Principles for Accreditation of Programs in Professional Psychology* (APA, 1997), set the foundation for 50 years of either progress or controversy, depending on one's perspective.

This chapter outlines the history of accreditation's attention or lack thereof to issues of diversity and multiculturalism in graduate education and training. Of particular interest will be the interrelationships of the criteria or standards for accreditation and the activities of the times (i.e., national conferences) that stimulated significant changes in the accreditation standards for graduate education, predoctoral internship training, and postdoctoral residency training.

HISTORICAL DEVELOPMENT OF ACCREDITATION STANDARDS

The first set of accreditation "standards" was published in 1947. These standards were not prescriptive in nature. Rather, the committee articulated what it termed *general principles* that it believed should characterize all accredited graduate programs irrespective of the details of implementation that would necessarily vary among programs. These standards had to do with curriculum (e.g., areas of study such as research methods and diagnostic methods) and with integration (e.g., contact with "normal material" as well as "clinical material").

Most relevant to our discussion of multicultural competencies were principles related to trainees' personal qualities and to the social implications of training. Because of their importance, these are quoted in their entirety:

> The general atmosphere of the course of training should be such as to encourage the increase of maturity, the continued growth of the desirable personality characteristics earlier considered.
>
> The program should do everything possible to bring out the responsibilities associated with the activities of the psychologist. There should be persistent effort to have the student appreciate that his findings make a real difference to a particular person and to the person's immediate group.

> In addition to the research implications of the data, he should become sensitive to their social implications; he must acquire the ability to see beyond the responsibilities he owes to the individual patient to those which he owes to society. (Committee on Training in Clinical Psychology, 1947, pp. 544-545)

Although these standards do not match with current emphases on diversity within training, they do argue that trainees should be personally mature and psychologically healthy and that trainees should be encouraged to think about and, indeed, emphasize the societal implications of their research and practice.

History tells us that the early emphasis on principles of quality training rather than prescriptive standards did not fare well within accreditation activities. In fact, departments were quickly arguing over the judgments of the then-named Committee on Training in Clinical Psychology. Because the principles were not specific, there was considerable room for the professional judgment of the committee in making accreditation decisions. These decisions, when made against programs, were controversial in that the committee had no clear criteria against which to defend its decisions. In addition, many in the larger psychological community questioned the need to make these judgments at all. This argument was that it should be up to each program to determine for itself what qualities it wished to possess and then to engage in such activities as were necessary to bring about desired outcomes. The committee responded with a vigorous defense: "We are convinced of the importance of setting standards and evaluating performance in clinical training. In fact, we see this process as inevitable if clinical psychology is to establish itself soundly and be a credit to psychology as a whole" (Committee on Training in Clinical Psychology, 1949, p. 340). Eventually, after much controversy, the committee itself came to believe that its work was ineffective and formally asked to be disbanded in 1960. As our continuing history of accreditation indicates, this request was refused.

In the middle stages of accreditation, during the 1960s and 1970s, a societal context began to exert considerable influence on accreditation standards and processes. In contrast to the early stages, when the committee attempted to determine principles of quality training, the practitioner community and the training programs began to articulate necessary changes during the middle stages. First, during these years, there was a dramatic increase in the number of accredited programs in all three areas of professional psychology then accredited: clinical psychology, counseling psychology, and school psychology. Second, there was an increase in activities related to the self-reflection of psychologists about their profession in the form of a series of national conferences. Each of these conferences (Greyston Conference: Thompson & Super, 1964; Chicago Conference: Hoch, Ross, & Winder, 1966; Vail Conference: Korman, 1976) resulted in position statements and advocacy activities that promoted various agendas. Third, the national landscape at this time was one of heightened attention to the rights of various groups of individuals and the responsibilities of psychology to be attentive to these rights.

In response, psychology promulgated two sets of criteria within a 10-year period, the 1973 criteria and the 1979 criteria. These criteria came about from the work of a commission on accreditation in psychology established in 1969. The commission articulated new values that should be fostered by specialized accreditation: that accreditation should stimulate effectiveness in the institution as a whole, foster innovation in training, clarify to the public what types of activities are performed by psychologists, and enable students to select programs that matched their own interests and training goals (e.g., facilitate good consumer choices among students). The 1973 criteria also contained the first explicative language regarding desired qualities for faculty and students:

> Faculty. The quality and diversity of the relevant faculty are perhaps the most important factors in the development of a professional psychologist.
>
> The faculty should include a sufficient number of mature, full-time persons who are clearly committed to and identified with the program.
>
> The director of the professional psychology training program should be a tenured member of the university faculty with broad training and experience in his area of specialization.
>
> Members of the professional faculty should not only have a sound background of training and experience, but should stay abreast of new developments in their field. . . .
>
> Students. The healthy growth of professional psychology over the past two decades has naturally led to the creation and development of diverse training programs. Consequently, each training program has the responsibility to inform prospective students of its specific goals and unique style and to provide continuous opportunity for its students to determine how their own professional aspirations can be achieved within the resources of the program. The materials used in the recruitment of students should convey information clearly and accurately about the goals of the program, the training resources available, and the requirements which the students are expected to meet. Selection procedures should reflect sound, ethical psychological practice. There should be no discriminatory practices by sex, race, religion, or ethnic background in any aspect of the program. (APA, 1973, pp. 15, 17)

These 1973 criteria contain the first instance of language governing program operation, approaching our current understanding of diversity within training. The nondiscriminatory clause applied only to students, not faculty or staff, and there were no standards on curriculum, practicum training, or internship training when multicultural competence was at issue. As was true for the earlier accreditation criteria, the standards were principled in nature, not prescriptive, and were meant to describe quality training in general. However, the 1973 criteria did reflect a growing interest in attending to nondiscriminatory practices in student selection and evaluation.

Two forces during the 1970s caused psychology to articulate a new set of accreditation criteria. The first force was an increased focus on credentialing. In the mid-1970s, the National Register and the APA cosponsored a conference on credentialing and licensure. Fretz and Mills (1980) outlined several distinct environmental pressures that led to the development of newer, more formalized, standards for evaluating both training programs and the credentials of their graduates. The first and perhaps most important pressure was the rise of third-party payments for the provision of psychological services. When health insurance companies began reimbursing providers other than physicians, both companies and state licensing boards experienced pressure to identify suitably prepared and credentialed practitioners. A related pressure was that psychologists were experiencing difficulties in establishing a right to practice. Individual states were addressing issues of practitioners' right to practice, and the substantive skills and credentials of those practitioners were of interest. A third environmental pressure was the changing job market. For most psychologists prior to the 1970s, job placements were either in academic settings, including counseling centers, or in institutional practice settings. However, as independent practice began to be an attractive option, the numbers of practitioners and of programs preparing practitioners also began to increase.

The second force behind the articulation of new accreditation standards was the outgrowth of the 1973 Vail Conference (Korman, 1976) on patterns of training in psychology. That conference gave voice to many psychologists who believed that traditional patterns of training discriminated against many people: persons of color, women, non-traditional-age students (e.g., returning adult learners), and people with practitioner-only career interests. Counseling psychology, as a specialty, was especially responsive to issues regarding empowering groups of people previously in disempowered status. As an example, counseling psychologists established an ad hoc committee on women that focused on the provision of support to women in various capacities: encouraging women to be authors and editors, encouraging the development of guidelines for providing counseling and psychotherapy to women clients, and initiating a job referral service (Newsletter, 1977).

In 1976, the APA convened another task force on accreditation. This task force considered several issues during its development of an alternate set of accreditation standards. The first issue was one of generality versus specificity. This issue had to do with the degree to which accreditation standards should be general (e.g., should articulate standards of quality training) or specific (e.g., should establish acceptable minimum levels of practicum training). The second issue was the model of training. Can standards for accreditation be established that will "work" for both traditional research-oriented programs in university settings as well as innovative practitioner-based programs in freestanding schools of psychology? The third issue, and the one most relevant to this chapter, is that of the best way for accreditation to promote attention to issues of diversity within training programs. This issue was articulated in ways that went beyond minimal nondiscriminatory language; rather, the issue was promoted as encompassing curriculum, faculty recruitment and retention, and student recruitment and retention. The result was the development of an accreditation criterion, Criterion II, which had far-reaching consequences.

Thus, the early history of accreditation criteria was one of a movement away from the articulation and adoption of principles presumed to underlie all quality training programs toward a set of specified, consensually defined standards and definitions. Although this movement had clear societal influences, as well as influences within the profession, its adoption had implications both for the practice of specialized accreditation within psychology and for the specific areas of focus. However, the early history, although considering relevant personal qualities of trainees as important, did not attend to what might be considered contemporary perspectives on multiculturalism.

CRITERION II

The 1979 criteria for accreditation for the first time attended explicitly to issues of diversity and multicultural competencies among faculty and students. The specific criterion is as follows:

> As a science and profession, psychology deals with the full range of human variability. It follows that social responsibility and respect for cultural and individual differences are attitudes which must be imparted to students and trainees and be reflected in all phases of the program's operation: faculty recruitment and promotion, student recruitment and evaluation, curriculum, and field training. Social and personal diversity of faculty and students is an essential goal if the trainees are to function optimally within our pluralistic society. Programs must develop knowledge and skills in their students relevant to human diversity such as people with handicapping conditions; of

differing ages, genders, ethnic and racial backgrounds, religions, and life-styles; and from differing social and individual backgrounds. These principles are embodied and elaborated in the specific guidelines and criteria that follow and are consistent with the purposes of the Association as stated in Article 1 of the Bylaws: "The objects of the American Psychological Association shall be to advance psychology as a science and profession and as a means of promoting human welfare by the encouragement of psychology in all its branches in the broadest and most liberal manner." (APA, 1980, pp. 4-5)

As such, Criterion II attempted to establish a set of principles related to diversity that were meant to amplify other criteria relevant to the faculty, students, curriculum, practicum and internship training, and institutional setting. These principles were that programs had the responsibility to select students and to recruit faculty who would embody a respect for cultural differences. These principles also mandated that programs construct curriculum and field experiences that would allow students to gain knowledge and skills relevant to clients of varying and diverse backgrounds: persons of color, persons with disabilities, persons of varying sexual orientation, persons of varying social class, and persons of varying religious and cultural background.

The Committee on Accreditation's decision making related to accreditation in general was governed by a set of procedures that are relevant to this discussion. First, the program to be evaluated engaged in a process of self-study, determining for itself and describing the degree to which and the means by which the program met the various required criteria for accreditation. Second, the program was site visited by a team of knowledgeable psychologists for 2 days. During that time, the site visitors endeavored to represent the Committee on Accreditation by determining the program's actual functioning in the required areas through discussions with program faculty and students and with institutional representatives. Third, the site visitors provided the committee with a report of their findings, to which the program was given an opportunity to respond. Finally, the committee reviewed the program's self-study, the site visitors' report, and the program's response and rendered a decision regarding the program's adherence to the required criteria.

Because programs, site visitors, and even committee members had occasional difficulties in determining how best to judge program compliance with the required criteria, the committee gave guidance to its various consumers in the form of comments meant to amplify their operating policies. In 1986, for example, the *Accreditation Handbook* contained the following guidance regarding compliance with Criterion II:

> In reviewing program's compliance with Criterion II, it is important for the Committee to obtain a clear understanding of the extent to which women, ethnic minorities, persons with disabilities, and self-identified gay and lesbian faculty and students are afforded equal treatment and status in the program and do not suffer discrimination.
>
> The Committee requires information about the procedures by which programs recruit women and ethnic minorities. In other words, what procedures does the program employ to recruit women and ethnic minorities? Were offers made to qualified women and ethnic minorities? If such offers were not successful, did the program investigate the reasons why there were unsuccessful? Has the program considered the creative use of consultants who are women or ethnic minorities? Has the program included materials in its brochure that might attract qualified women and ethnic minority students?
>
> The Committee also requires information about how a program's curriculum

offerings and the practicum and internship training experiences of their students address issues of cultural and individual differences. Since the Criteria do not require specific courses in this area, the method of addressing these issues is left to the discretion of the program. However, the program must demonstrate how that is accomplished.

> The site visitors should also obtain an impression of the climate of the program in regard to issues raised by Criterion II. One means of achieving this end is to speak candidly with students and faculty who represent special populations. Site visitors are also requested to question students about their assessment of the program's success in preparing them to teach and work with special populations. (APA, 1986, p. 24)

The time period of the 1980s and early 1990s was one of considerable tension over accreditation activities. Although this tension occurred over the boundaries of accreditation (what types of programs should be accredited) and the control of accreditation (which professional organizations should control accreditation of psychology graduate training programs and psychology predoctoral internships), it was especially present concerning judgments made by the Committee on Accreditation with regard to program compliance with Criterion II. The committee itself created a Subcommittee on Cultural and Individual Differences to review Criterion II in light of the considerable controversy over the criterion. This group was charged with identifying the rationale, meaning, scope, and implementation of Criterion II and reported to the accreditation publics in the summer 1991 *Capsule* newsletter (the newsletter sent by the Office of Accreditation to all accredited programs).

In this report, the subcommittee vigorously defended Criterion II as necessary to promote attention to issues of diversity among faculty, students, and training in predoctoral psychology programs. The subcommittee went on to offer thoughts about the implementation of Criterion II in areas of institutional context, faculty, students, and curriculum/field training. Although the tone of this report was constructive, the committee in general took a firm, affirmative view of the need for a focus on diversity in training:

> The key phrases in Criterion II are . . . "must be imparted," . . . "must be developed," and . . . "in all phases of a program's operation." How programs demonstrate this compliance will depend in part on how they are organized and structured, their model of training and specialty area of focus, and their setting; but compliance needs to be demonstrated. Not only do programs need to impart knowledge, skills, and productive attitudes about diverse populations, their accreditation should also be based in part on evidence that discriminatory policies pertaining to age, gender, ethnicity, race, sexual orientation, and religion do not exist in their institution, programs, and service settings, except as exempted by law. (*Capsule*, Summer, 1991, p. 3)

Despite the vigorous defense of a model of training that resembles the multicultural competency model predominant today, the committee came under ongoing criticism for its decisions regarding program compliance with Criterion II. In 1993, there was an exchange of opinion in *Professional Psychology* regarding the role of Criterion II in accreditation (Altmaier, 1993; Clements & Rickard, 1993; Payton, 1993; Rickard & Clements, 1993). The concerns regarding the implementation of Criterion II primarily revolved around the purported "vagueness" of the criterion and the corresponding degree to which site visitors and committee members must use their judgment in determining program compliance. An additional concern was that the then-shared understanding of the "minimal level of compliance" with the criterion was that programs must have at least one faculty member of color. Rickard and Clements (1993) specifically criticized the emphasis on racial diversity among faculty rather than a broad understanding of the types of diversity faculty could embody.

In response, Altmaier (1993) outlined three aspects of Criterion II. First, she argued that the criterion considers a range of program functioning: essential attitudes about social responsibility and respect for individual differences; social and personal diversity of faculty, students, and staff; and "intentional and systematic instruction in theory, research, and practice relevant to cultural and individual differences" (p. 127). Although Altmaier acknowledged that the committee must use professional judgment regarding the program's compliance with Criterion II, in reality, the committee used professional judgment for all the criteria as none were so prescriptive that judgment was avoided. Finally, Altmaier noted that the criteria themselves were going to be undergoing revision in a process that would allow a reexamination of all accreditation criteria.

The committee continued to rely on Criterion II as a means to encourage programs to promote attention to diversity among faculty and students and the inclusion of multicultural knowledge, skills, and attitudes among the curriculum and fieldwork required by the program. However, the broader psychological community was slower to embrace this aspect of accreditation. The tension over the 1979 criteria eventually gave rise to a complete reconsideration of scope, criteria, and procedures. However, it is important to note the progress made during the 1980s and 1990s in terms of the increased commitment of site visitors to closely examine this aspect of program compliance with accreditation standards, as well as the commitment of Committee on Accreditation members and many programs to bring issues of diversity among students and faculty as well as attention to multiculturalism to the forefront in judging the quality of training programs.

GUIDELINES AND PROCEDURES

In 1989, the Interim Board of Educational Affairs decided to reexamine the content and governance of accreditation within the APA. It convened, in 1990, a small group of people who represented the full spectrum of accreditation "constituencies": graduate education and academic departments and professional schools, public consumers of psychology's professional services, and professional practice, both institutional and independent. This group developed a proposal for a new governing body for accreditation, with an enlarged Committee on Accreditation, more representation on the new committee from defined constituent groups, and the charge of a complete overhaul of accreditation scope, criteria, and procedures. After governance groups both inside and outside of the APA had an opportunity for comment, the APA Council of Representatives voted in 1991 to establish a new body to govern accreditation matters within the APA. The new body was also named the Committee on Accreditation, and it was constituted to have 21 members representing a range of psychological constituencies, graduate students themselves, and the public.

This new group went to work on its assigned task and developed a new model for accreditation, with a new scope for accreditation activities, new criteria (the *Guidelines and Principles*), and new procedures for a variety of accreditation-related responsibilities (program review, site visitor training, site visitor evaluation, office operations). There were several definite changes in the new system of accreditation. First, the scope of accreditation was broadened to include "emerging substantive

areas of psychology" in addition to the then currently accredited school, counseling, and clinical psychology programs. Second, accreditation was continued for predoctoral internship programs and extended to postdoctoral residencies. Third, the philosophy of reviewing programs in their adherence to quite specific criteria was altered to an outcomes-based model in which programs articulated their model of training, the evidence on which they would decide that their model was "working," and the actual judgments made by faculty on program effectiveness.

The new guidelines also gave an enhanced role to the program's demonstrated effectiveness in the area of cultural and individual differences and diversity. The overall standard is that the program "recognizes the importance of cultural and individual differences and diversity in the training of psychologists." This standard must be demonstrated in two ways. First, programs must have made "systematic, coherent, and long-term efforts" to recruit and retain students and faculty of differing ethnic, racial, and personal backgrounds. The program must also "ensure a supportive and encouraging learning environment appropriate for the training of diverse individuals" (APA, 1997, p. 9). Second, programs must have a "thoughtful and coherent plan to provide students with relevant knowledge and experiences about the role of cultural and individual diversity in psychological phenomena" (p. 9) in both the science and practice of psychology. Each of these standards, as mentioned earlier, must be in the program's objectives as both a goal and as documented effectiveness. Thus, programs typically demonstrate the "thoughtful and coherent plan" in terms of curriculum, documented with course syllabi, and with practicum, documented with evaluation forms and with logs of experience with diverse clients.

In terms of multicultural competencies, how much closer are these accreditation standards to what might be considered ideal?

There are both definitional and structural improvements of the current system of accreditation over its predecessors regarding multicultural competencies. First, the standards "move" along with advances in thinking regarding multicultural competencies. As psychological knowledge about the roles of cultural and individual diversity increases, programs will be held accountable to enhance their curriculum and training in much the same way as they are held accountable to enhance curricula and training in testing, treatment, research methods, and so on as knowledge in those areas increases. Second, the program must provide both specific objectives for training and the means by which the faculty gather data on whether the objectives are met. Thus, advances in assessing multicultural competencies have a natural "home" in the most recent articulation of accreditation standards as these assessment methods can be incorporated into training programs for use as documentation of meeting training objectives.

However, as with previous systems of accreditation—and, in fact, more so than before—the enforcement of the *Guidelines and Principles* rests on the Committee on Accreditation's personal commitment to keeping the issue of high priority for the psychological community and in keeping site visitors current on evaluation methods. Thus, a program's planned objectives and evaluation methods in this area must be judged by site visitors and the committee itself with the same rigor as the other standards of the *Guidelines and Principles*. Thus, in a sense, the "jury is still out" on whether the new accreditation methods will enhance the acquisition of multicultural knowledge, skills, and attitudes among trainees more than was previously the case.

CONCLUSION

The best use of accreditation is as a voluntary system of peer review, whereby programs choose to explain themselves to peers within a set system of evaluation standards and receive helpful advice from peers on how to improve their functioning. However, with the increasing use of accreditation as a "gatekeeper" to licensing, third-party reimbursement, and other professional outcomes, the peer review aspect of accreditation may be left behind. Although the accreditation criteria themselves encourage creativity, innovation, and modernization in training methods and curricula, these innovations can only be achieved in an atmosphere that allows innovation to flourish. It is likely that the next 20 years will give psychology the best picture of how the activities of accreditation will enhance or detract from quality graduate education and internship and postdoctoral training. For psychologists committed to the need for increased attention to multicultural issues, the performance of the new system of accreditation will be a pivotal test of the impact of accreditation on training and education in psychology.

REFERENCES

Altmaier, E. M. (1993). The role of Criterion II in accreditation. *Professional Psychology: Research and Practice, 24,* 127-129.

American Psychological Association (APA). (1973). *Accreditation procedures and criteria.* Washington, DC: Author.

American Psychological Association (APA). (1980). *Accreditation handbook.* Washington, DC: Author.

American Psychological Association (APA). (1986). *Accreditation handbook* (Rev. ed.). Washington, DC: Author.

American Psychological Association (APA). (1997). *Guidelines and principles for accreditation of programs in professional psychology.* Washington, DC: Author.

Clements, C. B., & Rickard, H. C. (1993). Criterion II: A principle in search of guidelines. *Professional Psychology: Research and Practice, 24,* 133-134.

Committee on Training in Clinical Psychology. (1947). Recommended graduate training program in clinical psychology. *American Psychologist, 2,* 539-558.

Committee on Training in Clinical Psychology. (1949). Doctoral training programs in clinical psychology: 1949. *American Psychologist, 4,* 331-341.

Fretz, B. R., & Mills, D. H. (1980). Professional certification in counseling psychology. *The Counseling Psychologist, 9,* 2-17.

Hoch, E. L., Ross, A. O., & Winder, C. L. (Eds.). (1966). *Professional preparation of clinical psychologists.* Washington, DC: American Psychological Association.

Korman, M. (Ed.). (1976). *Levels and patterns of professional training in psychology.* Washington, DC: American Psychological Association.

Nelson, P. D., & Messenger, L. C. (2003). Accreditation in psychology and public accountability. In E. M. Altmaier (Ed.), *Fifty years of accreditation: Psychology's commitment to excellence in graduate education* (pp. 7-37). Washington, DC: American Psychological Association.

Newsletter for Division 17 Ad Hoc Committee on Women. (1977). *The Counseling Psychologist, 7,* 109-110.

Payton, C. R. (1993). Review of APA Accreditation Criterion II. *Professional Psychology: Research and Practice, 24,* 130-132.

Rickard, H. C., & Clements, C. B. (1993). Critique of APA Criterion II: Cultural and individual differences. *Professional Psychology: Research and Practice, 24,* 123-126.

Thompson, A. S., & Super, D. E. (Eds.). (1964). *The professional preparation of counseling psychologists: The report of the 1964 Greyston Conference.* New York: Columbia University Press.

20

Ethics and Multicultural Counseling Competence

EDWARD A. DELGADO-ROMERO

University of Indiana–Bloomington

ETHICS AND THE MULTICULTURAL COUNSELING COMPETENCIES

It is a time of change within the counseling profession. The Association of Multicultural Counseling and Development (a division of the American Counseling Association [ACA]) is updating the operationalization of the multicultural counseling competencies (Arredondo et al., 1996; Roysircar-Sodowsky et al., 2002; Sue, Arredondo, & McDavis, 1992), and the American Psychological Association (APA) is in the process of revising its ethics code (APA, 2002). The general issue of what constitutes multicultural counseling competency (MCC) is under discussion (Ridley, 2002), and the empirical basis and applicability of the MCCs are being challenged (Weinrach & Thomas, 2002). In the larger society, the United States continues to deal with the aftermath of

the September 11, 2001, terrorist attacks and the looming threat of both domestic and international conflict. Profound demographic changes in the United States are becoming evident as the results of the 2000 census demonstrate a rapidly changing ethnic and racial profile (e.g., U.S. Bureau of the Census, 2001). It is truly a time of uncertainty, conflict, and change.

In the midst of the fast-paced political, social, and demographic change, counseling professionals continue to aspire to provide competent services to their clients, design and implement research and training agendas, and implement programming. During times of change, ethics codes, ethical standards, and other guidelines (such as the MCCs) can provide the profession with guidance and a stabilizing influence.

The purpose of this chapter is to examine the intersection of professional ethics and the

MCCs. To achieve this objective, I have organized the chapter into three major sections. First, the domain of ethics and MCC is defined. Second, professional training and how professionals develop competence in the domain are examined. Third, evaluation and how competence in the domain is determined are discussed.

WHAT IS THE DOMAIN OF ETHICS AND MULTICULTURALISM?

General Ethical Principles

The practice of psychology has traditionally been guided by principle ethics. In their work in biomedical ethics, Beauchamp and Childress (1994) suggested that ethical decision making should be guided by four general, primary principles: respect for autonomy, nonmaleficence, beneficence, and justice. Respect for autonomy involves acknowledging and enabling the right of another person to act in accordance with his or her wishes; nonmaleficence involves the obligation to not cause harm to others intentionally; beneficence involves the obligation to help others, including preventing or removing harm; and justice involves the equitable distributions of burdens and benefits (Meara, Schmidt, & Day, 1996). In addition, Beauchamp and Childress suggested that there were two important secondary principles: fidelity and veracity. Fidelity involves keeping one's promise of trust in a relationship, and veracity involves telling the truth. Although Beauchamp and Childress suggested that fidelity was derived from respect from autonomy, Kitchener (1984) believed that fidelity was at the core of relationships between the therapist and client (Welfel & Kitchener, 1992). Therefore, Kitchener posited that fidelity should be elevated in importance to the status of a principle. Similarly, Meara et al. (1996) argued that veracity should also be elevated to a principle for psychologists.

Principle ethics can be described as a set of prima facie obligations one considers when confronted by an ethical dilemma (Meara et al., 1996). That is, principles are binding when considered in isolation; however when principles conflict, it is incumbent on the professional to make a determination on which principle will prevail. As Jordan and Meara (1990) noted, these dilemmas "typically emphasize the competing rights and claims of clients or institutions and the related responsibilities faced by service providers" (p. 107). For example, when a client reveals a concern to a psychologist in the course of therapy, in most cases, the psychologist is obligated to follow the principles of respect for autonomy by keeping the information confidential. However, if the client revelation consists of an imminent threat to the client (suicide) or others, then an ethical dilemma exists. The psychologist must balance the principle of respect for autonomy (keeping confidentiality) with the principle of nonmaleficence (preventing harm). Fortunately, in this case, the choice is clear as the psychologist is obligated (through ethics training and the force of law) to break confidentiality. However, as the reader can imagine, not all ethical dilemmas are this straightforward.

The aforementioned ethical principles are considered by many mental health professionals in the United States to be universal despite the principles being derived from a Western individualistic tradition (Meara et al., 1996). Therefore, the principles are applied to situations regardless of the backgrounds of the individuals involved. However, the universality of these principles has been called into question. Pedersen (1995) argued that ethical principles could be culturally determined or encapsulated:

Ethical principals generated in one cultural context cannot be applied to other substantially different cultural contexts without modification. In order to make these modifications, the counselor needs to distinguish between "fundamental" ethical principles, which are not negotiable, and "discretionary" aspects, which must be modified and adapted to each setting. . . . If the fundamental principles are compromised, the result will be a relativistic position in which justice is determined by whatever the common practice of a community may be. If the discretionary aspects are not modified, the result will be an absolutist domination by special interest groups that benefit from the status quo. (p. 34)

In response to the narrow focus on dilemmas and principles (Jordan & Meara, 1990), virtue ethics focuses on character traits and nonobligatory ideals that facilitate the development of ethical individuals (Meara et al., 1996). Meara et al. (1996) described the virtuous agent as one who is motivated to do what is good, possesses vision and discernment, realizes the role of emotion in ethical decision making, is self-aware, and is interdependent with her or his community or communities and understands the role of community in decision making. The reader will note that a virtue ethics perspective seems to be compatible with the multicultural counseling competencies, especially by emphasizing self-awareness and the role of community. The role of rules or principles is secondary to virtues. Examples of professional virtues include fidelity, prudence, discretion, perseverance, courage, integrity, public spiritedness, benevolence, humility, and hope (Jordan & Meara, 1990).

Meara et al. (1996) explained how an emphasis on principalism (DuBose, Hamel, & O'Connell, 1994) has the following effects: It leads to an overemphasis on individualism while de-emphasizing community, it accords a secondary status to religious traditions, it is dependent on rationality at the expense of emotion and care, and, far from being a universal perspective, principle ethics seems

firmly rooted in Western, U.S., Caucasian, and middle-class values. Meara et al. pointed out that virtue ethics is also derived from an individualistic tradition. However, they stated that the use of virtue ethics can provide a useful multicultural framework by making values explicit rather than implicit—thus fostering self-awareness and the examination of the differences and similarities between cultures—and a way to question and develop professional virtues while considering the virtues of other cultures. Ibrahim (1996) stated that both principle and virtue ethics are derived from a Western civilization perspective (focusing on Euro-Americans in the United States) and called for a paradigm shift in thinking about ethics and the creation of pan-cultural ethical assumptions.

Code of Ethics

Professional organizations in the mental health field attempt to find a balance between obligatory principles and aspirational character traits in their ethical codes of conduct (e.g., ACA, 1995; APA, 1992). For example, the ACA code instructs counselors to respect diversity (Section A.2), which includes both nondiscrimination (A.2.a) and respecting differences (A.2.b) as principles. Counselors are further instructed to actively understand the diverse cultural backgrounds of the clients with whom they work (A.2.b), which includes self-awareness. Thus, the ACA code instructs counselors to adhere to the principle of respecting diversity and aspire to have understanding of self and others.

Pedersen (e.g., 1995, 1997, 2002) has consistently addressed the ethical dilemma faced by multiculturally competent counselors as they attempt to follow ACA and APA ethical codes that aspire to be universal and address diversity issues but in reality reflect implicit (majority) cultural beliefs (see Pedersen, 2002, for a critique of APA and ACA ethical codes).

It is this dilemma that gave rise to the multicultural counseling competencies. Several authors (e.g., Sue et al., 1992; see Chapter 1, this volume) have pointed to the Vail conference of 1973 as the genesis of the MCC movement. At this conference, it was resolved that providing professional services to culturally diverse individuals is ethically inappropriate if the counselor is not competent to provide them and that cultural competence should be a part of graduate education in counseling (Korman, 1974). Therefore, the issues underpinning multicultural counseling competencies are issues of appropriate ethical conduct, which incorporate both obligatory behavior (principles, i.e., one should be competent to work with clients from a different culture) and aspirational traits (virtues, i.e., the development of an ethical individual).

Ethical Decision-Making Models

However, knowledge of ethical codes does not necessarily translate into appropriate ethical behavior (Blasi, 1980), nor do the APA or ACA ethics codes provide a hierarchical ranking of ethical principles to consider in the case of an ethical dilemma (interested readers should explore how the Canadian Psychological Association's code of ethics differs from APA and ACA codes, see Seitz & O'Neill, 1996; especially relative to multicultural issues, see Pettifor, 2001). Therefore, models of ethical decision making can provide a mechanism to translate ethical principles and virtues into action. Ridley, Hill, and Wiese (2001) proposed a model of reasoned application wherein competence is considered the superordinate ethical principle in multicultural assessments. Competence should also be the superordinate principle—that is, "the most crucial and relevant principle" (Ridley, Hill, et al., 2001, p. 31)—in multicultural counseling.

Ridley, Liddle, Hill, and Li (2001) have provided clarity in operationalizing terminology relative to ethical decision making, as well as both a descriptive and prescriptive model of multicultural ethical decision making. In this model, there are two dimensions: stages and processes. A *stage* is defined as a degree or level of development, and the two stages are critical reflection and creative problem solving. In the stage of critical reflection of the model, the decision maker evaluates the validity of the information, brings knowledge to bear on the situation, and recognizes the reality of reflection in action (i.e., the decision maker reflects on what she or he does while doing it). In the stage of creative problem solving, the decision maker practices flexibility in the representation of the problem, solicits suggestions, brainstorms with others involved in the situation about the problem and possible solutions, and analyzes the goodness of fit of each potential solution (e.g., by considering the ethical validity and pragmatic feasibility of each solution). A *process* is defined as a method of doing something involving steps or operations, and the two processes are the ethical consideration of cultural data and the ethical resolution of cultural conflicts. During the process of ethical consideration of cultural data, the decision maker explicates implicit assumptions about culture, identifies relevant cultural data, and considers all cultural data. During the process of ethical resolution of cultural conflicts, the decision maker attempts to prevent cultural conflicts; if and when conflict occurs, the decision maker defines cultural conflict contextually (rather than blaming the individuals involved), seeks solutions commensurate with treatment goals, and clarifies differences in cultural orientation. The two stages and processes overlap (respectively), meaning that they are separate but sometimes can occur simultaneously in an integrative fashion. Furthermore, the stages and processes interact with each other. For example, creative problem solving facilitates the ethical resolution of cultural conflicts. The Ridley, Liddle, et al. (2001) model also provides two entry points for ethical decision making—a potential ethical problem and an existing ethical problem—thus increasing the model's clinical utility. The authors underscored that making ethical decisions is a *"multicultural responsibility"* (p. 187).

Research

In this section, four issues related to research will be highlighted: Sue's (1999) criticism of psychology's emphasis on internal validity, concerns related to empirically supported treatments, research guidelines from ethnic minority psychological associations, and current directions in MCC research.

Stanley Sue (1999) pointed out that psychological research on ethnic minority populations lacks quality, quantity, and adequate funding. He argued that psychology's emphasis of internal over external validity was a limiting factor of ethnic minority research. Particularly salient to ethnic minority research is the assumption that research using White samples is universal, and research using ethnic minority samples is scrutinized for generalizability. Even within ethnic minority samples, the problem of inadequate participant specification is a potential problem. Sue advocated for greater emphasis on external validity while maintaining strong internal validity, in accordance with the scientific principles of skepticism and cross-validation. Sue stated that a wide range of research methodologies, including qualitative and ethnographic methods, should be used. At the heart of Sue's criticism is an ethical concern that flaws in the philosophy, methodology, and interpretation of psychological research can lead to inappropriate or negative outcomes for ethnic minority populations.

An example of the concern over the inappropriate generalization of research derived from White populations to ethnic minority populations is the debate regarding the empirically supported treatment (EST) movement. Wampold, Lictenberg, and Waehler (2002) documented the history of the EST movement, tracing the history of the movement both to the integration of science and practice and to the influence of managed health care. As the counseling profession attempts to define which interventions are empirically supported, there has been concern that ethnic and cultural issues are not being adequately addressed. Bernal and Scharrón-Del-Río (2001) asked, "Are empirically supported treatments valid for ethnic minorities?" (p. 328). Atkinson, Bui, and Mori (2001) stated a concern that EST will direct research attention away from cultural characteristics that might optimize counseling effectiveness. Quintana and Atkinson (2002) stated, in a reaction to a special issue of *The Counseling Psychologist*, that the proposed principles of empirically supported interventions (PESI) (Wampold et al., 2002) could possibly incorporate multicultural issues. However, they wondered how multicultural issues would actually be included in future intervention research, and they also expressed concerns about the first round of PESI research, which did not examine the effectiveness of interventions across cultural groups, and questioned whether the overemphasis on intervention research would draw attention away from cultural variables in the counseling process and outcome. Quintana and Atkinson made the strong statement that "multicultural counselors and therapists ignore the movement (EST), demanding more empirical accountability at their own peril because of the impact of this movement on the future funding of psychological services within and outside of managed care practices" (p. 289). One should note that the EST and PESI discussion is similar to the emic versus etic discussion in psychology. That is, are ESTs universal or culturally specific? Without sufficient emphasis on external validity and generality (Sue, 1999), researchers run the risk of assuming that treatments supported using majority participants will erroneously be applied to minority populations without modification.

One attempt to ensure that research is conducted in an ethically appropriate manner is the efforts by the Council of National Psychological Associations for the Advancement of Ethnic Minority Issues (CNPAAEMI). The CNPAAEMI is composed of the leaders of the five national ethnic minority psychological associations along with the APA, and the organization has published guidelines for research in ethnic communities (CNPAAEMI, 2000). This document is unique in that the authors are the representatives of the Society of Indian Psychologists, the Asian American Psychological Association, the Association of Black Psychologists, the Society for the Psychological Study of Ethnic Minority Issues (Division 45 of APA), and the National Hispanic Psychological Association. This document serves to supplement and expand on existing advisory principles and ethical considerations (i.e., Tapp, Kelman, Triandis, Wrightsman, & Coelho, 1974) for research with ethnic minority populations, with the added advantage of having members of the ethnic minorities in question generate the guidelines rather than outside experts. Although it is not inherently more ethically appropriate to have ethnic minority members participate in redefining guidelines for research, to the extent that the ethnic minority professional organizations accurately represent the cultures and concerns of ethnic minority populations, cultural encapsulation in regards to research can be prevented. CNPAAEMI is also producing guidelines for psychological practice.

Pope-Davis, Liu, Toporek, and Brittan-Powell (2001) highlighted what was missing from multicultural competency research, which they identified primarily as the client's perspective of multicultural counseling competencies. They recommended using real clients and real counseling situations and qualitative research methods. Doing so also requires the understanding that multicultural counseling often means multiple roles, and research needs to examine the counselor, client, and supervisor in multicultural counseling and training. Note that the concept of multiple roles can overlap with a culturally encapsulated view of "dual roles," and this recommendation in particular requires flexibility and cultural sensitivity (Pedersen, 2002). Pope-Davis et al. (2002) presented a study that examined the clients' perspectives of multicultural counseling competence and found that client experiences of MCC were contingent on their self-identified needs and how well their counselor met those needs. This study is important in several ways. Qualitative methods (grounded theory) were used, which, as Ponterotto (2002) pointed out, have the potential to "lead to a radical transformation and paradigm shift in the research-training components of counseling psychology programs" (p. 395). Specifically, Ponterotto identified the Pope-Davis et al. (2002) study as within the constructivist paradigm and elaborated the benefits of a constructivist paradigm to multicultural counseling research: entering the community of participants and becoming a cultural learner, describing the lived experience of participants in their own words, sensitizing the researcher to his or her own biases, and developing the potential for participant empowerment and researcher activism. These strengths are consistent with an emphasis on virtue ethics (Meara et al., 1996), which, as the reader might recall, emphasizes the virtuous agent as one who is motivated to do what is good, possesses vision and discernment, realizes the role of emotion in ethical decision making, is self-aware, and is interdependent with her or his community or communities and understands the role of community in decision making. In addition, the Pope-Davis et al. (2002) study, like the CNPAAEMI (2000) guidelines, gives voice to members of the ethnic minority population, which may help prevent cultural encapsulation in MCC research and produce ethically appropriate research and training.

Scope of Practice

This section generally focuses on issues related to the scope of practice of MCC and ethics issues and then specifically focuses on Weinrach and Thomas's (1996, 1998, 2002) criticism of MCC. Traditionally, the work in MCC has focused on the one-on-one counseling situation. However, with the expansion of the research and literature concerning MCC, the scope of practice issues has increased. This volume alone is testament to the broad range of practice issues being addressed: accreditation, consultation, private practice, managed health care, counseling centers, supervision, career counseling, school settings, health psychology, and rehabilitation counseling. One can find other practice issues and applications such as group counseling (Halcy-Banez, Brown, & Molina, 1999), family practice (Goodwin, 1997), racial ethical sensitivity (Brabeck et al., 2000), music therapy (Bradt, 1997), and undergraduate education (Estrada, Durlak, & Juarez, 2002) in the literature. In each case, careful consideration should be given to the ethical issues that accompany the particular application of the MCCs. For example, the limits of confidentiality are different in an individual therapy session than in conducting outreach in an ethnic minority community. Similarly, the limits of confidentiality differ from one-on-one sessions as compared to consultation or outreach. Therefore, it is strongly suggested that when authors explore the application of the MCCs into a new area of practice, they should specifically identify the unique ethical aspects that may arise. For example, Tozer and McClanahan

(1999) explicated ethical issues with regards to conversion therapy, Bradt (1997) explicated ethical issues with regards to music therapy, and Ridley, Hill, et al. (2001) explicated ethical issues in multicultural assessment.

Weinrach and Thomas (1996, 1998, 2002) have been outspoken critics of diversity-sensitive counseling generally and the MCCs specifically. In their latest work (Weinrach & Thomas, 2002), they criticized the MCC emphasis on race as an outdated concept, lacking empirical support for the efficacy of the competencies, and they subsequently strongly cautioned against the adoption of the MCCs by the American Mental Health Counselors Association (AMHCA). They argued that passage of the MCCs would adversely affect counseling practitioners. Furthermore, Weinrach and Thomas suggested that the adoption of the MCCs might be ethically inappropriate due to damage that might be caused to clients and the counseling profession.

Although it is essential for the counseling profession to continue to address and redefine the notion of multicultural competence, the majority of the Weinrach and Thomas (2002) criticism is unfounded and flawed. This section focuses on two issues that have ethical implications for practitioners: the assertion that race is an outdated issue in the United States and the politically charged and inaccurate characterization of multicultural psychology practice.

As mentioned earlier, the multicultural counseling competencies were created out of a desire to correct an ethically inappropriate situation: the provision of counseling service to racial and ethnic minority clients by racially and ethnically insensitive counselors. Racism and oppression based on race or ethnicity were a real phenomenon in the 1970s and continue to be challenging issues for counselors in a pluralistic society. Weinrach and Thomas's (2002) statement that the MCC emphasis on race is an "outmoded notion" (p. 24) is an indefensible assertion lacking any empirical basis. Although there have been changes in the manner in which oppression and racism have manifested themselves since the 1970s, work conducted on the modern manifestations of racism, such as aversive (Dovidio, Gaertner, Kawakami, & Hodson, 2002) or unintentional (Ridley, 1995) racism, highlights the continuing problem of race in the United States in the 21st century. The reader might be reminded of Helms's (1994) concern that an emphasis on multiculturalism, broadly defined, would obscure racial factors in the psychotherapy process and obscure race and culture as differential aspects of counseling competency (Helms & Richardson, 1997). It seems that Weinrach and Thomas, in attempting to broaden multiculturalism past the "outmoded" (p. 24) concept of race, are doing just that. Unless there is compelling evidence that racism and prejudice based on ethnicity are no longer problems that counselors and trainees deal with, the emphasis on race in multicultural competencies must be maintained to prevent ethically inappropriate professional behavior (i.e., practicing outside of one's competence, doing harm to others).

Weinrach and Thomas (2002) also warned practitioners against the "potential risks perpetuated in the name of multiculturalism" (p. 31) and cited female circumcision as an example. Nowhere in the MCC literature is this extreme practice advocated or endorsed. In fact, Nussbaum (1999) addressed the ethical aspects of this issue and found that relative to female genital mutilation, cultural sensitivity can exist and yet this cultural practice can be condemned. Unfortunately, using female genital mutilation as an example is typical of the highly politicized and sensationalistic rhetoric that characterizes Weinrach and Thomas's work. It is necessary to continue to question the philosophical, theoretical, and empirical basis of competency in general and MCCs specifically, and this matter should

continue to be addressed in the literature. If there is risk to clients, counselors, and counseling organizations in adopting the MCCs, these risks should be explicitly documented to prevent harm to clients, promote client welfare, and equitably distribute the burdens and benefits of MCC.

HOW DO PROFESSIONALS DEVELOP COMPETENCE IN THE DOMAIN?

Having defined a broad and expanding domain of ethics and MCC, we now turn our attention to how competency is developed in this domain by mental health professionals and trainees.

The authors of the original multicultural counseling competencies (Sue et al., 1992) were motivated by a general concern about the monocultural nature of training and, more specifically, by the findings that counselors were being therapeutically ineffective in working with racial and ethnic minority clients. If mental health practitioners are not competent to work with racial and ethnic minority clients, they run the risk of not helping clients or, even worse, harming clients. Clearly, this is ethically inappropriate, and as Sue et al. (1992) strongly stated, this situation might border on a violation of human rights. Arredondo (1999) later added, "In effect the profession was preparing individuals for unethical and potentially harmful behavior" and that a culturally competent counselor had to have the skill of providing "ethical and culturally relevant counseling through appropriate intervention strategies and techniques" (p. 103).

The original multicultural counseling competencies describe the attitudes and beliefs, knowledge, and skills necessary to become a culturally competent counselor (which the authors acknowledged was an active and ongoing process rather than an end state).

However, in describing the culturally skilled counselor, Sue et al. (1992) did not address how this competence was to be achieved. The operationalization of the MCCs and the addition of the dimensions of the personal identity model (Arredondo et al., 1996) included, as an appendix to the article, specific strategies to achieve the competencies and objectives (collapsed here from the original beliefs/knowledge and skills format of the original), which included the following:

1. familiarizing oneself with resources such as books, articles, and films;
2. attending conferences and workshops;
3. finding a mentor;
4. enrolling in ethnic studies courses;
5. spending time in other communities;
6. learning a second or third language;
7. seeking consultation from professionals or leaders within racial and ethnic minority communities;
8. conducting informal research;
9. communicating the need for cross-cultural training; and
10. joining professional organizations that have a cross-cultural focus.

Recently, Arredondo and Arciniega (2001) further refined strategies and techniques for counselor training based on the multicultural counseling competencies.

As Ridley and Kleiner pointed out in Chapter 1 of this volume, the articulation of MCCs was followed by efforts to define guidelines for multiculturally competent training programs and curricula. The research on guidelines, as well as the research and suggestions for best practices concerning the training, supervision, and education of multiculturally competent counselors, has been a major focus in the literature (e.g., Constantine, 1997; Ponterotto, Alexander, & Grieger, 1995; Pope-Davis & Coleman, 1997; Reynolds, 1995). However, relatively few publications have addressed the intersection of ethics education and MCC. It is often the case that ethical issues, such as competence, underlie the dimensions (beliefs, knowledge, and skills) of MCC, but rarely are those issues explicated clearly. Lack of definitional clarity and coherence (see Chapter 2, this volume) of multicultural counseling competence models also adds to the problem in explicating multicultural ethical issues.

Reynolds (1995) examined the challenges and strategies for teaching multicultural courses and examined ethical considerations in training. Reynolds cautioned that in undertaking multicultural education, faculty and other trainers should "strongly consider the ethical implications of their work" (p. 325), consider the quality of training and education (and the competence of those doing the training) being offered, attempt to infuse multicultural training within the curriculum, and focus on ethical concerns beyond competence. Reynolds then took the unusual step of addressing faculty multicultural competence. In the majority of the multicultural competency literature, the focus is usually on trainees, counselors, and supervisors and rarely on academic faculty. Reynolds argued, "Faculty competence is primary and most central to the issue multicultural training. It is vital that all counseling faculty members be retrained so that they may adequately address multicultural issues in their classroom and in their advising and dissertation mentoring" (p. 326). Reynolds then suggested that faculty need exposure to training design, group work, a systems perspective, cultural diversity content, an awareness of how multicultural issues affect the counseling process, and personal and professional experiences with multicultural populations. There seems to have been little follow-up in the multicultural counseling literature since Reynolds's (1995) work. Given that many counselors subscribe to a scientist/practitioner model of training, that academic faculty produce the majority of counseling research, and that there often exists power differentials between academic faculty, practitioners, and students, this lack of attention is troubling.

Trainees and practitioners hypothetically develop competence in the domain through a combination of coursework, clinical training, and supervision (e.g., Constantine, 1997; Daniels, D'Andrea, & Kyung, Kim, 1999; Hird, Cavalieri, Dulko, Felice, & Ho, 2001) at the prepracticum (see McCreary & Walker, 2001), practicum, internship, and postdoctoral levels; through the national licensure exam; and in continuing education necessary for licensure renewal. Although ethical and multicultural content is usually required for the development or demonstration of competence mentioned earlier, there is very little empirical evidence to demonstrate how (or how effectively) multicultural competency and ethics are combined in training.

Systemically, competence is reflected in the academic and training accreditation and credentialing process, as evidenced through accreditation through the American Psychological Association or Council for Accreditation of Counseling and Related Educational Programs (CACREP). Once again, it is unclear how or if the domain of ethics and MCC is taught, although each is a separate required component.

Several scholars (Ibrahim & Arredondo, 1986; Ridley, Espelage, & Rubinstein, 1997; Ridley, Mendoza, & Kanitz, 1994) have pointed out the need for multicultural ethical education. Ethics education is a required aspect of all counseling training, from coursework, clinical experience, licensure, and continuing education. MCC is fast becoming a required component of all levels of training and practice as well. However, of what would the teaching and training in the intersection of ethics and MCC (the domain of this chapter) consist?

Although many modern ethics texts and guides (e.g., Corey, Corey, & Callahan, 2003; Pope & Vasquez, 1998; Welfel, 2001) provide sections on multicultural issues within a general framework, there is a growing literature specifically on the topic of ethics and multicultural issues. A preliminary reading list for training in ethics and MCC would include the articles in Table 20.1.

Such a list serves as an important resource because of not only the wide range of issues covered but also the historical and developmental perspectives that one gains in review articles ranging from 1974 to 2002. The Internet can also provide valuable information regarding ethics, although specific Web sites relative to ethics and multicultural issues are lacking. Some examples of Web sites that address ethics issues are the APA Ethics Office (www.apa.org/ethics/), the ACA guide to ethical decision making (www.counseling.org/resources/pracguide.htm), and the Web site of author (Pope & Vasquez, 1998) and psychologist Kenneth Pope (kspope.com/), which features more than 40 different professional ethics codes. It is strongly suggested that organizations such as the APA (www.apa.org), the ACA (www.counseling.org), and specific multiculturally focused organizations such as the Association for Multicultural Counseling and Development (AMCD) (www.amcd-aca.org), Division 45 (the Society for the Psychological Study of Ethnic Minority Issues) of the APA (www.apa.org/divisions/div45/), and the Section of Ethnic and Racial Diversity (www.div17.org/serd) of the Society of Counseling Psychology (Division 17 of APA) include resources specific to ethics and multicultural issues. These preliminary suggestions of what specific training in this domain might consist of are primarily academic or informational. It is suggested that there must also be an experiential component to learning.

HOW IS COMPETENCE IN THE DOMAIN DETERMINED?

It seems that this area, the determination of competence in the domain of ethics and multicultural counseling competence, needs the

Table 20.1   A Reading List for Ethics and Multicultural Issues

Author(s)	Date
Bradt	1997
Burn	1992
Byington, Fischer, Walker, and Freedman	1997
Casas, Ponterotto, and Gutierrez	1986
Casas and Thompson	1991
Cayleff	1986
DuBose, Hamel, and O'Connell	1994
Evans and Foster	2000
Gil and Bob	1999
González	1997
Ibrahim	1996
Ibrahim and Arredondo	1986
Ivey	1987
Keitel, Kopala, and Adamson	1996
LaFromboise and Foster	1989
LaFromboise, Foster, and James	1996
La Roche and Turner,	2002
Lee and Kurilla	1997
May, Collins-Chobanian, and Wong	2002
Paradis	1981
Pedersen	1995
Pedersen	1997
Pedersen	2002
Pedersen and Marsella	1982
Pettifor	2001
Ridley	1985
Ridley, Hill, and Wiese	2001
Ridley, Liddle, Hill, and Li	2001
Ridley, Mendoza, and Kanitz	1994
Tapp, Kelman, Triandis, Wrightsman, and Coelho	1974
Vasquez	1996

most development and attention within the field. Without a mechanism to adequately determine competence, the study of ethics and MCC is open to charges that it lacks an adequate empirical basis (e.g., Weinrach & Thomas, 2002). Without a thorough definition and operationalization of competence, defining incompetence becomes extremely difficult, thus hampering efforts to prevent harm to clients or to identify or assist incompetent practitioners. In addition, the general question of how multicultural ethical competence differs from general ethics competence persists.

As Constantine and Ladany (2001) pointed out, very few programs that integrate multicultural issues into their academic curriculum are able to assess the effectiveness of the multicultural training they provide. This is the case for assessing MCC generally and the domain of ethics and MCC specifically. There are many available instruments to measure multicultural counseling competence (see Alexander & Suzuki, 2001; Constantine & Ladany, 2001), along with several methodological concerns (e.g., social desirability, Constantine & Ladany, 2000; the validity of supervisor ratings,

Constantine, 1997). However, there exists a need to empirically investigate the role of ethics education and training and ethical decision making relative to MCC.

For example, it seems that the process and outcome of using multicultural decision-making models (e.g., Ridley, Liddle, et al., 2001) are ideally suited for empirical investigation. One can hypothesize that training in multicultural ethical decision making should lead to better (more culturally sensitive, flexible, and creative) decision making. Previous empirical ethical decision-making research (e.g., Claiborn, Berberoglu, Nerison, & Somberg, 1994; Haas, Malouf, & Mayerson, 1988; Seitz & O'Neill, 1996) and multicultural moral development research (e.g., Evans & Foster, 2000) can serve as examples for the empirical demonstration of the efficacy of using a multicultural ethical decision-making model in training.

Rehabilitation counseling is one area that has provided an example of evaluating the effectiveness of a multicultural counseling ethics and assessment training workshop (Byington, Fischer, Walker, & Freedman, 1997). The training consisted of a 2-day, 15-hour workshop covering sociopolitical issues, ethical issues, and assessment. The authors created the Multicultural Counseling Ethics and Assessment Competency Scale (MCEACS) to evaluate the effectiveness of the training and also administered four established multicultural counselor assessments. Byington et al. also included a behavioral measure involving a written reaction (pretest and posttest) to a critical incident. The authors found significant differences between pretests and posttests on the MCEAS and higher posttest scores on the behavioral measure (but not significant differences). Although several of the methodological problems discussed above (i.e., the use of self-report measures) apply to this research, this study is one of the few examples in the literature to attempt to define, implement, and evaluate training in multicultural counseling and ethics.

The determination of competence in the domain of ethics and MCC is a challenge to the emerging field of MCC research and practice because it requires counselors, faculty, and trainees to think critically about both ethics and multiculturalism. It is also a challenge to create or adapt research methodology to operationalize, measure, and evaluate multicultural ethical competency. This task will require cognitive complexity (King & Shuford, 1996), creativity, flexibility, critical reflection, courage, and a willingness to consider and analyze all cultural data and possible solutions (Ridley, Liddle, et al., 2001), including alternate ethical guidelines (Pettifor, 2001), and it will involve both quantitative and qualitative methods of inquiry.

CONCLUSION

This chapter defined the domain of ethics and MCC, examined how professionals develop competence in this domain, and introduced how competence in this domain is evaluated. There was a great deal to say when defining the domain but less so about how competence is developed, and there were more questions than answers about evaluating competence. This situation parallels the state of inquiry into the developing field of ethics and multicultural competency. Ethical concerns gave rise to the multicultural counseling competencies, and careful attention to ethical aspects and ethical decision making in MCC will yield ethically appropriate outcomes and produce virtuous agents (students, clinicians, and faculty) who are self-aware, emotionally connected, community centered, and culturally sensitive.

REFERENCES

Alexander, C. M., & Suzuki, L. A. (2001). Measurement of multicultural constructs: Integration and research directions. In

J. G. Ponterotto, J. M. Casas, L. A. Suzuki, & C. M. Alexander (Eds.), *Handbook of multicultural counseling* (2nd cd., pp. 499-505). Thousand Oaks, CA: Sage.

American Counseling Association (ACA). (1995). *Code of ethics and standards of practice.* Alexandria, VA: Author.

American Psychological Association (APA). (1992). Ethical principles of psychologists and code of conduct. *American Psychologist, 47,* 1597-1611.

American Psychological Association (APA). (2002). Ethical principles of psychologists and code of conduct 2002. *American Psychologist, 57,* 1060-1070.

Arredondo, P. (1999). Multicultural counseling competencies as tools to address oppression and racism. *Journal of Counseling and Development, 77,* 102-108.

Arredondo, P., & Arciniega, G. M. (2001). Strategies and techniques for counselor training based on the multicultural counseling competencies. *Journal of Multicultural Counseling and Development, 29,* 263-273.

Arredondo, P., Toporek, R., Pack Brown, S., Jones, J., Locke, D. C., Sanchez, J., et al. (1996). Operationalization of the multicultural competencies. *Journal of Multicultural Counseling and Development, 24,* 42-78.

Atkinson, D. R., Bui, U., & Mori, S. (2001). Multiculturally sensitive empirically supported treatments: An oxymoron? In J. G. Ponterotto, J. M. Casas, L. A. Suzuki, & C. M. Alexander (Eds.), *Handbook of multicultural counseling* (2nd ed., pp. 542-574). Thousand Oaks, CA: Sage.

Beauchamp, T. L., & Childress, J. F. (1994). *Principles of biomedical ethics* (4th ed.). New York: Oxford University Press.

Bernal, G., & Scharrón-Del-Río, M. R. (2001). Are empirically supported treatments valid for ethnic minorities? Towards an alternative approach for treatment research. *Cultural Diversity and Ethnic Minority Psychology, 7,* 328-342.

Blasi, A. (1980). Bridging moral cognition and moral action: A critical review of the literature. *Psychological Bulletin, 88,* 1-45.

Brabeck, M. M., Rogers, L. A., Sirin, S., Henderson, J., Benvenuto, M., Weaver, M., et al. (2000). Increasing ethical sensitivity to racial and gender intolerance in schools: Development of the racial ethical sensitivity test. *Ethics & Behavior, 10,* 119-137.

Bradt, J. (1997). Ethical issues in multicultural counseling: Implications for the field of music therapy. *Arts in Psychotherapy, 24,* 137-143.

Burn, D. (1992). Ethical implications in cross-cultural counseling and training. *Journal of Counseling and Development, 70,* 578-583.

Byington, K., Fischer, J., Walker, L., & Freedman, E. (1997). Evaluating the effectiveness of multicultural counseling ethics and assessment training. *Journal of Applied Rehabilitation Counseling, 28,* 15-19.

Casas, J. M., Ponterotto, J. G., & Gutierrez, J. M. (1986). An ethical indictment of counseling research and training: The cross-cultural perspective. *Journal of Counseling and Development, 64,* 347-349.

Casas, J. M., & Thompson, C. E. (1991). Ethical principals and standards: A racial-ethnic minority research perspective. *Counseling and Values, 35,* 186-195.

Caylett, S. E. (1986). Ethical issues in counseling gender, race, and culturally distinct groups. *Journal of Counseling and Development, 64,* 345-347.

Claiborn, C. D., Berberoglu, L. S., Nerison, R. M., & Somberg, D. R. (1994). The client's perspective: Ethical judgments and perceptions of therapist practices. *Professional Psychology: Research and Practice, 25,* 268-274.

Constantine, M. G. (1997). Facilitating multicultural competency in counseling supervision: Operationalizing a practical framework. In D. B. Pope-Davis & H. L. K. Coleman (Eds.), *Multicultural counseling competencies: Assessment, education and training, and supervision* (pp. 310-324). Thousand Oaks, CA: Sage.

Constantine, M. G., & Ladany, N. (2000). Self-report multicultural counseling competence scales and their relations to social desirability and multicultural case conceptualization. *Journal of Counseling Psychology, 47,* 155-164.

Constantine, M. G., & Ladany, N. (2001). New visions for defining and assessing multicultural counseling competence. In J. G.

Ponterotto, J. M. Casas, L. A. Suzuki, & C. M. Alexander (Eds.), *Handbook of multicultural counseling* (2nd ed., pp. 482-498). Thousand Oaks, CA: Sage.

Council of National Psychological Associations for the Advancement of Ethnic Minority Issues (CNPAAEMI). (2000, January). *Guidelines for research in ethnic minority communities*. Washington, DC: American Psychological Association. Also available: www.apa.org/pi/oema/guidelinesremc.pdf

Corey, G., Corey, M. S., & Callahan, P. (2003). *Issues and ethics in the helping professions* (6th ed.). Pacific Grove, CA: Brooks/Cole.

Daniels, J., D'Andrea, M., & Kyung Kim, B. S. (1999). Assessing the barriers and challenges of cross-cultural supervision: A case study. *Counselor Education and Supervision, 38*, 191-204.

Dovidio, J. F., Gaertner, S. L., Kawakami, K., & Hodson, G. (2002). Why can't we just get along? Interpersonal and interracial distrust. *Cultural Diversity and Ethnic Minority Psychology, 8*, 88-102.

DuBose, E. R., Hamel, R. P., & O'Connell, L. J. (Eds.). (1994). *A matter of principles? Ferment in U.S. bioethics*. Valley Forge, PA: Trinity Press International.

Estrada, A. U., Durlak, J. A., & Juarez, S. C. (2002). Developing multicultural counseling competence in undergraduate students. *Journal of Multicultural Counseling and Development, 30*, 110-123.

Evans, K. M., & Foster, V. A. (2000). Relationship among multicultural training, moral development, and racial identity development of white counseling students. *Counseling and Values, 45*, 39-48.

Gil, E. F., & Bob, S. (1999). Culturally competent research: An ethical perspective. *Clinical Psychology Review, 19*, 45-55.

González, R. C. (1997). Postmodern supervision: A multicultural perspective. In D. B. Pope-Davis & H. L. K. Coleman (Eds.), *Multicultural counseling competencies: Assessment, education and training, and supervision* (pp. 350-386). Thousand Oaks, CA: Sage.

Goodwin, B. J. (1997). Multicultural competence in family practice. In D. T. Marsh &

R. D. Magee (Eds.), *Ethical and legal issues in professional practice with families* (pp. 75-93). New York: John Wiley.

Haas, L. J., Malouf, J. L., & Mayerson, N. H. (1988). Personal and professional characteristics as factors in psychologists' ethical decision making. *Professional Psychology: Research and Practice, 19*, 35-42.

Haley-Banez, L., Brown, S., & Molina, B. (1999). Association for specialists in group work principles for diversity-competent group workers. *Journal for Specialists in Group Work, 24*, 7-14.

Helms, J. E. (1994). How multiculturalism obscures racial factors in the psychotherapy process. *Journal of Counseling Psychology, 41*, 162-165.

Helms, J. E., & Richardson, T. Q. (1997). How "multiculturalism" obscures race and culture as differential aspects of counseling competency. In D. B. Pope-Davis & H. L. K. Coleman (Eds.), *Multicultural counseling competencies: Assessment, education and training, and supervision* (pp. 60-79). Thousand Oaks, CA: Sage.

Hird, J. S., Cavalieri, C. E., Dulko, J. P., Felice, A. A. D., & Ho, T. A. (2001). Visions and realities: Supervisee perspectives of multicultural supervision. *Journal of Multicultural Counseling and Development, 29*, 114-130.

Ibrahim, F. A. (1996). A multicultural perspective on principle and virtue ethics. *The Counseling Psychologist, 24*, 78-85.

Ibrahim, F. A., & Arredondo, P. M. (1986). Ethical standards for cross-cultural counseling: Counselor preparation, practice, assessment and research. *Journal of Counseling and Development, 64*, 349-352.

Ivey, A. E. (1987). The multicultural practice of therapy: Ethics, empathy and dialectics. *Journal of Social and Clinical Psychology, 5*, 195-204.

Jordan, A. E., & Meara, N. M. (1990). Ethics and the professional practice of psychologists: The role of virtues and principles. *Professional Psychology: Research and Practice, 21*, 107-114.

Keitel, M. A., Kopala, M., & Adamson, W. S. (1996). Ethical issues in multicultural assessment. In L. A. Suzuki, J. G. Ponterotto, &

Meller, P. J. (Eds.), *Handbook of multicultural assessment: Clinical, psychological, and educational applications* (pp. 29-38). San Francisco: Jossey-Bass.

King, P. M., & Shuford, B. C. (1996). A multicultural view is a more cognitively complex view. *American Behavioral Scientist, 40,* 153-164.

Kitchener, K. S. (1984). Intuition, critical evaluation and ethical principles: The foundation for ethical decisions in counseling psychology. *The Counseling Psychologist, 12,* 43-55.

Korman, M. (1974). National conference on levels and patterns of professional training in psychology: Major themes. *American Psychologist, 29,* 301-313.

LaFromboise, T. D., & Foster, S. (1989). Ethics in multicultural counseling. In P. Pedersen, J. Draguns, W. Lonner, & J. Trimble (Eds.), *Counseling across cultures* (3rd ed., pp. 115-136). Honolulu: University of Hawaii Press.

LaFromboise, T. D., Foster, S. L., & James, A. (1996). Ethics in multicultural counseling. In P. B. Pedersen, J. G. Draguns, W. J. Lonner, & J. E. Trimble (Eds.), *Counseling across cultures* (4th ed., pp. 47-72). Thousand Oaks, CA: Sage.

La Roche, M. J., & Turner, C. (2002). At the crossroads: Managed mental health care, the ethics code, and ethnic minorities. *Cultural Diversity & Ethnic Minority Psychology, 8,* 187-198.

Lee, C. C., & Kurilla, V. (1997). Ethics and multiculturalism: The challenge of diversity. In *The Hatherleigh guide to ethics in therapy* (Vol. 10, pp. 235-248). New York: Hatherleigh Press.

May, L., Collins-Chobanian, S., & Wong, K. (Eds.). (2002). *Applied ethics: A multicultural approach* (3rd ed.). Upper Saddle River, NJ: Prentice Hall.

McCreary, M. L., & Walker, T. D. (2001). Teaching multicultural counseling prepracticum. *Teaching of Psychology, 28,* 195-198.

Meara, N. M., Schmidt, L. D., & Day, J. D. (1996). Principles and virtues: A foundation for ethical decisions, policies and character. *The Counseling Psychologist, 24,* 4-77.

Nussbaum, M. (1999). *Sex and social justice.* New York: Oxford University Press.

Paradis, F. E. (1981). Themes in the training of culturally effective psychotherapists. *Counselor Education and Supervision, 21,* 136-151.

Pedersen, P. B. (1995). Culture-centered ethical guidelines for counselors. In J. G. Ponterotto, J. M. Casas, L. A. Suzuki, & C. M. Alexander (Eds.), *Handbook of multicultural counseling* (pp. 34-49). Thousand Oaks, CA: Sage.

Pedersen, P. B. (1997). The cultural context of the American Counseling Association code of ethics. *Journal of Counseling and Development, 76,* 23-29.

Pedersen, P. B. (2002). Ethics, competence and other professional issues in culture-centered counseling. In P. B. Pedersen, J. G. Draguns, W. J. Lonner, & J. E. Trimble (Eds.), *Counseling across cultures* (5th ed., pp. 3-27). Thousand Oaks, CA: Sage.

Pedersen, P. B., & Marsella, A. J. (1982). The ethical crisis for cross-cultural counseling and therapy. *Professional Psychology, 13,* 492-500.

Pettifor, J. L. (2001). Are professional codes of ethics relevant for multicultural counselling? *Canadian Journal of Counselling, 35,* 26-35.

Ponterotto, J. G. (2002). Qualitative research methods: The fifth force in psychology. *The Counseling Psychologist, 30,* 394-406.

Ponterotto, J. G., Alexander, C. M., & Grieger, I. (1995). A Multicultural Competency Checklist for counseling training programs. *Journal of Multicultural Counseling and Development, 23,* 11-20.

Pope, K. S., & Vasquez, M. J. T. (1998). *Ethics in psychotherapy and counseling: A practical guide* (2nd ed.). San Francisco: Jossey-Bass.

Pope-Davis, D. B., & Coleman, H. L. K. (1997). *Multicultural counseling competencies: Assessment, education and training, and supervision.* Thousand Oaks, CA: Sage.

Pope-Davis, D. B., Liu, W. M., Toporek, R. L., & Brittan-Powell, C. S. (2001). What's missing from multicultural competency research: Review, introspection and recommendations. *Cultural Diversity and Ethnic Minority Psychology, 7,* 121-138.

Pope-Davis, D. B., Toporek, R. L., Ortega-Villalobos, L., Ligiéro, D. P., Brittan-Powell, C. S., Liu, W. M., et al. (2002). Clients perspectives of multicultural counseling competence: A quantitative examination. *The Counseling Psychologist, 30,* 355-393.

Quintana, S. M., & Atkinson, D. R. (2002). A multicultural perspective on principles of empirically supported interventions. *The Counseling Psychologist, 30,* 281-291.

Reynolds, A. L. (1995). Challenges and strategies for teaching multicultural counseling courses. In J. G. Ponterotto, J. M. Casas, L. A. Suzuki, & C. M. Alexander (Eds.), *Handbook of multicultural counseling* (pp. 312-330). Thousand Oaks, CA: Sage.

Ridley, C. R. (1985). Imperatives for ethnic and cultural relevance in psychology training programs. *Professional Psychology: Research and Practice, 16*(5), 611-622.

Ridley, C. R. (1995). *Overcoming unintentional racism in counseling and therapy: A practitioner's guide to intentional intervention.* Thousand Oaks, CA: Sage.

Ridley, C. R. (2002). *Multicultural counseling competence: A construct in search of redefinition.* Manuscript under review.

Ridley, C. R., Espelage, D. L., & Rubinstein, K. J. (1997). Course development in multicultural counseling. In D. B. Pope-Davis & H. L. K. Coleman (Eds.), *Multicultural counseling competencies: Assessment, education and training, and supervision* (pp. 131-158). Thousand Oaks, CA: Sage.

Ridley, C. R., Hill, C. L., & Wiese, D. L. (2001). Ethics in multicultural assessment: A model of reasoned application. In L. A. Suzuki, J. G. Ponterotto, & P. J. Meller (Eds.), *Handbook of multicultural assessment: Clinical, psychological, and educational applications* (2nd ed., pp. 29-45). San Francisco: Jossey-Bass.

Ridley, C. R., Liddle, M. C., Hill, C. L., & Li, L.C. (2001). Ethical decision making in multicultural counseling. In J. G. Ponterotto, J. M. Casas, L. A. Suzuki, & C. M. Alexander (Eds.), *Handbook of multicultural counseling* (2nd ed., pp. 165-188). Thousand Oaks, CA: Sage.

Ridley, C. R., Mendoza, D. W., & Kanitz, B. E. (1994). Multicultural training: Reexamination, operationalization, and integration. *The Counseling Psychologist, 22*(2), 227-289.

Roysircar-Sodowsky, G., Toporek, R., Pope-Davis, D., Ponterotto, J. G., Coleman, H. L. K., Fuertes, J., et al. (2002, March). *2002 updating of the AMCD monograph: Operationalization of the multicultural counseling competencies.* Symposium presented at the annual meeting of the American Counseling Association, New Orleans, LA.

Seitz, J., & O'Neill, P. (1996). Ethical decision making and the code of ethics of the Canadian Psychological Association. *Canadian Psychology, 37,* 23-30.

Sue, D. W., Arredondo, P., & McDavis, R. J. (1992). Multicultural counseling competencies and standards: A call to the profession. *Journal of Counseling and Development, 70,* 477-483.

Sue, S. (1999). Science, ethnicity and bias: Where have we gone wrong? *American Psychologist, 54,* 1070-1077.

Tapp, J. L., Kelman, H., Triandis, H., Wrightsman, L., & Coelho, G. (1974). Advisory principles for ethical considerations in the conduct of cross-cultural research: Fall 1973 revision. *International Journal of Psychology, 9,* 240-249.

Tozer, E. E., & McClanahan, M. K. (1999). Treating the purple menace: Ethical considerations of conversion therapy and affirmative alternatives. *The Counseling Psychologist, 27,* 722-742.

U.S. Bureau of the Census. (2001, May). *The Hispanic population: Census 2000 brief.* Washington, DC: Government Printing Office.

Vasquez, M. J. T. (1996). Will virtue ethics improve ethical conduct in multicultural settings and interactions? *The Counseling Psychologist, 24,* 98-104.

Wampold, B. E., Lichtenberg, J. W., & Waehler, C. A. (2002). Principles of empirically supported interventions in counseling psychology. *The Counseling Psychologist, 30,* 197-217.

Weinrach, S. G., & Thomas, K. R. (1996). The counseling profession's commitment to diversity-sensitive counseling: A critical reassessment. *Journal of Counseling and Development, 74,* 472-477.

Weinrach, S. G., & Thomas, K. R. (1998). Diversity-sensitive counseling today: A postmodern clash of values. *Journal of Counseling and Development, 76,* 115-122.

Weinrach, S. G., & Thomas, K. R. (2002). A critical analysis of the multicultural counseling competencies: Implications for the practice of mental health counseling. *Journal of Mental Health Counseling, 24,* 20-35.

Welfel, E. R. (2001). *Ethics in counseling and psychotherapy: Standards, research and emerging issues* (2nd ed.). Pacific Grove, CA: Brooks/Cole.

Welfel, E. R., & Kitchener, K. S. (1992). Introduction to special section: Ethics education—an agenda for the '90s. *Professional Psychology: Research and Practice, 23,* 179-181.

21

Multicultural Competencies in Consultation

PATRICIA ARREDONDO
JEANNETTE GORDON REINOSO

Arizona State University

Attention and application of multicultural competencies to various professional endeavors continue to increase. Consultation is one domain of practice by counselors and psychologists, as well as individuals from other disciplinary or work histories (e.g., human resource personnel), that is sought after by a cross section of organizations for different reasons and objectives. Typically, organizations that intend to introduce a formal diversity initiative or a specific strategy that speaks to multiculturalism and diversity, such as a recruitment plan for employees of color or increasing the cultural competency of its clinical staff, seek the services of a consultant.

The focus on diversity and multicultural competencies has spawned a network of consultants who self-identify as diversity consultants. As with all counseling practitioners, there is a wide range of preparation and experience among consultants. Some may come with experience and skills in the headhunting or education and training domains but are not necessarily skilled in multiculturalism in an organizational context or appreciate that multicultural competencies are essential to guiding organizational change processes.

A related issue in the arena of diversity management and cultural competency consultation is the engagement of ethnic minority consultants. Although many ethnic minority consultants may have lived experiences of their own, it does not necessarily mean they are multiculturally competent. Finally, because most client organizations themselves are not schooled in the literature and research about workforce diversity, organizational theories, and multicultural competencies, they do not inquire about these skills of potential consultants. Thus, infusing multicultural competencies into consultation practices in the counseling literature is timely.

MY MULTICULTURAL CONSULTANT CONTEXT

As a "diversity management consultant" myself since the mid-1980s, there have been multiple opportunities to discuss the dynamics and historical presence of multiculturalism and diversity in all organizations (Adler, 1986; Arredondo, 1996; Cox, 1993; Sue et al., 1998). It has not always been easy to explain the interactions and effects of organizational culture and systems (policies, procedures, and other practices) on individuals, whether they are employees, customers, or other entities with some affiliation to the organization. Demonstrating the effects of organizational policies and practices on persons from different backgrounds (e.g., White, non-college-educated women secretaries or Chinese American gay male computer programmers) continues to be challenging, but inroads are slowly being made.

As a consultant, there are several premises I use to guide my work (Arredondo, 1996):

1. All organizations are multicultural and diverse and exist from a particular or conflicting worldview model.
2. Historical, sociopolitical, and financial influences operate for all organizations.
3. All organizations have competing issues of identity, masculinity/femininity, and power sharing.
4. Without people, organizations would not exist.

CHAPTER OVERVIEW

The purpose of this chapter is to promote the use of multicultural guidelines or competencies in consultation. The two foci for discussion are organizational diversity management and cultural competency. To achieve the chapter objectives, I introduce two case examples requiring the services of a consultant that will be discussed at the beginning and then analyzed at the end of the chapter. Contributing to this analysis will be other relevant topics: the context for multicultural consulting competencies, consultation models and theories that are psychological in orientation, a *blueprint* (Arredondo, 1996) to guide diversity management practices, cultural competency philosophies and models, proposed multicultural-centered consultation competencies, attributes of consultants practicing in the field of diversity management, and a process model, the *multicultural-centered consultation process* (see Figure 21.1).

Case Examples

Case Study 1: Family United Network

Family United Network (FUN) was an old, established human service agency in the middle of a small urban center. Dating back to the early 1900s, it was a multiservice organization, providing geriatric homemaker services, an employee assistance program (EAP) for employers, direct service to individuals and families, and group counseling for different issues. The latter included groups for substance abuse and incest survivors. Career counseling was also available. In the late 1980s, state-funded programs were suddenly cut, a by-product of the country's recession. Suddenly, a very proud organization found itself in the midst of a financial crisis. Services on a sliding scale, particularly to low-income and ethnic minority families, no longer were feasible. The homemaker program for low-income ethnic minority women was costly. Employees for this program also happened to be ethnic minority women who were not well paid but still employed for 10 years or more.

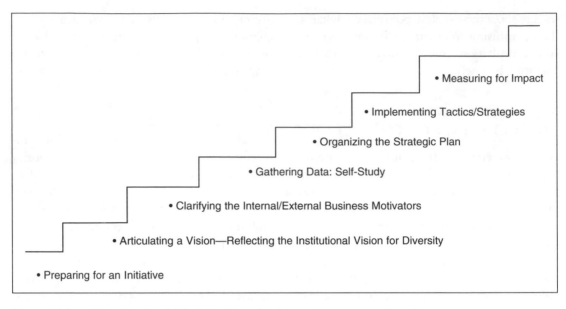

Figure 21.1 Organizational Diversity Blueprint

SOURCE: © Empowerment Workshops, Inc.

The multicultural agency administration and board of directors found itself confronting new challenges. Should programs and services for those most in need be eliminated because external funding was not as abundant? Should staff cuts be made? Salaries of senior clinicians, primarily White, would allow for the reallocation of precious agency money. The endowment fund was close to $15 million, but financial guidelines prohibited expenditures for operations. If only senior administrators remained, the message to clinicians and other personnel, including a clerical staff of primarily White women, would speak volumes about who was valued.

The emotional well-being of the staff was also a concern. This was the first time that the job security of employees with service of more than 20 years was threatened. The emergency came about so quickly that no one had a chance to prepare. External funding cuts led to a full-blown crisis for the agency at all levels. External consultation was sought.

Case Study 2: Middleton State College

In the mid-1990s, Middleton State College was experiencing a wave of prosperity. The public institution had reached an enrollment of 10,000, primarily undergraduates, and was the recipient of a bequest by a former alumna, a woman who endorsed the college's liberal policies during the civil rights era of the 1960s. One of the donor's stipulations was that the college should have a multicultural community building agenda. It was her belief that students, faculty, and staff needed to become good citizens together, thereby learning from one another's different cultural backgrounds in the process. The donor, Mrs. Samuels, was African American.

The board of trustees instructed the college president to move with haste to create this multicultural agenda. The president knew this was an opportunity for her institution. She espoused Mrs. Samuels's values and felt as though she now had a place to take action. Previous attempts with a diversity initiative had not advanced. Faculty and staff who had participated in mandatory diversity training found it to be a waste of time. The president wanted to have a different process, but she did not feel ready to go it alone. She decided that a consultant would provide guidance to a change-oriented process with which she had little to no experience.

THE MULTICULTURAL COMPETENCY CONTEXT

Multicultural counseling competencies (MCCs) have become guidelines, standards, and desirable competencies for education and training, assessment, research, and practice. Two primary documents (Arredondo et al., 1996; Sue, Arredondo, & McDavis, 1992) have served as the basis for guidelines in other areas of practice, including rehabilitation (Middleton, Rollins, & Sanderson, 2000), group, school, career, and family, and with gay, lesbian, and transgendered individuals (D'Andrea et al., 2001). Moreover, MCCs have influenced the resurgence of attention to a cross-cultural competency document (Sue et al., 1982) promulgated by Division 17 (Counseling Psychology) of the American Psychological Association (APA). Recently endorsed as policy is the APA's (2002) *Multicultural Guidelines on Education and Training, Research, Organizational Change, and Practice for Psychologists.* Consequentially, attention to consultation, another specialty area within counseling and counseling psychology, is appropriate.

Organizational Structure for Consultation and Multiculturalism

Why focus on consultation? Consultation is a practice area that falls under the purview of the "helping" profession. From this context,

practitioners would likely work from psychological principles about human and organizational development (Dougherty, 2000b; Morgan, 1997; Tobias, 1990). Principles of change specific to cognition, emotions, and behavior underlie consultation processes. Thus, understanding social learning, adult development, family systems, and cognitive-behavioral theories, among other psychological models, and their relevancy to consultation is essential.

Professional associations provide affiliations for individuals interested in consultation practice. Within the APA, there is Division 13 (Consultation Psychology), and within the Association of Counselor Education and Supervision (ACES) of the American Counseling Association (ACA), there has been a longstanding interest network for consultation. The professional attention by both entities suggests that consultation is a domain that counselors and psychologists move into as a primary or adjunct practice. In addition, there is the American Academy of Certified Consultants and Experts (AACCE), designed to validate consulting as an interdisciplinary profession.

With respect to multiculturalism and diversity, various organizations have emerged to give validation and support to an academic and research focus on multiculturalism. Noteworthy within the profession are the Association of Multicultural Counseling and Development (AMCD), established in 1971; Division 45, the Society for the Psychological Study of Ethnic Minority Issues, established in 1985; and other ethnic-specific psychological associations. Consulting in the area of multiculturalism and diversity is one of many applications sought after from these organizations. Non-psychology-specific associations for diversity practitioners/consultants include the National Multicultural Institute and the American Society of Training and Development, among others.

The Promise and Risks of Multicultural-Centered Consultation

Consultation is alive and well as a profession, and many individuals, recognizing that multiculturalism and diversity are increasingly on various organizational agendas, promote themselves as knowledgeable in these domains. This is not to diminish the content expertise of consultants assisting human resource personnel typically charged with addressing organizational diversity plans. Rather, it is to assert that because there is a knowledge base for multicultural organizational consulting, this must be formalized and grounded in more sophisticated multidimensional models, approaches, and research-based practices.

One of the unfortunate consequences of consultants who are not knowledgeable about multiculturalism from a systems and cultural perspective is the perpetuation of a demographic-specific approach (e.g., race, gender, or sexual orientation focus). This typically leaves organizational leaders and human resource personnel confused about the differences between affirmative action and diversity consultation. When consultants do not draw from theories that consider the historical and sociopolitical contexts for change processes and their impact on different constituencies, they are practicing in a culturally encapsulated (Wrenn, 1962) manner. Furthermore, when consultants are not knowledgeable about multicultural counseling competencies and other organizational cultural competency models, they are in fact practicing out of their realm of expertise. Thus, MCCs (Arredondo et al., 1996; Sue et al., 1992), *Multicultural Guidelines* (APA, 2002), and the Division 13 consulting psychology doctoral guidelines (APA, 2000) must guide practice.

CONSULTATION THEORIES/MODELS

Multicultural-centered consultation, similar to multicultural counseling, is interdisciplinary. Consultants must draw from counseling, psychology, business, and other social science research and practices. There are several fundamental premises to these theories and application:

1. Organizational change in some form is desired.
2. A "helping" relationship ensues between a consultant and a client or a client organization.
3. Consultation involves psychologically based approaches because all organizations are people-driven systems.
4. Affect in the form of tensions, conflict, stress, and other normative emotional reactions occurs.
5. Inherent in consultation are collaborative, developmental processes and practices that assist a client organization to reach its goals or expected outcomes.

Traditional Models

Traditional models of consultation seem to fall into three domains: scientific-technological, human development, and social political (Dougherty, 2000b; Gallessich, 1985). All three models may be reflected in multicultural-centered consultation practices.

Different consultation theories include organizational, mental health, and behavioral consultation (Dougherty, 2000b). The model to be followed in a consultation will be informed by a particular setting and presenting needs. For example, organizational consultation focuses on the entire system as the client and defines problems as they relate to the organization's structure and processes (Dougherty, 2000b). For mental health consultation, practitioners attend to agency programs and their work with clients. This often takes the form of case or program consultation (Dougherty, 2000a).

Psychological consulting is another framework to guide practice in the area of management (Tobias, 1990). Primarily a clinical approach, the consultant is the hub for the change process that occurs at multiple levels within an organization. Well known in the management literature and grounded in psychological principles is the process consultation model. Schein (1987) described three models of helping that may be applied by a consultant: expert, doctor-patient, and process consultation.

These theories provide various paradigms for approaching the consultation process on five dimensions: conceptualization of the problem, goals, methods and assumptions, consultant roles, and professional values (Dougherty, 2000b; Gallessich, 1982).

Another relevant framework is that of the learning organization (Morgan, 1997; Senge, 1990). Learning organization principles suggest tasks that will facilitate preparation and implementation of change management processes. These tasks include scanning trends in the external environment, analysis of those trends relative to the purpose or business of a given organization through self-study, and development of action plans to be proactive rather than reactive to projected changes. The learning organization approach complements the emphasis in multicultural counseling by factoring in sociopolitical context and other external forces.

Perhaps the most salient contemporary observation of the scanning process lies with census 2000 figures and projections. The numbers alone, reporting an increase in the population of ethnic minority groups and biracial individuals, are motivating organizational planning on short- and long-term bases. Colleges and universities, for example, now know that future student populations will have fewer White students than before. Thus, it is timely for institutions to examine the university culture and cultural competency to determine changes that may need to be made in policies and practices to ensure a climate that is open and welcoming.

Although the models discussed are often used to inform consulting practices, they all seem to be deficient in areas related to cultural diversity and gender issues (Dougherty, 2000b; Henning-Stout, 1994; Jackson & Hayes, 1993). In short, to be a multiculturally competent consultant, it would be insufficient to be guided only by these models.

Organizational Cultural Competency Models

Contemporary organizations, from mental health to financial institutions, are inquiring about their cultural competency status. Although there is insufficient empirical research on this topic, various models have been introduced for consideration. These models or frameworks provide concepts for examining structural, behavioral, and cultural factors that promote organizational performance as it relates to diversity management (Garcia, 2001).

Work in the field of child welfare by Cross and associates (Cross, Bazron, Dennis, & Issacs, 1989) led to the development of a cultural competency model with a six-stage typology ranging from cultural destructiveness to cultural proficiency. Cox (1993) proposed three types of organizational diversity—monolithic, plural, and multicultural—characterized by changes along six dimensions. The latter include culture, acculturation, structural integration, degree of formal integration, cultural bias in human resources, and process for resolving intergroup conflict. Tirado (1998) provided a five-stage typology of cultural competency, with stages ranging from cultural resistance to culturally versatile. Other stage models have emerged, using similar terminology.

Culture-Centered Competency Models

A review of the literature suggests that there is the beginning of a stream of publications on the topic of diversity and multicultural/cultural competency in consultation. The settings for these studies are schools, businesses, human service agencies, and all other types of work settings.

Different models for diversity-related consultation are being used. They have been referred to as the "valuing diversity" and the "diversity management" models. With diversity still widely associated with affirmative action, these models are typically dismissed because of their negative associations with quotas in hiring or the enrollment of women and persons of color. Even in organizations where there is an explicit mission toward inclusiveness and the valuing of human differences, the term *diversity* tends to introduce resistant responses.

Emerging literature describes cultural competence and multicultural competency as a developmental process for both individuals and organizations. The aforementioned MCCs posit an interdependent, multidimensional model of competency development in the areas of awareness, knowledge and skill, and strategy application. Adapted to consulting practice, the levels might refer to the counselor/consultant, the consultant in relation to the client and the client organization's worldview, and the synergistic application of culture-centered organizational change strategies.

Worldview-Based Models

In the multicultural counseling literature, the concept of "worldview" provides an invaluable lens for understanding and beginning to bridge cultural differences. Different worldview frameworks that can inform a consultant's practice will be briefly cited. Hofstede's (1984) research yields four constructs that are informative about organizational cultural values, behaviors, and attitudes: masculinity/femininity, power distance,

individualism versus collectivism, and uncertainty avoidance. Kohls (1987) discussed values that Americans subscribe to as a result of cultural/nationalistic socialization. Kluckhohn and Strodtbeck (1961) provided six value orientation dimensions of worldview. These are posed as perceptions of the individual, the world, human relations, activity, time, and space.

Another approach for understanding and measuring cultural issues in organizations offers four perspectives with defining features that describe the pros and cons of interpersonal interactions within a particular cultural context. Carter and Qureshi (1995) described these as universal, ubiquitous, traditional, and race based.

Identity-Based Models

Ethnic, racial, and gender identity are additional constructs for understanding organizational behavior. The Dimensions of Personal Identity (Arredondo & Glauner, 1992) (see Figure 21.2) was introduced in the AMCD multicultural counseling competencies (Arredondo et al., 1996) and complements the blueprint (Arredondo, 1996) for successful diversity management initiatives (see Figure 21.1). Essentially, the interdependent A, B, C model provides a profile of an organizational hierarchy based on the dimensions of the personal identity of different constituencies, particularly senior administrators, and the organization's history. The "C" dimension, for example, represents the contextual and external forces that drive organizational change.

For example, most dot.com companies were formed in the mid- to late 1990s by young (ages 20-30) entrepreneurs who were highly motivated to make money quickly by taking risks and using venture capital money. Referring to the "A" dimensions, the profile of these dot.coms indicates primarily heterosexual

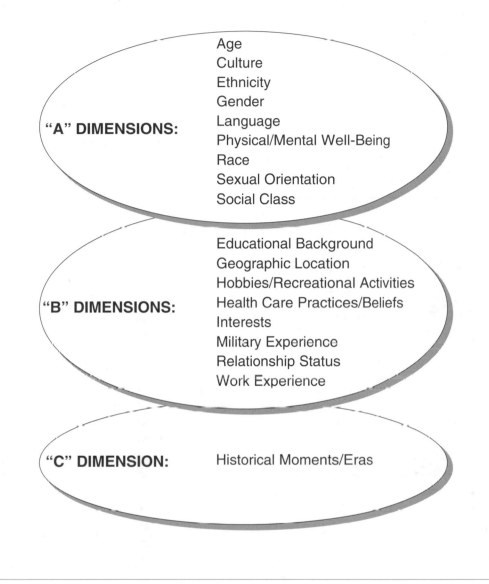

Figure 21.2 Dimensions of Personal Identity

SOURCE: Arredondo and Glauner (1992). © Empowerment Workshops, Inc.

White males, monolingual English speakers born in the United States, culturally American, and ethnically of Euro-American heritage. The "B" dimensions may suggest college-educated single persons, primarily in California, and recreation-minded individuals with interests in such areas as golf, hiking, and sailing as outlets for their hard-driving, get-rich-quick work ethos. The dot.coms came under fire for hiring very few persons of color.

Ethnic and racial identity models are also valuable references for examining organizational identity preferences, relationships, and business priorities. Although these models are typically stage based and individually centered, they can provide a composite view of the prevailing ethnic and racial identity that is valued. This value may be manifested through the presence, or lack thereof, of ethnic/racial minority persons across different workforce levels, financial allocations to address ethnic and racial minority issues, and so forth. The following models, among others, can be considered: Black and White identity (Helms, 1990), Mexican identity (Ruiz, 1990), and minority identity development (Sue & Sue, 1999).

CULTURAL COMPETENCY: AN ACCUMULATION OF WISDOM

Measurement of Multicultural Competence

From the various models and constructs about worldviews and identity, multiple instruments have emerged to assess organizational and individual cultural competency. Cross (1993) assessed behavior in policy management, services, and community relationships. The Cross Cultural Values Survey (Hofstede, 1984) has been widely used in more than 40 countries. Cameron and Quinn (1999) prepared a guide and validated instruments for diagnosing organizational culture. Finally, Arredondo and Woy (1997) have developed an employee-centered organizational climate survey adapted for use in various organizations.

The previous discussions indicate that organizational consultation with a focus on multiculturalism requires a competency-based approach. There is an expansive menu of data from which to draw, and all consultants must be informed by guidelines based on multicultural competencies and organizational change

principles, research, and practice. In addition, a body of knowledge about organizational and consultation theories and practices is also pertinent. Finally, attributes can enhance self-confidence for multicultural-centered consultants and be considered by organizations in their hiring of diversity consultants.

The sections that follow draw on close to 20 years of an active consulting practice that always includes a focus on multiculturalism and diversity, whether the desired changes are about cultural competency, sexual harassment, leadership development, or establishment of a diversity initiative.

AMCD Competencies Adapted

Borrowing from the AMCD MCCs (Arredondo et al., 1996; Sue et al., 1992), the following guidelines are proposed. They fall into the domains of awareness, knowledge, and skills. Not all are exact statements from the MCCs but are adaptations or new statements more specific to consultation. It is highly recommended that multicultural-centered consultants be knowledgeable about the MCCs and use them to guide consultation practices.

Awareness

Multicultural-centered consultants need to engage in self-exploration about who they are culturally and the influences on their worldviews. Understandably, biases and assumptions about the self cannot be generalized to others and to organizations; thus, attention to the MCC is a valuable first checkpoint. Multiculturally competent consultants do the following:

- believe that cultural self-awareness and sensitivity to one's own cultural heritage are essential (Arredondo et al., 1996, p. 57);
- can identify the culture(s) to which they belong and the significance of that membership—including the relationship of individuals in

that group with individuals from other groups—institutionally, historically, educationally, and so forth;

- recognize the impact of personal beliefs about others' cultural differences on their ability to respect others different from themselves in the consultation process;
- value bilingualism and do not view another language as an impediment to communication within an organization;
- recognize biases toward organizations that profit from the delivery of mental health services.

Explanatory Statement. To provide advice about multicultural issues and contexts, consultants have to know themselves, culturally speaking. In all consulting, there are multiple experiences within a client organization. Consultants are stimuli, and people in organizations are stimuli for consultants. In psychological terms, we call this *transference* and *countertransference.* No consultant is immune to this dynamic. Mature cultural self-awareness is necessary for individuals to provide advice or to facilitate difficult discussions during organizational processes of change. Consultants require honest objectivity to provide culturally competent and ethical services.

Knowledge

The breadth of knowledge that consultants must possess is vast. For those who dare to self-identify as diversity consultants, the yardstick is even longer. Multiculturally competent consultants are knowledgeable about the following:

- institutional barriers that prevent ethnic and racial minorities and others in underrepresented groups from having access to the organization either for services or for purposes of employment and advancement;
- the potential bias in standardized assessment instruments or other procedures they may recommend for data gathering within an intake process (e.g., employee screening);
- organizational worldview theories and how these manifest through policies, practices, and procedures;
- cultural competency models and guidelines and their relevance for application in particular organizational structures;
- the blueprint for guiding organizational diversity change processes;
- external and internal forces that influence an organization's mission and practices, including financial, sociopolitical, legislative, accrediting bodies, and so forth, and how these affect a diversity initiative;
- the experiences of different underrepresented cultural groups (gay and lesbian, women, ethnic and racial minorities, and the disabled) in different institutions as consumers, employees, and/or students; and
- identity development models that provide understanding of individual and organizational identities and interactions.

Explanatory Statement. A consultant must have a broad-based repertoire of knowledge specific to organizational culture, broadly speaking, and specific to the particular industry of a given organization. Several concepts such as worldview (Hofstede, 1984; Kohls, 1987; Sue & Sue, 1999) and dimensions of identity (Arredondo & Glauner, 1992) allow for a lens for conceptualizing about an organization's cultural status quo. Beyond this, however, consultants need to be knowledgeable about industry-specific practices. For example, there is a different emphasis on the not-for-profit versus the corporate world. Government agencies and public institutions also have different mandates. Although there may be similarities across these types of entities, the differences are even more important. Knowing the idiosyncrasies of a particular institution is also necessary. Consultants cannot assume to know all there is to know about all types of organizations. However, their preparation to be knowledgeable is essential.

Skills

The multicultural competencies and guidelines (Arredondo et al., 1996) indicate that a consultant's skills must be adaptable, relevant, and flexible for application in a given setting. As with all consultation, multiculturally centered consultants must engage in generic practices. According to Dougherty (2000b), these include four phases: entry, diagnosis, implementation, and disengagement. Consultants operating from a multicultural perspective must also know when to apply a particular model of helping. Schein (1987) described these as purchase of information or expertise, doctor-patient, and process-consultation models. The parallels between counseling and consultation practices can be exercised through specific skills and strategies. For example, collaboration is a skill embedded in the multicultural competencies. This indicates that interventions must be planned with a client organization as one's partner. Although a consultant's expertise is sought, the consultant will also learn in the process.

Communication skills and practices always have to be modified to fit within a particular cultural context. An understanding of worldviews and observation of communication practices will assist a consultant in recognizing relationship orientation (Kluckhohn & Strodtbeck, 1961)—hierarchical, collateral, or individualistic—high or low power distance (Hofstede, 1984), and the cultural competence paradigm that is operating. If the organization indicates it serves non-English-speaking clients, practices of bilingualism are expected. All of these data will assist a consultant with his or her communication practices (both verbal and written) with different client organizations. In consulting, one shoe does not fit all. Multicultural-competent consultants

- introduce a multicultural-based assessment process to the organization to inform change-management objectives,

- communicate to the client organization and colleagues the values and assets of bilingualism,
- reach out to resources that may assist the client organization in reaching its diversity objectives,
- can communicate to the client some of the institutional strengths with respect to diversity objectives, and
- can communicate to the client some of the possible institutional barriers to diversity objectives for inclusion and respect of different constituencies.

Explanatory Statement. It has been suggested that skill application must be grounded in multicultural awareness and knowledge, as well as counseling and consultation theories and models for practice. In addition, the role of language is significant. In a society with increasing numbers of speakers of English as a second language, particularly Spanish speakers, a consultant's bilingual abilities and knowledge about antibilingual legislation are essential. Outreach to community-based resources and knowledge about particular constituencies will enhance a consultant's credibility and facility to meet an organization's objectives.

CONSIDERATIONS FOR A MULTICULTURAL-COMPETENT CONSULTANT

The Context

In the early cross-cultural counseling literature, a statement indicated that all counseling relationships are cross-cultural (Sue et al., 1982). This premise also applies to consultation—all consulting relationships are cross-cultural or multicultural. That is, they involve individuals from different cultural backgrounds (with varying priority dimensions of personal diversity) in an organization that has its own culture, history, and sociopolitical practices (which has a consulting orientation based on psychological principles) at a point in time—the 21st century—when *multiculturalism, globalism,* and *pluralism* have become common terminology. In other words, contemporary consultants, whether they apply their skills in schools, corporate environments, or nonprofit centers, have to be broad based and multidisciplinary in their thinking and practice.

Everyone has a specialty area or areas. This content knowledge is typically what gets a consultant in the door in responding to a specific need of a client organization. Someone may request change-management consultation or communication skills training. However, to deliver this service in contemporary, diverse workforces or educational institutions in a way that reaches the individual and organizational goals, a consultant needs to be highly aware, knowledgeable, and multiskilled. The previous discussion proposed multicultural-centered competencies. Although not an exhaustive outline, these statements indicate that practice must be placed in "context" and that consultants need to be prepared on multiple levels, beginning with their own cultural self-understanding, the worldview of the client organization, and of course strategies and interventions that are culturally responsive. The next section proposes strategies to enhance professional development as a multicultural-centered consultant.

Consultant Peer Supervision

In my work as an organizational consultant, I have also provided in-service training to other consultants. At times, this has taken the form of supervision as we know it in counseling and as peer supervision with colleagues; yet another format has been to use workshops to teach strategies, techniques, or guidelines to enhance one's competency as a consultant. I will first comment on peer supervision.

Many multicultural-centered consultants work as solo practitioners. This is noted through membership in organizations such as the Diversity Leadership Forum, based in Washington, D.C. Working solo introduces many challenges, as clinicians in private practice would also acknowledge. As a supervisor and practitioner in the field of multicultural and diversity consulting, I can say that there are typically greater rather than fewer challenges. Reasons include resistance from organizations to the focus on multiculturalism and diversity, lack of commitment from organizational leadership, assumptions that magic can be performed by a consultant, and lack of clarity about root causes for organizational issues that may be labeled "diversity problems."

Many practitioners in this specialty area are White women and persons of color. To a resistant participant, these individuals are a stimulus, and it is not uncommon for frustrations and other hostilities to be directed to the consultant. Racist comments, naive or challenging in nature, are common. For example, one consultant reported that when training with a White male colleague, the White men in the group directed their comments only to her colleague. Another consultant, an African American woman, was asked, "What's your problem? You have a law degree. Why don't you practice law instead of bothering with this diversity (expletive)?"

One reason for establishing peer supervision groups is providing help to multicultural consultants who come under fire. Through this process, individuals can gain support and insights about their challenges. A group that I established in 1995 continued through 2001. Requirements were as follows: a commitment from participants to continue to learn from one another, a willingness to take responsibility for case- and research-based presentations, and a commitment to help in the development of a colleague's professional practice.

Personal and Professional Attributes

Not every counselor or psychologist will naturally move into the role of a multicultural-centered consultant. The previous discussion regarding competencies in consultation does not capture other intangibles or personality characteristics. In peer supervision, the consultants reported, through incidents and anecdotes, the type of "worldview" needed as it relates to multicultural-centered consulting. In-service workshops for diversity-related consultants were a second setting for generating these attributes. Typically in attendance were internal organizational consultants, charged with giving direction to a diversity initiative, and external organizational consultants, trying to advance their practice and learn more about the field.

The checklist that follows is a self-inventory used in workshop settings. It is designed to create awareness of desirable and necessary attributes for diversity consultants. Participants are invited to "agree" or "disagree" with the following statements:

- I enjoy being involved with change-related processes.
- I understand the organization's motivation for pursuing a diversity or cultural competency agenda.
- I can describe the organizational/institutional culture.
- I can describe the organizational enablers and barriers to the diversity agenda.
- I am knowledgeable about the history of workforce diversity in the United States.
- I am knowledgeable about the civil rights movement, affirmative action, and other legislation relevant to workforce diversity and education initiatives.
- I can articulate some of the best practices for organizational diversity.
- I am aware of multicultural competency literature and assessment tools.
- I can communicate with ease to a client the differences and similarities of cultural competency and diversity management practices.

- I can recognize forms of resistance to a diversity agenda.
- I can anticipate pitfalls to diversity goals in specific situations.
- I am seen by others (peers and previous clients) as a credible consultant.
- I consider myself to be a risk taker.
- I tend to be a supportive colleague or supervisor and give direct support.
- I recognize important dimensions of my personal identity and diversity.
- I have excellent listening skills.
- I am not conflict avoidant.
- I can facilitate disagreements or conflicts.
- I enjoy collaboration to get a project to completion.
- I am willing to learn from others.
- I recognize personal hot buttons in the area of cultural differences.
- I participate in ongoing experiences that promote more learning about diversity and cultural competency.
- I recognize my strengths and limitations as a communicator.
- I see myself as a change agent.
- I am comfortable in roles with designated power.

Summary

Many personal, multicultural, and technical competencies are relevant for a diversity consultant. The complexity and responsibility of consulting cannot be underestimated, nor can the skills and experience from multicultural perspectives. Consultants must not bring in their unresolved issues based on personal workplace or educational experiences—either idealized or bitter ones. To this end, the checklist of practices in addition to proposed multicultural consulting competencies may better prepare diversity consultants.

APPROACHES TO THE CASE STUDIES

Family United Network (FUN)

A consultant for Family United Network has many challenges because of the financial crisis and the need for the agency to take quick action. The entire system must be examined from multiple perspectives—behavioral system, change management, multicultural, psychological/ clinical, and sociopolitical. Having a big picture of the agency allows for zooming in on the interdependency of the various systems responsible for conducting the business of the agency. Is this an open or closed system? Given the purpose of FUN, a consultant might conclude that it is an open system, one that is interdependent and driven by an exchange of energy within and with the external environment (clients and communities) (Katz & Kahn, 1978). Some organizations that appear to be open are actually closed, which by definition means that they do not see themselves affected by external environments because of their own internal streams of energy. With FUN, a healthy endowment allowed it to be more autonomous than most not-for-profit human service agencies. However, it was not feasible to run the organization with endowment funds. A consultant for FUN would need to be knowledgeable about fiscal issues as well as change management practices.

Most organizations do not arrive at a crisis overnight; therefore, the possibilities for changes are likely present and now can be given more immediate attention. From a multicultural perspective, the worldview of the agency and its various constituencies; factors of ethnicity, socioeconomics, and gender; and the philosophy of the agency with respect to multiculturalism must also be queried. For a counselor or psychologist in the role of consultant, there may be hypotheses that FUN is being managed from a multicultural perspective with a high degree of cultural competence. Evidence for these two hypotheses must be tested. A counseling consultant may also expect that an organization with social work roots will be an ideal client organization. However, this is where seemingly like values with respect to helping others may not be

so congruent. When individuals, including even helping professionals, experience threat, subjectivity and self-preservation usually set in. The consultant must tread respectfully and compassionately among personnel, recognizing personal biases and assumptions and being mindful of not jumping to conclusions before having all of the facts (Tobias, 1990). Self-help may seem fine in theory, but when your job is threatened, reactions of panic and learned helplessness are not unusual.

There are many ways for a consultant to organize the facts to proceed with a multicultural-centered consultation. A number of elements must be considered and factored into the conceptualization process to proceed. For FUN:

1. Meta-systems are in crisis: Individual employees are experiencing a sense of shock, loss, and confusion; board members are having value conflicts confronting financial realities; administrators need objective feedback as they look at the changes for the entire organization; and consumers/clients accustomed to a particular relationship with the agency will likely face a change in services.

2. A number of psychological stressors are affecting different constituencies of the organization, causing emotions such as anxiety and fear to overpower "rational" thinking.

3. Employees of color, among the newest hires, question the board and the executive director's commitment to diversity because the homemaker service may be cut.

4. Structure through immediate interventions is desired to calm fears and introduce a sense of stability in the midst of enormous change.

Middleton State College

Consulting to Middleton State College (MSC) might appear to be straightforward.

There are no obvious crises occurring, and the concept of "community building" is easy to embrace by most groups on campus. If a consultant approaches with a more multicultural-centered lens, the following would be considered initially:

1. the culture of MSC: open or closed system;
2. administrative and organizational world-view in theory and practice: hierarchical, collateral or individualistic, a being or doing activity mode, high or low in power distance (Hofstede, 1984), predominant feminine or masculine orientation, and manifestation of the various values and beliefs;
3. dimensions of organizational identity: using the dimensions of personal identity model (Arredondo & Glauner, 1992) to determine representation of different dimensions of diversity among faculty, student, administration, and staff;
4. cultural competency continuum: based on prior and current practices, is this a more culturally aware or more culturally responsive institution (Garcia, 1996)?

There are other considerations to be made, and following the organizational diversity blueprint (Arredondo, 1996), a structure for planning and implementation can be followed. For example, for each phase in the blueprint, there are a number of tasks (see Figure 21.1) to undertake and best practices to follow. The ideal scenario is to constitute a representative diversity community-building taskforce to collaborate with the consultant. This inclusiveness opens more channels to communication across the MSC community once the process is officially launched. For MSC, baseline data from different constituencies with respect to campus climate and perceptions of community were gathered. These data then contributed to the development of a diversity-related action plan with measurable objectives. Without data, planning for action would have been less compelling.

Resistance is a natural occurrence when organizational change is proposed. When it is done so in the name of diversity or multiculturalism, the resistance tends to be stronger and more vocal. By following a systematic approach involving different constituencies, the consultant has allies to manage situations of difficulty and resistance. It had been noted that MSC's previous diversity initiatives had not gone "anywhere." Past history becomes relevant to the new approach so as not to re-create past situations that were unsuccessful. Naming of an initiative has become very important for different organizations. Quite often, it is preferable not to use the term *diversity* in the title of an initiative or education and training project because of the negative reaction it seems to engender. For MSC, the concept of community building reflected Mrs. Samuels's principles and also served as motivator to bring different groups together.

SUMMARY

Multicultural-centered consultation will continue to grow as a practice for counselors and psychologists. Rapidly changing demographics in the United States point to the increase of women, immigrants, and persons of color as employees, students, and consumers/clients. Educational institutions, from elementary to higher education, have to think about the relevance of their curriculum as well as systems of access and hiring practices. Employers also want to create environments of inclusiveness and respect for purposes of hiring and retention of underrepresented populations. For consultants, knowledge of the technical models to guide consulting, the multicultural competencies and guidelines, and industry-specific practices is essential.

There are many parallels between consultation and counseling processes. One major difference, however, is that the client organization is more complex. The proposed multicultural-centered consulting competencies are not exhaustive. Rather, they suggest that expertise as a diversity or multicultural consultant is comprehensive and multidimensional.

Consulting offers many growth opportunities for consultants. Diversity and multiculturalism are facts of life. Therefore, for the multicultural-centered consultant, the opportunities are infinite.

REFERENCES

Adler, N. J. (1986). *International dimensions of organizational behavior*. Belmont, CA: PWS-KENT.

American Psychological Association (APA). (2000). *Guidelines for education and training at the doctoral and post-doctoral level in consulting psychology*. Washington, DC: APA Division 13/Consulting Psychology.

American Psychological Association (2002). *Multicultural guidelines on education and training, research, organizational change, and practice for psychologists*. Washington, DC: Author.

Arredondo, P. (1996). *Successful diversity management initiatives*. Thousand Oaks, CA: Sage.

Arredondo, P., & Glauner, T. (1992). *Personal dimensions of identity model*. Boston: Empowerment Workshops.

Arredondo, P., Toporek, R., Brown, S. P., Jones, J., Locke, D. C., Sanchez, J., et al. (1996). Operationalization of the multicultural counseling competencies. *Journal of Multicultural Counseling and Development, 24*, 42-78.

Arredondo, P., & Woy, J. R. (1997). *Organizational climate survey*. Boston: Empowerment Workshops.

Cameron, K. S., & Quinn, R.W. (1999). *Diagnosing and changing organizational culture*. Reading, MA: Addison-Wesley.

Carter, R. T., & Qureshi, A. (1995). A typology of philosophical assumptions in multicultural counseling and training. In J. G. Ponterotto, J. M. Casas, L. A. Suzuki, & C. M. Alexander (Eds.), *Handbook of multicultural counseling and development* (pp. 239-260). Thousand Oaks, CA: Sage.

Cox, T. (1993). *Cultural diversity in organizations: Theory, practice and research*. San Francisco: Berret-Kochler.

Cross, T. (1993). *Organizational self-study on cultural competence in agencies: Addressing child abuse and neglect*. Portland, OR: Northwest Indian Child Welfare Association.

Cross, T., Bazron, B., Dennis, K., & Issacs, M. (1989). *Toward a culturally competent system of care: Vol. 1. Monograph on effective services for minority children who are severely emotionally disturbed*. Washington, DC: CASSP Technical Assistance Center, Georgetown University Child Development Center.

D'Andrea, M., Daniels, J., Arredondo, P., Ivey, A. E., Ivey, M. B., Locke, D. C., et al. (2001). Fostering organizational changes to realize the revolutionary potential of the multicultural movement: An updated case study. In J. G. Ponterotto, J. M. Casas, L. A. Suzuki, & C. M. Alexander (Eds.), *Handbook of multicultural counseling and development* (pp. 222-254). Thousand Oaks, CA: Sage.

Dougherty, A. M. (2000a). *Psychological consultation and collaboration: A casebook* (3rd ed.). Belmont, CA: Brooks/Cole.

Dougherty, A. M. (2000b). *Psychological consultation and collaboration in school and community settings* (3rd ed.). Belmont, CA: Brooks/Cole.

Gallessich, J. (1982). *The profession and practice of consultation*. San Francisco: Jossey-Bass.

Gallessich, J. (1985). Toward a meta-theory of consultation. *Counseling Psychologist, 13*, 336-354.

Garcia, I. (1996). *Preliminary findings of the hospital quality improvement project cultural competence measures*. Boston: McCormick Institute of Public Affairs, University of Massachusetts.

Garcia, I. (2001). *Improving systems of care for racial and ethnic minority consumers: Measuring cultural competence in Massachusetts acute care hospital settings*. Unpublished doctoral dissertation, Brandeis University.

Helms, J. (1990). *Black and White racial identity: Theory, research, and practice*. Westport, CT: Greenwood.

Henning-Stout, M. (1994). Consultation and connected knowing: What we know is determined by the questions we ask. *Journal of Educational and Psychological Consultation, 5*, 5-21.

Hofstede, G. (1984). *Culture's consequences.* Beverly Hills, CA: Sage.

Jackson, D. N., & Hayes, D. H. (1993). Multicultural issues in consultation. *Journal of Counseling and Development, 72*(2), 144-147.

Katz, D., & Kahn, R. L. (1978). *The social psychology of organizations* (2nd ed.). New York: John Wiley.

Kluckhohn, F. R., & Strodtbeck, F. L. (1961). *Variations in value orientations.* Evanston, IL: Row, Peterson.

Kohls, R. (1987). *Values Americans live by.* York, ME: Intercultural Press.

Middleton, R., Rollins, C. W., & Sanderson, P. L. (2000). Endorsement of professional rehabilitation competencies and standards: A call to action. *Rehabilitation Counseling Bulletin, 43*, 29-42.

Morgan, G. (1997). *Images of organization* (2nd ed.). Thousand Oaks, CA: Sage.

Ruiz, A. S. (1990). Ethnic identity: Crisis and resolution. *Journal of Multicultural Counseling and Development, 18*, 29-40.

Schein, E. H. (1987). *Process consultation: Lessons for managers and consultants.* Menlo Park, CA: Addison-Wesley.

Senge, P. (1990). *The fifth discipline.* New York: Doubleday.

Sue, D. W., Arredondo, P., & McDavis, R. J. (1992). Multicultural counseling competencies and standards: A call to the profession. *Journal of Counseling and Development, 70*, 477-483.

Sue, D. W., Bernier, J., Durran, A., Feinberg, L., Pedersen, P., Smith, E., et al. (1982). Position paper: Cross cultural counseling competencies. *The Counseling Psychologist, 10*, 45-52.

Sue, D. W., Carter, R. T., Casas, J. M., Fouad, N. A., Ivey, A. E., Jensen, M., et al. (1998). *Multicultural counseling competencies: Individual and organizational development.* Thousand Oaks, CA: Sage.

Sue, D. W., & Sue, D. (1999). *Counseling the culturally different: Theory and practice* (3rd ed.). New York: John Wiley.

Tirado, M. (1998). *Monitoring the managed care of culturally and linguistically diverse populations.* Vienna, VA: National Clearinghouse for Primary Care Information.

Tobias, L. L. (1990). *Psychological consulting to management: A clinician's perspective.* New York: Brunner/Mazel.

Wrenn, C. G. (1962). The culturally encapsulated counselor. *Harvard Educational Review, 32*, 444-449.

22

Multicultural Competencies in Managed Health Care

JEAN LAU CHIN

Alliant International University

The push for multicultural competencies arose out of ethnic and racial awareness during the early 1970s in response to Title VII of the Civil Rights Act of 1964. It made the integration of culture in clinical practice a matter of ethical practice and expanded cultural awareness and cultural knowledge in clinical practice toward skill-based, culture-centered clinical practice. Most important, it moved the discussion of cultural sensitivity to one of skills (i.e., the competencies providers must have to work cross-culturally and with diverse racial/ethnic populations). With multicultural competencies, we recognize that cultural considerations influence all levels of the client-provider encounter, including the communication process, health care practices and beliefs, treatment efficacy, utilization, cultural histories, and language.

In discussing multicultural competencies in managed health care, it is important, first, to use a systems viewpoint and, second, to consider the parallel concept of cultural competence as inclusive of system, clinical, and provider competencies. Two questions inform this consideration. What competencies do providers need to work with diverse racial/ethnic groups within managed care contexts? What do managed care organizations need to do to ensure that its system of care and providers are culturally competent? This chapter will distinguish between cultural competence and multicultural competencies. It will address multicultural competencies as a standard of care and what this means within a managed health care system. In effect, how do we view multicultural competencies as being core to quality of care within a system of care?

CULTURAL COMPETENCE VERSUS MULTICULTURAL COMPETENCIES

Some differences between cultural competence and multicultural competencies are worthy of note. The former came out of a systems perspective to assess the quality of mental health service delivery systems for children from racial/ethnic minority groups (Cross, Bazron, Dennis, & Isaacs, 1989). The latter arose out an awareness within the professions that psychologists and other mental health professionals need to move beyond monocultural, Eurocentric, and ethnocentric frameworks to provide quality care to persons from diverse and minority racial/ethnic groups (Sue, Arredondo, & McDavis, 1992; Sue et al., 1982). Both concepts presume that psychologists, clinicians, and providers need certain skills to practice competently with diverse groups and work with specific racial/ethnic groups; that diversity training and cultural competence training are necessary for the acquisition of these competencies; and that such training needs to be an ongoing process rather than a one-time workshop.

The evolution of multicultural competencies proceeded to delineate those provider skills and explicit competencies for ethical practice, as well as professional standards of care. Currently, professional multicultural guidelines have been adopted by the American Psychological Association to influence the practice and training of psychologists. The evolution of cultural competence, on the other hand, has proceeded toward developing performance-based indicators to assess and monitor both service delivery systems and providers. Common to both is the emphasis on accountability and standards of care.

Standards of Care

Justification for both multicultural competencies and cultural competence began with moral imperatives for ethical practice and concerns for social justice and equity. As advocates have become increasingly disenchanted with the slowness of change and met resistance to making cultural issues a priority, there has grown a push toward defining multicultural competencies as standards of care (i.e., competencies by which all must abide). With the growing diversity of the U.S. population, advocates for multicultural competencies focus on the ethical and legal risks for psychologists when working with diverse clients about whom they have little knowledge as they are practicing outside their scope of expertise. Advocates for cultural competence, on the other hand, have pushed to define provider competencies and to develop regulatory mandates for managed care organizations and service delivery systems (i.e., hospitals, state mental health systems, agencies), so they must demonstrate cultural competence as a quality-of-care issue (Chin, 2002).

Standards can address quality of care for either providers or systems. Provider standards include those defined by the profession (i.e., American Psychological Association's ethical code or credentialing standards used by managed care organizations or service delivery systems). System standards, on the other hand, include the National Committee for Quality Assurance (NCQA), which is used to govern managed care organizations, or the Joint Commission on Accreditation of Healthcare Organizations (JCAHO), which is used to govern service delivery systems.

Standards for Service Delivery Systems

The JCAHO standards address an organization's level of performance in specific areas (i.e., what organizations are actually doing; see Web site at www.jcaho.org/standards_frm. html). JCAHO standards set minimum achievable performance expectations for activities that affect the quality of patient care. The standards detail important functions relating to patient care and the management of health care organizations, framed as performance objectives that are unlikely to change substantially over time. Because the standards aim to improve outcomes, they place little emphasis on *how* to achieve these objectives. Networks and provider organizations can be flexible in meeting the expectations of the standards and can identify their own priorities and develop performance improvement activities that best meet their unique needs and those of their members. JCAHO develops all its standards in consultation with health care experts, providers, measurement experts, purchasers, and consumers. Standards are generally updated every 2 years and change only to improve clarity or reduce duplication.

During an accreditation survey, JCAHO evaluates a network's performance by using a set of standards that cross eight functional areas:

1. Rights, responsibilities, and ethics
2. Continuum of care
3. Education and communication
4. Health promotion and disease prevention
5. Leadership
6. Management of human resources
7. Management of information
8. Improving network performance

JCAHO accreditation has become the gold standard for an organization's or a network's standing in the health care market. Although its standards address quality of care, there is little or no reference in the standards to cultural competence or multicultural competencies.

Standards for Managed Care Organizations

The NCQA works with health plans, employers, and unions to develop standards that effectively evaluate the medical and quality management systems of managed care organizations (see Web site at www.ncqa.org). The NCQA review process examines a health maintenance organization's (HMO's) performance and commitment to continuous improvement in several important areas:

1. Quality improvement
2. Utilization management
3. Physician credentialing
4. Members' rights and responsibilities
5. Preventive health services
6. Medical records

Specific measures used include the Health Plan Employer Data and Information Set (HEDIS), a standardized, comprehensive set of indicators used to measure the performance of a health plan (i.e., a report card for managed care plans). HEDIS measures were developed by representatives from consumer groups, employers, health plans, and the NCQA; the measures address a variety of issues, including effectiveness of care, access/availability of care, member satisfaction, health plan stability, use of services, and cost of care. However, there are no measures on cultural competence; there is one on access/availability of care, but it does not require managed care organizations (MCOs) to report this by race/ethnicity of its members.

Provider Standards

Professional licensing standards defined by state statute govern psychologists and their license to practice. In addition, a credentialing process may also be required for reimbursement by MCOs or employment at hospitals and networks. This process involves verifying state licensure, hospital privileges, board certification, and malpractice insurance with primary sources. The licensing exam does require knowledge of social and multicultural bases of behavior, including how race, ethnicity, gender, sexual orientation, disability, and cultural differences factor into the psychosocial, political, and economic development of individuals, families, and groups. Most licensing standards do not have criteria for providers to be culturally competent, nor are there definitions of multicultural competencies. Massachusetts is one of the few states that require demonstration of competence on racial/ethnic bases of behavior, with a focus on people of color defined as a minimum of 3 graduate semester hours in courses such as cross-cultural psychology, psychology and social oppression, and racism and psychology.

Consumer Advocacy

With the increased emphasis on a consumer-centric approach and encouraging market forces and consumer satisfaction to drive the system, the Agency for Health Care Research and Quality (AHRQ) began a new initiative in October 1995 that involved building an integrated set of carefully tested and standardized questionnaires and reporting formats that could be used to collect and report meaningful and reliable information about the experiences of consumers enrolled in health plans. This resulted in the development of CAHPS® (Consumer Assessment of Health Plans) as an easy-to-use kit of survey and report tools that provides reliable and valid information to help consumers and purchasers assess and choose among health plans. The kit contains a set of questionnaires that asks consumers about their experience with their health plans, gives sample formats for reporting results to consumers, and provides a handbook to help purchasers implement the surveys and produce the reports. Although not a standard, these consumer satisfaction surveys or report cards are another way to monitor the system of care.

MULTICULTURAL COMPETENCIES AS A STANDARD OF CARE

A policy brief summarizes the movement of cultural competence, a concept that developed out of a systems perspective on service delivery systems (Chin, 1999). It addresses the question of mandating cultural competence, developing standards, and emphasizing outcomes and indicators as a means toward accountability and quality improvement. Multicultural competencies are increasingly emphasizing standards of care and the competencies needed to ensure high-quality services within a system of care; Figure 22.1 diagrams these relationships of the competencies needed to ensure a consumer-centric, culturally competent quality system of care. It includes three levels of competencies—systems, clinical, and provider competencies—based on the standards developed by the Center for Mental Health Services (Substance Abuse, Mental Health Services Administration [SAMHSA], 1998) for managed care organizations. It also includes who defines, regulates, and monitors the standards of the service delivery system, MCO, and providers. We cannot look at multicultural competencies in managed health care without looking at systems issues or considering the constraints influencing the development of standards. This raises several controversial issues.

Standards Versus Guidelines

Although there is a push for standards among advocates for multicultural competencies, the profession of psychology is increasingly moving away from standards of care that are too prescriptive toward guidelines that are suggestive in a risk management environment. Guidelines are a set of practices and implicitly recognized principles of conduct that evolve over the history of a profession. They are aspirational in nature and suggest or recommend specific professional behavior. In contrast, standards of a profession are mandatory and may be accompanied by an enforcement mechanism (American Psychological Association, 1993). Advocates for multicultural competencies

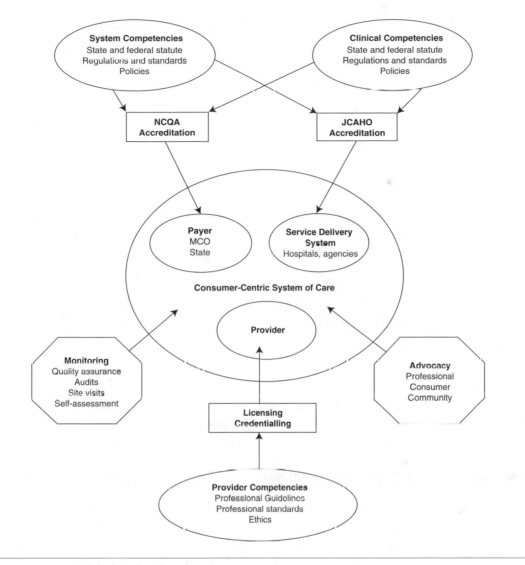

Figure 22.1   Model of Multicultural Competencies

are finding greater resistance to multicultural competency standards because they leave psychologists liable for lawsuits. In considering risk management issues and contracting with MCOs, providers are often cautioned to *avoid contracts that expose providers to a higher standard of care than what is normally required or standards with which the provider is unfamiliar* (U.S. Department of Health and Human Services, 1998).

Standards for Whom?
System Versus Provider

A second issue is for whom these standards are intended. Are they generic competencies intended for the service delivery system, for all providers, or for providers who choose as their specialization to practice with diverse populations? Many have argued against making multicultural competence a specialization because it would result in the adverse consequence of limiting the number of providers able and willing to practice cross-culturally while penalizing those who already practice with diverse and racial/ethnic groups.

Standards for service delivery systems under managed care either address accreditation of the service delivery system or credentialing of individual providers. They define what hospitals and outpatient agencies must do to monitor the competencies of their providers. Different MCO models have been developed to define and limit the provider network to control costs; Tufts Health Plan developed its network of providers by contracting with independent practitioners and group practices, whereas Harvard Pilgrim Health Care developed its network of providers using a staff model whereby members choose providers from staff employed by the MCO. Other provider networks were formed from mergers between hospitals, such as Massachusetts General Hospital and Brigham and Women Hospital; these networks were intended to enable hospitals to negotiate more favorable fees by commanding a significant market share. Initially, MCOs tended to limit their provider networks and used capitated payments to manage and control costs. In response to market demands, MCOs have expanded their networks and returned to fee-for-service arrangements to remain competitive. Although this results in less control over the providers with whom they contract, standards regulating provider practice shift from the MCO to the network. Service delivery systems increasingly use fee-for-service clinicians who are paid only for the units of service delivered as managed care reimbursement rates limit the ability to cover overhead costs of salaried employees. As emphasis on cost outweighs factors monitoring quality of care, cultural competence is given lower priority.

Performance-Based Outcomes

Although service delivery systems frequently include aspirational statements of cultural competence in their goals or mission statements, few have operationalized these into competencies, measurable objectives, or performance indicators (Chin, 2002). Even when they have, the failure of payers or managed care organizations to reimburse these costs usually means that they will not occur. Collection of race/ethnicity data is typically not required; some argue that this results in racial profiling and adverse consequences. Consequently, it is not possible to hold systems and providers accountable because it is not possible to monitor utilization and quality or to evaluate disparities among racial/ethnic groups.

Absence of a Population Focus

Currently, most regulatory mandates for provider or service delivery systems within managed care do not address cultural or multicultural competence. Managed care legislation or performance measures generally consider patients, clients, and members in the aggregate as a unitary group. A multicultural perspective or a consideration of diverse communities is lacking; there has not been a population focus in the development of regulations, standards, or guidelines. Contracts refer to the agreements between the provider and the service delivery system or the provider and the MCO. The consumer, client, or community has often been forgotten in the process.

Within a multicultural competency framework, the recognition of unique and diverse needs of clients and community (i.e., a population focus) is critical. Performance measures cannot strive to attain a uniform and normative criterion without attending to differential norms and targets for different communities and racial/ethnic groups. Health disparities and inappropriate utilization will result among minority groups when the system has failed to be culturally competent in serving all segments of a diverse population.

MULTICULTURAL COMPETENCE IN MANAGED HEALTH CARE

Managed care imposed a radical change on the health care system. Driven by the imperative to stem increasing health care costs, managed care seeks to save money by managing health care utilization and narrowing the choices available to health care consumers. The hardest part of this process was to formulate a set of viable guidelines that improves the ability of a MCO to meet high quality standards in all populations and translates into measures of accountability. (Lavizzo-Mourey & Mackenzie, 1996)

Use of a culturally competent framework is needed to address how population specific issues of health beliefs and cultural values, disease incidence and prevalence, and treatment efficacy are managed within a managed care environment.

Economic Imperative

Although a social justice perspective and moral imperative have dominated the push for multicultural competencies and cultural competence, many argue that an economic perspective will prevail as the U.S. population becomes increasingly diverse. As managed care increasingly dominates the market, many argue that market forces of changing population demographics will drive providers and systems to become culturally competent and to develop multicultural competencies; consumers will demand the quality of care that is responsive to specific cultural needs.

At the same time, many managed care strategies have raised concerns because of potential bias against racial/ethnic groups.

Risk selection (i.e., selecting against the possibility of loss associated with a given population) might have adverse consequences for racial/ethnic groups in which the need for interpreter services and case management services may be viewed as increasing risk.

Consumer Choice

The question of choice has been pivotal to the discussion in managed care. Critics of managed care have argued that managed care narrows the choice of providers and level of benefits such that the service delivery systems will be less competent and responsive to the diverse needs of racial/ethnic minority groups. From a multicultural perspective, the ability of clients to use race/ethnicity and cultural competence as criteria in their choice of therapists is crucial. Yet, most MCOs have not structured their provider directories to give consumers this choice in selecting a therapist by race/ethnicity. Choice is further reduced because provider networks are not always balanced to include providers from diverse racial/ethnic backgrounds mirroring the client population.

Costs Versus Quality

Managed care was created to achieve cost containment goals through managing care. Utilization review is intended to limit care to that which is medically necessary. Unfortunately, this emphasis on costs has potential adverse consequences on racial/ethnic groups. Interpretation of medical necessity criteria by reviewers who may not be culturally competent will result in a bias against racial/ethnic groups. The failure to collect or track utilization data by race/ethnicity further limits the ability of MCOs to evaluate disparities in utilization. Underutilization, commonly found among racial/ethnic groups unable to access the system, pits multicultural competence objectives against managed care objectives to reduce utilization or length of stays. Similarly, higher costs associated with delivering services to non-English-speaking populations are often not recognized or accepted within managed care. Reimbursement rates do not factor in interpreter costs; no incentives are given to bilingual providers in their reimbursement rates.

Payers and the consumer public are demanding that providers and service delivery systems be accountable for both quality and cost of services. Managed care has made a shift toward quality of care; this has resulted in an emphasis on performance outcomes and consumer satisfaction. At the same time, performance indicators specific to multicultural competencies tend to be limited to language access. Consumer satisfaction surveys rarely are conducted in languages other than English, and measures of access, availability, and appropriateness of services are not differentiated by racial/ethnic groups.

Provider Contracts

MCOs use provider contracts to monitor and regulate care. Contracts between MCOs and providers often hold providers accountable to reasonable and commonly accepted standards of care in providing services to its members; they also hold MCOs accountable for timely reimbursement when contracted services are delivered in the manner specified in the contract. From a multicultural perspective, exclusivity clauses limiting providers from participating in other networks have reduced consumer choice or limited the diversity of providers within a network. At the same time, as long as multicultural competencies are not standards of care, providers may object that they are being held to a higher standard of care than commonly accepted practice.

Medicaid

State contracts to MCOs, vendors, or counties for Medicaid patients frequently include provisions for cultural competence. Medicaid is part of the continuum of care for many clients in the public mental health sector. The Medicaid–Balanced Budget Act of 1997 requires that states and managed care entities provide information and instructional materials to enrollees "in a manner and form which may be easily understood." Proposed Medicaid Managed Care Regulations (1998) issued by the Health Care Financing Administration (HCFA) require states "to establish a methodology for determining the prevalent language or languages in a geographic area" and to ensure that materials are available in those languages. Cultural groups that represent at least 5% of the Medicaid population in a particular area is recommended as the criterion. Cultural competency requires awareness of the culture of the population being serviced; the network should include an adequate number of providers, commensurate with the population enrolled, that are aware of the values, beliefs, customs, and parenting styles of the community.

Approximately 48% of all Medicaid beneficiaries in the United States are now enrolled in a managed care program. In a survey of cultural competence in Medicaid managed care purchasing completed at George Washington University Medical Center, cultural competence is a general requirement for Medicaid purchasing in 29 of 50 states. Translated literature/interpreter assistance is reported as available in 35 of 50 states. On the other hand, only 9 of 50 states require cultural competency training for contractors and employees, only 12 states require language-proficient providers, and only 8 states have administration standards (Rosenblum, 1998).

MANAGED CARE INITIATIVES TO PROMOTE MULTICULTURAL COMPETENCE

Some managed care initiatives have promoted multicultural competence, but this has generally been limited to language accessibility to improve access for persons of limited English proficiency through translation or interpreter services. There is generally little emphasis on bilingual/bicultural providers or multicultural competencies of providers. Language translation of brochures and other educational materials, if available, is often available only in Spanish. Translations for Asian and other languages are often deferred for the future because of their costs and complexity. Sometimes, this is handled by providing a multilingual announcement asking members to get the notice translated because it is important. Several model initiatives in which definitions are clear and measurable have benchmarks that are responsive to racial/ethnic minorities, and these are described below.

California's County Cultural Competence Plans

California has an Annual Review Protocol for Consolidated Specialty Mental Health Services (Department of Mental Health, 2002) with implementation plan requirements and criteria for compliance; a number of the criteria require cultural and linguistic competence. All counties are required to have an approved Cultural Competence Plan (CCR, title 9, Chapter 11, Section 1810.410; DMH Information Notice No. 97-14 [see Department of Mental Health, 2002]). Plan elements include vision and mission, policies, data, measures and analysis of data to identify targets and benchmarks, training, and credentialing.

Thresholds are set for when linguistic services must be provided that state the following: The contractor will provide linguistic services to (a) a population group of mandatory Medi-Cal enrollees residing in the proposed service area who indicate their primary language as other than English and who meet a numeric threshold of 3,000 or (b) a population group of mandatory Medi-Cal eligibles residing in the proposed service area who

indicate their primary language as other than English and who meet the concentration standards of 1,000 in a single ZIP code or 1,500 in two contiguous ZIP codes. Thresholds are established by counties for the languages meeting criteria that require linguistically appropriate services and translated materials. Critics have argued that this puts the onus of responsibility on enrollees; the criterion is the number of enrollees or residents in the service area.

California's Medicaid contracting offered counties a choice to take a carve-out that could be either public managed care or privatized. Counties all submitted implementation plans to the state. Coye and Alvarez (1999) reviewed Medicaid managed care and cultural diversity in California. California has detailed requirements in health plan contracting, using a Cultural Index of Accessibility to Care to ensure effective services for a diverse Medicaid population; this is a system for rating culturally competent service requirements of HMOs when contracting for services. It includes two threshold and concentration standards for the provision of services to non-English-speaking beneficiaries/populations—that is, linguistic services must be provided in areas that meet either the threshold standard of 3,000 beneficiaries per language group or the concentration standard, defined as 1,000 beneficiaries in a single ZIP code or 1,500 in two contiguous ZIP codes.

California contracts with one local initiative and one commercial managed care plan in each county to give Medi-Cal beneficiaries a choice and promote competition among the MCOs. There are eight core contract provisions required by the state to ensure cultural competency, five of which specifically address interpretation and translation services (Coye & Alvarez, 1999). These include the following:

- provide persons with limited English proficiency (LEP) with 24-hour access to linguistic interpreter services over the phone or interpreters on site;

- provide linguistic services, including information on plan coverage, health education programs, provider orientation and training, appointment scheduling, medical advice phone lines, membership assistance, and satisfaction surveys;
- assess and report the linguistic capacity of interpreters employed or contracted by the plan;
- establish a community advisory committee to assist in developing and monitoring culturally competent services;
- conduct an internal needs assessment and formulate a plan to meet the cultural and linguistic service needs of enrollees within 12 and 18 months, respectively, of contracting with the state;
- monitor the provision of providers' linguistic services;
- develop and implement standards and performance requirements for the provision of linguistic services and monitor the performance of individuals offering such services;
- implement an interpreter coordination system and set standards for coordinating appointment scheduling with interpreter services.

This has had a favorable effect in stimulating the development of culturally competent initiatives by MCOs in California; the Alameda Alliance for Health Plan, for example, pays directly for interpreter services as a reimbursable service at about $70 per encounter. In addition, it is considering a financial incentive for physicians of about $15 per encounter to compensate for the additional time required for interpreter-supported services (K. Quan, Chief Financial Officer and General Counsel, Alameda Alliance for Health, personal communication, May 2001).

Language Thresholds in Contracting

Other states have used different definitions for these threshold levels compared to California. Missouri, for example, uses a threshold of 200 or 5% of program membership, whichever is less for interpreter services. Threshold criteria clearly define the point at which MCOs and service delivery systems must provide certain services such as bilingual providers and interpreter support.

Massachusetts includes a language threshold requirement to evaluate the cultural competency of bidders for state contracts: If a population reaches a threshold of 15%, then the vendor will be asked by the area office to respond to clinical vignettes related to that population in its applications. This will have the effect of clinically relevant criteria being developed that target racial/ethnic populations; evaluation tools are also currently being developed. This threshold, however, is probably too high and would exclude too many distinct racial/ethnic groups.

Contract language for contracting with managed care organizations in Massachusetts ensures that multilingual providers are available for the most commonly used languages in a particular service area (as defined by the state). The MCO shall ensure non-English-speaking enrollees a choice of at least two multilingual primary care providers. The compliance measure requires the MCO to provide (a) an analysis of where enrollees who require multilingual services reside within the MCO's service area and (b) a list of all multilingual primary care providers by ZIP code in the area. It is unambiguous, offers choice, and also asks the contractor to document where it cannot perform.

Washington's Parity Initiative

Washington has a parity initiative that is used to compare services to ethnic minority populations against the population residing in the county. *Parity has been used as a contract requirement for the accountability of services to ethnic minority populations since 1989.* It is a method to see who is enrolled and being served, comparing the general population demographics to the service population demographics based on 15 racial/ethnic categories. Differences can exist if it is demonstrated that this is appropriate to the population. Some flexibility is permitted; a county could build in a range if numbers are small or use the smaller number or percentage (e.g., 500 or 2% at the county level, or 1,000 or 5% at the regional service network [RSN] level). These requirements are not targets but rather are descriptive.

Originally, the concept of parity used percentages as contracting benchmarks (e.g., if an RSN was at 50% of parity, it needed to be at 75% in 2 years, 87.5% in 4 years, and 100% in 6 years). Currently, the concept of benchmark performance that is used states that payment to a contractor will be withheld in the amount of the lesser of $2,500 or 1% of the monthly capitated payment for each biennial quarter that the contractor fails to meet the minimum compliance levels but will be released if the minimum compliance is met (H. Balderama, Washington Department of Mental Health, personal communication, 2000). The intent of such parity initiatives is to ensure that racial/ethnic groups will be served in the system; it does not ensure quality.

Cultural Competence Self-Assessment Surveys

Self-assessment surveys have been developed in Oregon (Mason, 1995), New York (Chambers, 1998), and New Jersey (Weiss & Minsky, 1996) to assess the cultural competence of agencies and are used as monitoring and compliance tools for site visits. In New Jersey, the tool is sent to agencies before a site visit is made from the Bureau of Licensing and Inspections. Items on cultural competence are also included for the Patient Services Compliance Unit when it monitors compliance. The tool also is used informally at staff meetings for self-assessment.

Although these tools have the weight of audit tools, they are voluntary in nature and are recommended as self-assessment tools rather than mandatory standards. Statewide training of mental health staff (hospitals and agencies) often accompanies the dissemination of the tool to promote cultural competence skills training.

CULTURAL COMPETENCE STANDARDS

The U.S. Department of Health and Human Services, Office for Minority Health developed national standards for ensuring culturally competent and linguistically appropriate services in health care (i.e., CLAS Standards) in 2000 (U.S. Department of Health and Human Services, 2000). These include 14 standards that define culturally competent care, language access, organization supports, implementation guidelines, the relationship between the standards and existing laws, diverse and culturally competent staff, data collection, and information dissemination.

The Center for Mental Health Services developed cultural competence standards for managed behavioral health services provided to racial/ethnic populations (SAMHSA, 1998). These include overall system and clinical competencies, implementation guidelines, recommended performance indicators and outcomes or benchmarks, and provider competencies.

The Association for Multicultural Counseling and Development operationalized multicultural counseling competencies for providers using dimensions of personal identity and worldviews (Arredondo et al., 1996).

Although these standards describe specific benchmarks and indicators for assessing and monitoring the cultural competence of systems and providers, none of these standards is mandated by legislation. A version of these competencies is now part of the new guidelines for multicultural competencies approved by the American Psychological Association.

Cultural Competence Legislation

Several legislative mandates support the implementation of cultural competence initiatives. Title VI of the Civil Rights Act of 1964 prohibits entities that receive federal financial assistance from engaging in practices that have the effect of discriminating on the basis of race or national origin. State human rights laws prohibit forms of discriminatory practices that impair access by specific, identified subclasses of individuals (i.e., from racial and ethnic minority groups), and contractors have an affirmative obligation to ensure that services are accessible and "culturally competent." The Disadvantaged Minority Health Improvement Act of 1990 set the stage for cultural competence in health care systems with its intent to improve the health of racial/ethnic minority groups.

Several states, including Michigan, New York, California, and Washington, have cultural competency standards that are written into statute and result in criteria that states and counties or MCOs must implement in the form of cultural competency plans. A study out of Georgetown University summarizes contracting specifications used by different states in contracting with counties or vendors for the delivery of mental health services (Rosenblum & Teitelbaum, 1999).

The Washington parity initiative is analogous to affirmative action, whereas the California cultural competence initiative is more analogous to standards; both are set in statute. In Massachusetts, a bill has been filed requiring MCOs to have a culturally competent provider network or allow their members to go out of the network to access culturally competent providers.

SYSTEM COMPETENCIES

System standards domains include competencies of the system to ensure that services are accessible, available, appropriate, and adequate for all segments of the population. Components are fully described in the cultural competence standards for managed behavioral health services provided to racial/ethnic populations (SAMHSA, 1998) and include the following:

1. *Cultural competence planning.* Are there population assessments to identify demographic characteristics and user profiles by race/ethnicity to ensure that the needs of diverse groups are addressed? Does the needs assessment formulate a plan for meeting the cultural and linguistic needs of members using an incremental approach with concrete timelines?

2. *Governance.* Who is at the table when deciding on policies and protocols governing the system of care and its reimbursement? Are consumer voices and diverse voices of racial/ethnic groups represented in meaningful roles?

3. *Benefit design.* Is there equitable access and comparability of benefits across populations? Is there flexibility in the plan benefits to allow for culturally specific interventions such as alternative medicine?

4. *Prevention, education, and outreach.* Are plan materials and health education materials linguistically and culturally appropriate?

5. *Quality monitoring and improvement.* What indicators, benchmarks, and targets are relevant to diverse racial/ethnic groups and ensure access, availability, appropriateness, and adequacy of services? Is there a plan as well as the ability to monitor the MCO for its cultural competence?

6. *Utilization review.* Utilization review, prior authorization, and precertifications are all intended to limit coverage to those services that are medically necessary. Do reviewers

have training in cultural competence to ensure unbiased reviews?

7. *Decision support and management information systems.* Do data sources collect race/ethnicity data at all levels of care? Are racial/ethnic groups disaggregated? Can the MCO generate utilization and outcome reports by race/ethnicity with relevant indicators?

8. *Human resource development.* Are staffing patterns diverse and mirror the client population? Can the MCO identify providers by race/ethnicity to offer consumer choice? Is staff training and development in the area of cultural competence and racial/ethnic mental health offered or required for all staff?

CLINICAL COMPETENCIES

Clinical standards domains include competencies of the services that are delivered to ensure that they are accessible, available, appropriate, and adequate for all segments of the population. Components are described fully in the Center for Mental Health Services (CMHS) document (SAMHSA, 1998) and include the following:

1. *Access and service authorization.* Is there linguistic access for all groups, including both over the phone and on site? Are access criteria evaluated based on spiritual, social functioning, family, and community supports as well as medical and mental health?

2. *Triage and assessment.* Do triage and assessment criteria take into account individual, family, cultural, and community strengths?

3. *Care planning.* Are care plans compatible with cultural frameworks and community environments of consumers and family members?

4. *Treatment plan.* Are treatment plans relevant to culture and life experiences? Do they have input from consumer and family members?

5. *Treatment services.* Is the full array of services available and appropriate to the consumer's needs?

6. *Discharge planning.* Does discharge planning involve the consumer and family? Is it done within a culturally competent framework and communication style congruent with the consumer's values?

7. *Case management.* Are case management services consumer and family driven? Do they address specific and diverse needs for consumers who are uninsured, have different cultural perspectives, or lack familiarity with the system of care?

8. *Communication styles and cross-cultural linguistic and communication support.* Is linguistic access and cross-cultural communication support available at all points of entry and throughout the system?

9. *Self-help.* Is self-help part of the continuum of care? How does the plan address different strategies and needs of different racial/ethnic communities?

PROVIDER COMPETENCIES

Provider competency domains include competencies of the provider and the skills they bring to the clinical encounter. Three documents have attempted to define these skills specifically: the document from the CMHS, the document from the Association for Multicultural Counseling and Development, and multicultural guidelines approved by the American Psychological Association. Provider competency domains include the following:

1. *Knowledge, understanding, skills, and attitudes.* Providers must understand the

cultural backgrounds of the consumers with whom they work, as well as their implications for clinical issues, and develop treatment strategies that are effective and relevant for working cross-culturally and with diverse racial/ethnic groups. These include differences in symptom expression, communication styles, health beliefs and practices, psychosocial stressors and histories, and different pharmacological effects.

2. *Training.* Minimal baseline training and ongoing training as a continuing process are essential for providers to be culturally competent in preparing for licensure and credentialing.

Although professional associations such as the American Psychological Association have moved away from professional standards toward guidelines because of risk management concerns, advocates for multicultural competencies are moving toward professional standards to hold individuals and systems accountable. Many embrace the concept of multicultural competence, but many find the definition of competencies ambiguous or limited to cultural knowledge. Others are concerned that this concept is restrictive in advocating for concordance between client and provider based solely on race/ethnicity.

Definitions of provider competencies are only now being defined to include the above dimensions. Massachusetts is one of the few states to have a training requirement of 3 hours for professional licensure on racial/ethnic bases of behavior.

California's Policy on Workforce Diversity

Los Angeles County has a model policy on diversity, adopted by the Board of Supervisors in 1995, for its workforce that addresses provider competencies on a systems level. The objectives are to (a) create a high-performing, productive organization and an inclusive workplace environment in which each person is valued for his or her unique gifts and talents; (b) capitalize on the innovation inherent in diverse work groups; and (c) ensure that each person is valued based on individual characteristics rather than on stereotypes or assumptions.

The policy emphasizes workforce diversity and creating a nurturing environment. Departments are expected to develop opportunities; create policies to promote an open, flexible, responsive, and responsible work environment; monitor affirmative action compliance; consider bonus pay for bilingual staff; and promote diversity in recruitment, hiring, and training practices. This goal is reflected in the mission, vision, and strategic plan.

According to the goals of L.A. County's workforce training, there is an emphasis on managing diversity by achieving a full use of human resources (including White males), which is differentiated from affirmative action, and valuing differences, which is viewed as achieving representation and promoting quality interpersonal relationships. Training is conducted regularly, and all employees are required to attend diversity trainings. A bilingual bonus is offered to staff and included in the policy with eligibility criteria and measures of proficiency.

Washington's Initiative on Culturally Competent Providers

Washington defines culturally competent providers under its parity initiative. There is a contract requirement for agencies to have ethnic minority specialists—that is, they must have 100 hours of specialty training in cultural competence and be supervised for 2 years after obtaining a master's degree; these specialists ensure that the treatment plan is defined in relationship to the client's culture. The state has a 100-hour training program for mental health specialists, but this is no longer offered. The initiative is not tied to professional licensure but to agency licensure.

The standards for mental health specialists are specific, with three different levels—direct service provider, supervisor, and consultant—and include indicators to monitor compliance with these standards. Unfortunately, monitoring mechanisms for these standards remain weak. Mainstream providers often will attempt to sidetrack these standards, using cost as an excuse not to be monitored. Currently, these regulations are poorly monitored other than through self-report. For example, agencies providing services to racial/ethnic minorities by nonspecialists need to call in a consultant; however, they will only do it for an upcoming audit. Then, if the consultant does not give the report that they want, the agencies will not call him or her back. Some mainstream agencies do not have ethnic minority staff or supervisors. To be in compliance, they may have four people walk into a room and expect an outside consultant to evaluate all of them in an hour. Others will use providers qualified as specialists who sign off for clients from different racial/ethnic groups with whom they have had no experience (Focus group participant, interview, January 2001).

CONCLUSIONS

There is a window of opportunity to promote multicultural competencies as a standard of care within managed care. Changes in managed care have led to new organizational entities (i.e., integrated service networks), giving greater leverage to service delivery systems. There is a shift in emphasis toward quality of care, performance indicators, and accountability. There is also a growing disenchantment with managed care as a failed experiment to manage costs as health care premiums continue to soar.

Changing population demographics with racial/ethnic groups soon to become the majority should make both the public and the system of care reconsider consumer choice, economic imperatives, and accountability to prioritize cultural competence and multicultural competencies as a standard of care. Multicultural competencies have been operationalized for a managed care environment to address system, clinical, and provider competencies. These competencies need to be clearly defined and measurable, with monitoring mechanisms defined by indicators, benchmarks, and timelines.

MCOs, service delivery systems, and providers have yet to implement these competencies as a standard of care. Referring once again to Figure 22.1, this would require advocacy from consumer and professional groups in addition to legislative change, which would be integrated into regulations, accreditation standards, and professional licensure. Several considerations are offered to move the system toward cultural competence and providers toward multicultural competencies.

Maintain a Population Focus

Although cultural competence is increasingly included in mission statements and goals of organizations and MCOs, operationalization of these competencies within managed care has yet to occur. MCOs and service delivery systems often do not maintain a population focus on the premise that ignoring racial/ethnic differences is considered unbiased and equitable. However, MCOs should follow these guidelines:

1. *Population demographics.* MCOs should define the racial/ethnic groups in their target area and provide data on the population distribution by race/ethnicity for planning and resource allocation.
2. *Changing demographics.* When specific groups in the member population have

shown rapid growth by more than 10%, MCOs should demonstrate what they have done to ensure that services are appropriate and adequate to this population's needs. Population- and culture-specific indicators should be developed when rapid growth in the population is reported.

3. *Planning.* Needs assessments should include racial/ethnic groups that meet a population criterion of 1,500 or 3% in the member population.
4. Governance committees should mirror the racial/ethnic demographics of the member population.

Collect Race/Ethnicity Data

For managed care, there is often a disincentive to collect data by race/ethnicity because they can document managed care enrollment biases if underservice or utilization disparities exist. The following guidelines should be adopted:

1. A federal and common standard for the collection of race/ethnicity data with disaggregation of the five major race/ethnic groups using census 2000 categories should be set, as well as a timeline for implementation.
2. Representation of racial/ethnic groups on consumer satisfaction surveys and needs assessments should be ensured. When disaggregation results in numbers less than 50, there should be oversampling and secondary analysis to enable meaningful analysis of trends and results for specific racial/ethnic groups.
3. Consumer satisfaction surveys should be conducted in the client's primary language, and non-English-speaking groups should be included to the extent that they exist in the client population.

Cultural Competence
Performance Indicators

With the growing emphasis on performance-based contracting and indicators for quality assurance, cultural competence indicators need to be included in quality assurance monitoring of MCOs and service delivery systems, such as the following:

1. Utilization patterns by race/ethnicity should be reported to answer how ethnic minorities are represented in covered versus uninsured groups if there are differentials in referrals, types of intervention, and so forth.
2. Disparities in utilization by service type or in penetration rates among different racial/ethnic groups, to the extent that they exist within the target area, should be identified with a plan for eliminating the disparity.
3. Performance indicators targeting cultural/linguistic needs of specific racial/ethnic groups should be identified.

Promoting Workforce Development

1. Provider networks should be diverse and mirror the client population. A matrix of providers by geographic location, race/ethnicity, language, and expertise should be developed to identify the availability of culturally specific resources. These should be identified in a separate directory so as not to bias consumers in limiting racial/ethnic providers to racial/ethnic clients.
2. Credentialing should identify the multicultural competencies the providers should possess, and the curriculum modules for training providers should include the influence of culture in clinical practice, cross-cultural communication skills, culturally competent interviewing skills, and knowledge of clients' cultures.
3. MCOs can redesign their contracts with providers to expand cultural competence objectives and target racial/ethnic needs. They should expand provider networks and contracted vendors to include racial/ethnic providers that are culturally competent.
4. MCOs can require cultural competency plans from service delivery systems with whom they contract, and they should have sufficient enforcement mechanisms and incentives to ensure their success.

REFERENCES

American Psychological Association. (1993). *Legal risk management.* Washington, DC: Author.

Arredondo, P., Toporek, R., Brown, S., Jones, J., Locke, D. C., Sanchez, J., et al. (1996). *Operationalization of the multicultural counseling competencies.* Alexandra, VA: Association for Multicultural Counseling and Development.

Chambers, E. D. (1998). *Cultural competence performance measures for managed behavioral healthcare programs.* New York: New York State Office of Mental Health, The Research Foundation of New York State.

Chin, J. L. (1999). *Cultural competence and health care in Massachusetts: Where are we? Where should we be?* (Issue Brief No. 5). Waltham: Massachusetts Health Policy Forum.

Chin, J. L. (2002). Assessment of cultural competence in mental health systems of care for Asian Americans. In K. S. Kurasaki, S. Okazaki, & S. Sue (Eds.), *Asian American mental health: Assessment theories and methods* (pp. 301-316). New York: Kluwer Academic/Plenum.

Civil Rights Act of 1964, Pub. L. No. 88-352, Title VII, 42 U.S.C. § 2000e.

Coye, M., & Alvarez D. (1999). *Medicaid managed care and cultural diversity in California.* New York: The Commonwealth Fund.

Cross, T. L., Bazron, B. J., Dennis, K. W., & Isaacs, M. R. (1989). *Toward a culturally competent system of care.* Washington, DC: CASSP Technical Assistance Center, Georgetown University Child Development Center.

Department of Mental Health. (2002). *Addendum for implementation plan for phase II consolidation of Medi-Cal specialty mental health services—Cultural Competence Plan requirements* (DMH Notice No. 02-03). Sacramento, CA: Author.

Disadvantaged Minority Health Improvement Act of 1990, Pub. L. No. 101-527.

Lavizzo-Mourey, R., & Mackenzie, E. R. (1996). Cultural competence: Essential measurements of quality for managed care organizations. *The Annals of Internal Medicine, 124*(10), 919-921.

Mason, J. (1995). *The cultural competence self-assessment questionnaire: A manual for users.* Portland, OR: Portland Research and Training Center.

Medicaid–Balanced Budget Act of 1997, Pub. L. No. 105-33.

Proposed Medicaid Managed Care Regulations, 42 C.F.R. § 432.10(b)(1) (1998).

Rosenblum, S. (1998). *Negotiating the new health system: A nationwide study of Medicaid managed care contracts* (2nd ed.). Washington, DC: George Washington University Medical Center, School of Public Health and Human Services, Center for Health Policy Research.

Rosenblum, S., & Teitelbaum, J. (1999). *Cultural competence in Medicaid managed care purchasing: General and behavioral services for persons with mental and addictions-related illnesses and disorders* [Online]. Available: www.samhsa.gov/mc/managed%20care%20 contracting/issubr4/Issue_Brief4.htm

Substance Abuse, Mental Health Services Administration (SAMHSA), Center for Mental Health Services (CMHS), Center for Mental Health Services, The Western Interstate Commission for Higher Education. (1998). *Cultural competence standards in managed care, mental health services for four underserved/underrepresented racial/ethnic groups.* Rockville, MD: Author.

Sue, D. W., Arredondo, P., & McDavis, R. (1992). Multicultural counseling competencies and standards: A call to the profession. *Journal of Multicultural Counseling and Development, 20*(6), 64-88.

Sue, D. W., Bernier, J., Durran, M., Feinberg, L., Pedersen, P., Smith, E., et al. (1982). Position paper: Cross-cultural counseling competencies. *The Counseling Psychologist, 10,* 45-52.

U.S. Department of Health and Human Services, Office of Minority Health. (2000). *National standards on culturally and linguistically appropriate services (CLAS) in health care* [Online]. Available: www.omhrc.gov/clas/ frclas2.htm

U.S. Department of Health and Human Services, Substance Abuse and Mental Health Services

Administration. (1998). *Volume Nine: A guide for providers of mental health and addictive disorder services in managed care contracting* (DHHS Pub. No. 98-3242). Washington, DC: Government Printing Office.

Weiss, C. I., & Minsky, S. (1996). *Self-Assessment Survey Tool.* Trenton: New Jersey Division of Mental Health Services, Multicultural Advisory Committee.

23

Multicultural Competence in Counseling Centers

AMY L. REYNOLDS
Buffalo State College

RAECHELE L. POPE
University at Buffalo, State University of New York

College campuses today have a more diverse student body than ever before. The racial and ethnic diversity of college students will only continue to grow between now and 2015 (Carnevale & Fry, 2000). For many students, going to college means adjusting to a more diverse and complex environment than they experienced in their home communities. In fact, the majority of current college students attended high schools that were primarily one racial or ethnic group (Humphreys, 2000). In addition to the changing campus racial composition, multicultural issues, questions, tensions, and debates have become a hallmark of campus life today. To different degrees and in varying ways, multiculturalism is addressed on most college and university campuses. Evidence in the literature

suggests that increased racial diversity and multicultural initiatives on campus are linked to positive educational outcomes for all students. These outcomes are particularly noteworthy in the areas of cognitive development, critical thinking (Guthrie, King, & Palmer, 2000), and racial prejudice reduction (Chang, 2000). The literature also reveals, however, that more research is needed to fully understand the effects of diversity; gauge the degree of success, impact, and outcome of multicultural initiatives; ensure access; and develop inclusive curriculum. Regardless of how these issues are addressed, what is clear, according to Pope, Reynolds, and Mueller (2003), is that "new and innovative approaches are needed to address the individual needs of a diverse student body and the organizational demands of changing campuses" (p. 2).

On most college campuses, student affairs professionals, or those individuals responsible for addressing the co-curricular needs and concerns of college students, have often been asked to create and implement multicultural programs and services on campus (Cheatham, 1991; Pope & Reynolds, 1997). McEwen and Roper (1994) have suggested that a commitment to multiculturalism is the responsibility of all student affairs professionals; as such, student affairs practitioners are frequently the campus leaders in creating more welcoming and diverse campuses (Pope, 1993). However, many student affairs professionals have received minimal training or professional development in multicultural issues to prepare them for this important role (McEwen & Roper, 1994; Talbot, 1992). The complex cultural dynamics of higher education "have necessitated that student affairs professionals not only be prepared to address multicultural issues but also acquire the skills necessary to work effectively with culturally diverse populations and issues" (Pope & Reynolds, 1997, p. 266). Increasingly, mental health and student affairs professionals view multicultural competence as the most encompassing approach to addressing multicultural concerns.

Multicultural competence, although a vital and vibrant aspect of the counseling literature for the past 20 years, is a new addition to the student affairs literature and vernacular. Pope and Reynolds (1997), in an attempt to introduce the construct of multicultural competence to the student affairs literature, created a synthesized list of seven core student affairs competencies: (a) administrative and management, (b) theory and translation, (c) helping and interpersonal, (d) ethical and legal, (e) teaching and training, (f) assessment and evaluation, and (g) multicultural awareness, knowledge, and skills. The seven competencies were proposed to assist student affairs

professionals in their efforts to more effectively meet the complex and challenging demands of higher education.

College counseling center staff, who are often a bridge between the student affairs and counseling/psychology professions, work to strengthen their multicultural competencies to better meet the clinical needs of a diverse student body as well as assist in the efforts of campuses to become more multiculturally sensitive and inclusive. The intersecting histories and overlapping professional goals of the counseling psychology and student affairs professions assist college counselors in their efforts to effectively navigate the world of higher education as well as the counseling profession. Given their eclectic training as therapists, consultants, evaluators, and change agents, college counselors are well suited to address significant social and organizational change issues such as multiculturalism.

According to Zimmerman and Payne (1993), "The roles and functions of counseling centers have always changed in response to social needs" (p. 2). Stone and Archer (1990) and others (Constantine & Gloria, 1999; Murphy, Wright, & Bellamy, 1995; Yalof, 1997) believe that multicultural issues are central to the mission, functions, and future of counseling centers. Several studies have found that counseling centers emphasize multicultural issues more than other psychology training sites (Constantine & Gloria, 1999; Gloria, Castillo, Choi-Pearson, & Rangel, 1997); however, that finding may be more a statement about the omission of multicultural issues from the training curriculum of other clinical sites rather than an assumption about the successful inclusion of these issues within counseling centers. As such, Constantine and Gloria have underscored that all training sites, including college counseling centers, need to increase their commitment to multicultural issues.

Stone and Archer (1990) identified four unique periods in the history of counseling centers in which their roles and functions differed and changed according to societal needs (e.g., vocational guidance for World War II veterans coming to college) and concerns unique to particular institutions (e.g., whether the counseling center is part of the health center). Although Stone and Archer suggested that most counseling centers have moved away from an emphasis on career counseling to more attention on personal counseling and the campus environment, various external and internal demands and expectations in higher education have created diverse counseling centers that emphasize a variety of roles and functions. A common framework used to understand counseling centers is to identify their programs and services as taking a preventive, developmental, or remedial perspective (Phelps, 1992). Kiracofe et al. (1994) expanded this understanding:

> The counseling service should play three essential roles in serving the university and college community. The most prominent is providing counseling and therapy to students experiencing personal adjustment or psychological problems that require professional attention. Somewhat related is the preventive role of assisting students in identifying any learning skills that will assist them in effectively meeting their educational and life goals. The last goal is contributing to a campus environment that facilitates the healthy growth and development of students. (p. 38)

As attention in student affairs has turned toward participation in academic components of campus life, including student learning (cf. Astin, 1996; Blimling & Alschuler, 1996), counseling centers, through their counseling, outreach, and advocacy efforts, are increasingly serving an essential role in the educational mission of colleges and universities (Hotelling, 1990; Kiracofe et al., 1994). Although individual college counseling centers

serve different purposes, the most common functional areas for counseling center efforts are counseling (individual, group, crisis intervention, career), outreach and consultation, training and supervision, testing and assessment, and administration (Kiracofe et al., 1994; Stone & Archer, 1990). These diverse activities suggest that counseling center staff interact with a wide range of students, staff, and faculty, meeting their unique needs and addressing their distinct concerns. In all of these areas, counseling center staff have the opportunity to address multicultural issues and infuse multicultural competence as a standard for effective and ethical care on college campuses.

MULTICULTURAL COMPETENCE

Multicultural competence has become a significant force in the field of counseling (Sue, Bingham, Porche-Burke, & Vasquez, 1999). Despite its increasing relevance and application in clinical work, assessment, and training, a unified definition and theory of multicultural competence has not been created. Discussions and debates about the universal (etic) versus the culture specific (emic) nature of multicultural competence are ongoing, and D. W. Sue (2001) has argued the need for a conceptual framework to clarify, integrate, and enhance our understanding of multicultural competence. Although the Sue et al. (1982) position paper on cultural competence has continued to be a foundational work on which many research studies, models, and assessment tools have been based, multicultural competence as a construct has continued to evolve and change. At various times, key multicultural experts have argued for a revision, expansion, or redefinition of multicultural competence. Sue and Zane (1987) offered a reformulation of cultural competence by suggesting that therapists focus less on culture-specific knowledge or techniques and more on relational factors such as building credibility, relieving symptoms, and instilling hope. Speight, Myers, Cox, and Highlen (1991) argued for the need to reconceptualize multicultural skills by focusing less on culturally distinct or universal behaviors or values and more on self-knowledge and worldview. According to Sue and Zane, psychology must create new paradigms and practices to meet the diverse needs of clients.

S. Sue (1998) further suggested the need to specify between general counseling skills that are necessary for cultural competency and specific skills that increase one's counseling effectiveness with a particular cultural group. He proposed three orthogonal characteristics or skills necessary for cultural competence. The first characteristic is scientific mindedness or the ability to form hypotheses rather than rely on assumptions about clients. This skill also requires that one find creative ways to test hypotheses and gather more information. The second factor is dynamic sizing or "knowing when to generalize and be inclusive and when to individualize and be exclusive" (S. Sue, 1998, p. 446). This flexibility is necessary to combat the stereotyping that naturally occurs when individuals are trying to apply their understanding of group differences to work more effectively with individual clients. Being able to determine which individual and/or cultural factors are influencing a client requires a cognitive style that encourages complex and contextual reasoning (Reynolds, 2001). The final characteristic, culture-specific expertise, allows individuals to apply their knowledge of various cultures to effective and meaningful interventions. This type of counseling repertoire would include culture-specific interventions that could be applied appropriately to various clients based on the counselor's assessment of the client's cultural identity, needs, and concerns.

D. W. Sue (2001) recently expanded the construct of multicultural competence in his multidimensional model of cultural competence (MDCC). This dynamic framework provides important conceptual tools to broadly rethink our approach to multicultural counseling and competence. Sue introduced two significant expansions or enhancements of multicultural competence. First, he suggested that the multicultural counseling competence movement has focused almost exclusively on the individual level, with little attention on the organizational or institutional level. He recommended that cultural competence training and application efforts incorporate the counseling and psychology professions, organizations, and society. It is not enough to examine multicultural attitudes, knowledge level, and skills without also challenging the underlying values, policies, and structures of the profession, organizations, and society. Using the theories and tools of multicultural organization development is one way for organizations and professions to explore their underlying assumptions, values, and practices (D'Andrea & Daniels, 1995; D'Andrea et al., 2001; D. W. Sue, 1995, 2001).

A second and very crucial addition to the paradigm of multicultural competence was viewing social justice as a foundational component. According to D. W. Sue (2001),

> Multicultural counseling competence is defined as the counselor's acquisition of awareness, knowledge, and skills needed to function effectively in a pluralistic democratic society (ability to communicate, interact, negotiate, and intervene on behalf of clients from diverse backgrounds), and on a organizational/societal level, advocating effectively to develop new theories, practices, policies, and organizational structures that are more responsive to all groups. (p. 802)

D. W. Sue (2001) views advocacy within the workplace, the profession, and society as being central to multicultural competence and professional responsibility. Psychologists and therapists who address social policy issues have been arguing this point for years; what we do in our individual offices is not enough if it does not alter the social conditions that lead to sexual abuse, addiction, or depression. Sue stated, "Multicultural counseling competence must be about social justice—providing equal access and opportunity, being inclusive, and removing individual and systemic barriers to fair mental health services" (p. 801).

D. W. Sue (2001) and others (Archer & Cooper, 1998; Grieger & Toliver, 2001; Lee, 1998; Parham, 1999) have argued that it is not enough for counselors and psychologists to simply expand and change their counseling skills to help them meet the needs of individual clients who may be culturally diverse from them. These multicultural experts have emphasized the need to develop skills so counselors can intervene effectively, sometimes on a client's behalf, in a pluralistic society that includes advocating within the profession to develop new and more inclusive theories, practices, and organizational systems. This is a profoundly important shift in the definition of multicultural competence and offers new ways of thinking about and achieving multicultural transformation within the workplace, the profession, and society (Reynolds, 2001).

Exploring and understanding the dynamic and growing multicultural competence literature is an important first step when applying these philosophies, models, and strategies to the work of college counseling centers. A thorough and well-thought-out definition and application of multicultural competence at the individual, group, organizational, and professional levels must be considered. Grieger and Toliver (2001) stated,

> It is becoming increasingly clear that providing culturally sensitive counseling and psychotherapy is a necessary but not sufficient prerequisite for effectively addressing multiculturalism on campus (as well as in other settings). In fact, it can be argued that

counselors have a responsibility to move beyond in-the-office, conventional modalities of counseling and psychotherapy if they are to adequately challenge systems and environments that are oppressive to some of their constituents. (p. 828)

For college counselors to work effectively across all aspects of difference and assist their campuses in addressing multicultural issues, they must have a clear and concrete understanding of what constitutes multicultural competence. Further clarification and discussion are needed to ascertain what constitutes the multicultural competencies necessary to effectively and ethically address multicultural issues within higher education (Pope & Reynolds, 1997). Insight and knowledge about the specific components of multicultural competence in a counseling center context are vital for counseling center staff to meet the diverse needs of all individuals and the campus as a whole in meaningful and constructive ways.

COUNSELING CENTER APPLICATIONS AND IMPLICATIONS

Understanding multicultural competence in a counseling center context is most beneficial and productive when exploring the key functions of counseling centers. Grieger and Ponterotto (1998) have suggested that the functions of a counseling center counselor include (a) counseling; (b) outreach and consultation; (c) teaching, training, and supervision; and (d) testing and assessment. A fifth area—multicultural organization development, advocacy, and activism—is also emerging as a key aspect of multicultural competence that can assist counseling center staff and other higher education professionals in their efforts to combat prejudice and intolerance and cultivate culturally sensitive campus environments (Pope, 1995).

Counseling

The first function, counseling, is the most central responsibility of most college counseling centers. Counseling occurs with individuals, couples, and groups. In addition, career counseling is a function of some counseling centers. Much has been written about the multicultural awareness, knowledge, and skills that counselors need to work effectively with all clients. Jenkins (1999) argued that sensitivity to cultural and social variables is essential for ethical and competent practice in higher education. Expanding that notion, Grieger and Toliver (2001) stated that "providing effective and culturally sensitive counseling and psychotherapy to a diverse student population is the core mission of every counseling or university counseling center" (p. 831).

Multicultural scholars have identified many specific multicultural counseling competencies and offered suggestions about how to apply and implement these knowledge and skills (cf. Arredondo et al., 1996; Hansen, Pepitone-Arreola-Rockwell, & Greene, 2000; Sue, Arredondo, & McDavis, 1992; Sue et al., 1998). Offering a more parsimonious list specifically geared to multicultural counseling and advising in a student affairs context, Reynolds (1995, 1999) proposed six multicultural competencies:

1. Acquiring appreciation, knowledge, and understanding of cultural groups, especially those individuals and communities that have been historically underserved and/or underrepresented by the counseling profession.
2. Increasing content knowledge about important culturally related terms and concepts such as racial identity, acculturation, or worldview.
3. Enhancing awareness of one's own biases and cultural assumptions and assessing one's own multicultural skills and comfort level.
4. Developing the ability to use that knowledge and self-awareness to make more

culturally sensitive and appropriate interventions.
5. Developing an awareness of the interpersonal dynamics that may occur within a multicultural dyad.
6. Deconstructing the cultural assumptions underlying the counseling process. (Reynolds, 1999, p. 219)

In addition to these specific competencies, many multicultural scholars suggest that multiculturally competent counseling expands our understanding of what constitutes effective therapy. The traditional view of counseling begins and ends in the therapist's office. Some suggest, however, that culturally competent counseling begins before a client enters the counselor's office. Moreover, culturally competent counseling means moving beyond the safe parameters of our offices and more fully engaging with the diverse campus community. This expansion of what defines a therapeutic space not only is vital in building a reputation as a concerned and culturally sensitive person but is also essential in reaching those students who would never feel comfortable coming to a counseling center. Individual counseling center staff members who are most actively involved outside the counseling center with diverse student groups (e.g., international students; lesbian, gay, and bisexual students; and students of color) often have the most diverse caseload. This visibility and involvement with offices designed to serve the needs of these students often leads to more referrals from faculty and staff members and increases students' awareness of counseling services. Jenkins (1999) highlighted the importance of supporting the connection with students' natural support systems on campus (e.g., cultural organizations, churches, and spiritual organizations) as well as outreach to family and home community as appropriate.

It is important to highlight that such increased visibility and involvement on campus may lead to more complicated relationships with some student groups and clients. Students from various cultural groups may not understand or value the formality and ethical rules associated with the traditional counseling relationship. An example of this situation might involve a staff member who works closely with the women's center and trains its volunteers. If she is approached by one of the volunteers who asks to establish a therapeutic relationship, she will have to make sense of the traditional expectations and taboos around dual relationships. This counselor needs to balance these ethical rules with the importance of redefining therapeutic space and relationships in culturally appropriate ways. Jenkins (1999) highlighted the importance of being flexible in interventions to most effectively help clients and understand their worldview. Direct and honest conversations are needed to ensure open communication and common goals within the counseling relationship. Addressing the reality of dual relationships with clients who may want to engage with their counselors outside the context of the counseling relationship is another skill that counselors need to develop.

Outreach and Consultation

In a way that is qualitatively different from expanding the therapeutic space, many counseling centers devote significant time to providing conventional outreach and programming services across their campuses. Much of this outreach is focused on programming for intact student groups, such as residence halls or Educational Opportunity Program (EOP) students, or as campuswide programming on topics of significance to the entire campus, such as stress management or substance abuse education. Counseling center staff also provide ongoing training for many student groups such as resident assistants or orientation leaders. In addition to programming efforts, some counseling centers provide

programming and consultation services to administrators, staff members, and faculty. Programming oriented toward staff and faculty may be offered through the human resources department but is more likely part of a consultation effort. Much of the consultation may occur informally when staff members are asked to provide insight into a particular problem. Other times, there may be a formal request that involves all aspects of the consultation process from assessment to intervention. Such interventions may range from assisting staff in dealing with work-related stress to helping them develop effective working relationships with each other or with students. Many counseling center staff are also involved in providing crisis response and outreach for any traumatic or crisis situation on campus such as a student death or rape on campus.

Outreach and programming services can focus on diversity issues or broader psychological or campus concerns. Some counseling centers are actively involved in providing diversity programming on their campuses either because of multicultural expertise of individual staff members or as part of a campuswide diversity effort. Providing diversity programming and consultation is a vital campus service, and ideally, all counseling centers have staff members who can contribute to this important effort. In addition, it is vital that *all* outreach, regardless of the population or topic, address diversity issues. Assumptions should not be made about who the audience is or what their needs are. Programs must be designed with the most diverse audience in mind. For example, time management programs can acknowledge the significance of culture in how individuals view time, and workshops on relationships can openly discuss how everyone may not be heterosexual and that their relationship concerns may differ. Initiating dialogue with various cultural groups on campus and assessing their programming needs are an ideal way to build relationships and provide meaningful outreach programs. Counseling center staff also might consider getting feedback on their workshop designs from other staff members or various constituent groups on campus. In addition, program evaluations are an important way to gather information about the success and relevance of campus workshops.

Teaching, Training, and Supervision

According to Grieger and Toliver (2001), "Just as counseling center staff have a responsibility to further their own professional multicultural development, they carry an equal responsibility to provide multicultural training to all practicum students and interns at their site" (p. 833). Within a counseling center context, training occurs primarily through training seminars as well as group and individual supervision. The amount and type of training available is determined by the size and focus of the training program. Some counseling centers have well-developed predoctoral internship training programs, whereas others may use practicum students from both master's and doctoral programs in psychology, counseling, and social work. Accreditation standards from professional organizations such as the American Psychological Association (APA) or the Council for Accreditation of Counseling and Related Educational Programs (CACREP) emphasize the need for multicultural competence.

Practicum and internship experiences and their corresponding supervision are significant because they assist students in integrating and applying their theoretical knowledge of counseling and psychology. Some studies have shown that providing multicultural training to interns may increase their level of multicultural competence (Evans, Acosta, Yamamoto, & Skilbeck, 1984; Parker, Bingham, & Fukuyama, 1985; Pope-Davis, Reynolds, Dings, & Ottavi, 1994).

Such exposure to multicultural issues may happen within didactic and experiential seminars that are part of the practicum and internship experience. Some internship training programs provide multicultural counseling seminars as a means of educating their trainees about multicultural issues, whereas other training programs may infuse multicultural issues into other core seminars such as assessment or counseling theories.

Providing culturally sensitive supervision is another way to assist trainees in their appreciation and application of multicultural competence. According to Reynolds (in press), supervision is a significant and powerful relationship that provides students with the opportunity to integrate multicultural theory and techniques and receive feedback on their performance.

Ideally, supervision provides a supportive and developmentally oriented relationship in which supervisees can explore their own assumptions, attitudes, and biases toward working with particular individuals and groups. In addition, supervision provides a concrete opportunity to more fully examine and experience multicultural issues such as racial identity, power, and worldview. For supervision to be an effective medium for multicultural training, supervisors must be trained in multicultural issues and supervision. Unfortunately, Constantine (1997) reported that many supervisors have not been adequately trained to address multicultural issues in supervision and may not be equipped to effectively conceptualize the concerns of diverse clients and provide meaningful support to supervisees struggling to incorporate multicultural awareness and skills into their therapy. In fact, research has identified a significant training gap in multicultural issues, with many supervisees having more coursework and knowledge about multicultural issues than their supervisors (Constantine, 1997). Counseling centers must provide professional development opportunities for professional staff and possibly offer ongoing seminars and peer supervision so that professional staff can explore and enhance their ability to provide multiculturally sensitive supervision.

Testing and Assessment

According to Suzuki and Kugler (1995), assessment is the process that therapists use to gather information about clients. Assessment can occur through quantitative means such as tests or through qualitative means such as a clinical interview. Often, testing is not a significant function for many counseling centers. Some may provide minimal career and personality testing (e.g., Strong Interest Inventory, Myers Briggs Type Indicator), but many counseling centers offer minimal psychological testing. However, for those who do offer testing, counseling center staff need to be aware of the cultural biases inherent in standardized testing and work to provide testing experiences and interpret testing results in culturally appropriate and meaningful ways (Suzuki & Kugler, 1995). In recent years, significant writings in the area of multicultural assessment have occurred, and these resources should be reviewed by any counseling center staff who offer psychological testing (cf. Dana, 2000; Suzuki & Kugler, 1995; Suzuki, Meller, & Ponterotto, 2000).

For the many counseling centers that do not offer traditional testing programs, it is important to realize that clinical assessment is a central component of the counseling process. The process of gathering and making clinical meaning of information about clients and sometimes providing diagnosis also requires sensitivity to multicultural issues and knowledge about multicultural constructs. According to Grieger and Ponterotto (1995), "Successful counseling requires an accurate assessment of the client's concerns, which includes an in-depth understanding of the factors that influence the client's experience, perception, and presentation of his or her problems" (p. 357). Such assessments must include an understanding of the client as an individual, as a member of a family, and as a member of one or more cultural groups. Grieger and Toliver (2001) suggested that assessments incorporate factors such as "worldview, level of acculturation, racial/ethnic identity development, emotional intelligence, language dominance, and the equivalency of psychological constructs in the client's culture" (p. 834). Consideration of these factors is essential to honoring the individual and cultural uniqueness of each client.

Assessment is a complex process, and to accurately conceptualize and understand clients' presenting concerns and underlying issues, counselors must take great care in gathering information from a variety of sources, including the clients and significant people in their lives, as well as from observations during therapy. Counselors need to develop skills to make sense of the details, especially when there may be discrepant information. Assessment typically involves gathering data from clients and then comparing that knowledge to either standardized norm groups when using tests or clinical norms when completing intake interviews. In both situations, it is possible for cultural realities to be minimized, misunderstood, or ignored all together. A multiculturally competent counselor learns how to struggle with definitions of normal behavior and understands how to contextualize psychological problems without assuming pathology or ignoring strengths of clients.

Multicultural Organization Development, Advocacy, and Activism

Multicultural organization development (MCOD) provides a new paradigm for instituting multicultural changes within a college environment (Pope, 1995). MCOD, which was first developed as a theory in the early 1980s, emphasizes planned change as a way to create multicultural environments and organizations (Jackson & Holvino, 1988). Using organizational development strategies and practices, MCOD can create or transform organizations that support the key values of diversity and social justice. By questioning underlying cultural values and assumptions, MCOD encourages organizations and institutions to reexamine their beliefs, assess their practices, and transform how they work. According to Pope and Reynolds (1997), creating multicultural campuses demands commitment, reflection, expertise, and action. The use of MCOD theory and principles in higher education and psychology is relatively new, and the growing literature should be consulted as counseling center staff consider how to apply this innovative and dynamic theory to their work (cf. Grieger, 1996; Grieger & Toliver, 2001; Pope, 1993, 1995; D. W. Sue, 1995).

Multicultural organization development, advocacy, and activism are tasks that many counseling center staff may be uncomfortable with or feel ill prepared to address on their campuses. Multicultural organization development as a counselor center function has two unique goals. The first goal focuses on redefining what it means to provide counseling services for *all* students and incorporating an advocacy approach as appropriate. Grieger and Toliver (2001) stated, "It can be argued that counselors have an ethical responsibility to move beyond in-the-office, conventional modalities of counseling and psychotherapy if they are to adequately challenge systems and environments that are oppressive to some of their constituents" (p. 828). Although the majority of counseling is focused on the individual, all counselors are aware of how various systems (family, campus, and society) affect clients, their concerns, and their ability to succeed on campus. This function involves developing the commitment, programs, and

services to create change in the systems affecting clients, especially those on college campuses. This commitment entails active involvement with other offices and staff members on campus who typically advocate on behalf of students such as Minority Student Services, Disability Services, or EOP. Taking more of a community psychology approach to solving clients' problems increases the likelihood of client success and builds a stronger and more responsive network of concerned staff and faculty. For example, Buffalo State College Counseling Center has adopted a support coordination intervention on campus that involves gathering together key individuals within a client's support system such as family, staff members, and faculty to brainstorm and discuss how to work together more effectively to create a positive outcome for the student. The student is involved in these discussions, which helps reinforce their responsibility for helping to solve their problems. This type of approach is ideal for addressing the concerns of students who may be unable to get their needs met and have difficulty succeeding in college, and it is also an example of an intervention that focuses on expanding the role of the counseling center and the individual counselor.

The second goal of a multicultural organizational approach is to focus on the internal workings of the counseling center itself. MCOD uses various organizational theories, tools, and strategies to create systematic organizational change. Creating multicultural environments requires more than just the desire to be multiculturally sensitive. The process of cultivating counseling centers that are truly multicultural requires a willingness to fully engage in the process, take risks, develop specific competencies, and evaluate the quality and effectiveness of the counseling center. The first step in creating a multicultural counseling center is to establish commitment among the staff, especially the administrative leadership. Once a commitment has been made, a thorough assessment of the multicultural strengths and weaknesses of all aspects of the counseling center must be completed. Such assessment would include reviewing policies and procedures; services and programs; physical environment; staff recruitment, retention, and the evaluation and reward process; training curriculum; and other significant organizational factors. In addition, counseling center staff need to address any internal and external barriers to multicultural transformation. Through this process of reflection and assessment, counseling centers can create a long-term multicultural strategic plan that will enable them to develop culturally appropriate and relevant services as well as become a campus leader in multicultural change efforts.

Counseling centers cannot become multicultural overnight. In addition to commitment at all levels of the organization, there need to be models that can be used to guide and structure the multicultural change effort. Without such frameworks, it is difficult to assess the strengths and weaknesses of an organization, develop the necessary and appropriate interventions, and help those involved know whether their efforts have been successful. To illustrate the planning process and what a multicultural counseling center might look like, Grieger (1996) adapted and expanded an organization development checklist. This checklist is an ideal starting place for self-assessment and strategic planning and includes potential key components of a counseling center diversity plan. Table 23.1 identifies the 10 categories of the Template for a Multicultural Counseling Center, describes the purpose of each category, and identifies specific elements of how counseling centers may incorporate these key categories into their diversity plan.

Addressing the 10 factors identified within the multicultural counseling center template is an important step in developing a multicultural counseling center. Engaging in a process of reflection, assessment, and strategic planning

helps to provide a necessary model for understanding and managing change efforts. To understand the possibilities for using the Template for a Multicultural Counseling Center, we should explore potential applications. The first step to adopting this strategic planning process is to engage the staff in an open discussion about diversity and its role in the counseling center. Involving all staff, including support staff, counselors, graduate students, and administrative staff, in these early discussions is essential to creating openness and commitment to the process. This exploration can occur informally as a staff dialogue and more formally using an outside consultant. Vocal and active involvement from the counseling center administrative leadership sets a crucial tone. Counseling centers can use a committee approach or the staff as a whole to institute the strategic planning process. Both approaches have their pros and cons in terms of encouraging staff responsibility and having a manageable process. Regardless of whether a committee or staff as a whole is used, it may be useful if several staff members agree to coordinate the process so there can be organization and accountability. Once the plan is approved and in place, the goals, outcomes, and timelines will assist the staff in actually implementing the plan.

Once a strategic planning process is in place, the individuals involved can review the 10 factors identified in the template and explore significant concerns and issues. Although having an open-ended process encourages expression, it is also important to have a viable timeline for developing the strategic plan. Identifying the goals and timelines for the process in advance helps the staff know what to expect.

Ideally, dissent is encouraged, and if staff members seem hesitant to express contrary opinions, leaders might want to advocate ideas or attitudes that they believe might be present even if they are not spoken. It is hard to build

(text continued on page 379)

Table 23.1   Template for a Multicultural Counseling Center

MCOD *Category*	*Purpose*	*Specific Components*
1. Comprehensive definition of the term *multicultural*	In the interest of serving students, an inclusive and broad definition of *multicultural* should be chosen. Encouraging discussion of definitional issues is essential so there is agreement among staff members as to where diversity initiatives might be focused.	• Use an inclusive definition of diversity. • Identify the student groups that have historically been underserved or underrepresented in higher education (e.g., people of color, students with disabilities, nontraditional students, female students, religious minorities, international students, first-generation college students, and lesbian, gay, bisexual, and transgender students).
2. Mission statement	A counseling center mission statement identifies its values and priorities and ideally identifies diversity issues as central to the counseling center mission.	• Explicit use of words such as *multicultural* or *diversity* must be an essential part of the mission statement. • Incorporate the mission statement into all department publications and advertisements such as brochures and Web sites.
3. Leadership and advocacy	Multicultural change efforts in higher education are most successful when they involve the commitment of the top leadership within a college. However, when such top leadership is not available, individuals may take responsibility within their own sphere of influence and attempt to create change.	• Set short-term and long-term diversity goals for each year. • Give additional rewards and support to those staff members who fully participate in the multicultural vision of the counseling center. • Seek out additional multicultural training to assist efforts toward creating a multicultural counseling center. • Document how supervisors will assist their supervisees in the development of multicultural competencies.
4. Policy review	Multicultural organization development focuses on all significant subsystems of an organization such as mission, policies and procedures, training, and evaluation. Reviewing the current policies, procedures, and forms is one way to ensure that diversity issues are included in all aspects of an organization.	• Conduct a full review of departmental policies and procedures to assess their impact on diverse populations and make changes as appropriate.

(Continued)

Table 23.1   Continued

MCOD Category	Purpose	Specific Components
5. Recruitment and retention of a diverse staff	To have a truly multicultural counseling center, staff must be culturally diverse. Without a diversity of voices, life experiences, and cultural backgrounds, staff may be limited in their ability to meet the needs of some students. In addition to recruiting a diverse staff, addressing interpersonal and structural dynamics within the environment helps to create a welcoming and nurturing environment for all staff members.	• Develop and follow proactive diversity recruitment strategies that identify where advertisements will be sent and how a diverse candidate pool will be developed. • Include multicultural awareness, competence, knowledge, and skills as an integral part of the job description. • Evaluate all job candidates on those criteria. • Use ongoing supervision to explore retention-related issues.
6. Multicultural competency expectations and training	Multiculturally competent attitudes, knowledge, and skills are fast becoming the standard within counseling by which counseling center staff members are evaluated. It is no longer acceptable to have a multicultural expert on staff to meet the needs of specific student groups. Training or retraining staff members in multicultural counseling may help them feel more equipped to meet the needs of all students. Mentoring graduate students and encouraging the development of their multicultural awareness, knowledge, and skills are essential for effective supervision.	• Create opportunities for staff to attend local, state, or national conferences or workshops that address diversity issues. • Offer diversity training every year. • Provide effective multicultural supervision for all practicum students and interns. • Specify how multicultural tasks and responsibilities are part of graduate students' overall job expectations. • Assign diversity goals to each staff member and base their annual evaluation on how they contributed to the multicultural vision of the counseling center.
7. Scholarly activities	It is the responsibility of all professionals to contribute to the field of multicultural counseling through professional writing or presentations that reflect on their experiences. Such work instills more commitment to the process, creates a positive image for the counseling center, and provides opportunities for staff members to receive feedback and support from colleagues across the country.	• Encourage, support, and reward staff members who pursue any multicultural scholarly activities (either writing for publication or presenting at professional conferences).
8. Counseling center programs and services	Incorporating multicultural content and sensitivity into all counseling center programs and services from their advertisement to their implementation makes for accessible	• Review all programs, activities, forms, and services for multicultural content and values. • Develop plans for more thorough and deliberate infusion of diversity

(Continued)

Table 23.1   Continued

MCOD Category	Purpose	Specific Components
	and meaningful activities. It is also helpful to identify underserved student groups and develop ways to meet their needs more effectively, including the development of new and creative programs and services.	material in workshop agendas and materials. • Create at least one new and innovative program each year to contribute to the multicultural change efforts on campus.
9. Physical environment	The physical environment of a counseling center sends an important message about what it values. It is important to create an affirming and caring environment in which individuals of diverse backgrounds feel valued. Creating a setting that has music, artwork, and other visual images that are representative of diverse cultures not only makes those individuals feel welcome but also educates and expands the awareness of others. Center staff members need to be conscious and thoughtful in how they approach this issue, and ongoing dialogue is central to creating an inclusive and accepting environment.	• Review individual offices and public space to ensure they are void of offensive or insensitive materials. • Ensure that all offices and programs are accessible and welcoming to students with disabilities. • Display culturally inclusive artwork, music, and magazines in public spaces to create a welcoming environment. • Discuss how to respond to insensitive or offensive verbal or nonverbal conduct in any programs or services.
10. Assessment	To create a multicultural counseling center, staff must assess multicultural strengths and weaknesses. By knowing who it is serving and how satisfied clients are with the service, a counseling center is better able to develop effective programs and services. Once an accurate evaluation has been completed, it is easier to set goals and plan strategically. Self-evaluation is not enough. It is vital to gather information about the perceptions, attitudes, and experiences of the students, staff, and faculty who use the services for a more accurate picture of the type of changes needed. The goal of assessment is to ultimately create some accountability for the multicultural change efforts.	• Create an evaluation system that assesses the effectiveness of the center's services and outreach efforts to all students. • Assess student satisfaction with the multicultural sensitivity of the service or outreach effort as well as the multicultural competence of the staff. • Gather information about the demographic background of students who use any program or services. • Set yearly goals to either increase the percentage of students from underrepresented groups who use the office or improve the students' overall level of satisfaction with those services.

NOTE: MCOD = multicultural organization development.

trust for open dialogue, especially if it is a new norm within the counseling center. To be successful, staff members at all levels must genuinely believe they will not be penalized for suggesting unpopular ideas or resisting specific changes.

Finally, once a plan has been created and approved by the staff, it is important that all individuals take active responsibility for implementing some aspect of the plan. If everyone has some ownership in the plan, it is more likely to be successful. Creating a framework for ongoing review and evaluation will assist in the implementation of the plan and reiterate the idea that multicultural change is an ongoing and dynamic process.

Counseling centers cannot become multicultural overnight, and it is important to guard against the desire for quick change or immediate results. Using this template provides an overall structure with possible goals and target outcomes. In addition to this structure, more steps must be undertaken to create long lasting transformation in how a counseling center operates. Many of the changes vital to creating a multicultural counseling center are not easily described, instituted, or evaluated.

The most significant and meaningful aspect of a multicultural change effort occurs as specific organizational initiatives and multicultural interventions are being implemented. Changing the interpersonal culture and dynamic is as central to success as any concrete multicultural goals or outcomes could be. Developing a process whereby individual staff members are invested in addressing multicultural issues and differences of opinion are encouraged and supported provides as much ongoing incentive as organizational reward systems. Despite training in conflict resolution and other high-level communication skills, many counseling center staff have not developed the expertise or comfort level to engage in difficult dialogues around multicultural issues. By valuing these types of discussions

and emphasizing the process of understanding each other and building a multicultural community, counseling centers have the potential to create an enduring process that encourages a level of individual commitment and type of organizational dynamics essential to the development of a multicultural counseling center. Practicing authentic dialogue and diversity will also enhance the efforts of the campus community to embrace multiculturalism and allow the counseling center to play a significant role in the transformation process.

REFERENCES

Archer, J., & Cooper, S. (Eds.). (1998). *Counseling and mental health services on campus: A handbook of contemporary practices and challenges.* San Francisco: Jossey-Bass.

Arredondo, P., Toporek, R., Brown, S. P., Jones, J., Locke, D. C., Sanchez, J., et al. (1996). Operationalization of the multicultural competencies. *Journal of Multicultural Counseling and Development, 24,* 42-78.

Astin, A. W. (1996). Involvement in learning revisited: Lessons we have learned. *Journal of College Student Development, 37,* 123-134.

Blimling, G. S., & Alschuler, A. S. (1996). Creating a home for the spirit of learning: Contributions of student development educators. *Journal of College Student Development, 37,* 203-216.

Carnevale, A., & Fry, R. A. (2000). *Crossing the great divide: Can we achieve equity when Generation Y goes to college?* Princeton, NJ: Educational Testing Service.

Chang, M. J. (2000). Measuring the impact of a diversity requirement on students' level of racial prejudice. *Diversity Digest, 4*(2), 6-7.

Cheatham, H. E. (1991). *Cultural pluralism on campus.* Alexandria, VA: American College Personnel Association.

Constantine, M. G. (1997). Facilitating multicultural competency in counselor supervision: Operationalizing a practical framework. In D. B. Pope-Davis & H. L. K. Coleman (Eds.), *Multicultural counseling competencies:*

Assessment, education and training, and supervision (pp. 310-324). Thousand Oaks, CA: Sage.

Constantine, M. G., & Gloria, A. M. (1999). Multicultural issues in predoctoral internship programs: A national survey. *Journal of Multicultural Counseling and Development, 27,* 42-53.

Dana, R. H. (Ed.). (2000). *Handbook of cross-cultural and multicultural personality assessment.* Mahwah, NJ: Lawrence Erlbaum.

D'Andrea, M., & Daniels, J. (1995). Promoting multiculturalism and organizational change in the counseling profession: A case study. In J. G. Ponterotto, J. M. Casas, L. A. Suzuki, & C. M. Alexander (Eds.), *Handbook of multicultural counseling* (pp. 17-33). Thousand Oaks, CA: Sage.

D'Andrea, M., Daniels, J., Arredondo, P., Ivey, M. B., Ivey, A. E., Locke, D. C., et al. (2001). Fostering organizational changes to realize the revolutionary potential of the multicultural movement: An updated case study. In J. G. Ponterotto, J. M. Casas, L. A. Suzuki, & C. M. Alexander (Eds.), *Handbook of multicultural counseling* (2nd ed., pp. 222-254). Thousand Oaks, CA: Sage.

Evans, L. A., Acosta, F. X., Yamamoto, J., & Skilbeck, W. M. (1984). Orienting psychotherapists to better serve low income and minority patients. *The Clinical Psychologist, 40,* 90-96.

Gloria, A. M., Castillo, L. G., Choi-Pearson, C. P., & Rangel, D. K. (1997). Competitive internship candidates: A national survey of internship training directors. *The Counseling Psychologist, 25,* 453-472.

Grieger, I. (1996). A multicultural organizational development checklist for student affairs. *Journal of College Student Development, 37,* 561-573.

Grieger, I., & Ponterotto, J. G. (1995). A framework for assessment in multicultural counseling. In J. G. Ponterotto, J. M. Casas, L. A. Suzuki, & C. M. Alexander (Eds.), *Handbook of multicultural counseling* (pp. 357-374). Thousand Oaks, CA: Sage.

Grieger, I., & Ponterotto, J. G. (1998). Challenging intolerance. In C. C. Lee & G. R. Walz (Eds.), *Social action: A mandate for counselors* (pp. 357-374). Alexandria, VA: American Counseling Association and ERIC Counseling and Student Services Clearinghouse.

Grieger, I., & Toliver, S. (2001). Multiculturalism on predominantly White campuses: Multiple roles and functions for the counselor. In J. G. Ponterotto, J. M. Casas, L. A. Suzuki, & C. M. Alexander (Eds.), *Handbook of multicultural counseling* (2nd ed., pp. 825-848). Thousand Oaks, CA: Sage.

Guthrie, V. L., King, P. M., & Palmer, C. J. (2000). Higher education and reducing prejudice: Research on cognitive capabilities underlying tolerance. *Diversity Digest, 4*(3), 10-11, 23.

Hansen, N. D., Pepitone-Arreola-Rockwell, F., & Greene, A. F. (2000). Multicultural competence: Criteria and case examples. *Professional Psychology: Research and Practice, 31,* 652-660.

Hotelling, K. (1990). Taking the lead. *The Counseling Psychologist, 18,* 619-622.

Humphreys, D. (2000). The value of campus diversity: The emerging research picture. *Diversity Digest, 4*(3), 1, 32.

Jackson, B. W., & Holvino, E. (1988). Developing multicultural organizations. *Journal of Applied Behavioral Science and Religion, 9,* 14-19.

Jenkins, Y. M. (1999). Salient themes and directives for college helping professionals. In Y. M. Jenkins (Ed.), *Diversity in college settings: Directives for helping professionals* (pp. 217-238). New York: Routledge Kegan Paul.

Kiracofe, N. M., Donn, P. A., Grant, C. O., Podolnick, E. E., Bingham, R. P., Bolland, H. R., et al. (1994). Accreditation standards for university and college counseling centers. *Journal of Counseling and Development, 73,* 38-43.

Lee, C. C. (1998). Counselors as agents of social change. In C. C. Lee & G. R. Walz (Eds.), *Social action: A mandate for counselors* (pp. 3-14). Alexandria, VA: American Counseling Association and ERIC Counseling and Student Services Clearinghouse.

McEwen, M. K., & Roper, L. D. (1994). Incorporating multiculturalism into student affairs preparation programs: Suggestions from the literature. *Journal of College Student Development, 35,* 24-29.

Murphy, M. C., Wright, B. V., & Bellamy, D. E. (1995). Multicultural training in university counseling center predoctoral internship programs: A survey. *Journal of Multicultural Counseling and Development, 23,* 170-180.

Parham, T. A. (1999). Diversity and the helping professions: Lessons in understanding, advocacy, and sensitivity. In Y. M. Jenkins (Ed.), *Diversity in college settings: Directives for helping professionals* (pp. 239-246). New York: Routledge Kegan Paul.

Parker, W. M., Bingham, R. P., & Fukuyama, M. A. (1985). Improving cross-cultural effectiveness of counselor trainees. *Counselor Education and Supervision, 24,* 349-352.

Phelps, R. E. (1992). University and college counseling centers: One option for new professionals in counseling psychology. *The Counseling Psychologist, 20,* 24-31.

Pope, R. L. (1993). Multicultural organization development in student affairs: An introduction. *Journal of College Student Development, 31,* 201-205.

Pope, R. L. (1995). Multicultural organizational development: Implications and applications for student affairs. In J. Fried (Ed.), *Shifting paradigms in student affairs: Culture, context, teaching, and learning* (pp. 233-249). Lanham, MD: University Press of America.

Pope, R. L., & Reynolds, A. L. (1997). Student affairs core competencies: Integrating multicultural awareness, knowledge, and skills. *Journal of College Student Development, 38,* 266-277.

Pope-Davis, D., Reynolds, A. L., Dings, J. G., & Ottavi, T. M. (1994). Multicultural competencies of doctoral interns at university counseling centers: An exploratory investigation. *Professional Psychology: Research and Practice, 25,* 466-470.

Pope, R. L., Reynolds, A. L., & Mueller, J. A. (2003). *Multicultural competence in student affairs.* San Francisco: Jossey-Bass.

Reynolds, A. L. (1995). Multiculturalism in counseling and advising. In J. Fried (Ed.), *Shifting paradigms in student affairs: Culture, context,* teaching, and learning (pp. 155-170). Lanham, MD: University Press of America.

Reynolds, A. L. (1999). Working with children and adolescents in the schools: Multicultural counseling implications. In R. H. Sheets & E. R. Hollins (Eds.), *Aspects of human development: Racial and ethnic identity in school practices* (pp. 213-230). Mahwah, NJ: Lawrence Erlbaum.

Reynolds, A. L. (2001). Multidimensional cultural competence: Providing tools for transforming psychology. *The Counseling Psychologist, 29,* 833-841.

Reynolds, A. L. (in press). Illustrative applications in supervision. In R. T. Carter (Ed.), *Handbook of racial cultural counseling and psychology.* New York: John Wiley.

Speight, S. L., Myers, L. J., Cox, C. I., & Highlen, P. S. (1991). A redefinition of multicultural counseling. *Journal of Counseling and Development, 70,* 29-36.

Stone, G. L., & Archer, J. A. (1990). College and university counseling centers in the 1990s: Challenges and limits. *The Counseling Psychologist, 18,* 539-607.

Sue, D. W. (1995). Multicultural organization development: Implications for the counseling profession. In J. G. Ponterotto, J. M. Casas, L. A. Suzuki, & C. M. Alexander (Eds.), *Handbook of multicultural counseling* (pp. 474-492). Thousand Oaks, CA: Sage.

Sue, D. W. (2001). Multidimensional facets of cultural competence. *The Counseling Psychologist, 29,* 790-821.

Sue, D. W., Arredondo, P., & McDavis, R. J. (1992). Multicultural counseling competencies and standards: A call to the profession. *Journal of Counseling and Development, 70,* 477-486.

Sue, D. W., Bernier, J. B., Durran, M., Feinberg, L., Pedersen, P., Smith, E., et al. (1982). Position paper: Cross-cultural counseling competencies. *The Counseling Psychologist, 10,* 45-52.

Sue, D. W., Bingham, R. P., Porche-Burke, L., & Vasquez, M. (1999). The diversification of psychology: A multicultural revolution. *American Psychologist, 54,* 1061-1069.

Sue, D. W., Carter, R. T., Casas, J. M., Fouad, N. A., Ivey, A. E., Jensen, M., et al. (1998).

Multicultural counseling competencies: Individual and organizational development. Thousand Oaks, CA: Sage.

Sue, S. (1998). In search of cultural competence in psychotherapy and counseling. *American Psychologist, 53,* 440-448.

Sue, S., & Zane, N. (1987). The role of culture and cultural techniques in psychotherapy: A critique and reformulation. *American Psychologist, 42,* 37-45.

Suzuki, L. A., & Kugler, J. F. (1995). Intelligence and personality assessment: Multicultural perspectives. In J. G. Ponterotto, J. M. Casas, L. A. Suzuki, & C. M. Alexander (Eds.), *Handbook of multicultural counseling* (pp. 493-515). Thousand Oaks, CA: Sage.

Suzuki, L. A., Meller, P. M., & Ponterotto, J. G. (2000). *The new handbook of multicultural assessment: Social, psychological, and educational applications.* San Francisco: Jossey-Bass.

Talbot, D. M. (1992). A multimethod study of the diversity emphasis in master's degree programs in college student affairs. *Dissertation Abstracts International, 53*(07), 2198.

Yalof, J. A. (1997). Consolidating a professional identity in the 21st century: The changing landscape of education and training in psychology and its implications for counseling centers. *Journal of College Student Psychotherapy, 12,* 3-22.

Zimmerman, J. S., & Payne, J. P. (1993). The multicultural development of counseling centers: A model to promote self-study. *ACPA Commission VII Counseling and Psychological Services Newsletter, 20,* 2-5.

24

Multicultural Competence in Supervision

Issues, Processes, and Outcomes

MADONNA G. CONSTANTINE

Teachers College, Columbia University

Over the past few decades, scholars in the field of counseling psychology have developed a more disciplined focus in address ing issues of multicultural and cross-cultural counseling. Yet, even with the recent and concentrated attention to multicultural and cross-cultural counseling competencies, very little focus has been directed toward multicultural competence in clinical supervision. Supervision is not exempt from cross-cultural dynamics because the cultural worldviews of supervisors and their supervisees undoubtedly influence their actions within the supervision relationship (Brown & Landrum-Brown, 1995). Moreover, the dynamics that occur within supervisor-supervisee relationships inevitably have an effect on the development of supervisee-client relationships (Constantine, 1997).

The terms *multicultural supervision* and *cross-cultural supervision* often have been used interchangeably to represent cultural differences between supervisors and supervisees (Constantine, 1997; D'Andrea & Daniels, 1997; Fukuyama, 1994). According to Leong and Wagner (1994), the term *cross-cultural supervision* should be used and applied when describing supervisory relationships in which supervisors and supervisees are from different racial or ethnic groups (e.g., Black supervisor–White supervisee). *Multicultural supervision,* on the other hand, generally refers to supervisory relationships in which supervisors and supervisees are involved in examining a variety of racial, ethnic, and other cultural issues (e.g., gender, social class, religious affiliation, sexual orientation, etc.) that are important to effective counseling with clients from diverse backgrounds (Constantine, 1997; Stone, 1997). Furthermore, according to Garrett et al. (2001), multicultural supervision occurs when there are two or more people (i.e., supervisor, supervisee, and client) who are culturally different from one another. Multicultural supervision ultimately challenges both supervisors and supervisees to assess their worldviews and highlights how supervisors' and supervisees' racial, ethnic, and cultural identities affect counseling and supervision processes (D'Andrea & Daniels, 1997).

Multicultural supervision competence is characterized by supervisors' awareness, knowledge, and skills in addressing multicultural issues both within the context of supervision relationships and with regard to supervisees' relationships with their clients. Developing multicultural supervision competence should be viewed as a dynamic process (D'Andrea & Daniels, 1997; Martinez & Holloway, 1997; Porter, 1994) in that there are seemingly endless ways in which the intersections of cultural issues may be manifested within supervision and clinical relationships. Furthermore, because individuals are constantly undergoing various change and/or growth processes, some of which may affect certain components of their cultural group memberships (e.g., their cultural values), multicultural competence in the context of both counseling and supervision relationships is presumed to be an ongoing developmental process.

Several previous studies (e.g., Constantine, 2001; Pope-Davis, Reynolds, Dings, & Nielson, 1995) have reported that supervisees who receive higher amounts of multicultural supervision tend to perceive themselves as possessing higher levels of multicultural counseling competence. Because of the importance of multicultural supervision issues in facilitating the development of multicultural counseling competence in trainees and in meeting the needs of these trainees' clients, it seems vital to elucidate how supervisors can best achieve suitable levels of multicultural supervision competence.

This chapter discusses ways in which supervisors' levels of multicultural counseling competence and multicultural supervision competence may affect various processes and outcomes in supervisory relationships. In addition, this chapter examines recent multicultural supervision models and their potential role in the development of multicultural supervision competence. Last, future directions for the areas of multicultural supervision practice and research are offered.

HOW DO SUPERVISORS' LEVELS OF MULTICULTURAL COUNSELING COMPETENCE AND MULTICULTURAL SUPERVISION COMPETENCE AFFECT SUPERVISION RELATIONSHIPS?

Several studies to date have examined issues of multicultural competence within supervision dyads, and findings suggest that counselor trainees may be more prepared academically to work with culturally diverse clients than their supervisors. For example, Constantine (1997) found that 70% of the counselor supervisors in her study reported that they had *not* completed a formal course in multicultural counseling, whereas 70% of their supervisees had done so. Furthermore, Duan and Roehlke (2001), in their study of cross-racial supervisory dyads in university counseling center settings, found that supervisees were more sensitive to racial-cultural issues than were their supervisors.

Despite the possibility that some supervisors may lack high levels of multicultural counseling competence and because supervisors are typically in positions of power in supervisory relationships, it is important that they initiate discussions of cultural issues so as to create norms associated with open and forthcoming dialogues related to cultural similarities and differences (Constantine, 1997; Cook, 1994; Fong & Lease, 1997; Fukuyama, 1994). Rooney, Flores, and Mercier (1998) noted that it is beneficial for supervisees to learn from the demonstrated vulnerability of their supervisors in struggling to become multiculturally competent. Hence, supervisors' honest and meaningful explorations of their own personal values, cultural experiences, and cultural biases and stereotypes may provide supervisees with excellent models in discussing their own personal and professional challenges in working within counseling and supervision relationships.

Supervisors often set the pace and tone for how multicultural issues should be discussed in supervision, and if these discussions do not occur in this context, supervisees may surmise that it is inappropriate or unsafe to discuss such issues in supervision or even with their clients. The potential discrepancies between supervisors' and supervisees' levels of multicultural counseling competence may not only affect the development and quality of supervision relationships but may also limit the utility of supervisors' feedback related to trainees' interventions with clients. Arkin (1999) asserted that for supervisors to possess multicultural competence in supervision, they must (a) be aware of their own cultural and personal values, (b) know facts and information about their cultural selves, (c) examine their supervisory relationships in cultural terms, and (d) work on developing skills that ultimately facilitate multicultural competence.

One aspect of possessing multicultural supervision competence is supervisors' awareness of power dynamics that exist in both supervision and counseling relationships (i.e., between supervisors and counselor trainees and between counselor trainees and clients). For example, supervisors who neglect attending to power differentials across the triadic relationship with reference to race, ethnicity, sex, sexual orientation, and social class may perpetuate the institutional bigotry that multicultural competence writings have fought to combat. Moreover, whereas race, ethnicity, and sex can arguably be visible characteristics upon which power issues may be acknowledged, sexual orientation is frequently an invisible cultural group membership (Hitchings, 1999). Institutionalized homophobia and heterosexism run through our society in ways that may not be easily recognized by many heterosexual supervisors, counselors, and clients (Hitchings, 1999; Long, 1996). For supervisors, supervisees, and clients, discussions involving sexual orientation may raise issues around internalized homophobia, heterosexism, stereotyping, prejudice, and discrimination. Education in multicultural counseling tends to treat issues of sexuality in a cursory fashion, without active integration of such issues into academic coursework (Long, 1996), thereby limiting the opportunities for trainees and supervisors alike to explore biases within themselves and their environments. It is important that supervisors and their supervisees examine how sexual orientation issues may be affecting their own working relationship and the relationships between counselor trainees and their clients (Gatmon et al., 2001).

Supervisors must also be mindful not to either minimize or overly magnify cultural differences in supervision. Arkin (1999) noted that supervisors who avoid addressing cultural aspects of supervision might imply, both implicitly and explicitly, that supervisees adopt the perspectives, values, and behaviors associated with the mainstream or dominant culture. In these cases, the effectiveness of both supervisors and their supervisees could be impaired, potentially resulting in the provision of suboptimal mental health services to supervisees' clients (Haber, 1996). Conversely, supervisors who place excessive emphasis on unique cultural differences without recognizing universal or common factors run the risk of reinforcing social stereotypes of discrimination, deprivation, and disadvantage related to being members of minority or oppressed cultural groups (Arkin, 1999). In the latter case, the mental health needs of clients ultimately may be unmet because they may lose the benefit of obtaining helpful supervisory input because of supervisors' potential tendency to attribute actual pathology to unique cultural issues and syndromes (Lopez, 1997). The ability of supervisors and supervisees to recognize both similarities and differences among individuals will aid them in acknowledging the complexities of a pluralistic world and, simultaneously, connect divergent cultural backgrounds of all members of the supervisory triad. In a nutshell, supervisors' respect for cultural similarities and differences will increase the likelihood that they are aware of how aspects of clients' problems, problem-solving strategies, and coping behaviors might be culturally bound (Torres-Rivera, Phan, Maddux, Wilbur, & Garrett, 2001).

In sum, supervisory relationships may represent salient forums to explore intercultural and intracultural issues and may provide opportunities to disconfirm seemingly benign assumptions that could ultimately prove harmful in counseling settings. For supervisors and supervisees of differing cultural backgrounds, issues of power, communication, and treatment relevance may arise in supervision relationships. Such issues may provide fertile ground for progressive discussion of multicultural issues, as opposed to more superficial acknowledgments of cultural differences.

RECENT MULTICULTURAL SUPERVISION MODELS AND THEIR ROLE IN THE DEVELOPMENT OF MULTICULTURAL SUPERVISION COMPETENCE

Several contemporary models of multicultural supervision have been offered in the literature.

For example, Porter (1994) posed a four-stage model of clinical supervision for assisting supervisees of color to increase their multicultural counseling competence. In the first stage, supervisors work to increase supervisees' awareness of cultural issues and how supervisees' worldviews may affect the ways they perceive their own and others' experiences. Stage 2 explores how sociocultural factors (e.g., discrimination, oppression, and poverty) may be related to the mental health problems of people of color in the United States. In this stage, supervisees are also encouraged to move away from pathologizing certain symptoms or behaviors of clients of color to viewing some of these behaviors as culturally imbedded and/or adaptive ways of coping with problems. Stage 3 is perhaps the most challenging stage of the supervisory process in that supervisees are aided by their supervisors in exploring their own biases, stereotypes, racism, and classism. This stage requires supervisees to make themselves vulnerable in supervision by self-disclosing personal information, but it is equally important that supervisors themselves have engaged in their own self-reflection and self-examination related to these issues. In the last stage of Porter's model, supervisees are encouraged to expand their interventions beyond their individual clients to the realm of social action through mechanisms such as advocacy and empowerment. Supervisees operating in Stage 4 are also able to identify and promote indigenous or natural networks related to maintaining optimal mental health in individuals.

Brown and Landrum-Brown (1995) proposed a supervision model, the *worldview congruence model,* which addresses the supervisor, supervisee, and client triad. Their model, which was influenced by the work of Myers (1991), Nichols (1976), and Nobles (1972), consists of the following eight worldview dimensions: (a) psychobehavioral modality, (b) values, (c) guiding beliefs, (d) epistemology (i.e., how one knows), (e) logic (i.e., reasoning process), (f) ontology (i.e., nature of reality), (g) concept of time, and (h) concept of self (Brown & Landrum-Brown, 1995). Within this worldview model, these authors noted that patterns or configurations of convergent and divergent worldviews could result in various types of outcomes within triadic relationships. For example, marked worldview differences among clients, counselors, and supervisors could result in conflicts or mistrust within triadic relationships. Conversely, worldview similarities among members of triadic relationships could decrease opportunities for cultural misunderstandings and mistrust.

Constantine (1997) developed a multicultural supervision competence framework designed to aid supervisors and supervisees in actively discussing salient cultural issues within their relationships. She suggested that supervisors employ semistructured questions when working with supervisees to identify their cultural group identities and acknowledge the extent to which these identities may affect their interactions in both counseling and supervision relationships. Questions in her model included the following: What primary demographic variables comprise your identity? What worldviews (e.g., values, assumptions, and biases) do you bring to supervision relationships based on your cultural identities? What struggles and challenges have you faced in your work with culturally different clients? Constantine also noted that it would be beneficial for supervisors themselves to explore such questions with their supervisees to model ways to discuss these issues in supervision and to more deliberately share aspects of their cultural identities that affect supervisory relationships.

Holloway (1997) and Martinez and Holloway (1997) believed that using a systems approach to supervision (SAS) would be beneficial in addressing multicultural issues because it would naturally allow for the examination of various contextual factors that are germane to supervision processes and outcomes. There are seven interrelated factors in Holloway's SAS model: four contextual factors (i.e., the supervisor, the supervisee, the client, and the institution), supervision functions, supervision tasks, and the supervision relationship, which is considered to be the core factor. According to Holloway, the interrelationships among supervisors, supervisees, clients, and institutions converge to affect the nature, functions, and tasks of supervision relationships. Supervision relationships ideally become important forums in which trainees acquire multicultural knowledge and skills via discussions and explorations with their supervisors. Supervisory relationships may then also serve as models for how cross-cultural issues may be addressed in counseling relationships with culturally diverse clients.

Robinson, Bradley, and Hendricks (2000) suggested that it might not be necessary to develop new models of supervision to address cultural issues of diversity. They recommended that cultural concepts be integrated into preexisting models of counseling supervision. Hence, these authors proposed a four-step process for developing multicultural supervision competence. The first step for supervisors in becoming multiculturally competent is to develop an awareness of how cultural issues affect counseling processes. During this phase, supervisors may feel the need to consult with multiculturally competent supervisors, and they must begin to see themselves as cultural beings within the supervisory process. In the second step, supervisors recognize how cultural dynamics between supervisors and supervisees have an impact on supervision relationships. The third step is characterized by supervisors' exploration of the cultural limitations and contributions of existing counseling theories, and in the fourth step, supervisors are able to integrate effectively multicultural issues into existing counselor supervision models.

Ancis and Ladany (2001) asserted that traditional models of psychotherapy supervision, including psychodynamic, person-centered, and cognitive-behavioral models, tend to pay little attention to the relevance of cultural dynamics. Furthermore, these researchers maintained that existing models of multicultural supervision may focus primarily on supervisees' multicultural competence without attending to supervisors' own multicultural competence, and racial and ethnic issues are often emphasized in these models to the exclusion of other cultural identities (e.g., sexual orientation, social class, etc.). Hence, they presented a heuristic model of nonoppressive interpersonal development, which addresses identity development issues across a range of demographic variables in supervision. Ancis and Ladany's model provides an arena in which supervisors can explore patterns of thoughts, feelings, and behaviors about themselves, supervisees, and clients with regard to a range of demographic constructs. Included within this model is the belief that for any given demographic variable, an individual can be a member of one of two groups: a socially oppressed group (SOG) or a socially privileged group (SPG). Moreover, individuals can simultaneously be members of both a SOG and a SPG when delineating their multiple cultural identities (e.g., White and female). Ancis and Ladany also believed that for each demographic variable, individuals progress through phases called "means of interpersonal functioning" (MIF). MIF relates to the thoughts and feelings that individuals have about themselves, in addition to the behaviors they display as a result of their identification with a specific cultural group. There are four stages of MIF, including adaptation (i.e., complacency and apathy regarding socially oppressive situations), incongruence (i.e., previously held beliefs about various socially oppressive situations begin to be questioned), exploration (i.e., active examination of what it means to be a member of a SOG or SPG), and integration (i.e., recognition of and insight into socially oppressive situations, along with a proficiency in associating with multiple socially oppressed groups). According to Ancis and Ladany, every person has the ability to progress through each of these phases, which move from limited awareness of multicultural issues to increased awareness of such issues and their complexities. Naturally, depending on the stage at which both the supervisor and supervisee are located, different relationships and dynamics will present themselves. Each of these types of relationships and dynamics contributes to the quality of training that both supervisors and supervisees experience.

Because supervisory and counseling dyads often involve individual differences on more than one cultural dimension, and because individuals possess multiple reference (cultural) groups, some researchers (e.g., Constantine, 1997, 2001; Pope-Davis et al., 2002; Robinson, 1999) are increasingly recognizing the importance of examining the intersection of multiple cultural group memberships in supervision and counseling relationships. This area will continue to be important in future investigations and in future theoretical and conceptual models that address multicultural supervision issues.

FUTURE DIRECTIONS FOR MULTICULTURAL SUPERVISION PRACTICE AND RESEARCH

According to Batten (1990), supervisors desiring to further develop their multicultural supervision competence could benefit from seeking personal therapy to help understand themselves better and to better understand culturally diverse others. Supervisors might also best develop multicultural supervision competence by recognizing that the development of such competence is an ongoing, multifaceted, and multilayered developmental process

(Martinez & Holloway, 1997). However, to facilitate that process, supervisors must be active in multicultural activities. For example, helpful mechanisms for increasing supervisors' multicultural counseling and supervision competence include pursuing multiculturally relevant postgraduate coursework; reading professional materials related to augmenting one's multicultural awareness, knowledge, and skills; gaining applied clinical experience in working with culturally diverse clients; becoming active in professional multicultural counseling associations and organizations; attending professional workshops and conferences that highlight multicultural counseling competence themes; and identifying and working with individuals who could provide "expert" supervision and consultation related to multicultural issues (Constantine, 1997; Fukuyama, 1994; Hird, Cavalieri, Dulko, Felice, & Ho, 2001). It might also be beneficial for supervisors to familiarize themselves with the sociopolitical histories of their supervisees' cultural groups, which may provide them with frameworks from which to understand their supervisees' worldviews and perspectives (Hird et al., 2001).

In terms of future directions for multicultural supervision research, it will be important for investigators to explore the efficacy of supervision interventions and models in fostering the development of supervisors' multicultural competence. For example, Gainor and Constantine (2002) found that school counselor trainees who were exposed to multicultural supervision through either in-person or Web-based formats evidenced greater ability to integrate multicultural issues into their case conceptualizations of clients. In addition, researchers should explore the roles of culturally based supervisor and supervisee attitudes (e.g., their racial identity attitudes and worldviews) in the context of psychotherapy supervision activities (e.g., case conceptualizations). These types of cultural variables are likely to affect the ways in which supervisors and supervisees perceive and respond to a host of culturally based client variables. Furthermore, because multiculturally competent supervisors and supervisees are expected to possess (a) multicultural attitudes/beliefs in relation to working with culturally diverse individuals, (b) knowledge about the impact of various cultural group memberships on clients, and (c) appropriate intervention skills in the delivery of psychological services to culturally diverse clients, it may be important for future studies to systematically examine the processes by which supervisors and their supervisees develop competence in working with culturally diverse clients.

Finally, there is a need for both supervision practitioners and researchers to identify the types of multicultural supervision competencies that may be needed and used across various professional practice situations. That is, counseling is a multifaceted field, and the goals and responsibilities of supervisors in mental health, school, career, and rehabilitation counseling settings may differ significantly depending on the context. Thus, it will be critical for future supervisors and investigators to identify the degree to which both universal and context-specific types of multicultural supervision competencies can be applied to a range of counseling settings or environments.

REFERENCES

Ancis, J. R., & Ladany, N. (2001). A multicultural framework for counselor supervision. In L. J. Bradley & N. Ladany (Eds.), *Counselor supervision: Principles, process, and practice* (3rd ed., pp. 63-87). Philadelphia: Brunner-Routledge.

Arkin, N. (1999). Culturally sensitive student supervision: Difficulties and challenges. *The Clinical Supervisor, 18,* 1-16.

Batten, C. (1990). Dilemmas of "crosscultural psychotherapy supervision." *British Journal of Psychotherapy, 7,* 129-140.

Brown, M. T., & Landrum-Brown, J. (1995). Counselor supervision: Cross-cultural perspectives. In J. G. Ponterotto, J. M. Casas, L. A. Suzuki, & C. M. Alexander (Eds.), *Handbook of multicultural counseling* (pp. 263-286). Thousand Oaks, CA: Sage.

Constantine, M. G. (1997). Facilitating multicultural competency in counseling supervision: Operationalizing a practical framework. In D. B. Pope-Davis & H. L. K. Coleman (Eds.), *Multicultural counseling competencies: Assessment, education and training, and supervision* (pp. 310-324). Thousand Oaks, CA: Sage.

Constantine, M. G. (2001). Multiculturally-focused counseling supervision: Its relationship to trainees' multicultural counseling self-efficacy. *The Clinical Supervisor, 20,* 87-98.

Cook, D. A. (1994). Racial identity in supervision. *Counselor Education and Supervision, 34,* 132-141.

D'Andrea, M., & Daniels, J. (1997). Multicultural counseling supervision: Central issues, theoretical considerations, and practical strategies. In D. B. Pope-Davis & H. L. K. Coleman (Eds.), *Multicultural counseling competencies: Assessment, education and training, and supervision* (pp. 290-309). Thousand Oaks, CA: Sage.

Duan, C., & Roehlke, H. (2001). A descriptive "snapshot" of cross-racial supervision in university counseling center internships. *Journal of Multicultural Counseling and Development, 29,* 131-146.

Fong, M. L., & Lease, S. H. (1997). Cross-cultural supervision: Issues for the White supervisor. In D. B. Pope-Davis & H. L. K. Coleman (Eds.), *Multicultural counseling competencies: Assessment, education and training, and supervision* (pp. 387-405). Thousand Oaks, CA: Sage.

Fukuyama, M. (1994). Critical incidents in multicultural counseling supervision: A phenomenological approach to supervision research. *Counselor Education and Supervision, 34,* 142-151.

Gainor, K. A., & Constantine, M. G. (2002). Multicultural group supervision with preservice school counselors: A comparison of in-person versus Web-based formats. *Professional School Counseling.*

Garrett, M. T., Borders, L. D., Crutchfield, L. B., Torres-Rivera, E., Brotherton, D., & Curtis, R. (2001). Multicultural supervision: A paradigm of cultural responsiveness for supervisors. *Journal of Multicultural Counseling and Development, 29,* 147-158.

Gatmon, D., Jackson, D., Koshkarian, L., Martos-Perry, N., Molina, A., Patel, N., et al. (2001). Exploring ethnic, gender, and sexual orientation variables in supervision: Do they really matter? *Journal of Multicultural Counseling and Development, 29,* 102-113.

Haber, R. (1996). *Dimensions of psychotherapy supervision: Maps and means.* New York: W. W. Norton.

Hird, J. S., Cavalieri, C. E., Dulko, J. P., Felice, A. A., & Ho, T. A. (2001). Visions and realities: Supervisee perspectives of multicultural supervision. *Journal of Multicultural Counseling and Development, 29,* 114-129.

Hitchings, P. (1999). Supervision and sexual orientation. In M. Carroll & E. Holloway (Eds.), *Counseling supervision in context* (pp. 54-82). Thousand Oaks, CA: Sage.

Holloway, E. L. (1997). Structures for the analysis and teaching of supervision. In C. E. Watkins (Ed.), *Handbook of psychotherapy supervision* (pp. 249-276). New York: John Wiley.

Leong, F. T. L., & Wagner, N. S. (1994). Cross-cultural counseling supervision: What do you know? What do we need to know? *Counselor Education and Supervision, 34,* 117-131.

Long, J. K. (1996). Working with lesbians, gays, and bisexuals: Addressing heterosexism in supervision. *Family Process, 35,* 377-388.

Lopez, S. R. (1997). Cultural competence in psychotherapy: A guide for clinicians and their supervisors. In C. E. Watkins (Ed.), *Handbook of psychotherapy supervision* (pp. 570-588). New York: John Wiley.

Martinez, R. P., & Holloway, E. L. (1997). The supervision relationship in multicultural training. In D. B. Pope-Davis & H. L. K. Coleman (Eds.), *Multicultural counseling competencies: Assessment, education and training, and supervision* (pp. 325-347). Thousand Oaks, CA: Sage.

Myers, L. J. (1991). Expanding the psychology of knowledge optimally: The importance of worldview revisited. In R. L. Jones (Ed.), *Black psychology* (3rd ed., pp. 15-28). Berkeley, CA: Cobb & Henry.

Nichols, E. (1976, November). *The philosophical aspects of cultural differences.* Paper presented at the conference of the World Psychiatric Association, Ibadan, Nigeria.

Nobles, W. (1972). African philosophy: Foundation for Black psychology. In R. L. Jones (Ed.), *Black psychology* (pp. 18-32). New York: Harper & Row.

Pope-Davis, D. B., Reynolds, A. L., Dings, J. G., & Nielson, D. (1995). Examining multicultural competencies of graduate students in psychology. *Professional Psychology: Research and Practice, 26,* 322-329.

Pope-Davis, D. B., Toporek, R. L., Ortega-Villalobos, L., Ligiero, D., Brittan-Powell, C. S., Liu, W. M., et al. (2002). Client perspectives of multicultural counseling competence: A qualitative examination. *The Counseling Psychologist, 30,* 355-393.

Porter, N. (1994). Empowering supervisees to empower others: A culturally responsive supervision model. *Hispanic Journal of Behavioral Sciences, 16,* 43-56.

Robinson, B., Bradley, L. J., & Hendricks, C. B. (2000). Multicultural counseling supervision: A four-step model toward competency. *International Journal for the Advancement of Counselling, 22,* 131-141.

Robinson, T. L. (1999). The intersections of dominant discourses across race, gender, and other identities. *Journal of Counseling and Development, 77,* 73-79.

Rooney, S. C., Flores, L. Y., & Mercier, C. A. (1998). Making multicultural education effective for everyone. *The Counseling Psychologist, 26,* 22-32.

Stone, G. L. (1997). Multiculturalism as a context for supervision. In D. B. Pope-Davis & H. L. K. Coleman (Eds.), *Multicultural counseling competencies: Assessment, education and training, and supervision* (pp. 263-289). Thousand Oaks, CA: Sage.

Torres-Rivera, E., Phan, L. T., Maddux, C., Wilbur, M. P., & Garrett, M. T. (2001). Process versus content: Integrating personal awareness and counseling skills to meet the multicultural challenge of the twenty-first century. *Counselor Education & Supervision, 41,* 28-40.

25

Multicultural Competencies in Career Counseling

BYRON K. HARGROVE
MAUREEN G. CREAGH
DEBORAH B. KELLY

Seton Hall University

Career counseling must take place within a cultural context, helping clients set goals that are appropriate from their worldview (rather than the counselor's worldview) and using culturally appropriate techniques to best serve all clients. For their part, career counselors are willing to provide appropriate services but are often at a loss to learn how to be more culturally responsive to their clients.

—Swanson and Fouad
(1995, p. 172)

The need for the career counseling profession to proactively address multicultural and diversity issues in America's workforce has increased dramatically over the past decade. Numerous scholars have forecasted a number of future human resource changes that will inevitably force career counseling professionals to increasingly consider the role of cultural factors when providing career counseling interventions. The two most cited future trends appear to be the increased racial and ethnic diversity domestically and the globalization of the American economy (Judy & D'Amico, 1998). According to the U.S. Bureau of the Census (1998), the workforce is expected to increase in regard to members across the four major racial/ethnic minority groups: African Americans, Asian Americans,

Hispanic Americans, and Native Americans. By the year 2020, White Americans are expected to comprise less of the total proportion of the total population (64.3%). Conversely, persons of color are expected to comprise greater proportions of the population: African Americans (12.9%), Asian Americans (6.5%), and Latino/Latina Americans (16%). The labor force projections for the year 2020 are expected to be as follows: White (non-Hispanics) (68%), Hispanics (14%), African Americans (11%), and Asian Americans (6%). The workforce will continue to change slowly overall but more rapidly in the West and South regions of the United States. In particular, California will experience tremendous diversification, with Hispanic and Asian Americans rising rapidly in the population and workforce. Other notable changes expected by the year 2020 are gender diversification, with females accounting for half of the workforce, and an increasing share of immigrants in the workforce (Judy & D'Amico, 1998). As a result, career counselors need to be prepared to provide more multiculturally sensitive interventions (Fouad & Bingham, 1995; Leung, 1995; Swanson & Fouad, 1999).

In addition to domestic changes, the second major trend appears to be the need for American workers and career counselors to be concerned with workforce issues outside of the United States. That is, with the advent of globalization, automation, and information technology, there has been a growing trend toward the interdependence of the U.S. economy and workforce with other world economies and workforces, especially in Latin America and Asia. Simply put, the American workforce is no longer protected from the workforce events around the world. For example, automation and globalization will affect American manufacturing of exports, employment trends, opening and closing of markets, and competition for low-skilled jobs on an international

scale (Judy & D'Amico, 1998). In fact, global competition has been cited as the single most important issue facing corporate America, with cultural differences as the strongest challenge resulting from the acquisition of foreign businesses (Peterson & Gonzalez, 2000). Thus, given the increased racial and ethnic diversity within the American workforce and globalization of the American economy, career counselors have both the challenge and opportunity to assist a wider array of clientele with their career concerns.

The career counseling profession has made some strides toward conceptualizing and implementing services that meet the needs of diverse and multicultural clients. Beyond merely acknowledging the presence and importance of multicultural issues in career development, the career counseling profession has evolved to the point of articulating some methods of addressing cultural factors within the context of career counseling interventions. Likewise, exploring new training strategies for achieving minimum levels of multicultural career counseling competencies among career counselors has become a necessary next step in preparing career counselors for the current and future workforce.

The trend toward implementing specific multicultural competencies in career counseling appears to be the latest strategy for growth in the multicultural career counseling field. Although some advances have been made in the multicultural career counseling arena in preparation for these trends, much more work is needed in the assessment, research, and application of multicultural competence in the practice of career counseling. Therefore, the purpose of this chapter is to assist career counselors (and other career interventionists) to develop and implement more multiculturally sensitive career counseling interventions by providing a new framework for directly applying multicultural competencies to the practice of career counseling. We wrote this chapter with a wide range of educators and career interventionists in mind. Specifically, in this chapter, we discuss (a) the definition of career counseling, (b) the current status of multicultural career counseling, and (c) the multicultural guidelines offered in the newly revised 1997 career counseling competencies. At the conclusion of this discussion, we introduce our multicultural competencies model of career counseling. In this section, we express our ideas as to how the multicultural competencies developed and endorsed by the American Counseling Association (ACA) and the Association of Multicultural Counseling and Development (AMCD) might be adapted to career counseling in more specific terms than those endorsed by the National Career Development Association's (NCDA's) career counseling competency standards. Finally, we offer some future recommendations for the implementation of multicultural competencies in the training of career counselors and the practice of career counseling.

DEFINITION OF CAREER COUNSELING

In our review of the career literature, we found that the practice of career counseling has been defined in both narrow and broad terms. When defined more narrowly, career counseling has been described as "an ongoing, face-to-face interaction between counselor and client, with career- or work-related issues as the primary focus" (Swanson, 1995, p. 219). However, *career counseling* also has been used as an umbrella term, perhaps synonymous with the broader term of *career interventions*. A career intervention has been defined as "any activity or program intended to facilitate career development" (Fretz, 1981, p. 78). Similarly, the practice of career counseling has been referred to as a group of "counseling activities associated with career choices over the life span" (Zunker, 2002, p. 9). Although

career development courses and workshops have been found to have positive effect sizes, it is interesting to note that consistent empirical evidence demonstrates that individual career counseling continues to be the most effective career intervention method (Oliver & Spokane, 1988; Whiston, Sexton, & Lasoff, 1998).

The wide array of interventions subsumed under the practice of career counseling appears to be consistent with the definition provided by the NCDA, the recognized career development professional specialty within the American Counseling Association. According to the NCDA, the practice of career counseling encompasses a range of educational and career interventions with diverse clientele. For example, career counselors assist students all along the educational pipeline from K-12 to higher education, as well as employed and unemployed adults in the community. Career counseling professionals, nationally certified career counselors, career facilitators, and other clinical practitioners (e.g., counseling psychologists) provide the following types of interventions: (a) individual and group personal counseling, (b) administration and interpretation of tests and inventories, (c) career exploratory activities, (d) utilization of career planning systems and occupational information systems to understand the world of work, (e) improvement of individual career decision-making skills, (f) assistance in the development of individual career plans, (g) instruction in job-hunting strategies and skills, (h) resolution of on-the-job conflicts, (i) assistance in the integration of work and other life roles, and (j) support for persons experiencing job stress, job loss, and career transition (Engels, 1991). Thus, career development professionals who practice "career counseling" may be actively involved in treating a wide array of educational, career, leisure, and work-related symptoms and issues using a variety of person-to-person, group, paper-and-pencil, or computer-mediated interventions.

THE CURRENT STATUS OF MULTICULTURAL CAREER COUNSELING

In light of these trends, what progress has the career counseling field made toward addressing multicultural issues within the practice of career counseling and training of career counselors? For decades, career development scholars have widely criticized the use of traditional career development theories, career interventions, and career counseling training models for promoting the worldviews of able-bodied, heterosexual, middle-class, and English-speaking White American males. These cultural beliefs, attitudes, and values are aptly summarized in Neville, Gysbers, Heppner, and Johnston's (1998) five central tenets of traditional career counseling: (a) the importance of individualism and autonomy in decision making and vocational behaviors, (b) the assumption of a certain level of affluence and freedom to explore self-knowledge and training opportunities, (c) the assumption of educational and work environments that allow for opportunities available for all those who work hard, (d) a belief that work constitutes a central role in everyone's life, and (e) the assumption that the practice of career counseling should be based on linear models that focus on self-knowledge, world-of-work knowledge, and the true matching between the two using linear, rationale, and objective thinking.

Several decades ago, numerous scholars began arguing for the need for new models that were inclusive of alternative worldviews with respect to work, education, and career counseling processes, especially by individuals from racial and ethnic minority communities. In a commentary on previous discussions of the unique issues in racial and ethnic minority career development, Betz (1993) called for two areas for growth facing the career counseling specialty: (a) more commitment to address multicultural career counseling issues and (b) the development of multicultural sensitivity and competence among career counselors.

In regard to the first area, there has been tremendous growth in research and increased agreement among many professionals that the area of multicultural career counseling is at least viable and worthy of continued attention within the career counseling field. In fact, according to Pope (2000), the commitment of multicultural career counseling has evolved as one of the defining contemporary hallmarks of the career counseling field and a key aspect of the current (and sixth, respectively) phase of the practice of career counseling in the United States. Briefly, Pope summarized the career counseling history in six phases: The first stage represented job placement services (1890-1919), the second phase constituted educational guidance (1920-1939), the third phase emphasized colleges and universities and the training of counselors (1940-1959), the fourth phase focused on meaningful work and organizational career development (1960-1979), the fifth phase focused on independent practice and outplacement counseling (1980-1989), and the current sixth phase represents a focus on school-to-job transition, internalization of career counseling, increasing sophistication in the use of technology, and multicultural career counseling (1990-present).

With regard to practical interventions, career counselors can look to several contemporary writings to help guide career counseling practice. In our review of the career counseling literature, we found three approaches that reflect the profession's growth in thinking with respect to multicultural issues in the practice of career counseling: (a) group-specific guidelines for career counseling with racial and ethnic minorities, (b) culturally appropriate career counseling interventions applicable to all clients, and (c) the establishment of minimal competencies for career counselors when working with clients from "diverse populations."

Career Counseling With Racial and Ethnic Minorities

Outside of the women's career development literature, the major approach in career counseling dedicated to addressing multicultural issues in career counseling grew out of research into racial and ethnic minority career development. Although there continues to be no comprehensive model to explain the career development of racial and ethnic minorities (Betz, 1993; Leong, 1995), career counselors assisting clients of color in career counseling can look to various texts and journal articles published within the past decade for guidance. In fact, most new career counseling texts typically include one chapter titled either "multicultural career counseling" or "career counseling for racial and ethnic minorities." These chapters typically highlight specific cultural and contextual variables that may be useful when intervening with members from the four racial and ethnic minority groups (see Byars & McCubbin, 2001; Leung, 1995; Luzzo, 2000; Peterson & Gonzalez, 2000). Growth in this area is further evidenced by the publication of recent texts entirely devoted to racial and ethnic minorities' career behavior and interventions. Notable examples include the *Career Development and Vocational Behavior of Racial and Ethnic Minorities* (Leong, 1995) and *Career Counseling for African Americans* (Walsh, Bingham, Brown, & Ward, 2001). These resources are invaluable in increasing career counselors' awareness and knowledge of the worldviews and cultural factors (e.g., acculturation, cultural values, immigration issues, language preferences, racial identity) important to minority clients, as well as contextual variables (e.g., discrimination, access to role models, family and community) to consider when designing and implementing educational and career-related interventions. Despite some progress in this area, there continues to be inadequacy in the overall knowledge base, sparking additional calls for more empirical research with these minority populations and theoretical model building to better understand minority career development and culturally appropriate interventions (Betz & Fitzgerald, 1995; Byars & McCubbin, 2001; Pope-Davis & Hargrove, 2001).

The unique career counseling issues facing other "diverse" or "minority" groups, in addition to communities of color, have also garnered increased attention in the career counseling literature. For example, Peterson and Gonzalez (2000) emphasized the need for career counselors to know the career literature on gays, lesbians, and bisexuals, as well as persons with mental and physical disabilities. Drummond and Ryan (1995) noted specific interventions for immigrants and individuals representing a double minority status as well as training interventions that focus on promoting career counselor multicultural awareness and competence. Finally, Zunker (2002) discussed specific career assessment and counseling implications for women (White and women of color), men, immigrants, and racial and ethnic minorities; individuals with disabilities; and gay, lesbian, and bisexual clients. These group-specific efforts continue to dominate the landscape of what is typically referred to as "multicultural career counseling."

Culturally Appropriate Career Counseling

Beyond specific guidelines for certain groups, the second approach to addressing multicultural issues in the career counseling field focuses more on the application of culturally appropriate principles that may be applicable to all clients seeking career counseling services (Swanson & Fouad, 1999). As emphasized by Swanson and Fouad (1999), all career clients and career counseling interventions must be understood within a cultural context. In addition to having specific knowledge of the career behaviors of specific minority groups (see earlier section), Swanson and Fouad noted a number of other cross-cultural career counseling tenets such as the following: (a) Career counselors must attend to and incorporate a range of cultural and contextual factors, specifically discrimination, social class, acculturation, immigration issues, collective value orientations, and the role of the family with all clients; (b) career counselors must assess the degree to which cultural variables are salient to all clients; and (c) career counselors must be flexible enough to consider within-group variations. Swanson and Fouad provided several examples of career intervention models that represent this culturally appropriate approach to career counseling with minority (and majority) members (Fouad & Bingham, 1995; Leong & Hartung, 1997; Leung, 1995). Each of these models focuses on the themes of counselor self-awareness, understanding the culture and worldview of the career client, and creating culturally appropriate process and outcome goals. In the next section, we highlight two such examples focusing on individual career counseling and career interventions.

Within the context of individual one-on-one career counseling, career counselors are recommended to follow Fouad and Bingham's (1995) culturally appropriate career counseling (CACCM) model. Fouad and Bingham provided seven concrete steps. The first step requires the counselor to establish a culturally appropriate relationship with the client. The client-counselor relationship is critical in any counseling setting. Discussing the client's expectations and possible effects of differences between counselor and client can be instrumental in establishing rapport. The second step in their model consists of identifying the client's career issues. In addition to the client completing a career counseling checklist, career issues may be determined by familial, environmental, emotional, cognitive, and behavioral concerns. The authors emphasized the importance of defining external barriers that require the client's ability to balance factors within or outside of his or her control. The third step entails the career counselor assessing the impact of cultural variables on career issues. The counselor examines how the client is influenced by family, racial, and cultural interactions. The fourth step is when culturally appropriate process and outcome goals are set. The client clarifies interests, makes a career decision, and processes effects of that decision. During the fifth step, results from the checklist taken at Step 2 are considered, and needs are addressed. The counselor then determines and implements culturally appropriate interventions. For instance, the client may require family involvement and support, exposure to race- and gender-appropriate role models, or learning how to achieve a balance of individual and societal responsibility. The sixth step entails the counselor assisting the client in decision making and goal setting. At the seventh step, the client implements decisions formed during Step 6. The counselor follows up by making certain that the client is aware of whether or not the intended career plans satisfy the client's own worldview or are in opposition to traditional family values.

The CACCM is sensitive to the fact that external barriers of discrimination and prejudice may have a cumulative effect on minority clients, who may make career choices to avoid racial conflict or discomfort. The authors noted that their career counseling model is well rounded and applicable to the needs of individuals from diverse ethnic groups who are seeking assistance in career decisions. Future research, however, might include sexual orientation, within-group differences, and career behavior of racial and ethnic minority members (Fouad & Bingham, 1995).

A second intervention model that may be useful for career counselors is provided by Leong and Hartung (1997). These authors developed an integrative-sequential model (ISM) for cross-cultural career counseling. This is a five-stage model that assumes the crucial role of cultural factors both prior to and during career counseling intervention. The first stage is the emergence stage, whereby career and vocational problems are examined and assessed. Career and vocational problems are defined as issues that are partially influenced by an individual's concept of what is culturally normal and expected in his or her work life. Cultural differences in conceptions of normality and work will influence which experiences are perceived as a career problem (Leong & Hartung, 1997). The authors emphasize that individual clients follow cultural models that guide their own behavior, choices, and expectations. Career problems that may be culturally motivated include familial conflicts and obligations and work value conflicts (i.e., individualism vs. collectivism).

The second stage focuses on help-seeking attitudes and career services utilization. Leong and Hartung (1997) suggested that clients' help-seeking attitudes influence whether they seek help for career-related and other mental health problems. To assess attitudes toward seeking career counseling services, career counselors may want to use the Attitudes Toward Career Counseling Scale (ATCCS) (Rochlen, Mohr, & Hargrove, 1999). The ATCCS measures the degree of value and stigma attached to seeking career counseling. Leong and Hartung suggested that racial/ethnic minority clients in particular may not seek out career counseling services if they have negative attitudes toward career counseling and other mental health services. Negative help-seeking attitudes and underutilization of career services by racial and ethnic minority clients may stem from a lack of culturally sensitive programs and interventions, lack of bilingual staff, and perceptions of cultural mistrust (Leong & Hartung, 1997). To increase the likelihood of service utilization, career

counselors may need to assess and incorporate the client's worldview, provide culturally relevant outreach services and community-based programs, and use marketing group approaches (Leong & Hartung, 1997).

The third stage concerns evaluation of career and vocational problems. The career counselor assesses the career and vocational problems in a diagnostic interview, which often includes career and personality tests. The career counselor also examines the client's cultural identity, cultural factors related to the presenting problem, cultural factors in the environment, and cultural factors present in the client-counselor relationship. Finally, the counselor provides an overall cultural analysis and intervention plan. The fourth stage involves selecting culturally appropriate career interventions. Career interventions are presented in several forms and consist of any activity geared toward enhancing an individual's ability to make optimal career choices. Primarily, cultural elements between the client and counselor relationship are identified and comprehended. Such tactics help prevent barriers to effective counseling and positive outcomes. During this stage, cultural factors that surfaced in the evaluation process are again processed. Cultural elements typically considered include class-based, language-based, and culture-based barriers. In addition, much attention is given to the interpretation of vocational and personality test results.

The fifth and final stage entails an overall assessment of cultural factors that influence the diagnosis of the career problem and the career intervention plans. Finally, a follow-up with the client is necessary to ensure the client's ability to comprehend, integrate, and use assessment data. In summary, these two models emphasize the need for career counselors to integrate cultural factors along each phase of career counseling interventions.

Career Counseling Competency Standards Devoted to Diverse Populations

The third notable approach to addressing multicultural issues in career counseling has been the establishment of minimal standards of competency for career counselors by the NCDA. Although previous approaches have seemed to focus mostly on what to do with diverse career clients, the trend toward counselor competency reflects the need to also focus attention on the self-awareness, knowledge, and skills of the career counselor. The NCDA recently produced competency documents with demonstration statements to ensure the minimal quality of career counseling interventions (National Career Development Association Professional Standards Committee, 1992). Career counseling competency standards provide a useful measure of minimal professional ability within the specialty of career counseling for professional career counselors and other career interventionists (Mariani, 1998). In 1997, the NCDA revised the list of 10 minimum career counseling competencies and performance indicators and added an 11th competency. They are as follows: Career Development Theory; Individual and Group Counseling Skills; Individual/Group Assessment; Information and Resources; Program Promotion, Management, and Implementation; Coaching, Consultation, and Performance Improvement; Diverse Populations; Supervision; Ethical and Legal Issues; Research and Evaluation; and Technology. These minimum competencies were developed for career professionals (professional career counselors or persons in career development positions) with at least a master's degree. Thus, the career counseling specialty has increasingly moved toward specifying minimal competency areas to keep up and perhaps remain ahead of the workforce demands and trends.

Multicultural issues of career clients and multicultural competencies of career counselors are directly addressed under the "Diverse Populations" domain of the career counseling competencies. This domain emphasizes the need to establish minimal knowledge and skills in relating to diverse populations, meaning those individuals who may differ with respect to English-proficiency skills, gender, sexual orientation, ethnic group, race, and physical or mental capacity. Similar to guidelines for psychologists published by the American Psychological Association (1993), the general message from the published list of the nine competency statements under "Diverse Populations" suggests that career counselors must demonstrate an awareness of these diversity variables and take into consideration the unique situations raised by such diversity issues. For instance, career interventions must include advocacy, links to the community, and accommodations that respect the needs of the diverse populations.

Although these competency statements fill an important void in the career counseling practice, they continue to be rather vague and broad in nature with respect to integrating multicultural awareness, knowledge, and skills for career counselors. In fact, one of the first tenets under the "Diverse Populations" competency section indicates that career counselors must be familiar with "the developmental models and multicultural counseling competencies." Although the career counseling competencies acknowledge the importance of multicultural counseling competencies endorsed by the AMCD (Arredondo et al., 1996), we are uncertain to what extent career counselors are integrating these competencies into the practice of career counseling.

Thus, we believe the natural next step to advance the practice of multicultural competencies within career counseling is to discuss how the general multicultural competencies endorsed by the entire counseling profession specifically might apply to the practice of career counseling. This shift represents a change from "multicultural career counseling" or "culturally appropriate career counseling" to "multiculturally competent career counseling." Finally, this integration further addresses the second need emphasized by Betz (1993), that is, the call for more multicultural sensitivity and competence among career counselors.

A MULTICULTURAL COMPETENCIES MODEL OF CAREER COUNSELING

In this section, we offer a more specific framework for helping career counselors provide multiculturally competent career counseling by introducing a multicultural competencies (MCC) model of career counseling. We attempted to apply the operationalization of multicultural counseling competencies recently disseminated by the ACA and the AMCD. In two essential documents (Arredondo et al., 1996; Sue, Arredondo, & McDavis, 1992), the multicultural counseling competencies (i.e., hereafter referred to simply as multicultural competencies) were operationalized at the practice level for both counselors and clients. According to Arredondo (1998),

> The competencies articulate attitudinal and trait based statements/characteristics for three dimensions: (a) beliefs and attitudes, (b) knowledge, and (c) skills in three domains for development and practice. The skills are as follows: (1) counselor's self-awareness of personal beliefs and attitudes, knowledge, and skills for effective practice; (2) the counselors' understanding of beliefs/attitudes, and knowledge he or she holds about the worldview of the client; and (3) the counselor's ability to provide ethical and culturally relevant counseling through appropriate intervention strategies and techniques.

We propose that each of the multicultural competence attitudinal and trait-based statements/characteristics across the three domains

can be adapted to the practice of career counseling. Thus, using the three-part multicultural competencies model as the framework, we hope our MCC model of career counseling will (a) help career counselors better integrate multicultural factors in their career counseling interventions, (b) help stimulate future research on the applicability of the multicultural competencies model in career counseling, and (c) help career educators teach current and future career counselors how to become more multiculturally competent.

As Arredondo et al. (1996) suggested in their operational list, the first domain for counselors involves counselor self-awareness. Thus, we propose the following version for career counselors:

I. Career counselor awareness of own worldview toward educational and career-related behaviors, as well as career counseling interventions

    A. Attitudes and beliefs

        1. Career counselors believe in the importance of cultural self-awareness and the role of culture in the lives of clients and in the delivery of various career counseling interventions.

        2. Career counselors are aware of their own limits of their career counseling and multicultural counseling competencies (as defined by the NCDA and AMCD).

        3. Career counselors are aware of how their own cultural background, experiences, and role models influence their attitudes toward education and work, educational and career decision making, academic performance, and work-related behaviors.

        4. Career counselors are aware of how their own cultural background, experiences, and role models influence their own educational and work-related values and preferences related

to balancing life roles (e.g., homemaker, worker, parent, volunteer, citizen, etc.).

5. Career counselors are aware of how their own cultural background, experiences, and role models influence their attitudes toward seeking help for educational and career-related concerns.

B. Knowledge base

1. Career counselors have specific knowledge of how their own racial, ethnic, cultural, and national heritages affect their views on education, leisure, work, and retirement.

2. Career counselors have specific knowledge of how their own racial, ethnic, cultural, and national heritages affect their views on seeking help from different types of help sources.

3. Career counselors must have knowledge of sociopolitical and contextual variables such as racism, sexism, stereotyping, oppression, and discrimination and the affect they have on themselves, their work positions, educational levels, and future opportunities in the workforce.

4. Career counselors are knowledgeable of the impact that their educational statuses, places of employment, or professional positions have on their current and potential clients.

C. Self-awareness skills

1. Career counselors seek out educational and training experiences to improve their understanding and effectiveness when working with male and female racial and ethnic majority and minority clients.

2. Career counselors seek out educational and training experiences to improve their understanding and effectiveness when working with male and female clients with physical and mental disabilities.

3. Career counselors seek out educational and training experiences to improve their understanding and effectiveness when working with international clients and clients who are immigrants.

4. Career counselors seek out educational and training experiences to improve their understanding and effectiveness when working with clients who are heterosexual, gay, lesbian, or bisexual.

Similar to Arredondo et al. (1996), the second domain for counselors involves counselor awareness of the client's worldview. Thus, we propose the following version for career counselors:

II. Career counselor awareness of client's worldview toward education, work- or career-related behaviors, and career counseling interventions

A. Attitudes toward clients

1. Career counselors are aware of their own positive and negative emotional reactions associated with the educational and work-related choices and behaviors of members from racial and ethnic minority, linguistically different, and diverse groups.

2. Career counselors are aware of their own stereotypes and assumptions associated with the educational and work-related choices and behaviors of members from racial and ethnic minority, linguistically different, and diverse groups.

B. Awareness of client's worldview

1. Career counselors possess specific knowledge of the educational and work-related choices and behaviors typically associated with members from racial and ethnic minority, linguistically different, and diverse groups.

2. Career counselors understand how racial identity attitudes, ethnicity, immigration, acculturation, values,

and other cultural variables affect educational and work-related choices and behaviors.

3. Career counselors understand how current and historical sociopolitical issues (e.g., discrimination, oppression, sexism, and racism) affect access to and attainment of education and work for members from racial and ethnic minority, linguistically different, and diverse groups.

C. Awareness of client's worldview related to education, career, and life planning

1. Career counselors should familiarize themselves with the current research on the career behaviors of racial and ethnic minorities.

2. Career counselors should familiarize themselves with the current research on the career behaviors of women and men.

3. Career counselors should familiarize themselves with the current research on the career behaviors of people across socioeconomic and class lines.

4. Career counselors should familiarize themselves with the current research on the career behaviors of gays, lesbians, and bisexuals.

5. Career counselors should familiarize themselves with the current research on the career behaviors of people with mental and physical disabilities.

6. Career counselors should become actively involved in the educational, workplace, family, and community settings of members from racial and ethnic minority, linguistically different, and diverse groups.

Finally, the third domain for counselors involves developing culturally appropriate interventions (Arredondo et al., 1996). Thus, we proposed the following version for career counselors:

III. Culturally appropriate career counseling intervention strategies

A. Career counselor beliefs and attitudes

1. Career counselors respect the influence that gender, racial identity, level of acculturation, cultural values, worldviews, ethnic identity, socioeconomic status, sexual orientation, and religious and spiritual beliefs may have on their clients' educational and career behaviors.

2. Career counselors respect the influence the family and community may have on their clients' educational and career behaviors.

3. Career counselors respect the influence cultural factors may have on the attitudes their clients may have toward career counseling and other mental health services.

4. Career counselors need to be open to working in conjunction with alternative indigenous helping resources and help-giving networks in the family or community.

5. Career counselors need to value bilingualism in career counseling interventions.

B. Knowledge needed by career counselors

1. Career counselors need to know the values and attitudes associated with career counseling from their training perspective and their clients' perspective.

2. Career counselors need to know the perceived differences and similarities between career counseling interventions and other mental health services from their training perspective and their clients' perspective.

3. Career counselors need to know the potential biases in all forms of career counseling interventions, including group and individual assessment, computer-assisted guidance systems, career planning courses, career planning workshops, and individual career counseling.

4. Career counselors need to have training in career assessment and testing, as well as knowledge of the cultural

limitations of each assessment and testing procedure.

5. Career counselors need to have information on special work programs and policies, including school-to-work programs, welfare-to-work programs, affirmative action and equal opportunity policies, immigration policies, and discrimination policies in the workplace.

6. Career counselors need to have knowledge about the structure, hierarchy, values, and beliefs of the clients' families and/or communities.

7. Career counselors need to have knowledge about the structure, hierarchy, values, and beliefs of their clients' educational settings or workplaces.

C. Skills needed to implement interventions

1. Career counselors are able to communicate effectively and educate clients about career development theory and the profession of career counseling within the context of the United States.

2. Career counselors are able to advocate for clients at various individual, organizational, and institutional levels.

3. Career counselors can seek consultations with other helpers.

4. Career counselors can provide services using clients' preferred language or make an appropriate referral.

5. Career counselors have training in career assessment and testing and are aware of the cultural limitations of each assessment and testing procedure.

6. Career counselors can implement newly developed, culturally appropriate career counseling interventions in their career counseling practice.

CONCLUSION AND RECOMMENDATIONS FOR PRACTICE

If career counselors are to become more multiculturally competent in the practice of career counseling, more specific guidelines and training will be needed to meet the basic requirements of being a career counselor in the 21st century. As noted earlier, there continue to be domestic diversification and global changes that present unique multicultural and diverse challenges to the career counseling specialty. As noted earlier, there has been improvement and growth in the career counseling field's response to advancing multicultural career counseling knowledge and creating greater multicultural competence among career counselors. Advances in this area have moved our specialty from the analysis of the career behaviors of racial and ethnic minorities to more culturally appropriate career counseling interventions that may be applicable to all diverse clients seeking career counseling.

With professional organizations continuing to demand and standardize greater levels of competency, it is no surprise or coincidence that two divisions of the American Counseling Association, the NCDA and the AMCD, have almost simultaneously recently developed competency standards to "operationalize" particular attitudes and behaviors necessary for today's counselors and educators living and working in a global and multicultural society. However, as noted before, the competency statements endorsed by the NCDA remain global and lack behavioral consistency with the multicultural competencies developed by the AMCD. Therefore, we propose a new framework titled a multicultural competencies model of career counseling. This model attempts to directly translate the rich text of multicultural competencies to the audience of career counselors currently training or practicing in the United States. To further encourage greater specificity and integration of multicultural competencies in career counseling, we offer some future recommendations.

First, the MCC model of career counseling provided earlier needs to be expanded and fleshed out with more examples of career counseling interventions. For example, multicultural competencies across the three domains (counselor self-awareness, client worldview, and culturally appropriate interventions) can be expanded to each type of career intervention (workshops, computer-assisted programs, individual counseling, and especially career assessment). Second, there continues to be a surge of newly published articles that help career counselors better develop and implement either group-specific interventions or culturally appropriate process interventions. These studies need to be organized within the MCC model of the career counseling framework. Third, there needs to be more discussion as to how multicultural issues are addressed throughout the career counseling competencies and how these ideas are congruent with the multicultural competencies discussed throughout this text. Fourth, the MCC model of career counseling provides an organizational scheme that may be useful in organizing new research questions or studies on career counselor self-awareness strategies, awareness of clients' worldviews, or culturally appropriate interventions. Finally, career counseling educators may begin to assess how useful the MCC model is in regard to training career counselors to become more multiculturally aware, knowledgeable, and skilled during career counseling interventions. To actualize better multicultural competence, Swanson (1993) outlined numerous essential programmatic and individual components of multiculturally competent career counseling training programs.

In conclusion, it is our hope that this chapter stimulates further discussions and empirical research on the operationalization of multicultural competency standards within the realm of career counseling.

REFERENCES

American Psychological Association. (1993). Guidelines for providers of psychological services to ethnic, linguistic, and culturally diverse populations. *American Psychologist, 48*(1), 45-48.

Arredondo, P. (1998). Integrating multicultural counseling competencies and universal helping conditions in culture-specific contexts. *Counseling Psychologist, 26,* 592-601.

Arredondo, P., Toporek, R., Brown, S. P., Jones, J., Locke, D. C., Sanchez, J., et al. (1996). Operationalization of the multicultural counseling competencies. *Journal of Multicultural Counseling and Development, 24,* 42-78.

Betz, N., & Fitzgerald, L. (1995). Career assessment and intervention with racial and ethnic minorities. In F. T. L. Leong (Ed.), *Career development and vocational behavior of racial and ethnic minorities* (pp. 263-280). Mahwah, NJ: Lawrence Erlbaum.

Betz, N. E. (1993). Toward the integration of multicultural and career psychology. *Career Development Quarterly, 42,* 53-55.

Byars, A. M., & McCubbin, L. D. (2001). Trends in career development research with racial/ethnic minorities: Prospects and challenges. In J. G. Ponterotto, J. M. Casas, L. A. Suzuki, & C. M. Alexander (Eds.), *The handbook of multicultural counseling* (2nd ed., pp. 633-654). Thousand Oaks, CA: Sage.

Drummond, R. J., & Ryan, C. W. (1995). *Career counseling: A developmental approach.* Englewood Cliffs, NJ: Prentice Hall.

Engels, D. W. (1991). *The professional practice of career counseling and consultation: A resource document* (2nd ed.). Alexandria, VA: National Career Development Association.

Fouad, N. A., & Bingham, R. P. (1995). Career counseling with racial and ethnic minorities. In W. B. Walsh & S. H. Osipow (Eds.), *Handbook of vocational psychology: Theory, research and practice* (2nd ed., pp. 331-366). Mahwah, NJ: Lawrence Erlbaum.

Fretz, B. R. (1981). Evaluating the effectiveness of career interventions. *Journal of Counseling Psychology, 28,* 77-90.

Judy, R. W., & D'Amico, C. (1998). *Workforce 2020: Work and workers in the 21st century.* Indianapolis, IN: Hudson Institute.

Leong, F. T. L. (Ed.). (1995). *Career development and vocational behavior of racial and ethnic minorities.* Mahwah, NJ: Lawrence Erlbaum.

Leong, F. T. L., & Hartung, P. J. (1997). Career assessment with culturally different clients: Proposing an integrative-sequential conceptual framework for cross-cultural career counseling research and practice. *Journal of Career Assessment, 5,* 183-202.

Leung, S. A. (1995). Career development and counseling: A multicultural perspective. In J. G. Ponterotto, J. M. Casas, L. A. Suzuki, & C. M. Alexander (Eds.), *The handbook of multicultural counseling* (pp. 549-566). Thousand Oaks, CA: Sage.

Luzzo, D. A. (2000). *Career counseling of college students: An empirical guide to strategies that work.* Washington, DC: American Psychological Association.

Mariani, M. (1998). Career counseling and facilitating: Standards for a new century. *Occupational Outlook Quarterly, 42*(3), 30-31.

National Career Development Association Professional Standards Committee. (1992). Career counseling competencies. *Career Development Quarterly, 40,* 378-396.

Neville, H. A., Gysbers, N. C., Heppner, M. J., & Johnston, J. (1998). Empowering life choices: Career counseling in cultural contexts. In N. C. Gysbers, M. J. Heppner, & J. Johnston (Eds.), *Career counseling: Process, issues, and techniques.* Boston: Allyn & Bacon.

Oliver, L. W., & Spokane, A. R. (1988). Career-intervention outcome: What contributes to client gain? *Journal of Counseling Psychology, 35,* 447-462.

Peterson, N., & Gonzalez, R. C. (2000). *The role of work in people's lives: Applied career counseling and vocational psychology.* Belmont, CA: Wadsworth/Thomson Learning.

Pope, M. (2000). A brief history of career counseling in the United States. *Career Development Quarterly, 48,* 194-211.

Pope-Davis, D. B., & Hargrove, B. K. (2001). Future directions in career counseling:

Theory, research, and practice with African Americans. In W. B. Walsh, R. P. Bingham, M. T. Brown, & C. M. Ward (Eds.), *Career counseling for African Americans.* Mahwah, NJ: Lawrence Erlbaum.

Rochlen, A. R., Mohr, J. R., & Hargrove, B. K. (1999). Development of the Attitudes Toward Career Counseling Scale. *Journal of Counseling Psychology, 46,* 196-206.

Sue, D. W., Arredondo, P., & McDavis, R. J. (1992). Multicultural counseling competencies: A call to the profession. *Journal of Counseling and Development, 70,* 477-486.

Swanson, J. L. (1993). Integrating a multicultural perspective into training for career counseling: Programmatic and individual interventions. *Career Development Quarterly, 42*(1), 41-50.

Swanson, J. L. (1995). The process and outcome of career counseling. In W. B. Walsh & S. H. Osipow (Eds.), *Handbook of vocational psychology: Theory, research and practice* (2nd ed., pp. 217-259). Mahwah, NJ: Lawrence Erlbaum.

Swanson, J. L., & Fouad, N. A. (1999). *Career theory and practice: Learning through case studies.* Thousand Oaks, CA: Sage.

U.S. Bureau of the Census. (1998). *Statistical abstract of the United States: 1998* (118th ed.). Washington, DC: Government Printing Office.

Walsh, W. B., Bingham, R. P., Brown, M. T., & Ward, C. M. (Eds.). (2001). *Career counseling for African Americans.* Mahwah, NJ: Lawrence Erlbaum.

Whiston, S. C., Sexton, T. L., & Lasoff, D. L. (1998). Career-interventions outcome: A replication and extension of Oliver and Spokane (1988). *Journal of Counseling Psychology, 45,* 150-165.

Zunker, V. G. (2002). *Career counseling: Applied concepts of life planning* (6th ed.). Pacific Grove, CA: Brooks/Cole.

26

Multicultural Competence in School Settings

CHERYL C. HOLCOMB-McCOY

University of Maryland at College Park

The current demographics of U.S. schools have challenged school counselors to provide culturally appropriate services to students and their families (Coleman, 1995; House & Martin, 1998; Lewis & Hayes, 1991). In many states (e.g., Texas, California, Florida), ethnic minorities comprise 50% of the total state's population, and in major cities, ethnic minority students comprise the highest percentage of public school enrollments (Hacker, 1992; Sue & Sue, 1987). In addition to the increase in ethnic minority student enrollments, the influx of immigrants and non-English-speaking students poses a serious problem for school counselors who have been trained to use traditional, Eurocentric approaches to counseling and intervention (Lee & Richardson, 1991).

The literature regarding multicultural counseling competence of professional counselors has focused on three broad competency categories: (a) the counselor's own cultural self-awareness; (b) the counselor's understanding of the history, traditions, and values of persons from diverse cultural, ethnic, and racial backgrounds; and (c) the counselor's ability to develop and implement appropriate, relevant, and sensitive intervention strategies and skills when working with culturally different clients (Atkinson, Thompson, & Grant, 1993; Carney & Kahn, 1984; Sue et al., 1982). On the basis of these three categories, the Association for Multicultural Counseling and Development's (AMCD's) Professional Standards and Certification Committee elaborated on and promoted the set of multicultural competencies proposed by Sue, Arredondo, and McDavis (1992). Explanatory statements were later added to the competencies to further explain counseling interactions with culturally diverse clients (Arredondo et al., 1996). The American School Counselor Association (ASCA), the only national school counseling professional organization, adopted the competencies in 1997 (Locke, 1998).

In addition to adopting the competencies, the ASCA took a firm stance in support of multiculturalism by formulating a position statement encouraging school counselors to "take action to ensure students of culturally diverse backgrounds have access to appropriate services and opportunities which promote the maximum development of the individual" (ASCA, 1993, p. 3). Furthermore, numerous school counseling professionals (e.g., Lewis & Hayes, 1991) have suggested in the literature that cultural knowledge, sensitivity, and awareness be integrated into existing school counseling training programs. In response, the Council for the Accreditation of Counseling and Related Educational Programs (CACREP) included multicultural content into the "School Counselor Preparation Standards" (CACREP, 1994). CACREP now requires that school counseling students have curricular experiences that explore the implications of sociocultural, demographic, and lifestyle diversity relevant to school counseling.

Despite this adoption of multicultural content into the practice and training of school counselors, there is very little literature linking multicultural counseling competence and the services that school counselors provide. Hence, the primary purpose of this chapter is to describe how multicultural competence applies to the practice of school counseling. This chapter addresses multicultural competence as it relates to the essential services provided by school counselors: counseling, consulting, coordinating, assessment, classroom guidance, and family education. Also, a brief discussion regarding school counselor competence in understanding and identifying racism is given.

COUNSELING

The school counselor is the member of a school's full-time professional staff that will likely provide counseling interventions for students with educational, vocational, personal, and social concerns (ASCA, 1992). Herring (1997, p. 118) suggested that five preconditions for counseling ethnically and culturally diverse students in schools are directly related to the three categories of multicultural counseling competence previously stated. Herring's preconditions suggest that school counselors should do the following:

1. have faith in the students' ability to grow and to fully realize their potential, given responsive, supportive, and developmental intervention across both cultural contexts in which the students are immersed;
2. examine their own personal attitudes and personality style and how these characteristics influence how they behave with culturally diverse students;
3. understand that sociopolitical forces influence how culturally diverse students act;
4. become familiar with the differences in worldviews that characterize ethnic minority students and the implications for counseling; and
5. have a clear working knowledge of many approaches to counseling and be able to use the techniques that best accommodate cultural and ethnic differences without aggravating the presenting problems.

In essence, multiculturally competent school counselors are able to engage in counseling with culturally different students by integrating their cultural awareness, knowledge, and skills into every aspect of their practice (Pederson & Carey, 1994).

When implementing counseling interventions, multiculturally competent school counselors recognize that several factors must be considered before conceptualizing a student's problem or concern. Some of the factors school counselors will consider are students' racial and/or ethnic identity development, socioeconomic background, country of origin, bilingual/bicultural status, cultural expectations about counseling, family status, and social resources (Herr, 1989). Although many school counselors have been trained to look for sources of student problems within the individual, among culturally diverse students, the sources of the problem could be the result of external forces such as racial discrimination, social disadvantage, and/or poverty. Unless the school counselor is aware and culturally sensitive to the effects of these external forces, the school counselor will focus only on what may be perceived as the student's internal deficits when in fact the focus should be on external conditions for which the student is not responsible. School counselors need to incorporate this "paradigm shift" when conceptualizing student problems to provide culturally appropriate counseling interventions in schools.

Individual Counseling

Seeking individual counseling services emerges as a complex phenomenon for ethnic minority individuals (Canino & Spurlock, 2000). The literature documents that ethnic minorities underuse counseling services in part because their help-seeking behaviors and treatment expectations differ from those of the dominant culture (Giordano & Giordano, 1977; Tseng & McDermott, 1981). For instance, African Americans often mistrust mental health providers from traditional institutions other than their churches (Terrell & Terrell, 1984). Puerto Rican (Garcia-Preto, 1982) and Chinese (Tseng & McDermott, 1981) individuals often express distress by somatization and may seek physical rather than psychological assistance.

Although the help-seeking behaviors of ethnic minorities differ from the majority population, the majority of ethnic minority children still receive counseling services from school counselors who have been trained to expect traditional help-seeking client behaviors (Canino & Spurlock, 2000; Locke & Parker, 1994; Omizo & Omizo, 1989). Multiculturally competent school counselors, however, understand that students from culturally different backgrounds may have varying perceptions of counseling and, as a result, will modify their counseling programs to accommodate those perceptions.

According to D'Andrea and Daniels (1995), one of the most serious problems in school counseling rests in the fact that "most counseling theories and interventions, which are commonly used in school settings, have not been tested among students from diverse student populations" (p. 143). Very few individual counseling approaches have been specifically designed and validated for use with specific cultural groups. For this reason, multiculturally competent school counselors are constantly seeking and developing individual counseling methods and strategies that are effective with culturally different students.

It should also be noted that culturally competent school counselors incorporate traditional indigenous practices into their theoretical frameworks. School counselors who work with students from cultural backgrounds that use indigenous healing methods might consult with traditional folk healers regarding issues and problems of ethnic minority students (Koss-Chioino, 1995). Likewise, incorporating clergy and other religious leaders in the counseling process may be beneficial and advantageous when working with students from culturally different backgrounds.

Multiculturally competent school counselors are also aware of the pervasive influence that culture has on the counseling process (Wehrly, 1995). In the school setting, counselors should be aware of the impact of culture on students' way of thinking, belief systems, definitions of self, decision making, verbal and nonverbal behavior, and time orientation. For instance, some non-Westernized cultures place more emphasis on "being" than on "doing." In the Native American and Asian cultures, self is not seen as a separate entity from the group or from nature. In addition, African Americans and other nonmainstream Western cultures see family as an extended unit that does not necessarily limit itself to "blood" relatives. These varied cultural beliefs and practices can be significant in the helping process and have profound effects on the behavior of children and adolescents

Group Counseling

In school settings, group counseling is often the chosen form of counseling for many reasons. First, groups provide an opportunity for school counselors to observe social interactions among students. Groups also provide students with peer feedback, an opportunity to serve as role models for others, and an opportunity to bond with students experiencing similar issues (Myrick, 1993).

The effective multicultural group leader in the school setting must not only be sensitive to the distinct cultural differences between students but also be aware of his of her own cultural biases and prejudices. It is particularly important for group leaders to be accepting and nonjudgmental about the values, lifestyles, beliefs, and behaviors of others and to recognize the value of difference and diversity (Diller, 1999). School counselors who lead groups can learn much about other cultures by asking group members for information and assistance in understanding their diverse backgrounds. According to Holcomb-McCoy (2000), group counselors within the school setting must be able to facilitate the cultural development of group members by

1. understanding and acknowledging the reality that minority students are socialized within a society in which minorities have a history of suffering stereotyping, prejudice, and discrimination;
2. encouraging group members to explore their cultural heritages and experiences;
3. encouraging group members to explore their attitudes about their racial, ethnic, and cultural experiences; and
4. helping group members develop group norms that reflect the varying cultural values and perspectives of group members.

When composing a group, the school counselor should consider how students from differing cultural backgrounds are likely to relate to each other and to the group leader. The multiculturally competent school counselor should be familiar with the literature on selecting and planning for a culturally diverse group (e.g., Brown & Mistry, 1994; Davis, Galinsky, & Schopler, 1995). For instance, when reviewing the strengths of same-sex and same-race groups, Brown and Mistry (1994) noted that these groups have advantages when the group task is associated with issues of personal identity, social oppression, and empowerment.

School counselors who lead groups must also keep in mind that students bring diverse patterns of behavior, values, and language to the group (Axelson, 1999). Students might also bring experiences with oppression and particular feelings about themselves, their group identity, and the larger society. When problems such as student dissatisfaction or conflict among group members occur, the school counselor should keep in mind that the problems may be caused by cultural differences, not by an individual member's characteristics or flaws in the group process.

Group counselors in schools should assess how students' backgrounds are likely to affect the way they experience communication and interaction patterns, cohesion, and the overall group culture). It is important for school counselors to understand the language, symbols, and nonverbal communication patterns of people from different cultural backgrounds. As a result, school counselors must strive to become aware of the nuances of messages sent by group members, including how nonverbal messages differ across various cultures. In addition, the counselor should consider how cultural groups differ in their use of space (i.e., whether distance or closeness is the norm) and what other nonverbal communication norms govern interaction in the culture.

Regarding leadership, group leaders might have difficulty openly discussing the significance of their own cultural differences in the group process (Forsyth, 1999). School counselors, however, should not ignore or avoid multicultural topics when interacting with students in groups. It is imperative that multiculturally competent school counselors model positive cultural dynamics in group settings and use their own self-awareness to enhance students' levels of cultural sensitivity.

MULTICULTURAL CONSULTATION

Despite the attention focused on multicultural counseling, less emphasis has been placed on the significance of culture and ethnicity in the consultation process. Consulting is a significant responsibility for school counselors (Gerler, 1992; Kurpius & Fuqua, 1993; Strein & French, 1984). School counselors may be asked to consult with students, parents, teachers, student services specialists, administrators, or community agency professionals (Dougherty, 1992).

Given the amount of time school counselors spend consulting with parents, teachers, students, and administrators of diverse backgrounds, a discussion of multicultural competence of school-based consultants is warranted. Many of the traditional models of consultation (e.g., organizational, behavioral, mental health) fail to address how cultural

factors affect the consultation process. In one attempt to describe differences in the consultation process between African American and White teachers in school consultation, Gibbs (1980) found through multiple observations that African American teachers were more focused on the consultants' interpersonal skills, whereas White teachers focused more on instrumental skills demonstrated by the consultant. She concluded, as a result of this study, that culturally competent school-based consultants should pay close attention to building trusting relationships with Black teachers in the initial phase of consultation.

School counselors acting in the role of consultant should be sensitive to the cultural differences between the three parties in the consultation process: consultant, consultee, and client. School counselors who consult with culturally different teachers and parents should ensure that the teacher or parent (i.e., consultees) understands that his or her input is welcomed and, in many cases, necessary for the success of the intervention. It is just as important, however, to consider the cultural differences of the client. Although the consultation process involves indirect contact with the client, the consultant should not forget that the client is the focus of the consultee's problem; therefore, the culture of the client will have an impact on the change process.

In addition to being sensitive to the client's and consultee's culture, multiculturally competent consultants should also focus on conceptualizing the problem or concern of the consultee within a cultural context. Assessing the influence of culture on the consultee's and client's perceptions of the problem and interpersonal interactions is critical to the multicultural consultation process. Also, being aware of cultural variations in students', teachers', and parents' behaviors is important. For instance, a Taiwanese student who is overly concerned about involving her parents in her college choice should not be considered immature by a consultee because of his or her own cultural beliefs. Because the Taiwanese culture emphasizes parental respect, the consultant must ensure that the student is not penalized for behaving in a culturally appropriate manner.

Language, value differences, and prejudice may all lead to less than accurate information being obtained during the consultation process (Ramirez, Lepage, Kratochwill, & Duffy, 1998). School-based consultants should be cognizant of consultees' and clients' body language, eye contact, manner of speech, issues of biculturality, cooperation versus competition, punctuality, assertiveness, and family values (Jackson & Hayes, 1993). In addition, school-based consultants should be able to identify and challenge a consultee's (e.g., parents, teachers, school personnel) stereotypical beliefs and biases because ultimately these faulty perceptions can affect the consultation outcomes. Prejudicial attitudes within the consultation process may be manifested in outright rejection and/or the provision of inadequate interventions. Clearly, school-based consultants need to be vigilant about detecting and dealing with negative racial and/or cultural attitudes (Rogers, 2000). By identifying the consultee's biased and prejudicial statements and/or assumptions, the school-based consultant is more apt to eliminate negative racial and/or cultural attitudes that are possibly affecting the consultee's and/or client's problem. Oftentimes, for example, teachers will consult with a school counselor but fail to recognize their own biased beliefs that are directly and/or indirectly creating a problem for the student.

COORDINATION

As stated previously, school counselors provide a variety of services (e.g., group counseling, consulting) directly and indirectly to students, parents, and teachers. At the same time, however, school counselors are responsible for coordinating activities and services that involve individuals and programs outside the school. School counselors who serve as coordinators in their schools seek to bring various individuals together to share information, exchange ideas, set goals, and identify and implement interventions with students (Myrick, 1993). A school counselor's coordination activities may range from coordinating a school's peer mediation program to coordinating student assessment procedures. What follows is a brief description of common activities that school counselors might coordinate: test administration, child study teams, school-wide programs, and referrals. Aspects related to multicultural competence will be discussed for each.

Test Administration

School counselors are frequently required to coordinate school testing and assessment activities (Schmidt, 1991). This may include organizing testing materials, administering tests, and distributing and interpreting test results for students, teachers, and parents. Multicultural aspects of coordinating school testing include being knowledgeable about the cultural appropriateness of assessment instruments frequently used in schools, being aware of other cultures' perceptions of assessment, and having the skills to implement a culturally appropriate assessment procedure. When coordinating testing situations, multiculturally competent school counselors must pay careful attention to inappropriate or insensitive assessment techniques, test bias, and the purposes and/or goals for testing. For further information, see the "Multicultural Assessment" section later in this chapter.

In addition to fair testing procedures and administration, multiculturally competent school counselors should ensure that all students understand the purpose, process, and outcome of testing. This is particularly important for students who have recently migrated to the United States and do not understand testing practices in this country. Because parents from historically oppressed groups are unaware of the nature of tests, multiculturally competent school counselors attempt to ensure that all parents are educated on testing practices, testing assistance, and testing options. When coordinating test administration, multiculturally competent school counselors also must take responsibility for educating all parents of the types of tests used in their children's school.

Finally, multiculturally competent school counselors should be aware of the testing options for students whose first language is not English. Generally, the options for these students are to have a test translated, use interpreters, use tests that are norm referenced in their first language, or use a bilingual test administrator (Figueroa, 1990). Multiculturally competent school counselors ensure that bilingual students receive a fair and appropriate testing environment as well as an opportunity to receive a fair representation of their skills, abilities, and aptitudes.

Coordinating Child Study Teams

Child study teams or educational management teams are used in most schools to assemble a group of school professionals and parents (e.g., counselor, psychologist, nurse, classroom teacher, administrator) to review the status of a student who is experiencing some type of problem (e.g., reading problem, behavioral problem). School counselors are typically members of this team and help to coordinate them.

From a multicultural perspective, school counselors should be sensitive to the needs of culturally different parents of children who are being discussed in child study team meetings. For instance, multiculturally competent school counselors arrange for interpreters for non-English-speaking parents and make any other accommodations for parents who are culturally different. Also, multiculturally competent school counselors take special care to make sure culturally different parents understand the purpose, format, and possible outcomes of these meetings.

Multicultural school counselors are also aware of the possible bias of child study teams when making educational decisions about culturally different students. The process of decision making in special education, for instance, can be biased because of the subjectivity inherent in the process. Bias tends to influence observations, testing, and educational decision making (Rubin, 1992). In any case, it is critical for a multiculturally competent school counselor to identify when a student's culture is negatively affecting assessment procedures and, consequently, the decision-making process of a child study team.

Schoolwide Programs

Coordinating structured programs and special events that supplement educational programs has become a major responsibility of school counselors (Fall, 1994). Counselors may coordinate mentoring programs (Noll, 1997), coping skills training (Kiselica, Baker, Thomas, & Reedy, 1994), conflict resolution programs (Carruthers, Carruthers, Day-Vines, Bostick, & Watson, 1996), and prejudice prevention programs (Ponterotto & Pederson, 1993) for an entire school.

Multiculturally competent school counselors coordinate schoolwide programs that are relevant to the needs of all students, particularly those students from culturally different backgrounds. Baker (2001) emphasized that school counselors who plan and present schoolwide programs are more successful if they are able to make programs "meaningful to individuals representing all worldviews in their schools" (p. 153). Schoolwide programs that promote prejudice reduction and conflict resolution are excellent examples of programs that promote respecting others' worldviews. School counselors should also ensure that diverse students are active participants in all aspects of the schoolwide programs.

Coordinating Referrals

Often, school counselors refer students and their families to resources outside of the school (Downing, Pierce, & Woodruff, 1993; Hobbs & Collison, 1995). When students' problems are beyond the scope of the regular guidance and counseling services offered in a school, the counselor will refer the student to professionals in the community who have the time, experience, and resources to help. Many school counselors spend many hours building relationships and information about community mental health agencies, private practices in the community, and community leaders with expertise in areas relevant to the school.

Because of increasingly diverse school communities, school counselors must also take time to ensure that their referral sources are representative of their school communities. The ASCA (1989) specifically states that school counselors should develop resource lists of "educational and community support services to meet the socioeconomic and cultural needs of culturally diverse students and their families" (p. 322). Atkinson and Juntunen (1994) also recommended that school counselors be familiar with services offered both in ethnic communities and in the larger community. For instance, a school counselor in a community with a large percentage of Jewish students should contact and begin a working relationship with local synagogues. Or, a school counselor with a growing number of referrals from gay and lesbian students should contact and assess the services provided by local agencies that specialize in working with gay and lesbian youth.

Essentially, school counselors should be familiar with community services and referral agencies that are appropriate for all groups (e.g., economic groups, linguistic groups) of students and parents.

MULTICULTURAL ASSESSMENT

Given the prevalence of standardized achievement and aptitude tests in schools, it is imperative that school counselors understand the appropriateness of assessment instruments with culturally different students (Amour-Thomas, 1992; Howell & Rueda, 1996). The assessment of students from different ethnic and cultural backgrounds is complex and needs to be performed with professional care and consideration. School counselors need to be able to evaluate instruments that may be biased against certain groups and identify other methods for assessing these students. In addition, school counselors need to be competent in relaying assessment results to students and parents from diverse cultures.

In an effort to address cultural differences and disparities in educational opportunities, school counselors should be able to identify whether their schools' assessment process is culturally sensitive. According to Rodriguez (2000), the culturally sensitive counselor or administrator of tests should have the following qualities:

1. familiarity with professional standards for assessing culturally diverse children,
2. cultural self-knowledge,
3. inclusion of key elements in a culturally competent assessment (e.g., clearly defined referral question, record review, parent interview),
4. awareness of the strengths and limitations of assessment instruments,
5. knowledge of alternate assessment strategies,
6. understanding of the continuing evolution of intellectual assessment.

Although the culturally sensitive assessment process is an area in which school counselors should feel competent, the ability to identify and select culturally appropriate assessment instruments is not as easily attainable. Very few instruments have been developed to assess ethnic minority student populations. However, school counselors should be aware of instruments that have been restandardized to include a more representative sample of ethnically and linguistically diverse children. Examples of instruments that have been revised to minimize bias include the following: the Wechsler Intelligence Scale for Children–Third Edition (Wechsler, 1991), the Woodcock-Johnson Psycho-Educational Battery–Revised (Woodcock & Johnson, 1990) (has Spanish version), the Raven's Standard Progressive Matrices (Raven, Court, & Raven, 1947b), the Raven's Coloured Progressive Matrices (Raven, Court, & Raven, 1947a), and the Test of Nonverbal Intelligence–Third Edition (TONI-3) (Brown, Sherbenou, & Johnson, 1991). It is important to remember, however, that there is not one instrument that is totally unbiased. Therefore, multiculturally competent school counselors know that their judgments in assessing the cultural appropriateness of an instrument and providing unbiased interpretations are key in the process of culturally sensitive assessment. Biased interpretations, for instance, of a student's test results can lead to inappropriate decisions regarding the needs of a student. School counselors must also remember that biased test interpretations in student school records create an unfair and unjust educational process for students.

In addition to addressing the possible biases of the assessment process, school counselors should be aware of other aspects of assessment that might affect culturally/ethnically diverse students. For instance, Steele's (1999) research on the underperformance of middle-class African American students on standardized tests provides support that race is a depressing factor in the academic as well as test performance of these students. Steele and his colleagues found that African American students experienced "stereotype threat," which is "the threat of being viewed through the lens of a negative stereotype, or the fear of doing something that would inadvertently confirm that stereotype" (Steele, 1999, p. 47). In other words, African American students test poorly because they know that they are likely to be seen as having limited ability. Difficulty with a test, therefore, makes the negative stereotype relevant as an interpretation of their performance and of them. According to Steele, this phenomenon causes serious intimidation and may, in turn, impair the students' thinking and performance. To be multiculturally competent in student assessment, school counselors should be aware of research related to such concepts as "stereotype threat" to better understand student assessment.

CLASSROOM GUIDANCE

Classroom guidance, unlike group counseling, is used to relay information or to instruct a large group of students. The format for group guidance sessions is very similar to a regular lesson in which objectives are formulated and activities provide a means to achieving the objectives. One of the benefits to implementing group guidance is that the counselor is able to interact with large numbers of students (Nicholl, 1994). With that said, classroom guidance is an effective way for school counselors to address cultural sensitivity and issues pertaining to race, gender, sexual orientation, disabilities, or any diversity-related issue (Bruce & Shade, 1996). School counselors can help students become more culturally sensitive by implementing group guidance sessions focused on the following objectives: to accept and appreciate others' differences, to learn accurate multicultural terminology (e.g., racism, prejudice, ethnicity, oppression), to explore one's biases, and to learn about diverse cultures and ethnic groups.

Multiculturally competent school counselors develop guidance lessons with small group activities because student interaction and discussion are perhaps the best avenue to encourage students to interact with other students different from themselves (Corey & Corey, 1997). For instance, students can meet in small groups to talk about their ethnic and/or racial histories. Having students recognize each other's ethnic heritage can help them recognize the uniquenesses of all cultures and dispel stereotypical beliefs. School counselors can also use classroom guidance to discuss the impact of prejudiced behavior in our society. Lessons regarding such topics as racism, sexism, oppression, and prejudice should be well planned and geared for the students' developmental level. Sample classroom guidance lessons might include the following activities related to multicultural issues:

1. Case studies related to students of color and racism: Students are given cases and asked to discuss the feelings of characters and ways to solve problems dealing with prejudiced behavior.
2. Defining *stereotype* and brainstorming about stereotypes that students have or have heard about different groups of people. Discuss the danger of stereotypes.
3. Interviews of classmates about their experiences with prejudices and biases. This activity is then followed by a group discussion.
4. Invite people of color from the community to discuss their personal racial/ethnic histories. This activity can be done in a large auditorium with 60 to 65 students. Students should have prepared questions for the panelists about how they have dealt with prejudiced people, racism, and oppression.

FAMILY EDUCATION

School counselors are becoming more involved in family and parent education as a means to resolving persistent student problems in the schools (Amatea, 1989; Hinkle, 1993; Palmo, Lowry, Weldon, & Scioscia, 1988). Clearly, with such an increasingly diverse student population, school counselors need to pay more attention to the cultural contexts that influence students' family behavior and development. A comprehensive understanding of family development and functioning must take into account its cultural group's kinship networks, socialization experiences, typical interactive patterns, role of the extended family, and culturally linked attitudinal and behavioral arrangements (Goldenberg & Goldenberg, 1996). School counselors must never apply norms that stem from the majority culture when assessing attitudes, beliefs, and behaviors of students' parents and families. Multiculturally competent school counselors seek to have an understanding of a cultural group's traditional gender roles within the family, the rituals associated with the death of a family member, marriage practices, and parenting styles (Conoley, 1987; Widerman & Widerman, 1995). School counselors might also enlist assistance from cultural/ethnic communities when developing family and/or parent education programs. Developing family educational programs that are culturally relevant to the participants is important for its success.

UNDERSTANDING SYSTEMIC RACISM IN SCHOOLS

According to Carter (1990), race is an elusive, perplexing, and enduring aspect of life in the United States. Helms (1994), more specifically, argued that unresolved race issues are prevalent not only in society but also in the school system. Although racism can manifest in various forms ranging from stereotyping to committing acts of violence against ethnic minorities, multiculturally competent school counselors are able to identify and address the range of biased attitudes held by individuals in the school community. According to Gay (1993), issues related to race and racism are among the causes of discrepancies in student achievement among students of color and their White peers. Others (e.g., Delpit, 1995; Weiss, 1988) have also noted the presence of racist practices in schools such as tracking ethnic minority students in low-performing classes, excluding students of a particular ethnic/cultural group from school programs, and disproportionately referring ethnic minority students for special education services. Multiculturally competent school counselors have not only a clear understanding of systemic racism but also the ability to effectively challenge racist practices that occur in their schools.

CONCLUSION

With the increasingly diverse student population of today's schools, there is a critical need for school counselors who are able to effectively guide and counsel students of culturally diverse backgrounds. As school counselors work with larger numbers of culturally different students, they need to become more multiculturally competent. In so doing, school counselors may need to alter their perceptions, learn to counsel and consult with diverse populations, become knowledgeable of other cultures and the manifestations of racism, and, more important, use culturally appropriate counseling interventions with students and their families. Clearly, this chapter only touches on the beginning of a process of becoming multiculturally competent. However, engagement in this process provides for school counselors an unparalleled opportunity for personal as well as professional growth.

REFERENCES

Amatea, E. S. (1989). *Brief strategic intervention for school behavior problems*. San Francisco: Jossey-Bass.

American School Counselor Association (ASCA). (1989). American School Counselor Association statement: Cross/multicultural counseling. *Elementary School Guidance and Counseling, 23*, 322-323.

American School Counselor Association (ASCA). (1992). Ethical standards for school counselors. *School Counselor, 40*, 84-88.

American School Counselor Association (ASCA). (1993). *Position statements of the American School Counselor Association*. Alexandria, VA: Author.

Amour-Thomas, E. (1992). Intellectual assessment of children from culturally diverse backgrounds. *School Psychology Review, 21*, 552-565.

Arredondo, P., Toporek, R., Brown, S., Jones, J., Locke, D. C., Sanchez, J., et al. (1996). *Operationalization of the multicultural counseling competencies*. Alexandria, VA: Association for Multicultural Counseling and Development.

Atkinson, D. R., & Juntunen, C. L. (1994). School counselors and school psychologists as school-home-community liaisons in ethnically diverse schools. In P. Pedersen & J. C. Carey (Eds.), *Multicultural counseling in schools* (pp. 103-120). Boston: Allyn & Bacon.

Atkinson, D. R., Thompson, C. E., & Grant, S. K. (1993). A three-dimensional model for counseling racial/ethnic minorities. *The Counseling Psychologist, 21*, 257-277.

Axelson, J. A. (1999). *Counseling and development in a multicultural society* (3rd ed.). Pacific Grove, CA: Brooks/Cole.

Baker, S. (2001). *School counseling for the twenty-first century* (3rd ed.). Upper Saddle River, NJ: Prentice Hall.

Brown, A., & Mistry, T. (1994). Group work with mixed membership groups: Issues of race and gender. *Social Work With Groups, 17*, 5-21.

Brown, K., Sherbenou, R. J., & Johnson, S. K. (1991). The Test of Nonverbal Intelligence–2 (TONI-2). In R. C. Sweetland & D. J. Keyser (Eds.), *Tests: A comprehensive reference for assessments in psychology, education, and business* (p. 63). Austin, TX: PRO-ED.

Bruce, M. A., & Shade, R. A. (1996). Classroom-tested guidance activities for promoting inclusion. *School Counselor, 43*, 224-232.

Canino, I. A., & Spurlock, J. (2000). *Culturally diverse children and adolescents: Assessment, diagnosis, and treatment.* New York: Guilford.

Carney, C. G., & Kahn, K. B. (1984). Building competencies for effective cross-cultural counseling: A developmental view. *The Counseling Psychologist, 12,* 111-119.

Carruthers, W. L., Carruthers, B. J. B., Day-Vines, N. L., Bostick, D., & Watson, D. C. (1996). Conflict resolution as a curriculum: A definition, description, and process for integration in core curricula. *School Counselor, 43,* 345-373.

Carter, R. T. (1990). The relationship between racism and racial identity among White Americans: An exploratory investigation. *Journal of Counseling and Development, 69,* 46-50.

Coleman, H. L. K. (1995). Cultural factors and the counseling process: Implications for school counselors. *The School Counselor, 42,* 180-185.

Conoley, J. C. (1987). Strategic family intervention: Three cases of school-aged children. *School Psychology Review, 16,* 469-486.

Corey, M., & Corey, G. (1997). *Groups: Process and practice* (5th ed.). Pacific Grove, CA: Brooks/Cole.

Council for Accreditation of Counseling and Related Educational Programs (CACREP). (1994). *CACREP accreditation standards and procedures manual.* Alexandria, VA: Author.

D'Andrea, M., & Daniels, J. (1995). Helping students learn to get along: Assessing the effectiveness of a multicultural developmental guidance project. *Elementary School Guidance and Counseling, 30,* 143-154.

Davis, L., Galinsky, M., & Schopler, J. (1995). RAP: A framework for leadership of multiracial groups. *Social Work, 40,* 155-165.

Delpit, L. (1995). *Other people's children.* New York: New Press.

Diller, J. (1999). *Cultural diversity: A primer for the human services.* Belmont, CA: Wadsworth.

Dougherty, A. M. (1992). School consultation in the 1990s. *Elementary School Guidance and Counseling, 26,* 163-164.

Downing, J., Pierce, K. A., & Woodruff, P. (1993). A community network for helping families. *School Counselor, 41,* 102-108.

Fall, M. (1994). Developing curriculum expertise: A helpful tool for school counselors. *School Counselor, 42,* 92-99.

Figueroa, R. A. (1990). Assessment of linguistic minority group children. In C. R. Reynolds & R. W. Kamphaus (Eds.), *Handbook of psychological and educational assessment of children: Intelligence and achievement* (pp. 671-696). New York: Guilford.

Forsyth, D. (1999). *Group dynamics* (3rd ed.). Belmont, CA: Wadsworth.

Garcia-Preto, N. (1982). Puerto Rican families. In M. McGoldrick, J. K. Pearce, & J. Giordano (Eds.), *Ethnicity and family therapy* (pp. 164-187). New York: Guilford.

Gay, G. (1993). Building cultural bridges: A bold proposal for teacher education. *Education and Urban Society, 25,* 285-299.

Gerler, E. R., Jr. (1992). Consultation and school counseling. *Elementary School Guidance and Counseling, 26,* 162.

Gibbs, J. T. (1980). The interpersonal orientation in mental health consultation: Toward a model of ethnic variations in consultation. *Journal of Community Psychology, 8,* 195-207.

Giordano, G. P., & Giordano, J. (1977). *The ethno-cultural factor in mental health: A literature review and bibliography.* New York: Institute on Pluralism and Group Identity.

Goldenberg, I., & Goldenberg, H. (1996). *Family therapy: An overview.* Pacific Grove, CA: Brooks/Cole.

Hacker, A. (1992). *Two nations: Black and White, separate, hostile, unequal.* New York: Scribner's.

Helms, J. E. (1994). Racial identity in the school environment. In E. L. Herr (Ed.), *Counseling in a dynamic society: Opportunities and challenges* Alexandria, VA: American Association for Counseling and Development.

Herring, R. D. (1997). *Multicultural counseling in schools: A synergetic approach.* Alexandria, VA: American Counseling Association.

Hinkle, J. S. (1993). Training school counselors to do family counseling. *Elementary School Guidance & Counseling, 27,* 252-257.

Hobbs, B. B., & Collison, B. B. (1995). School-community-agency collaboration: Implications for school counselors. *School Counselor, 43,* 3-9.

Holcomb-McCoy, C. (2000). *Multicultural group counseling in schools.* Unpublished manuscript, University of Maryland at College Park.

House, R., & Martin, P. J. (1998). Advocating for better futures for all students: A new vision for school counselors. *Education, 119,* 284-295.

Howell, K. W., & Rueda, R. (1996). Achievement testing with culturally and linguistically diverse students. In L. A. Suzuki, P. J. Meller, & J. G. Ponterotto (Eds.), *Handbook of multicultural assessment* (pp. 253-290). San Francisco: Jossey-Bass.

Jackson, D. N., & Hayes, D. H. (1993). Multicultural issues in consultation. *Journal of Counseling and Development, 72,* 144-147.

Kiselica, M. S., Baker, S. B., Thomas, R. N., & Reedy, S. (1994). Effects of stress inoculation training on anxiety, stress, and academic performance among adolescents. *Journal of Counseling Psychology, 41,* 335-342.

Koss-Chioino, J. D. (1995). Traditional and folk approaches among ethnic minorities. In J. F. Aponte, R. Y. Rivers, & J. Wohl (Eds.), *Psychological interventions and cultural diversity* (pp. 145-163). Boston: Allyn & Bacon.

Kurpius, D. J., & Fuqua, D. R. (1993). Consultation I: Conceptual, structural, and operational dimensions. *Journal of Counseling and Development, 71,* 596-708.

Lee, C. C., & Richardson, B. L. (1991). *Multicultural issues in counseling: New approaches in diversity.* Alexandria, VA: American Association for Counseling and Development.

Lewis, A. C., & Hayes, S. (1991). Multiculturalism and the school counseling curriculum. *Journal of Counseling and Development, 70,* 119-125.

Locke, D. C. (1998). *Increasing multicultural understanding: A comprehensive model.* Thousand Oaks, CA: Sage.

Locke, D. C., & Parker, L. D. (1994). Improving the multicultural competence of educators. In P. Pederson & J. C. Carey (Eds.), *Multicultural counseling in schools: A practical handbook* (pp. 39-58). Boston: Allyn & Bacon.

Myrick, R. D. (1993). *Developmental guidance and counseling: A practical approach* (2nd ed.). Minneapolis, MN: Educational Media.

Nicholl, W. G. (1994). Developing effective classroom guidance programs: An integrative framework. *School Counselor, 41,* 360-365.

Noll, V. (1997). Cross-age mentoring program for social skills development. *School Counselor, 44,* 239-242.

Omizo, M., & Omizo, S. A. (1989). Counseling Hawaiian children. *Elementary School Guidance and Counseling, 23,* 282-288.

Palmo, A. J., Lowry, L. A., Weldon, D. P., & Scioscia, T. M. (1988). Schools and family: Future perspectives for school counselors. In W. M. Walsh & N. J. Giblin (Eds.), *Family counseling in school settings* (pp. 39-47). Springfield, IL: Charles C Thomas.

Pederson, P., & Carey, J. C. (1994). *Multicultural counseling in schools: A practical handbook.* Boston: Allyn & Bacon.

Ponterotto, J. G., & Pederson, P. B. (1993). *Preventing prejudice: A guide for counselors and educators.* Newbury Park, CA: Sage.

Ramirez, S. Z., Lepage, K. M., Kratochwill, T. R., & Duffy, J. L. (1998). Multicultural issues in school-based consultation: Conceptual and research considerations. *Journal of School Psychology, 36,* 479-509.

Raven, J. C., Court, J. H., & Raven, J. (1947a). *Coloured Progressive Matrices.* London: Lewis.

Raven, J. C., Court, J. H., & Raven, J. (1947b). *Standard Progressive Matrices.* London: Lewis.

Rogers, M. R. (2000). Examining the cultural context of consultation. *School Psychology Review, 29,* 414-418.

Rubin, D. (1992). Cultural bias undermines assessment. *Personnel Journal, 71,* 47-51.

Schmidt, J. J. (1991). *A survival guide for the elementary/middle school counselor.* Englewood Cliffs, NJ: Prentice Hall.

Steele, C. M. (1999). Thin ice: "Stereotype threat" and Black college students. *The Atlantic Monthly, 284,* 44-54.

Strein, W., & French, J. L. (1984). Teacher consultation in the affective domain: A survey of expert opinion. *School Counselor, 31,* 339-344.

Sue, D. W., Arredondo, P., & McDavis, R. J. (1992). Multicultural counseling competencies and standards: A call for the profession. *Journal of Counseling and Development, 70,* 477-486.

Sue, D. W., Bernier, J. E., Duran, A., Feinberg, L., Pederson, P., Smith, E. J., et al. (1982). Position paper: Cross-cultural counseling competencies. *The Counseling Psychologist, 10,* 45-52.

Sue, D. W., & Sue, S. (1987). Cultural factors in the clinical assessment of Asian Americans. *Journal of Consulting and Clinical Psychology, 55,* 479-487.

Terrell, F., & Terrell, S. L. (1984). Race of counselor, client sex, cultural mistrust level, and premature termination from counseling among Black clients. *Journal of Counseling Psychology, 31,* 371-375.

Tseng, N. S., & McDermott, J. F. (1981). *Cultural mind and therapy: An introduction to cultural psychiatry.* New York: Brunner/Mazel.

Wechsler, D. (1991). *Manual for the Wechsler Intelligence Scale for Children–3rd Edition.* San Antonio, TX: Psychological Corporation.

Wehrly, B. (1995). *Pathways to multicultural counseling competence: A developmental journey.* Pacific Grove, CA: Brooks/Cole.

Weiss, L. (1988). *Class, race, and gender in American education.* Albany: State University of New York Press.

Widerman, J. L., & Widerman, E. (1995). Family systems oriented school counseling. *School Counselor, 43,* 66-73.

Woodcock, R. W., & Johnson, M. B. (1990). *Woodcock-Johnson Psycho-Educational Battery–Revised.* Allen, TX: DLM Teaching Resources.

27

Implications of Social and Cultural Influences for Multicultural Competencies in Health Psychology

THOMAS V. MERLUZZI
KRUPA HEGDE

University of Notre Dame

Few statistics are more dramatic than those that indicate differences in life expectancies of men compared to women or African Americans compared to Whites (see Table 27.1). Equally dramatic are the incidence and mortality rates for specific diseases as a function of gender or ethnicity (see Tables 27.2 and 27.3). The sex and gender differences have been accounted for by investigating a number of biological, sociocultural, and behavioral differences between men and women. The ethnic differences have been accounted for by a contextual analysis that includes many factors. Racism (Clark, Anderson, Clark, & Williams, 1999) and socioeconomic status (Adler et al., 1994) may be associated with ecological stressors and social instability (Macera, Armstead, & Anderson, 2001). Physical vulnerability,

interactions of vulnerability and environmental conditions, and psychological variables such as anger suppression (Macera et al., 2001) may also contribute to ethnic differences in mortality. Cultural differences and intragroup variability may play a role in health and illness in that perceptions of health and illness, illness beliefs, and patterns of communication with health professionals may be informed by culturally specific attitudes and behaviors. These cultural attitudes, beliefs, and behaviors may, in turn, influence morbidity and mortality. Therefore, acculturation and biculturalism would also be important moderators of health behaviors. However, as in research on mental health, there is a paucity of research on culture and health (Sue, 1999). In this chapter, social and cultural influences on

Table 27.1 Age-Adjusted Mortality Rates Per 100,000 Population by Sex and Ethnicity for 1985 and 1995

Year	Sex	White	African American	Hispanic	Asian/Pacific Islander	American Indian
1985	Men	670	1,053	525	397	603
	Women	385	595	287	229	353
1995	Men	606	1,017	515	384	580
	Women	366	571	274	231	368

Table 27.2 Age-Adjusted Incidence and Mortality Rates for Cancer by Site, Sex, and Ethnicity (1990-1995): Rates Per 100,000 Population

Site	Caucasian	African American	Asian/Pacific Islander	American Indian	Hispanic
Incidence (number of new cases)					
All sites	405	446	278	154	278
Male	486	605	324	180	331
Female	352	336	243	136	245
Breast (female)	113	99	71	32	69
Prostate	150	224	82	46	104
Colon/rectum					
Total	44	51	38	16	29
Male	54	59	47	22	36
Female	37	46	31		24
Lung/bronchus					
Total	56	75	36	19	28
Male	74	114	52	25	40
Female	43	46	22	14	19
Mortality (number of deaths)					
All sites	168	225	104	103	105
Ratio	42	50	37	67	38
Male	210	311	130	123	133
Female	140	169	84	89	87
Breast (female)	26	32	12	12	15
Prostate	24	55	11	14	17
Colon/rectum					
Total	18	23	11	10	11
Male	22	28	14	11	13
Female	15	20	9	9	9
Lung					
Total	50	61	24	29	20
Male	71	102	35	40	32
Female	34	33	15	20	11

Table 27.3   Trends in 5-Year Relative Cancer Survival Rates (in percentages) by Ethnicity and Year
of Diagnosis (1974-1994)

	Caucasian			African American		
Site	1974-1976	1980-1982	1989-1994	1974-1976	1980-1982	1989-1994
Breast	75	77	87	63	66	71
Prostate	68	75	95	58	65	81
Colon	50	56	64	46	49	52
Rectum	49	53	61	42	38	53
Uterine cervix	70	68	72	64	61	59
Uterine corpus	89	83	87	61	54	54
Oral cavity/pharynx	55	55	55	36	31	32

health are viewed as layers of causes that are multiple determinants of health and illness.

Cancer is the second leading cause of death in the United States, accounting for nearly 25% of all deaths annually. Cancer incidence rates have increased over the past 20 years. However, the rise in breast and prostate cancers may be a function of more adequate detection and greater public awareness of those diseases. Nonetheless, relative incidence and mortality rates of breast and prostate cancer have been increasing at a faster rate among African Americans than Caucasians. The survival differences appear to be related to being diagnosed at a later stage of the disease and lower usage of screening among African Americans compared to Caucasians. Table 27.2 presents some summary statistics for cancer incidence and mortality as a function of site and ethnicity.

HEALTH CARE SYSTEM IN THE UNITED STATES

Access to health care is the largest contributor to the disparity in health care between dominant and nondominant groups. The nondominant groups include people of color, the working poor, and women. Universal coverage or viewing appropriate health care as a right, in the same class of rights as education, has met with opposition. The four components of the opposition are (a) the doctors and

medical schools, (b) insurance companies, (c) pharmaceutical companies, and (d) hospitals and health systems (Bayne-Smith, 1996). Each of these components has significant influence at the national level. Moreover, people of color and/or women are not admitted to the higher echelons of these industries despite the elevated diversity in medical schools (Bayne-Smith, 1996). Thus, it is not surprising that with the advent of managed care and the rollback and oversight of Medicaid spending, there has been consternation in all four components of medical care in the United States. As a result of those concerns, some physicians have chosen to limit the number of Medicaid patients they serve or have opted not to provide services to people on Medicaid. This further limits access to health care providers.

The technology that has driven advances in medicine may account for saving many lives, but the disparity in access to those procedures continues to grow. Relative to other developed countries, a large portion of the U.S. population is uninsured or underinsured, resulting in compromised access to basic health care (Bayne-Smith, 1996). Thus, poor people, particularly the working poor, and uninsured people have been excluded from access to medical care. Because disproportionately more minorities, women, and older people are poor in the United States, they will have less access to health care.

SOCIAL VERSUS CULTURAL INFLUENCES ON HEALTH

It is important to distinguish social influences on health from illness and cultural influences. Social influences include but are not limited to socioeconomic status, racism, and social stressors (e.g., crowding, high levels of crime). Cultural influences take form in culturally informed beliefs about health, illness, medicine, healers, health care, and emotional and physical reactions to symptoms of illness or markers of health (Wells & Black, 2000). There are three levels of analysis in the realm of social influences. The first level is the epidemiological analysis, which partitions the population in search of group differences. The thrust of this research has been to uncover disparities between genders or ethnic groups and Caucasians in morbidity and mortality. That the epidemiological analysis is descriptive suggests reasons why the disparities exist. The second level of analysis delves into explaining these disparities in terms of biological and social variables. These variables may influence health-related behaviors and, subsequently, morbidity and mortality. The final level of analysis is concerned with cultural influences on health. These influences may be moderated by social variables such as pressure for acculturation and increases in socioeconomic status.

EXPLAINING SOCIAL INFLUENCES ON HEALTH: RACISM, SEXISM, AGEISM, AND CLASSISM

It is clear that health is a multiply determined variable. However, the disparities noted above have some common features that revolve around social constructs such as racism, sexism, ageism, and classism.

Racism

Race has a longstanding history as a critical epidemiological variable in health statistics. Moreover, race has been used despite the lack of scientific consensus concerning the definition of race. There is also a strong tendency for Americans to confound race and ethnicity. For example, African Americans living in the United States have a wide variety of ethnic backgrounds that may affect how health and illness are perceived and may determine participation in health behaviors such as screenings for common diseases. This is one way in which the focus on race alone tends to mask what may be important intragroup differences. However, racism as a social force influencing access to and the delivery of health services, as well as the manner in which research is conducted, is clearly evident in the United States as it is in other countries.

A compelling example of the institutionalization of racism in health research is the Tuskegee syphilis experiment conducted from 1932 to 1972. Men who had latent syphilis were left untreated to test racial differences in the progression of the disease. Moreover, when effective treatments were available, they were deliberately withheld from these men. This and other less spectacular racially discriminatory research has built a climate of distrust (Whaley, 2001). That distrust has spilled over into the battle on AIDS (Jones, 1997) and cancer (Bayne-Smith, 1996). For example, incidence rates for AIDS among African Americans and Hispanics have increased at a greater rate than that for Caucasians. African American women are one of the fastest growing groups at risk for AIDS (Bayne-Smith, 1996). In 1990, 52% of women with AIDS were Black, 20.5% were Hispanic, and 26.5% were White (Centers for Disease Control and Prevention [CDC], 1990).

Clark et al. (1999) suggested that the effects of racism on health are far reaching and that several mechanisms account for these effects, particularly in African Americans in the United States. The exposure to acute and chronic stress due to racism is considered to be a significant and possibly unique risk for African Americans compared to other ethnic groups. Moreover, Clark et al. posited several moderating mechanisms that may exacerbate the effects of racism on health. These include constitutional factors (e.g., heightened vulnerability to hypertension), sociodemographic factors (e.g., socioeconomic status [SES]), and intragroup racism. In addition, they noted that mediating variables such as perceived racism, the subjective experience of racism, and coping responses may mitigate the effect of racism and promote resilience (Guyll, Matthews, & Bromberger, 2001).

Sexism

Women constitute 70% to 80% of health care consumers (Passau-Buck, 1994). Moreover, women take 50% more prescription drugs than men and are admitted to day surgery, hospitals, and outpatient clinics much more frequently than men. This use pattern may be based on a longstanding medical practice in which women have regular gynecological exams, mammogram screenings, and prenatal and postnatal care and give birth, for the most part, in hospitals. Thus, obstetric and gynecological care may account for most of the differences in medical utilization between women and men. However, the medical system traditionally has held a social view of women that reflects the dominant culture's perspective on women. Most of the research has focused on diseases that affect men. Medical practice is then extrapolated from research on men and applied to women.

Although the biological definitions of sex and the sociocultural definitions of social roles have been enmeshed, certain unique biological aspects of health separate men and women. There are the sex-specific illnesses such as ovarian and cervical disease, illness related to reproduction and pregnancy, prostate cancer, and the effects of hormones on the progression of disease or in the protection from disease. Also, some diseases are far more prevalent in women—for instance, certain autoimmune disorders such as multiple sclerosis, lupus, and rheumatoid arthritis. These gender-specific and gender-dominant illnesses have implications for different medical approaches and psychological reactions to the illnesses. For example, traditional approaches to coping with cancer involving support groups may have to be modified for men who typically have less of a penchant for emotional expression compared to women.

In the health professions, traditional sex roles have placed women in medical occupations that are supportive rather than in roles of leadership (e.g., nurses instead of doctors). Recently, the advent of nurse-practitioner clinics and the changing enrollments in medical schools portend changes in the role of women in medical care. However, research remains dominated by men.

Despite the increase of interest in women's health and the empowerment of women to influence the focus of research on issues such as breast cancer, the majority of health care and health research is being provided in the same male-dominated context as the medical profession itself (Passau-Buck, 1994). Generally, there is the role expectation for a patient to be compliant and dependent (Tagliacozzo & Mauksch, 1972). As you add "devalued" social labels to the patient, the expectations for compliance may increase; for example, in the case of women, there is double the expectation for compliance and dependence. For women of color, there may be triple the expectation.

Despite the differential use of medical services and the difference in life expectancy between men and women, the dominant thrust of medical research has been on men but applied to both men and women. It was not until recently that the disparities in medical research began to be remedied. The National

Institutes of Health has initiated policies to address the gender, ethnic, and age discrepancies in research.

Ageism

It has long been assumed that chronological age is associated with health. Although this may be true, the relationship between aging and health has been changing in the past few decades. The rates of mortality due to lung cancer and heart disease, the largest causes of American deaths, have been declining in the United States. As a result, the baby boomer cohort is expected to be much healthier in old age than previous cohorts, and the absolute number of older people will increase dramatically over the next two decades. Although there still may be a compression of illness in later life, which makes older people the largest consumers of medical services and dependent on physicians for quality of life, this conclusion is cohort based. The baby boomers will have access to more information and more resources than previous generations. Thus, the previous relationship between aging and health may be modified by the new cohort of older people. However, ethnicity and SES may be moderators of that general trend.

Gender and age interact with respect to the onset of disease. In general, men and women experience the same types of illness as they age; however, men tend to experience the onset of fatal conditions earlier than women, and women experience the onset of nonfatal conditions, particularly arthritis, earlier than men. For example, women experience the symptoms of coronary heart disease about 10 years later than men (Siegler, Bastian, & Bosworth, 2001) and the occurrence of myocardial infarction 20 years later than men. In fact, until relatively recently, heart disease in older women was not well understood; very little research had been done with respect to the disease in women, in general, and older

women, in particular. Because estrogen was a protective factor for women, there was the mistaken notion that rates of myocardial infarction were lower in women and that aggressive treatments were not warranted. These gender disparities were explored in the late 1980s in studies demonstrating that symptoms such as chest pain and coronary heart disease were treated less aggressively (Tobin et al., 1987) and that interventions such as cardiac catheterization and bypass surgery were used less often with women (Ayanian & Epstein, 1991) who had the same pathology as men.

The data with respect to the coping capacity of older people to deal with illness vary. Some researchers focus on the burden of poor health in old age and the impact of ageism on health. Others concern themselves with the lack of resources older people have to cope with the stress of ageism and poor health (Markides, 1989). Some recent evidence seems to counter the notion that older people cope more poorly. Merluzzi and Martinez Sanchez (1997) found that older people with cancer reported greater self-efficacy for coping than younger people with the disease. In addition, it appears that emotional stability is health protective across the life course (Aldwin, Spiro, Levenson, & Cupertino, 2001). It is clearly the case that illness increases with age and that there may be a compression of illness in old age, but the medical profession may underestimate the capacity of older people to cope with these illnesses.

Classism

Longevity is typically tied to socioeconomic status (Adler et al., 1994). However, the effects of SES may change somewhat in old age. Some data suggest that in older Americans, mortality from heart disease is uncorrelated with SES (Markides & Marchalek, 1984). Death from strokes is more common among people with lower SES, whereas mortality from cancer is higher in high-SES categories than in lower SES categories (Markides & Marchalek, 1984).

Despite the disadvantage of SES overall, at old age there is a crossover when African Americans exceed the life expectancy of Caucasian Americans. One explanation for this crossover is the selective survival hypothesis (Markides & Marchalek, 1984). The selective survival hypothesis states that people in groups that are at high risk for early mortality are more likely to die before old age, resulting in a relatively more health-hardy elderly population than people who are from groups that are not at risk. Also, high self-esteem and social support may have direct effects on health (Ritter, Hobfoll, Lavin, Cameron, & Hulsizer, 2000) that may counter the effects of SES. In addition, there may be some buffers in the relationship between income and health outcomes. Investigators have found that emotional (but not tangible) support may moderate the income-health outcomes relationship (Vitaliano et al., 2001).

EXPLAINING CULTURAL INFLUENCES

Cultural Views of Health and Illness

Perhaps one of the determinants of a person's approach to illness and the medical system is a culturally informed worldview of health and illness. Landrine and Klonoff (2001) presented a compelling account of the cultural beliefs and practices endemic to ethnic minorities in the United States. These cultural beliefs and practices have been meticulously studied by cultural anthropologists; however, the impact of these beliefs on health outcomes has not been as well studied (Landrine & Klonoff, 2001). The assumption that these beliefs and practices have an impact on health outcomes, regardless of the scarcity of outcome studies, is based on the notion that *acculturation*, which occurs when people adopt the dominant culture's beliefs and practices by people from nondominant cultures and eschew their own, has had a significant impact on morbidity and mortality. Landrine and Klonoff presented a treatise on the health-related cultural beliefs and practices and indicated that acculturation modifies these perspectives. Thus, the degree and type of acculturation represent an important facet of assessment in health psychology. Highlights of their work are presented to provide a context for the importance of culture in health psychology.

With respect to views of illness, many common minority cultures in the United States adhere to a view of health that is based on the integration of mind and body in which balance and harmony are evident. In causal explanations for illness, supernatural causes may be given as much credit as natural causes. In fact, in traditional Mexican, Southeast Asian, Chinese, and Native American cultures, biomedical factors are viewed as a very distal cause of illness. There are many culturally distinct folk disorders, and indigenous healers administer folk remedies for all of these cultures.

As an example of the cultural determinants of illness attribution, Landrine and Klonoff (2001) presented the concept of hot and cold as critical factors in the balance in conceptualizing health and illness, as perceived by the Mexican American culture. When illness occurs, it represents the dominance of one over the other. Hot and cold may refer to personality, foods, emotions, treatments, and so on (Landrine & Klonoff, 2001). For example, when cold dominates from too much night air, that may be implicated in catching a cold; a remedy that is "hot" (e.g., hot foods) would provide balance. Similarly, most Native American cultures view health as harmony between physical, spiritual, and social realms (Landrine & Klonoff, 2001). The three major causes of illness in traditional

Navajo culture are breach of taboo (i.e., doing things in the physical world that are forbidden), witchcraft (i.e., consorting with the dead to do evil on earth), and soul loss (e.g., premature death when the soul is firmly attached to the body, which may cause disease in others) (Landrine & Klonoff, 2001).

It is evident from the comprehensive presentation of culture and health by Landrine and Klonoff (2001) that there is a striking similarity among America's ethnic minorities with respect to the holistic assumptions about health and illness, the attributions about causes for illness, and the types of folk disorders and indigenous healers who tend to those disorders. Table 27.4 (from Landrine & Klonoff, 2001) summarizes the components of culture that represent traditional perspectives on health, illness, and medicine, and Table 27.5 (from Wells & Black, 2000) presents the underlying values that inform nondominant cultural perspectives on health in contrast with the dominant cultural perspective. These authors concluded that there are two distinct worldviews with respect to health. One worldview represents holism (i.e., integration of mind and body), which is consistent with sociocentric cultures, whereas the other worldview represents dualism (i.e., separation of mind and body) of egocentric Western European cultures. Landrine and Klonoff also noted that when there are thin boundaries between self, others, and the environment, "natural and supernatural entities and forces readily traverse it" (p. 877). That permeability allows spiritual and interpersonal factors to give rise to the social and moral implication of illness (Landrine & Klonoff, 2001). Thus, illness may have a shame and moral component in sociocentric cultures that is not present in most conceptualizations of Western medicine. In contrast, Western medicine may adopt the concept of holism (as in holistic medicine) but, in the final analysis, views illness as a physical event (Landrine & Klonoff, 2001).

CULTURALLY RELEVANT HEALTH PROMOTION AND DISEASE PREVENTION

One point of entry into health care is through participation in health promotion or disease prevention activities such as cholesterol, mammogram, prostate, or blood pressure screenings. Cultural issues may play an important role in the decision to participate in these types of prevention behaviors (Huff & Kline, 1999). The connection made through various types of communication needs to be persuasive to affect the behavioral intentions of the recipient who gets the information. Pasick, D'Onofrio, and Otero-Sabogal (1996) have presented a perspective on health promotion in which interventions may be culturally tailored for a specific cultural or ethnic group. They distinguished between merely targeting health promotions for specific groups and tailoring those promotion activities to include sensitivity to a particular target group's cultural beliefs, attitudes, and behaviors. The promotion intervention should be preceded by planning in which a thorough analysis of several dimensions is accomplished (Frankish, Lovato, & Shannon, 1999). Those dimensions might include components of the health beliefs model (Rosenstock, 1974), the theory of reasoned action (Ajzen & Fishbein, 1980), and other models that account for compliance with health promotion behaviors.

Frankish et al. (1999) presented the following dimensions, derived from the models noted above, as starting points for a cultural analysis that precedes the design of health promotion interventions that are culturally tailored:

Perceptions: These include knowledge, attitudes, values, and beliefs within a cultural context that may facilitate or hinder personal, family, and community motivations to engage in health-promoting or health-preventive behaviors. These aspects of culture may influence perceptions of vulnerability to the illness and the severity, cause, and duration of the illness.

Table 27.4 Similarities in Health Beliefs and Practices of American Minority Cultures

	Puerto Ricans	Mexican/Latinos	Southeast Asians	Chinese/Asians	African Americans	Afro-Caribbean	Native Americans
Basic assumption	Mind/body & person/ environment holism	Mind/body & person/ environment holism	Mind/body & person/ environment holism	Mind/body & person/ environment holism	Mind/body & person/ environment holism	Mind/body & person/ environment holism	Mind/body & person/ environment holism
Definition of health	Balance & harmony	Balance & harmony	Balance & harmony	Balance & harmony	Harmony	Balance & harmony	Harmony
Major proximal causes of illness	Supernatural factors	Emotions	Supernatural factors	Natural factors	Natural & supernatural factors	Supernatural factors	Breach of taboo (supernatural)
Other proximal causes	Natural factors & emotions	Natural factors	Natural factors & emotions	Emotions	Supernatural factors & emotions	Supernatural factors	Supernatural factors
Distal causes	Supernatural factors	Supernatural factors	Supernatural factors	Supernatural factors	Biomedical factors	Natural factors	Natural factors
Very distal causes	Biomedical factors	Biomedical factors	Biomedical factors	Biomedical factors	Supernatural factors	Biomedical factors	Biomedical factors
Folk disorders	Fright/soul loss Worry Evil eye Empacho States of blood Possession Hex/curse	Fright/soul loss Worry Evil eye Empacho Caida Hex/curse	Fright/soul loss Evil eye Nightmare Possession Hex/curse	Fright/soul loss Evil eye	Worry Falling out States of blood Possession/trance Hex/curse	Worry Falling out States of blood Possession/trance Hex/curse	Soul loss Possession Hex/curse
Indigenous healers	Spiritualists Herbalists Curanderas Pateras (midwives)	Herbalists Curanderas Pateras (midwives) Spiritualists	Chinese doctors Vaids Herbalists	Chinese doctors Herbalists	Ministers Herbalists Midwives Voodooists	Spiritualists Herbalists Midwives Voodooists	Ceremonialists
Folk cures	Magic rituals Tea, herbs Prayer Diet/rest Physical manipulation	Tea, herbs Prayer Diet/rest Physical manipulation Magical rituals	Magical rituals Diet change Tea, herbs Meditation	Tea, herbs Diet/rest Physical manipulation (acupuncture) Meditation	Prayer Tea, herbs Diet/rest Magical rituals	Magic rituals Tea, herbs Diet/rest Prayer	Magical rituals Herbs Diet/rest Prayer/chants Physical manipulation
Expectation of care providers	Charismatic Intuits problem Warm, personal	Charismatic Intuits problem Warm, personal	Charismatic Intuits problem Formal, polite	Charismatic Intuits problem Formal, polite	Charismatic Intuits problem Warm, personal	Charismatic Intuits problem Warm, personal	Charismatic Intuits problem Warm, personal
Cultural factors affecting health behavior	Distrust of Whites Language	Distrust of Whites Language	Distrust of Whites Fear of shame Language	Distrust of Whites Fear of shame Language	Distrust of Whites Dialect	Distrust of Whites Language	Distrust of Whites Noninterference

SOURCE: Landrine & Klonoff (2001, pp. 878-879). From "Cultural Diversity and Health Psychiatry," in A. Baum, T. A. Revenson, & J. E. Singer, *Handbook of Health Psychology*. Copyright

Table 27.5   Comparison of Values From Dominant and Nondominant Perspectives

Anglo-American	Other Ethnocultural Groups
Mastery over nature	Harmony with nature
Personal control over the environment	Fate
Doing/activity	Being
Time dominates	Personal interaction dominates
Human equality	Group welfare
Youth	Elders
Self-help	Birthright inheritance
Competition	Cooperation
Future orientation	Past or present orientation
Informality	Formality
Directness/openness/honesty	Indirectness/ritual/"face"
Practicality/efficiency	Idealism
Materialism	Spiritualism/detachment

SOURCE: Wells and Black (2000, p. 225).

Enablers: These include cultural, societal, systematic, and structural influences or forces that may either enhance or be barriers to engaging in the health-promoting or health-preventive behavior. These influences might include the availability of resources, accessibility, referrals, employers, government officials, skills, and types of services offered.

Nurturers: These represent the degree to which health beliefs, attitudes, and actions are influenced and mediated or nurtured by extended family, kin, friends, peers, and the community.

Positive behaviors: These behaviors are based on health beliefs and actions that are known to be beneficial and must be encouraged.

Existential behaviors: These are cultural beliefs, practices, and/or behaviors that are indigenous to a group and have no harmful health consequences and thus do not need to be targeted for change.

Negative behaviors: These are attitudes and behaviors based on health beliefs and actions that are known to be harmful to one's health (Frankish et al., 1999, pp. 67-68).

Based on this analysis, health promotion can proceed from a unique cultural perspective to promote healthy behaviors or practices. Conflicts might arise when the behaviors informed by culture present a barrier to health care interventions. For example, there is the cultural value of modesty among Latina women, such that exposing one's breast to a stranger would be considered a cultural taboo. This is especially true if that stranger is not female. Thus, mammogram screening may be a threatening procedure from a cultural perspective. In all interventions, whether they are health promotion or clinical in nature, there is the need to examine carefully the goals of the intervention and the cultural consequences.

Leininger (1991) suggested three strategies for assessing cultural consequences. The first strategy is *cultural preservation or maintenance*. If at all possible, the patient's cultural beliefs, attitudes, and behaviors should be maintained and used to enhance health promotion or compliance. The second strategy is *cultural negotiation or accommodation*. When there is apparent conflict between traditional medical practice and the patient's cultural beliefs, attempts should be made to negotiate an alternate solution, allowing both the health practitioner and the patient to feel comfortable without compromising the health of the patient (Wells & Black, 2000). The third strategy is *repatterning or restructuring*. This strategy is chosen when a cultural practice is a clear danger to the patient's health. If this option is chosen, then the health professional will need to explain to the patient why and how the cultural practice is a detriment to health and how the treatment may affect traditional cultural practices and vice versa. Ultimately, the choice of whether to participate in the treatment should rest in the patient (Wells & Black, 2000). However, this strategy requires the health psychologist to be very familiar with the patient's culture and clearly be able to explain and discuss the cultural as well as medical consequences.

A program of health promotion, called African American Women in Touch (AAWIT) in South Bend, Indiana, exemplifies a culturally tailored approach to prevention. Like most communities across the United States, mortality rates for African American women with breast cancer are higher than those in European American women. Moreover, at diagnosis, African American women usually are in a much later stage of the disease than European American women. With sponsorship from Memorial Hospital and with funding from the Avon and Komen foundations, a group of African American women, who were leaders in some capacity in the community, was assembled to form AAWIT. After some initial meetings, a plan was devised to promote breast health education and offer mammogram screenings. Based on focus group data and the research literature (Rimer, McBride, & Crump, 2001), barriers to and facilitators for obtaining a screening mammogram were identified. The barriers to early screening and

detection included the fear of cancer, the belief that the mammogram might be painful, transportation to the clinic, cost, desire not to expose one's body to strangers, distrust of the medical community, and lack of information about risk factors (i.e., underestimating risk). The facilitators included providing free mammograms (for those without insurance coverage), knowing someone who had been through the procedure, and having another African American woman guide them through the process (i.e., accompany them to their mammogram appointment).

Two African American nurses were employed to present educational programs on breast health, risk factors for breast disease, and breast self-examination and to facilitate appointments for mammograms. Dark skin-tone breast models were used in the educational workshops. The nurses made presentations at churches, neighborhood centers, and social organizations. Several videos were produced, with local women as actors, in which concerns about mammograms were discussed and resolved. Remuneration for transportation or child care was available to those in need. For those who were fearful, a facilitation model was used in which a woman from the AAWIT would accompany any woman to her appointment.

The AAWIT program has been in operation for approximately 8 years. Recent statistics indicate that early-stage diagnosis has increased by 12% over that time period, and late-stage diagnosis has decreased by 30%. Moreover, the sheer number of African American women getting first-time and repeat mammograms has increased 10-fold. Currently, the program is being extended to Latinas with the same approach to cultural tailoring.

In sum, health promotion and prevention activities represent a prime opportunity for using culturally informed and sensitive interventions to encourage health-protective or health-preventive behaviors. These types of interventions can also improve the credibility of the health care provider in addition to promoting access to and usage of health care services. These interventions also create a need to train health care providers to maintain a culturally sensitive stance so as to ensure compliance with medical regimens and for continued use of medical services that may maintain optimum health.

COMPETENCY ISSUES
IN HEALTH PSYCHOLOGY

Multiculturalism is a concept that emphasizes the diversity inherent in a pluralistic society, focusing on the importance of acceptance and respect for differences in race, religion, nationality, culture, language, and other factors on which people vary (Sue, Bingham, Porché-Burke, & Vasquez, 1999). Wells and Black (2000) cited Asante's (1991) proclamation that the goal of multiculturalism is to "achieve cultural pluralism without hierarchy." According to Wells and Black, multicultural educational goals fall into seven broad areas: ethnic and cultural literacy, personal development, attitude and value clarification, multicultural social competency, basic skills proficiency, educational equality and excellence, and empowerment for societal reform. Health psychologists are in a unique position to promote prosocial change, advocate for those in need, and contribute to the advancement of multiculturalism in the health care setting. First, however, there is a need to work on awareness of social and cultural factors in health care that are presented in this chapter.

Awareness

Multicultural competence occurs in three primary areas—self-exploration and awareness, knowledge, and skills. Culturally competent health psychologists have an awareness of their own cultural identity and how others perceive them. Health psychologists need to become aware of the power that may accrue just by their status in a medical setting. The hierarchy of power normally present in relationships with clients is exacerbated in a setting in which medicine is practiced. Thus, one area of competency is becoming aware of the social role and power vested in professionals in a health setting. Because that hierarchy of power traditionally has been used to the determent of poor, oppressed, and culturally different people (e.g., Tuskegee, Auschwitz, Bosnia), it is important to be knowledgeable about the existence of oppression, how it is perpetrated, and how it affects us as health psychologists. It is particularly important to be aware of the impact of the power hierarchy on the patients with whom we interact.

Power and privilege have traditionally been awarded to members of the dominant socio cultural group. That, coupled with the power vested in health care provision, leads to multiple levels of hierarchy that create a situation that challenges the culturally competent health care provider. It is important to have an awareness of the institutional racism, sexism, and classism that result in the disempowerment of culturally different persons seeking health care and the fostering of White privilege (Ancis & Szymanski, 2001). However, to be truly culturally competent in a health care setting, one needs to go beyond social analysis and gain some knowledge of the cultural beliefs that inform the explanation and expression of health and illness.

Health psychologists should strive to be aware of themselves as cultural beings, attending to preferences and biases that might enhance or impede the effective delivery of health care services. One must also strive to be aware of how worldview and cultural background can interact with individual, family, or group concerns, allowing the psychologist to recognize the "client in context." An awareness of socialization experiences and issues relating to discrimination and oppression of the underserved is necessary. With respect to health care, the vast majority of the research has been male dominated. There also exist many historical examples of racist, sexist, and homophobic influences in prior research. Accessibility to health care resources, insurance, and clinics may be strongly influenced by other factors in the individual's life.

Knowledge

Cultural characteristics and life experiences of racial and ethnic populations are important to know, as are similarities and differences among racial, ethnic, and culturally diverse groups. One should have a basic understanding of human development and the life cycle as it relates to ethnicity, race, gender, religion, sexual orientation, and disability. The primary goal should be to gain enough knowledge to know how to ask for information that is culturally relevant.

The culturally competent provider of health care should have the ability to generate, modify, and adapt a variety of intervention strategies to accommodate the particular needs of the client and his or her family (Shiang, Kjellander, & Bogumill, 1998). The knowledge and ability to be creative and resourceful in identifying and using cultural value systems on the behalf of the client is as important as the ability to use, send, and interpret a variety of communication skills—verbal and nonverbal—to bridge the gap between cultures. It is also important to have skills and the knowledge to learn about culture, as well as the capability to impartially evaluate discriminatory intent and effect in interactions and services (Pope-Davis & Coleman, 1997).

Health psychologists should also strive to make a lifelong commitment to continued learning concerning the multicultural bases of health care practice. For example, one should learn about cultural, ethnic, and racial groups and multiracial identity development as they relate to practice, theory, and research. We should learn about helping practices that are used in non-Western cultures that may affect the lives of our clients. Issues of acculturation in this realm might also apply. We should be aware and accepting of the limitations of our own multicultural and culture-specific proficiency and expertise and make referrals to appropriate experts should this prove necessary. Health psychologists should know and consider the validity of a given instrument or procedure with regards to biases, interpretational limitations, cultural equivalence, and so on.

Skill: Creating an Environment Conducive to Gathering Cultural Information

It is also important to create an environment that is conducive to gathering culturally relevant information that includes an assessment of the patient's culture, acculturation, and health-related cultural beliefs, attitudes, and behaviors.

Acculturation. A culturally competent health psychologist is familiar with the concept of acculturation and the complexities that concept brings to the health care setting. Acculturation refers to the degree to which and the contexts in which individuals adopt the behaviors of the dominant culture and the extent to which they eschew their own cultural traditions. The complexities come from the various types of groups that immigrated or were indigenous. Aponte and Crouch (1995) have identified the following groups: immigrants, who are voluntary migrants; refugees, who are involuntary; native people, who are indigenous and nonmigratory; ethnic groups, which are nonmigratory and less willing to interact with the larger society; and sojourners, who have temporary contact with society (e.g., students from other countries, temporary workers). Moreover, individuals in each of these groups may have some level of acculturation, which may have an impact on the presentation of the illness and the beliefs about the causes and cures for illnesses.

The following levels of acculturation have been offered by Lecca, Quervalú, Nunes, and Gonzales (1998, p. 33) with some slight modifications of wording:

1. Traditional: Retention of his or her original or traditional culture
2. Acculturated: Identification with the dominant Anglo-American culture
3. Bicultural: Identification with both the original and the adopted culture
4. Marginality: Rejection of both original and Anglo-American cultures
5. Transitional: A transitional orientation in which individuals are bicultural but question traditional values and religion

The guidelines from the American Psychological Association's (APA's) Office of Ethnic Minority Affairs (APA, 1993) stress the importance of seeking information about the client's culture and not solely relying on the client to provide the counselor with all the salient data (Pope-Davis & Coleman, 1997). Things worth documenting include but are not limited to the number of generations the client's family has been in this country, the number of years the client has been in this country (in the case of immigrants), the client's fluency in and comprehension of the English language, the level of education of the client, the acculturation stress experienced by the client, and the community resources accessed by the individual. This information assists the health care practitioner in being mindful of aspects of the client's culture that need to be treated with care and respect. Table 27.6 (from Wells & Black, 2000) provides some basic information that may be helpful in creating an environment that is conducive to gathering culturally relevant information. However,

health psychologists need to be mindful of how to communicate effectively to obtain that information.

Communication. Culturally competent health psychologists are conscious of their social effects on others, including awareness of their communication style, which is the basis of communication in health care settings. Because health care, including health psychology, has not taken into account the cultural bases for illness and health, there is a tendency to gloss over issues that may be easily resolved with some attention to the person's level of acculturation and his or her culturally informed beliefs, which may affect compliance and adherence. Kleinman, Eisenberg, and Good (1978) recommended the following line of questioning to ascertain the patient's conceptualization of his or her illness:

1. What do you think has caused your problem?
2. Why do you think it started when it did?
3. What do you think your sickness does to you?
4. How does it work?
5. Will it have a short or long course?
6. What kind of treatment do you think you need?
7. What are the most important results you hope to receive from this treatment?
8. What are the chief problems your sickness has caused for you?
9. What do you fear most about your sickness?

Understanding the patients' conception of illness and the role of acculturation contributes to an understanding of the patients' perspectives on illness and treatments. For more traditional, less acculturated people, there may be a need to delve further into their understanding of the intentions of the treatments that health psychologists propose, as well as have a respectful perspective on the ways that patients have traditionally dealt

Table 27.6   General Guidelines for Creating a Multicultural Approach and Environment

- Expect every client, family, colleague, or person to be different. (A client is not just a client.) Each person has his or her own identity, culture, ethnicity, background, experiences, and lifestyle.

- The culture and lifestyle of people do matter. Being aware of or respecting differences is not enough. Knowledge about and the effect of these differences must be integrated into all your interactions.

- Take into account the client's culture and how it affects and shapes the individual.

- Acknowledge that some health beliefs and practices are derived from basic needs and may have little basis in reality. Additionally, be aware that some practices you may consider to be primitive do serve a purpose for the person within the culture and must be respected.

- Be cognizant of gender and age. These characteristics affect the clinical approach used, as well as the perceptions held by the client, family, or caregiver about the practitioner.

- Use good basic health care practices, such as completing a thorough evaluation with the client and the family, checking diet restrictions before planning or initiating a cooking activity, involving the client and the family in the program, and doing an evaluation of the home environment.

- Look for cues, both verbal and nonverbal, that will help you involve the client in the treatment session.

- Be flexible and adaptable in your treatment of the client and, by all means, avoid a cookbook approach.

- Be aware of your personal biases and how they may affect the therapeutic relationship.

- Do not misjudge people because of their accents or grammar.

- Avoid being patronizing or condescending. Use language that fosters trust and alliance.

- Use an interpreter if you are not fluent in the client's preferred language. If an interpreter is unavailable, learn basic words, phrases, or sentences in that language. This will show that you are making an effort to identify with the client.

- Be an agent of change.

- Listening to the client and being responsive to his or her needs is a demonstration of cultural competency. It is important to understand the view of the world from the perspective of the client, family, and caregiver.

SOURCE: Wells and Black (2000, pp. 236-237).

with illness. The time it takes to become more familiar with patients' cultural beliefs, level of acculturation, and views on the causes and cures for illness will contribute to choosing treatments that will maximize compliance. Discounting traditional beliefs or not creating an atmosphere conducive to discussing them may deter the effects of the treatment. This situation is similar to the issue of health care professionals' acceptance of complementary therapies.

Giving short shrift to patients' overtures in this arena may undermine the patient-provider relationship and the attempts that the patients are making to cope with illness. An understanding of the patients' need for support for their coping attempts may provide for a different relationship with the health care provider, as well as supporting the attempts of the patients to cope with the illness. Understanding and working with culturally informed beliefs may also support a more trusting relationship with the health care provider and assist the patients' attempts to understand and cope with the illness and the treatments. Otherwise, patients might view the health care they are receiving as competing with their own perspectives on illness and

Table 27.7   Eliciting Cultural Information in Clinical Interaction

Proposed Opening Statement

Mr./Mrs./Ms. _____, sometimes clients and health care providers have different ideas about health and diseases as well as outcome expectations. To design and provide individualized care, it is important for me to have a clear picture and understanding of your thoughts and concerns about this illness. I would like to ask you some questions about your culture, values, and beliefs. This way we can work together to improve your health or function and address you concerns.

Questions Regarding Current Illness

- What is your general understanding about your illness?
- What do you think caused your problem?
- Why do you think it started?
- How severe is your illness? How long do you think it will last?
- What are the main problems your illness has caused for you?
- Have you tried any home remedies, medicines, folk, or traditional treatment for your illness? Did it help? Are you still using it or them?
- What type of treatment do you think you should receive?
- What results do you hope to receive from the treatment?
- Is there any other information that would be helpful in designing a workable treatment plan?

Questions Regarding Health Beliefs and Practices

- Do you adhere to a religious healing system (e.g., Seventh-Day Adventist, West African voodoo, Fundamentalist sect, Pentecostal)?
- Do you adhere to a cultural healing system (e.g., Asian healing system, Raza, or Latino *curanderismo*)?
- How is illness explained in your culture (e.g., germ theory, presence of evil spirits, imbalance between hot and cold, yin and yang, disequilibrium between nature and humans)?
- Do you rely on cultural healers (e.g., medicine men, shaman, *curandero*, Chinese herbalist, spiritualist, minister, *hougan* [voodoo priest])?
- What types of cultural healing practices or remedies do you [family] practice (e.g., massage to cure empacho, coining, wearing of talismans or charms for protection against illness)?
- How would you describe a state of wellness or good health? A state of poor health or illness?

Questions Regarding Cultural Beliefs and Values

- Are there any taboos or restrictions on who can see a woman's or man's body?
- Are there any taboos or other beliefs connected with mental illness?
- Describe your spirituality or religious practice or belief.
- What cultural, racial, or ethnic group do you identify with?
- How would you describe your family structure?
- What type of support system or network is available to you?
- Who is the primary decision maker in your family?

health. Thus, in most instances, a knowledge of the worldview of the patient may enhance the therapeutic relationship, foster compliance, and affirm the patient's own perspective.

Building on Kleinman et al. (1978), Wells and Black (2000) presented an interview protocol (see Table 27.7) for eliciting cultural information in a clinical interview. The integration of this information into a treatment plan can facilitate an understanding of how to intervene in the life of the patient. Culturally informed health psychologists may foster their role as the broker of cultural information in the staffing of cases. The effective communication of culturally relevant information may, on one hand, result in more appropriate medical treatment and, on the other hand, educate other health care professionals on the treatment team concerning the importance of culture in the optimal treatment of the patient.

DISENFRANCHISEMENT VERSUS EMPOWERMENT: A DELICATE BALANCE

Given the worldview of traditional sociocentric cultures, health psychologists face a challenge. There is the juxtaposition of traditional values and beliefs about health and the realities of disparities in the health system. Thus, many traditional beliefs support that fate or supernatural causes account for illness. At the same time, inherent in health care is the disenfranchisement of persons of color. Culturally competent health psychologists should strive to use culturally proficient awareness and knowledge in effective multicultural practice and, at the same time, contribute to the development of agency on the part of the client. Thus, there is a delicate balance between empowering patients to be better consumers and, at the same time, recognizing that self-advocacy may not be part of their conception of medicine. Finding ways to refute and dismantle this disparity in agency and reception of service and, simultaneously, fine-tuning skills that are sensitive to the unique worldview and cultural background of the clients may assist health care providers in determining if certain problems arise from biases in others so as to prevent the inappropriate internalization/personalization of the problem or victimization.

We should recognize that culture-specific interventions may require nontraditional interventions and apply this knowledge in practice by tailoring outreach programs and services to the local community, participating in a variety of cultural events, and seeking out natural leaders in local communities such as preachers, natural helpers, and nontraditional healers. Assessment of traditional interventions for contextual relevance and examination of interventions for cultural appropriateness are important activities by health psychologists on behalf of the underserved. We should also solicit ongoing feedback from knowledgeable persons through peer review, patient input, and review of current practices, with special attention paid to issues of multiculturalism. To accomplish these goals, health psychologists should seek out culturally diverse health professionals to foster a peer review process and consult with health care providers. A role that may not be familiar to most health psychologists emerges from this analysis—that of a culturally informed advocate not only for the optimal treatment of patients but also for systemic change. Thus, partnerships with providers that offer training in culturally sensitive health care delivery and culturally tailored health promotion may foster systemic change that will sustain the empowerment of those seeking health care and begin to reduce the disparities in health between men and women and between dominant and nondominant groups in the United States.

REFERENCES

Adler, N. E., Boyce, T., Chesney, M. A., Cohen, S., Folkman, S., Kahn, R. L., et al. (1994). Socioeconomic status and health: The challenge of the gradient. *American Psychologist, 49,* 15-24.

Ajzen, I., & Fishbein, M. (1980). *Understanding and predicting social change.* Englewood Cliffs, NJ: Prentice Hall.

Aldwin, C. M., Spiro, A., Levenson, M. R., & Cupertino, A. P. (2001). Longitudinal findings from the normative aging study: III. Personality, individual health trajectories, and mortality. *Psychology and Aging, 16,* 450-465.

Ancis, J. R., & Szymanski, D. M. (2001). Awareness of White privilege among White counseling trainees. *The Counseling Psychologist, 29,* 548-569.

American Psychological Association, Office of Ethnic Minority Affairs. (1993). Guidelines for providers of psychological services to ethnic, linguistic, and culturally diverse populations. *American Psychologist, 48*(1), 45-48.

Aponte, J. F., & Crouch, R. T. (1995). The changing ethnic profile of the United States. In J. F. Aponte, R. Y. Rivers, & J. Wohl (Eds.), *Psychological interventions and cultural diversity* (pp. 1-18). Boston: Allyn & Bacon.

Asante, M. (1991). Afrocentric curriculum. *Educational Leadership, 49,* 28-39.

Ayanian, J. Z., & Epstein, A. M. (1991). Differences in the use of procedures between women and men hospitalized for coronary heart disease. *New England Journal of Medicine, 325,* 221-225.

Bayne-Smith, M. (Ed.). (1996). *Race, gender and health.* Thousand Oaks, CA: Sage.

Centers for Disease Control and Prevention. (1990). *HIV/AIDS surveillance report.* Atlanta, GA: Author.

Clark, R., Anderson, N. B., Clark, V. R., & Williams, D. R. (1999). Racism as a stressor for African Americans: A biopsychosocial model. *American Psychologist, 54,* 805-816.

Frankish, C. J., Lovato, C. Y., & Shannon, W. J. (1999). Models, theories, and principles of health promotion with multicultural populations. In R. M. Huff & M. V. Kline (Eds.), *Promoting health in multicultural populations: A handbook for practitioners* (pp. 41-72). Thousand Oaks, CA: Sage.

Guyll, M., Matthews, K. A., & Bromberger, J. T. (2001). Discrimination and unfair treatment: Relationship to cardiovascular reactivity among African American and European American women. *Health Psychology, 20,* 315-325.

Huff, R. M., & Kline, M. V. (Eds.). (1999). *Promoting health in multicultural populations: A handbook for practitioners.* Thousand Oaks, CA: Sage.

Jones, J. M. (1997). *Prejudice and racism* (2nd ed.). New York: McGraw-Hill.

Kleinman, A., Eisenberg, L., & Good, B. (1978). Culture, illness, and care: Clinical lessons from anthropologic and cross-cultural research. *Annals of Internal Medicine, 88,* 251-258.

Landrine, H., & Klonoff, E. A. (2001). Cultural diversity and health psychology. In A. Baum, T. A. Revenson, & J. E. Singer (Eds.), *Handbook of health psychology* (pp. 851-891). Englewood Cliffs, NJ: Lawrence Erlbaum.

Lecca, P. J., Quervalú, I., Nunes, J. V., & Gonzales, H. F. (1998). *Cultural competency in health, social, & human services.* New York: Garland.

Leininger, M. M. (1991). *Culture, care, diversity and universality: A theory of nursing.* New York: National League of Nursing Press.

Macera, C. A., Armstead, C. A., & Anderson, N. B. (2001). Sociocultural influences on health. In A. Baum, T. A. Revenson, & J. E. Singer (Eds.), *Handbook of health psychology* (pp. 427-440). Mahwah, NJ: Lawrence Erlbaum.

Markides, K. S. (Ed.). (1989). *Aging and health.* Thousand Oaks, CA: Sage.

Markides, K. S., & Marchalek, R. (1984). Selective survival, aging and society. *Archives of Gerontology and Geriatrics, 3,* 207-222.

Merluzzi, T. V., & Martinez Sanchez, M. (1997). Assessment of self-efficacy and coping with cancer: Development and validation of the Cancer Behavior Inventory. *Health Psychology, 16,* 163-170.

Pasick, R. J., D'Onofrio, C. N., & Otero-Sabogal, R. (1996). Similarities and differences across cultures: Questions to inform a third generation for health promotion research. *Health Education Quarterly, 23,* S142-S161.

Passau-Buck, S. (1994). *Male ordered health care: The inequities of women.* Staten Island, NY: Power Publications.

Pope-Davis, D. P., & Coleman, H. L. K. (Eds.). (1997). *Multicultural counseling competencies: Assessment, education and training, and supervision.* Thousand Oaks, CA: Sage.

Rimer, B. K., McBride, C. M., & Crump, C. (2001). Women's health promotion. In

A. Baum, T. A. Revenson, & J. E. Singer (Eds.), *Handbook of health psychology* (pp. 519-540). Mahwah, NJ: Lawrence Erlbaum.

Ritter, C., Hobfoll, S., Lavin, J., Cameron, R. P., & Hulsizer, M. R. (2000). Stress, psychosocial resources, and depressive symptomatology during pregnancy in low-income, inner-city women. *Health Psychology, 19,* 576-585.

Rosenstock, I. M. (1974). Historical origins of the health beliefs model. *Health Education Monographs, 2,* 328-343.

Shiang, J., Kjellander, C., & Bogumill, S. (1998). Developing cultural competency in clinical practice: Treatment considerations for Chinese cultural groups in the United States. *Clinical Psychology: Science and Practice, 5,* 182-210.

Siegler, I. C., Bastian, L. A., & Bosworth, H. B. (2001). Health, behavior, and aging. In A. Baum, T. A. Revenson, & J. E. Singer (Eds.), *Handbook of health psychology* (pp. 469-476). Mahwah, NJ: Lawrence Erlbaum.

Sue, D. W., Bingham, R. P., Porché-Burke, L., & Vasquez, M. (1999). The diversification of psychology: A multicultural revolution. *American Psychologist, 12,* 1061-1069.

Sue, S. (1999). Science, ethnicity, and bias: Where have we gone wrong? *American Psychologist, 12,* 1070-1077.

Tagliacozzo, D. L., & Mauksch, H. O. (1972). The patient's view of the patient's role. In E. G. Jaco (Ed.), *Patients, physicians, and illness* (2nd ed., pp. 172-185). New York: Free Press.

Tobin, J. N., Wassertheil-Smoller, S., Wexler, J. P., Steingart, R. M., Budner, N., Lense, L., et al. (1987). Sex bias in considering coronary bypass surgery. *Annals of Internal Medicine, 107,* 19-25.

Vitaliano, P. P., Scanlan, J. N., Zhang, J., Savage, M., Brummett, B., Barefoot, J., et al. (2001). Are the salutogenic effects of social supports modified by income? A test of an "added value hypothesis." *Health Psychology, 20,* 155-165.

Whaley, A. L. (2001). Cultural mistrust and mental health services for African Americans: A review and meta-analysis. *The Counseling Psychologist, 29,* 513-531.

Wells, S. A., & Black, R. M. (2000). *Cultural competency for health professionals.* Bethesda, MD: American Occupational Therapy Association.

28

Multicultural Competencies and Rehabilitation Counseling/Psychology

PAUL LEUNG

University of North Texas

Roberto is 43 years of age, married with four children ages 5 to 20, and has worked as a construction laborer for almost 20 years. He has an eighth-grade education, was born in Mexico, and is bilingual in English and Spanish. He had a cerebral vascular accident (stroke) 2 years ago that resulted in paralysis of his left side, and he has not worked since that time. With Social Security disability payments as income and with his wife having to work, it has been particularly difficult for Roberto, and he says he feels much less of a "man" as a result.

Bok is 30 years of age and has the equivalent of a high school education in Korea, and although she understands some English, she is very uncomfortable using it. She had been in the United States for a little over a year and worked as a housekeeper in a Las Vegas hotel when she sustained a back injury. She is married, and her husband is a kitchen helper in a casino restaurant. With

two young children, finances are particularly stressed. Bok has little understanding of what she may be eligible for and how to obtain it. She has since sought help from a Korean church, but Bok is bewildered and confused about what to do next.

Alice is 37 years old and a single mother of three with a sixth-grade education. She has worked for 15 years in a poultry processing plant, where she developed carpal tunnel syndrome that has continued to plague her ability to continue working. Surgery is one option, although she is quite anxious about having surgery, given the conflicting reports of success from her fellow workers. Deeply religious, Alice believes that God will take care of her, but she is also very worried about how she will support her family.

Joseph is 52 years of age and currently lives in a rural area, although it is within an hour's driving time of a big city. His work

---

AUTHOR'S NOTE: Names have been changed and situations altered but are based on actual persons.

history has been sporadic as a ranch hand and as a municipal worker picking up trash and garbage. Joseph has a fifth-grade education at a Bureau of Indian Affairs school. Estranged from his wife and family, he has three adult children. Although an alcoholic, he has been sober for 4 years. Joseph has diabetes and believes that he no longer has the stamina or strength to continue working.

Carl, age 28, was hit by an automobile as he bicycled his way to work as a chef at a Chinese restaurant in a small midwestern town and acquired fairly significant brain damage. Following acute rehabilitation, he demonstrated the capability to perform most tasks of daily life. His wife continues to live in Hong Kong with their two young children. Carl currently resides with his brother and sister-in-law. Although it is almost 3 years since the accident, Carl spends most of his day watching television. His sister-in-law tends to his every need, not allowing Carl to do anything. When she was asked why, she explained that Carl is "sick" and should not do anything and that he is being cared for "by family."

Carl, Roberto, Bok, Joseph, and Alice are similar in that they have disabilities and are persons from diverse racial/ethnic backgrounds. Each undoubtedly has unique feelings, beliefs, and experiences that affect his or her ability to fully participate in his or her own racial/ethnic cultural community as well as the larger dominant community. Although from different cultures, background experiences, religious beliefs, and language, these five individuals are representative of the diverse populations that rehabilitation counseling and psychology will see as clientele.

THE CHALLENGE OF MULTICULTURAL CLIENTS

Although these individuals are similar in many ways to clients with whom we are already familiar as rehabilitation psychologists and

counselors, they are also very different from the more traditional rehabilitation client, patient, or consumer. Clients we are used to seeing in rehabilitation are most likely from a middle-class socioeconomic level and White, speak English as a first language, and are fairly well educated. But these five individuals present situations that challenge us and the rehabilitation process. They require not only multicultural competence but also disability competence or an awareness and understanding of disability quite different from what most rehabilitation practitioners have been confronted with up to now in practice.

It is not the intent of this chapter to rehash the need for multicultural competencies but rather to place them in another context. The chapter is an attempt to provoke dialogue and reflection about disability, rehabilitation, and diverse populations. It is hoped that questions will be raised about how we practice and relate to persons with disabilities from various ethnic and cultural groups. It would be impossible to cover all the information necessary to function effectively with persons with disabilities from various cultural backgrounds and experiences. We must also exercise caution in attempting to apply and use limited information. We must not further stereotype those from different ethnic and racial backgrounds and who have disabilities. Ideally, we need to be fully competent in all aspects of both culture and disability. The reality is that most of us will not be competent with both and will sometimes need to suspend long ingrained judgments and biases to be effective with clients quite different from ourselves.

This chapter explores disability and rehabilitation from the perspective of race, ethnicity, and culture. Beginning with a discussion of disability, the chapter goes on to look at how disability notions have evolved and are constantly changing. Besides exploration of disability as culture and how disability is perceived within the majority culture, perceptions of disability in various racial/ethnic communities are also presented. The chapter ends with some suggestions for the rehabilitation psychologist and practitioner.

DEFINING DISABILITY

Psychologists and/or counselors without specific education and training in rehabilitation have varying notions of what constitutes disability. Depending on the perspective of the service provider program, the particular individual provider, or purpose of the interaction between provider and client, there may be different guidelines of what disability entails. The definition of disability is especially critical for providing psychological service because the objective is to achieve "positive" outcomes whether it is in assessment, counseling, or psychotherapy with persons who have disabilities. How disability is defined is important and significant in forming the parameters of practice. Unfortunately, there is no one definition but many definitions of disability. Perhaps the best known is the World Health Organization's tripartite definition involving the notions of impairment, disability, and handicap. Known as the *International Classification of Impairments, Disabilities and Handicaps (ICIDH)*, it is currently being revised as the *International Classification of Functioning, Disability, and Health (ICIDH-2)* (World Health Organization [WHO], 2000), the result of pressure primarily from the disability community in the United States. The *ICIDH* originally used *impairment, disability,* and *handicap* to adequately describe the entire disability experience. *Impairment* meant abnormality or loss of physiological or anatomical structure or function. *Disability* meant the consequences stemming from the impairment, such as restrictions or lack of ability to perform activities within the range considered as appropriate for nonimpaired persons. *Handicap* meant the social disadvantage resulting from either the impairment or the disability. Although the term *handicap* reflected the social consequences rather than the individual impairment, it was perceived as pejorative enough, especially in the United States, to warrant the WHO to consider a revision and thus the *ICIDH-2*.

Another definition of disability currently used is from the Americans with Disabilities Act (ADA, 1990), whereby a person is considered as having a disability when (a) there is a physical or mental impairment that substantially limits one or more of the major life activities of that person, (b) there is a record of such an impairment, or (c) the person is regarded as having such an impairment. *Major life activities* are defined as caring for oneself, performing manual tasks, walking, seeing, hearing, breathing, learning, and working. One of the significant notions in the ADA and Rehabilitation Act definition is the phrase "regarded as having such an impairment" (Rehabilitation Act of 1973, p. 2). Although an individual may not now have a disability, he or she does have a disability under the definition if others perceive that person to have a disability.

Although laws such as the Rehabilitation Act and the Americans with Disabilities Act seem to stress the similarities of the impact of a disabling condition on an individual, others (Fine & Asch, 1988) believe that the differences among disabling conditions and their implications in the lives of persons who have them to be particularly important. Fine and Asch (1988) suggested that different conditions cause different kinds of functional impairment. For example, they described deafness, paralysis, blindness, and epilepsy as disabilities that pose problems of stigma, marginality, and discrimination but very different functional problems. Persons with epilepsy have no inherent limitations whatsoever, and yet they are regarded as having an impairment. Fine and Asch also pointed out that people with disabilities have differing degrees of impairment. Some persons with mobility impairment can walk in some situations, but others cannot. Fine and Asch concluded that factors of origin, experience, and effects of disability must be kept in mind when working with persons who have disabilities.

We must recognize that not only are there many definitions of what constitutes disability: What may be most significant is that the definition that we accept may dictate how we approach a client or patient. At the same time, specific legislation or objectives of a particular intervention, treatment, or program may dictate what we do. How we define disability provides clues as to what feelings we may have or how we approach individuals who have disabilities.

REHABILITATION COUNSELING AND PSYCHOLOGY

Combining rehabilitation counseling and psychology into one category of practice is probably unfair to both. There are some distinct differences in setting, credentials, and context. However, similarities of historical background and common assumptions warrant linking these two together. Perhaps like psychology, a major difference between counseling and psychology is the credentials of the practitioner. The rehabilitation psychologist is likely to have a doctoral degree, whereas the rehabilitation counselor will have a master's degree.

A rehabilitation psychologist will most likely be found in an acute rehabilitation setting and be involved earlier on in the rehabilitation process than a rehabilitation counselor. Rehabilitation counselors are more involved with the vocational rehabilitation process and are employed by government agencies administering the public state or federal vocational rehabilitation program. Some rehabilitation counselors are involved with private-sector vocational rehabilitation and may work with workers compensation programs.

For the most part, rehabilitation counseling and rehabilitation psychology share a common approach related to their history within counseling and psychology. Whether counseling or psychology, their practice involves persons with disabilities and working to assist persons with disabilities to cope with the effects of disability and chronic disease and to integrate fully into their communities.

DISABILITY AND MULTICULTURAL COMPETENCIES

The intersection of disability and multicultural competencies is complex and difficult to negotiate. Many different concepts with multiple nuances must be considered prior to taking action with our clients. The application of multicultural competencies in practice with persons with disabilities must be intertwined with disability awareness requiring more than knowledge and skill. In some ways, we must undergo a fundamental attitudinal change of ideas and notions that have been inherent in U.S. culture. We must understand the contextual and situational aspects of each individual with a disability. In addition, we must take into account the individual's family and the cultural context. We need to understand the societal changes that have occurred in the dominant culture related to disability and the cultural perspective of persons with disabilities within the majority culture. We must also understand and acknowledge the medical foundation of rehabilitation and its influence on practitioners and their relationships with persons with disabilities.

Scheer and Groce (1988) noted that "throughout human history, societies have defined what did and did not constitute a disability or handicap, and these definitions have changed over time" (p. 29). Rehabilitation with persons of varying backgrounds and experience must be seen as part of an ever-changing continuum often intertwined with what is happening within the majority culture and its often tenuous struggle to relate to disability. As practitioners in the rehabilitation process, we must both understand and incorporate such an understanding into our actions if we are to be effective in what we do.

Ethnic minority groups have developed a unique mix of roles, expectations, and conceptual frameworks that determine, "in part, how its members view its social networks, support systems, and communities," including the concept of disability (Groce & Zola, 1993, p. 1049). "These culturally based belief systems are not simply of scholarly interest, but are real social facts which help to shape the decisions made by individuals with a disability or chronic illness and their families" (Groce & Zola, 1993, p. 1049).

As rehabilitation is often a part of the health care system, providers—including rehabilitation counselors and psychologists—must recognize that the health care system has been dominated by the culture and values of socioeconomically empowered White America (Berger, 1998). For example, a primary assumption associated with rehabilitation psychology and counseling is behavior change and personal growth (Brems, 2001). This assumption is undoubtedly a positive driver and force for many people. Yet this assumption, examined in the context of disability, may also present an underlying conflict of what is at the heart of how people with disabilities view themselves and society.

There are at least two ways to explore disability from a multicultural perspective. Disability occurs in diverse ethnic populations, and persons with disabilities may be viewed as a cultural group. The former is the primary focus of this chapter, although it cannot be viewed in isolation from the latter. Using a definition of common experience as culture, some activists with disabilities trace the beginnings of disability culture to their recognition that persons with disabilities do have a

common experience and thus a distinct culture (Barnes & Mercer, 2001). Other American disability activists have linked the beginnings of this increased self-awareness and desire to take charge of their own lives to protests related to the implementation of regulations for Section 504 of the Rehabilitation Act in 1997 (Brown, 2000). Related to the perspective that disability is culture—although in some ways, it is a separate perspective—is the view that culture is disabling, given the prevailing cultural representations of disability in society (Barnes & Mercer, 2001; McDermott & Varenne, 1995). Regardless of whether it is the majority culture or any specific cultural group, some believe that culture promotes the "differential and unequal treatment of people because of apparent or assumed physical, mental, or behavioral differences" (Bogdan & Biklen, 1977, p. 14).

DISABILITY IN AMERICAN SOCIETY

How disability is viewed in American society has undergone tremendous change during the past few decades. How persons with disabilities perceive themselves has primarily driven these changes of perception. More than anything else, these changes are best illustrated by the passage of the Americans with Disabilities Act (ADA) of 1990, which can be seen as a watershed event in American disability history. But we must remember that the ADA is civil rights legislation and not welfare, Social Security, or even rehabilitation legislation. The ADA made it illegal to discriminate on the basis of disability in terms of employment, transportation, public accommodations, or telecommunications. The ADA is in many ways symbolic of changes in how persons with disabilities view themselves. That the ADA was signed into law in 1990 by President George Bush was the result of the ability of different and sometimes historically conflicting groups representing various categories of disabilities (Shapiro, 1993) to work together in a cooperative manner. Although there were precursors to the ADA, such as Section 504 of the Rehabilitation Act of 1973, the ADA nevertheless represented a "new" perspective both in terms of persons with disabilities and those who are seen as temporarily able bodied. As such, the ADA redefined how these two groups relate to each other.

The ADA, even with its affinity with the civil rights movement that was primarily driven by African Americans, has not had much impact on the lives of many individuals with disabilities from racial/ethnic minority populations. Many in racial/ethnic minority communities who have disabilities find themselves still ignored by both the mainstream disability community and their own communities (National Council on Disability [NCD], 1993; Smith, 2000). At the same time, all of the available evidence suggests that persons from diverse communities are much more likely to have a disability than persons from the majority population (Walker, Saravanabhavan, Williams, Brown, & West, 1996).

DISABILITY, ETHNICITY, AND RACE

Ethnicity and race in the United States generally follow the categories of the U.S. Bureau of the Census and include American Indian or Alaska Native, Asian, Black or African American, Native Hawaiian or other Pacific Islander, and White. A separate designation includes Hispanic or Latino and not Hispanic or Latino. In addition, the 2000 census included mixed racial groups. Disability status in these census categories is self-reported and, as such, may be conservative, not reflecting the true extent of disability in racial/ethnic populations. For example, the NCD (1993) pointed out that poverty, unemployment, and poor health status in Blacks or African Americans, Hispanics, and Asian Pacific Americans contribute to increased incidence and prevalence

of disability within them. Minorities would thus constitute a disproportionate share of the population of persons with disabilities, given higher rates of poverty, unemployment, and poor health. Wright (1994) and Olkin (1999) suggested that there are "synergistic effects of dual or triple minority status (disabled, racial or ethnic minority, female, elderly) which too often result in employment, poverty, and isolation" (Olkin, 1999, p. 23).

Race and ethnicity are among the factors that have "the strongest association with disability" (Smart & Smart, 1997, p. 13). Bradsher (1995) noted that, whether one is considering the overall disability rate in the United States, rates for people ages 15 to 64 (i.e., what is often considered "working age"), or rates of severe disability, African Americans and American Indians consistently have the highest rates of disability. Walker and Brown (1996), analyzing data from the National Center for Health Statistics, found African Americans and Hispanic Americans to be overrepresented in all disability categories, including chronic health conditions; physical, sensory, and language impairments; and nervous and mental disorders. Similarly, Walker et al. (1996), using data from the 1990 federal census, reported that although African Americans represent only 12.1% of the total U.S. population, they represent 14% of all persons with disabilities in the United States. Among African Americans who have a disability, 71.8% have a severe disability, as opposed to only 52% of White Americans with a disability. In addition, 78.2% of African Americans with disabilities are unemployed or not working, and 41% are at or below poverty-level income. Among Hispanic Americans with a disability, 67.8% have a severe disability, and 27% live at or below poverty-level income. Although the incidence and prevalence figures from the U.S. Bureau of the Census suggest a lower likelihood for disability for Asian Pacific Islander Americans, some have argued that this may be based on the use of aggregate statistics. Groups of Asian Pacific Islander Americans who immigrated perhaps on a refugee basis and who often find themselves in poverty or low socioeconomic straits may in fact have much higher rates of disability than normally reported (Yang, Leung, Wang, & Shim, 1996).

The bottom line is that disability within various diverse ethnic groups is an important and significant issue both in terms of their numbers and the fact that persons with disabilities have been marginalized, devalued, and ignored within their own communities. This is not to suggest that persons with disabilities are not accepted and loved by their families or even within the communities where they reside. Often, these relationships are complicated not only by views of disability of the majority population but also by perspectives on disabilities that have roots in religious and other cultural traditions.

EVOLVING VIEWS OF DISABILITY

Psychologists and counselors who work with persons with disabilities must have an understanding and sense of the historical evolution of how people with disabilities are viewed in society. As suggested already, notions of disability have changed tremendously in American society during the past few decades and are often not fully appreciated by individuals who do not see themselves as having disabilities. This evolution is best represented by the movement away from institutionalization and isolation of persons with disabilities to full inclusion in society. "Nothing about us without us" (Charlton, 1998, p. 3) and the development of a disabled identity (Linton, 1998) have led to a more contemporary model of disability (Hahn, 1988; Olkin, 1999). Ironically, it was a psychologist (Meyerson, 1948) sometime ago who, following a Lewinian perspective, commented that the primary problems

associated with having disability were not physical but rather social and psychological. In many ways, Meyerson's (1948) observation was far ahead of his time. The traditional psychological approach has been to focus on what persons with disabilities could not do and attempt to change individuals to fit into their community. The premise that people who live with disabilities have a unique and valuable identity (Cyganowski, 2000; Olkin, 1999) has been counter to the general views of disability held by the public as well the perspective of traditional psychological practice.

Those familiar with the civil rights movement undoubtedly see a parallel in this perspective to earlier struggles related to segregation and racial discrimination. In fact, many involved with the disability community view themselves as a "minority" group (Cyganowski, 2000; Olkin, 1999). At the same time, there is, however, an acknowledgment that there are also differences between what persons who are members of ethnic minority populations experience and what persons who have disabilities experience (Olkin, 1999). For example, Olkin (1999) believes that the core experience of prejudice, discrimination, and stigma with inferior status attributable to inherent traits and different physical appearance equates with ethnic minorities having a different skin color. At the same time, Olkin believes that there are differences between the disability population and other ethnic minorities in that the notion of separate is not viewed as inherently unequal and that one can join the disability community at any time (Cyganowski, 2000; Olkin, 1999) by becoming disabled. Reinforcing the concept that anyone can attain a disability, Davis (2001) expressed the notion that disability is "porous" and pointed out that it is also possible for a "person with disabilities to be 'cured' and become 'normal'" (p. 536).

Accepting the idea that persons who have disabilities have common characteristics and experiences in a nondisabled society, some (Barnes & Mercer, 2001) have raised the existence of a disability culture. Disability culture rejects the idea that disability is negative and the basis for self-pity and stresses solidarity and positive identity or consciousness. But the idea of disability culture is not without some controversy (Tucker, 1998) as there are persons with disabilities unwilling to acknowledge that such a culture exists. The most apparent disability culture is that found in some Deaf communities. The use of the capital *D* has sometimes served to differentiate the Deaf community from deaf with a lowercase *d*, which is simply recognition that a person has a hearing impairment. Given the use of American Sign Language and the reliance on isolated and segregated educational institutions of the past century, persons who are deaf have often lived and worked in largely deaf environments. Because communication is vital for survival and because members of the hearing majority refused to learn sign language, Deaf communities developed and flourished. Some writers suggest that Deaf people "like being deaf, want to be Deaf, and are proud of their Deafness" (Tucker, 1998, p. 6). The perspective that the deafness community can be categorized as a culture is not universal among deaf people, and there are some who feel that describing the deaf community as a *culture* is a misuse of the word (Tucker, 1998, p. 6).

Nevertheless, there is a movement to describe the disability experience as cultural. Its proponents believe that their common bond as persons with disabilities is their experience and relationship to the larger culture. This has led individuals to explore disability from artistic, literary, and other perspectives. In attempts to capture an identity that has been generally devalued, these individuals with disabilities view the disability experience as one that is not to be denigrated but to be celebrated. Much like African American studies, Latino studies, or Asian American studies,

disability studies have been put forward as a legitimate academic pursuit. What is interesting is that proponents of disability culture have been primarily members of the White majority in the United States (Backman, 1994).

DIFFERENCES OF PERCEPTION AND PARTICIPATION

Despite the fact that ethnic and racial minority populations have higher rates of disability than the majority, the leadership of the disability movement has been mostly White (Backman, 1994). Persons with disabilities who are not White have generally not involved themselves in the disability movement (Devlieger & Albrecht, 2000). One can only speculate as to why this has been so. Perhaps the combination of factors related to disability and culture in ethnic communities, with those who have disabilities in these communities having to also function in the larger majority community, is so formidable that survival has been their primary objective. Devlieger and Albrecht (2000) suggested as much in their interviews with African Americans with disabilities in Chicago:

> Disability is not the most critical life issue to inner-city African Americans, who daily face the more pressing problems of poverty; finding a place to live; feeding one's self and the children; guarding one's security against gangs, violence, and drugs; and confronting racism, which often results in inadequate education, unemployment, and denied benefits. (p. 58)

Disability culture notwithstanding, a general approach to working with persons with disabilities is that the disabling condition not be seen as the defining characteristic of the person. Often, this is easier said than done, especially for psychologists. Too often, the psychological focus has been on the individual and his or her need for change rather than what has become the prevailing disability perspective that the environment is where change is needed. It is often difficult for the psychologist to look beyond the individual for answers.

SOCIETAL PERCEPTIONS OF DISABILITY

Because we are part of our cultural tradition, our definitions of disability flow from society's definition. Our perceptions of disability are in part dependent on norms inherent within that culture. One way to understand disability perceptions, including how service providers relate to people with disabilities, is to understand more general paradigms or models accepted by the society in which we live. These models provide a framework for understanding how a particular society deals with disability among its members (Olkin, 1999; Smart, 2001). Although there are many models, three seem to stand out as significant. These are the moral, medical, and minority/social models of disabilities (Olkin, 1999), and they reflect partially the evolution and history of American society in relationship to disability. The oldest model, in which disability is seen as a defect, with an etiology in moral lapse or sin, is rooted in the Judeo-Christian perspective and has permeated American culture. The moral model contains within it the myth of disability as mysticism, whereby when disability impairs one sense, another is heightened "often to mythical proportions" (Olkin, 1999, p. 25). In many ways, the moral model continues to influence prevailing views of persons with disabilities. It is often in this context that Americans have pity for people with disabilities and yet adore the superhero who has overcome disability.

The medical model also has European historical roots and was introduced in the 17th century, when disability was seen as a medical problem. Rather than a defect of a moral source, it is a defect of the physical body. The goals of intervention or treatment are the cure and/or elimination of the "problem," with rehabilitation being the "adjustment" of the person to having the disability and to his or her surroundings. Because experts provide treatment and the person with disability is the passive recipient, persons with disabilities often see the medical model as paternalistic (Olkin, 1999; Smart, 2001). The moral and medical models both have some common assumptions that the majority culture has incorporated related to disability. Fine and Asch (1988) described these basic assumptions as the following:

1. Disability is biology, and disability is accepted uncritically as an independent variable.
2. Problems faced by persons with disabilities result from "impairment" rather than the larger environmental social context.
3. Persons with disabilities are victims, so treatment is aimed at changing the person.
4. Disability is central to an individual's identity, self-concept, and self-definition.
5. Disability is synonymous with needing help and social support.

A closely related approach posits that the functioning of an individual influences what is disabling (Smart, 2001). Smart (2001) cited the example of Stephen Hawking, the renowned physicist with amyotrophic lateral sclerosis, who considers limited mobility and difficulties with speech an advantage in allowing him more time to think. The functional perspective may serve to bridge the medical approach with the social or minority model, which has become the approach that many who have disabilities see as the most acceptable model to them.

The social model of disability begins with the assumption that disability is a social construct similar to constructs of race and ethnicity. This view reinforces the notion that cultural perspectives are important in understanding how persons with disabilities and their families relate to services such as rehabilitation.

Aside from issues related to how disability is perceived and how intervention is structured is the basic tenet that societal attitudes toward disability in the United States have their basis in Euro-American culture and, specifically, the notions of individualism and equality (McWhirter, 2000). McWhirter (2000) further noted that "in reality, rugged individualism is a myth; people with disabilities are merely more obviously inter-dependent" (p. 1). McWhirter viewed this as an "imposition of acceptable categories of interdependence," which "serves to minimize aspects of 'independence' that are often less available to people with disabilities" (p. 1).

Many of the basic tenets of multiculturalism and multicultural counseling certainly apply to psychologists and counselors who work with persons with disabilities. Most of the literature, however, has been focused on mental health and the recognition that the theories of counseling and psychotherapy and the standards used to judge normality, as well as the processes of mental health practice, are a reflection of a monocultural perspective (Sue et al., 1998). The guidelines on multicultural proficiency define cultural competence in a somewhat narrow fashion (American Psychological Association, 2002) in the sense that they do not address issues of disability.

The American cultural perspective has been that persons with disabilities are different (Scheer & Groce, 1988). Persons who fail to meet prescribed standards of physical attractiveness and functional independence are assumed to be inferior and exposed to stigma as less than human (Hahn, 1988). These views have been reflected in the institutions that have been established for persons with disabilities and are imbedded in our educational system. Although these views have been challenged, these views remain powerful forces that

continue to influence how society perceives persons with disabilities, regardless of whether they are from the majority European background or from other racial/ethnic populations. Persons with disabilities from various racial/ethnic communities thus confront not only these assumptions of the majority but also the influences that reflect their unique cultural heritage.

ETHNIC AND RACIAL PERSPECTIVES ON DISABILITY

How do ethnic communities view disability? Each ethnic community's perception of disability and what disability means is a reflection of its culture, religious beliefs, and traditions. In other words, there are as many varying perceptions as there are cultures, religions, and traditions. And, as has been mentioned, there are the influences of the majority culture, the nature of the disabling condition, and the acculturation of the individual and/or family members that affect the views of any given individual.

Anne Fadiman (1997) wrote a poignant account of a Hmong child who had a severe seizure disorder and the literal "collision" of cultures that occurred between the family and the medical establishment. Fadiman clearly demonstrates that it was fundamentally a refusal (not always a conscious decision) of both the family and the medical care providers to recognize they were not communicating that interfered with the care of the child. In many ways, similar incidents and events are played out daily as persons with disabilities, their families, and rehabilitation professionals attempt to bridge the differences of culture.

Groce and Zola (1993) have suggested that an individual's culture is not a diagnostic category in the sense that one's cultural heritage will wholly explain how a person will think or act. At the same time, several key issues may be considered almost universal (Groce &

Zola, 1993). For example, culturally perceived causes of chronic illness or disability are significant in all cultures, and the reason why an illness or disability is believed to have occurred will play a significant role in determining family and community attitudes. In addition, what social roles are considered to be appropriate for persons with disabilities may determine the amount of resources invested in the individual within that family and community.

Much of the literature dealing with cultural beliefs of ethnic groups has centered on concepts of health rather than disability. These concepts do provide some clues about the etiology of disease and thus disability from the perception of diverse populations. A great deal of care is necessary to ensure that stereotyping does not occur. Within-group differences are particularly important and yet often ignored. For example, Zavaleta (2000) suggested that terms such as *Hispanic* and *Latino* are catch terms lumping people together without regard to subcultural variation. He further illustrated that the Hispanic population in Texas draws from an incredibly diverse base from regions in Mexico, Central and South America, and a host of Caribbean countries. The term *Asian American*—in particular, *Asian Pacific Islander American*—is an artificial categorization in which more than 20 groups have been lumped together, with its origin in a presidential executive order (Wright, 1994). Each Asian group has its own unique cultural, religious, or other beliefs that may have an impact on how disability is perceived and accepted. Native Hawaiians have often bristled with their inclusion as Asian Pacific Islander because they are not fully recognized as the indigenous people of Hawaii. Blacks, too, are not homogeneous, with cultural variations of origin in Africa, the West Indies, or the Caribbean as well as geographical differences in the United States. Also, American Indians may refer to 500 or more tribal entities.

THE ETIOLOGY OF DISABILITY

Some of the various notions regarding disability within various cultural groups will be explored in this section. Rather than looking at each population separately, a more general approach has been taken, and some of the same cautions voiced earlier about application apply here as well.

Berger (1998) reported that many Caribbean Americans and southern African Americans believe that certain illnesses occur as a result of interpersonal conflict and supernatural activity. Some suggest that African Americans admire and have high regard for physical prowess and that there is great respect for athleticism, dance, size, and the way in which one walks and moves (Smith, 2000). Having a disability may diminish these outward signs and lead to persons with disabilities of African descent being stigmatized. With religion and the church a major influence in the lives of African Americans (Rogers-Dulan & Blacher, 1995), paternalistic treatment toward persons with disabilities may be the norm in the African American community as their "beloved, sick, and shut in" are prayed for at church (Smith, 2000). Within Hispanic community, a similar attitude is reflected in the common phrase about someone who is blind as *un pobre ciegito* or a poor blind man (Smart & Smart, 1991). Others (Rogers-Dulan & Blacher, 1995), however, believe that with the African American religious view that all people are "God's children," African Americans may be more accepting of disability. This perspective was reinforced in findings by Grand and Strohmer (1983). Associated with this perspective is the notion that a family may be given a family member who has a disabling condition because that family has the capacity to cope and deal with the added responsibility. An example of this is the Filipino family who believes that they are blessed with a child who has a disability (Ilagan, 2002). The significance is that disability is not a simplistic event but a complex and often conflicting one.

The belief in the role of a higher power and/or spirits is not limited to African Americans. A recent study of Hispanic Americans who were human immunodeficiency virus positive found a majority believing in spirits who had a causal role (Berger, 1998). Hispanic populations generally adhere to the belief that God or, at the very least, some supernatural forces are directly involved in illness (Zaveleta, 2000) and perhaps, by extension, disability. For example, deafness may be seen in some Hispanic cultures as a result of *mal de ojo* or an evil eye (Hernandez, 1999). At the same time, other writers point out that the individual is not to blame for disability in this framework, relying on the expression *si Dios quiere* or "God willing" (Pedemonte, 2001). Many cultures perceive disability to be a form of punishment (Gonzalez, 2001; Hernandez, 1999; Tsao, 2000). The person with the disability, his or her family, or an ancestor may be seen as having been cursed by God or Gods, sinned, or having violated a taboo (Groce & Zola, 1993). Illnesses and disabilities in some cultures are said to be the result of "bad" blood.

Some American Indians believe that illnesses are caused by evil spirits, witches, or animals that were mistreated (Berger, 1998). Health from a Navajo perspective may mean harmony with family, community, and nature as well as one's physical self (Berger, 1998). Concepts of health from an Asian perspective may also involve the idea of balance between individual, society, and the universe (Berger, 1998). Some Southeast Asian groups and Indians subscribe to beliefs of reincarnation, and disability may be seen as direct evidence of transgressions of a previous life, whether it is by the parents or the child (Groce & Zola, 1993). For example, Laotian culture is a blend of Hindu and Buddhist beliefs such as reincarnation along with values of selflessness and freedom from an attachment to material or worldly possessions (Moore, Keopraseuth, Leung, & Chao, 1997). Disability seen as punishment, an inherited evil, or personal impurity is reason enough to feel shame. Sucheng Chan (1995), an Asian American studies professor who had polio as a child, expanded on the belief that a person's physical status may be related to one's moral lapse in a previous life as well as to the Asian tendency to view the family as a single unit. She wrote, "It is believed that the fate of one member can be caused by the behavior of another" (p. 375). Because of this, there is often a desire not to call attention to himself or herself or to the individual with the disability, and the family member with the disability is kept at home away from public contact. Chan related an incident in her own life in which she was chosen to play in a music recital during which someone in the audience yelled, "Ayah! A *baikah* (cripple) shouldn't be allowed to perform in public" (p. 376). Filipino Americans, too, may share feelings of *hiya* or shame but at the same time embrace *bahalana* or a fatalistic attitude (Sustento-Seneriches, 1997). Although this fatalistic approach to life and, correspondingly, disability also has been associated with Hispanics, some have argued that associating fatalism with Hispanic culture is more the result of questionable research methodology and faulty generalization (Smart & Smart, 1991).

Cultural perspectives continue to have an impact on racial/ethnic individuals, sometimes in quite subtle ways. An example is a study involving the attitudes of health care professionals toward persons with disabilities. Paris (1993) found that ethnicity is related to attitudes and that Asians had the least positive attitudes, attributing them to reflecting collective shame. As rehabilitation professionals, we must evaluate our own traditions and culture and what their influence has been on our attitudes. At the same time, traditional perspectives no longer can wholly explain or provide a full understanding of disability in ethnic communities. Processes of assimilation and acculturation bring about change and add another dimension that must be taken into consideration. Lee (1997a, 1997b) reflected on the caution necessary in intervening with Chinese American families:

> There is no one typical Chinese American family. There are many individual differences, and they represent a wide range of cultural values from very traditional (such as newly arrived family from a rural area in China or Vietnam) to very "Americanized" (such as a third-generation American born professional family. (Lee, 1997a, p. 57)

The same caution applies to all of the populations mentioned in this chapter. Psychologists and counselors in rehabilitation settings must gauge carefully their use of cultural knowledge. We must be acutely aware that although changes have occurred related to societal views of disability and persons with disabilities are affected by these views, persons with disabilities from ethnic and racial communities have often not been considered within these perspectives.

As noted earlier, minority communities have not included disabilities as part of their mainstream (Smith, 2000), and little attention is generally given to disability issues. There is very little information and literature available about how disabilities are perceived in various ethnic communities. This is especially true for ethnic minority populations in the United States, where several forces are at work that have an impact on persons with disabilities. Obviously, the views and attitudes toward disability of the larger majority are also at least partially reflected in persons of different smaller ethnic groups. But as Groce and Zola (1993) pointed out, many ethnic and minority populations "do not define or address disability and chronic illness in the same manner as 'mainstream' American culture" (p. 1048). The culture "of origin" for racial/ethnic populations is also an influence.

Persons with disabilities from different ethnic and minority populations often also face double discrimination. Add gender to the equation, and discrimination often multiplies, perhaps even exponentially. This places additional stress on an individual as well as the families of which he or she is a part.

Finally, the rehabilitation process itself brings another confounding factor to the equation. Much of the dissatisfaction of persons with disabilities in the majority culture has focused on the inability of the medical model to allow persons with disabilities and medical practitioners to work as equals. Medicine has always focused on a cure and, coupled with the "fix-it" mentality of American society, has not been able to see that much of what constitutes barriers to persons with disabilities' ability to function is environmental and not an inherent problem of the individual person.

Rehabilitation providers have a particular task to bridge the gap between the medical and social models of disability. This, perhaps, is an impossible task in that the two models are in a constant state of tension. How psychology and counseling do business may mirror an ongoing tension that exists based on the philosophical assumptions that govern. For example, the practice of medicine has changed because of shifts that have occurred with regard to informed consent. The patient or consumer has become much more a player in determining what care he or she receives. This is certainly illustrated in the increasing number of advertisements by pharmaceutical firms suggesting that patients ask for certain medications through their physicians. Decisions of physicians are no longer sacrosanct and accepted without dissent. Although the model is still based on an authoritative expert base, it has moved away from only a one-sided perspective. The rise of alternative medical interventions and the acceptance of complementary approaches have come about from consumer awareness and assertiveness. These complementary approaches also include mainstream acceptance of what has traditionally been seen as ethnic or indigenous healing paradigms. The irony is that many racial/ethnic communities still confer status and expertise to the healing practitioner as the authority within the therapeutic process. We as service providers must understand these differences between the mainstream and some ethnic or racial populations.

Another aspect of cultural significance for those who work with persons with disabilities as part of the rehabilitation process relates to objectives and outcomes of rehabilitation. Olkin (1999) has focused on the difference between response and adjustment. She rightly noted that rehabilitation goals are often focused on return to work and adjustment to disability. But what should be the focus of our efforts? Grzesiak and Hicok (1994) pointed out that "coming to terms with the fact of being physically different requires significant adaptive effort" (p. 248). Olkin went on to suggest that psychology's approach is to look for and find differences and to pathologize those differences. On the other hand, Olkin suggested the need for a more positive approach in which variables that allow and promote resilience, hardiness, health, self-esteem, and adjustment are more central. Olkin believes that, too often, therapists "are primed to see the disability itself as the wellspring of the problems that come to clinical attention" (p. 49). This is not unlike that which occurs in psychological intervention, where the danger may be either equating mental disorder with difference or forming hasty judgments stereotypically imposed on phenomena observed across a cultural gulf (Draguns, 2000).

We have seen that perceptions and definitions of disability vary depending on culture.

Perhaps the only thing in common is that disability is not seen in most cultures as something positive, and persons with disabilities and their families are certainly subjected to more stress than individuals and families without disabilities. As providers of psychological services, we must acknowledge and understand these influences and incorporate them into our practice.

Groce (2000) has suggested that there is no single right way to look at disability in society, but there is a wrong way: "The wrong way is to mistake one's own disciplinary training as the sole approach to a complex problem and, with an almost missionary zeal, go forth to do battle with anyone who is not conversant in the tenets and terminology of one's particular discipline"(p. 7). The practice of rehabilitation with multicultural populations requires perhaps even more openness and flexibility in communication and in adapting what the provider has to offer with the needs and expectations of the consumer.

Another variable to consider is the notion of disability as culture. For persons who are temporarily able bodied, this may be difficult to accept, and, as suggested earlier, not even people with disabilities totally accept such an idea. Seeing disability from this perspective may help us understand why Christopher Reeve's almost obsessive need to walk again is viewed by many disability activists as negative or why there is opposition to cochlear implants in the Deaf community.

For professionals involved with persons with disabilities from various ethnic communities, these issues may be particularly significant. Notions that have been rallying cries of the disability movement have been seen by different ethnic groups as antithetical to values they hold. In addition, for those of us who practice in rehabilitation settings, using different decision-making mechanisms may actually hinder rehabilitation progress.

We must recognize that rehabilitation practice in the United States has followed the cultural tenets of Western value systems. In government-funded programs, these values have become entrenched in legislation putting additional barriers to persons with disabilities of different cultural orientations. *Independent living* has been the watchword for many persons with disabilities who have been activists in the disability community. That particular notion represents perhaps a uniquely Western philosophical approach that persons with disabilities wish to be as independent as possible and want to make decisions on their own. On the other hand, interdependence is often more of a value held in the majority of ethnic communities. The desire is to work together in concert with each other to achieve what the individual and the family perceive as their needs. There is much less of a competitive spirit but rather cooperation as the key element binding the individual to the larger whole.

In many ethnic communities, decisions not only for persons with disabilities but also for all persons are made in a collective manner, taking into consideration the larger community unit. An illustration of this is a Hispanic individual and family during rehabilitation. Team conferences are an integral part of acute rehabilitation, whereby an individual and perhaps some close family members meet with members of the treatment team to assess progress and develop plans. In this instance, rather than immediate family, the individual might want cousins and other extended family members to be involved in the process so that there are more persons from the family than in the treatment team. But for decisions to be implemented, rehabilitation counselors and psychologists must make this a necessary accommodation. For some individuals and families of Asian descent, decision making may be dictated by how it may affect not only the individual but also the larger family unit.

In summary, the ability of rehabilitation counselors and psychologists to work successfully with clients of differing experiences and backgrounds requires an open mind and flexibility that have sometimes been lacking in our training. Although attention to the individual is basic to rehabilitation, we must go beyond that to also take into account cultural views of disability, acculturation, and a host of factors associated with history, language, and immigration. Some concepts that have relevance to rehabilitation practice are generational status and level of acculturation, immigration history, and ethnic identification (Huang, 1997). Others have suggested that in work with Asian American adolescents, attention should be given to the following: (a) generation, gender, and birth order; (b) level of English comprehension and articulation; (c) socioeconomic status; (d) traumatic experiences; (e) coping strategies; (f) substance abuse; (g) sexual, physical, and emotional abuse; (h) sexual activity and sexuality; (i) suicidality; and (j) support system (Wong & Mock, 1997). Although Wong and Mock (1997) were writing about Asian Americans, their list of 10 items to address provides a framework for thinking about all racial/ethnic populations. Regardless of the particular racial or ethnic group, rehabilitation counselors and psychologists must be willing to go beyond their own stereotypic perspectives of their clients and embrace a perspective that truly understands where their clients are coming from in terms of individual and group experience and history. It is only when we are willing to set aside our own sometimes learned and ingrained perspectives that will we become effective with individuals who have disabilities and who belong to different ethnic and racial populations.

REFERENCES

American Psychological Association. (2002). *Guidelines on multicultural education,*

*training, research, practice, and organiza-
tional change for psychologists.* Washington,
DC: Author.

Americans With Disabilities Act (ADA), 42 U.S.C.
12101 et. seq. (1990).

Backman, E. (1994). Is the movement racist?
Focus, 10(2), 3-4.

Barnes, C., & Mercer, G. (2001). Disability
culture: Assimilation or inclusion? In
G. Albrecht, K. D. Seelman, & M. Bury
(Eds.), *Handbook of disability studies*
(pp. 515-534). Thousand Oaks, CA: Sage.

Berger, J. T. (1998). Culture and ethnicity in clinical care. *Archives of Internal Medicine, 158,*
2085-2090.

Bogdan, R., & Biklen, D. (1977). Handicapism.
Social Policy, 7, 14-19.

Bradsher, J. E. (1995). Disability among racial and
ethnic groups. *Disability Statistics Abstract,
10,* 1-4.

Brems, C. (2001). *Basic skills in psychotherapy
and counseling.* Belmont, CA: Brooks/Cole.

Brown, S. E. (2000). *Freedom of movement.*
Houston, TX: ILRU Publications.

Chan, S. (1995). You're short, besides. In M. L.
Anderson (Ed.), *Race, class, & gender* Belmont,
CA: Wadsworth.

Charlton, J. I. (1998). *Nothing about us without
us.* Berkeley: University of California Press.

Cyganowski, C. (2000). *Identifying characteristics: Diversity and distinction.* Cambridge,
MA: Harvard University Press.

Davis, L. (2001). Identity politics, disability, and
culture. In G. L. Albrecht, K. D. Seelman, &
M. Bury (Eds.), *Handbook of disability studies* (pp. 535-545). Thousand Oaks, CA: Sage.

Devlieger, P. J., & Albrecht, G. L. (2000). Your
experience is not my experience. *Journal of
Disability Policy Studies, 11*(1), 51-60.

Draguns, J. G. (2000). Psychopathology & ethnicity. In J. F. Aponte & J. Wohl (Eds.),
*Psychological intervention and cultural diver-
sity* (2nd ed., pp. 40-58). Boston: Allyn &
Bacon.

Fadiman, A. (1997). *The spirit catches you and
you fall down.* New York: Noonday Press.

Fine, M., & Asch, A. (1988). Disability beyond
stigma: Social interaction, discrimination, and
activism. *Journal of Social Issues, 44*(1), 3-21.

Gonzalez, R. (2001). *Being Hispanic* [Online].
Available: www.fathersnetwork.org/web/news/
connections/issues/32/gonz2.html

Grand, S. A., & Strohmer, D. C. (1983). Minority
perception of the disabled. *Rehabilitation
Counseling Bulletin, 27*(2), 117-119.

Groce, N. E. (2000). *Framing disability issues in
local concepts and beliefs* [Online]. Available:
www.dinf.ne.jp/doc/prdl/othr/apdrj/zl3jo030
0/zl3jo0303.html

Groce, N. E., & Zola, I. K. (1993). Multiculturalism, chronic illness, and disability. *Pediatrics,
91*(5), 1048-1055.

Grzesiak, R., & Hicok, D. A. (1994). A brief
history of psychotherapy and physical disability. *American Journal of Psychotherapy,
48*(2), 240-250.

Hahn, H. (1988). The politics of physical differences: Disability and discrimination. *Journal
of Social Issues, 44*(1), 39-47.

Hernandez, M. (1999). The role of therapeutic
groups in working with Latino Deaf adolescent
immigrants. In I. Leigh (Ed.), *Psychotherapy with
Deaf clients from diverse groups* (pp. 227-249).
Washington, DC: Gallaudet University Press.

Huang, L. N. (1997). Asian American adolescents.
In E. Lee (Ed.), *Working with Asian Americans*
(pp. 175-196). New York: Guilford.

Ilagan, V. (2002, May). *Understanding Filipinos in
the rehabilitation process.* Paper presented at the
Center for International Rehabilitation Research
Exchange Conference, Washington, DC.

Lee, E. (1997a). Chinese American families. In
E. Lee (Ed.), *Working with Asian Americans*
(pp. 46-78). New York: Guilford.

Lee, E. (1997b). *Working with Asian Americans.*
New York: Guilford.

Linton, S. (1998). *Claiming disability: Knowledge
and identity.* New York: New York University
Press.

McDermott, R., & Varenne, H. (1995). Culture as
disability. *Anthropology & Education
Quarterly, 26*(3), 324-348.

McWhirter, E. H. (2000). *Empowering people with
disabilities* [Online]. Available: www.counseling.
org/enews/volume_2/0207b.htm

Meyerson, L. (1948). Physical disability as a social
psychological problem. *Journal of Social
Issues, 4*(4), 2-9.

Moore, L. J. Keopraseuth, K., Leung, P. K., & Chao, L. H. (1997). Laotian American families. In E. Lee (Ed.), *Working with Asian Americans* (pp. 136-215). New York: Guilford.

National Council on Disability. (1993). *Meeting the unique needs of minorities with disabilities: A report to Congress.* Washington, DC: Author.

Olkin, R. (1999). *What psychotherapists should know about disability.* New York: Guilford.

Paris, M. J. (1993). Attitudes of medical students and healthcare professionals towards people with disabilities. *Archives of Physical Medicine and Rehabilitation, 74*(3), 818-825.

Pedemonte, M. (2001). Division 22. *Rehabilitation Psychology Newsletter, 28*(4), 16-17.

Rehabilitation Act of 1973, 87 stat.355, 29 U.S.C. 701 et seq.

Rogers-Dulan, J., & Blacher, D. (1995). African American families, religion, and disability. *Mental Retardation, 33*(4), 226-228.

Scheer, J., & Groce, N. (1988). Impairment as a human constant: Cross-cultural and historical perspectives on variation. *Journal of Social Issues, 44*(1), 23-37.

Shapiro, J. P. (1993). *No pity.* New York: Times Books.

Smart, J. (2001). *Disability, society, and the individual.* Gaithersburg, MD: Aspen.

Smart, J., & Smart, D. W. (1991). Acceptance of disability and the Mexican American culture. *Rehabilitation Counseling Bulletin, 34*(4), 357-367.

Smart, J. F., & Smart, D. W. (1997). The racial/ethnic demography of disability. *Journal of Rehabilitation, 63*(4), 9-15.

Smith, G. (2000). *Shedding light on African Americans with disabilities* [Online]. Available: www.accesslife.com/scripts/saisapi.dll/catalog.class

Sue, D. W., Carter, R. T., Casas, J. M., Fouad, N. Y., Ivey, A. E., Jensen, M., et al. (1998). *Multicultural counseling competencies.* Thousand Oaks, CA: Sage.

Sustento-Seneriches, J. (1997). Filipino American families. In E. Lee (Ed.), *Working with Asian Americans.* New York: Guilford.

Tsao, G. (2000). *Growing up Asian American with a disability* [Online]. Available: www.colorado.edu/journals/standards/V7N1/FIRSTPERSON/tsao.htlm

Tucker, B. P. (1998). Deaf culture, cochlear implants, & elective disability. *Hastings Center Report, 28*(4), 6-14.

Walker, S., & Brown, O. (1996). The Howard University Research and Training Center: A unique resource. *American Rehabilitation, 22*(1), 27-33.

Walker, S., Saravanabhavan, R. C., Williams, V., Brown, O., & West, T. (1996). *An examination of the impact of federally supported community services and educational systems on underserved people with disabilities from diverse cultural populations.* Washington, DC: Howard University Research and Training Center for Access to Rehabilitation and Economic Opportunity.

Wong, L., & Mock, M. (1997). Asian American young adults. In E. Lee (Ed.), *Working with Asian Americans* (pp. 196-208). New York: Guilford.

World Health Organization (WHO). (2000). *International classification of functioning, disability, and health: Prefinal draft version.* Geneva, Switzerland: Author.

Wright, L. (1994, July 25). One drop of blood. *New Yorker,* pp. 46-55.

Yang, H., Leung, P., Wang, J., & Shim, N. (1996). Asian Pacific Americans: The need for ethnicity-specific disability and rehabilitation data. *Journal of Disability Policy Studies, 7*(1), 33-54.

Zavaleta, A. N. (2000, June). *Do cultural factors affect Hispanic health status? Preface to proceedings.* Paper presented at the Rio Grande Valley Public Health Community Conference, Rio Grande, TX. Available: unix.utb.edu/~vpea/newarticle.html

29

Building Connection Through Diversity in Group Counseling

A Dialogical Perspective

ERIC C. CHEN
BRETT D. THOMBS
CATARINA I. COSTA

Fordham University

Yalom (1995) described interpersonal learning and the social microcosm as among the most influential explanations for change in group counseling. The maladaptive patterns in interpersonal relationships that prompt clients to seek counseling soon manifest themselves in their interactions with other members in the group (Slater, 1966). Accordingly, it has been suggested that the multicultural or diverse group provides a setting where racial and cultural stereotypes, prejudices, and misconceptions are likely to surface in a manner that can most effectively lead to active processing and efficacious interpersonal learning (Brook, Gordon, & Meadow, 1998; White, 1994). Group members bring their own social and cultural values, beliefs, and expectations into each interpersonal encounter (Ettin, 1994). As such, the diverse group affords its members a unique opportunity to identify and reflect on interpersonal perceptions, relationships, and conflicts that arise from sociocultural differences. Furthermore, the diverse group provides a setting in which members are able to improve their capacity to stay engaged in an intercultural dialogue that enhances interpersonal growth through dual concerns for self and others while exploring the intricacies of myriad levels of common and diverse human experiences (Coll, Cook-Nobles, & Surrey, 1997).

Ethical codes and guidelines of the American Psychological Association (1992, 1993, 2002) and the American Counseling Association (1995) mandate that mental health professionals develop and maintain competencies in the delivery of multicultural psychological services. A critical question facing group counselors is how to develop and implement multicultural competencies in the context of the complex sociocultural forces (Rutan & Stone, 2001) that affect group interaction, process, and outcome. Although the Multicultural Counseling Competency Model (MCCM) (Arredondo et al., 1996; Sue, 2001; Sue, Arredondo, & McDavis, 1992; Sue et al., 1982) has been widely recognized by the counseling and psychology professions and embraced in training programs (Ponterotto, Fuertes, & Chen, 2000), it has yet to be incorporated into the training of group counselors. The lack of a cohesive, theoretical structure for integrating multicultural competencies into group counseling practice presents a barrier that is likely to preclude otherwise motivated group counselors from maximizing the therapeutic potential of these groups.

The main goals of this chapter are to increase the group counselor's ability to identify and conceptualize the psychosocial influences of diversity on communication in the group counseling process and to assist the group counselor to develop an expanded repertoire of interventions grounded in theoretical structures of multicultural group counseling. In accordance with these goals, this chapter is predicated on three assumptions that warrant further clarification.

First, we adopt a psychosocial analysis of culture (e.g., Helms, 1994; Ho, 1995; Phinney, 1996). Defined as a network of domain-specific knowledge structures shared by members of a social-cultural group (Gudykunst & Kim, 1997; Hong, Morris, Chiu, & Benet-Martínez, 2000), culture is internalized and functions as a set of templates that guide and govern interpersonal expectations, perceptions, and interpretations across situations. These systems of knowledge or templates have been described as differing in terms of cultural individualism-collectivism (Triandis, 1989) and, by extension, low-context and high-context communication (Hall, 1976); cultural variability (Hofstede, 1980); and cultural value orientations (Kluckhohn & Strodtbeck, 1961). Although space limitations preclude a description of these dimensions, it is important to note that similarities and differences along these dimensions are linked to group affiliations and identities. These linkages, combined with variation between in-group (i.e., groups that are considered important to members, such as family and racial or ethnic groups) and out-group (i.e., groups that are less important to members) communication norms, exert considerable leverage on interpersonal communication.

A second assumption is that all interpersonal encounters in the counseling group context, although differing in degree and in kind, are multicultural in nature. Individuals in a counseling group may share common systems of group-based knowledge due to shared race, ethnicity, gender, or sexual orientation, for example. The degree to which systems of knowledge are shared and the specific application of these systems, however, may vary widely as a function of unique life experiences and the relative importance of in-group membership to identity. In effect, the group practitioner must be able to identify and appreciate three distinct but dynamically intertwined levels of personal identity variables: human or universal-level variables, social or group-level variables, and individual or personal-level identity variables (Kluckhohn & Murray, 1953; Leong, 1996; Turner, 1987), as well as the dynamic interactions between levels and their influences on interpersonal communication. By maintaining an integrated, dynamic perspective of human identity and motivation, the group practitioner minimizes the likelihood of ignoring the influence of diversity in an apparently homogeneous group.

Our third assumption is that diversity is best understood in a way that reflects the permeable boundaries and shifting borders of culture in the complexity of group life. As such, we conceptualize diversity in the context of group counseling as communicated through our interactions with others. As Frey (2000) contended,

> Diversity itself is not an inherent, predetermined condition per se; it is a symbolic concept that is created and sustained through interaction. In that regard, communication is not just a tool that can be used to manage diversity (although it certainly is such a tool); diversity itself, however it is defined, is best regarded as emerging from communication. Consequently, changing the form of communication (e.g., using dialogue instead of discussion) potentially has the power to change the very nature of what group members (and scholars) perceive to constitute diversity. (p. 226)

Similar to the assumptions made with respect to the multiple yet intertwined levels of individual identity functioning, the collective identity of the group is best conceived of in a flexible, evolving manner. The symbolic construction of the group identity influences both the unfolding of interpersonal dynamics and, ultimately, counseling outcomes. As such, the dual aspects of diversity as a *relationship* and diversity as a *process* are emphasized. Diversity as a relationship concerns how specific group constructs, such as cohesion, conflicts, impasses, and subgrouping, are affected by the diverse modes of communication of the group's members, as well as the sociocultural positions from which they communicate. Diversity as a process, on the other hand, reflects the group's evolving understanding of its own diversity and how diversity shapes interaction and

communication in the group over time. A group is a complex entity composed of multiple, interactive parts. Much more than the sum of its member, leader, subgroup, and whole-group identities, each group involves interactions at numerous levels, including the intrapersonal, interpersonal, and group-as-a-whole levels (Fuhriman & Burlingame, 1994; Kivlighan, Coleman, & Anderson, 2000). Understanding diversity as reflected in the group process therefore requires attention to and distinctions between the interplay of these parts, on one hand, and the connection of these interactions into the temporal matrix of the group, on the other.

In our attempt to understand how diversity is reflected in communication and how it affects the group outcome, we present a dialogical or interactional perspective that has, at its core, two related but different concepts: self-disclosure and interpersonal feedback. In the section that follows, we provide an overview of the dialogical perspective, with particular attention to prospects and challenges inherent in intercultural dialogues. These possibilities and perils are examined within the context of the theories of social cognition (e.g., Fiske & Taylor, 1991) and anxiety/uncertainty management (Gudykunst, 1995). The second section integrates these concepts with the processes of self-disclosure and feedback in the diverse group. We describe the specific roles and functions of self-disclosure and feedback relative to interpersonal learning in the group social microcosm and in the intercultural dialogue. In the third section, which suggests practice implications for the group counselor, we discuss the multicultural effectiveness and competence of the group leader in light of the four leadership roles described by Yalom (1995): participant-observer, norm shaper, historian, and technical expert. Then, a case vignette is presented to illustrate the dialogic perspective at work in the counseling group. This chapter concludes with training recommendations and some closing comments. It should be noted that detailed, comprehensive reviews of the extensive conceptual and research literatures are far beyond the scope of this chapter. Therefore, rather than providing exhaustive coverage, the chapter summarizes research and theoretical writings for illustrative purposes. Our overall goal is to stimulate research and clinical applications by promoting a view of diversity as a key part of a richly layered group fabric.

INTERCULTURAL DIALOGUE: PROSPECTS AND CHALLENGES

In the therapeutic context of the group system, each member's therapeutic work is inherently dependent on her or his relationship with other members. These symbiotic relationships may be described as one of three types: commensalistic, parasitic, or mutualistic. In commensalistic symbiosis, members simply happen to work in the group system with little interaction among them, either not communicating (i.e., the avoidance of interaction) or having severed communication (Gass & Varonis, 1991). In parasitic symbiosis, members accomplish their goals at the others' expense. It is in a system characterized by mutualistic symbiosis where members work collaboratively and benefit mutually from shared interaction. When members acknowledge their mutually beneficial interdependence, miscommunication problems, such as misunderstanding, incomplete understanding, and conflict, may be addressed more easily. By fostering a dialogical mode of communication, the group leader seeks to engender a symbiosis of mutuality and respect so that individual change is facilitated and monitored collaboratively within the context of the larger group dynamics.

Grounded in a collaborative communication process where personal experiences, assumptions, and predispositions are explored to deepen understanding, dialogue differs from other modes of communication, such as monologue or discussion, and more effectively facilitates the formation of mutually beneficial symbiotic relationships in the group. *Monologue,* as defined by Gudykunst and Kim (1997), refers to a conversation that is self-oriented and ignores the input or response of other interactants, thus leaving the speaker to control the direction and topics of conversation. *Discussion* is typically described as a problem-solving conversation emphasizing an analysis of opposing perspectives, opinions, or beliefs with the goal of reaching a compromise or a consensus (Frey, 2000). Dialogical interaction, however, allows group members, through a shared sense of control and ownership and the mutual confirmation of experiences, to establish a collaborative and mutually beneficial relationship. Facilitated and monitored effectively by the group leader, a dialogue about interpersonal connections in general and conflicts in particular offers an opportunity to avoid a power struggle and to forge a mutually growth-enhancing experience.

Frey (2000) described the dialogical process as one in which participation requires the suspension of closely held individual or sociocultural group assumptions. Basic moral and causal assumptions are exposed for examination, both by ourselves and by other participants in the dialogue. Especially crucial to the process is the substitution of a "both/and" mode of interaction for an "either/or" framework. In the either/or mode, the validity of a particular position rests on its proficiency in discrediting competing understandings. In the dialogue or both/and mode, group members are discouraged from engaging one another to collect information about competing viewpoints for the sake of persuasion. Rather, members seek to establish a more profound mutual understanding of one another through learning about their own and others' experiences, which have shaped self-concepts, values, worldviews, and, more immediately, assumptions about the group and its members.

Intercultural dialogues, however, introduce challenges not present in dialogical communication that is confined within a single framework of cultural knowledge. Two theoretical perspectives, those of social cognition (e.g., Fiske & Taylor, 1991) and anxiety/uncertainty management theory (Gudykunst, 1995), are useful for elucidating the particularities of these challenges. The social cognition literature attends to how individuals use social information about others, social situations, and groups to make inferences. Specifically, it examines processes and strategies employed to perceive, encode, and integrate social information to form impressions or conclusions about others (Markus & Sentis, 1982). Among many strategies we use to encode, monitor, store, retrieve, and evaluate information about others is categorization. Categorization is an important strategy because it allows us to structure and give coherence to our general knowledge about people and the social world, as well as to offer expectations and explanations about behavior patterns and common characteristic actions and attributes (Gudykunst & Kim, 1997). We categorize or classify based on physical (e.g., sex, race) or cultural (e.g., ethnic background) characteristics, as well as characteristics less immediately visible to the perceiver, such as attitudes or personality traits. Categorization processes, however, are subject to biases, and these biases lead to stereotypes, misunderstandings, or conflicts in a counseling group when, for example, there exists a discrepancy between a personal social identity with which a member defines herself or himself and the manner in which the others in the group have categorized the member based on her or his observed characteristics (Deaux, 1991).

The second perspective, Gudykunst's (1995) anxiety/uncertainty management theory, informs intercultural communication through its focus on the level of uncertainty and anxiety that accompanies interpersonal interaction. *Uncertainty* in this context refers to the lack of confidence in the prediction of another interactant's response, whereas *anxiety* is defined as an emotional reaction to the expectation of possible negative consequences. The amount of cognitive unpredictability and psychological stress in communication across sociocultural divides is a function of a broad range of factors, including prior contact with others of a similar group affiliation, knowledge and information about the sociocultural groups involved and their social identities, and the interactants' perceptions of similarities or differences between them. Uncertainty and anxiety may be reduced, for example, when one is given information, whether accurate or stereotypic, about the common attitudes, beliefs, value orientations, or norms of a particular sociocultural group. According to Gudykunst's theory, greater amounts of uncertainty and anxiety are associated with increased interpersonal risk perceived by interactants in the intercultural dialogue.

This interpersonal risk required of group members for interpersonal learning to occur has been identified by Yalom (1995) as a reason for which interpersonal learning is an important curative factor in group counseling. Through an examination of interpersonal perceptions and interactions, the counseling group provides opportunities for members to gain insight into their interpersonal problems and maladaptive interpersonal styles and to undergo the corrective emotional experiences that are crucial for change to occur (Chen & Mallinckrodt, 2002). This process is accelerated as counselors focus members on here-and-now interactions and communications that encourage self-disclosure and the exchange of feedback about mutual perceptions.

SELF-DISCLOSURE AND INTERPERSONAL FEEDBACK IN THE DIVERSE GROUP

In the context of the group social microcosm, self-disclosure and feedback promote interpersonal learning as members begin to identify their perceptual distortions of others and the effect that their distortions and stereotypes have on interactions with other group members across a host of sociocultural boundaries. Therefore, properly facilitated, self-disclosure and interpersonal feedback are effective in reducing categorization biases, as well as uncertainty and anxiety associated with intercultural encounters. Through thoughtful use of self-disclosure and feedback, misunderstanding is minimized, and change occurs more rapidly as members take interpersonal risks and use interpersonal learning to develop new ways of relating to others, first with fellow group members and subsequently with significant others outside of the group.

Self-Disclosure

Self-disclosure in group communication, which is central to group change processes (Corey & Corey, 2002; Yalom, 1995), has been defined as the willingness to share information about one's personal states, dispositions, events of the past, and plans for the future (Derlega & Berg, 1987). By virtue of its conceptualization as interactional or dialogical, self-disclosure is always an interpersonal act, requiring both a giver and a recipient. In the interpersonally oriented group, a continuous dialogue is more likely to occur when the content of disclosure focuses on personal experiences as opposed to beliefs or opinions. A discussion of one's views on religion, abortion, affirmative action, or other belief-based issues, for instance, tends to result in a heated debate that changes the tone of interaction from collaborative to combative

and from inclusive to divisive, regardless of the salience of the belief in question to particular members' social identities. Not only would this occurrence fail to deepen mutual understanding or change beliefs, but it would also run the risk of polarizing already divergent viewpoints and weakening connections within the group. Conversely, through the retelling of personal experiences, members learn about each other's histories, which serve as templates for construing the world and how these personal histories and experiences affect relations within the group. As a result of this process of exchanging experiences, each interactant's need for control and reactive defensiveness is minimized.

In the context of the diverse group, the concept of self-disclosure needs to be broadened beyond its traditional definition. Self-disclosure as a form of interpersonal communication is dictated by cultural group norms, and research evidence suggests that certain racial and ethnic minority group members may be less willing to disclose than White members (Shen, Sanchez, & Huang, 1984; Sue & Sue, 2003). Ridley's (1984) two-dimension typology of Black clients' nondisclosure offers a possible explanation of this finding. It assesses the nature of nondisclosure of ethnic minority clients to White counselors with respect to two dimensions: *cultural paranoia* and *functional paranoia*. The dimension of cultural paranoia refers to the degree to which minority clients' nondisclosure occurs due to fear of misunderstandings or negative responses from White counselors, suggesting a healthy and self-protective function in response to anticipated racism. Functional paranoia, conversely, pertains to the degree to which the nondisclosure of minority clients is motivated by their pervasive suspicion and distrust in others in general and counselors in particular, irrespective of race. On the basis of self-disclosure, a minority client may fall high or low on each dimension, yielding four possible disclosure styles:

(a) Trusting or intercultural nonparanoiac discloser: low on both dimensions

(b) Healthy cultural paranoiac: high on cultural paranoia, low on functional paranoia

(c) Functional paranoiac: high on functional paranoia, low on cultural paranoia

(d) Confluent paranoiac: high on both dimensions

Ridley's (1984) typology is helpful to group counselors when they facilitate a group in which there are visible minority group members. Following this assessment, group counselors may develop specific disclosure-focused interventions best matched to the nondisclosure mode of group counseling clients to decrease their mistrust and fear. A lack of awareness of the nature of nondisclosure by a minority group member would likely increase the risk of group counselors making erroneous attributions and implementing ineffective or counterproductive intervention strategies with potentially deleterious effects on group dynamics, cohesion, and future prospects of disclosure (Fenster & Fenster, 1998).

In discussing self-disclosure, Yalom (1995) distinguished between vertical and horizontal disclosures. Vertical disclosure is content based and focuses on the historical, outside-of-group information, whereas horizontal disclosure is here and now, is experience focused, and emphasizes the dynamic process of the feedback and disclosure cycle in the group. More specifically, horizontal disclosure centers on group members' internal feelings and thoughts, antecedent, concomitant, and consequent to the act of disclosing. Horizontal disclosure is therefore an exploration and expression of the discloser's normally unexpressed uncertainty and anxiety about the prediction and anticipation of others' reactions in the here-and-now group context. If a member of a women's group, for example, were to reveal that she is a lesbian, vertical disclosure would likely include information about when she first became

aware of her attraction to women, if she has come out to her friends or family, and other content details regarding her sexual orientation. Horizontal disclosure, on the other hand, would shift focus away from the content and onto her experience of disclosing at this moment to this group of women.

Although many writers and researchers (e.g., Slavin, 1993; Yalom, 1995) have emphasized horizontal disclosure over vertical disclosure, the value of vertical disclosure should not be overlooked in diverse groups. Because the interpersonal counseling group represents a microcosm of society, each member of the diverse group brings with her or him all of the experiences, feelings, and reactions surrounding prior encounters with out-group individuals outside of the group. The past oppression, prejudice, and discrimination encountered by members of visible or invisible minority groups in the United States may contribute to these individuals' mistrust of majority group members and counselors (Ridley, 1989). Similarly, they may perceive the group as a threat to reenact oppressive societal dynamics of invalidation, disempowerment, and lack of empathy and mutuality (Han & Vasquez, 1995). Consequently, at the beginning stages of group counseling, individuals who are members of minority groups may be more cautious about disclosing information to out-group strangers than to in-group strangers (Stephan, Stephan, Wezel, & Cornelius, 1991).

Both minority and majority members of diverse groups reap the benefits of vertical disclosure, however. For members who have experienced various forms of oppression, prejudice, and discrimination in society, vertical disclosure, in the form of narratives of personal histories, is invaluable. It allows their experiences to be acknowledged and validated. For majority group members, these disclosures provide opportunities for them to examine, recognize, and acknowledge their privilege and power as members of the majority group. Both minority and majority members may also begin to understand other members' past experiences that profoundly shape their personal and in-group identities.

When vertical disclosure is followed by horizontal disclosure, the group shifts the focus to how members' connections with others have been enhanced as a result. A delicate balance between vertical disclosure and horizontal disclosure during this dialogical process among minority and majority group members hence constitutes the cornerstone on which a counseling group can begin to construct meaning and deepen understanding about one another, thus facilitating a more positive and affirming sense of members' identities.

Self-disclosure in relation to visible diversity, as opposed to invisible diversity, tends to occur first in the group process (Fenster, 1996; White, 1994). If there were only two men in a counseling group of eight members, for example, the gender imbalance would typically be noted by both men and women. A dialogue that facilitated the exploration of personal experience in relation to communicating across gender divides (vertical disclosure), as well as the underlying uncertainty and anxiety that accompany the exploration (horizontal disclosure), would set the stage for later dialogue with respect to invisible diversity. Although self-disclosure at the horizontal and vertical levels may increase as the group progresses, self-disclosure is neither a static nor linear concept. It is, in essence, a cyclical process. Ideally, both disclosers and receivers build their trust and connections during this process, thus encouraging more interpersonal risks and a more fluid exchange of ongoing disclosure and feedback.

Interpersonal Feedback

The extant group counseling empirical literature, based on both subjective participant evaluation and process-outcome research, has consistently found feedback to be one of the most crucial variables to the change process in group counseling (Butler & Fuhriman, 1980; Flowers & Booarem, 1989; Kivlighan, 1985; Kivlighan et al., 2000; Tschuschke & Dies, 1997). Cohen (2000) defined interpersonal feedback as "sequences in which a participant, as feedback *donor,* responds to another, the *recipient,* so as to let the recipient know how her or his behavior has affected the *donor*" (pp. 167-168). An important element of Cohen's intersubjective conceptualization of feedback is the assertion that by emphasizing both the experience of the feedback donor and the behavior of the feedback recipient, group members are empowered to see other members as they see themselves. In the diverse group, an intersubjective understanding of the process of feedback allows members to understand events in the group through the eyes of other members. The focus of the group shifts from the content of the feedback provided by the donor member regarding another member's behavior, to the initial reaction of the donor member that led to the decision to share the feedback, and, finally, to the experiences of this member that have likely evoked the reaction. This bidirectional understanding of feedback assists members in creating mutual understandings of experiences and realities and, in doing so, correcting what Cohen referred to as "idealizing" or "demonizing" stereotypes.

Empirical research in social psychology focusing on the valence and timing of feedback suggests that positive feedback is important for building group cohesion in the initial stages of group formation. Early in the group, positive feedback tends to be more accepted by members than negative feedback in terms of credibility, desirability, and impact. Group members who receive high levels of both positive and negative feedback and who are able to provide both positive and negative feedback to other members are most likely to achieve positive change. Moreover, although initial positive feedback appears to be vital for creating group cohesion, the credibility difference between positive and negative feedback begins to vanish over time, and groups with higher levels of cohesiveness appear to be more capable of delivering negative feedback (Kivlighan, 1985).

In the diverse group, factors such as societal norms that discourage the exploration of divergent understandings between members of different sociocultural groups complicate the delivery and acceptance of both positive and negative feedback. Evidence suggests that differences between people from different sociocultural groups tend to be viewed as reflecting profound, immutable group-level differences rather than individual-level differences (Miller & Prentice, 1999). Crocker and colleagues (Crocker & Major, 1989; Crocker, Voelkl, Testa, & Major, 1991) have found that due to the attributional ambiguity of both positive and negative feedback delivered from White majority culture members, Blacks and other minority group members are likely to be wary of feedback from Whites. In the case of positive feedback, a member of a minority or stigmatized group may be uncertain whether the positive feedback occurred because of the merit of her or his behavior or, rather, from other motives, such as a desire not to appear prejudiced on the part of the White deliverer of feedback. When the feedback is negative, however, individuals of stigmatized groups may attribute the feedback to prejudice when such an attribution is plausible. This is consistent with Kelley's (1972) hypothesis that members of stigmatized groups tend to attribute negative feedback to prejudice rather than to a realistic appraisal of merit so as to protect self-esteem in a racist environment.

The findings from the aforementioned research are informative for leaders of diverse groups. Although positive feedback is a critical component in the development of group cohesion, it is a combination of negative and positive feedback delivery and receipt that is found to be predictive of change in group counseling (Kivlighan, 1985). Negative feedback delivered by majority group members or leaders, however, may not be well received by group members from minority or stigmatized groups due, in part, to uncertainty as to whether the criticism stems from their own actual behavior or because of negative stereotyping. Minority group members may also be reluctant to deliver corrective feedback due to uncertainty and anxiety about resultant negative stereotyping by majority group members. Spencer, Fein, Wolfe, Fong, and Dunn (1998), for instance, found that the receipt of negative feedback tends to make receivers of the feedback more likely to activate negative racial stereotypes when the feedback donor is a member of a minority group.

The exchange of feedback as a dialogue presents a formidable task for both the feedback donor and receiver and requires their willingness to stay engaged in this process. Unsolicited feedback from a group member with whom there is limited trust formed is likely to be rejected or devalued, regardless of whether the feedback is positive or negative. In a similar vein, a member may hesitate to give complete and honest feedback to another member in the presence of a high level of uncertainty and anxiety about the receiver's reaction. With the assistance of the group leader, however, members may develop skills that allow them to deliver and receive feedback that is specific, is contextualized, and focuses on one's experience and the experienced impact of other group members' behavior— cognitively, emotionally, and behaviorally.

Integration of Self-Disclosure and Interpersonal Feedback

Han and Vasquez (1995) focused on two sociocultural realities likely to be present in the context of group counseling involving racial and ethnic minorities: unique cultural needs and variations and the experience of minorities as members of underrepresented, stigmatized, and devalued groups in a predominately White society. The first sociocultural reality suggests that differences in worldviews among diverse groups would be expected to be evident in the divergent communication styles of group members. In a study of self-presentational misperceptions (Akimoto & Sanbonmatsu, 1999), for example, Japanese Americans responding to positive feedback described their own performances less favorably in public than in private, whereas there was no difference for European Americans between the two settings. European Americans who blindly evaluated the tape recordings, however, judged the Japanese American participants to be less competent and less likeable due to their comparatively self-effacing behavior consequential to receiving the positive feedback. In a counseling group with culturally diverse participants, conflicts and misunderstanding will inevitably occur without a mutual understanding of and respect for the behaviors that are culturally appropriate for all members, rather than just those behaviors that are sanctioned by the majority culture.

The second sociocultural reality may be understood as an interaction between the reality of the majority culture and the experience of the minority group within it. Specifically, implicit or explicit experiences of oppression, prejudice, discrimination, and stigmatization influence disclosure and the exchange of feedback between majority and minority culture members in the social microcosm of the group. In the here-and-now context of interpersonal group counseling, intermember learning depends greatly on the willingness of members to enter into one another's multiple realities. Yalom (1995) discussed the vital role of interpersonal feedback in the "self-reflective looping" process, through which here-and-now behavior in the group is examined and interpersonal learning occurs. Through feedback, a member's behavior and its effect on others are recognized and pointed out by other members, providing the member in question with an opportunity to better understand the behavior, as well as its interpersonal ramifications. Through self-disclosure, not only are members exposed to others' extragroup and intragroup experiences, but they are also called on to examine their conceptualization of what constitutes diversity, as well as their understandings of and reactions to similarity and dissimilarity.

In light of these sociocultural realities, dialogue provides opportunities for group members to share their experiences with each other in a manner that validates these experiences while challenging them to understand different realities. Within the dialogic framework, self-disclosure and feedback exchanges gradually blend into one another. In the process, members are challenged to alter or expand deeply held beliefs and assumptions that are found to be incongruent with previously unconsidered realities presented by other group members. Confronting one's stereotypes and established beliefs at the intrapersonal and interpersonal levels creates uncertainty and anxiety for the whole group as it endeavors to make a "risky shift" (Wallach, Kogan, & Bem, 1962) toward a meaningful web of interpersonal connections. The creation of a sense of trust that the experiences of each member are valid and will not be subjugated to the realities and experiences of others enables members to tolerate these cognitive and affective reactions to self-disclosure and feedback exchange. Under the guidance of the leader, members engage in a collaborative, reciprocal dialogue as they venture into identifying interior territories of other members.

IMPLICATIONS FOR MULTICULTURALLY COMPETENT GROUP COUNSELORS

The MCCM has been widely adopted as a yardstick against which the competence of mental health professionals may be measured (Ponterotto et al., 2000). The three components of the MCCM—awareness, knowledge, and skills—generally correspond with the sequence of increasing one's competence, beginning with awareness raising, followed by acquiring relevant factual knowledge and transferring that knowledge to actual counseling practice. Whereas competence implies general capacity or ability, effectiveness, which is specifically linked to a unique multicultural counseling encounter, results from cultural knowledge, clinical skills that are both general and theory specific, clinical judgment, and interpersonal attributes (Chen, 2001). The effort to increase the multicultural competence of the counselor will likely be thwarted in the absence of a thorough assessment of the sources of multicultural effectiveness or ineffectiveness.

Applied to the communication within the group, Chen's (2001) view is consistent with Howell's (1982) perspective that the process of improving one's communication with others progresses through four stages: (a) *unconscious incompetence*, whereby individuals misinterpret others' behavior but are not aware of the bias; (b) *conscious incompetence*, whereby individuals are aware of the misinterpretation of others' behavior but fail to correct this error; (c) *conscious competence*, whereby communication errors and behaviors are consciously and actively modified and improved; and (d) *unconscious competence*, whereby individuals practice the skills for effective communication to the extent that they need not think about them to use them. In this view, the multiculturally competent group counselor is characterized as a professional with both awareness and commitment to expand the boundaries of her or his multicultural competence.

Aside from awareness of one's own identity at the universal, group, and personal levels (Kluckhohn & Murray, 1953; Turner, 1987), the multiculturally competent group counselor

remains cognizant of how various forms of oppression, prejudice, discrimination, and stereotyping affect her or him personally and, thus, her or his interpretation of the group process. The group leader must challenge and appraise the preconceived impressions or assumptions about minority group members in the context of her or his own cultural upbringing and beliefs, discarding myths of universality or homogeneity of experience and understanding the effects of her or his own worldviews on the evaluation of group members and the group process (Brook et al., 1998; Tsui & Schultz, 1988). Through this process of self-examination, a sense of "mindfulness" (Langer, 1989) or "cultural sensitivity" (Ridley, Mendoza, Kanitz, Angermeier, & Zenk, 1994) helps the group leader to minimize the biases of categorization or stereotyping and to avoid operating in an automatic, habitual manner. When open to new information and characteristics associated with the cultural contexts of the members and group, the interventions of the group leader are less likely to be guided and constrained by her or his stereotypic beliefs and assumptions. In the remainder of this section, this process is further examined within the context of the four leadership roles described by Yalom (1995): the roles of participant-observer, norm shaper, historian, and technical expert.

Group Leader as Participant-Observer

Participant observation in the context of social science research is conceptualized not as a particular research technique but rather as a manner of "being-in-the-world" that is necessary for carrying out useful social research (Atkinson & Hammersley, 1994). The challenge for the researcher as participant-observer is to be able to understand an event from the perspective of an insider, including the effects of one's own involvement, while maintaining the ability to describe what is happening with as little bias as possible (Patton, 1980). Analogously, the group counselor in the dual roles of observer and participant constantly endeavors to strike a balance between data collected as an objective outsider versus that gleaned as a subjective insider, relative to the events both unfolding within and absent from the group. Self-understanding and consciousness of the leader's effect on the group process must be combined with an ability to arrive at an evaluation of what is happening in the group that reflects the experiences of the members rather than simply the biases of the group leader. In this role of participant-observer, attention is paid to forces at work in the group at three levels—member-leader, member-member, and the group as a whole—so that appropriate and effective interventions may be identified and implemented.

At the member-leader interaction level, the group leader attends to the significance of her or his role from the perspective of minority group members. For instance, group members who adhere to Asian cultural group norms may, compared with majority culture members, tend to relate to the group leader as an authoritative figure rather than as a process facilitator (Tsui & Schultz, 1988). Similarly, minority group members, whose reality often consists of experiences of oppression, prejudice, and discrimination in society (Han & Vasquez, 1995), may be particularly sensitive to the combined power of a leader who is a member of the majority culture as well as an authority in the group.

At the group level, the leader as a participant-observer of the dialogical process focuses on how uncertainty and anxiety affect the interaction or, more specifically, prevent an effective dialogue from taking place. Racial and ethnic minority group members, for example, may experience a sense of distrust, vulnerability, and lack of inclusion in a group composed predominantly of Whites, who may not attend to the racial or ethnic differences within the group, perhaps due to a lack of awareness or to fear of being labeled as culturally insensitive. Not surprisingly, then, in a racially mixed group, members may collude within their group to avoid an exploration of these issues by means of one of several strategies (Helms & Cook, 1999): (a) using imprecise terms such as *culture* and other euphemisms as opposed to *race* to depict out-group individuals; (b) using *they* and *we* to refer to specific racial out-group and in-group members, respectively; (c) shifting the group's focus to safer issues; and (d) neutralizing the topic to reduce consideration of the racial or cultural aspects of an interaction.

On the other hand, members may make an attempt to explore these differences, which, when not monitored appropriately, may lead to misunderstanding or conflicts due to differences in the recognition and expression of emotions or in cognitive and interpersonal styles.

Recognizing these potential difficulties, Cheng, Chae, and Gunn (1998) encouraged the leader with a focus on group-level interactions to explore questions such as the following: How might similarities and differences among group members influence the level or style of participation? Relative to maintenance functions, do certain members constantly interrupt or cut off other members from different cultures or backgrounds? Relative to task functions, to what degree is there an exchange of information, ideas, views, and feedback between members of different cultural backgrounds? Is there any unique connection formed based on similarities or differences in sociocultural identity? To what extent is the emphasis of interaction placed on seeking and giving information or opinions (discussion mode), as opposed to an exchange of personal experience and hidden meanings (dialogue mode)?

Group Leader as Norm Shaper

Yalom (1995) stressed the far-reaching, pervasive influence of the group leader on shaping norms. The foundation of group norms that are constructed early on will most likely guide the members' interactions throughout the life span of the group, influencing the processes of disclosure and feedback, as well as the level of acceptance and value allocated to diverse worldviews and life experiences. The therapeutic group norms designed to help members navigate the group experience, however, are typically in line with White majority culture values and expectations (Cheng et al., 1998; Tsui & Schultz, 1988). These norms resist intrusion and are likely to either exclude minority group members or demand that they adapt to interactional patterns that are incongruent with their own cultural norms. Although most group leaders have been trained to facilitate the discussion of feelings, disclosure, feedback, and direct confrontation of conflict, members of minority cultural backgrounds may not understand these norms or feel comfortable participating in interactions based on these expectations (Brook et al., 1998).

In light of the different realities of members, particularly those from minority cultural groups, it is incumbent on the multiculturally competent group counselor to ensure that the social microcosm of the group does not simply replicate societal norms of oppression, prejudice, and discrimination faced by both visible and invisible minority group members and that serve to denigrate, exclude, and silence members of these groups. By understanding how valence, timing, and cognitive and affective risk factors affect both the giving and receiving of feedback in a diverse group, the group leader facilitates the replacement of divisive societal norms with a dialogical norm of interaction through which the mutual comprehension of diverse experiences may take place.

In facilitating the development of mutual understandings, the multiculturally competent group leader endeavors to address the points of tension that exist in relation to norms on three different levels: those of the group, those of the majority culture, and those of minority cultures. Presenting the group with information about potential clashes or inconsistencies among these three norms would help group members to better understand other members' behaviors at the group, interpersonal, and intrapersonal levels, thus minimizing inaccurate attributions. To maintain a dialogical process and facilitate communication across diversity, group members need to acknowledge the norm of multiple realities. Instead of assessing the degree of validity of members' realities, the challenge for the group is to determine how to communicate in the context of a diversity of personal experiences. Through dialogue, group members can obtain information about other members without relying on stereotypes. The sharing of how different members experience the same group event differently, facilitated by a combination of descriptive horizontal and explanatory vertical disclosures, serves to reduce uncertainty and anxiety, triggering a spiraling process of open communication and interpersonal learning.

To mitigate the debilitating effects of monocultural norms on the cohesion of diverse groups, group leaders need to elicit reactions from all group members about their perceptions and expectations of group counseling. Group leaders should take an active role in forging functional group norms that are consonant with the various cultural backgrounds and expectations of group members, thus bridging the power differential between majority and minority group members (Tsui & Schultz, 1988). Through modeling intercultural curiosity, sensitivity to diversity, and self-disclosure, group leaders help the group develop norms under which differences across sociocultural boundaries are viewed as opportunities to confront stereotypical beliefs and assumptions. Throughout the group process, and particularly in the early stages most crucial for the development of group culture, they also encourage members to reflect on their own assumptions and stereotypes about others as manifested in their interpersonal encounters in the group.

Group Leader as Historian

As group historian, the group counselor maintains a temporal perspective, recalling the original goals of each group member, as well as serving to integrate the unfolding of related events over time in the group (Yalom, 1995). The skilled leader of the diverse group, however, needs to further expand on this role, both with respect to understanding the group process and individual members' behaviors, as well as facilitating the vertical disclosure necessary for mutual understanding of members' diverse experiences. Consistent with the MCCM, Fenster (1996) asserted that to determine the extent to which behaviors of group members are symptomatic or culturally congruent, the group counselor must have some familiarity with the cultural norms of the minority group members. Fenster compared the group counselor to an archeologist, who, prior to embarking on the excavation of a site, would not neglect to study the history of the people who lived there. An archeologist, however, studies historic cultures and is not interactive in her or his approach. For these reasons, the task of the group leader as historian is perhaps better described as similar to that of an anthropologist, who, based on the accumulation of observations as a participant-observer, must formulate theories of how moment-to-moment events and interactions are related to the histories of the members, individually and as a group.

A mere curiosity of the history of the member as an individual and as a member of the cultural group would not be of much use, however, if this history were not used to facilitate the type of vertical disclosure necessary for the formation of group dialogue and mutual understanding of diverse experiences. Although a here-and-now horizontal focus of disclosure is necessary for effective group counseling, vertical disclosure takes on a more important role in the diverse group, in which members are likely to have very different upbringings, experiences, values, and perspectives. The multiculturally skilled counselor hence has the responsibility of facilitating the sharing of members' past experiences so that other members can begin to relate emotionally to and understand these experiences. White members, who are unlikely to be able to identify with the experience of racial discrimination, for example, may more clearly understand a minority group member's disclosure concerning her or his difficulty trusting these members if the leader can facilitate the disclosure of life experiences that have provoked these feelings. Tsui and Schultz (1988) argued that acknowledging and validating the unique life experiences of minority group members and the connection of these experiences with the realities of our culturally diverse society prevent these experiences from being marginalized in the group and help group members move toward empathic, universal emotional response. They further argued that establishing the ability to respond in a unified manner to the often painful experiences of other members allows cohesion to develop in a group composed of members with diverse histories and life experiences.

Group Leader as Technical Expert

The role of the group leader as technical expert refers to the application of specific techniques used to shape the norms and direction of the group (Yalom, 1995). In the diverse group, the crucial role of the counselor as technical expert begins in the pregroup screening and preparatory process, in which potential members are informed that people from diverse backgrounds and groups, with varying issues to explore, will be present in the group. The group leader's preparation of individual members may include discussion of relevant sociocultural factors, and interventions by the group leader throughout the course of the group should reflect the leader's awareness and understanding of the effects of diversity on the group's interactions (Brook et al., 1998).

With the goal of facilitating the dialogical process, the leader deliberately plans and designs the conditions and norms necessary for self-disclosure and feedback to readily occur. Effective skills tend to fall into two major categories: caring and meaning attribution. *Caring* refers to those skills that allow members to experience warmth, support, and empathy from others in the group, whereas *meaning attribution* skills focus on gaining a cognitive understanding of meanings embedded in interpersonal interactions. When the interactions within the group seem to move toward the direction of nonengagement (Gass & Varonis, 1991), for instance, the leader may empathize with both majority and minority cultural group members' cognitive uncertainty and stress associated with self-disclosure and feedback. Through the increase of perceived similarity in this respect among the members, the curative value of universality in this context enables the members to open themselves to others' experience. Another skill in the meaning attribution category involves making process commentaries (Yalom, 1995) oriented toward difficulties that the group is having in addressing issues of diversity. Still another may be to educate the group as to how the norms and expectations—at the majority culture, minority culture, and group levels—may affect the nature and direction of interactions with others. In doing so, both caring and

understanding are communicated to members whose multiple realities are acknowledged and affirmed in the social microcosm of the multicultural group counseling experience.

CASE VIGNETTE

In the fifth session of an interpersonal counseling group led by a therapist in private practice and composed of five racial and ethnic minorities and three White members, Robert, a 39-year-old Black manager of a technology sales department, complained that he had been passed over for a promotion again. He further told the members, all in their late 30s to early 50s, that a young White man whose department had been less profitable than Robert's had received the promotion to which Robert had aspired. Robert concluded his description of the events by saying that he felt that he had been the victim of racist promotion practices by the management of his company and that this was not the first time that White colleagues with inferior track records to his had been promoted ahead of him. Several of the minority members of the group offered comments in support of Robert's assessment of what had happened. Rafael, a son of Ecuadorian immigrants, who taught math at a local community college, suggested that Robert investigate the possibility of a lawsuit against the company—Robert had nothing to lose in filing a lawsuit, as he was already "banging his head against the glass ceiling."

During the interchange, the three White members remained silent until the group counselor, Jessica, a 45-year-old White woman, noted their lack of participation and invited them to explore their reactions to Robert's complaint of racial discrimination. Susan, the manager of a local restaurant, stated that as a White woman, she did not feel it was her place to share her thoughts about racism as it did not affect her. She added that she was unsure that this was a case of racism and wondered if there was another reason why Robert had not been promoted. Rafael angrily demanded of Susan, "Can't you see what is happening here? You sit back without seeing anything and life goes on. Well, life going on means that you keep on reaping the benefits while we keep saying 'maybe next time!'"

After a long, awkward silence, the group leader, Jessica, acknowledged that although she had not personally experienced the negative effects of racism, she felt that it significantly affected the lives of the minority members of the group. She also suggested that, although often unrecognized, racism also limits the lives of majority members. She then asked group members if they would share their experiences with racism. In response, Rafael recalled an incident that occurred when he transferred schools at the age of 16 and his father, who spoke English with an accent, had attempted to enroll him in the honors classes at his new school. Despite his academic achievements and honors placement at his former school, the school administrator suggested that the academic level at the new school was "rigorous" and that Rafael would "surely do better" in the regular core curriculum. It was not until several weeks into the school year, when a teacher recognized Rafael's abilities and advocated for him, that Rafael was placed into the proper classes.

Other minority members described their experiences with racism. Robert reminded the group that these instances only scratched the surface and compared them to leaks in a pipeline, with the full current running hidden underneath. Jessica, the counselor, asked them how it felt to share these experiences with the group. Several of the minority members expressed concern that, although they felt supported by the other minority group members, they were still not sure how these stories would be received by the White members. Jessica then invited them to direct this question to the White members.

Geoffrey, one of the White members, disclosed that he was also uncomfortable and unsure about how to proceed. Although recognizing the stifling nature of racism, he typically tried to "walk around this issue" due, in part, to his own personal feelings of guilt. He gave the example of when he and a Black friend had gone separately to apply for a job at the same place during their college years. His friend had been grilled extensively about taking a year off from classes and asked to provide a thorough explanation of what he had done and where he had been during the year. In the end, his friend was not offered a job, but Geoffrey was quickly given a job despite having also been away for the past year. Robert thanked Geoffrey for recognizing the reality faced by him and other minority group members.

At this point, Linda stated that, although not a racial minority herself, she similarly experienced the adverse effects of oppression and discrimination as a lesbian woman. Rafael questioned whether Linda had experienced the same level of oppression as the racial and ethnic minorities in the group, arguing that nobody would know that she was a lesbian unless she decided to tell them. A heated debate began to develop until Linda, in response to the leader's invitation to recall some of her experiences, talked about feeling marginalized. For example, when she came out to people whom she had considered friends, they had assured her that "it didn't matter," only to later distance themselves from Linda. Several episodes like this had left her wary about forming close relationships with individuals outside of the lesbian and gay community. Jessica, the group counselor, then asked Linda what made her decide to come out to the group in this session. She responded that the manner in which the group had processed issues of racism and oppression encouraged her to disclose, despite her fears of the group keeping her at an arm's distance.

Following Linda's response, Rafael apologized to her for his insensitive comments.

Shortly before the end of the session, the group leader commented that the voices of minorities often go unheard and that dialogue on various forms of prejudice is typically avoided. For this reason, she was moved by their tangible support for one another and by their willingness to take risks through self-disclosure and feedback exchange, despite their anxiety and feelings of vulnerability.

Analysis

The interactions depicted in this interpersonal group are not uncommon in racially mixed groups. Societal norms in the United States typically discourage the open recognition of visible differences between members of different racial or ethnic groups, particularly between members of majority and minority groups. Following her observation of the emergence of subgrouping along racial lines, the group leader took a step toward shaping a norm of open communication about diversity by recognizing that the minority and majority group members may have been experiencing the interaction differently.

The group, replicating larger social norms, initially moved toward a discussion as to whether Robert's experience was indeed a case of racism or, on a larger scale, as to the dimensions of racism on a societal level. The leader, however, suggested that members share their experiences with racism, or vertically disclose. In a diverse group in which the members have had dissimilar experiences outside of the group, vertical disclosure is helpful in providing a context for understanding and empathy. Once minority members had disclosed their experiences with racism, the leader of this group encouraged horizontal disclosure, and members shared their feelings of vulnerability and fear that their experiences would not be validated. As a result of the process of moving

from vertical to horizontal disclosure, Geoffrey, one of the White members of the group, also expressed discomfort and feelings of guilt he had around the issue of race and oppression. This dialogue facilitated the additional disclosure and set the stage for beneficial interpersonal feedback to occur in future interactions.

As often occurs in diverse groups, this group addressed issues of visible diversity prior to realizing that they may have been diverse in less visible ways as well. Linda's disclosure as a lesbian was initially minimized by a racial minority member of the group. By seeking to determine if Linda's reported experience of oppression was comparable to that of the visible minority members, the group ran the risk of engaging itself in the communication mode of intellectual discussion. By inviting Linda to share some of her experiences, the leader helped move the group from a debate on the merits of her experience to a dialogue with the goal of simply understanding her subjective experience. As a consequence, Linda's disclosure was met with empathy and validation from other group members. The leader's process commentary further communicated her caring and helped members understand the meanings of these interactions. Furthermore, it shaped and underscored the importance of the norm of mutual respect and openness in future dialogues.

IMPLICATIONS FOR TRAINING

With the rapid demographic, social, and cultural changes in our society, group counselors can no longer afford to blindly employ theories that are disconnected from the realities of group counseling clients. As this chapter has demonstrated, group counselors face complex and, at times, overwhelming challenges as they strive to provide quality care in the murky context of diversity. For this reason, we emphasize the need for group counselors to keep abreast of multicultural counseling and group counseling literatures, both conceptual and empirical. Within the multicultural counseling field, the joint contributions of theorists, researchers, and clinicians over the past decade have proffered suggestions for infusing diversity-related issues into training programs, including didactic course, practice, and supervision (cf. Abreu, Chung, & Atkinson, 2000; Lopez et al., 1989; Pope-Davis & Coleman, 1997). In stark contrast to the recent emergence of a broad array of training models and perspectives in this literature, however, there has been a lack of conceptual work for multicultural training for group counselors. The group counseling literature on diversity or multicultural competence training consists largely of case studies or anecdotal accounts of training strategies that tend to lack conceptual coherence and empirical basis. Because training efforts to enhance multicultural competence of group counselors are not logically distinguished from research advances in these areas, the pressing need is for greater precision in the definition and assessment of multicultural competence (cf. Ponterotto et al., 2000; Ridley, Baker, & Hill, 2001; Suzuki, McRae, & Short, 2001), both generally and specifically in reference to group counseling practice.

Training programs that attempt to develop the multicultural competence of group counselors may build on conceptual work in the multicultural counselor training literature that falls into one of two categories. The first includes models that are comprehensive in focus and content, as exemplified by Ridley et al.'s (1994) Multicultural Program Development Pyramid (MPDP). The MPDP details a grid in which 10 learning objectives intersect with 10 instructional strategies. The MPDP may serve as a template for the development of a series of graded learning activities and experiences for group counselors. The second category includes approaches or models that are specific in goals, focus, and content.

Clinical supervision is a good example. For clinical supervisors who intend to enhance their supervisees' multicultural competence in group counseling, several approaches may be adapted for this purpose (e.g., Chen, 2001; Constantine, 1997; Martinez & Holloway, 1997). In designing training experiences for supervisees, the supervisor is concerned with questions that are both content focused and pedagogical (Chen, in press): "*How* do I help my supervisees know *what* they need to know and, further, transfer that knowledge into practice?"

Among the existing perspectives in the second category, Chen's (2001) interactional approach to clinical supervision may be a good link between the principles of our dialogical perspective and the multicultural training and supervision of group counselors. Central to this approach are interpersonal communications as a window into the nature of interpersonal relationships and into the character of the interacting participants. Adapted to the context of group counseling supervision, this approach may be modified by the supervisor in the supervision of group trainees, individually or as a group. The supervision group as a "social microcosm" (Yalom, 1995), in particular, provides a context whereby sociocultural roles and expectations may be explored and negotiated. The group supervisor of trainees hence has the benefit of fostering a multilayered analysis that penetrates interpersonal relationships and enhances the opportunity for increased sensitivity and appreciation for diversity issues (Chen, in press). With diversity-related "critical incidents" generated from the trainee for exploration, each supervision session is a reflective inquiry process that aims at helping group counselor trainees to develop a sense of intentionality and a reflective stance in their own practice. Within a supportive yet challenging supervision context, trainees may examine and challenge their tacit and unwarranted assumptions, stereotypes, and beliefs about their group members.

In closing, incorporating diversity into the practice and training of group counselors is not an easy task. In this chapter, we have proposed a perspective to working with diverse counseling groups that underscores the importance of communication as a means through which visible and invisible differences between members can be addressed. Integral to this perspective is the conceptualization of diversity in the group counseling process—not as an entity, but rather as sustained through interaction and moderated by self-disclosure and feedback. Counseling group members' conceptualizations of what constitutes diversity, as well as their understanding of and reactions to similarity and dissimilarity, cycle through the events of the group. The intense emotions that accompany diversity issues often leave the group reluctant and vulnerable in exploring their differences. Invariably, this dialogical process hinges on, to a large extent, the level of multicultural competence of the group counselor in assisting members in negotiating and managing interpersonal risks and vulnerabilities. Group counseling practice and, by extension, counseling supervision are embedded in multiple sociocultural realities and therefore have social and political consequences. In the presence of the group counselor who commits to the fostering of interpersonal learning through the exploration of diversity, group members will likely be rewarded with more meaningful connections rooted in the celebration of human similarities, as well as human differences.

REFERENCES

Abreu, J. M., Chung, R. H. G., & Atkinson, D. R. (2000). Multicultural counseling training: Past, present, and future directions. *The Counseling Psychologist, 28,* 641-656.

Akimoto, S. A., & Sanbonmatsu, D. M. (1999). Differences in self-effacing behavior between European and Japanese Americans. *Journal of Cross-Cultural Psychology, 30,* 159-177.

American Counseling Association (ACA). (1995). *Code of ethics and standards of practice.* Alexandria, VA: Author.

American Psychological Association (APA). (1992). Ethical principles of psychologists and code of conduct. *American Psychologist, 42,* 1597-1611.

American Psychological Association (APA). (1993). Guidelines for providers of psychological services to ethnic, linguistic, and culturally diverse populations. *American Psychologist, 48,* 45-48.

American Psychological Association (APA). (2002). Ethical principles of psychologists and code of conduct. *American Psychologist, 57,* 1060-1073.

Arredondo, P., Toporek, R., Brown, S. P., Jones, J., Locke, D. C., Sanchez, J., et al. (1996). Operationalization of the multicultural counseling competencies. *Journal of Multicultural Counseling and Development, 24,* 42-78.

Atkinson, P., & Hammersley, M. (1994). Ethnography and participant observation. In N. K. Denzin & Y. S. Lincoln (Eds.), *Handbook of qualitative research* (pp. 248-261). Thousand Oaks, CA: Sage.

Brook, D. W., Gordon, C., & Meadow, H. (1998). Ethnicity, culture and group counseling. *Group, 22,* 53-80.

Butler, T., & Fuhriman, A. (1980). Patient perspective on the curative process: A comparison of day treatment and outpatient counseling groups. *Small Group Behavior, 11,* 371-388.

Chen, E. C. (2001). Multicultural counseling supervision: An interactional approach. In J. G. Ponterotto, J. M. Casas, L. A. Suzuki, & C. M. Alexander (Eds.), *Handbook of multicultural counseling* (2nd ed., pp. 801-824). Thousand Oaks, CA: Sage.

Chen, E. C. (in press). Racial-cultural training for supervisors: Goals, foci, and strategies. In R. T. Carter (Ed.), *Handbook of racial-cultural psychology and counseling: Practice and training* (Vol. 2). New York: John Wiley.

Chen, E. C., & Mallinckrodt, B. (2002). Attachment, group attraction, and self-other agreement in interpersonal circumplex problems and perceptions of group members. *Group Dynamics: Theory, Research, and Practice, 6*, 311-324.

Cheng, W. D., Chae, M., & Gunn, R. W. (1998). Splitting and projective identification in multicultural group counseling. *Journal for Specialists in Group Work, 23*, 372-387.

Cohen, B. D. (2000). Intersubjectivity and narcissism in group counseling: How feedback works. *International Journal of Group Psychotherapy, 50*, 163-179.

Coll, C. G., Cook-Nobles, R., & Surrey, J. L. (1997). Building connection through diversity. In J. V. Jordan (Ed.), *Women's growth in diversity* (pp. 176-198). New York: Guilford.

Constantine, M. G. (1997). Facilitating multicultural competency in counseling supervision. In D. B. Pope-Davis & H. L. K. Coleman (Eds.), *Multicultural counseling competencies: Assessment, education and training, and supervision* (pp. 310-324). Thousand Oaks, CA: Sage.

Corey, M. S., & Corey, G. (2002). *Groups: Process and practice* (6th ed.). Pacific Grove, CA: Brooks/Cole.

Crocker, J., & Major, B. (1989). Social stigma and self-esteem: The self-protective properties of stigma. *Psychological Review, 96*, 608-630.

Crocker, J., Voelkl, K., Testa, M., & Major, B. (1991). Social stigma: The affective consequences of attributional ambiguity. *Journal of Personality and Social Psychology, 60*, 218-228.

Deaux, K. (1991). Social identities: Thoughts on structure and change. In R. Curtis (Ed.), *The relational self*: Theoretical convergences in psychoanalysis and social psychology (pp. 77-93). New York: Guilford.

Derlega, V. J., & Berg, J. H. (Eds.). (1987). *Self-disclosure: Theory, research, and therapy*. New York: Plenum.

Ettin, M. F. (1994). Links between group process and social, political and cultural issues. In H. I. Kaplan & B. J. Sadock (Eds.), *Comprehensive group psychotherapy* (3rd ed., pp. 699-716). Baltimore: Williams & Wilkins.

Fenster, A. (1996). Group therapy as an effective treatment modality for people of color. *International Journal of Group Psychotherapy, 46*, 399-416.

Fenster, A., & Fenster, J. (1998). Diagnosing deficits in "basic trust" in multiracial and multicultural groups: Individual or social psychopathology? *Group, 22*, 81-93.

Fiske, S. T., & Taylor, S. E. (1991). *Social cognition*. New York: McGraw-Hill.

Flowers, J. V., & Booarem, C. D. (1989). Four studies toward an empirical foundation for group therapy. *Journal of Social Services Research, 13*, 105-121.

Frey, L. R. (2000). Diversifying our understanding of diversity and communication in groups: Dialoguing with Clark, Anand, and Roberson (2000). *Group Dynamics: Theory, Research and Practice, 4*, 222-229.

Fuhriman, A., & Burlingame, G. M. (1994). Group psychotherapy: Research and practice. In A. Fuhriman & G. M. Burlingame (Eds.), *Handbook of group psychotherapy: An empirical and clinical synthesis* (pp. 3-40). New York: John Wiley.

Gass, S. M., & Varonis, E. (1991). Miscommunication in nonnative speaker discourse. In N. Coupland, H. Giles, & J. Wiemann (Eds.), *"Miscommunication" and problematic talk* (pp. 121-145). Newbury Park, CA: Sage.

Gudykunst, W. B. (1995). Anxiety/uncertainty management (AUM) theory: Current status. In R. L. Wiseman (Ed.), *Intercultural communication theory* (pp. 8-58). Thousand Oaks, CA: Sage.

Gudykunst, W. B., & Kim, Y. Y. (1997). *Communicating with strangers: An approach to intercultural communication* (3rd ed.). Boston: McGraw-Hill.

Hall, E. T. (1976). *Beyond culture*. New York: Doubleday.

Han, A. L., & Vasquez, M. J. T. (1995). Group intervention and treatment with ethnic minorities. In J. F. Aponte, R. Y. Rivers, & J. Wohl (Eds.), *Psychological interventions and cultural diversity* (pp. 110-130). Boston: Allyn & Bacon.

Helms, J. E. (1994). How multiculturalism obscures racial factors in the therapy process: Comment on Ridley et al. (1994), Sodowsky et al. (1994), Ottavi et al. (1994), and

Thompson et al. (1994). *Journal of Counseling Psychology, 41,* 162-165.

Helms, J. E., & Cook, D. A. (1999). *Using race and culture in counseling and counseling: Theory and process.* Boston: Allyn & Bacon.

Ho, D. Y. F. (1995). Internalized culture, culturo-centrism, and transcendence. *The Counseling Psychologist, 23,* 4-24.

Hofstede, G. (1980). *Culture's consequences.* Beverly Hills, CA: Sage.

Hong, Y., Morris, M. W., Chiu, C., & Benet-Martínez, V. (2000). Multicultural minds: A dynamic constructivist approach to culture and cognition. *American Psychologist, 55,* 709-720.

Howell, W. (1982). *The empathic communicator.* Belmont, CA: Wadsworth.

Kelley, H. H. (1972). Causal schemata and the attribution process. In E. E. Jones, D. E. Kanouse, H. H. Kelley, R. E. Nisbett, S. Valins, & B. Weiner (Eds.), *Attribution: Perceiving the causes of behavior* (pp. 151-176). Morrison, NJ: General Learning Press.

Kivlighan, D. M., Jr. (1985). Feedback in group counseling: Review and implications. *Small Group Behavior, 16,* 373-385.

Kivlighan, D. M., Jr., Coleman, M. N., & Anderson, D. C. (2000). Process, outcome, and methodology in group counseling research. In S. D. Brown & R. W. Lent (Eds.), *Handbook of counseling psychology* (3rd ed., pp. 767-796). New York: John Wiley.

Kluckhohn, C., & Murray, H. A. (1953). Personality formation: The determinants. In C. Kluckhohn & H. A. Murray (Eds.), *Personality in nature, society, and culture* (pp. 35-48). New York: Knopf.

Kluckhohn, F. R., & Strodtbeck, F. L. (1961). *Variations in value orientations.* Evanston, IL: Row, Peterson.

Langer, E. J. (1989). *Mindfulness.* Reading, MA: Addison-Wesley.

Leong, F. T. L. (1996). Toward an integrative model for cross-cultural counseling and psychotherapy. *Applied and Preventive Psychology: Current Scientific Perspectives, 5,* 189-209.

Lopez, S. R., Grover, K. P., Holland, D., Johnson, M. J., Kain, C. D., Kanel, K., et al. (1989). Development of culturally sensitive

psychotherapists. *Professional Psychology: Research and Practice, 20,* 369-376.

Markus, H., & Sentis, K. (1982). The self in social information processing. In J. Suls (Ed.), *Psychological perspectives on the self* (Vol. 1, pp. 41-70). Hillsdale, NJ: Lawrence Erlbaum.

Martinez, R. P., & Holloway, E. L. (1997). The supervision relationship in multicultural training. In D. B. Pope-Davis & H. L. K. Coleman (Eds.), *Multicultural counseling competencies: Assessment, education and training, and supervision* (pp. 325-349). Thousand Oaks, CA: Sage.

Miller, D. T., & Prentice, D. A. (1999). Some consequences of a belief in group essence: The category divide hypothesis. In D. A. Prentice & D. T. Miller (Eds.), *Cultural divides: Understanding and overcoming group conflict* (pp. 213-238). New York: Russell Sage.

Patton, M. Q. (1980). *Qualitative evaluation methods.* Beverly Hills, CA: Sage.

Phinney, J. S. (1996). When we talk about American ethnic groups, what do we mean? *American Psychologist, 51,* 918-927.

Ponterotto, J. G., Fuertes, J. N., & Chen, E. C. (2000). Models of multicultural counseling. In S. D. Brown & R. W. Lent (Eds.), *Handbook of counseling psychology* (3rd ed., pp. 639-669). New York: John Wiley.

Pope-Davis, D. B., & Coleman, H. L. K. (Eds.). (1997). *Multicultural counseling competencies: Assessment, education and training, and supervision.* Thousand Oaks, CA: Sage.

Ridley, C. R. (1984). Clinical treatment of the nondisclosing Black client: A therapeutic paradox. *American Psychologist, 39,* 1234-1244.

Ridley, C. R. (1989). Racism in counseling as an adversive behavioral process. In P. B. Pedersen, J. G. Draguns, W. J. Lonner, & J. E. Trimble (Eds.), *Counseling across cultures* (3rd ed., pp. 55-77). Honolulu: University of Hawaii Press.

Ridley, C. R., Baker, D. M., & Hill, C. L. (2001). Critical issues concerning cultural competence. *The Counseling Psychologist, 29,* 822-832.

Ridley, C. R., Mendoza, D. W., Kanitz, B. E., Angermeier, L., & Zenk, R. (1994). Cultural sensitivity in multicultural counseling:

A perceptual schema model. *Journal of Counseling Psychology, 41,* 125-136.

Rutan, J. S., & Stone, W. N. (2001). *Psychodynamic group psychotherapy* (3rd cd.). New York: Guilford.

Shen, W. W., Sanchez, A. M., & Huang, T. (1984). Verbal participation in group therapy: A comparative study on New Mexico ethnic groups. *Hispanic Journal of Behavior Sciences, 6,* 277-284.

Slater, P. E. (1966). *Microcosm: Structural, psychological, and religious evolution in groups.* New York: John Wiley.

Slavin, R. L. (1993). The significance of here-and-now disclosure in promoting cohesion in group counseling. *Group, 17,* 143-150.

Spencer, S. J., Fein, S., Wolfe, C. T., Fong, C., & Dunn, M. A. (1998). Automatic activation of stereotypes: The role of self-image threat. *Personality and Social Psychology Bulletin, 24,* 1139-1152.

Stephan, W. G., Stephan, C. W., Wezel, B., & Cornelius, J. (1991). Intergroup interaction and self-disclosure. *Journal of Applied Social Psychology, 21,* 1370-1378.

Sue, D. W. (2001). Multidimensional facets of cultural competence. *The Counseling Psychologist, 29,* 790-821.

Sue, D. W., Arredondo, P., & McDavis, R. J. (1992). Multicultural competencies and standards: A call to the profession. *Journal of Multicultural Counseling and Development, 20,* 64-88.

Sue, D. W., Bernier, J., Durran, M., Feinberg, L., Pedersen, P., Smith, E., & Vasquez-Nuttall, E.

(1982). Position paper: Multicultural counseling competencies. *The Counseling Psychologist, 10,* 45-52.

Suc, D. W., & Suc, D. (2003). *Counseling the culturally diverse: Theory and practice* (4th ed.). New York: John Wiley.

Suzuki, L. A., McRae, M. B., & Short, E. L. (2001). The facets of cultural competence: Searching outside the box. *The Counseling Psychologist, 29,* 842-849.

Triandis, H. C. (1989). The self and social behavior in differing cultural contexts. *Psychological Review, 96,* 506-517.

Tschuschke, V., & Dies, R. R. (1997). The contribution of feedback to outcome in long-term group counseling. *Group, 21,* 3-15.

Tsui, P., & Schultz, G. L. (1988). Ethnic factors in group process: Cultural dynamics in multiethnic therapy groups. *American Journal of Orthopsychiatry, 58,* 136-142.

Turner, J. C. (1987). *Rediscovering the social group.* Oxford, UK: Blackwell.

Wallach, M. A., Kogan, N., & Bem, D. J. (1962). Group influence on individual risk taking. *Journal of Abnormal and Social Psychology, 65,* 75-86.

White, J. C. (1994). The impact of race and ethnicity on transference and countertransference in combined individual/group therapy. *Group, 18,* 89-99.

Yalom, I. D. (1995). *The theory and practice of group counseling* (4th ed.). New York: Basic Books.

30

Racial and Ethnic Origins of Harassment in the Workplace

Evaluation Issues and Symptomatology

MARIA P. P. ROOT

Seattle, Washington

Ms. S, a 34-year-old Filipina American woman, came from a family of educators. She had worked successfully at a community college in Nevada but wanted less severe weather. Ms. S interviewed and successfully landed a job at a small-town community college that served several surrounding towns. She moved to this working-class community and started with high hopes of finding, if not a permanent home, a home that would be rewarding for a long time. Unfortunately, within 6 months, she was puzzled that she did not receive the support that seemed to be so forthcoming in her interviews. Colleagues, previously friendly, were more distant. She was not informed of department parties on multiple occasions. She tried harder to reach out, but to no avail. She had even changed her style of dress from blazers and trousers or skirts to more casual clothes and grew out her hair due to feedback that she dressed differently—looked different from other faculty on campus. Puzzled, because she saw her clothing as appropriate, she was willing to remove this as an obstacle.

Ms. S was puzzled at her difficulty connecting with the faculty. She had fit in well in her previous department and was able to communicate with even some of the most difficult people. She began to worry when her faculty mentor for promotion and tenure started giving her odd advice. More than a year later, when she asked to start her tenure review, as she was told she could when she was hired, she felt that she was penalized for being organized and going up for an early review. She received embarrassing reviews of her teaching methods, style, and content of her courses from two faculty members who sat in on some lectures. When she was assertive in asking for examples to understand the criticism, she received no further information but was admonished to watch her step. Ms. S was also placed in some difficult and worrisome situations during the course of three tenure committee meetings. One of the head administrators of the college would tell racist jokes, and the faculty would laugh. Ms. S felt the distance between her and committee members grow. Meanwhile, Ms. S started experiencing headaches, muscle spasms, hives, and strange itches. She had difficulty sleeping and felt anxious. Ms. S attempted to work within the system, making the changes that were recommended to her, but by early winter, it was clear that she would not make tenure. She became very anxious and depressed. Her love for teaching was not enough to sustain her in her job. Ms. S sought counseling and eventually sought an attorney. At the time of the evaluation, Ms. S was piecing together odd jobs and sustained a significant loss of income.

From another setting, Mr. R, a 50-year-old African American man, had worked for the same transit service for more than 10 years. Evidence supported his claim that he was respected and a good problem solver. He had repeatedly been voted to a shop steward position starting in his first year on the job. He spent extra time with employees he represented. He put in overtime, not always charging the company. With the hiring of a new employee whom he had helped to get a job, racial harassment toward him started. Graffiti with White supremacist messages appeared on the transit vehicles and in the restrooms. When he complained, he was told to clean it up. A noose had appeared by the water fountain that he drank out of each day. A death threat note with racist language had been slipped through a slot in his locker. He repeatedly tried to bring these events to the administration's attention but with little effective intervention. He began to lose sleep, become irritable with his family, socially withdraw, have panic attacks, and cry on

Sunday nights in anticipation of returning to work on Monday. He developed high blood pressure and gained weight. He felt that he was second-guessing the meaning of some coworkers' actions and comments. Eventually, his physician prescribed antidepressants and strongly encouraged him to enter counseling. As a last resort, he did enter counseling and, within 2 months, came to the conclusion that he had to take a leave from work to maintain his sanity and restore some sense of control over himself and his life. However, taking a leave added to his sense of helplessness. Eventually, he quit his job. This move, too, was difficult. He had difficulty looking for jobs, embarrassed that he was unemployed and fearful of being asked why he left his last job. He started having unpredictable panic attacks that contributed to his reluctance to leave his house. These symptoms started to significantly affect his wife and children. He felt he had failed them, which further contributed to his depression.

Ms. S's and Mr. R's stories provide a backdrop for looking at personal injury psychological evaluations within a culturally and racially appropriate manner. Both were sent by their lawyers for an evaluation of current functioning and possible damages associated with the experiences they sustained in the workplace. They had already filed lawsuits against their former places of employment.

A typical evaluation would consist of a review of the complaint with the Equal Employment Opportunity Commission (EEOC) if this occurred and its findings, a review of the legal complaint, a review of personnel files (including performance evaluations, memos, corrective action memos, commendations, and courses or trainings completed), and a review of medical and counseling records, possible collateral interviews, and the legal complaint. They would likely take the Minnesota Multiphasic Personality Inventory (MMPI-2) and perhaps some other psychological test. In addition, Mr. R and Ms. S would be interviewed. This interview would typically last 90 minutes to 2 hours, focusing on childhood, symptoms, brief prior job history, brief employment history related to the complaint, and an assessment of other possible stressors to account for psychological distress. Each of their attempts to explain that the obstacles and events felt racial or engendered in nature would receive, most likely, minimal probing. The line of interview probing might feel as though the interviewer was thinking that the client was overreacting. The report would provide a brief history, including a statement of the referral, procedures, demeanor during the interview, test results, and conclusions. These conclusions often state whether the person currently fulfills any psychological diagnoses and the certainty to which these can be attributed to the alleged workplace harassment.

This chapter provides theoretical explanations for why racial and ethnic origins of harassment in the workplace are particularly damaging to an individual and the extent of damage it may set in motion. It further outlines the relevant aspects of an evaluation for claims of this nature and the diagnoses that are common. Without this knowledge, many typical psychological evaluations may add injury to possible sustained injuries associated with the case for which the client is being evaluated, particularly when it involves racial, cultural, or ethnic origins of harassment. The reader familiar with sexual harassment will find much in common with the origins of distress caused by racial, cultural, or ethnic origins of harassment (O'Donohue, 1997). Race, in particular, as with gender, often represents a master status on which fears are projected. In addition, a secondary class status has been experienced that makes these individuals more vulnerable to maltreatment in the workplace. Allport (1954), in his classic text *The Nature of Prejudice,* defined racism as "an antipathy based upon a faulty and inflexible generalization.

It may be felt or expressed. It may be directed toward a group as a whole, or towards an individual because he is a member of that group" (p. 9). He also observed that anti-woman sentiments occur and survive with the same dynamic as racism. For many women of color who are harassed in the workplace, they are the recipients of the intersection of racism and sexual harassment.

With the passage of Title VII of the Civil Rights Act of 1964, which prohibits discrimination on the basis of minority status—specifically, race, sex, national origin, color, or religion—harassment policy guidelines have been set forth in the workplace. Nevertheless, there has been a delay in the appearance of lawsuits claiming racial or national origins of color discrimination in the courts, which have appeared in notable numbers only in the past decade. This delay may be due to several factors, including the fact that in 1991, the Civil Rights Act was amended to provide the foundation for recipients of discrimination to legally seek relief from the problem as well as damages (Lindermann & Kadue, 1999). Several high-profile racial suits have appeared in newspapers across the country since the Civil Rights Act of 1991 was amended. Some of these suits have awarded plaintiffs significant damages of more than $1 million (e.g., Haines, 1996).

The literature on racial or ethnic origins of harassment primarily documents discrimination against persons of African descent (e.g., Forman, Williams, & Jackson, 1997; Mays, Coleman, & Jackson, 1999), but it extends to all groups in which persons are deemed racially or ethnically different. Issues of accent, dress, type of food eaten, and language spoken other than English at work have been used as sources of discrimination. Loo (1994) has documented and defined racism against Asian American veterans in the service of their duty assignments in the Vietnam War. Nevertheless, the public is more familiar with the type of racism that is based on skin color and racism against persons of African descent. Forman et al. (1997) documented that African Americans report being the recipients of lifetime experiences of racism at approximately twice the frequency of White peers and almost three times the frequency compared to Whites in a 1-year reporting period. The work setting, as a source of discrimination, becomes important as it shapes the way in which discrimination, as well as its motives and consequences, takes place. Discrimination in the workplace is typically not life threatening, but it can be. At the very least, it threatens a personal sense of safety and, as time goes on, may threaten one's ability to earn a living as the debilitating effects of chronic harassment take a toll on one's spirit and ability to concentrate on work. Researchers report the workplace setting as among one of the most frequent sites of discrimination for African American men and women (Gary, 1995; Sigelman & Welch, 1991). Weiss, Ehrlich, and Larcom (1991-1992) interviewed a stratified random sample of 2,078 people in the United States in 1989 over the telephone. They found that 35% of respondents had experienced some form of the racial or ethnic origins of violence, although most incidences were not reported. The incidences tallied were not restricted to the workplace. However, they found that of 1,372 respondents who were working, 39% experienced some form of work-related violence attributed to acts of prejudice. The forms of prejudice were expressed through jokes and comments, many of which were oriented toward skin color or race and defamation of the reference group to which one belonged. Prejudice can also be expressed in the form of threats through notes and actions, the presence and tolerance for racist graffiti, verbal threats of harm, threatening phone calls, assignments to certain jobs, refusal to promote, workplaces and equipment being messed up, the presence of White supremacist literature and symbols, ridicule for lack of English-language fluency, and the presence of nooses, swastikas, racist cartoons, and other vehicles for racist expression.

RACISM IN THE WORKPLACE

Institutional racism and discrimination do not have to be intentional for them to have psychological and physical consequences (Weiss et al., 1991-1992). Defending the perpetrators or the institutions that ignore allegations of harassment often involves trying to suggest that if there was no intent, harm could not ensue or must be minimal. However, lack of conscious malicious intentions does not clinically correlate with the lack of significant negative effects on one's quality of life and psychological well-being. The consequences or effects of harassing behavior are the focus of the person affected. Because this type of stress or trauma is perpetrated by a person, the impact of such actions is greater than if one sustained injury in an industrial accident or natural disaster (Janoff-Bulman, 1992; Root, 1992).

Institutional racism is characterized by practices or policies that systematically limit opportunities for people who historically have been characterized as psychologically, intellectually, or physically deficient or limited in capacity by virtue of attributes assigned or assumed based on assumed race, ethnicity, or ethnic origins (Katz & Taylor, 1988). Although a company harassment policy provides an avenue for complaint and conveys a message of expectations of respectful behavior, it does not guarantee a harassment-free environment. Management must enforce policies to make it clear that racial or ethnic origins of harassment will not be tolerated. Although an agency or institution may have policies in place intended to remedy racial discrimination, individual representatives may nevertheless perpetuate discrimination. If they occupy positions of authority, such as a supervisor or a manager, employees find it very difficult to inform someone still higher up that the workplace has hostility or that inappropriate behaviors create obstacles to work. If superiors are the source of discrimination, this provides a message that harassment is okay to subordinates. Oftentimes, companies that have anti-harassment policies assume that the harassment is by an equal-status coworker and recommend that the employee inform his or her supervisor or "appropriate" personnel. When an agency does not take swift action either to investigate or correct the actions of the harassing persons, the institution or workplace colludes with the perpetrator and perpetuates institutional racism through the individual. Reporting may be that much more difficult when the harassment has a racial or gendered component because of potential power differences, isolation in the workplace as being part of a minority group, and reluctance to bring further attention or even retaliation on one's self.

The evaluator must challenge several assumptions about racial and ethnic origins of discrimination and harassment in the workplace. Although the behaviors that constitute harassment may not be obvious to everyone, particularly if they are not sensitive to its many faces, the insidious effects of racism and discrimination can be life changing. These experiences are situated historically in U.S. race relations. This history lays the foundations for the level of seriousness that the consequences of these types of processes, leveled at an individual, may have (Root, 1992).

In summary, at least five assumptions must be examined in doing an evaluation:

1. Poor treatment in the workplace, when it is intertwined explicitly with racial comments, even if occurring at different times but in the same workplace, can be impossible to separate from racial discrimination. It appears the same, regardless of intent.

2. Some people, no matter how overt their discriminatory or prejudiced actions may be, will be ignorant or defensive; they will be unwilling or unable to perceive their actions as discriminatory and harmful. At the extreme, they may feel entitled to discriminate.

3. Despite pervasive societal and legal efforts to undo racial prejudice, it still exists.

4. Supervisors may rely on White privilege in addition to their supervisory role to provide them the status to lie and be believed over other employees or to be perceived as more credible than their employees may be.

5. Although an agency or business may have a clear policy against racial discrimination, it does not preclude it or the persons representing it from operating in ways that are discriminatory and perpetuate institutional racism.

EXAMPLES OF HARASSING OR DISCRIMINATORY BEHAVIORS AND STRATEGIES

Harassing behavior can range from death threats with concomitant racially inappropriate remarks to stereotyping. It is impossible to provide an exhaustive list of examples to cover a broad range of potentially infinite discriminatory and harassing actions. Instead, common strategies are listed with an example. At its extreme, the combined strategies result in someone feeling tortured while held hostage. Although one solution is to quit the job, for some people, these are jobs they have held for 20 years, and it is unreasonable and difficult to think of quitting; it could be hard to find comparable work elsewhere, particularly if one has advanced in pay or status within the system. These advances may not automatically transfer to other employment.

Simple discrimination. This includes name-calling, racial epithets, stereotyped imitations of accents or vernacular speech, graffiti, racist cartoons, and racist jokes. For example, a

Chinese American firefighter is told by his chief, "There is a 'good Charlie Chan' movie on television tonight. You should watch it."

Administrative discrimination. Promotions are blocked. A less qualified White person is selected. For example, an African American man has been used to train the last three men promoted ahead of him but junior to him. He has even acted as the acting manager at various times when the position has been vacant.

Colonization strategy. A more insidious trauma is inflicted when other employees of color are used to perform the discriminatory actions. When a racial minority woman is involved, she may be compared to another minority woman whose behavior is held up as ideal. This is the Madonna/whore contrast used in racial stereotyping (i.e., the good minority vs. the bad minority). For example, an employee is told that she is not the recipient of racial discrimination because other minorities have been promoted. Another female colleague of color, who is particularly compliant, will be used as an example. It is either said directly or suggested that the complainant should try to be more like her. In a different setting, an African American manager may be used to tell an African American employee that he or she should not be affected by the racist actions and turn the other cheek.

Low expectations. Employees of color are assigned less desirable, less challenging, or dead-end assignments.

Bystander apathy. An employee is subjected to racial jokes and racial epithets daily. These may be directed at him or her or toward other persons. Repeated use in the workplace can reduce an employee's sense of safety. Vicarious psychological injury can result from the stereotyping as well as the diffusion of responsibility when no one else is willing to take action or sees a need for action. For example, a Cambodian American man told his coworkers that it was hurtful when people made fun of his accent. However, no one made attempts to stop other coworkers from this behavior.

Modern racism. A boss accused of discrimination or harassment will point out that they have hired other minorities and, in fact, done favors for these particular employees. Dovidio, Gaertner, Kawakami, and Hodson (2002) described aversive racism in the workplace as persons denying they would ever be prejudiced and, in certain circumstances, might be helpful in ways that support their claims. However, in laboratory settings, the data suggest that the subtle ways in which they behave and do or do not take action suggest that they are uncomfortable and may discriminate in an interracial setting. For example, a manager may provide some flextime to accommodate a young Latina mother's child care arrangements. Simultaneously, she provides messages that this employee has limited abilities and is untrustworthy.

Servant strategy. An employer expects the employee to baby-sit, do extra work, show up to facilitate some aspect of work on days off, and so forth, in line with a personal maid, butler, or baby-sitter.

Double standard. The employee has less room for errors. Errors count more than when a White employee makes them. Policies of confidentiality may be violated if negative information is sought.

Lack of training. A new employee is not offered the help offered to previous or other new employees, so this employee's performance will suffer and he or she will be at a disadvantage in performing the responsibilities of the job. An employee seeking a promotion may be denied classes, trainings, or other opportunities to keep him or her competitive for promotions.

Unrealistic expectations. These expectations may include meeting unreasonable deadlines or being assigned important projects in which failures or mistakes will be public. In this way, the public failure will allow other people to take over the harassment.

Mischaracterization. Stereotypes are imposed on the individual, positive or negative. When positive stereotypes exist, negative stereotypes may emerge. An employee's reactions to reports of racist events may then be characterized as overly sensitive, hysterical, and dramatic. Those who attempt to seek relief from the incidences may be characterized as unassertive with coworkers, overly dependent, and ineffective.

Isolation. Direct messages to coworkers or indirect messages may encourage previously friendly coworkers to avoid an employee. Subsequently, they are threatened even more by not knowing if they are believed and being watched or if reports are being made on their actions.

Lethal discrimination. At the extreme are death threats made verbally or in writing, attempts to run over people or hit people with vehicles, tampering with chemicals or equipment in the environment, and the presence of guns, knives, and other weapons that threaten bodily harm or death. For example, an African American man's anxiety escalated when an employee who had been harassing him for months showed up to work with a rifle in his car and made sure that he let him know that he hoped he "wouldn't be forced to use it."

SORTING OUT THE SEQUELAE TO EXPOSURE TO ENVIRONMENTS THAT ARE RACIALLY OR ETHNICALLY HARASSING

If someone is diagnosed as suffering acute or long-term harassment or discrimination, that person is likely to fulfill a diagnosis of some form of affective or anxiety disorder. Neither of these disorders, however, alone or together, can capture the full picture of those people who have recurrent intrusive thoughts, nightmares, and even flashbacks of work situations. Their tendency to socially withdraw, wish to die, or quit their line of work is not just depression or anxiety. It is related to suffering a trauma that rendered them tortured, helpless, and overwhelmed by their capacity to cope. In an interview situation, one might be perceived as particularly reactive, even with hysterical features, if the evaluator does not understand the potential destructiveness of racism. For many people, their symptoms are captured well by posttraumatic stress disorder (PTSD) and acute stress reaction except for Criterion A, threat of death or bodily injury to self or another (American Psychiatric Association, 1994, p. 427). However, when someone has been physically threatened, he or she may best be diagnosed with an acute stress reaction and, after a period of time, PTSD. In this section, conducting the assessment and understanding symptoms are core.

Approaching the Assessment

The evaluator has the difficult position of sorting out if the distress makes sense, given the meaning of the individual's experiences to them in the context of his or her life. The evaluator must have the experience and the means to sort out if the client's story and symptoms make sense. Evaluators must place their reactions in the context of the client's past history, the context within which the client works, and the meaning of being affected by the harassment or discrimination. Most often, clients, whether self-referred for therapy or referred by a lawyer for evaluation, are competent, motivated workers who take pride in their jobs and make a point of trying to excel. They often pursue a legal case for social justice reasons. Although the possibility of a monetary settlement is important, it is often secondary. Those persons who seek therapy often do so at the prompting of their families, physicians, or attorneys who have seen them symptomatic for an extended period of time with little improvement.

A frequent shortcoming of conventional personal injury evaluations that involve discrimination is that evaluators lack an understanding of the political context for comprehending discrimination in the historical context relevant to the personal life of the client. Agreeing that racism is uncivil and illegal in the workplace, they may not understand why it is important to have the clients tell their stories about what happened to them in the workplace. This approach to the evaluation heightens the fear by many minority status individuals that the evaluator does not understand them in context and may be vulnerable to stereotyping them. Furthermore, because the evaluator may reflect some characteristics of the harasser, the age, power differential in the evaluation setting, racial status, and gender of the evaluator may be triggers for defensive or cautious behavior. Without awareness by evaluators that some of their characteristics may be triggers for increased anxiety, cautiousness, and overgeneralization, the evaluators may proceed in a way that compromises their goals. It important for evaluators to inquire or assess if the client's cautiousness in the evaluation is possibly related to these factors. Evaluators may want to get physical, behavioral, and status descriptions of the persons who have been the alleged source of harassment or discrimination. By doing this, evaluators have a greater context within which to evaluate the client's defensiveness and behavior and may decrease the defensiveness in context rather than inadvertently heightening it.

Besides doing a standard evaluation that obtains some family history to put an individual in historical context, the evaluator also needs to obtain an education history and thumbnail sketch of work history. The meaning of these latter two histories is sometimes more significant if evaluators also know some of the educational history and employment or career history of their clients' families. This gives some sense of the clients' expectations of themselves and their families' expectations. Often, tremendous guilt and depression ensue because some may believe they have let their family down or have let their reference group down by being stereotyped or unable to be strong in the face of adversity. For example, an African American salesman was fired despite being a top performer for several evaluation cycles. He felt ashamed and embarrassed because of the stereotypes of unemployed Black men and, despite his strong work ethic, his fear of going out for interviews for new jobs while unemployed. His inability to cope contradicted his sense of being a strong and effective Black man.

It is important to remember that as the evaluator, one's job is not to assess whether the things they claim happened—unless there are obvious disparities in evidence and narrative. One determines if the clients' stories and symptoms are congruent; if the clients are competent to tell their stories, have sustained harm, or might be feigning symptomatology for secondary gain; the extent that their symptoms are seemingly caused by the events they report; the meaning of the events to them; how they have tried to cope to reduce their symptoms; and any relevant diagnoses.

The MMPI-2 is the gold standard of psychological evaluation, but it is not appropriate to use with persons who have grown up in a culture that is not of European origin and philosophy of thinking. For example, in evaluating a man who had grown up and schooled in Somalia through his young adult years, it was not appropriate to use the MMPI-2. Many of the items would have different meanings than are typically employed, and norms do not exist to help the interpretation of a profile configuration for someone from this cultural background. This means that the clinical interview will likely be longer. Testing is often conducted before the first session or immediately preceding it. The MMPI-2 is a source of hypotheses that must be confirmed and disconfirmed.

If possible, I suggest that the interview be conducted in two sessions. The interviews can take from 4 to 10 hours. The length is affected by the chronicity of events in the workplace, the age of the client, the level of distress the client is experiencing, and the client's style of narration. The evaluator will listen with a critical but compassionate stance. The interviews must include the range of information obtained in conventional evaluations: work history, educational history, family background, mental health history, alcohol and drug history, and the meaning of what happened to the client and his or her understanding or personal theory of why it happened. However, in evaluating someone who has been chronically harassed due to his or her ethnic origins or racial background, one must add elements to the evaluation to form an opinion on any psychological damages the client has sustained, make relevant diagnosis, and estimate what, if anything, the individual might need to do to overcome the harm he or she has sustained. These elements include allowing clients to tell their stories. Clients will more often than not spontaneously offer elements of their stories throughout other aspects of the interview. However, I suggest the evaluator only obtain enough information initially to provide an overview while reassuring the clients that they will be able to tell their stories. This reassurance will reduce interruptions and decrease anxiety when the evaluator attempts to ask clients to hold that part of the story until later.

The first session provides contextual background obtained in a typical evaluation described above. With this interview, the results of testing and a review of documentation

are discussed; the second interview is designed to ask clients to tell their stories, parts of which will already have emerged.

The second interview establishes diagnoses and possible other sources of explanation or origin for any diagnoses. Thus, this interview must include an exploration or inventory of the other stressors such as assaults outside of the workplace, relationship strife, or family problems that have occurred in a relevant time period that may be a likely or alternate source of explanation for symptoms. For many persons, telling a story of ethnic or racial harassment must be contextualized. It can take up to several hours to tell such a story, which may be longer than a typical evaluation. The evaluator is able to observe how the story seems to affect the client, as well as any changes in composure, emotion, language, coherence, or organization in telling the story. Any changes provide hypotheses to be explored.

When clients do tell their stories, there are typically discreet events that are particularly distressing. It can be useful to ask if there was anything significant about how, where, or who took the actions. What was at stake for them, or how helpless or powerful did they feel? Were there any witnesses? How did the witness act? Besides asking what action was taken to their knowledge to address this event, it is useful to ask what their expectation was for reporting the event. If they did not report the event, then why not? Ask for the personal meaning of the event. The evaluator can make a list of discreet events and ask the client to rate each event on a scale of 1 to 10, with 1 representing *slight distress* and 10 being *extremely distressing*. As a way of checking consistency and further understanding clients' source of distress, clients can be asked to indicate the three most distressing events to them. Again, assessing why each of these events was more distressing than an event with a lower rating is informative. During this part of the interview, there is often more visible distress, including crying, shaking, sweating, rapid breathing, and dissociating.

The other critical element typically not included in these types of evaluations is a history of experiences with racism or ethnic discrimination. This history necessarily goes back to childhood. These experiences can be elicited as most potent experiences, first experiences, and experiences that are irritants but do not feel damaging to their core. The therapist can also explore the meaning of these experiences and how and if they changed their worldview, coping, or approaches to certain situations. It is useful to find out the family value placed on silence or speaking out about this type of discrimination and the coping that was imparted. Another element of this interview is asking for the person's awareness of what environmental cues now serve as triggers for anxious feelings. The triggers are not always obvious as second-order conditioning may imbue certain people, places, actions, statements, sights, sounds, or smells with threatening value. Unfortunately, the consequence of racial harassment sometimes conditions "Whiteness" to serve as a trigger for anxiety or intrusive thoughts because, more often than not, White persons usually are the perpetrators of racial harassment in the workplace.

Last, symptoms need to be assessed. It is useful to ask when symptoms began and even to ask for ratings on a Likert-type scale for symptoms such as anxiousness, worthlessness, loss of drive, anxiety, and so on. A list of 10 common types of symptom clusters are described below that I have compiled after years of working with persons who have sustained harm from working in environments in which they have been discriminated against racially or ethnically.

Ten Common Sequelae

The following list of 10 symptoms has been gleaned over 15 years of working with persons who have specifically been self-referred for therapy or for evaluation due to workplace discrimination or harassment. I do not sense that the list of symptoms is different for these two populations. However, during litigation, the trauma story is kept alive through depositions, requests for documentation, meetings with attorneys, and settlement hearings or trial. Thus, the immediate distress may be more obvious and sometimes more acute.

Many persons subjected to acute or repetitive acts of discrimination experience several of the following clusters of symptoms. Weiss et al. (1991-1992) reported many of these symptoms in their survey of persons who had experienced ethnoviolence. The presence of several of these symptoms suggests that clients struggle against and with wounds to some core aspect of their spirit, reputation, or psychological defenses. Often, the harassment and discrimination are experienced as an attempt to destroy character. With chronic harassment, a client may start to manifest symptoms associated with being held hostage. Thinking about what has happened and what might happen next monopolizes his or her daily ruminations. The client may wonder what he or she could have done differently. This individual is acutely aware of his or her harasser's actions.

For clinical purposes, I suggest that the experience of any racism does stress an individual at some level. Chronic racial or ethnic origins of harassment have some lasting impact on the causation of symptoms that may last from months to years. One to three clusters of symptoms below represent the low end of psychological harm. However, if these are Clusters 1, 3, and 4 or 7 in any degree of moderateness, the effects are moderately severe. Endorsing four to seven clusters usually represents a moderate degree of psychological harm. Experiencing more than seven of the clusters represents severe impact. Often, Cluster 9 is one of the last to be manifested. Cluster 6 may be resistant to erosion for a long time, particularly in confident people. If clients tend to keep a multiracial or multiethnic support system, they are more resistant to experiencing Cluster 10.

1. *Anxiety*. The client may dread going to work. This is particularly notable when the client has been someone who has looked forward to going to work or has derived a considerable amount of identity from work. She or he may experience panic attacks, bad dreams, somatic symptoms, or an intensification of chronic physical or mental conditions. For example, someone with a tendency to have high blood pressure may manifest much higher blood pressure, blood sugar in diabetics may be harder to control, arthritis may be more painful and extensive, and migraine conditions may be more frequent.

2. *Paranoia*. The client manifests extreme self-consciousness or second-guesses others' intentions. She or he worries about the attributions that people make of her or him based on race or ethnicity. Similarly, there is focus on what misinformation people may have. This cluster of symptoms contributes to a desire to avoid people and makes it more difficult to seek other employment in the same city. Some clients may find themselves changing their routines of places they frequent such as the grocery, car wash, or church because of their extreme self-consciousness and worry about what other people might know and what misinformation they might believe. These symptoms are particularly acute in persons for whom the harassment is made public through news spots on television or radio or in published stories. She or he starts to fear a loss of positive reputation or fears damage to an otherwise neutral or positive reputation.

3. *Depression*. The following are symptoms of a major affective disorder for which the person may qualify: social withdrawal from friends, family, or pleasurable social activities; difficulty getting out of bed; difficulty keeping up with responsibilities and chores (or an awareness that accomplishing things feels exhausting); fatigue; and irritability. In general, a person may feel exhausted keeping up with life. At its extreme, one may wish to die to be relieved of misery and to relieve their families of the ripple effects or the toll their misery or unemployment takes on the family.

4. *Sleep Difficulties*. Although difficulty sleeping is a symptom of depression, it is considered a separate cluster because it is often one of the first symptoms. One may have difficulty falling or staying asleep or may wake up early. Often in trying to sleep, racing or intrusive thoughts persist about past events or anticipation of the next day of work.

5. *Loss of Confidence*. Previously confident people lose confidence in their ability to trust and evaluate people. Without this confidence, many interpersonal interactions become that much more difficult, which can increase anxiety in interpersonal interactions. This is particularly significant if someone's job has entailed interacting with the public, supervising people, or doing public relations work.

6. *Worthlessness*. This worthlessness reflects a loss of confidence in one's value or competence as a worker despite evidence to the contrary. This symptom cluster can reflect an extreme sense of humbleness to the extent that one truly believes he or she may have nothing to offer and is totally replaceable.

7. *Intrusive Cognitions*. Involuntary obsessional, intrusive replays and recollections of meaningful events are unpredictable at times and draining. Sleep may provide little escape from these intrusions, which may manifest in bad dreams or nightmares. Intrusions may impair work performance. The energy to stop intrusions may leave one more exhausted at the end of the day. Simply being at work, meeting deadlines, going to meetings, having

performance evaluations, seeing an item on the news, or passing by a manager's office can serve as a trigger for these intrusions.

8. *Helplessness.* Feelings of helplessness revolve around two things. One may feel helpless to stop the harassment with individual confrontation or the implementation of complaint procedures. Someone who does not want to quit his or her job may feel trapped. Second, systematic harassment often results in rewriting one's character or mischaracterizing that person's competence, values, and personality. This mischaracterization is often replete with racial or ethnic stereotypes such as *laziness, untrustworthy, sexually provocative, sneaky, addicted, accent too heavy,* and *unqualified.*

9. *Loss of Drive.* This cluster of symptoms often emerges after prolonged harassment and sometimes after one has left his or her job. A formerly ambitious person does not feel ambitious. Assumptions of how the world works have been shattered. An extreme but frequent manifestation of this cluster is the desire to abandon one's career or change one's line of work. Someone who has formerly initiated projects may not do so for an extended period of time. The loss of drive or ambition, coupled with other symptom clusters such as worthlessness, anxiety, and paranoia, makes seeking work very difficult. During job interviews, a person may have difficulty projecting competence and desire for the job.

10. *False Positives.* The interpersonal experience in the workplace may result in overgeneralizing certain characteristics and associating them with possible harm. In an effort to protect oneself against further harm, one may become suspicious or anxious of persons who resemble the harasser. Thus, the client may have become more suspicious of persons racially or ethnically similar to the person who has harmed him or her. This is more often the case with persons who have not previously experienced significant racism or discrimination than those who have had significant racist experiences over their lifetime.

Other typical symptoms include exacerbation of physical symptoms, such as migraines, acne, headaches, and skin conditions, or the development of physical conditions that are serious, such as high blood pressure, diabetes, asthma, and autoimmune conditions. Other physical responses may include hives, nausea, sweating, and chest pains. Williams and colleagues have documented the correlation of stress, minority status, racism, and physical health (e.g., Ren, Amick, & Williams, 1999). Fang and Myers (2001) and Mays et al. (1999) have demonstrated a correlation between physical response and symptomatology to the stress of racism. Landrine and Klonoff (1996) have studied the correlation of the increased tendency toward smoking and increased psychiatric symptomatology in African Americans who score higher on an inventory measuring exposure to racist events. Weiss et al. (1991-1992), in a random survey conducted in 1989, found that the perception of prejudice in different environments, including the workplace, resulted in both physical and psychological symptoms.

One common psychological consequence of chronic harassment in the workplace is the desire to abandon this line of work as the type of work and the conditions associated with it become triggers for many symptoms associated with the original harassment. Although it is not in the purview of the evaluator to help clients feel psychologically better after an evaluation, it is important for the evaluator to understand the feasibility of the client's changing work, the source of this desire, and the meaning of changing one's line of work. Sometimes, a change of careers may further exacerbate the trauma, with loss of income, status, and a profound sense of grief.

Diagnoses

The most common diagnoses given following the impact of racial, cultural, or ethnic origins of harassment are acute stress disorder, post-traumatic stress disorder, adjustment disorder with depressed mood or with mixed anxiety and depressed mood, major depressive disorder, generalized anxiety disorder, and panic disorder without agoraphobia, using the fourth edition of the *Diagnostic and Statistical Manual of Mental Disorders* (*DSM-IV*) as a guide (American Psychiatric Association, 1994). Although the experience of chronic racial or ethnic origins of harassment can be traumatic, it can be difficult to meet Criterion A1 of the diagnosis, which requires threat of bodily harm or fear for one's life or physical safety. In this case, PTSD is still a useful conceptualization, but a diagnosis of adjustment disorder, major depressive disorder, or one of the anxiety disorder diagnoses may capture most elements of the psychological distress.

Existing theories provide explanations for the symptoms that emerge in the context of chronic racial harassment. The social psychological theories that are useful, offered by Perloff (1983), Janoff-Bulman (1992), and Lerner (1980), suggest that damage comes from confusion when the person is confronted with a world that does not operate according to rules of justice or fairness. Although clients will typically agree that this is not a fair world, their psychological defenses, like those of most persons, are constructed to believe and make order out of how the world operates. When this is profoundly challenged, they become aware that they have less control over what happens to them than they thought. Perloff (1983) proposed a shift in vulnerability from unique to universal that creates confusion and disorientation in beliefs about causality. It is common for people to resort to believing that when bad things happen to a person, there is usually a rational explanation. Some "unique" characteristic of the person or his or her behavior must serve as at least a partial explanation of causing his or her vulnerability to victimization. Thus, an individual may believe that if a person does his or her job conscientiously and with pride, is collegial to coworkers, or goes the extra mile, bad things will not happen to that person in the workplace. This is belief in a "just world" (Lerner, 1980). When bad things do happen to an individual who holds this view, he or she does not have a way of comprehending causality. This creates anxiety. Quickly, this individual comes to believe that what operates is "universal vulnerability," which stems from merely being perceived as a member of a group that holds lower status and about which other workers attribute stereotypes. This essentially shatters assumptions about how the world works and causes significant disequilibrium (Janoff-Bulman, 1992) and a sense of helplessness. Helplessness has been causally linked to depression.

Behavioral conditioning theories also provide useful ways of understanding how helplessness develops and how environmental stimuli acquire threat value. Repeated exposure to harassment without effective intervention or ability to stop it creates learned helplessness. Out of self-preservation, certain cues associated with events can acquire threatening value; they become discriminative stimuli, causing significant anxiety. These triggers can result in false-positive responses to threat as a way of minimizing harm. The individual has to work very consciously to try to prevent this type of conditioning from taking place. Most individuals are not initially aware that this conditioning has taken place.

SUMMARY

When the workplace is the site of chronic discrimination, it has psychological consequences for most individuals. Although the Civil

Rights Act of 1964 was the foundation for civil liberties protection against discrimination on the basis of sex, race, color, national origins, and religion, it was the amended Civil Rights Act of 1991 that began the significant presence of lawsuits against these forms of discrimination in the workplace and forced many businesses and corporations to provide messages and training emphasizing that discriminatory behavior is not to be tolerated in the work environment. The proliferation of lawsuits based on discrimination related to race, color, or ethnic origins trails their emergence based on sex.

This chapter provides a foundation for elements of the evaluation process that can be converted into elements of history taking for therapy. These evaluations must necessarily ask for details of the story and take a history of experiences with racism. The psychological consequences and the explanations for the impact of symptomatology were offered.

In general, people are resilient. However, the damage of repeated racism in the workplace ensues from a sense of threat to one's means of a livelihood, sense of regard or value in the workplace, and disbelief that overt racism can exist on a repeated basis, even after brought to the attention of superiors. When it occurs in the workplace, one can be both trapped and shocked. It profoundly challenges a person's sense of causality in the world and his or her sense of safety. These experiences almost always move an individual from the prevailing sense of invulnerability for self and unique vulnerability for victims to a sense of universal vulnerability from which she or he is not exempt simply based on his or her minority status.

REFERENCES

Allport, G. W. (1954). *The nature of prejudice.* Reading, MA: Addison-Wesley.

American Psychiatric Association. (1994). *Diagnostic and statistical manual of mental disorders* (4th ed.). Washington DC: Author.

Civil Rights Act, Pub. L. No. 88-352, Title VII, 42 U.S.C. § 2000e (1964, 1991).

Dovidio, J. F., Gaertner, S. L., Kawakami, K., & Hodson, G. (2002). Why can't we get along? Interpersonal biases and interracial distrust. *Cultural Diversity and Ethnicity Minority Psychology, 8,* 88-102.

Fang, C. Y., & Myers, H. F. (2001). The effects of racial stressors and hostility on cardiovascular reactivity in African American and Caucasian men. *Health Psychology, 20*(1), 64-70.

Forman, T. A., Williams, D. R., & Jackson, J. S. (1997). Race, place, and discrimination. *Perspectives on Social Problems, 9,* 231-261.

Gary, L. (1995). African American men's perceptions of racial discrimination: A sociocultural analysis. *Social Work Research, 19*(4), 207-216.

Haines, T. W. (1996). J. C. Penney told to pay $1.5 million in race suit. *The Seattle Times,* pp. A1, A15.

Janoff-Bulman, R. (1992). *Shattered assumptions: Towards a new psychology of trauma.* New York: Free Press.

Katz, P. A., & Taylor, D. A. (Eds.). (1988). *Eliminating racism.* New York: Plenum.

Landrine, H., & Klonoff, E. A. (1996). The schedule of racist events: A measure of racial discrimination and a study of its negative physical and mental health consequences. *Journal of Black Psychology, 22*(2), 144-168.

Lerner, M. J. (1980). *The belief in a just world.* New York: Plenum.

Lindermann, B. T., & Kadue, D. D. (1999). *Sexual harassment in employment law: 1999 cumulative supplement.* Washington, DC: Bureau of National Affairs.

Loo, C. M. (1994). Race-related PTSD: The Asian American Vietnam veteran. *Journal of Traumatic Stress, 7*(4), 1-20.

Mays, V. M., Coleman, L. M., & Jackson, J. S. (1999). Perceived race-based discrimination, employment status, and job stress in a national sample of Black women: Implications for health outcomes. *Journal of Occupational Health Psychology, 1,* 319-329.

O'Donohue, W. (Ed.). (1997). *Sexual harassment: Theory, research, and treatment.* Boston: Allyn & Bacon.

Perloff, L. S. (1983). Perceptions of vulnerability to victimization. *Journal of Social Issues, 39,* 41-62.

Ren, X. S., Amick, B. C., & Williams, D. R. (1999). Racial/ethnic disparities in health: The interplay between discrimination and socioeconomic status. *Ethnicity & Disease, 9*(2).

Root, M. P. P. (1992). Reconstructing the impact of trauma on personality. In L. S. Brown & M. Ballou (Eds.), *Personality and psychopathology: Feminist reappraisals* (pp. 229-265). New York: Guilford.

Sigelman, L., & Welch, S. (1991). *Black Americans' views of racial inequality.* New York: Cambridge University Press.

Weiss, J. C., Ehrlich, H. J., & Larcom, B. E. K. (1991-1992). Ethnoviolence at work. *Journal of Intergroup Relations, 18,* 21-33.

PART V

Teaching

Education and counseling have enjoyed an enduring partnership. Recognizing this relationship, we believe that it is important for a book on multicultural competencies to give adequate attention to a variety of educational settings and educators. Although there are undoubtedly many more arenas we could include, we believe that this section provides a good foundation in the basic educational emphases. The goal of this section is to present an overview of critical issues related to the development of multicultural competencies for both educators and students at a range of levels and in a variety of educational settings.

This part is composed of six chapters. In Chapter 31, the author discusses the issues faced when addressing multicultural competence in an educational environment that stresses academic achievement. The current emphasis on academic achievement requires counselors and teachers to attend to a variety of goals, particularly given the great diversity of the student populations in many of our nation's schools. The need to foster students' development in this environment makes attention to multicultural competence critical.

The next four chapters in this section each focus on a different level of education to provide more specificity and attention to the diverse needs of each context. In Chapter 32, the authors consider the unique needs of the K-12 environment, and Chapter 33 presents strategies for teaching and enhancing multicultural competence for undergraduate students. Counselor training is described in Chapter 34 with specific attention to the issues involved in developing and offering curriculum that enhances and supports multicultural competence training. Issues in continuing education as a resource for psychologists are addressed in Chapter 35. Multicultural competence is particularly relevant for this arena, given that many professionals may have completed their initial training in programs that offered limited or no multicultural coursework or practicum. As the final chapter in this section, Chapter 36 provides an overview of the exciting new opportunities and complications in multicultural competence training available through the use of the Internet and other technology. New technology has the potential for increasing cultural self-awareness, expanding knowledge of domestic and international communities, and providing simulated interactions. This chapter aims to facilitate readers in using this tool while recognizing its limitations and unique demands.

31

The Multicultural Competence of Teachers and the Challenge of Academic Achievement

ERNEST D. WASHINGTON JR.

University of Massachusetts, Amherst

The multicultural movement and the school reform movement have evolved to address the underachievement of poor children. The multicultural movement set as its first priority to challenge the Eurocentric perspective in the schools. It is now widely accepted that the curriculum and instruction in schools should reflect a multicultural perspective. The first phase of challenging the hegemony of the Eurocentric perspective is now a fait accompli. This movement, led by people of color and their supporters, did have its successes. Nevertheless, a change to a multicultural perspective did not result in increased achievement. The multicultural movement is now facing its second major challenge, the problem of underachievement by children of color.

The school reform movement also set as its goal the improvement in achievement of poor and minority children. This movement is supported by legislation that includes mandatory academic standards and high-stakes testing. School reform is a recurring theme in American education, and this last iteration is overshadowing the multicultural movement. Politicians and policymakers provide the sustenance for this movement, and the setting of academic standards and high-stakes testing in elementary and secondary education are now accepted practice. The insistence that standards and benchmarks are essential is a contribution from the educational reform movement. Research indicates, however, that the setting of standards is neither a simple strategy nor one certain to improve achievement, and it is sometimes controversial (Apple, 2001). At the same time, the multicultural and school reform movements are not kindred spirits, even though both aim to change current educational practice. Each harbors deep reservations about the other movement (Stotsky, 1999; Vavrus, 2001). In a climate of skepticism about the efficacy of multicultural education and school reform, we hear the following question increasingly asked: Can multicultural education and school reform be combined to improve educational achievement?

It is possible for multiculturalists to dismiss the question of improving academic achievement by insisting that it was never the purpose of multicultural education to improve academic achievement. Although that may be true, it is a deliberate distraction to claim success in helping students to become knowledgeable about themselves as cultural beings while ignoring the challenges of a rigorous set of academic standards. There is also a further danger in the dismissive stance. Lurking in the background is the stereotype that students of color are capable of learning complex emotional and cultural knowledge without the ability to achieve high academic standards. Acknowledging the success of the infusion of a multicultural perspective into schools without academic success amounts to an acceptance of academic incompetence for children of color.

At first glance, it appears that there are conflicts between creating multicultural classrooms and school reform. Such concerns turn out to be groundless. A careful scrutiny of multicultural competencies and academic content reveals a common epistemology. When both are viewed through a common lens, it will be clear that they are not in conflict but have a common underlying structure. It will be shown that multicultural education is a cognitive enterprise and that the cognitive element in teaching is a multicultural experience.

The steps to integrating multicultural competencies and academic standards are straightforward once it is acknowledged that the identification of academic and multicultural competencies includes a theoretical framework. The first step is to recognize that knowing, believing, and understanding are the common grounds through which to examine competence. (In the section that follows, I will show the relations between knowing, believing, and understanding and how central these three concepts are to explaining multicultural education. The next step is to compare three models of multicultural competence: a cultural model advanced by Sue, Ivey, and Pedersen (1996); an identity model put forward by McAllister and Irvine (2000); and a model of instruction by Vygotsky (see Ball, 2000). These three models have a common background that is amenable to description in terms of the knowledge, belief, and understanding that are necessary elements of instruction.

A new set of multicultural/academic competencies is described below: understanding the self, understanding the other, and multicultural instruction. The first two competencies, understanding the self and understanding others, are found in the work of Sue et al. (1996). The identity model of multicultural competencies (McAllister & Irvine, 2000) also contributes to the first set of competencies, understanding the self, by elaborating on stages of identity. The third set of competencies introduces a new dimension of multicultural/academic teaching, and this requires a set of competencies that are particular to instruction. Finally, a rationale is presented that the competencies lend themselves to the placement of teachers along a continuum from novice to expert multicultural teacher. Critical competencies mark each step along the way to multicultural competence in teaching.

KNOWING, BELIEVING, AND UNDERSTANDING: THE COMMON GROUNDS

Academic achievement and multicultural education have common grounds in the interrelated cognitions of knowing, believing, and understanding. These forms of cognition are the underlying structures of practical and theoretical knowledge that are the foundations of achievement and social actions. Cognitive theories usually emphasize knowing while ignoring believing and understanding. Even in research that emphasizes knowing and believing, the interconnections between knowing, believing, and understanding go unreported. This approach begins by examining the roles of knowing, believing, and understanding in McAllister and Irvine (2002), Sue et al. (1996), and Vygotsky's approach (Ball, 2000; Wells, 2000). The patterns that emerge from these analyses reveal the essential elements to the structure of competence.

Requisite to comparing the three models of multicultural competence is a model of knowledge based on the work Franklin (1981) and Washington (2000) that links knowing, believing, and understanding. It is not fortuitous that these different forms of knowledge correspond to the cultural theory developed by Sue et al. (1996). Similar knowledge structures have been identified by LaFromboise, Coleman, and Hernandez (1991); D'Andrea, Daniels, and Heck (1991); and Sadowsky, Taffe, Gurkin, and Wise (1994). The practice of counseling has produced knowing, believing, and understanding as key concepts in the development of multicultural competence, and this raises the question of the theoretical linkages between these forms of knowledge. This approach brings to the conceptual foreground a teacher and students who are engaged in the social construction of knowledge based on their beliefs in each other and their evolving understanding of knowledge.

During the course of these discussions, the relations between knowing, believing, and understanding will be clarified, and their roles in practical and theoretical knowledge will be explained.

Understanding rises above the content of knowing and believing as it provides appraisal and structure to a learning situation. During the appraisal process, a judgment is made with regard to good and bad and right and wrong. Minsky (1986) defined understanding as a frame, a data structure for representing a stereotyped situation. Several kinds of information are attached to the frame: how to use the frame, what to expect new or next, a theory of thinking, a schema for reasoning by analogy, and ways to jump to conclusions based on partial similarity matching. This last point is worth remembering; that is, our understandings are always provisional and based on partial similarity matching.

Only recently have researchers recognized the multiple forms of understanding (Gardner & Boix-Mansilla, 1994; Simmons, 1994). As indicated in Figure 31.1, understanding has three different forms: understanding that (theoretical knowledge), understanding how (practical knowledge), and systems knowledge or understanding why. Practical and theoretical knowledge are narratives that provide structure and appraisal through the process of understanding. These two forms of understanding rise above the content of knowing and believing across multiple situations.

It is also my intention to emphasize the relations between theoretical and practical knowledge while recognizing that most of our attention has been given to theoretical knowledge. The remarkable progress of the physical sciences over the past three centuries has provided theoretical knowledge with a revered status. A definition of theoretical knowledge is in the standard account of knowledge as justified true belief (Gettier, 1963). As an example, at one time it was sensible to say that we believe that men did not walk on the moon. Now that men have gone to the moon, we have new evidence. We now *know that* men have walked on the moon. The change from *believing that* to *knowing that* is determined by evidence and circumstance.

Practical knowledge is created in the collaboration between two individuals as they solve

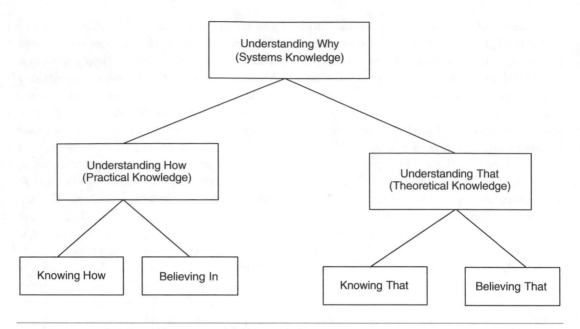

Figure 31.1   The Three-Element Model of Knowledge

a problem in the real world. Practical knowledge is created in school when students learn how to demonstrate new skills in collaboration with a teacher who they *believe in*. As children learn a skill, they *know how* to do something new, and to accomplish this, they need a teacher, someone to *believe in*. They learn such practical skills as how to read, count, get along with their peers, make friends, and be patient. The student believes in her teacher, and this belief is required if learning is to take place. Children learn a myriad of different forms of practical knowledge during their early years of school. Theoretical knowledge grows out of practical knowledge as collaborators search for and find the principles and solutions to problems. The separation of abstract principles from practical experiences takes place as knowledge is codified, and after some time has passed, it appears as if theoretical knowledge is separate from the very experiences that were its progenitors This is the way that theoretical knowledge develops in the real world, and it is no different in school.

Today, the concept of belief is much changed from its original meaning. The uses, power, and complexity of belief can be partially explained by the history of the concept (Smith, 1977). The original use of belief was similar to what today is the concept of "belief in." In Old English, the words that evolved into the modern *believe* (*geleofan, gelefan, geliefan*) meant "to belove"—to hold dear, to cherish, to regard as lief. They were the equivalent of what the German *gelefan* means today and show the same root as the Latin, *libet*, "it *pleases.*" In Chaucer's (1386/1979) *Canterbury Tales*, the words *accept my belief* mean simply "accept my loyalty." With the approach of modernity, the concept of belief evolved from a belief in the person to a *belief that* the word of the person is true. Even though the practice of using the expression "believe in" has faded from our discourse, the practices that gave rise to the original concept remain with us.

As Figure 31.1 indicates, practical understanding and theoretical understanding have different accompanying belief structures.

Theoretical understanding is connected to *believing that,* and practical knowledge is connected to *believing in* someone. Theoretical knowledge does not stand alone; a network of beliefs accompanies it. The scientist who investigates theoretical knowledge also retains a set of *beliefs that* the artifacts of her profession—the instruments, the conversations, the publications and methods—are appropriate and necessary for making science. The artifacts, instruments, conversations, and methods that are integral to theoretical knowledge are also connected to practical knowledge. Practical knowledge is the foundation from which theoretical knowledge develops. In typical fashion, in the real world, there are real problems that are encountered by teachers and students, and it is necessary that students have a teacher who they *believe in* to solve the problem. Theoretical knowledge refers to the principles that are the distillation of their practical knowledge.

In the 1980s, new research on understanding came to the fore as researchers emphasized "teaching for understanding." To get beyond rote memorization to achieve true understanding of new information, students need to develop and integrate a network of associations linking new information to preexisting knowledge and beliefs anchored in informative appropriate experience (McCaslin & Good, 1992).

This definition of systems understanding includes knowing and believing in an activity (a practice) that is anchored in preexisting knowledge and belief. Teachers, too, recognize that theory grows out of practice. Systems understanding is created when practical understanding and theoretical understanding come together. The mastery of the practical and the theoretical has always been the ideal. The ideal teacher is someone who has mastered a practical and theoretical understanding of the classroom: She has well-rehearsed routines that allow lessons to flow smoothly, that provide students and teachers with established

routines that maintain student attention, and that reveal the difficulties students are encountering (Leinhardt & Greeno, 1986). These practical routines are automatic and are implemented without recourse to debate and reflection. Expert teachers have overarching theoretical conceptions of content and the process of instruction. Experienced teachers build on their practical understanding with theoretical understanding to achieve a deep or systems understanding of the classroom.

MODELS OF MULTICULTURAL COMPETENCIES

Models of multicultural competence by McAllister and Irvine (2000), Sue et al. (1996), and Vygotsky (Ball, 2000; Wells, 2000) will be compared to explicate their underlying cognitive structures. Identity theory (McAllister & Irvine, 2000) as the basis for multicultural competence is causal and points to the past, cultural theory (multicultural counseling) (Sue et al., 1996) is multicausal and emphasizes the present (phenomenological), and a Vygotskian approach is goal oriented and points to the future. The three perspectives share a common grounding in knowing, believing, and understanding. However, comparing these perspectives reveals a methodological divide that appears as three different time perspectives. Understanding plays different roles in the process of explanation for the different models, and these different roles result in different time orientations.

Identity theory is the most familiar theory in multicultural competence because it answers that perennial American question, "Who am I?" McAllister and Irvine (2000) answered this question by advancing the view that cultural identity can be understood as ascending stages of self-awareness until the individual reaches a level of systems understanding. The second model of cultural competence and standards is central to the field of multicultural counseling (Sue et al., 1982). The methodology includes a widening circle of understanding that begins with understanding the individual self, understanding others, and becoming a multicultural counselor. The Vygotskian perspective (Ball 2000; Wells, 2000) is directed toward the goal of teachers and students solving problems during the course of daily life.

Understanding is a methodological marker that separates the three models. At each stage of identity development, the individual has a new encounter that has consequences, and this new learning results in a new understanding. One stage builds on another, and the resulting understanding links the past with the present. By contrast, the Vygotskian approach is teleological, and it begins with an understanding of the situation or problem and answers the question, "What is going on?" Once the student and teacher agree on an initial understanding of the problem, it is possible to set the goals and then determine the actions that are necessary to reach the goal. The Vygotskian approach begins with an understanding of the present problem and sets a course of action to reach a future goal. Implicit in this approach is the idea of human agency—what is human is the power to evaluate our desires, to regard some as desirable and others as undesirable. This capacity to evaluate desires is bound up with our powers of self-evaluation, which in turn is an essential feature of agency (Taylor, 1985). The cultural model is an intermediate position, a phenomenological approach that focuses on understanding the present. Understanding of the present begins with understanding the self in relation to the other. Both individuals live lives in which they experience multiple realities, and understanding is an ever-widening circle in which new understandings of the different realities are taking place.

IDENTITY DEVELOPMENT AS MULTICULTURAL COMPETENCE: UNDERSTANDING THE SELF

The ideal teacher in this model is someone who traverses the stages from being naive in matters of race and ethnicity to one who is skilled in cross-cultural communication. Each stage is characterized by an encounter with racial or ethnic conflict that results in a new level of understanding. The focus is on a succession of understandings through which the individual moves on to the next stage of development. Identity development as a form of multicultural competence is included in Phase 1 of multicultural and academic competencies for teachers (see Table 31.1).

McAllister and Irvine (2000) used identity theories by Cross (1991) and Helms (1995) and theories of White privilege by Sleeter (2000) in fashioning a view of multicultural competence. The focal interest of these researchers is the changing self-understanding of the individual or teacher with regard to race and racism. Identity theory focuses on the minority or White teacher moving from a state of lack of awareness of his or her cultural identity and racism to an awareness and acceptance of his or her cultural identity and later of a multicultural world. Banks (1994) takes a firm position that individuals do not understand other ethnic groups until they develop a positive sense of self, including an understanding and acceptance of their own ethnic group. Sleeter (2000) and Tatum (1997) share this view and focus on the changing self-perception of Whites with regard to their identity and privileges as White citizens. The encounters with racism result in a psychological movement toward a new state of awareness. These changes within the self are necessary before the individual is able to intervene in multicultural affairs.

Understanding the self is a narrative of practical and theoretical knowledge. The most

Table 31.1   Multicultural and Academic Competencies for Teachers

Cultural Clarification: Self-Understanding

Understanding
- A culturally skilled teacher has moved from naive to understanding her cultural heritage.
- A culturally skilled teacher understands how her background influences instruction.
- A culturally skilled teacher respects the differences between herself and students who differ with regard to race, ethnicity, culture, and belief.

Knowledge
- A culturally skilled teacher has specific knowledge about her own racial/cultural heritage, and she can participate easily in the culture.
- A culturally skilled teacher has knowledge of racism, discrimination, and stereotyping affects on instruction.
- A culturally skilled teacher has knowledge of how her style of teaching affects the instructional process.

Beliefs
- A culturally skilled teacher understands how her beliefs about her own culture make her the person she is.
- A culturally skilled teacher understands how her beliefs in herself influence the ways in which she teaches.
- A culturally skilled teacher understands how her students' beliefs about racism influence the instructional process.

Cultural Literacy: Understanding the Culture of the Other

Understanding
- A culturally skilled teacher understands the lives of her students.
- A culturally skilled teacher understands the ways in which their cultural experiences affect their understanding of the cultures of their students.
- A culturally skilled teacher understands how prejudices influence the instruction of students.

Knowledge
- A culturally skilled teacher is knowledgeable about the family and religious and social practices of her students.
- A culturally skilled teacher is knowledgeable about the history of the religious and social practices of her students.

Beliefs
- A culturally skilled teacher believes in her students.
- A culturally skilled teacher understands the beliefs of her students.

Understanding Academic and Multicultural Competence

Understanding
- A culturally skilled teacher understands that all teaching is cultural.
- A culturally skilled teacher understands how to incorporate the cultural backgrounds of her students into the curriculum.
- A culturally competent teacher understands the relations between practical and theoretical knowledge.
- A culturally skilled teacher understands the importance of teaching critical thinking skills.

Continued

Table 31.1   Continued

Knowledge
- A culturally skilled teacher is knowledgeable about the subject matter she is teaching.
- A culturally skilled teacher has well-rehearsed routines that help the lesson to flow fluidly and provide teacher and students with a structure for their planned actions.
- A culturally skilled teacher knows how to teach critical thinking skills.

Beliefs
- A culturally skilled teacher helps her students to see the role of beliefs in the curriculum.
- A culturally skilled teacher believes in herself as a competent teacher.
- A culturally skilled teacher has a role model who serves as a mentor.
- A culturally skilled teacher believes that all children can learn.
- A culturally skilled teacher believes that critical thinking skills are necessary for the consciousness raising of majority and minority students.

important form of practical knowledge is the narrative, according to Geertz (1997). Telling stories about ourselves to others and ourselves is the earliest and most natural way in which we organize our experiences and our knowledge. In keeping with narrative knowledge as concrete specific and interpersonal, narratives include characters, settings, institutions, intentions, emotions, and actions (Bruner, 1996). There is much practical knowledge that is taught to members of minority groups by other group members about prejudice and racism. When the principles and abstractions of this practical knowledge take places, theoretical knowledge begins to come into being. These forms of knowledge are passed on in the stories that are integral to the culture. Sleeter (2000) made the point that Whites do not hold conversations (practical knowledge) about racism. By contrast, narratives of racism are a routine topic of conversation for African Americans.

How does the multicultural teacher acquire knowledge of her self? Even though the self is hidden from view, a claim that she knows herself is a claim that can be verified. It is possible to validate this statement in the same way that we validate other statements. We have to stop and look as she is engaged in teaching to determine if we can infer from her narratives of the self that she does understand her self. If she claims to know her ethnic identity as an African American teacher, and if we see no evidence of it in the narratives of her teaching, then it is plausible for us to conclude that she does not understand herself. On the other hand, if we see that she includes narratives of African American culture throughout her classroom and teaching and places herself within those narratives, then we can infer that she has knowledge of her identity. Our observations provide a method by which we determine if our African American teacher is knowledgeable about her identity. The books, artifacts, and methods that explain the self provide the *knowledge that* is theoretical knowledge.

Freudian theory links the past and the present as one stage of the self builds on a preceding stage. The connections between the past and present are the linkages between the stories that we tell about ourselves and that others tell about us. Identity theories emphasize the multiple stages of the development of the self. It is a mechanistic approach in which conflict causes movement to the next and more comprehensive level of awareness. As identity theory links the past and the present, it is almost invariably grounded in the fiction of the halcyon days of the past.

Understanding one's self or identity is a narrative in which conflict is the major motivating factor for change from one stage to the next. Theories of identity remind us that narratives of racial conflict are a part of daily life in America. The appeal of identity theory is in its continuity and the sympathy that we share with others. We are naturally drawn toward narratives that are similar to our own. Our sympathies emerge when we become engaged with the narratives of others who are experiencing similar conflicts and problems. This causal model links the past and the present, and it leaves to the imagination or interpretation the relations between narratives of the self and narratives of the other. The empirical support for the efficacy of identity theory as a way of explaining behavior is not well widespread, and yet its appeal tells us more about the universal appeal of narratives than it does about our subjective worlds.

A CULTURAL APPROACH TO MULTICULTURAL COMPETENCE: UNDERSTANDING THE SELF AND UNDERSTANDING THE OTHER

The ideal teacher understands her culture as well as the cultures of her students. Cultural theory begins with the premise that understanding another culture requires that we understand our culture in relation to the other (Sue et al., 1996). There are multiple realities for the self and the other. The cultural approach is phenomenological, and it joins the self and the other into a full description of the present world. The totality and interrelationships of experience and contexts are emphasized. The ideal teacher is able to give a full description and understanding of the complexities of her cultural world as well as those of her students. She is well grounded in the methods and routines that enable her students to acquire the knowledge, beliefs, and understandings that are integral parts of the curriculum.

In a bold and prescient article, Sue et al. (1982) initiated the multicultural competency movement in counseling psychology. Their approach fits within the larger educational competency movement that was gathering momentum across the nation. This seminal paper was further developed and extended by LaFromboise et al. (1991); D'Andrea et al. (1991); Sue, Arredondo, and McDavis (1992); Sadowsky et al. (1994); and Sue et al. (1996). This led to a systemic volume, *Multicultural Counseling Competencies: Assessment, Education, and Training and Supervision* (Pope-Davis & Coleman, 1997). These writers have collectively set counseling psychology on a path that takes for granted that multicultural competence is an important element in the education and training of counseling psychologists.

From this approach, a consensus has emerged that knowledge, belief, and awareness (understanding) are critical forms of knowledge in multicultural competence (Fassinger & Richie, 1997; LaFromboise et al., 1991; Sue et al., 1982; Sue et al., 1996). The ubiquitousness of these three facets of knowledge is evident and not in dispute. The fact that these writers have found it necessary to deploy these terms as essential to multicultural competencies confirms their importance. They have taken the additional step of identifying specific competencies that are crucial to multicultural competence. A recent statement by Sue et al. (1996) provides a cogent example that offers guidance in developing multicultural competence for teachers. The authors identify three broad areas of competence: counselor awareness of his or her own cultural values and biases, counselor awareness of the client's worldview, and culturally appropriate intervention strategies. Within each of these three areas, they also list the specific attitudes/beliefs, knowledge, and skills that are relevant to that domain. It is this model that is modified and used in identifying a set of multicultural competencies for teachers (see Figure 31.1).

The division of multicultural competencies into the domains of understanding the self, understanding the other, and professional skills separates the self and the other. This has the theoretical consequence of requiring a mechanistic or transmission model of knowledge in which knowledge is transferred from one person to another. Of course, Sue et al. (1996) recognized this division, and their approach includes multiple realities in the self and the other. The self in relation to the other is the frame they used to explain this relationship. Their model reaches beyond the self and other to include the cultural artifacts, knowledge, and beliefs of the different cultures. These disparate and complex sets of knowledge are joined together through systemic understanding of relationships. The central role of language, multiple causation, and grasping the complexities of cultural understanding leads to the recognition that this approach is phenomenological. As a correlate of this view, there is an emphasis on understanding the present in all its fullness and complexity.

As in our previous discussion of understanding the self, understanding others can be conceptualized as a narrative approach to inquiry. Understanding the other amounts to understanding the stories that we tell about others, the stories they tell about themselves, and the artifacts and methods that have accumulated to help us understand the other. There is practical and theoretical knowledge in understanding the other. The practical knowledge about the other comes to us via the stories that we hear from family, friends, and neighbors about the other. We *believe in* these informants, and they shape our knowledge of the other. The theoretical knowledge that we have about the other comes to us from the media and the artifacts of our culture.

Understanding the self in relation to the other is the guiding theme of the multicultural approach to counseling. The emphasis is on widening the circle of understanding to be more and more inclusive. This approach is phenomenological in orientation, and it is directed at understanding the present. Counseling has as its benchmarks the success or failure of the therapeutic process. These empirical benchmarks direct the counseling enterprise. An unsuccessful counseling experience reflects a failure to widen the circle of understanding.

A VYGOTSKIAN APPROACH TO MULTICULTURAL AND ACADEMIC COMPETENCE

The Vygotskian teacher understands the web of theoretical concepts and principles such as internalization of the social, dialogical learning, skills as psychological tools, community of practice, and the zone of proximal development. She also considers the classroom as a community in which students and teachers work toward solving everyday problems while en route to shared goals (Ball, 2000; Wells, 2000).

Understanding comes first. Before there is action, the teacher and student have to understand the situation and then make appropriate plans. The transformation of the student takes place while participating in activities that are real and meaningful. Activities bring together individuals and artifacts in a problem-solving and goal-oriented situation. The curriculum refers to the specified knowledge and skills that make up the cultural tool kit that is used to carry out activities of personal and social significance. The outcome of these activities cannot be known in advance because human actions are directed toward goals. The zone of proximal development is the setting in which the individual is able to achieve more with assistance than alone. The teacher is guide, coach, and support for the learner in the Vygotskian approach.

Vygotsky and his followers were engaged in the task of promoting literacy and scientific development in a country with millions of illiterate people in a time of revolution. The rapid rate of industrialization and social transformation provided a sense of urgency to their work that is matched today as we face the challenge of educating an increasingly diverse student population and where new instructional strategies are imperative. Vygotsky's work introduced a number of synergistic innovations that are applicable to our educational predicaments today.

His first major contribution was the recognition that knowledge is not something that is created in the heads of students. Against the transmission model, knowledge is based on relations between knowing and acting as knowledge is created and re-created between people as they bring their personal experience and information from other sources to bear on a problem. Knowledge is the enhanced understanding of the problem situation gained by the participants and the representation of the knowledge that is produced in the process (Wells, 2000). Following in this tradition, Ball (2000) made these points about knowledge and learning. Knowledge is culturally and socially mediated, temporary, developmental, and internally constructed. Learning is a self-regulatory process of struggling with conflicts between existing knowledge and beliefs and discrepant new experiences and going on to construct new representations and models. Systems knowledge is the enhanced understanding of the problem situation gained by the participants and the representation of the knowledge that is produced in the process (Wells, 2000). Learning takes place within an activity that is part of a community of practice. Learning is a lifelong activity as each new situation creates new demands and opportunities for change, learning, and development.

Like other approaches to cognition, Vygotsky and his followers recognized that theoretical knowledge evolved over the millennia when several conditions were met: a visuographic means of giving a permanent representation to the meanings expressed in speech and an ideological shift toward the objectification of the material world. At the same time, the European Renaissance contributed three inventions: the controlled experiment, the register of scientific writing, and the technology of printing. When these conditions were satisfied, theoretical knowledge came into being with its artifacts of scientific reports, theories, and models (Wells, 2000).

Practical or procedural knowledge is the fundamental form of knowledge, and it arises in the process of solving problems in the real world. This last point is a matter that can be disputed, and some privilege theoretical knowledge. This is not a debate that we can entertain at this time; suffice it say that few dispute the central importance of practical knowledge. Problem-solving activities are goal directed and involve practical reasoning. It is critical to keep in mind that practical knowledge is teleological. Although practical reasoning is teleological, it takes the form that there is a wanted goal or end of an action, there is some action to secure this goal, and, in conclusion, the action is used to secure the goal (von Wright, 1964).

The concept of belief is not integral to the descriptions and explanations of Vygotsky's approach; it is included in the concept of the zone of proximal development. The *zopod,* as it is now known, refers to a context and activity in which an individual is able to achieve more with assistance than he or she can manage alone. Personal coaching is the closest parallel to the idea of assisted development that we find in Vygotskian theory. The very point of personalized coaching is that the student believes that the coach can make him or her perform better and, moreover, that the student can achieve more with a competent coach.

Increasingly, educators recognize that it is important to go beyond knowledge and belief to apprehend the ways in which students and teacher construct understanding (Brophy & Good, 1986; Gardner & Boix-Mansilla, 1994). Understanding is the creation of something new; it is the result of internalization. The process of internalization is not the transferal of an external activity to a preexisting, internal "plane of consciousness": It is the process in which the plane is formed. When someone has internalized something, she or he can go beyond the initial idea or activity and beyond previous levels of functioning to expand on a concept and relate it to new situations (Ball, 2000).

Within the Vygotskian tradition, understanding comes first. The process begins when teachers and students come into shared agreement about their goals. Ball (2000) described the process as follows:

> As pre-service and practicing teachers come into teacher education programs with their own literacy histories, they discuss, read, write, reflect on theories and practice, and challenge preconceived notions about literacy with the learning context. Within such an environment where it is safe to take risks, their utterances come into contact with the theoretical and practical utterances of others. Understanding begins to occur when these teachers begin to understand themselves with respect to the theory and practical ideas that are presented. (p. 232)

Perhaps the most intriguing aspect of Vygotsky's approach is that it provides an alternative view of the future in multicultural development. In the area of identity, such a view suggests that identity is a problem-solving, goal-oriented activity. We are not simply who we used to be or even who we are today; rather, we are also in the process of becoming and achieving a new identity. Education, broadly conceived, can be thought of as a striving to reach a new identity. Our cultural role models and teachers guide us as we learn the skills that are necessary to reach our goals. This model of instruction is oriented toward the future, and it is a model of evolving knowledge in which we take for granted that knowledge is temporary and changing.

UNDERSTANDING ACADEMIC AND MULTICULTURAL COMPETENCE

This set of competencies is not a logical framework; instead, these competencies are a loose network of knowledge, beliefs, and understandings that are appropriate for academic/multicultural instruction. There is no pretense of completeness, but the concern is with the identification of appropriate skills that were supported by the research literature. The argument quite simply is that a teacher who demonstrates these competencies is a professional who can be trusted to teach all of our children.

One of the important questions left untouched by these discussions is the importance of racial and ethnic differences between teachers and students. In the area of multicultural counseling, it is taken for granted that racial/ethnic issues are critical to a successful outcome (Ponterotto, Casas, Suzuki, & Alexander, 1995). The research literature does show that ethnic and racial differences are significant variables in therapeutic success. In contrast, educators as a profession tend to reject the view that racial and ethnic differences are pivotal to the success of teaching. At present, the research literature is equivocal with regard to the question of whether the race and ethnicity of the teacher is a significant factor in educational success. The most likely prospect is that outcomes, in teaching and counseling, are influenced by race and ethnicity.

It is hoped that the specification of the multicultural and academic competencies for teachers will help to focus discussion on the issues that are central to teacher competence and the education of children. Up to this point, we have identified a set of competencies that are essential to academic and multicultural competence; now we need to provide a framework that can be used to help in the education of teachers.

FROM NOVICE TO EXPERT: MULTICULTURAL COMPETENCIES FOR TEACHERS

An important question for those who are involved in improving the multicultural competence of teachers is the following: How can we conceptualize the progress that teachers make in improving the multicultural competencies of teachers? A milestone in research into the development of expertise is the work of Dreyfus and Dreyfus (1986), who identified five stages of development in the movement from novice to expert. In the "novice" stage, the commonplaces of a situation are learned, context-free rules of behavior are followed, behavior is relatively inflexible, and experience must be gained. The "advanced beginner" melds knowledge with on-the-job experience, building up case or episodic knowledge to go along with semantic knowledge, but is still not very flexible in behavior. The "competent performer" of a skill is rational and flexible, can articulate goals, and can employ sensible means to achieve them. The "proficient performer" has a heightened sense of pattern recognition, has a holistic understanding of the processes involved, and recognizes similarities between apparently quite different situations. The "expert" not only has a holistic, integrated view of the situation but can also respond effortlessly, fluidly, and appropriately to the demands of competence and expertise.

Berliner (1988, 1989) applied the Dreyfus and Dreyfus (1986) approach to the development of teacher expertise because it provided a useful template for organizing and explaining the sequential organization of the development of teacher competence. He proposed that the routes from a novice instructor to expert reveal many of the challenges facing the neophyte teacher. It also brings to light the recognition that every profession has a set of implicit and explicit skills and knowledge that are used to guide professional development. In a discussion of well-practiced skills in the hands of expert teachers, Berliner (1988, 1989) identified examples of practical knowledge and belief in the instructional process. To fully appreciate the complexities involved in developing expertise, we must examine each of the stages.

Novice teachers are suddenly faced with a classroom of 25 or so children, and their first concern is survival. Their knowledge of the subject matter is disjointed without clear connections between the different areas of the curriculum (Calderhead, 1996). They claim that categorical differences among students do not matter in teaching. The only differences that do matter (i.e., have a role in teaching), they thought, are individual differences such as personality characteristics. These teachers see student diversity as a problem to be overcome or solved, rather than a feature of all classrooms. Individualized instruction is a solution to the problem, and they are uncritical of that solution. There is no evidence of substantial changes in knowledge or beliefs about diversity (Borko & Putnam, 1996). At the novice level, the neophyte teacher has not mastered practical knowledge of running a classroom or the theoretical knowledge of subject matter. He has difficulty believing in himself or his students.

Advanced beginners emerge from the survival phase of their first years in the profession, and they eagerly search for the new knowledge that will make them more competent. They are very often overwhelmed by the complexity of the task; there is a tendency to search for simple answers, and they struggle with establishing consistent routines. Advanced beginners inadvertently use the transmission model of instruction in which they assumed that teaching is the transmission of knowledge from the teacher to the student. They are beginning to understand themselves and their students as cultural beings. The advanced beginner is mastering the practical routines of the classroom but is not yet able to apply theory to practice. She is starting to believe in herself as a teacher and begins to recognize that she is knowledgeable about subject matter.

The competent teacher develops a series of routines and ways of perceiving classroom events based on past experiences, and these past experiences become fluid and automatic practical knowledge (Berliner, 1988). Management problems have faded from view. Berliner (1988) makes the point that as a teacher acquires the ability to routinize the activities in the classroom, she is freed to think about other things. She anticipates that students will have difficulty, and they have worked out routines that will help the students. There is a recognition that the student plays an important part in the learning process. As students develop expertise, they begin to regulate their own learning by asking questions and working on complex applications more independently. The teacher is knowledgeable about the cultures of her students.

The breakthrough comes when the teacher has acquired the ability to orchestrate well-honed and appropriate routines in the classroom. Competent though he is in practical knowledge, his instructional practices are not yet supported by theoretical knowledge.

The proficient teacher not only has well-organized sets of routines at her disposal (practical knowledge), but she also structures and restructures these activities to fit the situation (theoretical knowledge). The proficient teacher begins with an understanding of the instructional situation. Instructional scaffolding and a range of task assistance or simplifications are used to bridge the gap between what students are capable of doing and what they can accomplish with help, and this becomes a part of her repertoire. The teacher's plans include herself and the students' actions as well as the corresponding goal sequences (Leinhardt & Greeno, 1986). The teacher listens to students and incorporates their ideas and understandings into the instruction. She believes in her students, and she encourages them to think for themselves. She uses her knowledge of the cultures of her students to help them explore the intricacies of their cultures.

Expert teachers are capable of completing the circle of understanding. They begin with an understanding of the instructional process, themselves, and their students, and when the instructional process is completed, they have helped create a new and deeper understanding. These teachers are problem solvers, and they initiate their students into a mind-set whereby they are able to enjoy the challenge of solving problems. These teachers are able to monitor and interpret simultaneous, multiple cultural events within a classroom. They also describe and interpret the events and behaviors and also draw conclusions about their meaning and make evaluative judgments. Lessons are scaffolded and adapted to fit the instructional skills of students. Understanding is constructed in the process of people working together to solve the problems that arise in the course of shared activity. The organization of classroom resources, the resolution of interpersonal disputes, the planning of field trips, and curriculum-based activities are approached in the same open-ended exploratory way (Wells, 2000). The classroom becomes a collaborative community in which each individual becomes a party to the search for understanding.

SUMMARY AND CONCLUSIONS

Two alternative approaches to multicultural competence for teachers were described. The first approach—Multicultural and Academic Competencies for Teachers—identifies three different areas of competencies: self-understanding, understanding the culture of the other, and academic-multicultural competence. Each of these areas divides into knowledge, beliefs, and understanding, and within each of these cognitive forms, specific competencies are specified. The second approach—From Novice to Expert: Multicultural Competence for Teachers—defines multicultural competence for teachers as a continuum from novice to expert. As the teacher progresses in her practical and theoretical knowledge, she improves in incremental steps. These incremental steps are changes in knowledge, beliefs, and understanding. Underlying both approaches to multicultural competence are theoretical and practical knowledge that, in turn, are composed of the cognitive states of knowing, believing, and understanding. The novice to expert strategy and the multicultural competence approach are simply different ways of looking at the developing multicultural competencies of teachers.

REFERENCES

Apple, M. W. (2001). Markets, standards, teaching and teacher education. *Journal of Teacher Education, 52*(3), 182-196.

Ball, A. F. (2000). Teacher's developing philosophies on literacy and their use in urban schools: A Vygotskian perspective on internal activity and teacher change. In C. D. Lee & P. Smagorinsky (Eds.), *Vygotskian perspectives on literacy research: Constructing meaning through collaborative inquiry* (pp. 226-255). Cambridge, UK: Cambridge University Press.

Banks, J. A. B. (1994). *Multicultural education: Theory and practice.* Boston: Allyn & Bacon.

Berliner, D. C. (1988). *The development of expertise in pedagogy.* Report No. 0-89333-1 35 P, February.

Berliner, D. C. (1989). Knowledge is power: A talk to teachers about a revolution. *Equity and Excellence, 24*(2), 4-19.

Borko, H., & Putnam, R. T. (1996). Learning to teach. In D. C. Berliner (Ed.), *Handbook of educational psychology* (pp. 673-798). New York: Simon & Schuster.

Brophy, J. G., Good, T. L. (1986). Teacher behavior and student achievement. In M. C. Wittrock (Ed.), *Handbook of research on teaching* (3rd ed.). New York: Macmillan.

Bruner, J. S. (1996). *The culture of education.* Cambridge, MA: Harvard University Press.

Calderhead, J. (1996). Teachers: Beliefs and knowledge. In D. C. Berliner (Ed.), *Handbook of educational psychology* (pp. 709-725). New York: Simon & Schuster.

Chaucer, G. (1979). *The Canterbury tales.* New York: Ballantine. (Original publication 1386)

Cross, W. E., Jr. (1991). *Shades of Black: Diversity in African-American identity.* Philadelphia: Temple University Press.

D'Andrea, M., Daniels, J., & Heck, R. (1991). Evaluating the impact of multicultural training. *Journal of Counseling and Development, 70,* 143-150.

Dreyfus, H. L., & Dreyfus, S. E. (1986). *Mind over machine: The power of human intuition and expertise in the era of the computer.* New York: Free Press.

Fassinger, R. E., & Richie, B. S. (1997). Sex matters: Gender and sexual orientation in training for multicultural counseling competency. In D. Pope-Davis & H. L. K. Coleman (Eds.), *Multicultural counseling competencies: Assessment education and training and supervision* (pp. 83-110). Thousand Oaks CA: Sage.

Franklin, R. L. (1981). Knowledge, belief and understanding. *The Philosophical Quarterly, 31,* 193-207.

Gardner, H., & Boix-Mansilla, V. (1994). Teaching for understanding: Within and across the disciplines. *Educational Leadership, 51*(5), 14-17.

Geertz, C. (1997). Learning with Bruner. *New York Review of Books, 44*(6), 22-24.

Gettier, E. (1963). Knowledge as true belief. *Analysis, 23,* 121-123.

Helms, J. (1995). An update of Helm's White and people of color identity models. In J. G. Ponterotto, J. M. Casas, L. A. Suzuki, &

C. M. Alexander (Eds.), *Handbook of multi-cultural counseling* (pp. 181-198). Thousand Oaks, CA: Sage.

LaFromboise, T. D., Coleman, H., & Hernandez, A. (1991). Development and factor structure of the Cross-Cultural Counseling Inventory–Revised. *Professional Psychology: Research and Practice, 22*, 380-388.

Leinhardt, G., & Greeno, J. (1986). The cognitive skill of teaching. *Journal of Educational Psychology, 78*, 75-95.

McAllister, G., & Irvine, J. J. (2000). Cultural competence and multicultural teacher education. *Review of Educational Research, 70*(1), 3-24.

McCaslin, M., & Good, T. L. (1992). Compliant cognition: The misalliance of management and instructional goals in current school reform. *Educational Researcher, 21*(3), 4-17.

Minsky, M. (1986). *The society of mind.* New York: Simon & Schuster.

Ponterotto, J. G., Casas, J. M., Suzuki, L. A., & Alexander, C. M. (Eds.). (1995). *Handbook of multicultural counseling.* Thousand Oaks, CA: Sage.

Pope-Davis, D., & Coleman, H. L. K. (Eds.). (1997). *Multicultural counseling competencies: Assessment, education and training and supervision.* Thousand Oaks, CA: Sage.

Sleeter, C. E. (2000). Multicultural education and the standards movement: A report from the field. *Phi Delta Kappan, 82*(2), 156-159.

Simmons, R (1994). The horses before the cart: Assessing for understanding. *Educational Leadership, 51*(5), 22-24.

Smith, W. C. (1977). *Belief and history.* Charlottesville: University of Virginia Press.

Sodowsky, G. R., Taffe, R.C., Gurkin, T. B., & Wise, S. L. (1994). Development of the Multicultural Counseling Inventory: A self report measure of multicultural competencies. *Journal of Counseling Psychology, 41*, 137-148.

Stotsky, S. (1999). *Losing our language: How multicultural classroom instruction is undermining our children's ability to read, write and reason.* New York: Free Press.

Sue, D. W., Arredondo, P., & McDavis, R. J. (1992). Multicultural counseling competencies and standards: A call to the profession. *Journal of Counseling and Development, 70*, 477-486.

Sue, D. W., Bernier, J. E., Durran, A., Feinberg, L., Pedersen, P. B., Smith, E. J., et al. (1982). Position paper: Cross-cultural counseling competencies. *The Counseling Psychologist, 10*, 45-52.

Sue, D. W., Ivey, A. E., & Pedersen, P. B. (1996). Research, practice, and training implications of MCT theory. In D. W. Sue, A. E. Ivey, & P. B. Pedersen (Eds.), *A theory of multicultural counseling & therapy* (pp. 30-52). Pacific Grove, CA: Brooks/Cole.

Tatum, B. D. (1997). *Why are all the Black kids sitting together in the cafeteria? And other conversations about race.* New York: Basic Books.

Taylor, C. (1985). *Human agency and language: Philosophical Papers 1.* New York: Cambridge University Press.

Vavrus, M. (2001). Deconstructing the multicultural animus held by monoculturalists: A review of: Stotsky (1999). Losing our language: How multicultural classroom instruction is undermining our children's ability to read. *Journal of Teacher Education, 52*(1), 70-77.

von Wright, G. H. (1964). *Explanation and understanding.* Ithaca, NY: Cornell University Press.

Washington, E. D., Jr. (2000). Knowing, believing and understanding: The social construction of knowledge in the O. J. Simpson criminal trial. *Journal of Black Psychology, 26*(3), 302-316.

Wells, G. (2000). Dialogic inquiry in education: Building on the legacy of Vygotsky. In C. D. Lee & P. Smagorinsky (Eds.), *Vygotskian perspectives on literacy research: Constructing meaning through collaborative inquiry* (pp. 51-85). Cambridge, UK: Cambridge University Press.

32

Teachers' Multicultural Competencies (K-12)

GENELLA M. TAYLOR
STEPHEN M. QUINTANA
University of Wisconsin–Madison

Interviewer:	What does it mean to be African American?
White child (10 years):	I don't know. It doesn't mean you are different 'cept how you look.
Latino child (11 years):	My teacher's racist. She likes the White kids better than the Mexicans.
Interviewer:	How can you tell?
Child:	She treats the White kids better. She doesn't think nobody notices, but everybody knows she don't like the Mexican kids.
Interviewer:	Why are some people prejudiced?
Black child (12 years):	They think we're just unintelligent. They think they're better than we are just because they can make the honor roll and Black people don't make the honor roll because they don't study hard.

How can teachers respond to children like those quoted above? What curriculum could engage children who may believe that the educational system favors other children? If the educational system becomes more multicultural, what benefits would the changes have for White children? We review important facets of multicultural education that teachers need to understand if they are to develop multicultural curriculum and instructional practices. We review the purposes of multicultural education guiding the implementation of this kind of educational reform, the various approaches to multicultural education, and dimensions of multicultural competence.

PURPOSES OF MULTICULTURAL EDUCATION

To properly implement multicultural education, teachers must understand the purposes underlying its implementation. Teachers tend to identify implicitly or explicitly objectives to be accomplished before adopting an approach to multicultural education. Multicultural education may be implemented improperly or incompletely if teachers have misconceptions about the purposes for multicultural education. Some teachers, for example, may assume multicultural education is designed only for children of color and may be unnecessary for White children. We have identified five purposes for teachers in implementing multicultural education (see Table 32.1).

Importance of Multicultural Education for All Children

We believe teachers need to understand that all children, including White children, have much to gain from multicultural education programs, if implemented effectively. Given the accelerating diversification of the populations in the United States and other countries,

most White children no longer live in monocultural or monoracial environments (Pollard & O'Hare, 1999). Consequently, they increasingly need to develop cross-cultural and cross-racial skills to succeed in the larger U.S. society. More than ever, White children need multicultural education to be productive and skilled members in contemporary society.

Many teachers, like a majority of the U.S. population, are relatively unaware of the prevalence of racism (Pollard & O'Hare, 1999). As teachers consider adopting multicultural forms of education, they should understand the nature of socialization affecting all children, particularly White children. White children are socialized into a society that, despite strides in civil rights legislation, continues to be racist in many of its social institutions, not the least of which are schools. Although so-called "old fashioned racism" is, arguably, less prevalent today than it was 40 years ago, other forms of racism are alive and well in U.S. society. The "old-fashioned" version refers to categorical racism or discrimination against another group of people based on their racial status (e.g., "I don't like them because they are Black [Mexican, Indian, Asian]."). This kind of racism fell out of fashion largely during the civil rights movements but still occurs, as evidenced in the racial harassment many people of color experience in mundane activities, such as being followed while shopping, poor or no service in restaurants, and racial profiling while driving. Children experience overt forms of ethnic and racial bias during their school years from peers as well as teachers and other educators (e.g., Quintana, 1994). Teachers and other educators are more likely to respond directly to these overt forms of racism, when they see it happening on school grounds, but show reluctance in response to more subtle expressions and manifestations of racism (Davidson, 1996).

Table 32.1   Purposes of Multicultural Education

General Purposes	Specific Purposes
Expose all children to multicultural education	Redress bias in children's racial socialization
	Address old-fashioned and modern forms of prejudice
	Counterbalance children's ethnocentric perspectives and beliefs
Redress failure of U.S. schools	Address numerous indicators of racial disparities in education
	Redress the scapegoating of children, families, or cultures for educational disparities
	Identify characteristics of schools associated with school failure and success
Address unique needs of diverse children	Address educational needs associated with primary cultural characteristics (e.g., linguistic skills, social norms)
	Address educational needs associated with secondary cultural characteristics (e.g., oppositional identity, academic disidentification, and self-handicapping)
Redress ethnocentrism in U.S. schools	Recognize that the implicit purpose of schools is to culturally socialize children
	Acknowledge and reduce pressure on children to assimilate to dominant norms
Redress racism in education	Eliminate discriminatory teaching practices

Other forms of racism—alternatively called "modern," "subtle," and "symbolic"—may be more prevalent today than the "old-fashioned" versions. We refer to these other forms of racism as "modern" despite the fact that these modern forms of racism have been around for a while, perhaps as long as the old-fashioned ones. We consider these forms of bias "modern" because they are not out of style like the old-fashioned ones. In short, these modern forms represent a rejection of the categorical forms of racism based on genetic or biological features that characterized old-fashioned racism. Nonetheless, racial superiority is still presumed in modern racism but is based on cultural features rather than genetic or biological dimensions. The modern form of racism is illustrated as follows: "I don't dislike him because he is Black but

because he acts so 'Black.'" In this example, acting "Black" is usually represented as those characteristics that are perceived as violating dominant values (e.g., work ethic), norms (e.g., law abiding), and ideology (Jhally & Lewis, 1992; Sears, 1988).

Teachers need to realize that children are socialized early in racial ideology. Before the civil rights movement, children's socialization into an old-fashioned racist ideology may have been, in many cases, explicitly communicated. In contrast, contemporary socialization into the more modern forms of racism is much more implicit and subtle (Quintana & Johnson, 2001). Research continues to demonstrate that children show marked pro-White/anti-Black bias (see Aboud, 1988). This bias occurs early in life and may be formed even before children have the cognitive capacity to differentiate among racial groups (Hirschfeld, 1994). How this prejudice emerges at such an early age remains unknown. Speculations suggest that young children are sensitive to racial bias within the larger society and that racial inequities are subtly communicated to young children—in many cases, unwittingly—by parents, other adults, and peers (Quintana, 1998).

It is important to note that young White children's racial bias tends to reflect *ethnocentrism,* preference for one's own racial group, more so than it reflects negative or hostile attitudes toward other racial groups. Moreover, there is an attenuation, or lessening, of the pro-White/anti-Black bias during elementary school. However, this attenuation occurs because of a decrease in the ethnocentrism and not because of decreases in negative attributions toward other racial groups (Doyle & Aboud, 1995). Indeed, White children during elementary school tend to be influenced by the explicit socialization messages of many parents, teachers, and children's media that appear to promote an ideology of racial equality. To most White children, like the child quoted at the beginning of this chapter, to be Black or any other ethnic/racial minority status is to be no different than it is to be White, except for some superficial aspect of physical appearance—a form of color blindness. This color blindness may be a result of the attempts to explicitly socialize children according to principles of racial equality by teachers, parents, and other authorities. Nonetheless, most children also notice racial or ethnic disparity in the proportion of children assigned to advanced classes and in the proportion of children being disciplined for behavioral problems (Davidson, 1996). These observations leave White children in a quandary, given the apparent contradiction between their "color blindness" and the racial disparities that are apparent in school, community, and society. White children's apparent color blindness also

leaves little room for understanding the extent to which racism and prejudice continue to affect children of color (Quintana & Johnson, 2001).

How do children solve this quandary between being encouraged to believe in racial equality and noticing racial inequities? We believe that, ironically, attempts to promote "color blindness" in children actually may encourage the development of modern forms of racism. Many children may believe in equality of *opportunity* that exists across racial groups but may also notice racial inequities with respect to *outcomes* (e.g., occupational, educational forms of success). The dissonance between perceived equality of opportunity and observed racial disparity in outcomes may leave children in a quandary between what they feel they should think and what they observe about racial differences. Children resolve this quandary by attributing the disparity in outcomes to perceived inferiorities related to individual or cultural characteristics rather than to genetic or hereditary sources. These attributions, we believe, form the beginnings of modern racism.

Multicultural curriculum could help the educational system to serve its implicit mission of preparing children and youth, particularly White children, to be informed, skilled, and knowledgeable citizens in their country by redressing problems in the socialization of children. In short, the educational system is failing to serve the citizenship needs of White children. Houser (1996) provides a useful description of how multicultural education could encourage the development of a multicultural sense of self in White children. Among other things, developing into a multicultural person involves engaging "in critical self-reflective examination of the effects of their beliefs (e.g., the American work ethic, Manifest Destiny, and social Darwinism)" (Houser, 1996, p. 127). Indeed, many of the adult students in our multicultural classes report feeling as if their public school education had deceived them in matters dealing with race. The ability to develop this critical self-reflective perspective can be developed during late elementary and secondary school years with the implementation of multicultural education (Banks, 1993).

Failure of U.S. Schools

A second important justification for multicultural curriculum and multiculturally competent teachers to implement this curriculum is the obvious indicators that schools are failing to educate adequately a large proportion of ethnic and racial minority children. The statistics about ethnic or racial disparities in education between children of color and White children are staggering (for a review, see National Center for Education Statistics [NCES], 2000, 2001; Osborne, 1999; President's Advisory Commission on Educational Excellence for Hispanic Americans, 1996). For example, gaps in achievement and school completion, among other indicators, continue to show racial disparities (NCES, 2001). Although some indicators suggest that the disparities are lessening, others suggest that the disparities are widening (NCES, 2000). It is clear, however, that no indicators suggest that the disparity in educational success is going to disappear anytime soon.

To briefly illustrate, the report from the President's Advisory Commission on Educational Excellence for Hispanic Americans (1996) indicated that the educational attainment for most Hispanic Americans is in a state of "crisis," with an "intolerable" number of Hispanic students enrolled below grade level. Gaps in the educational achievement level between Black and White children do not disappear, even after controlling for the previous level of educational achievement (NCES, 2001). In other words, the gap in achievement is widening during the school years. The

dropout rates for Hispanic children are around 30%, nearly four times higher than Whites and more than twice the percentage of Black children (NCES, 2000). These examples are merely the tip of the iceberg in the problems facing ethnic and racial minority children in schools in the United States.

Such statistics are often taken to imply that children of color and their supporting networks are failing (e.g., Moynihan, 1965). We are beginning to realize that these statistics indicate that the schools are failing to educate effectively children of color. Research, for example, by Rumberger and Thomas (2000) has shown that characteristics of schools are predictive of indices of school failure above and beyond the characteristics of children (e.g., income levels, educational levels of parents, etc.). Numerous solutions have been proposed to address these widespread indices of schools' failure to educate adequately children of color—these lists of proposed solutions usually include recommendations about improving teachers' multicultural competence (e.g., Banks, 1995).

Unique Needs for Diverse Children

A third, yet related, purpose for multicultural education is to address specific or unique educational needs of children of color. Practices that have been developed for educating White children are insufficient for educating children of color because of important differences in children's background, culture, and approach to school. These differences fall into two broad categories, described by Ogbu (1994) as differences due to primary and secondary cultural differences. Primary cultural differences describe cultural features of ethnic and racial minority children that derive from their cultural of origin, including linguistic patterns, cultural traditions, cultural norms for social relations, and religious beliefs, among many dimensions. The sources of the primary cultural differences can be traced to ancestral patterns before the cultural minority group had contact with the dominant cultural groups. In contrast, secondary cultural differences refer to those features associated with ethnic or racial groups that have emerged as a result of contact between the minority group and dominant majority group. Types of secondary cultural characteristics include ethnic or racial responses to stigmatization, expressions of resistance to assimilation pressures, and assertion of identity separate from that of the dominant group. Teachers should understand important differences between primary and secondary cultural characteristics.

Primary cultural characteristics are most evident in immigrant groups that have recently traveled from other countries to the United States. Children from these groups may lack some prerequisite cultural or linguistic skills necessary for success in schools in the United States. Bilingual programs are perhaps the best example of programs designed to directly address primary cultural differences. These programs can be highly effective, particularly if they are funded and designed according to the latest educational technology and research. For example, late-exit bilingual programs in which immersion in English occurs after 4 to 5 years have been shown to be associated with elevated achievement scores in math and reading, when compared to early (after 1-2 years) immersion into English instruction (see Padilla et al., 1991). Importantly, the advantages of the late-exit programs have been demonstrated on tests conducted in the children's second language (i.e., English). To reiterate, children who have substantial involvement in bilingual education, receiving much of their instruction in their first language and gradually transitioning to English-based instruction, tend to perform better on tests of math and reading *that are in English,* when compared to children who have had most of their instruction in their second language. This research

exemplifies an important point in how skill deficits may be misidentified in culturally diverse children. In this case, the deficits for many language minority children are not their English language skills per se but their limited opportunities to receive linguistically appropriate instruction. Teachers can develop multicultural curriculum tailored to their students' linguistic as well as other primary cultural differences in recent immigrants and other children of color.

When considering cultural differences across various groups of children, teachers think mostly in terms of primary cultural characteristics. Nonetheless, secondary cultural characteristics are equally important considerations for teachers adopting multicultural education. Ethnic and racial minority populations that have been exposed historically to discrimination and prejudice have developed responses to this oppression. According to Ogbu (1994), secondary characteristics are attempts to resist or oppose pressures for assimilation into dominant norms and values. He argued that minority students' acquiescence to these norms would force them to participate in systems that are oppressive to them and their ethnic or racial group. Instead of acquiescence, many students develop strategies for resisting this perceived oppression. Theorists have suggested that the developments of oppositional identities for children of color are indicative of secondary cultural characteristics (e.g., Boykin, 1986; Cross, 1995; Davidson, 1996; Fordham, 1988; Ogbu, 1994). Oppositional identities are characterized by a sense of identity that is the opposite of the perceived characteristics of the dominant group. For example, academic achievement may be seen as reflective of the dominant culture, and an oppositional identity would involve a disidentification with academic achievement (Steele & Aronson, 1995). Academic disidentification occurs when there is a disengagement of general self-esteem from academic performance for students who are stigmatized. Consequently, students may have little psychological investment in their academic success. Osborne (1999) found that academic disidentification began to appear for some African American boys at eighth grade.

In a seminal article, Boykin (1986) described a "triple quandary" for African American children in U.S. schools that White children do not experience. African American children are enculturated by three disparate realms in their lives: mainstream or White culture, minority culture, and African American cultures. Each of these realms encourages and reinforces different values and behaviors: the individualistic orientation of White cultures, which tends to value reason over emotion, or the collectivistic nature of African American cultures, which often values integrations of affect and cognition (Boykin, 1986). The enculturation into the third realm, minority culture, refers to the experience of historical and contemporary oppression and hegemony. Years ago, Allport (1954) identified characteristics common to victims marginalized by stigmatization. Contemporary research has identified some of the these characteristics for minority students. For example, Steele and Aronson (1995) found that African American students were vulnerable to stereotype threat, which occurs when negative stereotypes are made salient. One consequence of stereotype threat is that students from stigmatized groups will underperform on academic tests, relative to their ability, when experiencing stereotype threat. The quote from the African American child at the beginning of this chapter is a compelling example of children's knowledge of stereotypes against their group.

Similarly, Midgley, Arunkumar, and Urdan (1996) found support for the view that stigmatized groups may handicap themselves in anticipation of poor performance on, for example, academic assignments. Examples of handicapping strategies include procrastinating in doing homework and allowing peers to distract the student during class. These self-handicapping strategies function to offer an external source of attribution (e.g., "I didn't have the chance to do well"), rather than an internal attribution (e.g., "I am unable to do well"), which may threaten self-esteem or self-image. The development of oppositional identities and other coping strategies reflects a response to stigmatization. Importantly, these strategies are not only found in groups that are stigmatized because of racial status. Indeed, Crocker and Major (1989) reviewed social psychological research on the tendency for stigmatized groups to devalue those domains on which nonstigmatized groups are perceived to have superior performance (e.g., academic achievement). These responses have been found to emerge in a wide variety of stigmatization contexts—disability, physical unattractiveness, obesity, sexual orientation, and mental illness—but all reflect experiences of a minority culture that has been stigmatized.

African American children in particular, but also other children of color, face this kind of triple quandary, whereas White children experience greater consistency between school and home cultures. Teachers adopting multicultural education can assist children of color with negotiating the competing influences on them. For example, some multicultural education strategies explicitly teach children how to negotiate the school culture (e.g., Delpit, 1995). Analogously, Afrocentric curriculum provides instruction within African-based cultural orientations (e.g., Asante, 1991), in part to avoid the triple quandary that is manifested for African American children in a Eurocentric curriculum.

Consequently, teachers need to be aware of some of the characteristics and experiences that are specific to children of color and tend not to be present for most White children. Clearly, traditional approaches to education that have been developed for majority group children must be modified to address the unique educational needs of children of color. Multicultural education approaches respond to some of these unique needs.

Ethnocentrism in U.S. Schools

A fourth purpose for multicultural education is to redress the Eurocentric cultural orientation to which most children of color are exposed in U.S. schools. U.S. schools usually reflect assimilation orientations toward ethnic or racial minority populations (Delpit, 1995; Fordham, 1988). An assimilation orientation is reflected in pressure within schools for ethnic and racial minority groups to assimilate to the behavior, language, values, and norms of the dominant group (Davidson, 1996; Delpit, 1995; Fordham, 1988). This pressure to assimilate takes the forms of encouraging behaviors that conform to dominant cultural and linguistic norms (Delpit, 1995) or discouraging the maintenance of ethnic or racial minority culture or languages (Fordham, 1988). Fordham (1988) found that many Black students, to be academically successful, had to sacrifice their racial identity as well as their in-group racial pride. Often, Black students need to develop a sense of "racelessness" to succeed in U.S. schools (Fordham, 1988). This racelessness takes a significant psychological and interpersonal toll on children. Importantly, it robs the larger society of important sources of diversity if success for minorities comes at the cost of losing their cultural identities. Teachers could implement principles of multicultural education to allow Black and other children of color to maintain positive forms of racial identity and maintain positive contact with their own racial group while also succeeding in school.

Through curriculum, instruction, assessment, and administration, the educational system in the United States has propagated a system in which those who fit the status quo are groomed for success (McCarthy, 1990). The standard curriculum followed in most public elementary and secondary educational institutions in the United States fails to integrate accurate and representative information of the many cultural groups who populate them. There is a biased commitment in school curricula that disproportionately focuses on Eurocentric values and history. This biased focus tends to perpetuate oppressive stereotyping that has historically disenfranchised ethnic and racial minority populations. As stated by McCarthy (1990),

> Through the school curriculum and its centerpiece, the textbook, [North] American schoolchildren come to know a kind of make-believe world made by European ancestors and white people generally. From this vantage point, the real present-day world comes to seem out of kilter—overpopulated by minorities and Third World people. (p. 119)

Examples of this ethnocentric bias can be found in the rudimentary attention paid to the history and culture of people of African descent in the United States. If addressed at all through curriculum, the units covering minority populations are usually dedicated to cultural arts, selected aspects of slavery, or a select few heroes or heroines, which are, by definition, exceptions. It is rare that an integrative curriculum coalesces the full spectrum of existence of minority populations with all aspects of North American society. Even less common is a curriculum that addresses issues of power, privilege and control, or the social, political, and economic injustices and inequalities that these and other nonmajority populations face (Bell, 1997).

Because they are in constant contact with the increasingly culturally diverse populations being served by educational institutions, educators have critical opportunities to teach in a culturally and socially balanced manner.

Table 32.2   Approaches to Multicultural Education

Approach	Description
Teaching the culturally different	Identify individual learning styles of all children Emphasis given to developing multiple instructional tools to accommodate differences
Human relations training	Teach children sensitivity to all forms of individual differences
Single-group studies	Focus on teaching about the cultural history of major ethnic or racial groups
Comprehensive multicultural education	Educational reform redressing discrimination in interpersonal, curricular, and educational contexts Emphasis on social justice
Social reconstruction through multicultural education	Broad social action agenda Educate students to enact activism agenda

Consequently, teachers and other educators have as their responsibility to redress the ethnocentrism that contributes to the disenfranchisement of children of color.

Bias in the Educational System

A final reason for the need for competent teachers to implement multicultural curriculum is to redress discriminatory or biased teaching practices. Authorities within the school system are not likely to be immune to the biases and prejudices characteristic of the larger society. Research suggests that teachers may respond differently to minority children than to White children (e.g., Aaron & Powell, 1982; Simpson & Erickson, 1983). Dusek and Joseph (1983) conducted a meta-analysis that included 77 studies and found that teacher interactions with children of color reflected lower expectations, less praise, and greater criticism when compared to teacher interactions with White children. Olsen (1988) reported that a third of her sample of Mexican American students reported being victims of prejudice from teachers. Children, like the Latino child quoted at the beginning of this chapter, become aware of prejudice affecting their lives during elementary school (Quintana,

1994, 1998). Adopting multicultural educational practices can help teachers redress bias in this instruction and bias in the school system that further undermines the educational success of children of color.

APPROACHES TO MULTICULTURAL EDUCATION

Multicultural education has passed through many stages of development, and various approaches have been developed to meet different goals related to multicultural education. Christine Sleeter (1996) described five main approaches to multicultural education: teaching the culturally different, human relations, focus on individual cultural groups, comprehensive multicultural education, and social action through multicultural education approaches. We review the five approaches delineated by Sleeter and others in Table 32.2.

Teaching the Culturally Different

Sleeter (1996) characterized this approach by its focus on raising student achievement and self-esteem through adapting instructional procedures to meet the needs of students who do not benefit from traditional classroom procedures. Implicit within this approach is a view of minority children as "culturally different" from White or majority children. Diverse learning and educational needs are believed to be a result of the cultural differences of these children. Teachers respond to these diverse needs by implementing different curricular techniques purportedly designed to accommodate these different needs. This is a favored approach by many teachers. For example, Goodwin's (1994) survey indicated that a majority of teachers viewed multicultural education as a collection of instructional tools to address the diverse learning styles of children, many of whom are children of color. The task for teachers, therefore, is to find what strategies work with which children. The positive aspect of this approach is that teachers are encouraged to consider the individual needs of children and provide individualized instructional plans. The limitation of this approach is related to the reluctance to match children's cultural values with culturally congruent instruction, given that this approach is focused narrowly on individual differences. This shortcoming is addressed in a somewhat more advanced variant of this approach involving culturally congruent instruction for children (e.g., Tharp, 1989). In this approach, teachers match instructional strategies, such as cooperative learning, with the culture of origin for children (e.g., collectivistic cultural values). The positive aspect is that the culturally based nature of traditional instruction is identified, which in turn allows for integration of indigenous cultural strategies into educational practices. The culturally congruent instruction often occurs when there is a high density of ethnic or racial minority children, such as native Hawaiians in Hawaii or African American children in predominately African American schools. These approaches may be particularly well suited to addressing primary cultural characteristics, as described above. The shortcoming involved even in the more advanced variant of this approach is related to the need to address the secondary cultural characteristics of children. Moreover, these approaches do not address the racism in the educational system that underlies may of the educational challenges faced by children of color (Sleeter, 1996).

Human Relations Approach

The human relations approach to multicultural education is likened to sensitivity training to individual differences (Sleeter, 1996). Through this approach, all forms of human diversity (gender, race, etc.) are given equal status. There is often emphasis given to similarities rather than differences. That is, once differences are acknowledged, there is a somewhat naive emphasis on finding commonalities across children: "We're all the same because we're all different" (Sleeter, 1996, p. 6). This approach is consistent with social psychological research suggesting that interracial relations tend to be more harmonious when there is an emphasis on similarities across the different groups (e.g., Pettigrew, 1998). Indeed, greater harmony among different groups of students is often the main objective for teachers using the human relations approach to multicultural education. However, social psychological research also identifies some of the limitations for this emphasis on similarities (Pettigrew, 1998). Specifically, although interracial contexts in which similarities are emphasized are associated with little racial conflict, these contexts do little to change the more generalized racial attitudes of participants. In a sense, children learn to like each other *in spite of* their racial group differences, but they may not learn to appreciate the value of racial or ethnic differences—similar to the color-blind orientation described earlier. In contrast, contexts in which racial group differences are salient are associated with reductions in generalized ethnic prejudice or racism

(Pettigrew, 1998). In these contexts, children learn to respect and, in some cases, value these cultural differences.

Single-Group Studies

A third approach tends to focus on the history and cultural characteristics of a particular cultural group. The prototype of this approach is often found in colleges and universities in which an entire curriculum is devoted to gender studies or a specific ethnic group. In elementary or secondary schools, this kind of approach is illustrated as different sections, often in social studies courses, devoted to gender issues or to a specific ethnic or racial group. The advantages of this approach are that the history and roots of specific cultural groups may be covered in some depth. There can be, however, a danger of trivializing cultural groups through "tourist" approaches in which only superficial aspects of a culture (e.g., food, music, and dance) are emphasized (Sleeter, 1996).

Comprehensive Multicultural Education

The fourth approach to multicultural education is the primary focus of this chapter, in part because it incorporates the five purposes previously reviewed and also extends some of the approaches to multicultural education reviewed above. For our purposes, we will refer to this approach as *comprehensive multicultural education*. This approach—associated with the works of scholars such as James Banks, Geneva Gay, Carl Grant, Sonia Nieto, Christine Sleeter, and others—focuses on reform of the classroom and entire educational systems with two ideals: equal opportunity and cultural pluralism for all.

The comprehensive multicultural education approach requires specific competencies to be implemented properly, rather than a collection of instructional techniques. Multicultural education competencies require social awareness on multiple levels: the personal or individual educator level, the classroom level (e.g., curriculum and instruction), and the institutional level (e.g., administration, policy, etc.). Of primary focus for this approach is the educator and classroom. This level refers to the nature of the educator's values, cultural identity, and bicultural skills (e.g., ability to communicate, motivate, understand, and develop rapport with children from different cultural backgrounds). An intense focus on creating changes at the educator and classroom levels is thought to provide momentum for more extensive institutional changes. The direction of changes from the educator and classroom levels to institutional changes is a "bottom-up" process. Nonetheless, it is inevitable that institutional change, across levels, occurs for changes to be made at the educator and classroom levels (Grant & Sleeter, 1999).

Over the past 30 or so years, a coherent sense of themes has merged defining a comprehensive approach to multicultural education. Sonia Nieto (1999) captured these themes in a conceptual framework that we use in this chapter as a broad definition of multicultural education. In her book, *Affirming Diversity: The Sociopolitical Context of Multicultural Education*, Nieto (1999) called for "comprehensive school reform and basic education for all students that challenges all forms of discrimination, permeates instruction and interpersonal relations in the classroom, and advances the democratic principles of social justice" (p. 7). This statement provides a meta-framework that will be essential to the current dialogue presented on culturally competent K–12 education. We discuss the competencies needed for such practice in the next section of this chapter after briefly discussing the fifth approach to multicultural education. A discussion of this fifth approach allows us to further define the current comprehensive approach by distinguishing it from an even more ambitious fifth approach.

Social Reconstruction
Through Multicultural Education

The fifth approach to multicultural education has been described as multicultural education with social reconstruction. This approach makes explicit attempts for reconstructing the entire educational, social, and political systems as they currently exist in the United States. This approach to education addresses political and economic oppression, discrimination, and institutional racism, preparing young people to use social action skills to bring about a more just world. Although logical as the next step in the progression toward a culturally pluralistic nation that educates its youth through a system that engenders equality, this approach to education has been challenged because of its explicit political agenda (Sleeter, 1996). In some ways, this approach can be viewed as the outgrowth of a political agenda that focuses on education as one of its means of bringing about broad political changes. In important ways, this movement supplements the comprehensive multicultural education approach with a significant social action agenda. Given that the broad social action agenda is beyond the scope of this chapter, we will focus on the fourth approach in greater depth by describing the multicultural competencies for teachers that are involved in the comprehensive multicultural education approach described earlier.

MULTICULTURAL
EDUCATION COMPETENCIES

As mentioned earlier, the comprehensive multicultural education approach requires a set of competencies rather than technical expertise. A comprehensive approach to multicultural education depends not only on what is taught or how it is taught but also on who is teaching. By this, we mean that personal qualities, convictions, awareness, and consciousness

give a foundation for the comprehensive implementation of the principles of multicultural education. According to some estimates, only about 8% of teachers are multiculturally competent. There are several important characteristics of culturally competent educators. These competencies, based on Banks (1991), are briefly presented in Table 32.3 but are elaborated as follows.

Educating from a culturally competent perspective requires teachers to have a clear sense of their own cultural identity. This identity is not only made up of awareness of static cultural features such as cultural ancestry but also includes consciousness of contemporary components of cultural identity. This consciousness includes exploration of self-ascribed features as well as socially ascribed features of cultural identity. The self-ascribed features of cultural identity include a formulation of the personal and social meanings of the teacher's own cultural heritage and values. The socially ascribed components of identity include awareness of how others perceive and react to the teacher's expression and sense of cultural identity. Typically, the formulation of cultural identity involves sometimes an emotionally intense and personally challenging exploration of the role of culture in the teacher's personal and professional life. When performed properly, this exploration will occur to a significant degree in a social context, rather than in isolation. Teachers can use their social experiences and social resources to elicit feedback and stimulate authentic exploration of their identity. Such an exploration will lead to teachers' understanding of how they transmit their own cultural characteristics, biases, and assumptions. This awareness strengthens teachers' ability to identify potential inconsistencies and incompatibilities with those of their students. An additional outcome is that educators, through self-exploration, will find ways to balance self-needs with the needs of culturally similar and culturally different students.

Table 32.3 Competencies for a Comprehensive Multicultural Education

Competency Level	Examples of Competencies
Personal/individual level	• Exploration of personal cultural identities • Knowledge of histories associated with personal cultural identities • Assessment of levels of personal racism and ethnocentrism • Awareness of abilities to use bicultural communication skills
Classroom level	• Ability to stop seeing minority students as "the other" • Understanding of classroom culture and how this affects learning for all students • Creating an classroom environment that is respectful of multiple cultures represented in classroom and school • Use of multiculturally based curriculum and instructional methods (e.g., cooperative learning strategies for children with collectivistic orientations) • Use of multiculturally inclusive instruction materials • Respect, valuing, and infusing of student's cultural and linguistic characteristics into the instruction • Ability to communicate with all students and facilitate communication between students • Ability to offer an academically challenging curriculum that children understand and that is related to their own lives
Institutional/school level	• Explicit mission or philosophy that addresses issues of multiculturalism and that is reflected in school policies and practices • Explicit measures of accountability for instructor and classroom levels of multicultural education practices • Policy and advocacy for multicultural populations • Administrative and financial support for multicultural educational practices

Culturally competent educators who engage in ongoing self-exploration in the context of culture will also explore the cultural experiences and orientations of their students, communities, and institutions around them. Within the context of race and ethnicity, there are important characteristics ascribed to various ethnic and racial groups. Teachers should recognize that their ethnic or racial minority students and parents are also members of other cultural groups, making each student and parent truly a multicultural person. In these ominous times, religious and spiritual affiliations are cultural features sharply targeted for oppression. Nevertheless, most cultural features play a large role in the ways in which teachers interact with colleagues, students' parents, and students. The first step for teachers is to identify the cultural dimensions underlying their mundane interpersonal and professional activities.

Educational institutions possess a cultural embodiment of their own. Teachers should recognize the explicit and implicit role that the cultural orientation of the school plays in the education of students. Teachers should be able to recognize when the institution's cultural orientation is incompatible with that of some students. When incompatibilities exist between the cultural orientations of an institution and a student, multiculturally competent teachers recognize this early and effectively mediate the incompatibilities.

Many students who are educationally disadvantaged are often left feeling that educational environments are not intended for them. We believe that these feelings result from an exclusionary nature to school cultures that supports and encourages some students to the exclusion of others. A culturally competent educator works to transform the cultural orientation of the school, particularly the classroom. Such an educator is committed to achieving an equitable system of education and a network of educators who view all students as being capable of learning the fundamentals of education and understanding the histories of the systems that put these fundamentals in place. A culturally competent educator teaches students explicitly about the culture of the school environment and seeks to maintain environments that respect students' cultural, ethnic, and racial pride and identity.

Culturally competent educators are personally committed to achieving equity for all students and believe that they are capable of making a difference in their students' learning. This requires not only that educators develop a bond with their students but also that they cease seeing their students as the "other." Such educators will offer an academically challenging curriculum, communicating high expectations for all students, and a belief that all students can succeed. Furthermore, culturally competent educators employ instructional methods that build on the cultural and linguistic strengths and accommodate diverse learning styles of students (Banks, 1991). Capturing the spirit of multicultural education is a quote from the guidelines on ethnic studies curriculum written by the Task Force on Ethnic Studies Curriculum Guidelines, chaired by James A. Banks (1991): "The multicultural curriculum should promote values, attitudes, and behaviors that support ethnic pluralism and cultural diversity as well as build and support the nation-state and the nation's shared national culture. E. Pluribus Unum should be the goal of the schools and the nation" (p. 15).

Culturally competent educators belong to an empowering school culture and social structure. They encourage and assist community members and parents in becoming involved and having significant voices in educational activities, including classroom and school administration—namely, decision-making processes that affect the children and families of the community.

These competencies are presented as components of teaching from a culturally competent manner. Few educational institutions have successfully employed this comprehensive approach to education because its multiple components have been found difficult to arrange and implement under existing educational structures. Consequently, there is need for further educational reform in the future.

CULTURALLY PLURALISTIC EDUCATIONAL REFORM IN THE FUTURE

Mass educational systems in the United States, such as the modern public elementary and secondary educational systems, were founded as a means of producing future contributors to the nation's economic and political systems as well as upholding the cultural capital of the United States (Cheng, Brizendine, & Oakes, 1979; Yeakey & Bennett, 1990). Cultural capital refers to the values and beliefs commonly associated with the foregoing success of the United States. It is quite evident that there is a stratified system inherent in educational contexts. Those who are among the elite of the population are tracked into the top tiers of education, and the working classes are often tracked into the more technical vocations (Mehan, 1992; Yeakey & Bennett, 1990).

The primary responsibility of educational institutions is to prepare future citizens for their positions in society. The task of school administrators is to facilitate this preparation through management of the institutions. Unfortunately, an underlying agenda of school administrators is to ensure that the institution upholds the cultural capitalist values of the major shareholders (i.e., tax payers, politicians, and economic investors) (Fowler, 1999). In upholding these values, there is a perpetuation of the historical disenfranchisement of ethnic and racial minority populations.

In developing arguments for the reform of educational systems and structures, we must look at the impact that educational institutions have on the identity development processes of children. Superimposing historical and modern educational practices over social and racial identity development theories, it is no surprise that the picture created is one of despair in which many children, particularly children of color, are potentially stripped of the tools necessary for developing ambitious academic identities. Education is still considered as one of the major pathways to success social, political, and economic advancement is absolutely imperative in the process of leveling out the hierarchical system that fosters oppression.

REFERENCES

Aaron, R., & Powell, G. (1982). Feedback practices as a function of teacher and pupil race during reading groups instruction. *Journal of Negro Education, 51,* 50-59.

Aboud, F. E. (1988). *Children and prejudice.* Cambridge, UK: Blackwell.

Allport, G. W. (1954). *The nature of prejudice.* Cambridge, UK: Addison-Wesley.

Asante, M. K. (1991). The Afrocentric idea in education. *Journal of Negro Education, 60,* 170-180.

Banks, J. A. (1991). *Curriculum guidelines for multicultural education.* Prepared by the NCSS Task Force on Ethnic Studies Curriculum Guidelines, Silver Spring, MD.

Banks, J. A. (1993). The canon debate, knowledge construction, and multicultural education. *Educational Researcher, 22*(5), 4-14.

Banks, J. A. (1995). Multicultural education and curriculum transformation. *Journal of Negro Education, 64,* 390-400.

Bell, L. (1997). Theoretical foundations for social justice education. In M. Adams, L. Bell, & P. Griffin (Eds.), *Teaching for diversity and social justice: A sourcebook* (pp. 3-15). New York: Routledge Kegan Paul.

Boykin, A. W. (1986). The triple quandary and the schooling of Afro-American children. In V. Neisser (Ed.), *The school achievement of minority children* (pp. 57-92). Hillsdale, NJ: Lawrence Erlbaum.

Cheng, C. W., Brizendine, E., & Oakes, J. (1979). What is "an equal chance" for minority children? *Journal of Negro Education, 48,* 267-287.

Crocker, J., & Major, B. (1989). Social stigma and self-esteem: The self-protective properties of stigma. *Psychological Review, 96,* 608-630.

Cross, W. E., Jr. (1995). Oppositional identity and African American youth: Issues and prospects. In W. D. Hawley & A. W. Jackson (Eds.), *Toward a common destiny: Improving peace and ethnic relations in America* (pp. 185-204). San Francisco: Jossey-Bass.

Davidson, A. L. (1996). *Making and molding identity in schools.* Albany: SUNY Press.

Delpit, L. (1995). *Other people's children: Sociocultural conflict in the classroom.* New York: New Press.

Doyle, A., & Aboud, F. E. (1995). A longitudinal study of White children's racial prejudice as a social-cognitive development. *Merrill-Palmer Quarterly, 41,* 209-228.

Dusek, J. B., & Joseph, G. (1983). The bases of teacher expectancies: A meta-analysis. *Journal of Educational Psychology, 75,* 327-346.

Fordham, S. (1988). Racelessness as a factor in Black students' success. *Harvard Educational Review, 58,* 54-84.

Fowler, F. C. (1999). Curiouser and curiouser: New concepts in the rapidly changing landscape of educational administration. *Educational Administration Quarterly, 35,* 594-614.

Grant, C. A., & Sleeter, C. E. (1999). *Turning on learning: Five approaches for multicultural teaching plans for face, class, gender and* disability. Englewood Cliffs, NJ: Prentice Hall.

Hirschfeld, L. A. (1994). The child's representation of human groups. *The Psychology of Learning and Motivation, 31,* 133-185.

Houser, N. O. (1996). Multicultural education for the dominant culture: Toward the development of a multicultural sense of self. *Urban Education, 31,* 125-148.

Jhally, S., & Lewis, J. (1992). *Enlightened racism.* Boulder, CO: Westview.

McCarthy, C. (1990). Multicultural education, minority identities, textbooks, and the challenge of curriculum reform. *Journal of Education, 172,* 118-130.

Mehan, H. (1992). Understanding inequality in the schools: The contribution of interpretive studies. *Sociology of Education, 65,* 1-20.

Midgley, C., Arunkumar, R., & Urdan, T. C. (1996). "If I don't do well tomorrow, there's a reason": Predictors of adolescents' use of self-handicapping strategies. *Journal of Educational Psychology, 88,* 423-434.

Moynihan, D. P. (1965). *The Negro family in America: A case for national action.* Washington, DC: U.S. Department of Labor.

National Center for Education Statistics. (2000). *Digest of educational statistics, Table 106.* Washington, DC: Author.

National Center for Education Statistics. (2001). *Educational achievement and Black-White inequality.* Washington, DC: Author.

Nieto, S. (1999). *Affirming diversity: The sociopolitical context of multicultural education.* Boston: Addison Wesley Longman.

Ogbu, J. U. (1994). From cultural difference to differences in cultural frame of reference. In P. M. Greenfield & R. R. Cocking (Eds.), *Cross-cultural roots of minority child development* (pp. 365-392). Hillsdale, NJ: Lawrence Erlbaum.

Olsen, L. (1988). *Crossing the schoolhouse border: Immigrant students and the California public schools.* Boston: California Tomorrow.

Osborne, J. W. (1999). Unraveling underachievement among African American boys from an identification with academics perspective. *Journal of Negro Education, 68,* 555-565.

Padilla, A. M., Lindholm, K. J., Chen, A., Durán, R., Hakuta, K., Lambert, W., et al. (1991). The English-only movement: Myths, reality, and implications for psychology. *American Psychologist, 46,* 120-130.

Pettigrew, T. F. (1998). Intergroup contact theory. *Annual Review of Psychology, 49,* 65-85.

Pollard, K. M., & O'Hare, W. P. (1999). America's racial and ethnic minorities. *Population Bulletin, 54,* 3-48.

President's Advisory Commission on Educational Excellence for Hispanic Americans. (1996). *Our nation on the fault line: Hispanic American education* [Online]. Available: http://www.ed.gov/pubs/faultline/call.html

Quintana, S. M. (1994). A model of ethnic perspective taking ability applied to Mexican-American children and youth. *International Journal of Intercultural Relations, 18,* 419-448.

Quintana, S. M. (1998). Children's developmental understanding of ethnicity and race. *Applied & Preventive Psychology, 7,* 27-45.

Quintana, S. M., & Johnson, D. J. (2001, August). *How racism and prejudice influence children.* Paper presented at the annual convention of the American Psychological Association, San Francisco.

Rumberger, R. W., & Thomas, S. L. (2000). The distribution of dropout and turnover rates among urban and suburban high schools. *Sociology of Education, 73,* 39-67.

Sears, D. O. (1988). Symbolic racism. In P. A. Katz & T. Dalmas (Eds.), *Eliminating racism: Profiles in controversy* (pp. 53-84). New York: Plenum.

Simpson, A. W., & Erickson, M. T. (1983). Teacher's verbal and nonverbal communication patterns as a function of teacher race, student gender, and student race. *American Educational Research Journal, 20,* 183-198.

Sleeter, C. E. (1996). *Multicultural education as social activism.* Albany: SUNY Press.

Steele, C. M., & Aronson, J. (1995). Stereotype threat and the intellectual test performance of

African Americans. *Journal of Personality and Social Psychology, 69,* 797-811.

Tharp, R. G. (1989). Psychocultural variables and constants: Effects on teaching and learning in schools. *American Psychologist, 44,* 349-359.

Yeakey, C. C., & Bennett, C. T. (1990). Race, schooling, and class in American society. *Journal of Negro Education, 59,* 3-18.

33

Walking a Tightrope

Strategies for Teaching Undergraduate Multicultural Counseling Courses

ALVIN N. ALVAREZ
San Francisco State University

MARIE L. MIVILLE
Teachers College, Columbia University

From the student eager to learn exactly how to deal with her roommate, to the student who eyes the instructor warily and wonders how his community will be portrayed, and to the student who is fearful that this will be yet another forum for blaming him as the source of oppression, the challenges of teaching an undergraduate multicultural counseling course are clear. Indeed, with all eyes on the instructor, teaching a course on such emotionally charged topics is akin to walking an academic version of a tightrope. In maintaining this delicate pedagogical balance, instructors must negotiate both the reactions of students with varying, if not conflicting, attitudes toward the course as well as the expectations of a department trying to fulfill any number of potentially unrealistic, curricular requirements. No less important, the instructor also must balance her own expectations by designing a course that she considers to be ethical, professionally competent, and pedagogically sound.

Yet, in light of the clear challenges that such a course presents, the paucity of literature that explores the actual teaching of multicultural counseling is particularly striking for a profession that has worked diligently to promote multicultural competence as a professional standard (American Psychological Association,

1993; Sue, Arredondo, & McDavis, 1992). Indeed, although the literature on multicultural competence has focused on defining standards of multicultural competence (Sue et al., 1992), operationalizing and developing measures of multicultural competence (LaFramboise, Coleman, & Hernandez, 1991; Sodowsky, Taffe, Gutkin, & Wise, 1994), and measuring outcomes of multicultural experiences and curriculum (Pope-Davis, Reynolds, Dings, & Nielson, 1995; Sodowsky, Kuo-Jackson, Richardson, & Corey, 1998), it is surprising to find that little attention has been devoted to the practice of teaching such courses at either the undergraduate or graduate level. Nevertheless, both logic and intuition suggest that the components involved in actually teaching such courses (i.e., pedagogical approach, course goals, group facilitation, etc.) are critical to effectively realizing the standards of multicultural competence promulgated by our profession. To this end, the present chapter was written with the intent of challenging instructors to examine key areas for consideration in designing and teaching effective multicultural counseling courses for undergraduate students.

Although multicultural competence as a professional imperative has focused primarily on defining standards for graduates in training and professionals in practice, the underlying dimensions of multicultural competence (Sue et al., 1992) may be as educationally valuable to undergraduates as they are to graduate students and professionals. Although multicultural competence at the undergraduate level may have less to do with the training of culturally skilled helpers, the value of such courses for these students may have more to do with facilitating their development as critically thinking individuals. Departments may differ in types of multicultural courses offered to undergraduates, with some offering more counseling-oriented courses (in preparation for graduate study) and others offering courses

focusing more on psychology. Although both types of courses may have differing agendas, the general focus, as it relates to this chapter, is the same—dealing with multicultural issues or collective differences as based on race/ethnicity, gender, socioeconomic class, and so forth in practice and research. Particularly in light of the diversification of higher education and the infusion of multicultural perspectives into academia (Turner, Garcia, Nora, & Rendon, 1996), undergraduates and graduates alike stand to benefit from courses that facilitate their awareness of themselves, as well as their biases and assumptions; foster an awareness of culturally different worldviews; and challenge them to compare and critique multicultural perspectives on psychological functioning. Given that developing multicultural competence is clearly a lifelong process and that graduate programs have often been criticized for their insufficient training on such a complex topic, it stands to reason that counseling as a profession can only benefit from promoting multicultural competence at earlier points in the educational pipeline. Consequently, the present chapter has been written to serve as a catalyst for an ongoing dialogue among instructors about teaching practices that have been effective in facilitating the multicultural competence of their undergraduates.

To this end, we have chosen to focus the present chapter on teaching stand-alone, introductory multicultural counseling courses, not as an endorsement of this particular curricular format but as an acknowledgment of the prevalence of such courses in academia (Reynolds, 1995; Ridley, Mendoza, & Kanitz, 1994). Indeed, although the prevalence of such a format may be more reflective of institutional expediency rather than sound pedagogical rationale, a central challenge still remains for instructors of such courses. That is, how does one teach the sole multicultural counseling course in a curriculum where students may receive little to no formal exposure to the

Table 33.1   Issues for Developing a Multicultural Counseling Course

I. Pedagogical Assumptions
    a. Role of the instructor
    b. Role of students
    c. Content and process

II. Structural Considerations
    a. Focus of the course
    b. Course content
    c. Course format and assignments
        i. Activities
        ii. Discussion formats
        iii. Journals
        iv. Noncounseling readings
        v. Experiential exercises
        vi. Scholarly presentation

III. Process
    d. Group norms
    e. Formative feedback
    f. Expectations and reactions
    g. Conflict and resistance
    h. Planning for change
    i. Instructor's process

topic? To address this question, we begin with a discussion of the pedagogical assumptions that inform an instructor's design and goals for his or her course and an articulation of our own assumptions within our courses. The second section of the chapter addresses how the design and implementation of a multicultural counseling course follows from the instructor's pedagogical assumptions. Last, we conclude with an examination of both the structural and process dimensions for consideration in such a course (see Table 33.1).

PEDAGOGICAL ASSUMPTIONS

A central premise of the current chapter is that the design of a multicultural counseling course is directly related to an instructor's pedagogical stance on teaching (Adams & Marchesani, 1992; Bonwell & Sutherland, 1996). That is, the structure, content, and the process of the course are directly reflective of the instructor's answers to questions about his or her role, the role of the students, and ultimately the process of learning (i.e., how students learn in the course). Indeed, it is our belief that the instructor's pedagogical assumptions influence key dimensions of a multicultural counseling course such as the role of the instructor as expert versus facilitator, the role of students as active versus passive learners, and the extent to which the course is content versus process driven.

Hence, as an initial step in designing their course, instructors need to reflect on their role in the classroom as well as their stance on authority, particularly as it relates to students. For example, answers to questions such as, "Do you regard yourself as a facilitator?" "To what extent do you assume the role of a multicultural expert?" and "What does the instructor contribute to the course?" may be directly reflected in instructors' preferred instructional methods (i.e., lectures, experiential exercises, classroom discussion, etc.), as well as the quality of interaction between instructors and their students. Relatedly, questions about one's expectations of students and their role in the classroom may be critical in shaping the dynamics of the course. For instance, questions such as, "Do you regard students as active or passive learners?" "What do students contribute to the course?" "How do you incorporate the experiences and values of students into the course?" and "What do you expect students to learn from each other?" influence the manner in which instructors encourage dialogue in the course as well as the extent to which class assignments and exercises are designed to engage students actively in the course material. Last, instructors also may need to address their expectations of both course content and process. Answers to questions such as, "To what extent does the course focus on theory and research?" "Does the course maintain a balance between facilitating an understanding of oneself and understanding other individuals and their respective communities and cultures?" "To what extent do lectures, assignments, and discussions challenge students to learn on affective, cognitive, and behavioral dimensions?" and "How are classroom conflicts addressed?" challenge instructors to examine both what students learn and how they learn.

Although the answers to such questions clearly fall along a continuum, to the extent that an instructor regards himself or herself as an expert, students as passive learners, and learning as a primarily cognitive exercise, there is a greater likelihood that the course may focus more on class lectures and the comprehension and analysis of theories and concepts and less so on class discussion and student input. Conversely, a course in which the instructor regards himself or herself as a facilitator, students as active learners, and learning as having affective, cognitive, and behavioral dimensions will more likely involve alternative

instructional methods (in addition to lecturing) such as experiential exercises, role-plays, and simulations that challenge students on affective as well as cognitive levels. Thus, the instructor's willingness to examine such pedagogical questions in a reflective and intentional manner is an initial step in creating an effective instructional experience for students.

Authors' Assumptions

Consistent with the challenge that instructors examine their own pedagogical assumptions, an articulation of our pedagogical assumptions in our own courses may provide a context for what follows in the current chapter. Although the goal of such an articulation is not to define how instructors should do their work, it is our intention to stimulate the reader to examine his or her own position in regards to the issues at hand. Specifically, we address how we have designed our own multicultural counseling courses in terms of our assumptions about (a) the role of students and instructors, (b) the value of students' experiences and biases, (c) the nature of learning, (d) the role of identity development, and (e) counseling in a sociopolitical and sociohistorical context.

Role of Students and Instructors

With respect to our assumptions about the roles of students and instructors, we believe that the process of learning multicultural competency is both interpersonal and multidirectional. That is, learning potentially comes as a result of interactions from instructor to student, student to instructor, and student to student. Contrary to a course in which the instructor is regarded as the "expert" and, by extension, regarded as the primary "source" of information, we believe that all participants bring potentially instructive experiences, values, and beliefs to a multicultural counseling course. The experiences and assumptions about race, class, gender, sexual orientation, prejudice, and oppression that both students and instructor(s) bring into such courses are potentially instructive experiences that may be starting points for both self-exploration and discussion. Thus, we believe that the role of the instructor has less to do with being the primary "expert" on multicultural counseling and more to do with being a facilitator in creating a forum and a classroom climate that allows for a constructive exchange of ideas and experiences.

Student Experience and Biases

Consequently, a pedagogical stance that values the experiences and ideas of students is integral to a classroom experience that encourages students to actively engage in the course material through self-reflection and self-disclosure. Contrary to the expectation of instructors as experts or "givers of knowledge" and students as "receivers of knowledge" (Perry, 1999), we believe that a pedagogical approach that minimizes hierarchies and positions of authority while emphasizing a sense of collaboration and interaction will be far more effective in creating a classroom environment that encourages a genuine exchange of experiences, ideas, and opinions. Indeed, in a course where students clearly bring their own experiences and opinions, facilitating rather than neglecting or repressing such an exchange will prove to be a key step in engaging students to use their experiences as a starting point for examining themselves and their assumptions about others. Although students typically enter such courses with an implicit goal of learning about the nuances and traditions of "other" cultures, we believe that a focus on learning about oneself is a critical step in developing multicultural competence. That is, an explicit premise of multicultural counseling courses, particularly for undergraduates, is that a genuine understanding and

appreciation for individuals from culturally different backgrounds is directly related to their understanding of their own assumptions, values, and beliefs regarding issues of gender, sexual orientation, race, and so on (Sue & Sue, 1999).

More than with many courses within a curriculum, we believe that students enter multicultural counseling courses with their own, perhaps unexamined, experiences, assumptions, and biases about many of the topics being discussed. Although the emotional charge of a multicultural counseling course may come from students' experiences and their anticipatory anxiety about how such experiences may be respected or disrespected, supported or challenged, or acknowledged or ignored in the course, we regard such experiences as potentially instructive in engaging students to recognize the instructional relevance of the material. For students to engage themselves emotionally as well as intellectually in the course, instructors will need to acknowledge the value of the experiences and assumptions that students bring with them into the course.

Nature of Learning

Thus, both the content and process of learning in our courses are grounded in the explicit goal of bridging the gap between the abstract and intellectual dimensions of the course and the more personal and affective dimensions. Unlike more traditionally structured courses, we would argue that the power of a multicultural counseling course comes from its potential to be personally relevant and emotionally evocative (Weinstein & Obear, 1992), as opposed to being simply an intellectual exercise involving the comprehension and critique of abstract concepts and theories. As a result, the learning process in a multicultural counseling course will need to involve instructional strategies (Bonwell & Sutherland, 1996) that address and engage students on both affective and cognitive domains. Indeed, to the extent that instructors can create an affectively and cognitively challenging learning environment that encourages self-reflection, it seems likely that students will be better able to recognize the personal relevance of abstract concepts and "objective" histories and how their own cultural socialization and assumptions influence their worldviews.

Identity Development

Relatedly, we believe that coming to an awareness of oneself and one's assumptions is a developmental process that involves qualitatively distinctive shifts in a student's awareness, understanding, and reactions to multicultural issues. Extrapolating from the literature on racial identity theory (Helms, 1990; Tatum, 1992), one can argue that the manner in which both students and instructors respond to multicultural issues is reflective of their own point of development in terms of their identities regarding race, gender, sexual orientation, and so forth. Furthermore, Helms (1990) has argued that interpersonal dynamics are reflective of the racial identity of the participants. Hence, instructors may need to be cognizant of the fact that classroom dynamics between students, as well as between students and instructors, may be influenced by the multiple levels of identity development among the individuals in the class.

Consequently, an ability to assess both a classroom's and the individual student's developmental maturity will be critical in creating a developmentally responsive learning experience. In other words, instructors may need to recognize that due to differing levels of developmental maturation, what is developmentally appropriate for one student, in terms of exercises, assignments, and verbal responses, may not be appropriate for another student. For instance, immersing a group of students who have had minimal exposure to multicultural

issues in an exercise on oppression, during their first day of class, may be less effective than doing the same exercise with a group of students who have had more exposure to such topics. Hence, the challenge for an instructor will be to create an instructional experience for a student that is responsive to his or her particular point of development (Alvarez, 2002).

As a corollary to the importance of assessing student development, an equally critical skill for instructors involves an assessment of their own identity development (Adams & Marchesani, 1992; Hardiman & Jackson, 1992). In particular, it may be important for instructors to recognize that their comments in the course, the manner in which they frame assignments and exercises, and their responses to their students may all be reflective of their own developmental maturity with regards to the material at hand. Particularly in a course that deals with potentially provocative material, an awareness of and perhaps the ability to articulate one's assumptions, views, and limitations are critical in establishing a sense of trust and genuineness among the students (Weinstein & Obear, 1992). Moreover, the ability to articulate one's own developmental process and struggles is an ideal opportunity to model the learning process expected of our students. As Weinstein and Obear (1992) observed,

> Unless I can admit to the students that I [the instructor] am still in the process of learning and unlearning and that there are areas about which I still need to be educated, I may give the impression that there are simple solutions. . . . This attitude places great pressure on us as instructors to have "the answer." (p. 45)

Sociopolitical Context

With regard to the content of effective multicultural counseling courses, we believe that effective multicultural counseling courses are designed within a sociopolitical and sociohistorical framework. That is, an understanding of a community's history and its history of oppression within a dominant society is integral to working effectively with cross-cultural differences. Although multicultural counseling courses clearly need to address the differences in communities with regard to values, belief systems, traditions, and so on, we strongly believe that it is critical to address how such cultural differences have been regarded and devalued within a larger social context. As various authors have noted (Helms & Cook, 1999; Sue & Sue, 1999), the dynamics of oppression have been and continue to be the fuel that underlies the interactions and relationships between various cultural communities. We concur with Sue and Sue's (1999) contention that a history of oppression within various cultural communities, as well as the professional history of psychology as a perpetrator of oppression (Guthrie, 1997), provides a context for what they defined as "sociopolitical considerations of mistrust" in counseling. That is, an individual's experience with oppression, both directly and indirectly as a historical legacy, is relevant to understanding not only how individuals perceive themselves, others, and the environment and institutions in which they live but also how they regard both the counselor and counseling process. Consequently, to the extent that multicultural counseling courses strive to expose students to the life experiences of various cultural communities, an understanding of the dynamics of oppression, both historical and contemporary, will be critical.

STRUCTURAL CONSIDERATIONS

Focus of the Course

Although the overall structure of the course depends on how the instructor addresses a number of issues described above, instructors may want to consider additional factors as well. For instance, a critical issue involves whether the focus of the course will be on one community or multiple communities. Relatedly, the instructor needs to decide the nature of the communities to be studied. The term *multicultural* has a variety of meanings: It can focus uniquely on race and ethnicity, even a single racial/ethnic community (e.g., Asian American psychology course), or a have a broader emphasis that involves overarching issues of oppression, access, and social justice (Bell, 1997). This latter emphasis can focus on multiple group memberships, even multiple oppressions, based on race, ethnicity, gender, socioeconomic status, sexual orientation, abilities, age, and religion. The advantage of choosing a more narrow focus (e.g., only race and ethnicity) is that it allows students to grasp a more in-depth understanding of relevant topics for a single group, whereas disadvantages include a lack of understanding of cultures beyond that single group. The advantage of a broader perspective allows students to understand global issues of oppression and their interconnections; disadvantages include having too broad a perspective such that students end up with little substantive knowledge of the individual groups. Regardless of the approach that one chooses, it is important to make a realistic appraisal about what can be adequately covered in a single semester, particularly if the course is more broad based.

In choosing one approach over another, one factor for consideration may be the extent to which multicultural issues are already included within the university and departmental curricula. Insofar as multicultural issues are genuinely infused into the broader curriculum, an instructor may have greater license to create a more focused course; conversely, a curriculum with minimal attention to multicultural issues more likely increases the pressure on an instructor to create a broad-based multicultural counseling course. Relatedly, instructors may need to be mindful of the ethical considerations of designing a course within their scope of expertise. Although instructors may face institutional and departmental pressures to create a course with a certain format, we believe it is also critical that instructors explicitly define the boundaries of their expertise and the scope of the course. Indeed, we would suggest that agonizing over the pros and cons of a broad-based versus focused course is not as important as ensuring that the course has clearly articulated goals. Regardless of the focus that instructors ultimately choose, it will be critical for them to articulate both the scope of the course and the rationale for such a decision. Given that students will most likely enter such a course with clear, albeit unspoken, expectations about what the course "should" address, we believe that it is the responsibility of the instructor to clarify the goals of the course, what the course can and cannot address, and the advantages and disadvantages of their chosen approach.

Another aspect in deciding course content is weighing the extent to which basic knowledge should be covered as well as including a skills component. Although skills acquisition often may be regarded as being less salient for undergraduate students, we also have found that multicultural courses can suffer by focusing exclusively on providing knowledge (the proverbial "dos and don'ts" with people of color) and consciousness-raising activities, such that students may be left feeling angry, confused, and without any new way of dealing with cultural differences. In fact, Tatum (1992) has argued that consciousness raising without raising students' awareness of the possibility for change is a "prescription for despair" (p. 20). Thus, we believe a skills component is essential for multicultural counseling, whether the course is broad based or more specific in focus.

Although a multicultural skills component for undergraduates will clearly not address the assessment and intervention skills required of graduate-level counseling students, it may be useful to address how many of the basic communication skills that are taught in undergraduate interpersonal skills or personal growth courses can be applied to interacting with culturally different people. One of the authors has often included a variety of "how-tos" for students that she has gathered from readings over the years. For example, critical cultural differences in such areas as proxemics, kinesthetics, and paralinguistics (Sue & Sue, 1999) that affect the very space and tone of effective communication across cultures can be applied to role-plays. As with communication skills in general, we cannot provide scripts of the "perfect" interaction, but we can provide some guiding questions or suggestions to students. Indeed, a major part of having one's consciousness raised is freeing oneself to bring up normally "taboo" topics, such as racism and culture, by applying and adapting basic communication skills.

Course Content

One of the most important structural components of a multicultural course is in providing accurate knowledge of the groups to be studied. Sadly, it is still safe to assume that most students have little accurate knowledge or understanding about most of the groups to be studied in multicultural courses. Indeed, what knowledge or understanding students have is in the form of stereotypes and misinformation, fed to them from birth by multiple sources, not the least of which include parents, extended family, friends, school teachers, the government, and, of course, the ever present media. Borrowing from DuBois's famous phrase, one might describe this socialization process as "the miseducation of the American!" Thus, we believe that a major goal of the course is to provide accurate information, such as the numerical disparities via the U.S. Census about racial and gender differences in critical areas such as education, salary, and poverty.

From this starting point, an instructor may want to consider how to address the histories of various communities in the United States. Although a primary theme is for students to learn the existence of discriminatory policies and legislation, an equally critical rationale for providing a historical context is to help students to understand the impact of oppression on both the collective and individual psyches of targeted communities. In focusing on histories, instructors may generally use a variety of techniques, ranging from experiential exercises (e.g., Power Shuffle) to videos and films to discussions of current topics (e.g., the Elian Gonzalez story as told from several vantage points).

Although discussions of racism, sexism, and so on are integral to the effectiveness of such courses, it is equally important for students to explore how topics such as race and gender may be sources of pride and personal enrichment. Given that discussions about racism (and other "isms") may be similar to discussing other traumatic events, thereby evoking strong emotions or feelings of helplessness, instructors may want to consider how to instill balance into their class discussions. That is, part of deconstructing the "taboo" aspects of race, gender, and other similar topics may involve an openness to discussing the positive as well as negative associations and consequences of such topics.

An equally important piece to address in course content are cultural values, customs, ways of knowing, ways of behaving, social mores, social organization, and so forth of particular communities. Courses that are more focused (e.g., specific racial group) are generally advantaged in adequately covering this kind of content, at least beyond the laundry list approach. Instructors may find that students underestimate information about cultural values and beliefs as overly simplistic, in both content and application. Thus, a major challenge for students in these courses is learning and applying the information about specific communities in an accurate, albeit nonstereotypical manner. For example, in addressing the topic of collectivistic values, students may grapple with understanding how therapy or research would differ from a collectivist culture versus a Western individualistic culture.

One author typically presents this dilemma to students at the beginning of the course in the following manner—that the information to be learned here is unique in that it centers on social information about which much prejudice and stereotypes already exist (e.g., based on race, gender, or sexual orientation). Thus, the challenge for a student is to learn the information without losing the humanity and individuality of the people being studied. Indeed, a major instructional accomplishment is achieved if students can walk away from the course with an understanding of the multiple levels of psychological functioning (collective and individual) that affect individuals. This extends to understanding both between-group differences in social expectations and norms, as well as individual within-group variance from these norms (both healthy and unhealthy).

Using information learned in a multicultural counseling course is not only unique but also similar to other areas of knowledge. A comparison that one author usually makes is with learning about making diagnoses (i.e., abnormal psychology). In this area, students learn that psychologists use checklists of symptoms to diagnose people. Given a diagnosis, how then do professionals maintain their understanding of the client in question as a unique individual? We propose that a similar situation exists in learning cultural information, though at a more profound level. That is, an understanding of general norms or tendencies as well as values, customs, and mores of social groups provides a context and starting point for distinguishing between that which is cultural versus that which is reflective of the individual.

Course Format and Assignments

In addition to making decisions regarding course content (the "what" question), instructors must decide the manner in which information will be learned (the "how" question). Given the emotionally evocative nature of the course content, an implicit goal of designing course activities is to provide several outlets for discussion, analysis, and self-growth. For detailed resources regarding potential course activities and active learning techniques, readers are referred to Katz (1978), Pfeiffer and Jones (1972-1981, 1982-present), Silberman (1998), Singelis (1998), and Adams, Bell, and Griffin (1997). In structuring the course, instructors may want to consider a variety of activities, such as

- traditional didactic lectures;
- small- and large-group discussions;
- self-reflective assignments (e.g., keeping a journal, writing thought or reaction papers);
- readings related to multicultural theories, concepts, and skills;
- non-counseling-related readings and essays from history, literature, political science, gender studies, ethnic studies, and so forth;
- experiential activities;
- simulations and role-plays; and
- critical analysis assignments and presentations (i.e., critiquing a body of literature or a construct).

Activities. Consistent with the spirit of a multicultural course, using a variety of activities helps ensure that the course will be responsive to the variety of learning styles that students bring into the class (Adams & Marchesani,

1992), whether the style is visual or auditory, collectivistic or individualistic, and so on. Indeed, alternative learning strategies may provide implicit cross-cultural lessons for students. For instance, emphasizing cooperative learning techniques places the onus of growth squarely on students' shoulders and de-emphasizes the teacher as the "expert" while providing students with an exercise in collectivism, rather than individualism. Group activities also establish that learning occurs for everyone in the class, including the instructor, and that a general norm for the class is collaboration, rather than competition.

Discussion Formats. Realizing that a multicultural course is certain to evoke student opinions and reactions, incorporating sufficient time for discussions, both in large and small groups, will be essential to the success of the course. Although a large-group discussion has the benefit of allowing a broader range of students to participate, we have found that small-group discussions are more effective in building cohesion, trust, consistency, and safety in a manner that is far more difficult in the larger class. Particularly in a course where topics are potentially volatile, it is critical that instructors examine how to provide students with alternative and safer arenas for self-disclosure. Options for creating small groups include the following: (a) using the same small groups throughout the semester or (b) creating new small groups with each activity. The advantage of the former is that group members, over time, can come to know each other and can better confront/challenge the members as the semester proceeds. The advantage of the second option is that changing the group means not getting "stuck" with the same people and learning from new people. This is important if the makeup of the small group can differ in terms of ethnicity and other variables of diversity.

Journals. As an additional opportunity for self-disclosure and self-reflection, keeping a journal or writing reaction papers is an effective means for allowing some private or confidential space for students to process through what they are learning and understanding what are the pockets of resistance for each person. It has been the experience of both authors that the cumulative effect of the readings, exercises, assignments, and discussions in such a course evokes far more reactions from students than what can be adequately addressed in an all-too-brief 50-minute class. Moreover, such an assignment implicitly conveys to students that developing multicultural knowledge involves an ongoing process of self-reflection that occurs long after either the class or the course is finished. In fact, one of the authors has had several students tell her that they continued to write in their journal after the course was over because it was still personally powerful for them.

Noncounseling Readings. Although course readings typically focus on providing basic knowledge and theoretical information (e.g., journal articles, book chapters) from the field of psychology, instructors also may want to consider readings of a more personal/autobiographical nature (e.g., Andersen & Collins, 1998; Anzaldua, 1990; Hong, 1993). This type of reading helps shift the focus away from purely abstract and intellectual concepts and helps expose students to the opinions and experiences of others from a lived perspective (i.e., understanding where someone is coming from, understanding their "soul"). Indeed, we would argue that such personal essays and autobiographical readings give life to much of what is taught in a multicultural course. For example, reading the autobiography of Malcolm X is an excellent illustration of racial identity theory (Helms, 1990). Moreover, assigning such readings also helps professionals-to-be value the contributions of areas beyond

psychology, such as political science, gender and ethnic studies, anthropology, and sociology. In effect, these readings help students move beyond the "box" of psychology by recognizing that the development of multicultural competence is an interdisciplinary process.

Experiential Exercises. Also in line with moving beyond the cognitive focus of traditional lectures, instructors may want to consider incorporating structured experiential activities and simulations that result in a heightened level of consciousness and affective growth. As Bonwell and Sutherland (1996) noted, "Students are simply more likely to internalize, understand, and remember material through active engagement in the learning process" (p. 3). Although topics such as discrimination or stereotypes clearly can be treated as abstractions in a lecture, it is our belief that an exercise that allows students to experience discrimination, stereotyping, or a sense of being "different" can be a far more transformative and powerful learning experience. For instance, a classic activity to use at the beginning of the course is the "Power Shuffle," in which the class stands together on one side of the room. Then, the instructor calls out a variety of labels (such as being female, gay, person of color, etc.). As each of these labels is called, students must decide if the label applies to them and, if so, move to the other side of the room. The activity is done in total silence, after which there is small-group discussion, followed by a large-group discussion. The class members generally experience the activity with much emotion and great enthusiasm. It is an excellent way to open up discussion about the experience of being "different" while modeling inclusion and self-expression. Yet as Joplin (1995) keenly observed, "Experience alone is insufficient to be called experiential education, and it is the reflection process which turns experience into experiential education" (p. 15). Thus, to the extent that instructors decide to incorporate experiential exercises into their courses, they will need to provide students with both the structure and the time to process thoroughly their observations and reactions.

Scholarly Presentations. Another important activity for instructors to consider is having students write a scholarly paper and/or presentation on a multicultural topic. This is generally an enjoyable part of the class because it allows students to take on something of an expert role in an area of their choosing. Initially, students are uncomfortable about this part of the class but generally come to embrace it with enthusiasm. A primary learning goal of the assignment is that students learn to deal with their own discomfort in learning and leading a discussion about an "other" group while taking primary responsibility for passing on accurate information (nothing better signifies higher learning than this kind of activity!). In essence, the assignment exposes students as well as challenges them to critique the existing professional literature on a given topic or community.

PROCESS

Group Norms

To the extent that the course is taught correctly, there will no doubt be a number of strong reactions by students. Thus, in addition to structural considerations, it is important to plan for and address the process issues related to such reactions and the need to create a safe environment that helps students to process these reactions. As an initial step toward such an environment, it may be important for instructors to consider the group norms necessary in creating such an environment, as well as the process by which such norms are established in the class. To foster a more collaborative

classroom environment, as well as to increase students' investment into the course, instructors and students may find it helpful to establish group norms together, rather than having the instructor generate norms by herself or himself. For instance, an initial class may be devoted to a discussion about students' expectations of themselves, their peers, and the instructor in regards to creating a successful course. In addition to the norms established by students, instructors may need to be prepared to contribute their own suggestions to this process. For instance, one of the authors begins the course by reviewing three basic rules Tatum (1992) has set forth: (a) all class discussion is confidential (use no identifying information outside of class), (b) speak from one's own perspective (use of "I" statements), and (c) no "zaps" or use of hostile humor about other groups.

Although the process of developing group norms typically results in guidelines centered on honesty, respect, and so on, most classes typically overlook what to do when group norms are violated and/or conflict arises. Thus, a class may want to explore their expectations of both the students as well as the instructor in addressing and facilitating such episodes in the class. For instance, when is it appropriate to bring up problems in the class? Should conflict be addressed in the class or as individuals? Given the emotionally charged nature of such a course, we believe that it is equally important to address how the class will deal with an unsafe or tension-filled environment as it is to discuss how to create such a safe environment in the first place.

Formative Feedback

Although group norms are essential in establishing a common set of expectations about how a class will conduct itself, instructors may want to consider creating formative feedback mechanisms that allow them to monitor the "pulse" of the course on an ongoing basis, rather than waiting for summative feedback at the end of the term. One method may involve brief reaction papers in which students are asked to explore their reactions to exercises, readings, and discussions within the classroom. Alternatively, borrowing from the corporate world, regular meetings of "quality circles," consisting of three to four volunteers in each class who will be responsible for meeting with the instructor, allows students to voice their impressions and concerns about the course directly to the instructor. Specifically, one of the authors typically asks the quality circle to provide formative and anonymous feedback based on their own experiences and the experiences of their peers in the course. Through such feedback, instructors may increase their likelihood of obtaining an accurate assessment of the progress of the course, as well as increase their responsiveness to any existing or impending concerns. More important, such feedback mechanisms promote a collaborative teaching environment that conveys to students that their input is not only valued but also critical to the success of the course.

Expectations and Reactions

As a course instructor, it is paramount to understand that students have a variety of fears evoked by the course content. These include the following:

- Hurting/offending others
- Being hurt/offended by others
- Appearing racist, sexist, homophobic, and so on
- Looking stupid or ignorant
- Losing respect of others
- Losing own self-respect
- Having to explain self to others
- Others not understanding
- Not understanding the material, readings, exercises, and so forth

At the same time, students also hold a number of hopes:

- Learning something new
- Being changed in a positive way
- Helping or understanding others/society better
- Helping or understanding self better
- Making a difference

Although many instructors would prefer to teach courses where learning is a pleasant and comfortable experience for all students, the reality of teaching a multicultural course is that such courses elicit students' fears and emotional defenses. Thus, instructors may do well to remind themselves that the success of such a course may not necessarily be gauged by the happiness of the students, nor does conflict and tension necessarily suggest that the course is a failure (Weinstein & Obear, 1992). Indeed, classroom conflicts and defensive reactions by students may prove to be some of the most "teachable" moments in a course. One of the authors teaches a multicultural counseling course in a predominantly White rural area. As a result, students in the classes are generally open about their lack of knowledge, even biases, toward other people. At first, the author was concerned about the difficulty of teaching these students about oppression and culture, until another instructor framed the situation in an unforgettable way: These students' openness actually provided valuable opportunities to confront and challenge their belief systems. These opportunities might not ordinarily be present if students were attempting to present themselves in a socially desirable (i.e., accepting or "tolerant") way. The basic lesson of the situation for the author was this: No matter who or where you teach, it is essential to be open to your students, their unique perspectives, and how they express themselves.

Conflict and Resistance

Relatedly, in the course of class discussion, it is important to not eliminate or shut down all class conflict. Instead, instructors may be instrumental in facilitating discussion about the nature of the conflict and helping students to dialogue respectfully with one another. The experience of openly discussing controversial, even "taboo," topics provides a greater opportunity to learn than perhaps any other aspect of the course. Indeed, such moments are rare and valuable teaching opportunities precisely because in the course of daily life, people are more apt to walk away from these moments with anger, fear, and perhaps hostility. Unfortunately, such conflicts typically signal the end, rather than the beginning, of a dialogue. Thus, learning how to discuss "hot-button" topics such as race or sexual orientation gives students a valuable "live" experience that, it is hoped, will generalize to their daily lives.

Nevertheless, dealing with resistance is a primary part of the class process, regardless of whether that resistance arises from an examination of one's socialization around race, gender, sexual orientation, and so forth. Griffin (1997) noted that

> when we raise social justice issues in a classroom, we unsettle both unconscious and deeply held beliefs about society, self, and social relations. This disequilibrium can create resistance, as familiar ground shifts and students encounter doubt, and self-questioning as they attempt to regain their balance. (p. 292)

As a result, resistance may be manifested in reactions such as invalidating another's experience, claiming that the status quo is part of the natural order, invalidating the teacher, and evoking a hostile silence (Griffin, 1997). In addressing such resistances, instructors must acknowledge the difficulty of participating in such a course early on while ensuring that students are provided with a variety of avenues for disclosing their reactions (i.e., small groups, reactions papers, etc.) without sanction. Moreover, Helms's (1992) notion of the ethical dilemma of privilege (from the White racial identity model) may be used as a basis for contextualizing this resistance because the course likely highlights these very dilemmas for many students. That is, by participating in the course, students for the first time may be struggling with tough but genuine answers to questions such as, "How can I be a moral or religious person and still be accepted by Whites who treat people of color immorally?" "How can I believe in freedom and equality without relinquishing White privilege?" "How can I say that I treat others with respect and dignity if I act as though people of color are not worthy of such basic human concern?" Framing resistance as resolving ethical dilemmas enables students to grapple with privilege honestly, personally, and without blame.

Another aspect of resistance is in helping students differentiate between agreement and understanding. Resistance to course material sometimes comes from assuming that learning the information and hearing the experiences of others means that one must agree with it. Consequently, it is critical to help students to distinguish between agreeing with a point of view versus understanding it—its sources, its motivation, in essence, the nature of its existence. In effect, one of the implicit goals of most multicultural counseling courses is to expose students to both the existence and validity of various points of view. Ideally, this shifts the tenor of the discussion from agreement versus disagreement to understanding another's experience or perspective, which is ultimately critical to developing the empathy that forms the basis of multicultural competence.

Planning for Change

Although discussions of multicultural topics can clearly be stressful for some students, instructors may need to be particularly mindful when students are overwhelmed with feelings of anger, guilt, and confusion (they come to take on the "deer in the headlights" look). Given the scope of the materials being addressed in such a course, students often report feeling somewhat paralyzed by the historical and institutional enormity of what they are learning, as well as the insidious nature of oppression in daily life. Hence, students will find themselves grappling with the question of what to do with their new-found consciousness. Although such questions clearly have no single answer, it may be helpful, as Tatum (1992) described, to assist students in recognizing the possibilities for change that can occur at a variety of levels, among family and friends, as well as within various "spheres of influence" (e.g., work, church, school, etc.). Moreover, students also may benefit from learning to weigh both the risks and gains they may encounter in raising issues of oppression beyond the classroom (say, at the next family reunion or school board meeting) and how they may face some potential social and familial losses in doing so. In effect, students may bene-fit from a discussion that helps them to distin-guish which "battles" to fight as they begin to take personal responsibility for acting on their awakened consciousness. Relatedly, it also may be important to address the role of self-care, particularly when students adopt the role of a change agent. Although students may find their multicultural courses as their own personal cat-alyst for "changing the world," instructors may want to encourage students to take a break periodically (particularly because the world will be there when they get back).

Instructor's Process

Although the emphasis of much of this chapter has focused on students and their process of learning, instructors should be reminded that they are not immune to the stresses of teaching such a course. Indeed, in interviews with faculty members about what makes them nervous in raising issues of racism in the classroom, Weinstein and Obear (1992) found that instructors raised significant con-cerns about confronting their own identity conflicts, having to confront or being con-fronted with their own biases, responding to biased comments in the classroom, grappling with their own competency, wanting the approval of students, and facilitating intense emotions and conflict. Although space limita-tions do not permit a fuller discussion, readers are referred to Bell, Washington, Weinstein, and Love (1997) for a more in-depth discus-sion. Particularly in an academic culture where being the instructor is equivalent to being the "expert," fears related to one's competence, image, and stature will prove to be a signifi-cant struggle for many instructors.

Yet, to the extent that instructors are open to acknowledging, both to themselves and to their students, their own socialization processes and the continuous unlearning and relearning that accompanies this awareness, then perhaps students and instructors may learn from the parallels in their own experi-ences. In particular, it may be helpful for instructors to reflect on those areas in their own lives that they still find challenging and how they may be manifested in their courses. For instance, as an instructor, are you as will-ing to discuss your limited awareness of your privileges as an able-bodied individual as you are in discussing your heightened conscious-ness as a person of color? Do you present yourself as a teacher who is as willing to be challenged by students as you are in challeng-ing them? Are you as open to discussing the homophobic environment in which you were socialized as you are in discussing the antisex-ist environment for which you now advocate? In effect, the challenge for instructors is whether or not they are open to engaging in the very same process they expect of their students. Insofar as instructors are open to this challenge, we believe that they will find their own identities changing and growing as they teach the course, particularly as they examine both their own reactions and the reactions of their students.

Nevertheless, even with such openness (and perhaps because of it), instructors still face the emotional and intellectual toll of teaching such a course. Subsequently, instructors may want to examine how they process their own thoughts and feelings, not only to the material and to the students but also to the nature of the discussion that occurs during the course. For instance, instructors may want to consider their own journal as a means of exploring and monitoring their own development as a multicultural counseling instructor. Indeed, it is our belief that being cognizant of our own reactions as teachers will better inform and influence the manner in which we teach.

Moreover, particularly in departments where being the sole "multicultural expert" translates into professional isolation, it is essential for instructors to have their own network of allies and colleagues, if not locally then nationally. Instructors may want to ask themselves who they can turn to, both within and outside of their departments, for support and feedback. Do you have a colleague who can help you with an exercise you are planning? Is there someone who can help you work through your reactions to one particular student? Relatedly, instructors may need to be mindful of the extent to which support is provided both within the department and the larger institution. To illustrate, Bell et al. (1997) observed that faculty who teach such courses often face multiple risks in that they are often untenured faculty members advocating for information that questions the status quo and using alternative teaching methodologies, all in a course that may have tenuous support from within the department as well as the larger institution. Thus, learning to develop support and self-care can ultimately be the difference between surviving and thriving as an instructor of a multicultural counseling course.

CONCLUSION

As one of our colleagues shrewdly pointed out (Andres Consoli, personal communication, April 1998), one of the central ironies of being a faculty member is that, for many of us, we have the least amount of training in one of the areas we do the most—teaching. In a field that has upheld the notion of the scientist-practitioner as a model for our profession, perhaps the role of teaching should be considered as equally worthy. For without further dialogue and debate about what constitutes effective teaching, the gap between standards of multicultural competence and the practice of multicultural competence will be that much harder to bridge.

REFERENCES

Adams, M., Bell, L. A., & Griffin, P. (1997). *Teaching for diversity and social justice: A sourcebook.* New York: Routledge Kegan Paul.

Adams, M., & Marchesani, L. S. (1992). Dynamics of diversity in the teaching learning process: A faculty development model for analysis and action. In M. Adams (Ed.), *Promoting diversity in college classrooms: Innovative responses for the curriculum, faculty, and institutions* (pp. 9-20). San Francisco: Jossey-Bass.

Alvarez, A. N. (2002). Racial identity and Asian Americans: Supports and challenges. In J. H. Schuh (Series Ed.) & M. K. McEwen, C. M. Kodama, A. N. Alvarez, C. Liang, & S. Lee (Vol. Eds.), *New direction for student services: Working with Asian American college students* (pp. 33-43). San Francisco: Jossey-Bass.

American Psychological Association. (1993). Guidelines for providers of psychological services to ethnic, linguistic, and culturally diverse populations. *American Psychologist, 48,* 45-48.

Andersen, M. L., & Collins, P. H. (1998). *Race, class, and gender: An anthology* (3rd ed.). Belmont, CA: Wadsworth.

Anzaldua, G. (1990). *Making face, making soul, Haciendo caras: Creative and critical perspectives by feminists of color.* San Francisco: Aunt Lute Books.

Bell, L. A. (1997). Theoretical foundations for social justice education. In M. Adams, L. A. Bell, & P. Griffin (Eds.), *Teaching for diversity and social justice: A sourcebook* (pp. 3-15). New York: Routledge Kegan Paul.

Bell, L. A., Washington, S., Weinstein, G., & Love, B. (1997). Knowing ourselves as instructors. In M. Adams, L. A. Bell, & P. Griffin (Eds.), *Teaching for diversity and social justice: A sourcebook* (pp. 299-310). New York: Routledge Kegan Paul.

Bonwell, C. C., & Sutherland, T. E. (1996). The active learning continuum: Choosing activities to engage students in the classroom. In T. E. Sutherland & C. C. Bonwell (Eds.), *Using active learning in college classes: A range of options for faculty* (pp. 3-16). San Francisco: Jossey-Bass.

Griffin, P. (1997). Facilitating social justice education courses. In M. Adams, L. A. Bell, & P. Griffin (Eds.), *Teaching for diversity and social justice: A sourcebook* (pp. 279-298). New York: Routledge Kegan Paul.

Guthrie, R. V. (1997). *Even the rat was white: A historical perspective of psychology* (2nd ed.). Needham Heights, MA: Allyn & Bacon.

Hardiman, R., & Jackson, B. W. (1992). Racial identity development: Understanding racial dynamics in college classrooms and on campus. In M. Adams (Ed.), *Promoting diversity in college classrooms: Innovative responses for the curriculum, faculty, and institutions* (pp. 21-37). San Francisco: Jossey-Bass.

Helms, J. E. (1990). *Black and White racial identity: Theory, research, and practice.* Westport, CT: Greenwood.

Helms, J. E. (1992). *A race is a nice thing to have: A guide to being a White person or understanding the White persons in your life.* Topeka, KS: Content Communications.

Helms, J. E., & Cook, D. A. (1999). *Using race and culture in counseling and psychotherapy: Theory and process.* Needham Heights, MA: Allyn & Bacon.

Hong, M. (1993). *Growing up Asian American.* New York: William Morrow.

Joplin, L. (1995). On defining experiential education. In K. Warren, M. Sakofs, & J. S. Hut Jr. (Eds.), *The theory of experiential education* (pp. 12-26). Dubuque, IA: Kendall/Hunt.

Katz, J. H. (1978). *White awareness: Handbook for anti-racism training.* Norman: University of Oklahoma Press.

LaFramboise, T. D., Coleman, H. L., & Hernandez, A. (1991). Development and factor structure of the Cross-Cultural Counseling Inventory–Revised. *Professional Psychology: Research and Practice, 22,* 380-388.

Perry, W. G. (1999). *Forms of ethical and intellectual development in the college years: A scheme.* San Francisco: Jossey-Bass.

Pfeiffer, J., & Jones, J. (Eds.). (1972-1981). *The annual handbook for group facilitators.* La Jolla, CA: University Associates.

Pfeiffer, J., & Jones, J. (Eds.). (1982-present). *The annual handbook for facilitators, trainers, and consultants.* La Jolla, CA: University Associates.

Pope-Davis, D. B., Reynolds, A. L., Dings, J. G., & Nielson, D. (1995). Examining multicultural counseling competencies of graduate students in psychology. *Professional-Psychology: Research and Practice, 26*(3), 322-329.

Reynolds, A. L. (1995). Challenges and strategies for teaching multicultural counseling courses. In J. G. Ponterroto, J. M. Casas, L. A. Suzuki, & C. M. Alexander (Eds.), *Handbook of multicultural counseling* (pp. 312-330). Thousand Oaks, CA: Sage.

Ridley, C. R., Mendoza, D. W., & Kanitz, B. E. (1994). Multicultural training: Reexamination, operationalization, and integration. *The Counseling Psychologist, 22,* 227-289.

Silberman, M. (1998). *Active training: A handbook of techniques, designs, case examples, and tips.* San Francisco: Jossey-Bass.

Singelis, T. M. (1998). *Teaching about culture, ethnicity, and diversity: Exercises and planned activities.* Thousand Oaks, CA: Sage.

Sodowsky, G. R., Kuo-Jackson, P. Y., Richardson, M. F., & Corey, A. T. (1998). Correlates of self-reported multicultural competencies: Counselor multicultural social desirability, race, social inadequacy, locus of control racial ideology, and multicultural training. *Journal of Counseling Psychology, 45*(3), 256-264.

Sodowsky, G. R., Taffe, R. C., Gutkin, T. B., & Wise, S. L. (1994). Development of the Multicultural Counseling Inventory: A self-report measure of multicultural competencies. *Journal of Counseling Psychology, 41*(2), 137-148.

Sue, D. W., Arredondo, P., & McDavis, R. J. (1992). Multicultural counseling competencies and standards: A call to the profession. *Journal of Multicultural Counseling and Development, 20,* 644-688.

Sue, D. W., & Sue, D. (1999). *Counseling the culturally different* (3rd ed.). New York: John Wiley.

Tatum, B. D. (1992). Talking about race, learning about racism: The application of racial identity development theory in the classroom. *Harvard Educational Review, 62*(1), 1-24.

Turner, C., Garcia, M., Nora, A., & Rendon, L. I. (1996). *Racial and ethnic diversity in higher education.* Needham Heights, MA: Simon & Schuster.

Weinstein, G., & Obear, K. (1992). Bias issues in the classroom: Encounters with the teaching self. In M. Adams (Ed.), *Promoting diversity in college classrooms: Innovative responses for the curriculum, faculty, and institutions* (pp. 39-50). San Francisco: Jossey-Bass.

34

Teaching Multicultural Competence in the Counseling Curriculum

LUIS A. VÁZQUEZ
ENEDINA GARCÍA-VÁZQUEZ
New Mexico State University

The psychology of multiculturalism, a sociopolitical phenomenon that refers to differences and similarities in the field of psychology, has received strong opposition from conservative psychologists and strong affirmation by liberal psychologists (Redding, 2001). Both parties have used the phenomenon against each other to defend their points of view. The true understanding of multiculturalism is inclusive of diverse points of view, whether they are the same as or different from each other. Many authors in the area of multiculturalism are examining mainstream psychology through the view of those who have been omitted, the oppressed (Ponterotto, Casas, Suzuki, & Alexander, 2001). The oppressed constitute such populations as minorities; gay, lesbian, bisexual, and transgendered

individuals; the disabled; and the poor, to name a few.

The pedagogy of multicultural psychology articulates a self-reflective process that challenges the view of psychology toward oppressed populations. The inclusion of this process creates a critical view of the current state of psychology. The application of a critical pedagogy in the teaching of multiculturalism in psychology would advance the field in its views toward diversity. Such pedagogy entails an understanding of the major theories in multicultural psychology and the application of these theories in a self-reflective process leading to the deconstruction and reconstruction of the disciplines in psychology, as we know them today. It is through the application of multicultural theories that students can develop a self-reflective process of understanding psychology.

POWER AND DISCRIMINATION

The major theories in the study of multiculturalism embed the understanding and integration of the concepts of power and discrimination. It is through the understanding of these two concepts that students can begin the process of critically examining the knowledge in the various disciplines of psychology. Power can be described as the ability to control, influence, and have authority over others (Ramsey, 1997). According to Pedersen (1994), power correlates highly with dominance, leading to the disparaging treatment toward such groups as ethnic/racial populations and minority group status populations. Naisbitt and Aburdene (1990) described power from three different levels: individual, group, and societal.

At the individual level, power is related to a person's internal locus of control and how the person conceives his or her abilities to be successful. Power at the group level involves the expression of influence and its use toward others in the same group. At the societal level, it involves the dominance and use of authority to regulate those who are less dominant. However, the role of power in the discipline of psychology has been used to discriminate against the ideology of truth among less dominant populations and maintain mainstream psychology's spoken "truths."

Discrimination can be described as the act of making or perceiving differences, similarities, and distinctions, leading to a showing of favoritism toward one-sided perspectives used to define the realities of a minority culture, whether real or not (Swim, Cohen, & Hyers, 1998). This type of discrimination is often developed by a culture of dominance. Only seeing the world from a Western worldview that defines psychology is in itself a discriminatory perspective (Albert, 1988). Neglecting the experiences of people of color and other minority status populations in psychology has allowed the discipline to develop a narrow focus of interpreting reality in its various disciplines. Power and discrimination, along with the dominance of the majority culture as the point of reference for comparison to other cultures, has been part of psychology's political history and also formulates the foundation in the following major multicultural theories: worldview, racial/ethnic identity, and acculturation.

WORLDVIEW, RACIAL/ETHNIC IDENTITY, AND ACCULTURATION

Worldview

Worldview pertains to how we see, experience, and interpret the world. It is a representation about our activity in the world; our beliefs, values, assumptions about the world; and our assumptions about people, relationships, nature, and time (Dana, 1993). Worldview is often used to create individual understanding in relationships of persons from diverse cultures. However, of strong interest and rarely addressed is how domains of worldview are described from the point of reference of the majority culture. This point of reference is often called the Western worldview. The Western worldview sets the standard of comparison that is used to distinguish how people deviate from this perspective. Those individuals differing in worldviews from the Western worldview are often described as "abnormal" (Sue, 1978). For example, if a person were more collective than individualistic in relationships, psychology would interpret this perspective as dependency rather than independence. In the scientific research, there is more emphasis on the internal validity of measures, rather than the external validity or generalizability of these measures to minority populations. In fact, these measures have been developed and validated from a Western worldview. This view, in and of itself, illustrates a position of power inherent in the scientific research in psychology as the "right" view or, at the very least, "the" point of reference. The research is used to provide evidence for discriminatory perceptions toward people of color and those with minority status in the field of psychology. In the majority of studies measuring worldview, there is a comparison of the minority culture to the majority culture (Hall & Barongan, 2002). This methodology is another example of the Western worldview dictating the points of comparison in psychology, leading to misperceptions toward minority group populations.

Racial/Ethnic Identity

Racial/ethnic identity is described as reactions to societal psychological dynamics of oppression based on phenotypic features and stereotypic perceived behaviors of minority populations (Helms, 1996). At the individual level, racial/ethnic identity is defined as "that part of an individual's self-concept which derives from knowledge of his/her membership of a social group (or groups) together with the value and emotional significance attached to that membership" (Tajfel, 1981, p. 255). Several models have been developed to conceptualize racial/ethnic identity into stages, levels, statuses, or states of being (Fischer & Moradi, 2001). In many of the models, the point of reference in describing the process of growth is based on minorities' interactions with the majority culture, along with power and discrimination as the foundational base of these interactions. Racial/ethnic identity models have been developed with the concepts of power and discrimination as points of reference in describing how minority and majority populations develop identities of

being the oppressed or oppressor, leading to a critical consciousness of liberation. This process of growth for oppressed populations is based on the interaction with the majority culture in the process of negotiating issues of power and discrimination in their interpersonal relationships within their culture of origin and the majority culture.

For the oppressor, the process involves the acknowledgment of privilege based on power and discriminatory practices toward minority populations to maintain such a status. These conceptualizations illustrate the positions of inherent power in the ability of the majority culture to dictate how people negotiate their identities with the mediating variable of discrimination, along with the inherent risk of challenging this process by minority populations. Several researchers have proposed that racial/ethnic minorities and White populations experiencing the full-growth process of identity development reach the highest positive levels of self-awareness, self-esteem, self-concept, and mental health (Ponterotto & Pedersen, 1993). This level of understanding allows for critical examination and dialogue about the interpretation of research results, pathology, assessment, and the "truths" in the field of psychology.

Acculturation

Acculturation is a phenomenon that results when groups of individuals sharing different cultures come into continuous firsthand contact, with subsequent changes in the original cultural patterns of either group or both groups (Redfield, Lenton, & Herskovits, 1936). In this phenomenon, a view of change is proposed based on the inherent influence of one culture over another. Such changes may occur through wars, missionaries, and education. The general definition, various conceptualizations, and measures of acculturation are evidence of the complexity associated with the phenomenon. However, in the literature, various factors such as generational level, language usage, and ethnic identification appear to be consistently used by researchers as points of comparison to the majority culture (Padilla, 1980).

Acculturation has often been used to describe the process of the immigrant experience of adapting to the majority culture in the United States. However, the phenomenon has been extended to indigenous minority populations adapting to their educational experiences, professional employment experiences, and cultural experiences in a multicultural social structure of existence (LaFromboise, Coleman, & Gerton, 1993). The majority of the research in the area of acculturation has been conducted examining minority culture experiences in comparison to the majority culture in the United States (Kim & Abreu, 2001). This type of research has contributed to understanding the disposition of power—a basic need to change a minority culture to the dominant culture's definitions of acceptable behavior. This body of research has also shown the types of behaviors and norms that minority populations have adopted from the majority culture in the United States (Rogler, Cortes, & Malgady, 1991; Vega & Rumbaut, 1991). However, there has been a paucity of research conducted on within-group cultural experiences.

What is rarely discussed is how the experience of acculturation is a phenomenon based on the differential use of power in creating change in less dominant cultures. In the United States, the Western culture has been the culture of dominance that is often dictated as the point of reference to describe change in another culture's acculturation process. Central to this view is the discriminatory bias that the "best" culture is the Western culture. This perspective is reinforced through the methodology of using the majority culture as the point of comparison to describe the minority

culture. A fascinating phenomenon rarely studied is how the majority culture has adopted behaviors from other cultures and has established them as "normal" activities. An example would be the medical profession's integration of natural cultural healing practices along with traditional medicine. At one time, natural healing practices were assumed not to be valid medical practices.

Throughout the previous discussion of the three multicultural theories, a common thread integrates the issues of power and discrimination as a foundation in describing the development and interactions of relationships within and between people. The understanding of these theories across the disciplines of psychology is of utmost importance in developing a foundation of objectivity in understanding the subjectivity in each discipline. The obligation of professors to educate students in psychology about the three multicultural theories will help them engage in multiple perspectives and self-reflective understanding that creates critical thinking, reasoning, and understanding about the development of attitudes among majority and minority cultures.

THE TRADITIONAL MULTICULTURAL COURSE

Professors of psychology have the ethical responsibility to foster understanding of the complexity of power and discrimination in teaching psychology across the various disciplines. To be pedagogically objective, professors must be able to thoroughly understand and apply the multicultural theories in a self-reflective process, as well as teach the students how to understand and experience these theories. Each of these theories gives a complex understanding of human nature. However, most multicultural courses in psychology are taught from a traditional perspective of focusing on specific minority groups and do not deal with the self-evaluation of power and discrimination in the development of self-understanding for each student to experience throughout the curriculum and in the classroom.

Ponterotto and Pedersen (1993) have pointed out in their research of multicultural curriculum development that White students often feel guilty and angry, whereas minority students feel validated and empowered throughout this intellectual process of multiculturalism. The traditional focus of a multicultural course usually begins with the history of discrimination toward minority populations in the field of psychology, focusing on how this history has developed discriminatory practices, followed by cursory exposure to the theories of worldview, identity, and acculturation. This process is usually followed with exposure to the knowledge base of the multicultural competencies and how they are applied to the field of counseling and psychology. Various activities are interspersed throughout the multicultural curriculum, resulting in an intellectualizing, superficial base of knowledge, along with politically correct responses to issues of diversity. Students become well versed in how to articulate issues of diversity from an intellectual level of understanding with the stereotypic views presented in the curriculum about how minority group members interact with each other.

The process that is experienced by the students in a traditional multicultural psychology course has some common elements. For some students, the belief that addressing issues of multiculturalism is a "politically correct" response in support of minority students is developed. Others believe that it is not necessary and a waste of time to their academic progress. Yet others believe that what they have learned in the course has "met" the level of competence necessary to work with minority populations. Our interviews with students who have taken multicultural courses across the United States show that students have not learned enough to be competent, but they have learned enough to develop a false sense of security in their practices toward minority populations.

The lack of integration and use of multicultural theories throughout the students' degree program is still a common practice (Ponterotto et al., 2001). Due to this void of an integrated multicultural curriculum in psychology, students' views often result in anger and resentment—anger for some of the students in having to take such a course, resentment for others not having the multicultural theories integrated throughout their coursework.

These feelings toward multicultural courses are growing stronger across disciplines of psychology. Resistance continues—if not active, then at least passive—within multicultural courses and across psychology courses. Students may be apprehensive expressing their true beliefs for fear of what others may think of each other's attitudes toward diverse populations. Some of the students have a great distrust toward the instructor and the "hidden agendas," whereas others feel that such expectations from their instructors are unfair and ludicrous at best. All students—regardless of race, ethnicity, sexual orientation, (dis)ability, and various worldviews, identity levels, and acculturation levels—often struggle with being defensive and feeling threatened.

Clark (1991) discussed defense mechanisms as an unconscious distortion of reality used to reduce painful affect and conflict through habituated responses. Ponterotto and Pedersen (1993) described eight common defense mechanisms that students may exhibit, such as color blindness, color consciousness, cultural transference, cultural countertransference, cultural ambivalence, pseudo-transference, over-identification, and identification with the culture of power.

All of these responses, without a self-reflective process, perpetuate the lack of learning in the classroom and the entrenchment of preexisting attitudes of power and discrimination. The professor must educate as well as have a flexibility to create a facilitative discussion about power and discrimination and how it affects those who perpetuate it and those who receive these messages. Yet, the requirements for accreditation by the American Psychological Association (APA) include strong support for multicultural issues but not how they are to be taught in the classroom or what rights the instructor has (Pope-Davis & Coleman, 1997). The APA Code of Ethics (APA, 1993a) also includes standards related to the training of students when working with issues of diversity. The "Guidelines for Providers of Psychological Services to Ethnic, Linguistic, and Culturally Diverse Populations" (APA, 1993b) also gives statements regarding the ethics of working with diversity. None of these documents explores "how" training in multiculturalism should occur in the classroom across the various courses of psychology. Multicultural instruction must challenge and yet support these diverse views within the classroom across all courses.

In our countless interviews with both majority and minority students, these students consistently state that the traditional approach has taught them how to stereotype minorities as well as majority culture students; keep the issues of diversity at a superficial, intellectual level; and not have to deal or explore their own issues of power and discrimination. The failure of traditional multicultural courses in helping students come to terms with their own discriminatory practices or with a process to help them engage such issues across all of their courses is severely lacking, perpetuating the lack of a self-reflective critical process across the disciplines of psychology.

A NONTRADITIONAL MULTICULTURAL COURSE

It is proposed that students of the various disciplines of psychology experience a nontraditional multicultural critical pedagogical process. The fundamental elements consist of educating students in a self-reflective process of understanding power and discrimination regardless of ethnic/racial background. The self-exploratory experience will enable the students to understand how their worldview, racial/ethnic identity, and acculturation affect their attitudes in their discipline of psychology. The multicultural course would be based on the three theories of worldview, racial/ethnic identity, and acculturation. These three theories form the foundation of understanding the within- and between-group differences and similarities within each student. The course would be sequenced in a developmental perspective, engaging each student in his or her self-reflective process of understanding each of the three multicultural theories (Vázquez, 1997). All the experiential exercises, readings, and assignments would focus on each of these theories. The theories would be presented in a developmental perspective, beginning with worldview, racial/ethnic identity, and acculturation with the underlying foundational constructs of power and discrimination (see Appendix 34.A).

Two requirements must be met in teaching a multicultural course: It must be experientially based and process oriented. These two requirements are the basis for self-exploration and self-awareness. These types of courses have specific criteria that must be met to ensure a competent level of understanding human development. Such criteria would include appropriate communication skills, openness to self-awareness exercises, and facilitation of an open, nonthreatening environment so that those participating in the interaction can discuss issues that are at times difficult to hear.

If the students are not able to show competency in performing these skills, then they have not met the criteria established for the multicultural course. These requirements for teaching a multicultural course are the foundation of skills necessary in developing a multiculturally aware student. The difficult issues arise in developing appropriate criteria for assignments, experiential exercises, and open risk-taking behaviors that are measurable for evaluation. The following assignments have been the most productive in ensuring a multicultural open environment that facilitates and encompasses affirmation of diversity, as well as an opportunity for racist views to be discussed with responsibility. These assignments include journaling, multicultural genogram, identity awareness, and acculturation awareness self-reflective papers, along with group experiential exercises appropriately sequenced throughout the course.

The course would begin with an exploration of the student's worldview. *Worldview* is defined as a person's perceptions of culture, universality, and individuality (Sue & Sue, 1990). One method to accomplish this task is through the use of the multicultural genogram (Vázquez & Vázquez, 2001). The assignment includes an exploration of family history dating back three generations. The unique quality of this particular genogram is the descriptors that are used as variables of exploration for the student. For example, some of the variables would include perceptions of the student's family across generations toward diversity and positive and negative interactions. In addition, students can explore their ethnic group's historical perceptions of people diverse from themselves. This area of the assignment may include all the ethnicities that are identified by the student. Another section would include an integration of these two areas, ending with a section that includes areas for improvement, exploration, and probable limitations to the biases toward diversity. The integration of this assignment with the concept of worldview would create historical and personal awareness, as well as possibly emotional conflicts for the student to examine, especially in the discipline of psychology.

In conjunction with these assignments would be the integration of videotaped interviews. For example, the video *Voices* (Daniel, Aden, Davidson, & Ellis, 1990) interviews several diverse individuals and how they have experienced their interactions with other people of diversity. The interviews are honest, heartfelt experiences that students are more apt to relate to in the classroom. These assignments create an excellent catalyst for discussion and process. Other examples may include diversity awareness exercises that would involve having the students trace their experiences chronologically from kindergarten to their current age about such issues as race, ethnicity, gender, disability, and sexual orientation. Once this is done, the students can share with each other in a group format what these experiences were like for them and give each other feedback. This exercise would help the students accept responsibility and be accountable for their attitudes toward diversity. In addition, it provides the opportunity to learn from those similar and different from them. The process affords the students a multicultural experience with each other. Once students have experienced and processed these exercises, they can begin to examine their identity development.

Simply defined, *identity* is how people feel about themselves in relation to their own racial/ethnic group and those groups diverse from themselves (Sue & Sue, 1990). Perceptions of skin color are explored at this level and addressed to deal with perceptions toward skin color (Carter, 1995). An exercise that has generated great success is the analysis of the film *Malcolm X* (Worth, Lee, & Lee, 1993) in relation to Black, gender, and religious identity development. The integration of the multiple dimensions of identity develops students' deep awareness of the complexity of a person. The student watches the film in small groups with other students, applies the appropriate identity development models and the concept of skin color to the main character, and at the same time responds in journal format to each phase of development from his or her own multiple dimensions of identity development. This exercise allows students to explore how skin color and multiple group identifications mitigate their own relationships with people of color. The exercise also serves as a reflection of the students' own development and interactions with their own history of developing intimate relationships with populations diverse from themselves. This assignment has often created very strong emotional reactions. These emotions are often processed during experiences in the small groups during and after the film. The reactions are also processed in the classroom environment with the instructor as the facilitator.

Learning the concepts of worldview and identity development sets the stage for integrating the concept of acculturation. *Acculturation* refers to the contact an individual has with a different culture and the traits adopted from that culture (Redfield et al, 1936). The complexity of the concept of acculturation makes it difficult to choose a comprehensive model of application. However, the multidimensional model developed by Keefe and Padilla (1987) provides a very comprehensive conceptual picture of acculturation. This model is thoroughly explored and presented by the professor in class. The students are taught how to operationalize the constructs of the model in relation to themselves. Once this is accomplished, the students are assigned the movie *Mi Familia* (Thomas & Nava, 1995) and asked to select a character from the movie. The comprehensiveness of the multidimensional model engages the student in an integrative process of examining the various dimensions of acculturation and how these concepts apply to the character and himself or herself. This allows the student to assess how she or he has been affected by the experience. The exercise is assigned as a group task.

Four to five students watch the movie together while they process the dimensions of the acculturation model. In addition, the assignment is processed in class with the other students to exchange similar and different experiences that each group encountered. These are only a few examples that can be used in providing experiential exercises for students to integrate the various multicultural constructs.

While the students are engaged in these various activities, they are also journaling their reactions to their experiences each week and handing them in to receive feedback from the professor. Journal entries include such information as a description of an incident or reaction to an incident during class, the immediate emotional reaction to the incident, where the emotional reaction developed (personal history, family history, etc.), and possible suggestions to resolve or explore these reactions. The journal allows the professor to monitor progress in the student's critical consciousness and awareness to multicultural issues. As long as the students follow the format to the journals, they receive full credit regardless of the personal views that are expressed.

To ensure an appropriate level of competency, the professor could administer a pretest and posttest inventory. Such inventories may include the Multicultural Awareness-Knowledge-Skills Survey (MAKSS) (D'Andrea, Daniels, & Heck, 1991), the Multicultural Counseling Inventory (MCI) (Sodowsky, Taffe, Gutkin, & Wise, 1994), or the Multicultural Counseling Awareness Scale (MCAS-B) (Ponterotto, Rieger, Barrett, & Sparks, 1994). These instruments and other forms of self-assessment would become part of an ongoing multicultural assessment portfolio (Coleman, 1996). Different types of multicultural assessments could be used throughout each course in the students' curriculum. They would provide areas of strength as well as areas of growth for the students to set goals throughout their psychology courses.

In our experiences, students consistently have shown a marked increase in self-awareness and confidence in the ability to apply the three multicultural theories to themselves and their field of study. There is also a thorough understanding of how a person's perception of the three theories can affect interpersonal communication. In addition, there is an awareness of how power differentials and perceptions of discrimination directly affect interpretations of results in research and human interactions. These experiences set the foundation for the other courses in the students' curriculum.

AN INTEGRATION OF MULTICULTURALISM ACROSS THE CURRICULUM

The ability to understand and apply the three multicultural theories sets the stage for their application to the various courses in any discipline of psychology. In counseling psychology, several courses are required to meet accreditation standards (see Appendix 34.B). The integration of the three multicultural theories into each course forms the various perspectives of diversity necessary for multicultural competency. The following discussion will include brief examples of three courses: theory, research, and practicum. In theory courses, the application of these multicultural concepts to the autobiography of each theorist, such as Freud, Adler, Rogers, and others, along with the study of their generational struggles, helps the students deconstruct and reconstruct their theories of human behavior. The richness of these explorations provides the rationale for the foundations of each theory and their applicability to human nature. In turn, students can develop a higher level of competency in applying these theories to the diversity of clients and the cultural assumptions of each theory.

In the research courses, issues of objectivity, bias, and universal principles are very important.

The integration of the three multicultural theories would provide the balance necessary to enhance the objectivity of a researcher. The researcher's awareness of his or her worldview would lessen the bias in the methodology chosen or the scientific method applied to test research questions. For example, one of the authors was asked to be a consultant for a study measuring self-esteem in successful Chinese graduate students that included measures of self-esteem, academic satisfaction, and advisers' perceptions, along with demographic information. The study yielded results that showed that the students were very successful academically but had a low self-esteem. On further examination of the study, it was discovered that the self-esteem measure was developed with majority culture students. An item analysis of the scales for the study indicated that the Chinese students had endorsed items related to group support, nondirectness, and cooperation. Several of these items lowered the overall scores of the participants, indicating low self-esteem. Investigating the reliability of the instruments used in the study for the worldview presented in the constructs and using a measure of acculturation as a predictor variable would have resulted in a more objective study. If the results had not been reviewed for these biases related to the multicultural theories, they would have added to the misinterpretations of self-esteem in successful Chinese graduate students.

Equally important are the interpretations of research results when they include the worldviews, identity, and acculturation levels of the researcher. A review of the autobiographies of researchers, along with the spirit of the times, can give students a wealth of knowledge into understanding the researchers' intent in developing instruments and interpreting the results of their studies. Even how a research question is posed comes from the many cultural implications of the three multicultural theories. The research examples provided are just a few of the hundreds of examples to explore the application of the three multicultural theories to the field of research.

In practicum courses, it is a necessity for counselors and supervisors to be well aware of their worldview, identity, and acculturation levels, along with the ability to assess these multicultural theories in their clients and supervisees. Studies have shown how differing worldviews and identity levels can affect the therapeutic process, leading to inappropriate goals for the client. Issues of conflict and credibility have also been shown to affect the progress for clients in counseling. Supervisors also face similar issues when working with supervisees in supervision. Supervisees from diverse cultures and languages can be very challenging to supervisors who are unaware of their cultural biases and how they impose them on their supervisees. The knowledge and the ability to assess for worldview, identity, and acculturation can become the catalyst in developing credibility and trust in the supervision relationship. A multicultural assessment that integrates the theories of worldview, identity, and acculturation is an ethical requirement so that a counselor or supervisor can provide appropriate process and outcomes to the client or the supervisee.

Even though the discussion of integrating the multicultural theories in three courses has been brief, it has provided examples of the use of worldview, identity, and acculturation in the curriculum. To develop the knowledge, skills, and awareness necessary to apply the multicultural theories in their courses, faculty in the department would need to discuss collaboratively how they would integrate these three theories in their curriculum. In addition, the faculty would have to agree that the multicultural class needs to be taken first by the students in their sequence of courses. This develops the foundation for using the multicultural theories in the other classes. Once this is accomplished, outcome assessments can be integrated into class exams, written and oral comprehensive exams, and clinical competencies.

CONCLUSION

The development of self-awareness and understanding of how information is integrated creates a powerful zeitgeist in the paradigm shift of how students learn about their disciplines in psychology. It creates a knowledge base of sociopolitical values that must be considered in cultural diversity. These values reflect the core beliefs within the chosen disciplines in psychology. Sensitivity to diverse cultural beliefs and the cultural milieu of any chosen discipline of psychology helps students develop a critical consciousness of their field and how it has influenced issues of diversity from positive and negative perspectives.

The field of psychology prides itself in its "nondiscriminatory" research methods in developing answers to society's difficult challenges with diversity. The examination of worldview, identity, and acculturation processes before engaging in investigating issues of diversity often leads to the intent and interpretation of the curriculum presented in research and psychology classes. The understanding and application of the three multicultural theories allow for the development of an understanding of versus a frustration toward faculty's views about diversity in the various disciplines of psychology. The lack of faculty's self-awareness in psychology only perpetuates the lack of self-examination of how courses of psychology are taught to future psychologists. This lack of self-examination and self-evaluation can only lead to the destruction of a diversity of ideas in the profession of psychology while preserving the "status quo" to the exclusion of diversity. Admittedly, it is difficult to fathom every discipline in psychology engaging in a process of learning that includes an open, critical process of a consciousness of liberation that helps students critically examine their chosen field of psychology. Such a process would lead to challenges in teaching and accountability for the university professor. Professors of psychology would have to expose their biases and intent versus expecting a regurgitation of knowledge passed from one generation to another in the field of psychology. This type of interactive process would create a sociopolitical deconstruction of the disciplines of psychology—a long overdue and awaited process if psychology is truly to incorporate a diversity of ideas and people. Through the development of these competencies with the multicultural theories discussed, the students are continually in a process of self-evaluation in their chosen field of psychology.

APPENDIX 34.A

THE PSYCHOLOGY OF MULTICULTURALISM: CEP 517

Monday & Wednesdays: 3:00-7:00 p.m.
Room 300-A O'Donnell Hall

Instructor:	Dr. Luis A. Vázquez	**Office:**	205 O'Donnell Hall
Phone:	646-2121	**Office Hours:**	By Appointment

Required Texts: Ponterotto, J. G., Casas, M. J., Suzuki, L. A., & Alexander, C. M. (Eds.). (2001). *Handbook of multicultural counseling* (2nd ed.). Thousand Oaks, CA: Sage. Pope-Davis, D. B., & Coleman, H. L. K. (1997). *Multicultural counseling competencies: Assessment, education, and training, and supervision.* Thousand Oaks, CA: Sage.

Required: Reading packet available at LRC and readings on reserve at third floor of O'Donnell Hall.

Purpose of Course

This course is designed to assist students in the understanding and valuing of diversity. It is based on the principles of awareness, knowledge, and skills as they relate to the areas of worldview, identity, and acculturation. The first portion of the course, awareness, will assist students in identifying some of their cultural assumptions in relation to people diverse from themselves. This will be accomplished through modeling, observations, readings, and experiential exercises.

The second portion of the course, knowledge, will consist of "what is" multiculturalism in various types of roles and relationships. It will begin with the examination of the psychology of multiculturalism and the requirements of multicultural competencies in the field of counseling. In addition, there will be a review of Western theories and various theories of diversity (identity development, acculturation, worldview, bilingualism, and disability), including an exploration of various diverse populations.

The last portion of the course, skills, will focus on the "how-tos" of multiculturalism in practice. Students will learn basic issues related to assumptions that are used in communicating in intracultural and intercultural interactions. This will be accomplished through the use of mock interview experiences, video vignettes, and role-plays.

Course Format

Class sessions will include discussions, experiential exercises, and presentations.

Course Evaluation

Grading Criteria:
Class Participation   10 pts.

Journal   25 pts.
Multicultural Genogram   25 pts.
Reaction Papers   20 pts. each × 2   40 pts.
                                              _____

                                    100 pts. Total

Grades will be assigned on the following basis: A = 90-100, B = 80-89, etc. Plus (+) and minus (−) will also be given. A grade of "B" in this course means that a student has completed all assignments at a high level of proficiency. A grade of "A" signifies that all assignments have been completed at a level of excellence. A grade of "A" will not be "a given" in this course, and it may not even be the norm.

Note

Considerable risk taking, hard work, sensitivity, and honesty are essential for successful completion of this course.

The department has prepared the following statement for process/didactic courses such as CEP 517:

This course has been identified as an experiential/didatic course. This means that the major focus of evaluation will be determined by the instructor's professional judgment of the following criteria as they pertain to this course: ethical judgment, interpersonal characteristics (i.e., openness to feedback), interpersonal skills, and effective application of communication techniques, along with the written assignments and exams. These components have been identified as necessary prerequisites to assure a student's ability to function effectively and ethically in a multicultural professional role implied by this degree program. Students who are not meeting minimal competence in these areas will receive grades reflecting the deficiencies.

Class Participation: 10 points total

Class discussion and participation are extremely important given the nature of this course. On the basis of the readings, presentations, and experiential activities, you are required to assume an active role in this course. From time to time, you may be assuming roles of leadership or support in group activities. After the first absence or (not and) late arrival/early departure, absences or late arrivals/early departures will cost 5 points each. In the case of an unexpected development or crisis (e.g., pregnancy, severe illness, death of a significant other), arrangements can be made with the instructor. Interruptions by cell phones will also result in a loss of 5 points.

Journal: 25 points total

A journal will be kept on a weekly basis exploring issues of diversity throughout the course. The focus here should be on how the issues of diversity presented throughout the class impact you. I will also provide feedback on your journal entries on a weekly basis. You are required to have one entry per each class meeting. Journals are kept completely confidential. They will consist of four components: Each component is worth 2 points.

1. Present the issue you had a reaction to in class or readings.
2. What was your emotional reaction to the issue (anger, happiness, etc.)?
3. Where do you believe your reaction came from (historically, etc.)?
4. What are ways you believe that you could work with these issues?

Multicultural Genogram: 25 points

Your history of relationships with people of diversity will be explored in this assignment to create a greater self-awareness. Further information will be given in class.

Reaction Papers: 20 points each

Write two 7- to 10-page papers using APA style. Misspellings, grammatical mistakes, or not using APA style will result in a lack of credit for the assignment.

1. An identity development model to the film *Malcolm X* and your own identity
2. An acculturation model to the film *Mi Familia* (*My Family*), *El Norte, Joy Luck Club, Remember the Titans,* and your own process

More information will be presented in class about these two assignments.

Students With Disabilities

If students enrolled in this course have or think they may have disabilities that interfere with their performance as students in this course, they are encouraged for academic reasons to make this known to the instructor. You may discuss this on a confidential basis with the instructor, the Disabled Student Programs Coordinator (646-1921), and/or the Americans With Disabilities Act Coordinator (646-7795). If students have conditions that may affect their ability to exit from the premises in case of emergency, they are urged, for safety reasons, to notify any of the above persons.

Reading Schedule

July 10   Introduction: Course Requirements: Life History
The Politics of Counseling: Sue & Sue, Chapter 1
Traditional Approaches to Counseling & Psychotherapy: Atkinson & Hackett, Chapter 1
Treatment of Diversity: A Historical Overview: Atkinson & Hackett, Chapter 2
A Redefinition of Multicultural Counseling: Speight et al.
Cultural Coat of Arms: Exercise
How Multicultural Is My Life: Name 5/Exercise

July 12   *Handbook of Multicultural Counseling*: Part I: Chapters 1, 2
Part III: Chapters 12, 15
Operationalization of the Multicultural Counseling Competencies
White Privilege: Unpacking the Invisible Knapsack: McIntosh
Racial/Ethnic Awareness: Exercise

July 13   **Last day to drop a course without record of a grade**

July 17   Downsizing & Cost-Effective: Exercise
Multicultural Video: *Voices*
Handbook of Multicultural Counseling: Part II: Chapter 4
Outcome of Training in the Philosophy of Assessment: MC Competencies, Chapter 1
Barriers to Effective Cross-Cultural Counseling: Sue & Sue, Chapter 2
The Role of Culture & Cultural Techniques in Psychotherapy: Sue & Zane

July 19   Portfolio Assessment MC Competencies/Differential Aspects of MC, Chapters 2, 3
Worldviews: The Human Connection: Exercise
Dimensions of World Views: Sue & Sue, Chapter 7
Social Identity Development: Jackson & Hardiman
Minority Identity Development & Prejudice Prevention: Ponterotto & Pedersen
White Racial Identity Development & Prejudice Prevention: Ponterotto & Pedersen
Handbook of Multicultural Counseling: Part II: Chapters 9, 10, 11
Multidimensional Identity Development: Reynolds & Pope
Multicultural Genogram Paper Due

July 24   Spirituality/Religiosity & Identity Development/Instructor
Sex Matters: Gender & Sexual Orientation, Chapter 4
Handbook of Multicultural Counseling: Part VI: Chapter 21
Gay-Lesbian Identity Development
Definitions & Myths/Facts of Homosexuality & Bisexuality
Revisioning Sexual Minority Identity Formation: McCarn & Fassinger
Why Are We Gay?: Video

July 25   **Last Day to Drop With a "W"**
July 26   **Identity Reaction Paper Due**

	Gender Awareness: Exercise/Sex Matters: Gender & Sexual Orientation in Training for Multicultural Counseling Competency

Gender Awareness: Exercise/Sex Matters: Gender & Sexual Orientation in Training for Multicultural Counseling Competency

The "New" Relationship Models of Women's Development: A Review & Critique for Counselors: Enns

Multicultural Counseling Video: *Amy*

July 31-   *Handbook of Multicultural Counseling*: Part VI: Chapter 2
August 2   Acculturation: Vázquez

History of Bilingualism in the U.S.

The English-Only Movement: Padilla et al.

Bilingual Issues in Mental Health Assessment & Treatment: Bamford

Handbook of Multicultural Counseling: Part IV: Chapters 16, 17, 18

Part V: 19: Translator/Interpreter: Exercise

August 7   MC Training Model: Competency Model, Chapter 5

Cultural Ambience: Culturally Aware Learning Environment, Chapter 11

Handbook of Multicultural Counseling: Part II: Chapters 5, 6, 7

Multicultural Video: *Exercises*

Personal/Group Contract

Acculturation Paper Due

August 9   Multicultural Curriculum Development: Vázquez, Chapter 7

Toward Defining a Multicultural Training Philosophy: Leach & Carlton, Chapter 8

Multicultural Video: *Exercises*

Part VII: Chapter 26, Appendices I, II, III

Last Day of Classes

APPENDIX 34.B

CORE COURSES IN TYPICAL PSYCHOLOGY PROGRAMS

(POWER AND DISCRIMINATION)

	Worldview	*Identity*	*Acculturation*
Multicultural			
Supervision			
Theories			
Individual practicum			
Group			
Group practicum			
Family counseling			
Assessment			
Diagnosis			
Professional issues			
Social psychology			
Statistics			
Research design			
Ethics			
Psychopathology			
Human development			
Career			
History and systems			

Journal for the Advancement of Counselling, 19, 277-291.

Redding, R. E. (2001). Sociopolitical diversity in psychology: The case for pluralism. *American Psychologist, 56*(3), 205-215.

Redfield, R., Lenton, R., & Herskovits, M. J. (1936). Memorandum for the study of acculturation. *American Anthropologist, 38,* 149-152.

Rogler, L. H., Cortes, D. E., & Malgady, R. G. (1991). Acculturation and mental health status among Hispanics: Convergence and new directions for research. *American Psychologist, 46,* 585-597.

Sodowsky, G. R., Taffe, R. C., Gutkin, T. B., & Wise, S. I. (1994). Development of the multicultural counseling inventory: A self-report measure of multicultural competencies. *Journal of Counseling Psychology, 41,* 137-148.

Sue, D. W. (1978). Worldviews and counseling. *Personnel and Guidance Journal, 56,* 458-462.

Sue, D. W., & Sue, D. (1990). *Counseling the culturally different: Theory and practice.* New York: John Wiley.

Swim, J. K., Cohen, L. L., & Hyers, L. L. (1998). Experiencing everyday prejudice and discrimination. In J. K. Swim & C. Stangor (Eds.), *Prejudice: The target's perspective* (pp. 37-60). San Diego: Academic Press.

Tajfel, H. (1981). *Human groups and social categories.* Cambridge, England: Cambridge University Press.

Thomas, A. (Producer), & Nava, G. (Director). (1995). *Mi familia* (My family) [Film]. (Available from New Line Productions, Inc., New Line Home Video, Turner Home Entertainment)

Vázquez, L. A. (1997). A systemic multicultural curriculum model: The pedagogical process. In D. B. Pope-Davis & H. L. K. Coleman (Eds.), *Multicultural counseling competencies: Assessment, education and training, and supervision* (pp. 159-183). Thousand Oaks, CA: Sage.

Vázquez, L. A., & Vázquez, E. G. (2001). The impact of phenotype on gender and class for southwestern Hispanic Americans: Implications for counselor training. In D. B. Pope-Davis & H. L. K. Coleman (Eds.), *The intersection of race, class, and gender in multicultural counseling* (pp. 323-340). Thousand Oaks, CA: Sage.

Vega, W. A., & Rumbaut, R. G. (1991). Ethnic minorities and mental health. *Annual Review of Sociology, 17,* 351-383.

Worth, M., Lee, S., (Coproducers), & Lee, S. (Director). (1993). *Malcolm X* [Film]. (Available from Warner Home Video, 4000 Warner Blvd., Burbank, CA 91522)

35

Teaching Multicultural Competencies in Continuing Education for Psychologists

THOMAS A. PARHAM
University of California at Irvine

LISA WHITTEN
State University of New York/College at Old Westbury

Education is the passport to the future, for tomorrow belongs to those who prepare for it today.

—Malcolm X

Beyond the notion of supplemental education, professionals are often confronted with new challenges that stretch the limits of their professional training. In some cases, new scenarios are beyond the capacity of one's existing repertoire to accommodate because the situations are so new. In such cases, continuing education provides the latest cutting-edge information that can assist professionals in meeting those demands. Owing to the belief that learning is not a plateau that one arrives at but a process one engages in over the life span, continuing education is a necessary vehicle to achieve that end. Philosophically, then, continuing education ought to provide an important supplement to the knowledge and skill base professionals have acquired through their academic training.

Historically, preparation of yesterday's leaders, academicians, and practitioners within the fields of counseling and psychology was a primary undertaking of undergraduate and graduate programs on college and university campuses and in professional schools. Traditionally, the congruence between the educational curriculum and the requisite knowledge and skills required to be a competent professional seemed to be quite high, given professional standards.

With the surge in licensing and certification requirements over the past two decades, as well as the changes in what was thought to be requisite skill, the profession seemed no longer able to count on academic training programs alone to meet advanced training needs within the few years of traditional graduate education. Clearly, more training hours and additional courses are now required to meet the demands of clinicians and academicians. Unquestionably, continuing education is a must to be considered a competent professional.

Helping to fuel the demand for additional training is the multicultural counseling competency movement (D'Andrea et al., 2001; Sue, Arredondo, & McDavis, 1992). However, unlike other courses or programs of instruction in areas such as psychopharmacology, ethical and legal issues, substance abuse, testing and assessment, and even child abuse, increasing knowledge, awareness, and skills in the areas of cultural competence has been a more difficult outcome to achieve. Several reasons appear to account for this trend in resistance to culturally specific education. First, few programs have training curriculum that adequately infuses multicultural content into courses. This trend is nearly a decade old, as Ridley, Mendoza, and Kanitz (1992, 1994) pointed out. In identifying six models of diversity and multicultural training that could be incorporated into graduate training (traditional, workshop design, separate course, interdisciplinary cognate, subspecialty cognate, and integrated program), they argued that the model that seemed the most ideal was the least used. Ponterotto (1997) made a similar point when discussing the notion of cultural

competency. He developed a Multicultural Competency Checklist, with a list of 22 items that could be used as a separate template for programs to measure training standards. Unfortunately, his data revealed that few counseling programs met the stated criteria.

Second, faculty who are charged with teaching multicultural competency are themselves lacking proficiency in the areas of diversity and multiculturalism. Undoubtedly, their own graduate training reflected less of a diversity curriculum than is available today. Also, literature and other resources on diversity issues were less plentiful, making studying multicultural materials difficult. Third, the yardstick that measures adequate multicultural training is often restricted to a single course, in which issues of race, ethnicity, gender, class, physical ability, and sexual orientation are accorded a week's worth of topical coverage within a given semester or quarter (Parham, 2002). In fact, Parham (2002) has argued that the standard or "bar of competence" is so low that measures of progress toward diversity may be artificially inflated. For example, some authors have suggested that "interest in diversity issues" is a measure of progress, where counseling psychology programs have been shown to have more interest in diversity-related issues and research when compared to other programs in clinical psychology (Norcross, Sayette, Mayne, Karg, & Turkson, 1998). Ponterotto's (1997) analysis has shown that of those programs sampled, 89% of them offer at least one multicultural course. However, Hill and Strozier (1992) found that only 59% of the programs they sampled had a multicultural course as a core requirement for graduation at the master's or doctoral level. Clearly, measures of progress that focus solely on interest in multiculturalism, in our opinion, are simply inappropriate, insufficient, and bordering on unethical.

In part, the demands for more culturally rich curricula and training experiences are instigated by a population that is growing increasingly diverse and presenting themselves frequently for counseling and mental health services. In fact, although some argue that training needs are influenced by market forces (Goodyear et al., 2000), they also recognize that the changing demographics and diversity needs seem to have had less influence on training requirements than other comparable market forces such as managed care. Without adequate training in graduate programs to demonstrate cultural competence and proficiency, continuing education courses and seminars take on a greater level of importance in professional and ethical standards of practice. Therefore, the purpose of this chapter is to discuss the importance of continuing education for psychologists and counselors, within the context of preparation for increasing levels of cultural proficiency.

THE NEED FOR CONTINUING EDUCATION IN MULTICULTURAL ISSUES

Twenty years ago, Bernal and Padilla (1982) documented the need for greater attention to issues related to people of color in graduate counseling and clinical psychology programs. At that time, chairs of graduate programs acknowledged that there was a wide range of opinion regarding the inclusion of material related to "ethnic minority" populations. Research and experience reveal that this is still the case. Quintana and Bernal (1995) found that only a few counseling psychology programs have designed programs that will yield culturally competent psychologists. The findings were similar for clinical psychology programs. A survey conducted by Rogers, Ponterotto, Conoley, and Wiese (1992) discovered that school psychology programs accredited by the American Psychological Association (APA) were more active in relation to providing multicultural content, hiring

faculty who are people of color, and arranging placements with multicultural populations. Yet, 40% of the programs sampled did not include specific courses on minority issues or infuse multicultural content into core school psychology courses.

Identifying psychological literature that addresses continuing education related specifically to multiculturalism is no easy task. In addition to the lack of exposure to these issues in graduate school, there are a number of possible reasons for this difficulty. First, the existence of White privilege (McIntosh, 1998) means that the concerns related to multiculturalism such as inclusion, racism, and other forms of discrimination might not have directly affected the lives of psychologists. Therefore, because it was not a concern in these psychologists' lives, they may believe these issues are irrelevant for everyone. Often, this difference in experiences results in the stereotype that the clinicians who do believe culture is important are pathologically concerned about oppression and race relations. Moreover, bringing issues of multicultural inclusions to the attention of faculty, colleagues, and training directors can be a source of stress for both students and professionals.

Given the current state of affairs related to producing culturally competent psychologists, it is clear that the knowledge, awareness, and skills of many psychologists are inadequate. Some graduate training programs may offer courses at the end of students' coursework, but this "add-on" course makes it difficult for students to integrate and apply the concepts and techniques into their understanding of the process of working with clients throughout training. This occurs because add-on courses tend to marginalize content as less germane to the core course of study. Furthermore, the exposure to programs that do not validate the importance of diversity issues could convince these psychologists that diversity and multicultural issues are, indeed, irrelevant. Comprehensive and thorough continuing education related to diversity issues is one mechanism by which the problem of multicultural competency can be rectified. Highlen (1994) argued persuasively that universal psychology (one psychology fits all cultures) in graduate school programs should be abandoned for approaches that recognize a wider range of worldviews. As a result, psychologists can be trained to be effective with a broad range of patients and can use cultural and other diversity information to the benefit of all of their clients.

RESISTANCE TO CONTINUING EDUCATION

Although there has been an explosion of articles on multicultural competence and multiculturalism during the past 20 years, very few address continuing education as a focal point. The paucity of articles on diversity issues in continuing education is indicative of the fact that some practitioners and scholars believe that once psychologists have their degrees, there is no need to continue to build multicultural competence. There are, however, several authors who offer a slightly different perspective on the topic of multiculturalism in continuing education.

According to Lee and Kurilla (1996), practitioners who cannot open-mindedly and effectively treat clients from different cultures or with different worldviews are ethically obligated to seek consultation or refer clients. Because many clinicians may be more likely to attend a continuing education seminar than they are to obtain individual supervision, continuing education can be an avenue for clinicians to learn about other cultures and their own resistance to understanding people from groups other than their own.

The importance of continuing education in various counseling professions has been addressed. Rubin, Davis, Noe, and Turner (1996) have written about methods of assessing outcomes of multicultural continuing education for rehabilitation counselors. School counselors have also recognized the importance of multicultural education in continuing education. For instance, Carey, Reinat, and Fontes (1990) surveyed 719 school counselors to determine their training needs. They found that counselors wanted additional training to assist them in promoting students' academic achievement and to enhance counselors' cross-cultural communication and racism awareness.

But even though some programs invite multiculturalism into their curriculum, resistance remains. In addition, challenges to multicultural continuing education are not limited to student resistance. Indeed, instructors themselves must navigate their way through walls of resistance. In fact, one of the greatest challenges facing those interested in diversity teaching continuing education is that compared to graduate training programs, psychologists can exercise choice in their selection of courses. Hence, even if a multicultural competency course is offered, at this point, it is not mandatory that they learn about multiculturalism. For example, at many psychology conferences, the sessions on race, racism, and other diversity issues are noticeably underattended by White psychologists. This could change as licensing boards begin to require multicultural knowledge on licensing exams. Therefore, strategies should be designed to encourage people, perhaps for the first time, to take multicultural courses. Efforts must be made to make multicultural and diversity-related courses more accessible and attractive to resistant or skeptical clinicians. For example, among clinicians, training materials demonstrating how multicultural competency will be useful in their work with all of their clients, not just people of color, could be a draw for some psychologists.

CURRICULUM AND PEDAGOGY

Psychologists who are diversity trainers may find that although it is easy to obtain curriculum materials, it is sometimes difficult to manage the intense reactions participants can have to the concepts they present. Pedagogical strategies should take into account that participants will need time to process what they are learning, possibly in small groups, and to work collaboratively with their colleagues. A major premise of adult education is to connect with and use the "life experience" of the participants. Yet at the large majority of conferences and training sessions, participants sit and listen passively for most of the program and are allotted 2 or 3 minutes at the end to "ask questions." In addition, multiculturalism is often marginalized into a session with few, if any, references to it along the way. Material on culture should appear throughout all training sessions to achieve a greater level of integration of content into the entire curriculum. Again, the literature on these issues focuses on undergraduate and graduate students (Fairchild, Richard, & Whitten, in press; Jackson, 1999; Whitten, 1993a, 1993b). Whitten (1993b) discussed student reactions to controversial issues surrounding race and culture and suggested strategies for managing both attitudes and affect. Jackson (1999) analyzed her experiences teaching graduate students about diversity issues, focusing on a range of responses from students of color.

The basic idea, as in other areas of clinical skill, is that it is essential that clinicians continue to develop and hone their skills in relation to multiculturalism (Livneh & Livneh, 1999). They must keep up with the research and theory as it relates to working with culturally diverse clients. In addition, it is important to learn about changes in the demographic makeup of certain groups. For example, it would be important for psychologists to know that in the past, Latinos in the New York area were overwhelmingly from Cuba, the Dominican Republic, and Puerto Rico. Recently, there has been an influx of immigrants from Central and South America, with different concerns and cultures, and knowing about one Latino group is not enough to work with other Latino cultures. Fortunately, in most states, continuing education is required of psychologists, and if they see a workshop or paper focusing on a pertinent issue for their practice, they will be likely to participate.

Within the context of diversity issues, a unit in the continuing education workshop should also focus on resources and strategies for obtaining additional information about groups with whom clinicians work and about groups representing their own ethnic background. There are many journals, for example, that many psychologists may not have been exposed to in graduate school due to the absence of a real commitment to education about culture and race in many graduate programs (a list of these journals could be provided).

In these continuing education sessions, participants can be encouraged to consider culture, social class, and other diversity issues in all of their professional endeavors. When designing research projects, interpreting results, working with clients, teaching and working with students outside of the classroom, and interacting with colleagues, participants can consider how culture and race affect their practice, relationships, and self-understanding. Psychologists can also benefit from reflecting on their own cultural and racial experiences since within-group variation and similarity are sometimes overlooked. This within-group exploration may be important for White people especially. Finally, social class is another issue that is often ignored yet may yield benefits to learning and self-understanding when explored.

WHAT DOES A CLINICIAN NEED TO BE CULTURALLY COMPETENT?

The first step toward cultural competence is the awareness and recognition that continuing growth and development of professional skills is a priority for every professional psychologist. Within that recognition is the duality of the responsibility for continuing education. On one end of the continuum is the responsibility of institutions that must anticipate and identify the needs of professionals and create forums to share and deliver the information. On the other end of the responsibility continuum are professionals who must recognize gaps in their existing skill and information base and avail themselves of the opportunities to enhance their personal, professional, and intellectual capabilities. In the middle are the professional associations and state licensing boards, which must regulate the conduct and training requirements of professional psychologists and counselors, with an eye on protecting the consumer of the services rendered by these professionals.

The determination of what constitutes cultural competence is far from an objective standard. And yet the norm for cultural competency training is so variable that adherence to any standard becomes difficult. Sue et al. (1992), in citing the ethical codes of professional counseling associations, were clear that competency related to the possession of three attributes: *awareness, knowledge,* and *skill.* These three characteristics were thought to be the cornerstone of a more culturally sensitive professional practice of counseling and psychology. This is particularly true when a clinician seeks to examine his or her own values and biases, understand culturally different clients worldviews, and develop appropriate intervention strategies and techniques.

Subsequent revisions to the competency model have been provided by Arredondo et al. (1996). In fact, Abren, Chung, and Atkinson (2000) argued that the Arredondo et al. revision may be a more advanced approach because it seeks to translate the competency document into behavioral norms. Irrespective of which version is called for here, questions still remain about the most viable and appropriate form to affect multicultural skills, knowledge, and attitudes.

Regardless of which form is used to acquire and sustain enhanced awareness, knowledge, and skills, it is clear that competencies cannot be achieved without those three attributes. Clearly, continuing education has an important role to play in facilitating access to these increased levels of competence. Beyond the attributes listed above, however, other didactic and experiential training must be acquired for professional competence to be achieved, and continuing education has a role to play in assisting professionals with these goals.

DEFINING CULTURE

No level of competence can ever be achieved in a multicultural context without being able to define and understand the variables of culture. Because superficial definitions of culture have dominated the popular literature, professionals learn to accept superficial explanations for what should be more "deep structure analysis." For example, some professionals accept the idea that culture is synonymous with food. Others prefer to associate culture with music, dance, or even dress or attire. Even more sophisticated attempts to understand culture link it with race and ethnicity, believing that racial background serves as the anchor point for one's cultural identity. Although each of these variables can be considered a manifestation of culture, they do not form the core of what constitutes culture. Culture is a complex constellation of mores, values, customs, and traditions that provide a general design for living and a pattern for interpreting reality (Nobles, 1986). Culture is like the DNA of human consciousness through which the transmission of information is carried and processed. This element, an understanding of culture, is an essential ingredient in the acquisition of multicultural competence.

ABILITY TO SELF-ASSESS

Perhaps no skill in the clinician's repertoire is more important than the ability to self-assess. In this regard, we are referring to the ability to render a realistic appraisal about one's own strengths and limitations as a therapist. Indeed, many therapists and academicians have advocated that self-awareness serves as the cornerstone of competency models (Arredondo et al., 1996; Sue et al., 1992). We fear that the rush to acquire newfound knowledge or learn a specific technique does place less salience and, consequently, less priority, on the awareness dimension. This can be a serious mistake.

Equally important is the understanding of how specific skills used in a particular situation affect culturally different clients. Parham (2002) has invited us to consider the older wisdom that says, "Life at its best is a creative synthesis of opposites in fruitful harmony." This statement reminds us that our greatest strength can also be our greatest weakness, depending on the context. Relatedly, a clinician's awareness must also extend to a recognition of how personal strengths and weaknesses may differentially affect culturally different clients, based on those clients' culture and worldview.

FLEXIBILITY TO ADAPT

Among the variables that provide a clinician with an important support is the ability to be flexible and adaptive with culturally different populations. Flexibility and adaptability are important for several reasons. Primarily, it is believed that many clinicians approach client concerns guided by theoretical orientation. Beyond a template for helping to conceptualize client dynamics, theories and constructs provide a road map in directing therapeutic interventions designed to address client distress identified by the clinician. Unfortunately, most theories of psychotherapy are not normed on culturally diverse populations. Thus, interventions identified by clinicians may need to be adjusted to better address the issues presented by a culturally different client. This flexibility and adaptability variable is something traditional graduate training rarely teaches. This is why continuing education will be challenged to create models that allow professionals to acquire these skills.

CULTURALLY SPECIFIC COURSEWORK

Amid the desire to provide informative instructional sessions of a multicultural nature is the teaching of multicultural counseling and therapy itself. Typically, graduate students and professionals alike are exposed to a single-course format in which diversity is broadly defined by a host of demographic (race, ethnicity, gender, sexual orientation, physical ability, etc.) variables. The course is then designed in a format that is usually didactic in nature, where each demographic characteristic or group within a category is given topical consideration. Thus, over the course of the semester, students in the class can expect to spend some fraction of the course (e.g., 1 week) covering each topic.

Unfortunately, generic courses do little to enhance cultural competence, beyond the superficial exposure to each variable covered. What is needed is a curriculum regiment that provides instruction in courses such as African American, Asian American, Chicano/Latino, and American Indian psychology and counseling. Generic multicultural counseling courses can serve as a good primer but must be supplemented with coursework that is culturally specific in nature. Continuing education curriculum must account for both necessities.

ABILITY TO USE SPECIFIC INTERVENTION STRATEGIES

Much like traditional therapeutic techniques that are guided by theoretical orientations, intervention strategies that are culturally based must be similarly anchored. For example, Parham (2002) and Parham, White, and Ajamu (1999) have likewise argued that those who work with people from African descent need to ground their therapy techniques in a set of culturally based assumptions that inform both the direction of therapy intervention as well as the role and task of the practitioner (healer).

In addition, Parham (2002) proposed the learning and incorporation of specific techniques that are designed to enhance the success of a therapeutic interaction whereby African Americans are the clients being served. His model assumes that therapy as a whole can be broken down into specific categories of skill sets. These skill sets include specific suggestions on how to connect with clients, conduct assessments, facilitate awareness, set goals, take action and instigate change, and seek feedback and accountability. Given this range of knowledge and skills, it is clear that culturally specific coursework is necessary to help practitioners develop and increase skills that are culturally competent. Continuing education must design instructional curriculum and methodologies that teach these basic skills over the course of several weeks or even months.

CONTINUING EDUCATION: A LAST STANCE

If the skills discussed above are necessary to increase cultural competence, professionals will need to rely on continuing education to meet this demand. Indeed, continuing education may be the last stance for professionals to achieve a level of professional competence, given the failure of traditional graduate training to adequately prepare professionals to meet the challenges of serving the mental health needs of culturally different populations. Yet, as we examine the literature, it appears that there are no models of multicultural training for psychologists in a continuing education setting. In this section, we propose some guidelines for curriculum and pedagogy and suggestions related to the type of environment that promotes learning about working with people who are culturally diverse.

A review of the available periodicals reveals that multicultural continuing education is an area that has not received much attention in the literature. However, Wheaton and Granellor (1998) found that in a group of practicing rehabilitation counselors, those who participated in a greater number of multicultural counseling workshops obtained significantly higher test scores on the Multicultural Competency Inventory (MCI) and higher scores on the MCI Skill, MCI Knowledge, and MCI Awareness subscales of the instrument. Scores on the Relationships subscale did not increase significantly with the amount of training. However, this research appears to support the notion that continuing education can have a positive impact on how counselors view their own multicultural counseling skills.

CHALLENGES TO MULTICULTURAL CONTINUING EDUCATION

At this point, psychologists who must obtain continuing education units or credits do not have any requirements specifically related to multicultural coursework. Because required coursework on diversity issues is still a relatively new phenomenon in graduate programs, it is safe to assume that many psychologists have not been trained in this area. Thus, continuing education represents an opportunity to enhance the multicultural competency of psychologists in ways that potentially increase their effectiveness. Another significant challenge to multicultural continuing education is the fact that courses are rarely evaluated and/or graded. Grades and evaluation have a tendency to both incite a different level of motivation to engage the subject matter and promote a greater level of accountability to meet course requirements. If, however, evaluation criteria and grades are absent from the educational experience, this could potentially foster a lack of engagement of the subject matter on the part of the trainee and communicate that the content is less important than topics where testing is required.

Another challenge to multicultural continuing education has to do with the notion of curriculum. Based on our own experiences, we have seen how in some graduate programs, professors give scant or limited attention to issues of multiculturalism by referring briefly to the need for different techniques in working with diverse populations. If this practice is repeated within the context of continuing education sessions as well, obvious problems will continue. It is our belief that multicultural curriculum materials should be infused into courses that are acceptable for continuing education credits. As in undergraduate and graduate settings, these courses ideally will not be marginalized by being distinct or separate from the rest of the curriculum but will be a part of a regimen of courses in a series related by a common theme. In this regard, we are suggesting that continuing education should include generic courses about multicultural counseling and psychology, specific courses at a more advanced level on multicultural counseling and diversity, and the infusion of multicultural content into existing courses (i.e., assessment, ethics, etc.).

When designing instructional methodology for continuing education programs, educators and instructors should also attend to one of the fundamental aspects of adult education: using student experiences. Clinicians should be assisted in relating the new learning to their own personal experiences as cultural beings, especially their own cultural and racial identity. This type of training should engage students in active learning rather than allowing them to be detached from the learning experience in ways that only require passive participation. The relevance of multicultural education to all people and the impact on each of our lives should be strongly emphasized.

Another component of multicultural continuing education and training should assist the participants in discovering how they will actually apply their learning to their work with clients. This step is essential in helping clinicians to develop concrete plans of how they might implement newly developed skills. In addition, time in the course can and should be devoted to illuminating the assumptions, beliefs, knowledge, and attitudes of psychologists about multicultural training. For example, some psychologists may be insulted by the basic notion of being labeled "incompetent" after earning their doctoral degrees. They may resent the suggestion that their work with culturally different populations may be less than adequate. Some counselors and psychologists are passionate about the idea that "we all are human beings" or "we are all Americans," so culture, race, gender, and other diversity issues are less germane. Certainly, some may assert that if their graduate school faculty and administrators did not deem the topic important, it must not be significant enough to attend continuing education courses to cover the subject matter. Obviously, teaching professionals with resistant and dismissive attitudes can be difficult at best.

Another concern is that educational sessions on diversity-related issues are generally conducted by people who represent the particular group being discussed. Tisdell (1998), in writing about poststructural feminist pedagogies, contended that it is crucial to pay attention to issues of positionality of all the participants, including the instructor. Instructors, Tisdell believes, must take into account the impact of their "Blackness" or "gayness" in the context of teaching. She knows that there is less risk involved in the endeavor for those on the privilege side of the equation.

Psychology and counseling instructors in continuing education may also need to move outside of the discipline to learn and/or enhance their skills in disseminating instructional information. Perhaps some of that learning should come from continuing education departments themselves. Queeny, Smultz, and Shuman (1990) argued that each professional's continuing education should be a cumulative, integrated process directed toward optimum performance, rather than a series of unrelated events. This is an interesting suggestion, given that the way much of continuing education for psychologists and counselors is currently structured seems to create and foster a climate where each course is seen to be separate and distinct from the other. Smultz and Queeney also asserted that professionals must be trained to be informed consumers of continuing education. In this regard, continuing educators must help professionals learn to value continuing education and to develop the skills needed to coordinate their own personal growth and development as professionals.

THE ABPsi MODEL

Despite the absence of training models for psychologists in continuing education, a few organizations have taken on the role and responsibility. One such organization is the National Association of Black Psychologists (ABPsi), and the training model it has incorporated is the *African Psychology Institute* (API). Rowe and Webb-Msemaji (2002) have detailed the components of the API, which is a systematic training paradigm for preparing psychologists of African descent to work more effectively with African American people.

The API includes as its mission (a) establishing parameters of a common fund of knowledge necessary for articulating African-centered psychology, (b) offering a training program in African-centered psychology, and (c) certifying and/or credentialing psychologists to meet the psycho-cultural needs of African people. Rowe and Webb-Msemaji (2002) also outlined the domains of instruction that form the core of the API curriculum that is thematically related. The training begins with an introductory course, followed by a course reflecting one of four domains: (a) historical moments and movements; (b) spiritness, including ethics and human development; (c) epistemology/research, and (d) applications and contributions. Rowe and Webb-Msemaji also reported that each course is 6 hours in length and emphasizes receptive, participatory, and demonstrative styles of learning. Clearly, the Association of Black Psychologists is one organization that is setting a new standard for how continuing education can be structured so that the ability to achieve greater levels of cultural competence is promoted.

Last, we want to reinforce the notion of pedagogy. As you can see from the API example, the methodology by which instructional information is delivered is extremely important. In this regard, we are suggesting that continuing education around multicultural counseling and therapy and/or culturally specific psychology should be varied and flexible in its methodology. The standard lecture format should not be the dominant methodological technique used by most instructors. It is also important that students have time to process their experiences and changing awareness. In this way, a continuing educator can assess the progress, or lack thereof, of the participants involved in the class. It is hoped that the sessions will consist of dynamic interchange among the participants and the instructor such that each benefits from the other's expertise.

CLOSING THOUGHTS

The challenge of providing continuing education to psychologists, counselors, and other mental health providers is enormous. Given the lack of training in multicultural counseling and competencies at the graduate level, professionals will need to rely on continuing education forums to be able to meet their demands and needs. Because education and training should be about more than simply course instruction and logging hours in the classroom, we close this chapter with some thoughts on contextualizing that perspective on the need for continuing education.

1. *First, learning should be a process rather than a plateau.* Thus, the awarding of degrees and certifications should not be the only goal of a professional. Rather, learning should be viewed as a lifelong process of self-discovery and information enhancement.

2. *Much like the purpose of education should never be to get a job, continuing education should not be acquired simply to accommodate licensing requirements.* Education, in its truest form, should be about the cultivation of the human spirit in all aspects. Thus, we would invite mental health personnel and professionals to enlighten their minds, develop value sets that are more principled, and develop a set of professional behaviors and conduct that is more culturally congruent.

3. *Learning in a culturally different context cannot be relegated to the classroom or even a training facility.* Learning about African Americans, Asian Americans, Chicanos/Latinos, American Indians, and so forth must come from real experiences in

living, sharing, and bonding outside of the classroom setting.

4. *Last, continuing education should focus less on acquiring hours and more on the principal of mastery.* Therefore, what one professional needs to demonstrate mastery may be different from what his or her colleague requires. Thus, we urge professionals, licensing boards, and certification bodies alike to consider the notion that cultural competence requires not simply hours of instruction but mastery of the skills and knowledge necessary to be effective service providers.

REFERENCES

Abren, J. M., Chung, R. H. G., & Atkinson, D. R. (2000). Multicultural counseling training: Past, present, and future directions. *The Counseling Psychologist, 28,* 641-656.

Arredondo, P., Toporek, R., Brown, S. P., Jones, J., Locke, D. C., Sanchez, J., et al. (1996). Operationalization of the multicultural counseling competencies. *Journal of Multicultural Counseling and Development, 24,* 42-78.

Bernal, M. E., & Padilla, A. M. (1982). Status of minority curricula and training in clinical psychology. *American Psychologist, 37*(7), 780-787.

Carey, J. C., Reinat, M., & Fontes, L. (1990). The multicultural counseling competencies of state vocational rehabilitation counselors. *Counselor Education and Supervision, 29*(3), 155-169.

D'Andrea, M., Daniels, J., Arredondo, P., Bradford Ivey, M., Ivey, A., Locke, D., et al. (2001). Fostering organizational changes to realize the revolutionary potential of the multicultural movement: An updated case study. In J. Ponterotto, J. M. Casas, L. A. Suzuki, & C. M. Alexander (Eds.), *Handout of multicultural counseling* (pp. 222-253). Thousand Oaks, CA: Sage.

Fairchild, H. H., Richard, H. W., & Whitten, L. (in press). Teaching African American psychology: Resources and strategies. In P. Bronstein & P. Kat (Eds.), *Teaching a psychology of people* (2nd ed.). Washington, DC: American Psychological Association.

Goodyear, R. K., Cortese, J. R., Grizzardo, C. R., Allison, R. D., Clairborn, C. D., & Packard, T. (2000). Factors, trends, and topics in the evolution of counseling psychology training. *The Counseling Psychologist, 28*(5), 603-621.

Highlen, P. S. (1994). Racial/ethnic diversity in doctoral programs of psychology: Challenges for the twenty-first century. *Applied and Preventive Psychology, 3*(2), 91-108.

Hill, H. I., & Strozier, A. L. (1992). Multicultural training in APA approved counseling psychology programs: A survey. *Professional Psychology: Research and Practice, 23,* 43-51.

Jackson, L. C. (1999). Ethnocultural resistance to multicultural training: Students and faculty. *Cultural Diversity & Ethnic Minority Psychology, 5*(1), 27-36.

Lee, C. C., & Kurilla, V. (1996). Ethics and multiculturalism: The challenge of diversity. In *The Hatherleigh guide to ethics in therapy* (pp. 235-248). Long Island City, NY: Hatherleigh.

Livneh, C., & Livneh, H. (1999). Continuing professional education among educators: Predictors of participation in learning activities. *Adult Education Quarterly, 49*(2), 91-106.

McIntosh, P. (1998). White privilege: Unpacking the invisible knapsack. In M. McGoldrick (Ed.), *Re-visioning family therapy: Race, culture, and gender in clinical practice* (pp. 147-152). New York: Guilford.

Nobles, W. W. (1986). *African psychology: Toward its reclamation, reascension, and revitalization.* Oakland, CA: Institute for the Advanced Study of Black Family Life and Culture.

Norcross, J. C., Sayette, M. A., Mayne, T. J., Karg, R. S., & Turkson, M. A. (1998). Selecting a doctoral program in psychology: Some comparison among Ph.D. counseling, Ph.D. clinical, and PsyD clinical psychology programs. *Professional Psychology: Research and Practice, 29,* 609-614.

Parham, T. A. (2002). *Counseling persons of African descent: Raising the bar of what passes for competence.* Thousand Oaks, CA: Sage.

Parham, T. A., White, J. L., & Ajamu, A. (1999). *The psychology of Blacks: An African centered perspective.* Upper Saddle River, NJ: Prentice Hall.

Ponterotto, J. (1997). Multicultural counseling training: A competency model and national survey. In D. B. Pope-Davis & H. L. K. Coleman (Eds.), *Multicultural counseling competencies: Assessment, education, training, & supervision* (pp. 111-130). Thousand Oaks, CA: Sage.

Queeney, D. S., Smutz, W. D., & Shuman, S. B. (1990). Mandatory continuing professional education. *Continuing Higher Education Review, 54*(1), 11-25.

Quintana, S. M., & Bernal, M. E. (1995). Ethnic minority training in counseling psychology: Comparisons with clinical psychology and proposed standards. *Counseling Psychologist, 23*(1), 102-121.

Ridley, C. R., Mendoza, D. W., & Kanitz, B. E. (1992). Program designs for multicultural training. *Journal of Psychology and Christianity, 11,* 326-333.

Ridley, C. R., Mendoza, D. W., & Kanitz, B. E. (1994). Multicultural training: Re-examination, operationalization, and integration. *The Counseling Psychologist, 22,* 221-289.

Rogers, M. R., Ponterotto, J., Conoley, J. C., & Wiese, M. (1992). Multicultural training in school psychology: A national survey. *School Psychology, 4*(21), 603-616.

Rowe, D. T., & Webb-Msemaji, F. (2002, August). *African Psychology Institute training modules.* Paper presented at the annual meeting of the Association of Black Psychologists, San Diego.

Rubin, S. E., Davis, E. L., Noe, S. R., & Turner, T. N. (1996). Assessing the effects of continuing multicultural rehabilitation counseling education. *Rehabilitation Education, 10*(2-3), 115-126.

Sue, D. W., Arredondo, P., & McDavis, R. (1992). Multicultural counseling competencies and standards: A call to the profession. *Journal of Counseling and Development, 70,* 477-484.

Tisdell, E. J. (1998). Poststructural feminist pedagogies: The possibilities and limitations of feminist emancipatory adult learning theory and practice. *Adult Education Quarterly, 48*(3), 139-156.

Wheaton, J. E., & Granellor, D. H. (1998). The multicultural counseling competencies of state vocational rehabilitation counselors. *Rehabilitation Education, 12*(1), 51-64.

Whitten, L. (1993a). Infusing Black psychology into the introductory psychology course. *Teaching of Psychology, 20*(1), 13-21.

Whitten, L. (1993b). Managing student reactions to controversial issues in the college classroom. *Transformations, 4*, 30-44.

36

Teaching Multicultural Competencies Using the Internet and Other Technologies

JULIE R. ANCIS

Georgia State University

One of the challenges of training mental health professionals involves teaching multicultural competencies within an increasingly diverse and technologically advanced society. Counseling programs have an ethical responsibility to train professionals who can meet the needs of a culturally, racially, and ethnically diverse clientele (Altmaier, 1993). To meet the needs of a diverse clientele, counseling trainees must develop the awareness, knowledge, and skills required of a multiculturally competent counselor (Arredondo et al., 1996; Sue, Arredondo, & McDavis, 1992). Such competencies are essential to accurate assessment, interpretation, and treatment (Sue, Ivey, & Pedersen, 1996). In conjunction with the demands to address issues of diversity, educators and trainers are confronted with technological innovations that are changing the nature of teaching and higher education. Technological innovations, such as the Internet, present opportunities to further trainees' multicultural counseling competencies.

Both multicultural counseling competencies and technical competencies are continually being defined and reconceptualized. The Division 17 of the American Psychological Association (APA) publication outlining cross-cultural counseling competencies (Sue et al., 1992) serves as one of the key educational, research, and training documents in the field of multicultural counseling. This document has subsequently been refined and the contents operationalized (Arredondo et al., 1996; Sue et al., 1992). Similarly, professional associations and organizations continue to develop technical standards and competencies for learners and educators. For example, the Association for Counselor Education and Supervision (ACES, 1999a) has developed technical competencies for counselor education students and guidelines for online instruction. ACES's (1999b) Technology Interest Network has outlined technical competencies that counseling students should master before graduation. The standards of the Council for Accreditation of Counseling and Related Educational Programs (CACREP) include technology and distance learning as a component of preservice preparation.

The prevalence of both multicultural competency training and technologically based instruction in higher education is evident. Approximately 89% of APA-accredited counseling psychology and counselor education programs have a multicultural counseling course (Ponterotto, 1997). Similarly, there has been an increase in the number of higher education institutions offering distance-based courses. In 1997-1998, approximately 44% of all higher education institutions offered distance-based courses, an increase of one third since 1994-1995 (Council for Higher Education Accreditation, 2000). Seventy-eight percent of public 4-year and 62% of public 2-year institutions offered some form of distance-delivered courses. The majority of the growth in distance-delivered courses involved asynchronous computer-based technology (primarily over the Internet) rather than video-based technology. In the past several years, there has been a dramatic growth in the use of computer resources in instruction in the form of Internet resources, multimedia technology, and CD-ROM programs (Murray, 1999). The advent of technological advances has provided great potential for developing trainees' multicultural counseling competencies.

Various approaches to multicultural counseling training have been employed and reviewed in the literature. These approaches represent diverse philosophical frameworks regarding the definition of *multicultural,* the definition of *multicultural counseling competence,* the goals of multicultural training, and the content and process of training. The details of the diverse approaches to developing multicultural counseling competencies are beyond the scope of this chapter (for a review, see Enns, Sinacore, Ancis, & Phillips, in press). Rather, in this chapter, I will discuss how particular aspects of multicultural counseling competence—that is, self-awareness, knowledge, and skills—can be augmented by the use of the Internet and other technologies.

As many approaches to multicultural counseling training exist, there are also many modes of technologically driven education. The following section briefly describes distance education delivery modes and related issues associated with multicultural competency training.

Electronic College Courses. Students who are geographically distant from an institution's main campus complete courses for academic credit. Typically, students complete computer-packaged lessons and assignments that are returned to the institution electronically (using computer systems such as e-mail or Web sites) or through the mail. Prepackaged audiotapes, videotapes, and printed material often accompany the computer programs. Instructors evaluate the completed material and assign a grade or provide directions for further work.

Electronic courses are also delivered via the World Wide Web or Internet (i.e., online). In this format, students enroll in a course and log on to an Internet Web site containing the class syllabus, readings, assignments, and other course-related material. In addition to independent work, students often are required to log on to Web site discussions at designated class times. In addition, e-mail and chat rooms are used for discussion outside of class time.

Broadcast Television. Courses are offered by community colleges, colleges, and universities through commercial or public television and are broadcast or cable-delivered into students' homes. Live classes may be delivered at designated time periods, or videotaped lectures may be shown repeatedly several times. This mode of delivery often involves one-way audio-video so that students can hear and see the instructor, but the instructor cannot hear or see the student. Several programs allow for two-way audio, whereby students are allowed to telephone the instructor during class broadcasts to offer reactions, respond to material, and ask questions.

Teleclasses. These classes are similar to the broadcast television class and involve students enrolled in the course meeting together in a specially wired classroom where they view lectures by an instructor. Sometimes, a teaching assistant or clinical instructor leads the discussion.

Broadcast courses and teleclasses are often part of larger, more comprehensive distance learning package that includes videotapes, videoconferencing, audiotapes, printed materials, and Web-based instruction.

Interactive Audio-Video Classrooms. This is the most technically advanced form of distance learning. Classrooms are transmitted by an integrated system of video, audio, and computer signals from the main campus to off-campus locations. Students at multiple sites interact with each other and with the instructor through closed-circuit television or limited-access satellite television. The instructor typically conducts class from a central studio where "in-house" students are present. Video monitors are located at each site, and verbal communication is accomplished through a specially wired audio system. The classroom provides one-way or two-way video interaction and two-way audio interaction.

Several challenges are associated with the above forms of distance learning. The one-way video format, whereby students may view the instructor but students lack visual access to the instructor and other students, creates limitations in the multicultural classroom. For example, faculty lack access to the students' nonverbal behavior, which often provides cues to student comprehension, interest, and anxiety. Instructors often rely on these nonverbal cues as a means to structure multicultural material, offering support or challenge as needed. Second, the geographic dispersion of students and faculty may limit students' ability to form support groups and interact directly with a diverse peer group (Willis, 1994). Third, the increased learner access associated with distance education frequently results in televised courses with larger student enrollments compared to traditional classrooms (Willis, 1994). The larger class size may affect classroom interaction, student participation, and the amount of individualized attention provided to students. The degree to which experiential exercises, common in multicultural counseling classrooms, may be processed with each student is limited. However, the demographic diversity associated with increased educational access, particularly the inclusion of non-traditional-age students, often results in a student body possessing diverse perspectives. Remote site students, as a function of their age and life experience, can offer viewpoints that may enliven multiculturally relevant discussions. Despite these challenges, flexibility and creativity on the part of an instructor may result in innovative learning opportunities (Ancis, 1998).

This chapter focuses on the use of technology in traditional multicultural classroom settings rather than distance education classrooms (see Ancis, 1998, for a review of cultural competency training via distance education).

THE INTERNET AND MULTICULTURAL COMPETENCIES

One of the most exciting features of the Internet is the ability to facilitate interaction between students and educators within the classroom, as well as with individuals outside of the classroom both nationally and internationally (Gorski, 2001). Students and faculty can engage in dialogue via electronic mail, listservs, and discussion groups with others worldwide. Such forums provide opportunities for resource sharing, cross-cultural communication, and coalition building. Through these forums and interactions, trainees are directly confronted with how their own background influences their attitudes and values, are able to increase their understanding of their own and others' cultural heritage and experiences, and actively engage in cross-cultural communication—dimensions of self-awareness, knowledge, and skills. The Internet also provides access to a multitude of multicultural information regarding diverse groups and related research, thus promoting multicultural knowledge. Moreover, the Internet and the multimedia format of the World Wide Web (WWW) (the graphical interface for the Internet that combines text, photographs, discussion forums, and exercises) requires active participation and engagement, resulting in greater learner motivation (Price, Repman, & White, 1994) and learning outcomes (Jonassen & Hannum, 1987; Keller, 1983), particularly in distance education classrooms (Schwitzer, Ancis, & Brown, 2001).

Often, multicultural material is digested and processed beyond the actual class meeting. Students in multicultural counseling courses often report that the assigned reading, lectures, exercises, and class discussions prompt them to process issues beyond the class time. Providing students with tools to continue this developmental process beyond the confines of the classroom may help to facilitate continued

and more in-depth learning. Students develop an understanding that cultural competence, like technical proficiency, is not necessarily mastered in one course or workshop but requires lifelong learning (Ancis, 1998). Students also learn that they need not rely solely on the instructor for access to such material.

The following section discusses the use of electronic mail, listservs, and interactive Web sites for teaching multicultural competencies.

Using Electronic Mail and Listservs With Class Members

Electronic mail, or e-mail, refers to text messages and documents transmitted over telephone lines, cable, or satellite to a receiving computer. Listservs, also known as Internet mailing lists or bulletin board discussions, allow all subscribed participants to simultaneously view each other's e-mail messages. Subscribers may choose to respond to the entire mailing list or to individual members via personal e-mail. Both faculty and students may benefit from online communication. Online discussion may provide the instructor with information regarding students' level of awareness and knowledge. Such information allows the instructor to adapt the curriculum accordingly as well as provide material for continuing dialogue or clarification in class. Faculty may encourage e-mail discussion among students or set up a listserv, creating a collective space to dialogue about course-related issues. E-mail and listservs allow students to continue processing with their peers and faculty members outside of the classroom, thus allowing for greater opportunities to foster personal and professional growth. This is particularly useful in multicultural courses as students often report that exposure to multicultural material results in increased self-exploration, self-questioning, and behavior change as they begin to develop an appreciation for its personal and professional relevance (Ancis & Szymanski, 2001).

Depending on course goals, instructors may structure online discussions in a variety of ways. The instructor must decide whether free-flowing dialogue, discussion in response to specific material, or a combination of both best meets course goals. In addition, the instructor must decide whether he or she will be an active participant or moderator in online interchanges. Structured material may include the presentation of a multicultural case study and related questions. Students may engage in online discussion of these questions. At the conclusion of the online discussion, the duration of which may vary from 1 to several weeks, the instructor may facilitate an in-class debriefing session, which includes discussing the value of the activity. Alternatively, the instructor may post questions about particular issues, such as the degree to which professional ethical guidelines are multiculturally relevant, and students may engage in online discussion around this issue. Issues that are not fully explored in the classroom due to time constraints may also be pursued online.

Students are often apprehensive about vocalizing personal viewpoints in multicultural discussions. Open and productive multicultural conversations are more likely to occur in classrooms in which students respect each other and feel relatively comfortable challenging others' viewpoints. This is often difficult to achieve in a time-limited classroom where students are unfamiliar with each other. In addition, multicultural material is often processed outside of the classroom as students have time to reflect on the material and dialogue with others. E-mail and listservs remove many of the boundaries imposed by time limits and provide an opportunity to facilitate greater rapport, group cohesion, and reflective thinking among students (Hiltz, 1994). Moreover, given the sensitive nature of many multicultural discussions, students may feel less restrained in communicating openly about multicultural issues via e-mail and listservs (Ancis, 1998; Kiesler, Siegel, & McGuire, 1984; Wizer & Beck, 1996). Relatedly, in-class conversations about multicultural issues may become less strained following online interaction. In fact, students who have participated in such online discussions report that in contrast to face-to-face discussions, dialogues are more open and less restrained (Wizer & Beck, 1996). Moreover, students report that such discussions help minimize the tension related to controversial issues. As such, students' more personal attitudes and beliefs may be pursued.

Alternatives to e-mail and listservs include chat rooms, which involve synchronous communication. The instructor may set up specific times when class members may dialogue around a particular issue using simultaneous communication. In large classes, members may be divided into two or more groups. Each group may work on an assigned homework project such as designing a culturally relevant intervention for a particular population presenting with a specific problem. Synchronous online communication allows for immediate feedback and challenge with diverse individuals, critical components of promoting self-awareness and understanding. In addition, scheduling and logistical difficulties associated with outside-of-classroom group projects are minimized with synchronous online communication.

As instructors set ground rules for in-class discussion, such as maintaining confidentiality, it is essential that the importance of respecting others and asking for clarification when needed in online formats is also discussed. The potential for miscommunication and misunderstanding in multicultural conversations is often compounded with no access to visual or nonverbal cues, as well as response delay due to asynchronous communication (Ancis, 1998).

Using Electronic Mail and Listservs to Connect Globally

E-mail and listserv connections can provide students and faculty with exposure to diverse individuals and groups outside of the classroom. For example, the site Intercultural E-Mail Classroom Connections (IECC) provides an innovative use of e-mail for multicultural classrooms. This site, facilitated by two psychology professors and a UNIX systems specialist at St. Olaf College in Minnesota, provides a free service to help faculty link with partners in other countries and cultures for e-mail classroom pen-pal and project exchanges. Partner classrooms are provided for instructors seeking cross-cultural e-mail exchanges with institutions of higher education and K-12 classrooms. Fifty-nine countries currently participate in the higher education connection. Although international connections are available, rural and urban schools and those in geographically distant locations within the United States also develop partnerships. The potential for fostering self-awareness and knowledge is enhanced as students engage with peers globally. Moreover, communication skills are developed as students learn to dialogue with others who differ along dimensions of race, ethnicity, language, class, and geographic location. Critical thinking is encouraged as students are exposed to their e-mail partners' behavior, thoughts, and values beyond those reported by books and media representations. Students may participate in this e-mail interchange and journal their feelings, thoughts, and discoveries throughout the experience or write a paper describing what they have learned about themselves and others, as well as counseling implications. Faculty may also benefit from this site, which enables teachers at all levels to connect with colleagues nationally and internationally to discuss issues related to the use of electronic mail in intercultural classroom connections, seek assistance on projects, and exchange ideas.

The instructor may also encourage students to subscribe to a listserv. Listservs provide an opportunity for students to dialogue with other students and professionals outside of the classroom. Such listservs facilitate students' multicultural awareness and knowledge by providing access to information, the opportunity to engage in conversations with others about advances in the field, and opportunities to pursue issues and questions with individuals invested in the field. Moreover, listserv participants often include educators, researchers, clinicians, and community activists, thereby bridging the gap between theory and practice (Gorski, 2001).

Instructors must decide how listservs can best meet course goals, including the degree to which they prefer to monitor students' activity on the listserv. Students may participate in a multicultural listserv discussion for a specified period of time and then write a review of the content and process of discussion threads, as well as what they have gained from the interactions.

In addition to benefiting students, listservs also provide an opportunity for faculty to dialogue with other professionals. This helps minimize feelings of isolation that multicultural counseling faculty often experience, in addition to receiving advice and support. Many listservs focus on multicultural issues specific to counselors and other mental health professionals. Related APA listservs include those of Division 17's (Counseling Psychology) Section on Ethnic and Racial Diversity (SERD) at SERD-L@LISTSERV.UGA.EDU and Division 45 (Society for the Psychological Study of Minority Issues) at LISTSERV@LISTS. APA.ORG. DIVERSEGRAD-L at listserv@listserv. american.edu provides a forum to discuss diversity issues in counseling. POWR-L (POWR-L@pete.uri.edu) focuses on women's issues within psychology.

Interactive Web Sites

One of the more powerful exercises for students enrolled in multicultural counseling classes involves reading about the personal experiences and autobiographies of diverse individuals. Such readings give "life" to the course, moving the material beyond an intellectual exercise. The Internet offers a host of Web sites offering first-person accounts, such as one developed by Steven Mintz at the University of Houston (vi.uh.edu/pages/mintz/primary.htm), which provides excerpts of slave narratives. Unlike many existing hard-text personal accounts and autobiographies, several sites on the Internet provide an opportunity to e-mail and dialogue with authors. For example, Holocaust survivors Sidney Finkel (members.aol.com/ghetto1942/) and David Katz (members.home.net/captainhall/david_e.html) have Web sites that describe their experiences in concentration camps and encourage correspondence via e-mail. Access to such information and interactions helps to augment concepts and perspectives presented in class.

The most obvious opportunity provided by the Internet is that of facilitating knowledge via its informational resource base. The Internet contains many Web sites with multiculturally relevant information in the form of video, audio, graphics, and text. Such multimedia presentations help to maintain student interest as well as accommodate varied learning styles. For example, the Indian Health Service has a site with links to information about Native American Resources (www.his.gov/GeneralWeb/Links/AmericanIndian/index.asp) in the areas of art, business, education, genealogy, history, and so on. Ethnic NewsWatch is a full-text database that provides a comprehensive collection of articles, reviews, and editorials of the ethnic, minority, and native presses not well covered in the mainstream media. Both English- and Spanish-language search options are available. This is a subscription-based site. The Multicultural Web Links page (www.isomedia.com/homes/jmele/mcultlink.html) provides access to a variety of Web sites containing information about diverse racial and ethnic groups and educational resources.

All of the major counseling and psychology professional organizations have Web pages. For example, the American Counseling Association's (ACA's) Association for Gay, Lesbian, and Bisexual Issues in Counseling (AGLBIC) has a Web site (www.aglbic.org/) containing links to a compendium of useful readings. The National Congress for Hispanic Mental Health has a Web site (www.mental-health.org/cmhs/SpecialPopulations/HispMH Congress2000/) that includes the contents of the 2000 Proceedings of the National Congress for Hispanic Mental Health. This site includes detailed materials outlining such issues as the mental health needs of Hispanics in the United States and a directory of relevant federal resources.

Although multicultural counseling resources are available via the WWW, multicultural information on the Internet tends to be dominated by Web sites in the field of multicultural education such as the Multicultural Forum (curry.edschool.virginia.cdu/go/multicultural/pavboard/pavboard.html) and McGraw-Hill's Multicultural SuperForum (www.mhhe.com/socscience/education/multi/discussion/index.html). The latter site houses information about multicultural curriculum transformation and intercultural activities, a discussion board for educators, and exercises for facilitating multicultural awareness and understanding.

Web pages could be used to supplement traditional classroom material with links to relevant sites. Students may be encouraged to use Internet sources for assignments and papers. Alternatively, students may be asked to identify relevant Web sites and present a critique of their strengths and limitations. Because the information presented on various

Web sites varies in its degree of accuracy, this exercise may assist students in reviewing material critically.

Last, the instructor may create a Web site for the course. The instructor may use the Web site to post assessment tools at the beginning of the course to obtain an estimate of students' multicultural competence. This information may be used to develop course assignments and direct the course content and process accordingly. The instructor may also post exercises and multicultural counseling assessment instruments on the course Web site, whereby students may engage in skill building as well as obtain feedback regarding their level of self-awareness, knowledge, and skills. The course Web site may also contain links to relevant sources of information that students can pursue to enhance their understanding of related material.

OTHER TECHNOLOGIES

Interactive Videodisc Programs, CD-ROMs, and Counseling Simulations

One of the more innovative technological advances in the area of counseling is computer and interactive videodisc programs that simulate clinical situations. Students can actually practice interventions and develop counseling skills using these programs (Seabury, 1994). Within a simulated environment, students can experiment with a range of interventions not always possible in an actual counseling situation. Computer applications have been developed for basic counseling interview skills training (Hummel, Lichtenberg, & Shaffer, 1975), counseling response skills training (e.g., Alpert, 1986), teaching problem-solving strategies (Lichtenberg, Hummel, & Shaffer, 1984), teaching diagnostic and treatment decision making (e.g., Semmel, Varnhagen, & McCann, 1981), and teaching case

management skills (e.g., Chubon, 1986). In the Great Therapists Program (Halpain, Dixon, & Glover, 1987), students are presented with a client statement. After the student types his or her response to the client, the computer displays a response from a master therapist from three different counseling orientations, allowing the student to compare his or her own response. The purpose of this program is to teach students to apply a theory to a client statement. Other programs, such as the SuperShrink program (Lowman & Norkus, 1987), allow the student interviewer to question the computer as client.

Videodisc and computer programs specifically designed to facilitate the development of multicultural counseling competencies are limited in number. Pacino and Pacino (1996) developed videodisc (titled "Intercultural Communication") and CD-ROM (titled "Exploring Cultural Diversity") versions of a menu-driven, interactive computer program. This courseware provides film clips of intercultural interactions and stereotypical portrayals with accompanying questions and alternative responses. When students provide inaccurate answers, they are prompted to try again by reviewing the clip or scenario and making another selection. Students actively integrate and apply multicultural knowledge to relevant situations and receive continuous and instant feedback. Another interactive videodisc program with relevance to the development of multicultural competencies simulates a social work agency in which the student works to uncover patterns of institutional racism and sexism (Seabury, 1994). The program, titled "Organizational Assessment," requires the student to perform the role of an internal advocate and collect information from three areas of organizational life. The organization is intentionally designed to provide significant obstacles to students so that they are prepared for any agency they may encounter.

The continued development of counseling simulation programs to foster multicultural competencies is much needed. Such programs allow students to actively engage in the instructional process at their own pace, experiment with a range of interventions, and receive immediate feedback. Programs that allow students to receive feedback by practicing alternative counseling interventions and code both counselor and client behavior, such as the degree to which a particular counselor intervention attends to the client's sociocultural context, are invaluable tools in developing multiculturally effective and sensitive skills. Computer programs can simulate clients representing diverse cultural backgrounds and presenting with a range of counseling issues.

Computer programs may be developed based on the extensive work on Intercultural Assimilators or Sensitizers (Fiedler, Mitchell, & Triandis, 1971), which were originally conceived as viable computer programs. Intercultural Assimilators were designed to teach students to perceive situations from the perspective of members of that culture. Intercultural scenarios are presented, followed by a series of alternative attributions or interpretations of the situation. After participants select the attribution they believe is made by persons in the target culture, culturally relevant feedback is provided. The premise of the Intercultural Sensitizer may be applied to computer simulations with even greater interactivity. Similarly, multicultural computer simulations may be developed based on the work of Lambert (1987a, 1987b) to train counselors to integrate client information and intervene accordingly. For example, students may be presented with a description of a client and presenting problem, select assessment and intervention strategies, and receive computer feedback. Alternatively, following a description of a client and a presenting problem, the trainee may view, via the videoscreen, various interventions based on different approaches.

Such tools have already been developed in the fields of medicine and nursing and in the training of airline pilots (see Seabury, 1994).

In addition to facilitating skill development, some authors have described the use of computer-assisted feedback for increasing counselor self-awareness (e.g., Froehle, 1984). Counselors' emotional state may be recorded through electromyograph (EMG), skin conductance level (SCL), and skin temperature (ST) tests. During an actual session, trainees may also report their own comfort level and provide an assessment of the client's comfort level and the quality of the relationship. Self-reports are made by activating a numeric keyboard built into the armrest of the counselor and client chairs, and the data are fed into the computer. As multicultural counseling interactions often elicit trainees' apprehension, confusion, and fear, such feedback can be employed to increase students' awareness of emotional reactions experienced in these interactions, help them to examine the cognitive messages associated with these feelings, and challenge them to resolve those affective and cognitive reactions that may interfere with effective helping (Ancis & Szymanski, 2001). One primary advantage of such feedback is that both the instructor and the student do not have to rely on delayed recall, which may prove inaccurate or incomplete.

Videos

Videos can be used in traditional classrooms or in Web-based courses. Films may be used to further validate course concepts among students who are skeptical about the material presented by the instructor or text. Films are also helpful in stimulating class discussion. In Web-based courses, students may view videos or portions of existing movies that have been integrated onto a Web page. Many multicultural counseling videos exist that facilitate self-awareness and knowledge, such as

Ethnic Notions by Marlon Riggs (1986) and *The Color of Fear* by Lee Mun Wah (1994). *Ethnic Notions* uses educators, artists, films, and movies to present the depiction of African Americans from slavery to the present. *The Color of Fear* presents a multiracial group of eight men who meet for a weekend to explore race and racism. Both films are powerful facilitators of trainees' exploration of their biases, values, and assumptions. Other videos may be used to facilitate counselor knowledge of the history and experiences of diverse groups. The film titled *The Shadow of Hate* (Carnes & Robertson, 1995) is a documentary on the history of intolerance in America. Religious, ethnic, and racial intolerance is reviewed. Microtraining Associates also produces a series of films developed by leading multicultural experts on counseling specific populations.

Faculty may also benefit from viewing videotapes focused on multicultural issues. For example, in the videotape titled *Difficult Dialogues* (Jones & Young, 1996), produced by the Annenberg/CPB Project, faculty from various campuses of California State University describe their experiences and strategies in teaching and facilitating discussions related to race, culture, class, gender, and sexual orientation via distance learning. Faculty engage in open dialogue about moderating the affective as well as cognitive dimensions of "difficult" conversations. Such media are valuable to faculty who are developing the tools needed to effectively engage in multicultural dialogues with students who demonstrate a range of attitudes and participatory levels.

Videotapes

Videotapes are particularly useful in distance learning courses when visual limitations exist. Skill development requires that instructors monitor students' verbal and nonverbal behavior. Distance learning students can submit videotaped

role-plays with diverse clients, allowing the instructor to assess progress and provide feedback regarding students' level of sensitivity to nonverbal cues, recognition of direct and indirect communication styles, and ability to intervene effectively (Ancis, 1998). Videotapes may be viewed in both distance learning and traditional classrooms and critiqued. In distance learning classrooms, videotapes provide students with visual access to their distant classmates, allowing for feedback from a diverse peer group as well as the instructor. Such reviews also encourage student participation. Videotapes are also useful for the supervision of students in field placements.

Multicultural demonstration videotapes are also available for students to view. The Society for the Psychological Study of Ethnic Minority Issues (Division 45) of the APA, with the support of Microtraining Associates, has developed videotape demonstrations of multicultural counseling and therapy. Professionals in the field demonstrate culturally consistent counseling approaches with clients of African, Asian, Latin, and Native American Indian descent. These videotapes are useful for discussions of skill development.

Teleconferencing

Teleconferencing refers to any conferencing system that uses telecommunication technologies to facilitate meetings, workshops, courses, and conversations among groups or individuals at two or more locations (Willis, 1993). Teleconferencing includes videoconferencing, computer conferencing, and audio conferencing and facilitates synchronous, real-time communication among participants. Instructors may use such technology to connect faculty and students regionally, nationally, or worldwide. Opportunities for interactions with individuals outside of the classroom who may serve as guest lecturers and consultants or participants in a classroom project are limitless.

CAVEATS

As described earlier, the Internet and other technologies offer many opportunities for facilitating counseling and psychology trainees' multicultural competencies. However, certain caveats must be considered. First, the use of the Internet requires that students have access to computers in their residence hall, apartment, workplace, or on campus. Students who cannot afford computers or work full-time must rely on on-campus access. Thus, students with limited finances compared to their more financially comfortable peers do not have easy access to the Internet. Moreover, much technology is costly and requires a significant amount of time to set up and learn. Many colleges and universities lack the financial resources and technological staff to support such efforts (Council for Higher Education Accreditation, 2000).

Second, many faculty lack training and expertise in computer use and technology (Lambert, 1988), thus preventing them from taking advantage of alternative educational methods and sources of information. Relatedly, given the time and effort required to integrate technology into the curriculum, educators must be supported and rewarded by their respective institutions of higher learning.

Third, educators and students must be aware that much of the information presented on the Internet is not screened for accuracy and credibility. Educators must be vigilant about reviewing the information presented and training students to be critical evaluators of the material. Moreover, information on the Internet is not static, and the content or design of Web sites may change. Before referring students to a particular Web site, educators must ensure that they keep up to date with the information available.

More important, although the Internet and other instructional technologies offer enormous potential for facilitating multicultural competencies, I do not believe that they can replace the level of development that occurs via meaningful human contact. The one-on-one, live interactions that occur within classrooms between students and between students and the instructor, which include the opportunity for verbal and nonverbal challenge, questioning, self-examination, clarification, and active dialogue, cannot be replaced by technology, at least not at the present time.

Moreover, multicultural competence requires consideration to multiple client contexts, such as the individual, family, community, and society. Accurate assessment must derive from an understanding of these contexts as well as the unique style and perceptions of the individual client. Live human interaction, which contains the physical and spiritual presence of all individuals involved, seems essential to such accurate assessment and successful intervention. Computer programs are often limited to what can be conveyed verbally. More complex interactions and the presentation of both verbal and nonverbal behavior may be difficult to present (Albert, 1983). Similarly, research indicates that personal interactions and experiences increase students' awareness of multicultural issues, particularly racism and discrimination (Ancis & Szymanski, 2001). At this point, it is not possible to simulate all of the realities of an actual counseling interaction. As such, the ability to receive immediate feedback regarding one's verbal and nonverbal behavior, practice active listening skills, and gain access to nonverbal communication within a realistic clinical setting—opportunities essential for the development of multicultural competencies—are not fully available via the Internet and other technologies.

Despite the above stated limitations, the Internet and other technologies can be used to enhance the development of multicultural self-awareness, knowledge, and skills. These technological advances provide the opportunity to interact with a diverse group of students, educators, clinicians, researchers, and community activists, both nationally and internationally. A plethora of multicultural information is also available. Moreover, computer programs allow students to practice counseling skills and receive immediate feedback. Technological advances also provide access to varied learning approaches, which enhances the promotion of multicultural counseling competence among diverse students (Schwitzer et al., 2001). Educators must become proactive in incorporating these advances into their teaching practices to maximize students' multicultural counseling competencies.

REFERENCES

Albert, R. D. (1983). The intercultural sensitizer or culture assimilator: A cognitive approach. In D. Landis & R. W. Brislin (Eds.), *Handbook of intercultural training: Vol. 2. Issues in training methodology* (pp. 186-217). Elmsford, NY: Pergamon.

Alpert, D. (1986). A preliminary investigation of computer-enhanced counselor training. *Computers in Human Behavior, 2,* 63-70.

Altmaier, E. M. (1993). Role of Criterion II in accreditation. *Professional Psychology: Research and Practice, 24,* 127-129.

Ancis, J. R. (1998). Cultural competency training at a distance: Challenges and strategies. *Journal of Counseling and Development, 76,* 134-143.

Ancis, J. R., & Szymanski, D. M. (2001). Awareness of White privilege among White counseling trainees. *The Counseling Psychologist, 29*(4), 548-569.

Arredondo, P., Toporek, R., Brown, S. P., Jones, J., Locke, D. C., Sanchez, J., et al. (1996). Operationalization of the multicultural counseling competencies. *Journal of Multicultural Counseling and Development, 24,* 42-78.

Association for Counselor Education and Supervision (ACES), Technology Interest Network. (1999a). *Guidelines for on-line instruction in counselor education* [Online]. Retrieved from www.chre.vt.edu/f-s/thohen/acesweb.htm

Association for Counselor Education and Supervision (ACES), Technology Interest Network. (1999b). *Recommended technical competencies for counselor education students* [Online]. Retrieved from www.chre.vt.edu/f-s/thohen/competencies.htm

Carnes, J., & Robertson, H. (Writers), & Southern Poverty Law Center (Producer). (1995). *The shadow of hate: A history of intolerance in America* [Videotape]. (Available from Teaching Tolerance, 400 Washington Avenue, Montgomery, AL 36104)

Chubon, R. A. (1986). Genesis II: A computer-based case management simulation. *Rehabilitation Counseling Bulletin, 30,* 210-217.

Council for Higher Education Accreditation. (2000, June). *Distance learning in higher education* (CHEA Update No. 3). Washington, DC: Author. Retrieved from /www.chea.org

Enns, C. A., Sinacore, A. L., Ancis, J. R., & Phillips, J. (in press). Toward integrating feminist and multicultural pedagogies. *Journal of Multicultural Counseling and Development.*

Fiedler, F. E., Mitchell, T., & Triandis, H. C. (1971). The culture assimilator: An approach to cross-cultural training. *Journal of Applied Psychology, 55,* 95-102.

Froehle, T. C. (1984). Computer-assisted feedback in counseling supervision. *Counselor Education and Supervision, 24,* 168-175.

Gorski, P. C. (2001). *Multicultural education and the Internet: Intersections and integrations.* New York: McGraw-Hill.

Halpain, D. R., Dixon, D. N., & Glover, J. A. (1987). The great therapists program: Computerized learning of counseling theories. *Counselor Education and Supervision, 27,* 255-260.

Hiltz, S. A. (1994). *The virtual classroom: Learning without limits via computer networks.* Norwood, NJ: Ablex.

Hummel, T. J., Lichtenberg, J. W., & Shaffer, W. F. (1975). CLIENT 1: A computer program which simulates client behavior in an initial interview. *Journal of Counseling Psychology, 22,* 164-169.

Jonassen, D. H., & Hannum, W. C. (1987, December). Research-based principles for designing computer software. *Instructional Technology,* pp. 7-14.

Jones, T., & Young, G. A. (Writers). (1996). *Difficult dialogues* [Videotape]. (Available from California State University, Hayward)

Keller, J. M. (1983). Motivational design of instruction. In C. M. Reigeluth (Ed.), *Instructional-design theories and models* (pp. 383-436). Hillsdale, NJ: Lawrence Erlbaum.

Kiesler, S., Siegel, J., & McGuire, T. W. (1984). Social psychological aspects of computer-mediated communications. *American Psychologist, 39,* 1123-1134.

Lambert, M. E. (1987a). A computer simulation for behavior therapy training. *Journal of Behavior Therapy & Experimental Psychiatry, 18,* 245-248.

Lambert, M. E. (1987b). MR. HOWARD: A behavior therapy simulation. *The Behavior Therapist, 10,* 139-140.

Lambert, M. E. (1988). Computers in counselor education: Four years after a special issue. *Counselor Education and Supervision, 28,* 100-109.

Lichtenberg, J. W., Hummel, T. J., & Shaffer, W. F. (1984). CLIENT 1: A computer simulation for use in counselor education and research. *Counselor Education and Supervision, 24,* 155-167.

Lowman, J., & Norkus, M. (1987). The SuperShrink interview: Active versus passive questioning and student satisfaction. *Computers in Human Behavior, 3,* 181-192.

Murray, B. (1999). Technology invigorates teaching, but is the pizzazz worth the price? *APA Monitor, 30*(4), 36-37.

Pacino, M. A., & Pacino, J. L. (1996). Multimedia and cultural diversity. *Technological Horizons in Education Journal, 23*(6), 70-71.

Ponterotto, J. G. (1997). Multicultural counseling training: A competency model and national survey. In D. B. Pope-Davis & H. L. K. Coleman (Eds.), *Multicultural counseling competencies: Assessment, education and training, and supervision* (pp. 111-130). Thousand Oaks, CA: Sage.

Price, R. V., Repman, J., & White, D. (1994, February). *Producing effective graduate-level distance education courses for interactive television.* Paper presented at the 1994 National Convention of the Association for Educational Communications and Technology, Nashville, TN.

Riggs, M. (Writer/Director/Producer). (1986). *Ethnic notions.* [Videotape]. (Available from California Newsreel, 500 Third Street, #505, San Francisco, CA 94107)

Schwitzer, A. M., Ancis, J. R., & Brown, N. (2001). *Promoting student learning and student development at a distance: Student affairs concepts and practices for televised instruction and other forms of distance learning.* Lanham, MD: University Press of America.

Seabury, B. (1994). Interactive videodisc programs in social work education: "Crisis Counseling" and "Organizational Assessment." *Computers in Human Services, 11*(3-4), 299-316.

Semmel, M. I., Varnhagen, S., & McCann, S. (1981). MICROGAMES: An application of microcomputers for training personnel who work with handicapped children. *Teacher Education and Special Education, 4,* 27-33.

Sue, D. W., Arredondo, P., & McDavis, R. J. (1992). Multicultural counseling competencies and standards: A call to the profession. *Journal of Counseling and Development, 70,* 477-486.

Sue, D. W., Ivey, A. E., & Pedersen, P. B. (1996). *A theory of multicultural counseling and therapy.* Pacific Grove, CA: Brooks/Cole.

Wah, L. M. (Writer/Producer). (1994). *The color of fear* [Videotape]. (Available from Stir Fry Productions, 1904 Virginia Street, Berkeley, CA 94709)

Willis, B. (1993). *Distance education: A practical guide.* Englewood Cliffs, NJ: Educational Technology Publications.

Willis, B. (Ed.). (1994). *Distance education: Strategies and tools.* Englewood Cliffs, NJ: Educational Technology Publications.

Wizer, D. R., & Beck, S. S. (1996). Studying diversity issues in teacher education using online discussions. *Journal of Computing in Teacher Education, 13*(1), 6-11.

CONCLUSION

Reflections and Future Directions

37

The Future of Multicultural Counseling Competence

DONALD R. ATKINSON
TANIA ISRAEL

University of California at Santa Barbara

The multicultural counseling competence (MCC) movement—that is, the movement to identify and propagate counseling competencies that enhance counseling process and outcome with diverse clients—is currently riding a groundswell of popularity in the mental health professions. This has not always been the case; in the past three decades, the MCC movement has moved from the fringes to the mainstream of professional counseling and psychology. By some measures of accomplishment, the movement is one of the great success stories in contemporary professional psychology. In other respects, however, the movement has made little progress, particularly in the area of research on the competencies themselves. This chapter reviews the history of the MCC movement, examines reasons why the movement may wane, and

suggests research that could help sustain the movement. In particular, we focus on the development of, research on, and limitations of the most widely used definition of multicultural counseling competencies, those identified initially by Sue et al. (1982) and expanded on by Sue, Arredondo, and McDavis (1992). For the MCC movement to continue to make meaningful contributions to the profession, we must move beyond those knowledge, attitude, and skill components that have intuitive appeal and begin developing a strong empirical base for the future of MCC.

HISTORICAL OVERVIEW OF MCC ACHIEVEMENTS

Groundwork for the current MCC movement was laid in the 1960s, 1970s, and 1980s

591

(Jackson, 1995). In the 1960s, a few articles appeared in the professional literature pointing out that psychologists were ill prepared to serve ethnic minority clients (Arbuckle, 1969; Calia, 1966; Smith, 1967). In the 1970s, a number of publications appeared that further elaborated on this theme (e.g., Bryson & Bardo, 1975; Harper, 1975; Mitchell, 1971). Although not using the current terminology of multicultural competence, these early publications did argue that special skills were needed to work with diverse populations.

In 1982, the Education and Training Committee of Division 17 of the American Psychological Association (APA) published a landmark article (Sue et al., 1982) that had a profound effect on the subsequent MCC movement in psychology. In that article, the Education and Training Committee identified 11 knowledge, attitude, and skill competencies needed for work with culturally diverse clients. In an article published a decade later, Sue et al. (1992) expanded the list of MCCs to 31 and challenged the profession to adopt specific standards for training in MCC. The Sue et al. (1992) article also helped to shape much of the MCC movement; the 31 knowledge, attitude, and skill competencies identified in the article have been endorsed by three divisions (17, 35, and 45) of the APA and six divisions (ACES, AADA, AGLBIC, ASCA, ASGW, and IAMFC) of the American Counseling Association (D. W. Sue, personal communication, August 26, 1997).

Even prior to Sue et al. (1982), the concerns raised by earlier authors began to have an affect on policy within the APA. In 1979, the APA Council of Representatives adopted Criterion II as part of the APA accreditation policy, stipulating that "programs must develop knowledge and skills in their students relevant to human diversity" (APA, 1986, p. 4). Concern for psychologist preparedness has been reflected in subsequent revisions of the accreditation criteria. The most recent accreditation policy (APA, 1995) integrates the need for training to work with diverse populations into several accreditation domains. Domain B, in particular, stipulates that accredited programs must implement curriculum plans that will ensure student competence in cultural and individual diversity as it relates to the science and practice of psychology (APA, 1995, pp. 6, 7).

The MCC movement also has had a dramatic impact on APA ethical and practice standards. The 1992 version of APA's "Ethical Principles of Psychologists and Code of Conduct" made it unethical to discriminate against ethnic and other minority groups and reinforced the concept that psychologists need to be aware of cultural, individual, and role differences (APA, 1992). Under the principle of competence, the code stipulates that "psychologists are cognizant of the fact that the competencies required in serving, teaching, and/or studying groups of people vary with the distinctive characteristics of those groups" (p. 1599). Furthermore, "Guidelines for Providers of Psychological Services to Ethnic, Linguistic, and Culturally Diverse Populations" was published in 1993 in the *American Psychologist,* stipulating that "issues of language and culture do impact the provision of appropriate psychological services" and that psychological service providers need special "knowledge and skills for multicultural assessment and intervention" (APA, 1993, p. 45).

Thus, through policies manifested in its accreditation procedures, ethical code, and practice guidelines, the APA has acknowledged that psychologists need special training and skills to provide services to ethnic minority populations. By the early 1990s, 87% of APA-accredited counseling psychology programs offered one or more classes that addressed multicultural issues (Hills & Strozier, 1992), and 70% of counseling and clinical psychologists had attended postdoctoral seminars on diversity issues (Allison,

Table 37.1   MCC Publications in PsychINFO
by Year

Year	Number of Publications
2001	40
2000	31
1999	29
1998	33
1997	24
1996	15
1995	12
1994	11
1993	10
1992	4
1991	5
1990	1
1989	1
1988	1
1987	1
1986	1
1985	0
1984	0
1983	2
1982	0

Crawford, Echemendia, Robinson, & Knepp, 1994). A plethora of articles have appeared since the publication of Sue et al. (1992) designed to help training programs by identifying the key components of training and supervision for multicultural competence (APA, 2001; Constantine, 1997; D'Andrea & Daniels, 1997; Hansen, Pepitone-Arreola-Rockwell, & Greene, 2000; Kiselica, 1998; Leach & Carlton, 1997; Ponterotto, 1997; Ponterotto, Alexander, & Grieger, 1995; Reynolds, 1995; Ridley, Mendoza, & Kanitz, 1994; Speight, Thomas, Kennel, & Anderson, 1995; Sue et al., 1998).

Also, by the late 1990s, the concept and terminology of multicultural competence began to have a significant impact on the broader professional literature. A search of the PsycINFO database reveals that an average of only 1 article per year included *multicultural competence* as a keyword in the 8 years

immediately following the publication of Sue et al. (1982). This number jumped to 5 articles in 1991 and increased steadily to 33 in 1998 (see Table 37.1). In 2001, *multicultural competence* was a keyword for 40 publications (by way of comparison, *empirically validated treatment* was a keyword for 23 publications in 2001), providing further evidence that the MCC movement has become a mainstream force in applied psychology.

LACK OF EMPIRICAL SUPPORT FOR MCC

Unfortunately, however, the policy achievements of the MCC movement have taken place without a strong research base. The reality is that very little research actually supports either the policy changes that have been implemented by the APA and other professional organizations or the MCC training models that have been an important feature of the movement. In part because of this lack of research on MCCs, none of the APA professional policy statements to date incorporates any definitions or standards for such competence.

Given the widespread acceptance of the MCCs identified in Sue et al. (1982) and Sue et al. (1992), it may come as a surprise to many readers that they are only hypothesized MCCs. The Sue et al. (1982) MCCs were established by committee consensus (D. W. Sue, personal communication, August 26, 1997), and the Sue et al. (1992) MCCs were written by three knowledgeable authors (Sue et al., 1992) and subsequently endorsed by a number of APA and ACA divisions (D. W. Sue, personal communication, August 26, 1997). However, despite the powerful impact they have had on the counseling and psychology professions, the 31 MCCs of Sue (1992) have never been linked to counseling process and outcome, nor have they been validated by surveys of multicultural experts or consumers.

The research base for MCCs that we judge to be missing or inadequate can be grouped into three categories: (a) research designed to empirically *identify* MCCs, (b) research designed to empirically *validate* theoretically hypothesized MCCs, and (c) the development of instruments that accurately *measure* the validated MCCs. The research designed to empirically identify MCCs would start with a blank slate and use qualitative and/or quantitative research procedures to identify counseling competencies judged or found to be related to counseling process and/or outcome with ethnically diverse clients. For example, open-ended surveys (e.g., Delphi studies) of those knowledgeable about the topic might be one way to identify MCCs. Qualitative analyses of multicultural counseling to determine verbal and nonverbal counselor behaviors that are related to counseling process and outcome variables with ethnic minority clients might be another. Two decades after the original MCCs were

identified by Sue et al. (1982), a single study of this type (Pope-Davis et al., 2002) finally appeared in the counseling literature.

The status of research designed to validate theoretically hypothesized MCCs is hardly any better. Although a few studies have examined the validity of hypothesized micro-MCCs (Atkinson, Casas, & Abreu, 1992; Gim, Atkinson, & Kim, 1991; Pomales, Claiborn, & LaFromboise, 1986), none have validated the macro-MCCs hypothesized by Sue et al. (1982) and Sue et al. (1992). Furthermore, MCC research has bypassed the missing identification and validation studies and plunged ahead with investigations that have examined predictors of MCC and/or evaluated MCC training elements. For example, researchers have studied the relationships between self-reported multicultural counseling competencies and counselor demographic variables (Ottavi, Pope-Davis & Dings, 1994; Pope-Davis & Ottavi, 1994; Pope-Davis, Reynolds, Dings, & Nielson, 1995), racial identity development (Ladany, Inman, Constantine, & Hofheinz, 1997; Ottavi et al., 1994), and training experiences (D'Andrea, Daniels, & Heck, 1991; Neville, Heppner, Thompson, Brooks, & Baker, 1996; Ottavi et al., 1994; Pope-Davis et al., 1995; Pope-Davis, Reynolds, Dings, & Ottavi, 1994; Sodowsky, Kuo-Jackson, Richardson, & Corey, 1998). Thus, without being validated, the Sue et al. (1982) and Sue et al. (1992) MCCs (or instruments based on them) have begun turning up as dependent variables in studies that have important implications for the selection and training of counselors and psychologists.

How could this happen? Why would the MCC movement bypass the foundation research needed to identify and validate MCCs and begin treating them as desired counselor competencies? The first and foremost reason is the extraordinary success of the Sue et al. (1982) and Sue et al. (1992) landmark publications. Sue et al. (1982) and Sue et al. (1992)

were innovative, bold attempts to move psychology beyond the general, often vague criteria for training psychologists to work with culturally diverse clients that were appearing in the professional literature. It is doubtful that anyone, even the authors of these articles, could have imagined how successful they would be. The knowledge, attitude, and skill categories of competencies described in both publications have been, for the most part, accepted without question by proponents of MCC. The 11 competencies identified in Sue et al. (1982) were operationalized in several self-report instruments that all but monopolized the measurement MCC in the 1990s. The 31 specific competencies identified in Sue et al. (1992) are reflected in subsequent attempts to operationalize MCC (APA, 2001; Arredondo et al., 1996), and they are studiously memorized by counseling and psychology trainees across the United States in preparation for comprehensive examinations. Ironically, the fact that these two publications were so widely endorsed and embraced may have contributed to our current lack of empirical support for MCCs because researchers were not motivated to either look further for additional competencies or validate those identified in Sue et al. (1982) or Sue et al. (1992). As suggested by Pope-Davis, Liu, Toporek, and Brittan-Powell (2001), it is almost impossible for MCC researchers to identify research questions, measure counseling process, or develop research methodology without being biased by the Sue et al. (1992) competencies.

The appearance of four MCC assessment instruments (Multicultural Awareness-Knowledge-Skills Survey, D'Andrea, Daniels, & Heck, 1990; Cross-Cultural Counseling Inventory–Revised, LaFromboise, Coleman, & Hernandez, 1991; Multicultural Counseling Awareness Scale–Form B, Ponterotto, Sanchez, & Magrids, 1991; and Multicultural Counseling Inventory, Sodowsky, Taffe, Gutkin, & Wise, 1994) in the professional literature by the early 1990s also may have contributed to the lack of research identifying and validating MCCs. Like the MCCs identified in Sue et al. (1982) on which they were based, these instruments were widely adopted and used without hesitation. The validity of each of the four instruments was questioned but not seriously challenged by Ponterotto, Rieger, Barrett, and Sparks (1994). Ponterotto et al. also raised concerns about the self-report nature of three of the instruments, but that did not deter their widespread use as measures of MCC. Furthermore, despite the appearance and widespread acceptance of the 31 competencies subsequently identified by Sue et al. (1992), these instruments based on Sue et al. (1982) remained popular as measures of MCC throughout the 1990s. By the end of the 1990s, however, studies examining the validity of the self-report measures of MCC began to appear that suggest that when social desirability is accounted for, there is no relationship between MCC as measured by these instruments and multicultural case conceptualization ability (Constantine & Ladany, 2000; Ladany et al., 1997). As suggested by Worthington, Mobley, Franks, and Tan (2000), it appears that these instruments actually measure self-efficacy for MCC, not MCC itself.

A third factor contributing to the lack of research identifying and validating MCCs is the relatively small pool of researchers who have been interested in researching MCC. When the pool of researchers examining any topic is limited, the creative thinking that can be brought to bear on the topic is limited. There are several reasons why, until recently, the pool of doctoral students and new Ph.D. graduates interested in researching MCCs has remained small. For one, ethnic minority students, many of whom are interested in multicultural issues, have been historically underrepresented in psychology. Furthermore, many ethnic minority students, for a variety of reasons, have been more interested in practice

than in research. And for many European
American students, there has been either little
interest on their part or a perception of prohi-
bition against doing such research.

These and other factors have probably contributed to the MCC movement's failure to
empirically identify and validate MCCs.
However, it is not too late to rectify the situation. Bingham (2001) has suggested that psychology's failure to include marginalized
groups is both understandable and fixable; we
can acknowledge there are gaps in our field
and move on to fill those gaps without
dwelling on blame for creating the gaps.
Similarly, the empirical oversights in multicultural counseling competence are both understandable and fixable. It is understandable
that Sue et al. (1982) developed a conceptual
framework in the absence of a research base
because neither a research base nor a conceptual framework for multicultural counseling
existed at the time. It is also understandable
that this framework was so readily embraced
by a fledgling field anxious to provide competent care to traditionally underserved populations. It is understandable that researchers
accepted the Sue et al. (1982) conceptual
framework as valid given their desire to begin
researching multicultural counseling process
and outcome. Although this oversight has
potentially negative implications for the future
of the movement, it is fixable. In the next section, we discuss some of the forces that could
derail the MCC movement, given the lack of a
solid research base. Afterward, we discuss
what we believe needs to be done to develop
the kind of research base needed if the MCC
movement is to survive in the future.

RESEARCH SUPPORT NEEDED
IF THE MCC MOVEMENT IS
TO THRIVE IN THE FUTURE

The availability of research support distinguishes
those theories and techniques in psychology
that become part of the underlying knowledge
base from those movements and fads that fade
away into relative obscurity. Without extensive research support, we predict that the
MCC movement will subside as quickly as it
arose. A number of forces at work inside and
outside psychology lead us to this pessimistic
prediction.

Pressures in Larger Society
That Oppose Multiculturalism

It is important to recognize that societal
pressure on ethnic groups to acculturate
remains a powerful force that directly and
indirectly works against multiculturalism. The
United States has a long history of acculturat-
ing ethnic minorities into an English-speaking
society that is based on Grecian and Roman
laws and cultural norms. Although full assimilation, which includes acceptance without discrimination, has been largely reserved for
immigrants from Western Europe, acculturation to U.S. norms has been promoted for all
immigrant groups. Schools have historically
been the primary instrument of acculturation
and, despite the interest shown for bilingual
education in the 1970s and 1980s, remain the
primary instrument of acculturation. Along
with schools, the media (particularly television
and, more recently, the Internet) have been
powerful instruments of acculturation.

Although some institutions in the United
States have demonstrated a willingness to recognize and accept diversity (e.g., the Census
Bureau's increasing willingness to recognize
ethnic diversity within the general population),
the forces that promote amalgamation and
acculturation remain strong. The success of
ballot initiatives in California in the late 1990s
targeting illegal immigration (Proposition 187)
and eliminating affirmative action (Proposition
209) and bilingual education (Proposition
227) provides recent evidence that the general
public, even an ethnically diverse constituency

such as that found in California, continues to support acculturation and oppose any kind of "special status" for ethnic minority groups. In fact, it can be argued that a backlash against multiculturalism germinated in the larger society in the mid-1980s and continues to motivate legal, legislative, and administrative efforts to eliminate cultural and ethnic distinctions.

Backlash Against Multiculturalism in Professional Psychology

Several authors have argued that professional psychology, rather than being proactive, is reactive to the values and goals of the larger society (Halleck, 1971; Prilleltensky, 1989). Social changes in society are often reflected in psychology after a delay of a decade or more; the time it took after the civil rights movement of the 1960s for the APA to incorporate civil rights values in its ethics code and accreditation criteria is a good example. We believe the political backlash against diversity and affirmative action that started in the larger society in the 1980s is just beginning to have an impact on professional psychology publications. Several articles appeared in psychology journals near the turn of the century that were highly critical of affirmative action procedures used to admit undergraduate (Detterman, 2000) and graduate (Thomas & Weinrach, 1998a, 1998b) psychology students. A few articles have also appeared challenging multiculturalism itself, suggesting that it violates the principles of psychology (Fowers & Richardson, 1996; Thomas & Weinrach, 1998b). More recently, one article constructively addressing failings of the MCCs (Pope-Davis et al., 2001) and another denouncing professional adoption of the MCCs (Weinrach & Thomas, 2002) appeared in psychological journals.

Multicultural psychology may learn from the experience of feminist psychology. Although feminist psychology grew rapidly in

the wake of second-wave feminism (Enns, 1993), backlash against feminism in the United States (Faludi, 1991) has shifted the cultural context within which feminist psychological research is conducted and received. In this less-than-hospitable environment, criticisms of feminist research have focused on the rigor of the research methods employed (Crawford, 1997; Sommers, 1994). Multicultural competence theorists and researchers may want to heed the warning that intuitively appealing constructs are insufficient when the political climate is not supportive of the conclusions.

Thus, although the MCC movement has had a significant impact on APA policy as stipulated in the ethics code and accreditation procedures, increasing attacks on multiculturalism within the professional literature may undo or weaken many of the policy advances that have been made to date.

Conflict With the EVT Movement

The empirically validated treatment (EVT) movement is another driving force within psychology that has gained considerable momentum in recent years. The EVT movement arose in part as a response to the rapidly rising medical costs of the 1980s and early 1990s and the desire on the part of health maintenance organizations to have a list of empirically validated psychotherapy treatments for the purposes of insurance reimbursement. In 1993, Division 12 of the APA established the Task Force on Promotion and Dissemination of Psychological Procedures, whose goals were to develop criteria for identifying EVTs, provide examples of EVTs, and make recommendations for incorporating EVTs in the training of psychologists. The task force published its first report in 1995 in *The Clinical Psychologist* (Task Force, 1995); subsequent reports have appeared in the same publication in 1996 (Chambless et al., 1996) and 1998 (Chambless et al., 1998).

Like the MCC movement, the EVT movement has begun to affect APA policy in the form of accreditation criteria. The task force recommended in 1995 that training in EVTs be a criterion for program accreditation (Task Force, 1995). Later that same year, the Accreditation Committee came out with new accreditation criteria specifying that accredited programs must provide (a) instruction in "formatting and implementing interventions strategies (including training in empirically supported procedures)" and (b) practicum experiences that "provide a wide range of training and educational experiences through applications of empirically supported interventions procedures" (APA, 1995, p. 7). It seems likely that the EVT movement will, in time, also affect the wording of ethical and practice standards.

According to Atkinson, Bui, and Mori (2001), the EVT movement is on a collision course with the MCC movement because the former ignores the effects of client and counselor characteristics, whereas the latter emphasizes these effects. Atkinson et al. detailed a number of criticisms that have been leveled against the EVT movement, including the criticism that the task force failed to take ethnicity and culture into consideration in identifying EVTs (Doyle, 1998; Sue, 1999). Recognizing this limitation in their initial (1995) document, the task force subsequently recommended that EVTs be validated across various ethnic groups (Chambless et al., 1996). However, replicating validation studies across ethnic groups still ignores the powerful role that cultural values play in counseling and psychotherapy. Therefore, Atkinson et al. expressed concern that multicultural researchers may be beguiled into testing the validity of EVTs across the various ethnic populations and thus be drawn away from basic research on ethnic and cultural factors that affect counseling process and outcome. Furthermore, by ignoring the role of culture and promoting training of EVT competence, the EVT movement will serve to undermine

the training of MCC. For an expanded discussion of the collision course between these two movements, the reader is referred to Atkinson et al. (2001).

RISE AND FALL OF MOVEMENTS WITHIN PSYCHOLOGY

Since the beginning of psychology as a discipline and profession, psychological movements (some theory based and some not) have waxed and waned with regularity. Psychoanalysis, trait-factor theory, existentialism, transactional analysis, group therapy, and feminist therapy, for example, have all risen to positions of considerable prominence within psychology only to recede in popularity and influence. Some of these movements have been little more than fads that come and go with the influence of a single outspoken proponent. Others have had broad-based support and only recede in popularity when a more forceful and persuasive movement takes its place.

Some movements have continued to influence psychology long after their creators and initial proponents have left psychology's jousting field of professional publications. Those movements that have withstood the test of time have been able to marshal empirical support for the theory underlying the movement. Behaviorism, for example, in the current cloth of cognitive-behavioral psychotherapy, has a fairly extended longevity due to its strong foundation in research. No movement has maintained a prominent role in psychology without research to back it up. We believe that the MCC movement is in danger of waning in the coming decades due to the lack of empirical support for some of the concepts underlying multiculturalism.

DEVELOPING A STRONG RESEARCH BASE FOR MCC

If the MCC movement is to maintain and possibly enhance its influence on psychology, it is imperative that multicultural competence be linked empirically to counseling process and outcome. To do that, we need to retrace our steps and begin building a strong foundation for MCC based on research. As a starting point, we need to empirically validate the MCCs developed by Sue et al. (1992), as well as empirically develop other valid MCCs.

Empirically Validate
Sue et al. (1992) MCCs

There is every reason to believe that the MCCs developed by Sue et al. (1982) and Sue et al. (1992) are valid, efficacious competencies for counselors working with culturally diverse clients. However, there is currently no research evidence to support the validity of the 31 MCCs described in Sue et al. (1992). To encourage such validation research, we suggest the following as examples of research methodologies that could be useful.

Surveys of Experts. Experts in multicultural counseling could be identified based on their scholarly contribution to, or direct service experience with, diverse client populations. These experts could be asked to rate the importance or effectiveness of the 31 MCCs when working with particular client populations (it may be that some competencies are more important or effective when working with some populations than others). Furthermore, the experts could be asked to judge whether these are generic competencies that are helpful in counseling any client versus those that are specific to ethnic minority clients. This process would provide a primary level of validation for the Sue et al. (1992) MCCs.

Surveys of Consumers. Various client and/or potential client populations could be surveyed to determine how helpful they perceive the Sue et al. (1992) competencies to be. In addition to

validating their efficacy across various ethnic populations, the competencies could be validated across types of concerns (e.g., emotional, interpersonal, academic, and career concerns). The 31 MCCs could be imbedded with other counseling competencies to determine if they are perceived to be more, as, or less helpful than generic counseling competencies. Surveys of consumers and/or potential consumers would also provide a primary level of validation.

Analog Studies Linking Competencies to Process and Outcome. Analog studies conducted in laboratory settings could be used to determine if the experimentally manipulated presence versus absence of the 31 MCCs affects counseling process and outcome with diverse clients varying in client characteristics (e.g., level of acculturation, stage of identity development, degree of cultural mistrust) under controlled conditions. The effect on counseling process might be measured by such variables as strength of working alliance, client willingness to self-disclose, and perceived counselor credibility. The effect on counseling outcome might be measured by such variables as client ratings of self-esteem, retention in counseling, ratings of counselor effectiveness, and behavior changes. Analog studies linking MCCs to counseling process and outcome could provide a secondary level of validation for the Sue et al. (1992) competencies.

Field Studies Linking Competencies to Process and Outcome. Although it would be difficult, and possibly unethical, to manipulate Sue et al.'s (1992) 31 MCCs with actual clients, audiotapes and videotapes of actual counseling sessions with diverse clients could be rated for the presence of the competencies to determine if they are predictive of counseling process and outcome. The same process and outcome variables as used with analog studies could be used with field study participants but would require counseling agencies to pursue a more rigorous assessment of counselors and counseling services than is typical of most at this time. Field studies linking the Sue et al. competencies to counseling process and outcome would provide the tertiary, or highest, level of validation.

Develop Appropriate Instruments to Measure Knowledge, Attitudes, and Skills Developed by Sue et al. (1992). After, and only after, some or all of the MCCs identified by Sue et al. (1992) have been validated, instruments could be developed that validly measure these competencies. In doing so, it will be important to not rely too heavily on self-report instruments to assess knowledge and skills, as was done with the first round of MCC assessment instruments based on Sue et al. (1982). The instrument developed by LaFromboise et al. (1991) serves as one model of the kind of observer-scored instrument that could provide an objective assessment of MCC. Another model would involve the use of different assessment procedures to measure attitudes, knowledge, and skills.

Attitudes. Although observers can be used to assess attitudes, observer ratings are usually assessments of assumed attitudes based on the counselor's verbal and nonverbal behaviors because observers do not have direct access to the counselor's attitudes. Therefore, the assessment of attitudes is probably best accomplished with a self-report method. However, self-report instruments are needed that will measure actual MCC attitude competence, not self-efficacy for competence. Also, self-report instruments are needed that minimize or account for socially acceptable response sets. At a minimum, they will need to include items designed to assess the respondents' desire to give socially acceptable responses.

Knowledge. MCC knowledge should be assessed through instruments that measure actual knowledge, rather than assessing self-efficacy of MCC knowledge. MCC knowledge assessment instruments might consist of items that measure the counselor's knowledge of information identified in the knowledge competencies, such as knowledge of factors that make ethnic groups unique (e.g., language, culture, discrimination) and contribute to within-group differences (e.g., acculturation, stages of identity development, levels of cultural mistrust). Like standardized achievement and aptitude assessments, MCC knowledge could be measured using self-report instruments or interview assessments.

Skills. Rather than assessing counselors' self-efficacy ratings for MCC skills, instruments are needed that objectively assess skill in working with culturally diverse clients. In all probability, this will involve client, observer, or supervisor ratings of skills with clients or role-played clients. This process can be standardized by using written, audio, or audio-visual vignettes, which might serve as stimuli that require the counselor to respond in some way that demonstrates the presence or absence of the skill being assessed. As in measuring generic counseling competence, it may be important to break MCC skills into micro- and macro-units (Heppner, Kivlighan, & Wampold, 1999).

The 31 MCCs identified in Sue et al. (1992) are examples of macro-MCCs. Examples of micro-MCCs that could be investigated include (a) counselor responsiveness to racial, ethnic, and cultural content introduced by client; (b) counselor-initiated discussion of racial, ethnic, and cultural issues related to the client's problem; (c) counselor-introduced racial, ethnic, and cultural content; and (d) counselor acknowledgment and processing of racial, ethnic, and cultural differences and similarities that may create barriers to counseling. Three studies that serve as models of micro-MCC research are Atkinson et al. (1992), Gim et al. (1991), and Pomales et al. (1986).

Empirically Assess and Validate Competencies From Multicultural Models

A number of multicultural counseling models have appeared to date, and it is hoped that more will be forthcoming in the future. These models, in effect, define MCCs, some of which are incorporated in the Sue et al. (1992) list of competencies and some of which have not. We will cite one example of how MCCs associated with a model not cited by Sue et al. (1992) have been validated and assessed. A similar process could be applied to other multicultural models.

Ruelas (2001; see also Chapter 17, this volume) used written vignettes to assess psychologists' skill at matching counselor roles with client characteristics. According to the 3-D model of multicultural counseling (Atkinson, Thompson, & Grant, 1993), counselors need to consider at least three client characteristics when choosing a helping role to use with a culturally diverse client. The three characteristics (visualized as continua) to be considered are the etiology of the client's problem (internal vs. external), client goal for counseling (prevention vs. treatment), and client level of acculturation (low vs. high). Atkinson et al. (1993) hypothesized that the eight intersection points of these three continua prescribe which of eight counselor roles best address the client's problem. For example, the 3-D model postulates that a low-acculturated client who is currently being discriminated against at work (problem with external etiology that needs treatment) is best served by a counselor who functions as an advocate. Although Atkinson et al. acknowledged that client goals for counseling, problem etiology, and acculturation level seldom fall at the extremes of the continua, they suggest that the model can be useful to help counselors identify the role or roles they might assume when working with a culturally diverse client. Atkinson, Kim, and Caldwell (1998) subsequently validated six of the eight roles in a survey of multicultural counselors and three of the eight roles in a survey of Asian American students.

Ruelas (2001) defined the ability to match validated counseling roles with the appropriate client characteristics as a MCC skill. She developed four vignettes for the four nontraditional counselor roles validated in Atkinson et al. (1998); the four vignettes described a culturally diverse client's goals for counseling, problem etiology, and level of acculturation. She then developed a questionnaire in which respondents could rate the helpfulness of various counselor roles for each of the four vignettes. Respondents who gave their highest ratings to the validated role for each vignette were judged to be competent in matching roles with the three client characteristics.

Although the primary purpose of the Ruelas (2001) study was to examine the relationship between multicultural training and ability to match validated counselor roles with client characteristics, an important component of her study was the development of a MCC assessment instrument. The Ruelas study provides a blueprint for the development of MCC skill assessment instruments for other MCC models: operationalization of the MCC skills described by the model, validation of these MCC skills, and development of an instrument to assess them.

Empirically Identify MCCs Using Qualitative and Quantitative Methodology

The Sue et al. (1982) and Sue et al. (1992) MCCs were developed as a result of committee consensus. As indicated earlier, their efforts have been so widely accepted that they may have discouraged the use of empirical methods to identify MCCs. We agree with Ponterotto (2002) that both qualitative and quantitative methods are needed to empirically validate the MCCs specified by Sue et al. (1992) as well as to identify other additional multicultural competencies.

Qualitative Methods. Qualitative methods of identifying MCCs might include interviews with diverse clients following counseling to determine those counselor behaviors that they found most helpful. An example of this research methodology is provided by Pope-Davis et al. (2002). Another approach might involve qualitative analysis by experts of counselor behavior in counseling sessions that are judged by ethnic minority clients to be productive. Both of these methods would be particularly helpful in identifying MCC skills.

Quantitative Methods. Quantitative methods that would be particularly helpful in identifying MCCs would be surveys of experts and consumers (or potential consumers). Surveys of multicultural experts would be particularly helpful in identifying MCCs that apply across diverse groups. Surveys of specific cultural groups would be helpful to determine MCCs that these groups consider most helpful.

CONCLUSION

The MCC movement has enjoyed considerable success in recent years, particularly with respect to influencing policy in professional psychology. However, the foundation of the movement is based on MCCs identified by committee consensus, not empirical investigation. Furthermore, these committee-identified MCCs have never been subjected to validation studies. As a result, the MCC movement is vulnerable to detractors, such as those in the EVT movement who choose to ignore the counselor and client characteristics that are at the heart of the MCC movement.

To provide the kind of research support that will be needed if the movement is to remain in a position of prominence, MCC advocates will need to go back to the drawing boards and design research to identify and validate MCCs. We have suggested a few research methodologies and topics that could be useful in validating MCCs. To generate a large pool of researchers studying MCCs, psychologists and students in training of all ethnic and cultural backgrounds should be encouraged to participate in this research effort. Also, if the movement is to succeed, researchers must be willing to challenge each other's ideas and theories without fear of being ostracized by the community of multicultural scholars. In this vein, new instruments are needed to replace the first generation of MCC assessment measures, especially those self-report measures that may be assessing self-efficacy for MCC, not MCC. Finally, because most of the existing instruments have measured self-efficacy for MCC, earlier studies examining correlates of MCC will need to be revisited when more valid measures of competency are available.

REFERENCES

Allison, K. W., Crawford, I., Echemendia, R. J., Robinson, W. L., & Knepp, D. (1994). Human diversity and professional competence. *American Psychologist, 49,* 792-796.

American Psychological Association. (1986). *Criteria for accreditation of doctoral training programs and internships in professional psychology.* Washington, DC: Author.

American Psychological Association. (1992). Ethical principles of psychologists and code of conduct. *American Psychologist, 47,* 1597-1611.

American Psychological Association. (1993). Guidelines for providers of psychological services to ethnic, linguistic, and culturally diverse populations. *American Psychologist, 48,* 45-48.

American Psychological Association. (1995). *Guidelines and principles for accreditation of programs in professional psychology.* Washington, DC: Author.

American Psychological Association. (2001). *Guidelines for multicultural counseling proficiency for psychologists: Implications for education and training, research and clinical practice* [Online]. Retrieved April 26, 2001, from www.apa.org/divisions/div45/guidelines.pdf

Arbuckle, D. S. (1969). The alienated counselor. *Personnel and Guidance Journal, 48,* 18-23.

Arredondo, P., Toporek, R., Brown, S. P., Jones, J., Locke, D. C., Sanchez, J., et al. (1996). Operationalization of the multicultural counseling competencies. *Journal of Multicultural Counseling and Development, 24,* 42-78.

Atkinson, D. R., Bui, U., & Mori, S. (2001). Multiculturally sensitive empirically supported treatments: An oxymoron? In J. G. Ponterotto, J. M. Casas, L. A. Suzuki, & C. M. Alexander (Eds.), *Handbook of multicultural counseling* (pp. 387-414). Thousand Oaks, CA: Sage.

Atkinson, D. R., Casas, A., & Abreu, J. (1992). Mexican American acculturation, counselor ethnicity and cultural sensitivity, and perceived counselor competence. *Journal of Counseling Psychology, 39,* 415-520.

Atkinson, D. R., Kim, B. S. K., & Caldwell, R. (1998). Ratings of helper roles by multicultural psychologists and Asian American students: Initial support for the 3-dimensional model of multicultural counseling. *Journal of Counseling Psychology, 45,* 414-423.

Atkinson, D. R., Thompson, C. E., & Grant, S. K. (1993). A three-dimensional model for counseling racial/ethnic minorities. *The Counseling Psychologist, 21,* 257-277.

Bingham, R. P. (2001, March). *The power of inclusion: A counseling psychologist's perspective.* Keynote address presented at the 2001 Counseling Psychology Conference, Houston, TX.

Bryson, S., & Bardo, H. (1975). Race and the counseling process: An overview. *Journal of Non-White Concerns in Personnel and Guidance, 4,* 5-15.

Calia, V. F. (1966). The culturally deprived client: A re-formulation of the counselor's role. *Journal of Counseling Psychology, 13,* 100-105.

Chambless, D. L., Baker, M. J., Baucom, D. H., Beutler, L. E., Calhoun, K. S., Crits-Christoph, P., et al. (1998). An update on empirically validated therapies II. *The Clinical Psychologist, 51,* 3-16.

Chambless, D. L., Sanderson, W. C., Shoham, V., Johnson, S. B., Pope, K. S., Crits-Christoph, P., et al. (1996). An update on empirically validated therapies. *The Clinical Psychologist, 49*(2), 5-18.

Constantine, M. G. (1997). Facilitating multicultural counseling competency in counseling supervision: Operationalizing a practical framework. In D. B. Pope-Davis & H. L. K. Coleman (Eds.), *Multicultural counseling competencies: Assessment, education and training, and supervision* (pp. 310-324). Thousand Oaks, CA: Sage.

Constantine, M. G., & Ladany, N. (2000). Self-report multicultural counseling competence scales: Their relation to social desirability attitudes and multicultural case conceptualization ability. *Journal of Counseling Psychology, 47,* 155-164.

Crawford, M. (1997). Agreeing to differ: Feminist epistemologies and women's ways of knowing. In M. M. Gergen & S. N. Davis (Eds.), *Toward a new psychology of women* (pp. 267 284). New York: Routledge Kegan Paul.

D'Andrea, M., & Daniels, J. (1997). Multicultural counseling supervision: Central issues, theoretical considerations, and practical strategies. In D. B. Pope-Davis & H. L. K. Coleman (Eds.), *Multicultural counseling competencies: Assessment, education and training, and supervision* (pp. 290-309). Thousand Oaks, CA: Sage.

D'Andrea, M., Daniels, J., & Heck, R. (1990). *The Multicultural Awareness-Knowledge-Skills Survey.* Honolulu: University of Hawaii–Manoa.

D'Andrea, M., Daniels, J., & Heck, R. (1991). Evaluating the impact of multicultural counseling training. *Journal of Counseling and Development, 70,* 143-150.

Detterman, D. K. (2000). Tests, affirmative action in university admissions, and the American way. *Psychology, Public Policy, & Law, 6,* 44-55.

Doyle, A. B. (1998). Are empirically validated treatments valid for culturally diverse populations? In K. S. Dobson & D. D. Craig (Eds.), *Empirically supported therapies: Best practice in professional psychology* (pp. 93-103). Thousand Oaks, CA: Sage.

Enns, C. E. (1993). Twenty years of feminist counseling and therapy: From naming biases to implementing multifaceted practice. *The Counseling Psychologist, 21,* 3-87.

Faludi, S. (1991). *Backlash: The undeclared war against American women.* New York: Crown.

Fowers, B. J., & Richardson, F. C. (1996). Why is multiculturalism good? *American Psychologist, 51,* 609-621.

Gim, R. H., Atkinson, D. R., & Kim, S. J. (1991). Asian American acculturation, counselor ethnicity and cultural sensitivity, and ratings of counselors. *Journal of Counseling Psychology, 38,* 57-62.

Halleck, S. L. (1971). Therapy is the handmaiden of the status quo. *Psychology Today, 4,* 30-34, 98-100.

Hansen, N. D., Pepitone-Arreola-Rockwell, F., & Greene, A. F. (2000). Multicultural competence: Criteria and case examples. *Professional Psychology: Research and Practice, 31,* 652-660.

Harper, F. D. (1975). What counselors must know about the social sciences of Black Americans. *Social Work, 20,* 379-382.

Heppner, P. P., Kivlighan, D. M., & Wampold, B. E. (1999). *Research design in counseling* (2nd ed.). Belmont, CA: Brooks/Cole.

Hills, H. I., & Strozier, A. L. (1992). Multicultural training in APA-approved counseling psychology programs: A survey. *Professional Psychology: Research and Practice, 23,* 43-41.

Jackson, M. L. (1995). Multicultural counseling: Historical perspectives. In J. G. Ponterotto, J. M. Casas, L. A. Suzuki, & C. M. Alexander (Eds.), *Handbook of multicultural counseling* (pp. 3-16). Thousand Oaks, CA: Sage.

Kiselica, M. S. (1998). Preparing Anglos for the challenges and joys of multiculturalism. *The Counseling Psychologist, 26,* 5-21.

Ladany, N., Inman, A. G., Constantine, M. G., & Hofheinz, E. W. (1997). Supervisee multicultural case conceptualization ability and self-reported multicultural competence as functions of supervisee racial identity and supervisor focus. *Journal of Counseling Psychology, 44,* 284-293.

LaFromboise, T. D., Coleman, H. L. K., & Hernandez, A. (1991). Development and factor structure of the Cross-Cultural Counseling Inventory–Revised. *Professional psychology: Research and Practice, 22,* 380-388.

Leach, M. M., & Carlton, M. A. (1997). Toward defining a multicultural training philosophy. In D. B. Pope-Davis & H. L. K. Coleman (Eds.), *Multicultural counseling competencies: Assessment, education and training, and supervision* (pp. 184-208). Thousand Oaks, CA: Sage.

Mitchell, H. (1971). Counseling Black students: A model in response to the need for relevant counselor training programs. *The Counseling Psychologist, 2,* 117-122.

Neville, H. A., Heppner, M. J., Thompson, C. E., Brooks, L., & Baker, C. E. (1996). The impact of multicultural training on White racial identity attitudes and therapy competencies. *Professional Psychology: Research and Practice, 27,* 83-89.

Ottavi, T. M., Pope-Davis, D. B., & Dings, J. G. (1994). Relationships between White racial identity attitudes and self-reported multicultural counseling competencies. *Journal of Counseling Psychology, 44,* 284-293.

Pomales, J., Claiborn, C. D., & LaFromboise, T. D. (1986). Effects of Black students' racial identity on perceptions of White counselors varying in cultural sensitivity. *Journal of Counseling Psychology, 33,* 57-61.

Ponterotto, J. G. (1997). Multicultural counseling training: A competency model and national survey. In D. B. Pope-Davis & H. L. K. Coleman (Eds.), *Multicultural counseling competencies: Assessment, education and training, and supervision* (pp. 111-130). Thousand Oaks, CA: Sage.

Ponterotto, J. G. (2002). Qualitative methods: The fifth force in psychology. *The Counseling Psychologist, 30,* 394-406.

Ponterotto, J. G., Alexander, C. M., & Grieger, I. (1995). A multicultural competency checklist for counseling training programs. *Journal of Multicultural Counseling & Development, 23,* 11-20.

Ponterotto, J. G., Rieger, B. P., Barrett, A., & Sparks, R. (1994). Assessing multicultural counseling competence: A review of instrumentation.

Journal of Counseling and Development, 72, 316-322.

Ponterotto, J. G., Sanchez, C., & Magrids, D. (1991, August). *Initial development and validation of the Multicultural Counseling Awareness Scale (MCAS-B).* Paper presented at the annual convention of the American Psychological Association, San Francisco.

Pope-Davis, D. B., Liu, W. M., Toporek, R. L., & Brittan-Powell, C. S. (2001). What's missing from multicultural competency research: Review, introspection, and recommendations. *Cultural Diversity and Ethnic Minority Psychology, 7,* 121-138.

Pope-Davis, D. B., & Ottavi, T. M. (1994). Examining the association between self-reported multicultural counseling competencies and demographic variables among counselors. *Journal of Counseling and Development, 72,* 651-654.

Pope-Davis, D. B., Reynolds, A. L., Dings, J. G., & Nielson, D. (1995). Examining multicultural counseling competencies of graduate students in psychology. *Professional Psychology: Research and Practice, 26,* 322-329.

Pope-Davis, D. B., Reynolds, A. L., Dings, J. G., & Ottavi, T. M. (1994). Multicultural competencies of doctoral interns at university counseling centers: An exploratory investigation. *Professional Psychology: Research and Practice, 25,* 466-470.

Pope-Davis, D. B., Toporek, R. L., Ortega-Villalobos, L., Ligiero, D. P., Brittan-Powell, C. S., Liu, W. M., et al. (2002). Client perspectives of multicultural counseling competence: A qualitative examination. *The Counseling Psychologist, 30,* 355-393.

Prilleltensky, I. (1989). Psychology and the status quo. *American Psychologist, 44,* 795-805.

Reynolds, A. L. (1995). Challenges and strategies for teaching multicultural counseling courses. In J. G. Ponterotto, J. M. Casas, L. A. Suzuki, & C. M. Alexander (Eds.), *Handbook of multicultural counseling* (pp. 312-330). Thousand Oaks, CA: Sage.

Ridley, C., Mendoza, D., & Kanitz, B. (1994). Multicultural training: Re-examination, operationalization, and integration. *The Counseling Psychologist, 22,* 227-289.

Ruelas, S. R. (2001). Multicultural counseling competencies (Doctoral dissertation, University of California, Santa Barbara, 2000). *Dissertation Abstracts International, 62,* 2499.

Smith, D. H. (1967). The White counselor in the Negro slum school. *School Counselor, 14,* 268-272.

Sodowsky, G. R., Kuo-Jackson, P. Y., Richardson, M. F., & Corey, A. T. (1998). Correlates of self-reported multicultural competencies: Counselor multicultural social desirability, race, social inadequacy, locus of control racial ideology, and multicultural training. *Journal of Counseling Psychology, 45,* 256-264.

Sodowsky, G. R., Taffe, R., Gutkin, T., & Wise, S. (1994). Development of the Multicultural Counseling Inventory: A self-report measure of multicultural competencies. *Journal of Counseling Psychology, 41,* 137-148.

Sommers, C. H. (1994). *Who stole feminism: How women have betrayed women.* New York: Simon & Schuster.

Speight, S., Thomas, A. J., Kennel, R. G., & Anderson, M. E. (1995). Operationalizing multicultural training in doctoral programs and internships. *Professional Psychology: Research and Practice, 26,* 401-406.

Sue, D. W., Arredondo, P., & McDavis, R. J. (1992). Multicultural counseling competencies and standards: A call to the profession. *Journal of Counseling and Development, 70,* 477-486.

Sue, D. W., Bernier, J. E., Duran, A., Feinberg, L., Pedersen, P., Smith, E. J., et al. (1982). Cross-cultural counseling competencies. *The Counseling Psychologist, 10,* 45-52.

Sue, D. W., Carter, R. T., Casas, J. M., Fouad, N. A., Ivey, A. E., Jensen, M., et al. (1998). *Multicultural counseling competencies: Individual and organizational development.* Thousand Oaks, CA: Sage.

Sue, S. (1999). Science, ethnicity, and bias: Where have we gone wrong? *American Psychologist, 54,* 1070-1077.

Task Force on the Promotion and Dissemination of Psychological Procedures. (1995). Training in and dissemination of empirically validated psychological treatments: Report and recommendations. *The Clinical Psychologist, 48,* 3-23.

Thomas, K. R., & Weinrach, S. G. (1998a). Ethnic parity and race-based quotas: Some ethical and legal concerns. *The Counseling Psychologist, 26,* 124-128.

Thomas, K. R., & Weinrach, S. G. (1998b). Multiculturalism, cultural diversity and affirmative action goals: A reconsideration. *Rehabilitation Education, 12,* 65-75.

Weinrach, S. G., & Thomas, K. R. (2002). A critical analysis of the multicultural counseling competencies: Implications for the practice of mental health counseling. *Journal of Mental Health Counseling, 24,* 20-35.

Worthington, R. L., Mobley, M., Franks, R. P., & Tan, J. A. (2000). Multicultural counselor competencies: Verbal content, counselor attributions, and social desirability. *Journal of Counseling Psychology, 47,* 460-468.

Author Index

Subject Index

Note: "MCC" is used throughout the index as an abbreviation for multicultural counseling competencies.

About the Editors

Donald B. Pope-Davis, Ph.D., is a Professor of Psychology at the University of Notre Dame. His primary research interests are in the areas of multicultural psychology, counseling, and education. Specifically, he is interested in cultural and racial identity development, cultural competency training, development, and assessment. Other areas of research include multicultural supervision in professional psychology, acculturation, and issues of mental health for persons of color. He received his doctorate from Stanford University.

Hardin L. K. Coleman, Ph.D., is a Professor of Counseling Psychology at the University of Wisconsin–Madison. His research and clinical interest focus on the role that cultural identity development and bicultural competence play in the process of psychological well-being and resilient outcomes. He received his doctorate from Stanford University.

William Ming Liu, Ph.D., is an Assistant Professor of Counseling Psychology at the University of Iowa. His research areas are men and masculinity, social class and classism, and multicultural competency. He received his doctorate in Counseling Psychology at the University of Maryland in 2000.

Rebecca L. Toporek, Ph.D., is an Assistant Professor in the Department of Counseling at San Francisco State University. Her research interests include clients' experiences in multicultural counseling, race and poverty attitudes in counseling training, the role of systemic interventions in addressing discrimination, advocacy and social justice, multicultural issues in career counseling, and multicultural counseling supervision. She received her doctorate degree in 2001 from the University of Maryland, College Park.

About the Contributors

Elizabeth M. Altmaier, Ph.D., is a Professor in the Division of Psychological and Quantitative Foundations, College of Education, University of Iowa. She has a secondary appointment in the Department of Community and Behavioral Health, College of Public Health, University of Iowa. Her areas of research are in the applications of counseling psychology to problems of physical health, with a particular emphasis on oncology and chronic pain. She is Principal Investigator of the Adult Health Quality of Life Substudy of the T Cell Depletion Trial funded by National Health Lung and Blood Institute. She served on the Committee on Accreditation of the American Psychological Association from 1990 through 1994, chairing the committee in 1993 and 1994.

Alvin N. Alvarez, Ph.D., is an Assistant Professor and Coordinator of the College Counseling program at San Francisco State University. He was born in the Philippine Islands and raised in Southern California. He holds M.S. and Ph.D. degrees in Counseling Psychology from the University of Maryland at College Park. His professional interests are in the area of Asian American racial identity development, anti-Asian racism and ethnoviolence, and college student affairs.

Julie R. Ancis, Ph.D., is an Associate Professor in the Department of Counseling and Psychological Services at Georgia State University. She has published numerous articles and presented nationally and internationally in the area of racial and gender attitudes, multicultural competency training, career and educational development of women and students of color, and distance learning. She has served on the editorial board of the *Journal of Counseling and Development* and is the Diversity Chair of the APA Guidelines for Counseling/Psychotherapy With Women. She is currently working on a book on culturally based interventions.

Patricia Arredondo, Ed.D., is an Associate Professor in Counseling Psychology at Arizona State University and President of Empowerment Workshops, Inc. of Boston. She has dedicated her career to promoting organizational change through a focus on multiculturalism and cultural competencies. Her extensive publications focus on organizational diversity initiatives, immigrant and Latino issues in counseling, the development and application of multicultural competencies, and counselor education and professional development. She is president of the National Latino Psychological Association and Chicano Faculty and Staff Association of Arizona State University and past president of the Association for Multicultural Counseling and Development (ACA) and the Society for the Psychological Study of Ethnic Minority Issues (APA). Her graduate degrees are from Boston College and Boston University, and she is a licensed psychologist.

Donald R. Atkinson, Ph.D., is a Professor of Education in the combined Counseling, Clinical, and School Psychology program at the University of California, Santa Barbara. He received his Ph.D. from the University of Wisconsin in 1970. He is a Fellow in the American Psychological Society and Divisions 17 and 45 of the American Psychological Association. He is coauthor of three books: *Counseling American Minorities: A Cross-Cultural Perspective* (now in its 5th edition); *Counseling Non-Ethnic American Minorities, Counseling Diverse Populations* (now in its 2nd edition); and *Counseling Across the Lifespan.* He is also author or coauthor of more than 130 journal articles and book chapters, most of which report the results of research on cultural variables in counseling.

Thomas Baskin is a doctoral student in Counseling Psychology at the University of Wisconsin–Madison. His practical experience includes full-time work as a school counselor with ethnically diverse middle school students. His research interests include investigating the link between the basic psychological need of belongingness and student mental health, school achievement, and need fulfillment across cultures.

Lonette Belizaire is completing her doctoral degree in Counseling Psychology at Fordham University. She has worked as a mental health educator and is currently a retention counselor, researcher, and career development instructor in the New York City university system. Her research interest includes the impact of acculturative stress on the adjustment of refugees, immigrants, and international students. She earned her master's degree in counseling from the University of Miami.

Sharon L. Bowman is a Professor and Chair of the Department of Counseling Psychology and Guidance Services at Ball State University in Muncie, Indiana. She received her Ph.D. in counseling psychology from Southern Illinois University–Carbondale in 1989. She is a member of the American Psychological Association (Division 17), the American College Personnel Association, the Association of Black Psychologists, and the American College of Counselors. Her research interests are in multicultural counseling and development, the intersection of feminism and multiculturalism, and mentoring for ethnic minority students.

Eric C. Chen, Ph.D., is an Associate Professor in the Division of Psychological and Educational Services in the Graduate School of Education at Fordham University. He was born and raised in Taiwan and received his doctorate in Counseling Psychology from Arizona State University in 1995. His research interests and publications have encompassed topics of clinical supervision, group counseling, multicultural issues and competencies, and career choice and development of immigrant youth. He is a member of the editorial boards for the *Group Dynamic: Theory, Research, and Practice;* the *Journal of Counseling and Development;* the *Journal of Counseling Psychology;* and the *Journal of Multicultural Counseling and Development.*

Jean Lau Chin is the Systemwide Dean of the California School of Professional Psychology at Alliant International University. She is a licensed psychologist and Associate Professor at Boston University School of Medicine, where she was core faculty for the Center for Multicultural Training in Psychology. She has 30 years of clinical and management experience that includes president of CEO Services, regional director of Massachusetts Behavioral Health Partnership, executive director of South Cove Community Health Center, and codirector of Thom Child Guidance Clinic. She has consulted to and advised national, state, and community organizations on policy, advocacy, and program development related to cultural competence, community health, substance abuse, and mental health for underserved communities. She has done extensive work on ethnic minority, women, and Asian American issues. She is currently president of the Society for the Psychology of Women, Division 35, of the American Psychological Association with a presidential initiative on feminist leadership.

Devika Dibya Choudhuri, Ph.D., is an Assistant Professor in the Department of Counseling and Leadership at Eastern Michigan University. Originally from India, she received her doctorate in Counselor Education from Syracuse University in 2001. Her specialization is in multicultural counseling, and she has worked clinically with populations of color in community and college settings. Her research interests include the impact of social identities within the counseling relationship and the pedagogical issues inherent in the teaching of counseling.

Madonna G. Constantine, Ph.D., is a Professor of Psychology and Education in the Department of Counseling and Clinical Psychology at Teachers College, Columbia University. She received her Ph.D. in Counseling Psychology from the University of Memphis and her bachelor's and master's degrees from Xavier University of Louisiana. She has more than 75 publications related to her research interests. She also has held national and local leadership positions in counseling psychology, and she currently serves as Senior Editor of the *Journal of Multicultural Counseling and Development* and Associate Editor of the *Journal of Black Psychology.* Her research and professional interests include multicultural competence issues in counseling, training, and supervision and career development issues of people of color and psychologists in training.

Catarina I. Costa, M.S.Ed., is a doctoral student in Counseling Psychology in the Graduate School of Education at Fordham University. She holds an M.S.Ed. degree from Fordham University. She has taught high school psychology and advanced placement psychology through the Americorps program in Brownsville, Texas. She immigrated from the islands of the Azores at the age of 12, and her research interests lie primarily in the area of multicultural issues in individual and group counseling and include issues of adjustment, coping, and resiliency within diverse settings.

Maureen G. Creagh is completing her Ph.D. degree in Counseling Psychology from Seton Hall University and was a predoctoral intern at the University Counseling Center of the University of Notre Dame. Both programs are APA accredited. She received her M.A. in Education (counselor preparation) from Seton Hall University. Her clinical interests include multicultural issues, career exploration, interpersonal concerns, and developmental issues among the college population.

Michael D'Andrea, Ed.D., is a Professor in the Department of Counselor Education at the University of Hawaii, Manoa. He is a nationally recognized multicultural advocate who is well known for his efforts in eradicating various forms of institutional racism and cultural oppression that continue to be perpetuated in the fields of counseling and psychology, as well as his work as a social justice advocate in the broader communities of which he is a part. He has more than 100 professional publications, most of which focus on issues related to multicultural diversity and social justice counseling.

Judy Daniels, Ph.D., is a Professor in the Department of Counselor Education at the University of Hawaii. She is well known for her work in multicultural and social justice counseling. She has authored 2 books and more than 50 publications focusing on diversity issues.

Edward Delgado-Romero, Ph.D., is an Assistant Professor in the Department of Counseling and Educational Psychology in the School of Education at the University of Indiana–Bloomington. Previously, he was a clinical assistant professor, assistant director, and licensed psychologist at the Counseling Center of the University of Florida. He received his doctorate in Counseling Psychology from the University of Notre Dame. He is the chair of the Section of Ethnic and Racial Diversity (SERD) of Division 17 (Counseling) of the American Psychological Association and the bylaws chair of the Association of Multicultural Counseling and Development (AMCD) of the American Counseling Association. His research interests include the relationship between ethnicity and burnout among faculty of color, Latino/a issues in higher education, Latino identity development, and narrative psychology.

Enedina García-Vázquez is an Associate Professor in the Department of Counseling and Educational Psychology at New Mexico State University and training director for the school psychology program. Her research interests are in the areas of acculturation, skin color, academic achievement, and various psychological factors such as self-esteem, self-expressiveness, self-perception, and social support. Other publications have addressed language proficiency, acculturative stress, and reading. She is on the executive council of Division 45's Society for the Psychological Studies of Ethnic Minority Issues and the editorial review board of the *Hispanic Journal of Behavioral Sciences* and serves as a senior program reviewer for the National Association of School Psychologists. She received her Ph.D. in school psychology from the University of Iowa.

Gregory Gard, Psy.D, is a recent graduate of Antioch New England Graduate School's Department of Clinical Psychology. As a graduate student, he worked closely with Gargi Roysircar as her research assistant, and he has collaborated with her on several published works and conference presentations. His areas of interest include multicultural process and outcome, psychometrics, and psychotherapy outcomes research particularly related to the development of practice research networks.

Byron K. Hargrove, Ph.D., is a counseling psychologist specializing in career development and career counseling with adults. He currently works at the 1199 Employment, Training, & Job Security Program in New York City, where he provides career counseling with diverse adult learners returning to school. He has worked at several college and university counseling centers and served as a faculty member at Seton Hall University. He has published a number of articles and chapters on career counseling and has served on the editorial board of the *Journal of Multicultural Counseling and Development.* His research interests include the family systems approach to career development, multicultural issues in career counseling, and help-seeking attitudes. He holds M.A. and Ph.D. degrees in Counseling Psychology from the University of Maryland at College Park.

Julie M. Hau, M.S., is a graduate student in Counseling Psychology at the University of Wisconsin–Madison and is a career intern in the Counseling and Career Services at the University of California, Santa Barbara. Her research interests include college student career development and counselor training issues, with a specific focus on first-generation college students' career development and portfolios as a means of evaluating multicultural competency for counselors.

Krupa Hegde is a doctoral student in Counseling Psychology at the University of Notre Dame. She holds master's degrees in psychology from Boston University and the University of Notre Dame. Her research interests include multicultural issues in psychology, health-related behaviors, neuropsychology, and methodological concerns in research. She recently completed a 10-year follow-up study of survivorship in women with breast cancer.

Carrie L. Hill works for the Alzheimer's Association and is Adjunct Instructor of Psychology for Dixie State College of Utah. Her scholarly interests include clinical judgment, multicultural issues, and geropsychology. She received her Ph.D. in Counseling Psychology from Indiana University.

Cheryl C. Holcomb-McCoy, Ph.D., is an Assistant Professor in the Department of Counseling and Personnel Services at the University of Maryland at College Park. Her areas of research and scholarly interest include multicultural competence of school counselors, counseling African American female adolescents, and urban school counselor reform. She is the author of numerous articles and chapters on multicultural counseling competence in schools. Her experiences as a counselor educator at Brooklyn College of the City University of New York give her a unique perspective on school counseling issues and the "transformed role" of school counselors in today's urban schools. She is a former public school teacher and school counselor and is currently involved in the implementation of the first professional development school for school counselors in the Washington, D.C. area.

George S. Howard is the Morahan Director, Core Course and Professor in the Department of Psychology, and he twice served as chairman of Notre Dame's psychology department.

He has served as the president of both the Division of Theoretical and Philosophical Psychology and the Division of Humanistic Psychology of the American Psychological Association. Author of 9 books and more than 150 professional articles and chapters, his research focuses on philosophical and methodological issues in counseling and clinical, educational, sports, and ecological psychology. He was named the 1998 recipient of the Notre Dame Faculty Award. He received his Ph.D. in Counseling Psychology in 1975 from Southern Illinois University.

Robert Hubbell is a doctoral student in the Department of Clinical Psychology, Antioch New England Graduate School, Keene, New Hampshire. He earned an M.Ed. in Counseling at the College of Saint Rose, Albany, New York. His research interests include outcome assessment, program evaluation, community-based interventions, and issues of social justice. He has worked primarily with adults around problems of interpersonal difficulty, anxiety, trauma, and depression.

Tania Israel, Ph.D., is an Assistant Professor in the Counseling, Clinical, and School Psychology Program at the University of California, Santa Barbara. She received her Ph.D. in counseling psychology from Arizona State University in 1998. Her professional interests include diversity training, feminist therapy, multicultural counseling, and sexuality education and counseling. Her current research focuses on the development and assessment of counselor competence with lesbian, gay, and bisexual clients.

Deborah B. Kelly is a fourth-year doctoral student in the Counseling Psychology program in the Department of Professional Psychology and Family Therapy at Seton Hall University. Her interests include multicultural counseling and group counseling.

Keisa D. King is a doctoral student in Counseling Psychology at Ball State University in Muncie, Indiana. She is a student member of the American Psychological Association, the American College Personnel Association, and the Indiana Association of Black Psychologists. She is a graduate student representative to ACPA's Counseling and Psychological Services Commission (Commission VII). Her research and clinical interests include racial identity scale comparison, ethnic minority women's identity development, and multicultural counseling and development for college students.

Amy J. Kleiner is a doctoral student in Counseling Psychology at Indiana University–Bloomington. She earned her bachelor's degree from Cornell College and her master's degree from Northeastern University. Her professional interests include change processes, critical pedagogy, and the implications of social justice issues on counseling and teaching practices.

Paul Leung, Ph.D., is a Professor in the Department of Rehabilitation, Social Work, and Addictions at the University of North Texas in Denton, Texas. He has held previous academic and administrative appointments at Deakin University (Melbourne, Australia), University of Illinois at Urbana-Champaign, University of North Carolina at Chapel Hill, and the University of Arizona. His doctoral degree is from Arizona State University. His research interests are related to racial/ethnic populations, disability, and rehabilitation.

Laurie McCubbin, M.A., is a doctoral candidate at the University of Wisconsin–Madison and is currently a psychology intern at The Ohio State University. Her areas of research interest include resilience, Asian Americans/Pacific Islanders, Native Hawaiians, career development, and racial/ethnic identity development.

Jaclyn Mendelsohn is completing her doctoral degree in Counseling Psychology at Fordham University. She has worked as a medical counselor and associate manager of a health clinic and has also has worked and externed in the New York City public school system. She is currently training in a college counseling center. Her research interests include multicultural counselor training and women's health/psychological issues.

Thomas V. Merluzzi, Ph.D., is a Professor of Psychology at the University of Notre Dame, codirector of the doctoral program in counseling psychology, and a Fellow of the Society of Counseling Psychology (Division 17). He conducts research on resilience processes in coping with cancer from the perspective of self-regulation and self-efficacy theories. He has developed the Cancer Behavior Inventory, a widely used measure of self-efficacy for coping with cancer (http://www.nd.edu/~tmerluzz). His current research interest is developing methods for the cultural analysis of coping measures. He received a master's degree in Experimental Psychology (human learning and memory) and a Ph.D. in Counseling Psychology from The Ohio State University.

Gina E. Miranda, Ph.D., M.S.S.W., is a faculty member in the School of Social Service Administration and an affiliate of the Center for the Study of Race, Politics, and Culture at the University of Chicago. Her most recent study focuses on the adult identity work of mixed race (Black-White) transracial adoptees, interpreting findings in the sociopolitical context of race and multiraciality both within child welfare and society at large. This multisystemic approach to examining race, culture, and identity is also reflected in her methodological orientation, as she is exploring innovations through her research to better "measure" these constructs in all their contextual complexity. Her work ultimately seeks to reframe theories of race, culture, and identity development in ways that have relevance to policy and practice with populations, including multiracial persons and interracial family systems both biological and adoptive.

Debra Mollen is a doctoral candidate in Counseling Psychology at Indiana University in Bloomington. She earned her bachelor's degree from Adelphi University and her master's degree from the University of Denver. Her research and practice interests include multiculturalism and feminism. Her dissertation is titled "Voluntarily Childless Women: Choices and Challenges."

Marie L. Miville, Ph.D., is an Associate Professor of Psychology and Education in the Department of Counseling and Clinical Psychology at Teachers College, Columbia University. She earned M.S. and Ph.D. degrees from the University of Maryland at College Park. Her professional interests are in Latino/a psychology, the integration of multiple collective identities, and universal-diverse orientation.

Mary Jo Noonan, Ph.D., is a Professor of Special Education at the University of Hawaii, Manoa. She prepares special education preschool and elementary teachers to work with students who have severe and multiple disabilities. Most of her research has focused on the inclusion of children with disabilities in typical preschool classrooms located in multicultural settings. She has also studied coteacher interactions in multicultural preschool settings.

Romana A. Norton, M.A., is a doctoral candidate in Counseling Psychology at the University of Wisconsin–Madison. Her research and teaching interests broadly focus on how social constructions of race influence individual and interpersonal functioning. Her research focuses on cultural identity

development, particularly the identity development of people of mixed racial heritage, and multicultural supervision processes and outcomes.

Lideth Ortega-Villalobos is a doctoral student in the Counseling Psychology program in the Department of Psychology at the University of Notre Dame. Her research interests include the assessment of multicultural competence in counseling, supervision and training, and the assessment of cultural identity development.

Thomas A. Parham, Ph.D., is an Assistant Vice Chancellor for Counseling and Health Services and Director of the Counseling Center, as well as an adjunct faculty member at the University of California, Irvine. He is a past president of the National Association of Black Psychologists and past president of the Association for Multicultural Counseling and Development (a division of ACA). He is currently president of the 100 Black Men of America–Orange County Chapter and architect of their "Passport to the Future" Rites of Passage programs. He is the coauthor of *The Psychology of Blacks: An African American Perspective* (2nd ed., 1990) and author of *Psychological Storms: The African American Struggle for Identity* (1993). His most recent book, *Counseling African Descent People: Raising the Bar of Practitioner Competence,* is now available. He has also coauthored *The Psychology of Blacks: An African Centered Perspective,* now in its third edition. He has written more than 20 journal articles and/or book chapters and has also produced several videotapes on counseling African Americans.

Joseph G. Ponterotto, Ph.D., is a Professor of Education and Director of Training in the Counseling Psychology Program at Fordham University in New York City. His primary teaching interests are in multicultural counseling, career development, psychological measurement, and qualitative research methods. He is an associate editor of the *Journal of Counseling Psychology* and coeditor of the International Forum section of *The Counseling Psychologist*. He has written extensively in the area of multicultural counseling, and he is the coeditor or coauthor of a number of books on the topic, including the recently released second editions of the *Handbook of Multicultural Counseling* (2001) and the *Handbook of Multicultural Assessment: Clinical, Psychological, and Educational Applications* (2001).

Raechele L. Pope, Ed.D., is an Associate Professor in the Higher Education program in the Department of Educational Leadership and Policy at the University of Buffalo, State University of New York. With more than 20 years of experience in college student affairs, she has written numerous articles and book chapters. She has provided expertise on multicultural interventions, multicultural competence, and multicultural organization development to both higher education and corporate clients.

Jodi C. Potere is a doctoral student in Counseling Psychology at Fordham University. She earned her M.S. (2002) in Counseling and Personnel Services from Fordham University. She currently works as a counselor on a research project that investigates the effectiveness of a counseling intervention with HIV-positive mothers who are substance users. Her research interests include women's issues, health psychology, the multicultural personality, and social learning theory of career decision making.

Stephen M. Quintana, Ph.D., is a Professor and Chair in the Department of Counseling Psychology at the University of Wisconsin–Madison. He is Associate Editor of *Child Development* and received a Gimbel Child and Family Scholar for promoting ethnic,

racial, and religious understanding. He received a Ford Foundation Postdoctoral Fellowship, 1993-1994. He earned his Ph.D. from the Department of Psychology at the University of Notre Dame, with a specialization in Counseling Psychology. His area of research includes development of children's perspective-taking ability for social status (ethnicity, race, nationality, gender, etc.).

Jeannette Gordon Reinoso is a doctoral student of Counseling Psychology at Arizona State University.

Amy L. Reynolds is a Senior Psychologist at the Buffalo State College Counseling Center. She received her doctorate in counseling psychology from The Ohio State University. She has been working in higher education as a psychologist and professor for 15 years. Her work as a scholar and teacher focuses on multicultural counseling and training; multicultural competence in counseling and student affairs; and feminist and lesbian, gay, bisexual, and transgender issues. She has published numerous journal articles and book chapters addressing multicultural issues, which include race/ethnicity, gender, and sexual orientation, in counseling or student affairs.

Charles R. Ridley, Ph.D., is a Professor in the Counseling Psychology Program and Associate Dean of Research and the University Graduate School (RUGS) at Indiana University. His primary interests are multicultural counseling, assessment, and training; organizational consultation; integration of psychology and theology; and therapeutic change. He is the author *of Overcoming Unintentional Racism in Counseling and Therapy: A Practitioner's Guide to Intentional Intervention* (1995). He is a Fellow of the American Psychological Association and a licensed psychologist. He received his Ph.D. from the University of Minnesota.

Maria P. P. Root, Ph.D., is a clinical psychologist in Seattle, Washington. She has edited and authored six books, two of which have won awards. She is recognized for her expertise on culturally sensitive assessment issues, race and ethnic identity models, trauma, and women's mental health. She has served as an expert witness for 15 years on lawsuits alleging racial and ethnic origins of harassment and/or sexual harassment in North America.

Gargi Roysircar, Ph.D., is the Founding Director of the Antioch New England Multicultural Center for Research and Practice (www.multiculturalcenter.org) and Professor in the Department of Clinical Psychology (APA accredited), Antioch New England Graduate School, Antioch University. She does research on the interface of acculturation and ethnic identity with the mental health of immigrants and ethnic minorities, worldview differences between and within cultural groups, multicultural competencies and training in professional psychology, and multicultural assessment and instrumentation. She was awarded the 2002 Extended Research Award of the American Counseling Association for having consistently furthered and broadened the counseling profession's understanding of diversity through research in a variety of areas. She is a Fellow of the American Psychological Association (APA), president of the Association for Multicultural Counseling and Development, and editor of APA's Division 17 Counseling Psychology Newsletter. She is on the editorial board of several professional journals. At the Antioch MC Center, she integrates research with clinical services, consultation, and education.

Shelley Ruelas, Ph.D., is a psychologist in the Department of Counseling and Consultation at Arizona State University. Specializing in diversity issues, her work includes individual and group psychotherapy, counselor training and supervision, and outreach programming and consultation. Her current professional endeavors include conceptualizing and implementing a multicultural counseling training seminar for psychology interns, preparing university students to work with culturally diverse communities via service learning initiatives, and working with women who have survived sexual trauma and abuse. She is also involved in addressing diversity issues in organizational settings and works extensively with university programs oriented toward the recruitment and retention of underrepresented college students.

Genella M. Taylor is a doctoral candidate in the Department of Counseling Psychology at the University of Wisconsin–Madison. Her current research and professional focus are on the impact of curriculum and instruction on identity development, self-efficacy, academic attainment and achievement, and risk and protective factors for African American youth living in poverty. She also serves as a member of the research and evaluation team at the Madison center of the Pacific Institute of Research and Evaluation (PIRE).

Brett D. Thombs, M.A., is a doctoral candidate in Clinical Psychology and Psychometrics at Fordham University and a psychology intern at Cornell University Weill Medical College, Payne Whitney Clinic. He received a master's degree in special education from the University of Arizona in 1995 and, prior to his doctoral studies, taught primary and middle school special and regular education students in Tucson, Arizona and Mexico City, Mexico. His research interests include culturally sensitive research methods and psychotherapy, bilingualism in psychotherapy and assessment, cross-cultural measurement, and child maltreatment.

Enedina García Vázquez, Ph.D., is Associate Dean of the Graduate School at New Mexico State University. Her research interests are in the areas of acculturation, skin color, academic achievement, and various psychological factors such as self-esteem, self-expressiveness, self-perception and social support. Other publications have addressed language proficiency, acculturative stress and reading. She is on the executive council of APA Division 45's Society for the Psychological Studies of Ethnic Minority Issues. She received her Ph.D. in school psychology from the University of Iowa. Her areas of emphasis included special education and counseling.

Luis A. Vázquez, Ph.D., is an Associate Professor and the Department Head of the Counseling and Educational Psychology Department at New Mexico State University. His areas of special interest and research include dealing with the three major constructs of worldview, ethnic identity, and acculturation in multicultural competencies and curriculum. His greatest interest is the "empowering" focus versus the "deficit" focus of research on diverse populations. He has published in the areas of acculturation and educational development, as well as on issues of phenotype and privilege, and has developed multicultural training videos used across the country in counseling programs. He received his doctorate in Counseling Psychology from the University of Iowa. He has also served as a consultant to higher education, school districts, and agencies in their multicultural development and policies.

Bruce E. Wampold, Ph.D., ABPP, is a Professor of Counseling Psychology at the University of Wisconsin–Madison. He is a Fellow of the American Psychological Association, diplomate of the American Board of Professional Psychology (Counseling Psychology), and past associate editor of the *Journal of Counseling Psychology*. His area of interest is in modeling the effectiveness of psychotherapy, and he is the author of *The Great Psychotherapy Debate: Models, Methods, and Findings.*

Ernest D. Washington Jr. is a Professor of Education at the University of Massachusetts, Amherst. He received his Ph.D. from the University of Illinois in Educational Psychology. His current interests are in culture, methodology, and the philosophical foundations of education. His current research is focused on the use of aesthetics as the foundation of methodology in education.

Lisa Whitten, Ph.D., is an Associate Professor of Psychology at the State University of New York, College at Old Westbury. Active in the Association of Black Psychologists for more than 20 years, she served two terms as president of the New York chapter, was the Eastern Regional representative, and currently serves on the Strategic Planning Committee. An early proponent of bringing race and culture to the center of undergraduate instruction, her 1993 article, "Infusing Black Psychology Into the Introductory Psychology Course," was the third article on race or culture published in the first 19 years of the journal *Teaching of Psychology.* She was a member of the APA Textbook Guidelines Initiative Work Group of the Commission on Ethnic Minority Recruitment, Retention and Training Task Force, which developed recommendations for introductory psychology textbook publishers and authors on enhancing coverage of diversity issues. She maintains a private practice in Queens, New York, and is president of Maximixing Excellence, an educational and psychological consulting firm. Her scholarly interests center on the development of African American college and graduate students, parent education, and African American women's attitudes about hair.